Marine Life
of the Pacific Northwest

Marine Life
of the Pacific Northwest

A Photographic Encyclopedia of Invertebrates, Seaweeds and Selected Fishes

  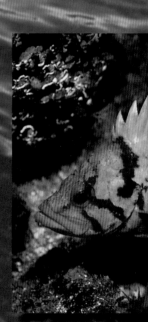

Andy Lamb and Bernard P. Hanby

Seaweed and Annelid Worm Sections in Collaboration with
Dr. Michael W. Hawkes and Sheila C. Byers respectively.

Photography by Bernard P. Hanby

HARBOUR PUBLISHING

QUICK REFERENCE GUIDE

Flowering Plants *Phylum Anthophyta* p.17

Sea Asparagus p.17

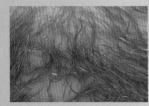
Eelgrasses p.17

Surfgrasses p.18

Marine Algae p.18

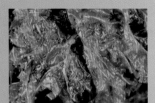
Green Algae p.20
Phylum Chlorophyta

Yellow-Green Algae p.24
Phylum Tribophyta

Brown Algae p.24
Phylum Ochrophyta

Diatoms p.37
Class Bacillariophyceae

Red Algae p.37
Phylum Rhodophyta

Miscellaneous and Undetermined p.58

Sponges *Phylum Porifera* p.60

Calcareous Sponges p.61

Siliceous Sponges p.63

Demosponges p.64

Undetermined p.76

Sea Anemones, Corals, Hydroids, Hydrocorals, Jellies *Phyla Cnidaria, Ctenophora* p.80

Sea Anemones p.81

Zoanthids p.88

Hard Corals p.89

Soft Corals p.90

Sea Anemones, Corals, Hydroids, Hydrocorals, Jellies *continued*

Sea Pens p.92

Gorgonians p.93

Hydrocorals p.95

Hydroids p.96

Jellies p.105

Stalked Jellies p.111

Sea Gooseberries and Comb Jellies p.112

Worms p.113

Flatworms p.113
Phylum Platyhelminthes

Ribbon Worms p.116
Phylum Nemertea

Arrow Worms p.121
Phylum Chaetognatha

Peanut Worms p.122
Phylum Sipunculida

Segmented Worms p.123
Phylum Annelida

Spoon Worms p.162
Phylum Echiura

Phoronids, Moss Animals, Nodding Heads and Lampshells p.162

Phoronids p.162
Phylum Phoronida

Moss Animals p.163
Phylum Bryozoa (Ectoprocta)

Nodding Heads p.173
Phylum Entoprocta

Lampshells p.173
Phylum Brachipoda

Chitons, Bivalves, Univalves, Bubble Shells, Nudibranchs, Octopus *Phylum Mollusca* p.175

Chitons p.176

Mussels p.184

Scallops p.187

Oysters p.189

QUICK REFERENCE GUIDE

Chitons, Bivalves, Univalves, Bubble Shells, Nudibranchs, Tuskshells, Octopus *cont'd*

Clams p.191

Limpets p.212

Coiled Snails p.219

Bubble Shells p.247

Nudibranchs p.251

Tuskshells p.272

Octopuses and Squids p.273

Shrimps, Crabs, Hermits, Barnacles, Sea Fleas, Sea Spiders *Phylum Arthropoda* p.275

Mites p.276

Amphipods p.276

Isopods p.280

Opposum Shrimps p.283

Sea Lice p.284

Krill p.285

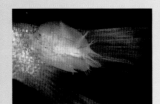
Fish Lice p.285

Shrimps p.285

Miscellaneous p.298

True Crabs p.299

Porcelain Crabs p.307

Galatheid Crabs p.308

Lithode Crabs p.308

Hermit Crabs p.313

Barnacles p.318

Sea Spiders p.323

Sea Stars, Brittle Stars, Feather Stars, Sea Urchins *Phylum Echinodermata* p.324

Sea Stars p.325

Brittle Stars p.334

Feather Stars p.338

Sea Urchins p.338

Sea Cucumbers p.340

Tunicates, Salps, Acorn Worms and others *Phyla Chordata, Hemichordata* p.346

Solitary Tunicates p.346

Social Tunicates p.351

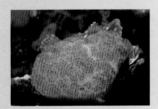

Compound Tunicates p.352

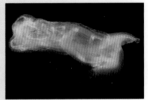

Salps p.360

Acorn Worms p.360

Vertebrates p.361

Selected Fishes p.361

Garter Snake p.386

TABLE OF CONTENTS

7 8 9 10 19 18 17

Harbour Publishing
P.O. Box 219
Madeira Park, BC
V0N 2H0
www.harbourpublishing.com

Design by Roger Handling, Terra Firma Digital Arts.
Photography by Bernard P. Hanby unless otherwise noted.
Printed in China through Colorcraft Ltd, Hong Kong.

Harbour Publishing acknowledges financial support from the Government of Canada, through the Book Publishing Industry Development Program and the Canada Council for the Arts, and from the Province of British Columbia through the British Columbia Arts Council and the Book Publisher's Tax Credit through the Ministry of Provincial Revenue.

Library and Archives Canada Cataloguing in Publication

Lamb, Andy, 1947-
Marine life of the Pacific Northwest : a photographic encyclopedia / Andy Lamb and Bernard P. Hanby.

Includes bibliographical references and index.
ISBN 1-55017-361-8

1. Marine biology—Northwest Coast of North America—Pictorial works. 2. Marine biology—Northwest Coast of North America—Encyclopedias. I. Hanby, Bernard P., 1934– II. Title.
QH104.5.N6L34 2005 578.77'09711'1022 C2005-903599-4
FC3803.R35 2005   971.1'1   C2005-903628-1

This book, reflecting a shared curiosity, is dedicated to all who
are interested in the magic and wonder of the marine world, with the hope
that increased interest will result in its preservation.

PREFACE

This extraordinary encyclopedia of Pacific Northwest marine life includes descriptions of some 1,400 species of seaweeds and animals and about 1,700 colour photographs. While it is particularly relevant to the coast of Oregon, Washington and British Columbia, the ranges of most of the included organisms extend from Alaska to central California, where Point Conception (just northwest of Santa Barbara) is the northern boundary to a southern California faunal region.

It is surprising to realize that coastal water temperatures from Alaska to California are amazingly uniform. You might think that California waters are warm, but they are not. They are cool and temperate, like the waters along the coast of BC. (August water temperatures along the coasts of Baja California, San Francisco, Victoria BC and southern Alaska are usually between 13° and 15°C.) This is brought about by the nature of water currents in the North Pacific. Warm North Pacific currents sweep in a great arc clockwise across the ocean to Oregon and Washington where they turn partly to the north and partly to the south. This warms the northern regions and, together with upwelling of deep water, cools the California coast, thus balancing temperatures north and south. Even the winter temperatures vary only a few degrees along the coast. This thermal uniformity, relatively stable across 22 degrees of latitude and over a long period of time, has brought about a diverse and extensive fauna, the temperate marine fauna of the American North Pacific. These species are restricted to temperate conditions and are intolerant of warmer or cooler water.

Of course the Pacific Northwest itself is differentiated by the inland waters of Puget Sound, the Strait of Juan de Fuca, the Strait of Georgia and all the associated channels and fiords. Locally summer temperatures may be elevated and winter temperatures may be lowered in comparison with the outer coast. This is particularly true for areas around the mouths of streams and rivers. Such areas usually have fewer species than are found on the open coast. On the other hand, swift tidal currents agitate and mix the waters and create habitats rich in marine life.

Half of the species within this very large temperate west coast fauna are endemic (found nowhere else) as compared with less than one quarter of the European North Atlantic species. Unique genera and even families are conspicuous along the Pacific coast. Notable are the lithode crabs of which there are 13 genera and 26 species. Among the molluscs, chitons and octopod cephalopods have numerous species, more than in other oceans. Sea stars are exceedingly numerous in this region. No other region in the world has so many species, genera and families. Some scientists estimate there are as many as 92 species here. The fishes are interesting and unusual also. The live-bearing sea perch (Family Embiotocidae) contains 21 species in 20 genera. These fish give birth to large young. The two-metre-long wolf eel is related to the wolf fish of the North Atlantic. The greenlings, lingcod and sable fish, closely associated with the Pacific sculpins (Family Cottidae) are characteristic of northern seas. Many of them are endemic to the Pacific coast, and over 100 species exist here. Conspicuous and numerous are the rockfishes, cool water members of the scorpion fish family (Scorpaenidae) of which there are about 60 species along the Pacific coast.

While we are discussing the abundance and the diversity of the marine animals we must not forget the seaweeds—the great kelp forests and the rich intertidal algal and plant growth that provide habitat for so many marine animals. The great intertidal amplitude and the cool summer climate in the northern waters are conducive to abundance and good health in intertidal organisms.

Author Andy Lamb, as a biologist with the Canadian Department of Fisheries and Oceans and later at the Vancouver Aquarium, has been scuba diving and taking notes for almost 40 years. For 28 of these years he has teamed up with noted underwater photographer Bernie Hanby who has provided the illustrations for the text. Together they have created this significant new work.

The book is designed to be useful to beachcombers, divers, students and professional biologists and anyone interested in marine life. It is easy to use. The Quick Reference Guide and its diagnostic colour photographs smoothly direct you to the proper pages. Each phylum is introduced by a few descriptive paragraphs and then the numbered species and the photographs follow. Each species is given a common name, a scientific name, size, range, depth, description and natural history note. Appropriate and useful references are listed throughout the text. Species identification has been checked and rechecked by leading scholars. Dr. Michael Hawkes of the University of British Columbia contributed a substantial number of photographs of seaweeds and co-authored the botanical section of the book. Dr. Bill Austin of the Marine Ecology Centre in Sidney, BC, generously gave his advice concerning the difficulty in trying to identify sponge species. Sheila Byers shared her expertise and co-authored the extensive section on polychaete worms.

While we like to talk about the abundance of west coast marine life it must be said that the rapidly growing human population together with overfishing, coastal development and pollution have seriously reduced the richness. Let us hope that this comprehensive work will increase appreciation of marine life and contribute to its conservation. The book is a milestone in the photographic documentation of west coast marine life.

Murray A. Newman, PhD
Director Emeritus
Vancouver Aquarium

INTRODUCTION

The Pacific Northwest

The abundance and diversity of its marine life has been a source of amazement throughout the history of the Pacific Northwest (or "Northeast Pacific," as it is known in scientific circles). This marine world provided First Nations peoples with cultural inspiration as well as being a source of food. It sustained the first European settlers and gave rise to many of the region's first major industries. Naturalists were drawn to it from the earliest days, diligently cataloguing and documenting these

living treasures during the great voyages of discovery in the 1700s and 1800s. The marine environment of the Pacific Northwest is home to more than 10,000 life forms, and the task of identifying them is a great challenge. Many species are still being discovered and classified as the 21st century begins.

The purpose of this volume is to facilitate species identification for everyone interested in Pacific Northwest marine life—amateur and professional, novice and expert. It would be impossible to represent every species in one volume, but it is safe to say that, with more than 1,400 species and 1,700 images, *Marine Life of the Pacific Northwest* contains the most comprehensive and up-to-date photographic record of marine life in this region so far published. We originally set out to document invertebrates, because marine vertebrates such as finfish and marine mammals have

been treated adequately in other works. In the end we did add some selective coverage of finfish, but we have concentrated on invertebrates and seaweeds.

We have also emphasized image over text. "A picture is worth a thousand words" is the premise that guided us in our 25-year quest to craft a photographic record of all such organisms that most observers of Pacific Northwest marine life are likely to encounter.

This project has been a labour of love that both of us feel privileged to have been able to carry out. With each successive intertidal trek, boating excursion and scuba dive, our sense of wonder has grown. But it would be irresponsible to record this marvellous undersea world without mentioning that it is seriously threatened by climate change, environmental degradation and overharvesting. As resources dwindle, more harvesting pressure is placed on the remaining marine life. This has resulted in population crashes of lingcod (VB57), rockfishes (VB36-53) and northern abalone (MC165), among others. Time is running out. Over the last 100 years or more, various North American governments have had the foresight and commitment to create national, provincial, state and municipal terrestrial parks, but this vision and resolve have not been extended to the creation of No-Take Marine Protected Areas. Action is needed, now.

That is why in 1989 we founded the Marine Life Sanctuaries Society of British Columbia, a non-government organization whose primary objective is the establishment of a network of No-Take Marine Protected Areas. Within protected areas it would be forbidden to extract any living organism, but non-consumptive users would be welcomed and encouraged. A growing number of countries embrace this approach, and there is ample evidence that it has significant positive effects.

Pacific Northwest marine life raises major challenges for us, but its richness is still cause for celebration. We urge you to assist in the work of protecting the flora and fauna of this area, and at the same time to enjoy its magnificent diversity.

The Authors

 Recent scientific discoveries, up-to-date nomenclature as well as new photographs and enhanced content are available online at www.knowbc.com/marine.

USING THIS BOOK

We have spent many enchanted hours sightseeing among the undersea wonders of the Northwest Coast and readers may enjoy an armchair version of the diving or beachcombing experience simply by browsing the pages of this book. We hope our work will serve to spread appreciation of this region's remarkable marine life far and wide. However, we also intend it to serve a more specific function in helping readers to efficiently identify organisms they encounter. Here are some simple steps to follow:

1. If you already know the name of the organism you wish to identify, or can make a good guess, the quickest way is to look up the name (scientific or common) in the index at the back of the book. Scientific names are indexed by genus, followed by species (e.g., *Crassostrea gigas*). Common names are listed the way they are normally spoken, as in "giant Pacific chiton" (not "chiton, giant Pacific"). Variant names are not indexed but are listed in the entries. Turn to the page or pages indicated and confirm your identification. (See more on naming conventions below.)

2. If you do not know the exact name of the organism you wish to identify but know the general group it belongs to, turn to the Table of Contents and look for the scientific or common name of the group, then turn to the appropriate section of the book. Match the colour coding of the group to the coloured tabs at the tops of the pages for easy location.

3. If you don't have the name or general group but have a specimen, a photo or a mental picture, turn to our Quick Reference Guide and match your organism to the photo that it most closely resembles. Note the group name and turn to the page indicated, using the colour coding, then browse through the group of related organisms until you find a match. Remember that individual size, markings and colouration may vary.

4. If you are unable to find an exact match, it is possible your specimen is not among those we have catalogued. Keep in mind, though, that there are few omissions among seaweeds and invertebrates likely to be encountered by the non-professional, and the reader should examine all possibilities in this book. The one category in which coverage is not intended to be exhaustive is that of fishes. More complete reference for these species may be found in *Coastal Fishes of the Pacific Northwest* by Andy Lamb and Phil Edgell (Harbour, 1986) or *Pacific Fishes of Canada* by J.L. Hart (Fisheries Research Board of Canada, 1973).

—Andy Lamb and Bernie Hanby

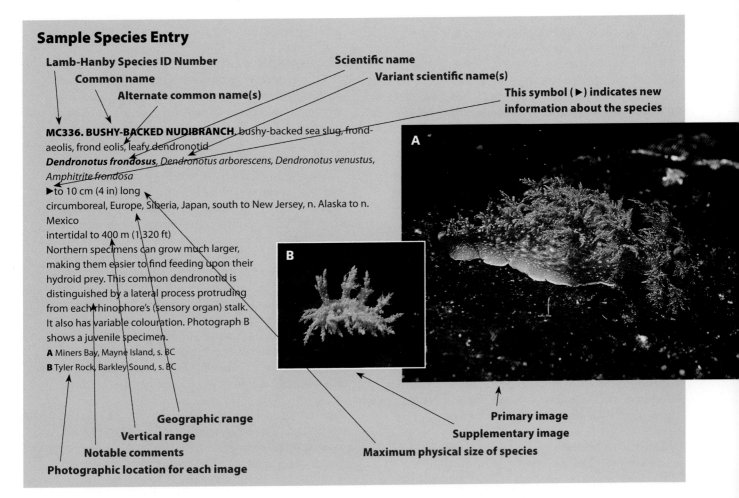

Sample Species Entry

Lamb-Hanby Species ID Number

Common name

Alternate common name(s)

Scientific name

Variant scientific name(s)

This symbol (▶) indicates new information about the species

MC336. BUSHY-BACKED NUDIBRANCH, bushy-backed sea slug, frond-aeolis, frond eolis, leafy dendronotid
Dendronotus frondosus, Dendronotus arborescens, Dendronotus venustus, Amphitrite frondosa
▶to 10 cm (4 in) long
circumboreal, Europe, Siberia, Japan, south to New Jersey, n. Alaska to n. Mexico
intertidal to 400 m (1,320 ft)
Northern specimens can grow much larger, making them easier to find feeding upon their hydroid prey. This common dendronotid is distinguished by a lateral process protruding from each rhinophore's (sensory organ) stalk. It also has variable colouration. Photograph B shows a juvenile specimen.
A Miners Bay, Mayne Island, s. BC
B Tyler Rock, Barkley Sound, s. BC

A

B

Geographic range

Vertical range

Notable comments

Photographic location for each image

Primary image

Supplementary image

Maximum physical size of species

Organization

We have organized the species in this volume by scientific category. Each organism is placed in a phylum, which is described briefly. We have not divided these phyla into lesser ranks, such as classes and orders, but have arranged species more informally, following external similarities. The phyla are arranged from simple to complex, with some general headings, such as Chitons and Crabs, to indicate familiar subgroupings.

One significant exception is the polychaete worms, which are introduced by family. This book features the first extensive treatment of these species for the general audience, including a new taxonomic system and description of common characteristics that define family groupings.

A Further Reading list in many sections notes additional information sources.

Names

Each organism has a scientific name, consisting of a genus and a species, which can vary considerably. The initial name (in boldface type) listed for each species is the most widely used or the most current. That name is followed by alternatives, including those that have been misspelled or used incorrectly, for cross-referencing purposes with other books, scientific papers and local usage.

Established common names are also listed. Where no common name exists, we have assigned one, marked with the symbol ▶. We hope these newly minted names will provide a bridge between experts and other interested people, encouraging the exchange of more information on the organisms. For some species, the Scientific Committee for the Establishment of Common Names has assisted in this process. We believe that this consistent dual tracking system not only enables easier engagement with Pacific Northwest marine life, but also facilitates more communication by all concerned.

Some species illustrated here were previously unknown. Others, while already "found," present such formidable challenges to classification that formal designation is still pending. Where the genus (first name) of such an organism is known but the species (second name) is not, the genus is followed by the abbreviation sp. or spp. Less precisely identified organisms are presented in a more narrative form. We have included them to indicate what information we do have, and to encourage all students of marine life to gather more data.

Numerous species in certain groups, such as sponges and bryozoans, cannot be identified readily without access to sophisticated instruments and jargon-laden scientific keys. In an effort to be inclusive rather than exclusive, we present such organisms with a basic name and letter, such as sponge A or sponge B.

Maximum Sizes

Maximum sizes are referenced from scientific literature combined with the authors' field observations (also noted by the symbol ▶). Species that grow in an irregular mat or carpet-like fashion, such as encrusting sponges, bryozoans and compound tunicates, are difficult to size precisely. In such instances we provide approximations or descriptive comments. Measurements of some species may have been documented from preserved specimens; therefore, dimensions shown are likely smaller than the living organisms' true maximum sizes—particularly for soft-bodied forms. Optimally justified metric/imperial equivalents are supplied for this and the following categories.

Distributions

We have made our best effort to provide accurate geographic and vertical ranges for all species, drawing on published records and direct previously undocumented observation (again noted by the symbol ▶). Information may be approximate due to several factors. Imprecise depth estimates have sometimes entered the literature because sampling equipment was limited or tide level was not considered. As more naturalists study with ever-improving technologies, documentation will improve. Amateurs can contribute to this process as well as professionals, and all are encouraged to make accurate observations and place them on record.

Comments

In addition to brief biological descriptions, entries include incidental information, usually on behaviour and ecology, to aid identification.

Photograph locations

Each entry concludes with a line noting where the organism in the photograph was encountered. These locations were taken directly from nautical charts or topographical maps so that readers can pinpoint sites.

A Changing World

The information in this book is current as of 2005, but like everything else under the sun, the marine world is subject to constant change. As we were going to press, a non-indigenous tunicate, *Didemnum* sp. (CH43), was spreading rapidly in the Pacific Northwest. This adaptable species, which originated in Europe, was first found colonizing the Atlantic seaboard, and then was recorded from Puget Sound, Washington, in 2004. Less than a year later, we were shocked to find it carpeting extensive areas of rocky subtidal shoreline in Agamemnon Channel, 200 kilometres (120 miles) to the north. Recent scientific discoveries, up-to-date nomenclature, new photographs and enhanced content are available online at www.knowbc.com/marine.

About the Photography

Several generations of cameras, strobes and housings were used by Bernie Hanby in the 25 years during which the photographs included here were accumulated.

In the late 1970s and early 1980s, photographs were

taken using a Canon F1 camera with 50 mm macro lens in an Oceanic housing. Lighting was provided by Oceanic 2001 and 2003 strobes. Successive systems included both Canon F1N and Nikon F4 cameras in Aquatica housings combined with Ikelite 200 and 225 strobes, as well as a Nikonos V system. More recently a Nikon F90 camera in a Sea & Sea housing with YS 350 underwater strobe was also used.

Most images were captured with Nikon F4 systems using 60 mm macro lenses and 25 ASA Kodachrome film. As a result of the "digitizing" of photography, Kodak recently discontinued this excellent film, whose consistent and true colour rendition, together with outstanding archival qualities, made it a favourite of many professional and amateur photographers for more than 40 years. As the project neared completion, Kodachrome 64 ASA film was substituted. Wide-angle photographs were taken primarily using Kodachrome 200 ASA film. For some intertidal subjects, including many smaller species, a Nikon ring light and extension rings augmented the equipment.

All of Bernie Hanby's images have been reproduced without digital alteration.

The close-up images of seaweeds contributed by Dr. Michael W. Hawkes were produced using a Contax camera with Zeiss 60 mm macro lens. With the aid of a Bencher copy stand, these subjects were placed in shallow, seawater-filled Plexiglas trays, which were illuminated from below with quartz halogen lights. The film used was Ektachrome EPY 50 ASA Tungsten.

During this project, Andy Lamb evolved into the role of photographer's assistant—a necessity considering the number of species recorded, many of which presented special challenges. Our photographic adventures would likely provide the basis for another book!

Notes on Marine Exploring
Tides and Tidal Zones

Tides—the alternating rise and fall of sea level in oceans and other bodies of water—are caused by the gravitational effects of the sun and moon. In the Pacific Northwest, the difference between high and low tide may exceed 7 metres in some areas. Tides are regular events that can be forecast, and they are recorded and published as tide tables or calendars.

The band of shoreline that lies between the terrestrial and oceanic (subtidal) environments—that part of the land that is exposed at low tide and submerged at high tide—is called the intertidal zone, and it consists of upper, mid- and lower sub zones. It is a glorious place that contains various unique habitats that are fascinating to explore.

With this wonderful opportunity comes a responsibility to protect the organisms living there. If you turn over a rock to see what is underneath, put it back where it was—creatures locate on either side for good reason. Leave no refuse. Better yet, carry a bag and remove foreign materials as a mini beach cleanup. For snorkellers and divers, good behaviour underwater is equally important. Move carefully through the water, along the sea bottom and near reefs, pilings and other natural or manmade structures. Many years' worth of stability and growth of some organisms can be destroyed in a few minutes of carelessness near a reef or wall.

Harvesting Food

Gathering the ocean's bounty for recreational and commercial reasons is a long-established tradition. Over time, as some species have become scarcer, governments have imposed more limits on such activities. If you plan to harvest organisms to eat, check with local fisheries and wildlife officials first. They will give you information on gathering limits, necessary permits, presence of marine biotoxins such as Red Tide (PSP) and other local considerations.

Safety

Whether you are exploring marine life in the intertidal zone or in deeper water with scuba equipment, exercise caution—Pacific Northwest environments are often challenging. Weather, tides and currents can all be hazardous, so find out about them before planning an outing. Wear suitable clothing and footwear, and always be alert for slippery or jagged surfaces, unexpected wind or wave action, boat traffic and so on.

Donna Gibbs photograph

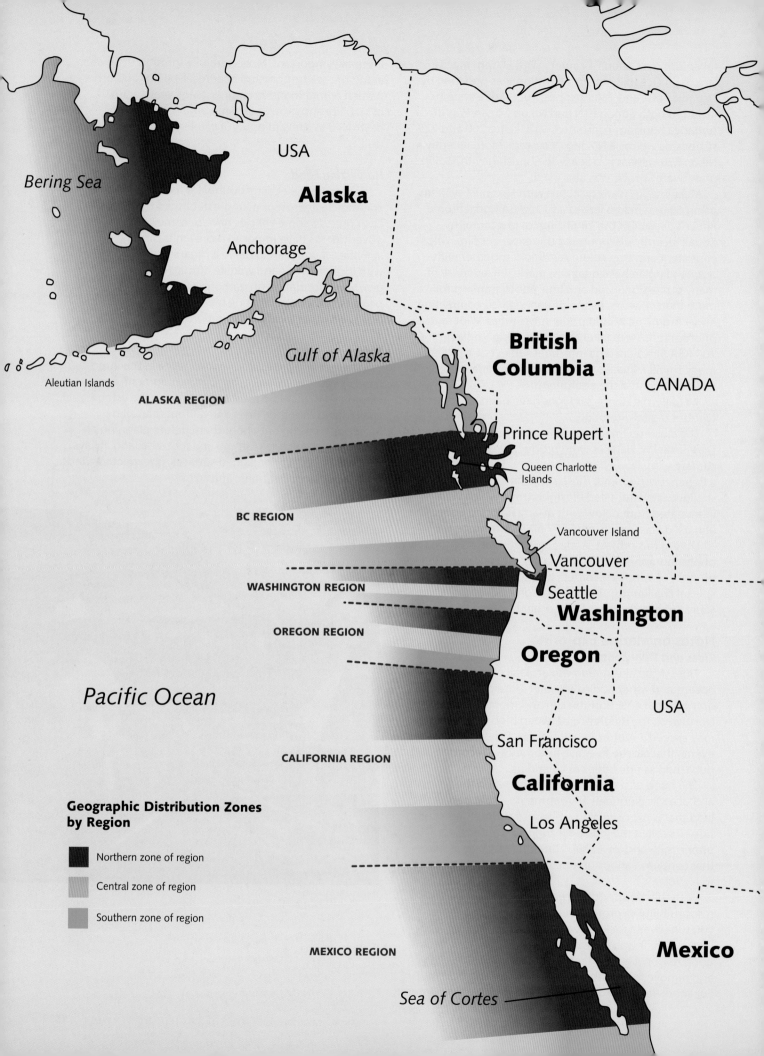

USA

Bering Sea

Alaska

Anchorage

Gulf of Alaska

Aleutian Islands

ALASKA REGION

British Columbia

CANADA

Prince Rupert

Queen Charlotte Islands

BC REGION

Vancouver Island

Vancouver

Seattle

WASHINGTON REGION

Washington

Pacific Ocean

OREGON REGION

Oregon

USA

San Francisco

CALIFORNIA REGION

California

Los Angeles

Geographic Distribution Zones by Region

Northern zone of region

Central zone of region

Southern zone of region

MEXICO REGION

Mexico

Sea of Cortes

SEAGRASSES & SEAWEEDS

FLOWERING PLANTS *Phylum ANTHOPHYTA*

Dominant in the terrestrial realm, flowering plants are familiar to everyone. In the marine environment, however, they are definitely in the minority. Only a few truly marine species—the seagrasses—live in the Pacific Northwest. Members of this group all have flowers (see photograph of *Phyllospadix* **sp., SW4**), leaves, stems and roots. Their roots derive nutrients from surrounding soft sediments such as sand and mud.

Seagrasses are flowering plants that have migrated from the land back into the ocean. In this sense, they can be considered the whales of the flowering plant world! Actually they are not true grasses and consequently are not placed in that family, the Poaceae. Rather, they are placed in two families: the Potamogetonaceae (34 species) and the Hydrocharitaceae (14 species), for a total of 48 species of grass-like marine flowering plants worldwide. Seagrasses are especially diverse in tropical to warm temperate seas.

Ecologically, seagrass meadows play several important roles. Their root systems stabilize bottom sediments, and their leaves slow water currents and promote sedimentation. Seagrasses are also important primary producers, and they provide crucial habitat for fish, invertebrates and marine birds.

Other flowering plants encroach into the marine environment, primarily as salt-marsh inhabitants. This topic is outside the mandate of this book, but two species are included primarily because they also dwell in coastal salt marshes, along rocky shores.

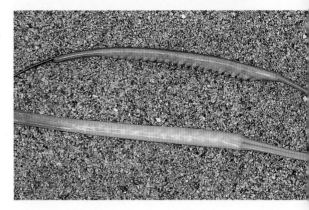

Highest Intertidal and Beyond

SW1. ANNUAL SEA ASPARAGUS, pickleweed, glasswort, saltwort, samphire
***Salicornia depressa**, Salicornia virginica*
to 25 cm (10 in) long
Alaska to Mexico
high intertidal
This plant lives in coastal salt marshes and tidal flats. It has flower heads (inflorescences) terminating all stems. Rich in oils, the seeds of this plant could be economically important in the future. Its leaves make a great salty salad ingredient.
The perennial sea asparagus, *Sarcocornia perennis,* is also found in the Pacific Northwest. It differs from *Salicornia depressa* in its stems, of which many are strictly vegetative and only some are terminated by flower heads.
Kleindale, Pender Harbour, s. BC

Low Intertidal–Shallow Subtidal

SW2. EELGRASS, eel-grass, eel grass
Zostera marina
leaf blades to 2 m (6.6 ft) long, 1.5–12 mm (0.06–0.4 in) wide
Alaska to n. Mexico
low intertidal to shallow subtidal
Characteristic of shallow, muddy or sandy-bottomed estuarine bays, this plant anchors itself in sand or mud via a rhizome—a stem that has numerous hair-like white roots. Eelgrass beds are very productive and are important areas for juvenile fish and invertebrates.
A B Ucluth Peninsula, w. Vancouver Island, s. BC

SW3. DWARF EELGRASS
***Zostera japonica**, Zostera nana*
leaf blades to 30 cm (12 in) long, 1.5 mm (0.06 in) wide
s. BC to s. Oregon, accidentally introduced from Japan
mid-intertidal
This species grows in similar sheltered, tidal-flat habitats as *Zostera marina* (SW2), but it occurs higher in the mid-intertidal zone and usually in much smaller beds. It can easily be differentiated by its much shorter, narrower leaves, as shown in the photograph. Dwarf eelgrass is an annual species. It also grows in brackish coastal lagoons.
The name *Zostera nolti* has unfortunately been applied to this species in some references, but it is the name of a European species.
Crescent Beach, Boundary Bay, s. BC

SW4. SURFGRASSES, basket grasses, green surfgrasses, surf-grasses, surf grasses, including Scouler's surfgrass, Torrey's surfgrass, ►serrated surfgrass
***Phyllospadix spp.**, including Phyllospadix scouleri, Phyllospadix torreyi, Phyllospadix serrulatus*
leaf blades to 2 m (6.6 ft) long, 4 mm (0.15 in) wide
s. Alaska to n. Mexico
mid-intertidal to shallow subtidal
Although surfgrasses grow on rock, their roots and rhizomes (root-like stems) may be covered in sand. These plants thrive along exposed coasts in moderate to strong surf. *Phyllospadix scouleri* is featured in photograph A. Two other species found in the Pacific Northwest are *Phyllospadix torreyi* (photograph B) and *Phyllospadix serrulatus*. The former species has narrower leaves than *Phyllospadix scouleri* and grows lower on the shore. *Phyllospadix serrulatus* has tiny marginal serrations that can be felt when stroking the leaf from its tip or apex to its point of origin. Note the flowering heads in the lower portion of photograph C.
A Frank Island, w. Vancouver Island, s. BC
B Slip Point, Olympic coast, n. Washington
C Sooke, s. Vancouver Island, s. BC. Michael Hawkes photograph

Marine Algae

Marine algae are organisms living in the sea that utilize sunlight, via a process called photosynthesis, to sustain themselves. An arbitrary (not scientific) division of this huge group into microscopic and macroscopic components can be made.

The vast majority of microscopic, unicellular marine algae collectively comprise the vital community of life known as phytoplankton. Phytoplankton form the base of most marine food chains and, as such, have an impact on all other life in many ways.

A significant oceanic phenomenon is the phytoplankton bloom, essentially a gigantic reproductive occurrence that happens primarily in response to increases in nutrients and sunlight. Such blooms usually occur in spring and summer. In the Pacific Northwest, they generally cause seawater to become cloudy, which affects the marine naturalist's underwater visibility.

Two types of phytoplankton bloom are of particular interest to commercial and recreational users of the Pacific Northwest's marine environment. One, popularly called red tide (photograph A), involves several species of single-celled algae called dinoflagellates. One of

these algae, *Alexandrium catenella*, contains a toxin that can become concentrated in the tissues of clams and mussels—bivalve mollusc predators of the alga—and cause severe illness or even death for those who consume them, including humans. This is known as paralytic shellfish poisoning (PSP). If planning to harvest these shellfish, you are well advised to consult local authorities or postings before consuming them. A tingling sensation in the lips is an indication of PSP.

At night, a second, more benign type of phytoplankton bloom produces spectacular bioluminescence. The single-celled organism involved in this bloom has the capacity to chemically generate a flash of light. In an intense bloom, any moving object—such as a diver—is illuminated in the surrounding darkness.

Macroscopic marine algae, typically referred to as seaweeds, are readily visible to the naked eye and are almost always attached to solid substrata. Unlike the complex flowering plants *(Phylum Anthophyta)*, seaweeds have no flowers, stems or leaves. A superficially root-like holdfast merely attaches the alga to a solid substrate and derives no nutrients.

In the following section, seaweeds are presented in three major groupings (photograph B, by Michael Hawkes): *Phylum Chlorophyta*—green algae, *Phylum Ochrophyta*—brown algae, *Phylum Rhodophyta*—red algae. A few miscellaneous entries appear at the end.

In general, the colour distinction for recognizing the three main seaweed groups works well with the green and brown algae. The brown algae are typically a characteristic olive-brown colour, whereas some shade of green is seen in the green algae. Red algae are more problematic: those living in the intertidal zone are often black, brown-red, or even yellowish. Subtidal species are easier to recognize as red algae, being bright red or pinkish—most of the time. The colour in these plants varies because of the dominance of different photosynthetic and accessory pigments within them.

In this book, the marine flowering plants and seaweeds are arranged according to the vertical tidal zones they inhabit: high intertidal, mid-intertidal, low intertidal and subtidal. Some species live within very narrow bands, whereas others frequent a wider vertical distribution. This listing is somewhat arbitrary, as wave exposure, surge channels, shading, tidepools and other factors affect vertical distribution from site to site.

More than 600 species of macroscopic seaweeds and seagrasses live in the Pacific Northwest.

Further Reading

Conner, Judith, and Charles Baxter, 1989, *Kelp Forests,* Monterey Bay Aquarium, Monterey, CA, 64 pp.

Druehl, Louis, 2000, *Pacific Seaweeds: A Guide to Common Marine Seaweeds of the West Coast*, Harbour Publishing, Madiera Park, BC, 190 pp.

Graham, L.E., and L.W. Wilcox, 2002, *Algae*, Prentice-Hall, Upper Saddle River, NJ, 640 pp.

Mondragon, Jennifer, and Jeff Mondragon, 2003, *Seaweeds of the Pacific Coast: Common Marine Algae from Alaska to Baja California,* Sea Challengers, Monterey, CA, 97 pp.

O'Clair, Rita, and Sandra Lindstrom, 2000, *North Pacific Seaweeds*, The Plant Press, Auke Bay, AK, 161 pp.

Technical References

Gabrielson, P.W., T.B. Widdowson, S.C. Lindstrom, M.W. Hawkes and R.F. Scagel, 2000, *Keys to the Benthic Marine Algae and Seagrasses of British Columbia, Southeast Alaska, Washington and Oregon,* Phycological Contribution #5, UBC, Department of Botany, Vancouver, BC, 189 pp.

Gabrielson, P.W., T.B. Widdowson and S.C. Lindstrom, 2004, *Keys to the Seaweeds and Seagrasses of Oregon and California: North of Point Conception,* Phycological Contribution #6, PhycoID, Hillsborough, NC, 181 pp.

Scagel, R.F., P.W. Gabrielson, D.J. Garbary, L. Golden, M.W. Hawkes, S.C. Lindstrom, J.C. Oliviera and T.B. Widdowson, 1993, *A Synopsis of the Benthic Marine Algae of British Columbia, Southeast Alaska, Washington and Oregon*, Phycological Contribution #3, UBC, Department of Botany, Vancouver, BC, 535 pp.

GREEN ALGAE *Phylum CHLOROPHYTA*

Like land plants and seagrasses, green algae contain chlorophylls a and b, the dominant pigments that provide these organisms with their characteristic colour. These special pigments are used to capture sunlight and convert it to chemical energy used to fix carbon dioxide into sugars (photosynthesis). Green algae store excess sugars as starch.

Macroscopic species are featured in this section, but numerous green algae are microscopic, single-cell forms. One of these is *Chlorella*-like zoochlorellae, which live in the tissues of certain anemones (CN13–15) along with the single-celled zooxanthellae (dinoflagellates) belonging to the genus *Symbiodinium*. These symbionts give the burrowing anemone (CN15), shown in the photograph, a green colour. Another single-cell alga, the free-floating *Tetraselmis*, is responsible for the "pea soup" colour in some seashore pools just above the direct influence of the tides.

Although most green algae live in fresh water, at least 130 species inhabit Pacific Northwest marine waters.

NOTE: Identification of many green algae to species can be difficult, and usually requires microscopic examination.

High Intertidal

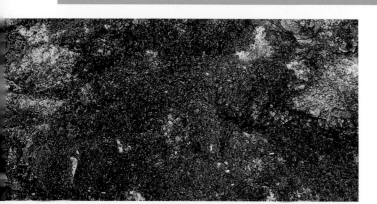

SW5. SHORT SEA LETTUCE, bird-guano alga
Prasiola meridionalis
to 1 cm (0.3 in) long
n. Alaska to s. California
highest intertidal
This alga forms green mats on rocks frequented by marine birds and is nearly always coated by their droppings! Such a nitrogen-rich habitat is tolerated by very few other seaweeds.
Four other species of *Prasiola* are reported to occur in the Pacific Northwest.
Wizard Islet, Barkley Sound, s. BC. Michael Hawkes photograph

SW6. ▶TINY-TUBE SEA LETTUCES
Blidingia spp.
to 3 cm (1.3 in) long
Alaska to California, depending on species
high intertidal
Members of this genus form extensive carpets of tiny, green, unbranched tubes arising from a basal green cushion. Precise identification is difficult without careful microscopic examination because *Blidingia* spp. are easily confused with one another, as well as other tiny, green, blade-like seaweeds such as *Prasiola meridionalis* (SW5). One species, *Blidingia minima* var. *vexata*, is dark green to olive-green, with distinctive brownish to black wart-like protuberances on the surface caused by a fungal infection.
Laura Point, Mayne Island, s. BC

SW7. ▶TINY GREEN BALLS
Collinsiella tuberculata
to 3 mm (0.2 in) in diameter
s. Alaska to c. California
high intertidal
Easily overlooked, these tiny green spheres can form extensive carpets on flat rock outcrops or boulders, particularly where there is slight water accumulation. Recent research demonstrates that this phase of the species, as shown in the photograph, alternates with a shell-boring unicellular 'Codiolum' phase, indicating that it has a heteromorphic (taking different forms at different stages) life history. The 'Codiolum' phase is the diploid, sporophyte generation (having two sets of chromosomes and producing spores) in the life history.
Shushartie Bay, n. Vancouver Island, c. BC

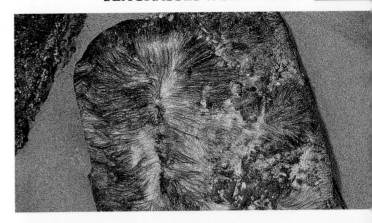

SW8. GREEN HAIR, Hanic's green barrels
Urospora penicilliformis, *Urospora mirabilis*, *Hormiscia penicilliformis*
to 30 cm (12 in) long
n. Alaska to s. California, cosmopolitan in temperate waters, Japan, Arctic
Ocean, n. Atlantic Ocean, s. Australia
high intertidal
This species grows on logs as well as rock. A total of five *Urospora* species
have been reported along Pacific Northwest coasts; however, some have
very restricted geographical distribution or are doubtfully distinct. Further
study is required. Also complicating the issue are several other similar-
looking species.
God's Pocket Resort, Hurst Island, c. BC

SW9. SEA MOSS, green tuft, green dome seaweed
***Cladophora* sp.**
to 6 cm (2.5 in) long
s. Alaska to n. Mexico
high to mid-intertidal
This species forms a characteristic moss-like turf on rocky shores. Seven
other *Cladophora* species inhabit Pacific Northwest waters. Microscopic
examination is required to distinguish them.
Frank Island, w. Vancouver Island, s. BC

SW10. GREEN EXCELSIOR
***Chaetomorpha* sp.**
to 30 cm (12 in) long
c. BC to n. Mexico
high to mid-intertidal
This species' very "stringy" texture is due to the large cells that constitute
the unbranched filaments. Eight *Chaetomorpha* species have been reported
from the Pacific Northwest. Further detailed research is required to verify
their validity.
Bremner Islet, Burnett Bay, c. BC

SW11. CORNROW SEA LETTUCE, green string lettuce, tubeweed, tube
weed, sea hair, hair weed, link confetti, sea felt
Ulva intestinalis, *Enteromorpha intestinalis* (Note: the genus *Enteromorpha*
is no longer recognized as distinct from *Ulva*)
to 20 cm (8 in) long
to 6 mm (0.3 in) tube diameter
n. Alaska to Mexico, cosmopolitan along temperate coasts
intertidal to subtidal
This alga forms long, typically unbranched hollow tubes, which can
become contorted, constricted or occasionally flattened. Often associated
with fresh-water runoff channels, it is a preferred food for the sea slater
(AR24).
Frank Island, w. Vancouver Island, s. BC

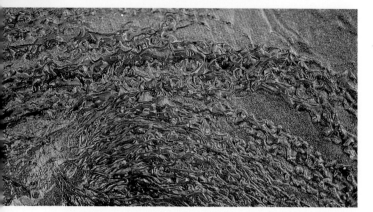

SW12. ▶FLAT-TUBE SEA LETTUCE
Ulva linza, Enteromorpha linza
to 20 cm (8 in) long, 10 cm (4 in) wide
Alaska to Mexico, Chile, s. Australia, n. Atlantic
intertidal to subtidal
This sea lettuce forms a hollow tube near the base and then flattens out into a sheet that is two cell layers thick. Microscopic examination is required to see this.
Ucluth Peninsula, w. Vancouver Island, s. BC

Mid-Intertidal

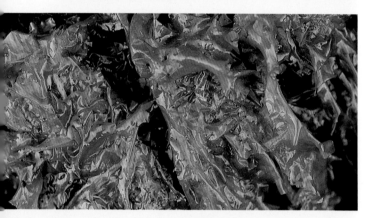

SW13. SEA LETTUCES
Ulva **spp., including** *Ulva lactuca* (*Ulva fenestrata* is no longer considered to be a Pacific Northwest inhabitant)
to 1 m (39 in) long
Japan, Kamchatka, n. Alaska to n. Mexico
mid-intertidal to shallow subtidal
Summer blooms of various green algae, including sea lettuce, often dominate shallow, sheltered bays. Sea lettuces are edible. The holes in the blade of *Ulva lactuca* are natural and not the result of invertebrate grazing. A recent molecular study of sea lettuces recognized a total of 11 Pacific Northwest species.
Ucluth Peninsula, w. Vancouver Island, s. BC

SW14. GREEN ROPE, tangle weed
Acrosiphonia coalita, Spongomorpha coalita, Acrosiphonia mertensii, Chlorochytrium inclusum
to 46 cm (18 in) long
n. Alaska to s. California
mid- to low intertidal
When handled, this alga feels like knotted nylon fishing line that has become badly snarled. It has a heteromorphic life history: the plant shown in the photograph is the large, gamete-producing stage, which alternates with a single-celled, spore-producing stage known as the 'Chlorochytrium' or 'Codiolum' phase. Intriguingly, this single-celled stage lives inside some red algae, such as the various *Mazzaella* species.
The Pacific Northwest is home to six other *Acrosiphonia* species.
Bremner Islet, Burnett Bay, c. BC

Low Intertidal

SW15. SEA FERN, green sea fern
Bryopsis **sp.**, probably *Bryopsis corticulans*
to 15 cm (6 in) long
s. BC to c. Mexico
low intertidal to shallow subtidal
Two *Bryopsis* species occur in the Pacific Northwest, and microscopic examination is required to tell them apart. Most common and easily observed in early spring, the two are readily recognized by their feathery appearance. A close-up view of this species' characteristic branching is shown in photograph B.
A Stanley Park, Burrard Inlet, s. BC
B Dixon Island, Barkley Sound, s. BC. Michael Hawkes photograph

SW16. SEA STAGHORN, green sea velvet, felty fingers, finger sponge weed, sponge weed

Codium fragile

to 40 cm (16 in) long

s. Alaska to n. Mexico

low intertidal to shallow subtidal

Though superficially very sponge-like, this species is definitely an alga! Certain tiny species of bubble shells, such as Hedgpeth's sea hare (MC289), ingest the chloroplasts (organelles containing chlorophyll) from this plant and incorporate them into their tissues—and amazingly, photosynthesis continues for a brief time. A subspecies of *Codium fragile* was accidentally introduced to the east coast of the United States from Japan. Spreading easily via asexual reproduction, it has become quite invasive and caused severe economic problems because of its tendency to disturb shellfish beds. The reddish tinge visible in the photograph is a filamentous red seaweed.

Slip Point, Olympic coast, n. Washington

SW17. SPONGY CUSHION, green spongy cushion, green cushion weed

Codium setchellii

to 25 cm (10 in) across, 2 cm (0.8 in) thick

n. Alaska to n. Mexico

low intertidal to shallow subtidal

This alga is a thick, dark green, almost black species. To the uninitiated, it looks and feels more like a sponge than an alga.

The very similar ▶northern spongy cushion, *Codium ritteri*, has been reported in northern BC and once from Botanical Beach on the southwest coast of Vancouver Island, BC.

Sutton Islets, Egmont, s. BC

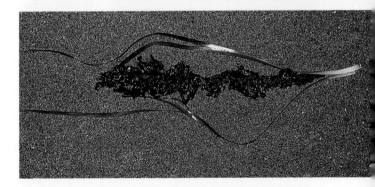

SW18. EPIPHYTIC SEA LETTUCE

Kornmannia leptoderma, *Monostroma zostericola*, *Kornmannia zostericola*

to 5 cm (2 in) long

Japan, n. Alaska to s. California; Arctic Ocean, North Atlantic Ocean

low intertidal to shallow subtidal

Visible as small, thin blades, usually ragged in outline, this alga most often grows epiphytically, and is most noticeable on *Zostera marina* (SW2), *Phyllospadix* spp. (SW4), *Fucus gardneri* (SW23) and *Halosaccion glandiforme* (SW80). This seaweed is named in honour of Peter Kornmann, a marine botanist who worked in Helgoland, Germany, and did much to clarify our understanding of seaweed life histories.

Ucluth Peninsula, w. Vancouver Island, s. BC

Subtidal

SW19. SEA PEARLS, green sea grape, sea bottle

Derbesia marina, *Halicystis ovalis*

to 5 cm (2 in) long (filamentous phase)

to 1 cm (0.3 in) in diameter (spherical 'Halicystis' phase)

n. Alaska to n. Mexico

low intertidal to 20 m (66 ft)

In this species, a filamentous, spore-producing phase (photograph A) alternates with a giant, single-celled, gamete-producing stage (photograph B). Whereas the latter phase ('Halicystis') is readily recognized, the former (sporophyte) may be easily confused with other small filamentous green algae. Indeed, early algal taxonomists believed two species were involved.

A Bamfield, w. Vancouver Island, s. BC. Michael Hawkes photograph

B Moore Point, Francis Peninsula, s. BC

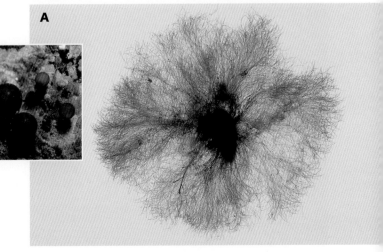

YELLOW-GREEN ALGAE *Phylum TRIBOPHYTA*

SW20. BLACK FELT MAT
***Vaucheria* spp.**
indeterminate, irregular size
BC to c. California
intertidal
Four species in the Pacific Northwest form mats in salt marshes and mudflats. Microscopic examination is required to identify the various species—a task that is beyond the interest and patience level of most readers.
Grice Bay, Tofino, s. BC

BROWN ALGAE *Phylum OCHROPHYTA*

(Class Phaeophyceae)

Recent investigations of plant and plant-like organisms using DNA data have altered our understanding of their relationships and therefore their classification at the highest levels. The brown algae, previously treated as *Phylum Phaeophyta*, are now Class Phaeophyceae in the *Phylum Ochrophyta*.

The golden-brown pigment fucoxanthin masks the green of chlorophyll. Consequently brown algae range in colour from yellow through golden brown to almost black. Energy required by these organisms is stored as a polysaccharide called laminarin. Brown algal cell walls are made up of cellulose, which is often combined with fucans or alginates. This provides structural flexibility and prevents rapid drying.

All of the approximately 2,000 species of brown algae are multicellular. The greatest diversity occurs in cool, temperate marine waters: 150 or more species inhabit the Pacific Northwest, the centre of diversity for kelps, such as *Macrocystis integrifolia* (SW59), shown in the photograph. Two kelps in particular, *Nereocystis luetkeana* (SW60) and *Macrocystis integrifolia* (SW59), are very important components of nearshore, rocky coastal ecosystems. All kelps are brown algae but not all brown algae are kelps—a fact that has led to some species being incorrectly named kelp.

High Intertidal

SW21. BROWN TUFT, navel-lint algae
a variety of species within the genera ***Ectocarpus, Feldmannia, Hincksia and Pilayella,* among others**
to 3 cm (1.3 in) long
Alaska to n. Mexico
high intertidal to subtidal
Many small, filamentous brown algae look like fuzzy growths when viewed with the naked eye. Detailed microscopic examination of vegetative and/or reproductive features of the specimen is required for identification.
Stanley Park, Burrard Inlet, s. BC

SW22. SKINNY ROCKWEED
Fucus **sp.?**
at least 18 cm (7 in) long
BC
intertidal
The status of this peculiar, narrow form of rockweed, found in the vicinity of Newcastle Island and Texada Island in southern BC, is currently under investigation. Indeed, it may actually be a species of *Silvetia*, a genus associated with more southern latitudes such as California. Skinny rockweed occurs lower in the intertidal than *Fucus gardneri* (SW23) and is reproductive earlier in the year. Also shown in the photograph is *Ulva* sp.
Newcastle Island, Nanaimo, s. BC. Michael Hawkes photograph

SW23. ROCKWEED, rock weed, common brown rockweed, bladderwrack, bladder wrack, popping wrack, popweed
Fucus gardneri has been synonomized by some scientists with the Atlantic species
Fucus distichus, Fucus evanescens
to 25 cm (10 in) long
n. Alaska to s. California
high to mid-intertidal
Perhaps the most familiar Pacific Northwest brown alga, rockweed usually dominates sheltered shorelines, where it characteristically forms a dense intertidal band. The "popper" swellings, so popular with youthful beachcombers, contain reproductive structures (photograph B) that produce eggs and sperm. Photograph A features immature specimens.
A God's Pocket Resort, Hurst Island, c. BC
B Georgina Point, Mayne Island, s. BC

SW24. LITTLE ROCKWEED, dwarf rockweed, small rock weed, spindle-shaped rockweed
Pelvetiopsis limitata
to 15 cm (6 in) long
c. BC to s. California
high intertidal
This species lacks the distinctive midrib of *Fucus gardneri* (SW23) and is restricted to rocky shorelines along wave-exposed outer coasts. It is often found growing in association with the yellow-green turf formed by *Mazzaella parksii* (SW72).
Frank Island, w. Vancouver Island, s. BC

SW25. DARK SEA TUBES, twisted soda straws
Melanosiphon intestinalis, Myelophycus intestinalis
to 15 cm (6 in) long
Japan, Siberia, n. Alaska to n. Mexico, n. Atlantic Ocean
high to mid-intertidal
This species is seasonal, making an appearance in the late winter to early spring, typically on coasts sheltered from direct wave action. Frequently found at the edges of tidepools, it often grows in association with *Petalonia fascia* (SW26) and *Scytosiphon lomentaria* (SW31).
Ucluth Peninsula, w. Vancouver Island, s. BC

SW26. FALSE KELP, sea petals
Petalonia fascia, Petalonia debilis, Ralfsia californica
to 30 cm (12 in) long, typically much shorter
Korea, Japan, Siberia, n. Alaska to n. Mexico, Chile, n. Atlantic Ocean
high to mid-intertidal
Thin blades appear in the late winter to early spring along shores sheltered from direct wave action. It is often associated with *Melanosiphon intestinalis* (SW25), but this brown alga also frequently attaches to and grows on *Zostera marina* (SW2) and surfgrasses (SW4), as shown in the photograph. This is an epiphytic relationship, in which the attaching organism causes no harm to the host.
Bamfield, w. Vancouver Island, s. BC. Michael Hawkes photograph

SW27. SEA CAULIFLOWER, cauliflower seaweed, brain seaweed, golden spongy cushion, sea potato
Leathesia difformis, Leathesia nana
to 7.5 cm (3 in) across, rarely larger
Korea, Japan, Siberia, n. Alaska to n. Mexico, Chile, New Zealand, Australia, s. Africa, n. Atlantic Ocean
high to mid-intertidal
This brown alga looks like *Colpomenia peregrina* (SW28), particularly when young. The thicker, convoluted, mucilaginous wall of *Leathesia difformis* contrasts with the thin, smooth outer layer of both *Colpomenia peregrina* and *Colpomenia bullosa*. Tear a piece and feel the difference. If it is slimy, it is sea cauliflower.
Clarke Island, Barkley Sound, s. BC. Michael Hawkes photograph

Mid-Intertidal

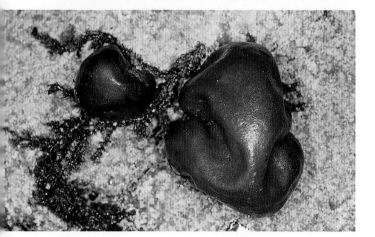

SW28. ►ROUND BROWN BAG
Colpomenia peregrina
to 12 cm (5 in) across
Japan, n. Alaska to s. California, New Zealand, Australia, n. Atlantic Ocean
mid-intertidal to shallow subtidal
Hollow and somewhat similar to *Leathesia difformis* (SW27), this brown alga occurs singly, is more or less spherical and usually grows much larger. It also attaches to the substrate with a small base. Small clusters of colourless hairs festoon this species.
A similar species is the oyster thief, *Colpomenia bullosa*, which has a broad, contorted base.
Ucluth Peninsula, w. Vancouver Island, s. BC

SW29. STUDDED SEA BALLOON
Soranthera ulvoidea
to 7 cm (2.8 in) across
Siberia, n. Alaska to n. Mexico
mid- to low intertidal
Typically, this brown alga grows epiphytically on *Neorhodomela larix* (SW77) and *Odonthalia floccosa* (SW115). This species is a hollow sac, and if one holds it in front of a bright light, the characteristic dark spots covering its surface are obvious. These features distinguish *Soranthera ulvoidea* from both *Colpomenia* species.
Cape Beale, Barkley Sound, s. BC. Michael Hawkes photograph

SW30. FIR NEEDLE, fir branch, sea fir, thickly leaved rockweed
***Analipus japonicus**, Heterochordaria abietina*
to 35 cm (14 in) long
Korea, Japan, Kuril Islands, n. Alaska to c. California
mid- to low intertidal
Look for this species along rocky shores directly exposed to Pacific surge.
The upright alga grows from an extensive basal crust that acts as the
overwintering stage. Whereas the crust may survive for several years, the
more obvious erect growths are ephemeral, lasting only part of a year. In
Japan this alga is called *matsumo* and is an important culinary item.
Wizard Islet, Barkley Sound, s. BC. Michael Hawkes photograph

SW31. WHIP TUBE, leather tube, soda straws
Scytosiphon lomentaria (*Scytosiphon simplicissimus* was proposed as a
substitute name for this alga, but *Scytosiphon lomentaria* was recently
confirmed as the correct one)
to 50 cm (20 in) long, typically much shorter
Korea, Japan, Siberia, n. Alaska to n. Mexico, n. Atlantic Ocean
mid- to low intertidal
Hollow tubes with distinctive sausage-like constrictions make this species
easy to identify. In Japan it is a soup ingredient. This brown alga has a
heteromorphic life history (taking different forms at different stages)
involving alternate crusts resembling *Ralfsia fungiformis* (SW37) or other
tiny structures called microthalli.
A second smaller species without constrictions, ▶southern whip tube,
Scytosiphon dotyi, lives from s. Oregon to n. Mexico. It is a winter annual and
is restricted to the high intertidal zone.
Frank Island, w. Vancouver Island, s. BC

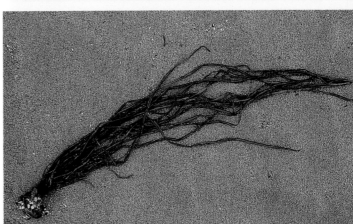

SW32. SEA PALM, sea palm kelp, palm kelp
Postelsia palmaeformis
to 60 cm (24 in) tall
c. BC to c. California
mid- to low intertidal
This annual kelp is restricted to the most wave-exposed headlands along
the outer coast. Wave impacts rip mussels and barnacles off the rocks,
preventing them from competing with the sea palm for space. Arguably
this is *the* most spectacular kelp! But be careful when observing it, as you
are vulnerable to incoming waves.
Frank Island, w. Vancouver Island, s. BC

SW33. SEA CABBAGE, sea cabbage kelp
***Hedophyllum sessile**, Hedophyllum subsessile*
to 1 m (39 in) long
n. Alaska to c. California
mid- to low intertidal
This is the only kelp that lacks a stipe (stem-like structure). Young plants
have a strap-shaped blade, whereas older plants develop thick, leathery
blades that are bullate (blistered) near the base and torn toward the
end. Individuals growing in more sheltered areas are usually shorter and
highly corrugated; those in wave-pounded locales are usually longer and
smoother.
Tongue Point, Olympic coast, n. Washington

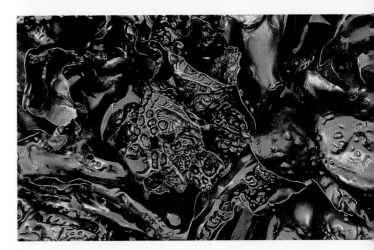

SW34. FEATHER BOA KELP, feather-boa kelp, feather boa
Egregia menziesii, *Egregia laevigata*
to 10 m (35 ft) long
n. BC to Baja, n. Mexico
low intertidal to shallow subtidal, along moderately exposed coasts
This kelp's resemblance to a woman's fashion accessory from a bygone era inspired its common moniker. The scientific name, in part, honours Archibald Menzies, Captain George Vancouver's surgeon and naturalist, who found it. Many small gas-filled floats located along the fronds of this massive species lift it off the bottom, creating a sheltering canopy for many creatures.
Ucluth Peninsula, w. Vancouver Island, s. BC

SW35. NARROW-WINGED KELP, winged kelp, long-bladed alaria
Alaria nana
to 1 m (39 in) long
Alaska to California
mid- to low intertidal
The various winged kelps are characterized in mature specimens by a double row of sporophylls ("wings") arising from the stipe at the base of the blade. This species prefers exposed, rocky shores and, as a result, often has a ragged end.
The ▶float-bearing winged kelp, *Alaria fistulosa*, is a subtidal Alaskan species, distinguished by a hollow mid-rib that contains gas-filled chambers.
Bremner Islet, Burnett Bay, c. BC

SW36. SAND-SCOURED FALSE KELP
Phaeostrophion irregulare
to 40 cm (16 in) long, usually much shorter
from an extensive crustose base to 20 cm (8 in) in diameter
n. Alaska to s. California
mid- to low intertidal
Typically this species grows attached to rocky outcrops adjacent to sandy, surf-swept beaches and consequently may be subjected to seasonal sand-burial. The ragged ends of its blades are the result of life in such an environment.
Frank Island, w. Vancouver Island, s. BC. Jeff Mondragon photograph

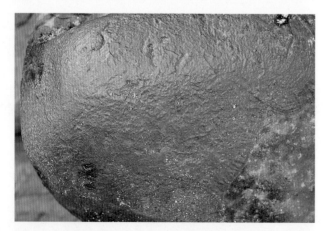

SW37. ▶FUNGIFORM TAR SPOT ALGA, tar spot alga, tar spot seaweed, tar spot, sea fungus
Ralfsia fungiformis
to 20 cm (8 in) across
Korea, Japan, Siberia, n. Alaska to n. California, n. Atlantic Ocean
mid-intertidal to shallow subtidal
The specific name *fungiformis* refers to the prominently overlapping lobes that make this crust resemble some bracket fungi. *Ralfsia*-like crusts occur in the life histories of some other brown algae such as *Petalonia fascia* (SW26) and *Scytosiphon lomentaria* (SW31).
Ucluth Peninsula, w. Vancouver Island, s. BC

Low Intertidal

SW38. BROAD-WINGED KELP, ribbon kelp, angel wing kelp, wing kelp, ribbed kelp, edible kelp
Alaria marginata
to 3 m (10 ft) long
c. Alaska to c. California
low intertidal to 8 m (26 ft)
This species is distinguished from *Alaria nana* (SW35) by its broader sporophylls (wing-like blades near the base of the main structure). Known as "North American Wakame" (wakame is a Japanese kelp, *Undaria pinnatifida*), this alga is a popular consumable—fresh, dried or cooked. Very similar is the ▶hairy-winged kelp, *Alaria taeniata*, which has tufts of tiny hairs on its blade. A total of seven *Alaria* species exist in the Pacific Northwest.
Slip Point, Olympic coast, n. Washington

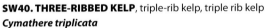

SW39. SEERSUCKER KELP, seersucker, five-ribbed kelp, five-rib kelp, ribbed kelp, rib kelp
Costaria costata
to 3 m (10 ft) long
Korea, Japan, Siberia, n. Alaska to c. California
low intertidal to shallow subtidal
This kelp is often very bullate (blistered) and has five distinct ribs along its length. Intriguingly, its form and shape is influenced by the wave activity in its surroundings. Specimens inhabiting rocky shores exposed to heavy surf are generally narrow and thick (photograph A), whereas those in quieter locales tend to be broad and thin (photograph B). Younger plants also tend to be narrow.
A Ucluth Peninsula, w. Vancouver Island, s. BC
B Moore Point, Francis Peninsula, s. BC

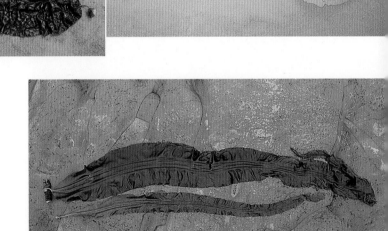
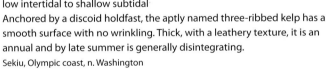

SW40. THREE-RIBBED KELP, triple-rib kelp, triple rib kelp
Cymathere triplicata
to 4 m (13 ft) long
n. Alaska to n. Washington
low intertidal to shallow subtidal
Anchored by a discoid holdfast, the aptly named three-ribbed kelp has a smooth surface with no wrinkling. Thick, with a leathery texture, it is an annual and by late summer is generally disintegrating.
Sekiu, Olympic coast, n. Washington

SW41. ▶DARK-BROWN WRACK KELP
Laminaria bongardiana, formerly *Laminaria groenlandica*, a name that refers to another species from the Atlantic Ocean
to 2 m (6.6 ft) long
n. Alaska to c. California
low intertidal to high subtidal
Although this species has a somewhat flattened stipe (stem-like structure), is darker and often lives in more exposed locales than *Laminaria saccharina* (SW42), only microscopic examination can definitively distinguish the two. Special mucilage ducts are present in the stipe of *Laminaria bongardiana* but not in *Laminaria saccharina*.
Point George, Shaw Island, n. Washington. Michael Hawkes photograph

SW42. SUGAR WRACK KELP, sugar wrack, sugar kelp, sea belt
Laminaria saccharina
to 3 m (10 ft) long, stipe usually shorter than 20 cm (8 in)
Siberia, n. Alaska to s. California, Arctic Ocean, n. Atlantic Ocean
low intertidal to shallow subtidal
Sugar wrack kelp has a shorter, more cylindrical stipe (stem-like structure) and is somewhat lighter in colour and often more ruffled than *Laminaria bongardiana* (SW41). Microscopic examination for the presence or absence of mucilage ducts in the stipe is required to distinguish the two species.
Point Cowan, Howe Sound, s. BC

SW43. SPLIT KELP, split blade kelp
Laminaria setchellii
to 1.5 m (5 ft) long
c. Alaska to n. Mexico
low intertidal to shallow subtidal
Found on exposed outer coasts, this kelp has a rigid but flexible stipe (stem-like structure) and a split blade that droops when exposed at low tide. Photograph A shows a bed of split kelp and photograph B illustrates one specimen in detail. Microscopic examination of blade anatomy is required to distinguish split kelp from northern split kelp, *Laminaria dentigera*, which occurs in northern BC and Alaska.
A Seal Rock, Oregon. Michael Hawkes photograph
B Frank Island, w. Vancouver Island, s. BC

SW44. DENSE-CLUMPED KELP, dense clumped laminarian
Laminaria sinclairii
to 1 m (39 in) long
c. BC to s. California
low intertidal to shallow subtidal
Two characteristic features of this species are the numerous blades arising from a single holdfast and its persistence on surf-exposed rocks typically associated with sand scour. When viewed under a microscope, this kelp has mucilage ducts in the stipe, whereas *Laminaria longipes* lacks them. The very similar ▶northern dense-clumped kelp, *Laminaria longipes*, is primarily an Alaskan species, with an isolated population off San Juan Island, n. Washington. This report requires verification.
Seal Rock, Oregon. Michael Hawkes photograph

SW45. SUCTION-CUP KELP
Laminaria yezoensis
to 2 m (6.6 ft) long
Japan, Siberia, n. Alaska to c. BC
low intertidal to shallow subtidal
The holdfast, featured in the photograph of this rugged perennial species, is a characteristic suction cup-like disc. Growing subtidally in sheltered areas, this kelp has not been reported south of northern BC.
Another Pacific Northwest species, ▶annual suction-cup kelp, *Laminaria ephemera*, has a similar holdfast but is annual, rather delicate and uncommon.
God's Pocket Resort, Hurst Island, c. BC

SW46. BROAD-RIB KELP, broad rib kelp, sea spatula
Pleurophycus gardneri
to 1.5 m (5 ft) long
n. Alaska to s. California
low intertidal to 30 m (100 ft)—in southern part of its range
This kelp is a deciduous perennial species (as are most kelps) in which the stipe (stem-like structure) and holdfast persist for some years. The blade portion erodes away over the winter, regrowing from the meristem (apex of stipe) the following season. Darker patches visible on the blade in late summer are spore-producing sites. The wide mid-rib is characteristic of this kelp.

Eagle Point, San Juan Island, n. Washington

SW47. STRAP KELP
Lessoniopsis littoralis
to 2 m (6.6 ft) long
c. Alaska to c. California
extreme low intertidal to shallow subtidal
This sturdy kelp is restricted to outer coasts directly exposed to Pacific surge. Its massive holdfast and stipes (stem-like structures) become tough and wood-like. Some old individuals may have as many as 500 blades! Be careful when examining this kelp, because there is a very real danger of being washed off the rocks by heavy surf.

Frank Island, w. Vancouver Island, s. BC

SW48. ▶NET-OF-CORDS KELP
Dictyoneurum californicum
to 1 m (39 in) long
s. BC, Oregon, n. California to s. California
extreme low intertidal to 10 m (33 ft)
A few isolated BC populations of this primarily California species exist along the west coast of Vancouver Island, south of Bamfield. Blades of this kelp look similar to the fronds of both giant kelps—*Macrocystis integrifolia* (SW59) and *Macrocystis pyrifera*—but are thicker and arise from a very short, usually rhizome-like stipe (stem).

Monterey, c. California. Michael Hawkes photograph

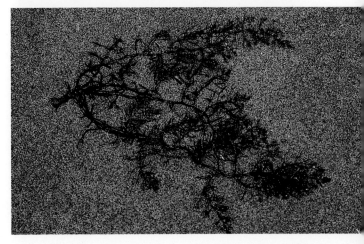

SW49. NORTHERN BLADDER CHAIN, bladder leaf, chain bladder
Cystoseira geminata
to 8 m (26 ft) long, but usually much shorter
Japan, Kuril Islands, n. Alaska to n. Oregon
low intertidal to shallow subtidal
Each tiny, individual oval float usually has a pointed tip on it that distinguishes this brown alga from the superficially similar *Sargassum muticum* (SW51).

Laura Point, Mayne Island, s. BC

SW50. BLADDER CHAIN
Cystoseira osmundacea, *Cystoseira expansa*
to 8 m (26 ft) long
n. Oregon to n. Mexico
low intertidal to shallow subtidal
This brown alga has a woody, erect stipe (stem-like structure) that is triangular in cross-section. Its tiny floats are in regular chains of five or more, and the one at the end has a pointed tip. The holdfast and woody stipe usually overwinter, but the upper portions erode due to severe seasonal conditions.
Point Lobos, c. California. Michael Hawkes photograph

SW51. WIREWEED, sargassum, Japanese seaweed, Japanese weed, Jap weed
Sargassum muticum
to 2 m (6.6 ft) long
s. Alaska to n. Mexico
low intertidal to 6 m (20 ft)
This exotic species was accidentally introduced on oyster spat from Japan

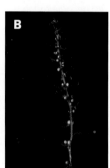

in the 1930s. A very successful "Japanese import," it is difficult to believe this alga is not native given its abundance in many locales. It undoubtedly has affected the distribution of native seaweed species. *Sargassum muticum* has also been accidentally introduced in the English Channel. The close-up of a young specimen, shown in photograph B, nicely features the species' tiny gas-filled floats.
A Ucluth Peninsula, w. Vancouver Island, s. BC
B Moore Point, Francis Peninsula, s. BC

SW52. SEA CHIP
Coilodesme californica
to 40 cm (16 in) long
c. Alaska to n. Mexico
low intertidal to shallow subtidal
Typically this brown alga grows attached to *Cystoseira geminata* (SW49), *Cystoseira osmundacea* (SW50) or *Sargassum muticum* (SW51), making it difficult to notice (three flattened pale brown sacs in photograph). It can also adhere directly to solid rock substrate. One to several fragile, flattened sacs can arise from one holdfast.
Dinner Point, Mayne Island, s. BC

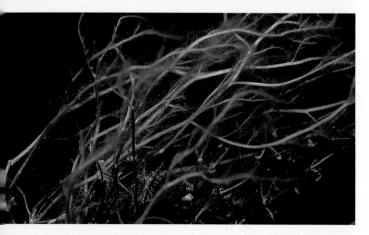

SW53. ▶HAIRY BROWN SEAWEED
Haplogloia andersonii
to 50 cm (20 in) long
Alaska to Mexico
lower intertidal
A spring annual, this seaweed is distinguished by hair-like filaments and a soft, slimy texture. It is usually profusely branched. South of Alaska, this species is the only common branched, mucilaginous species of brown alga.
God's Pocket Resort, Hurst Island, c. BC

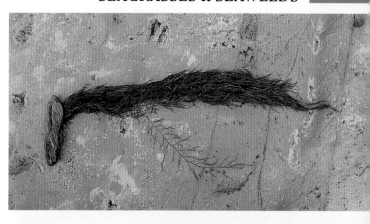

SW54. WIRY ACID WEED, witch's hair, landlady's wig, crisp color changer

Desmarestia aculeata, *Desmarestia intermedia*

to 2 m (6.6 ft) long

Siberia, n. Alaska to s. Oregon, n. Atlantic Ocean

low intertidal to shallow subtidal

Close inspection shows that this brown alga has an alternate branching pattern, whereas the similar-looking *Desmarestia viridis* (SW55) is oppositely branched. The various *Desmarestia* species contain sulphuric acid in their cells, probably as a defence against invertebrate grazers, especially sea urchins. The large plants—spring–summer annuals—are the spore-bearing phases that alternate with a microscopic, filamentous, gamete-producing phase. Some experts believe the very similar *Desmarestia latifrons* may be the same species.

Sekiu, Olympic coast, n. Washington

SW55. STRINGY ACID WEED, stringy acid hair

Desmarestia viridis, *Desmarestia media* var. *tenuis*

to 60 cm (24 in) long

Korea, Japan, Siberia, n. Alaska to n. Mexico, Chile, Argentina, n. Atlantic Ocean

low intertidal to shallow subtidal

This brown alga has an opposite branching pattern (see photograph B), which distinguishes it from *Desmarestia aculeata* (SW54). Whether you are collecting seaweeds to eat or as a tool to create beautiful prints, keep all species of *Desmarestia* separate, because the sulphuric acid they contain will destroy other algae.

A Eagle Point, San Juan Island, n. Washington

B Tzartus Island, Barkley Sound, s. BC. Michael Hawkes photograph

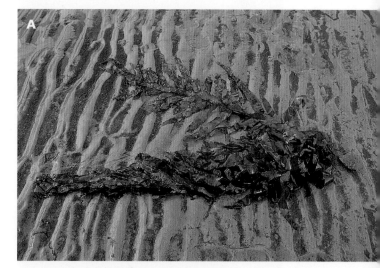

SW56. BROAD ACID WEED

Desmarestia ligulata, *Desmarestia herbacea*

to 3 m (10 ft) long, branches to 5 cm (2 in) wide

Korea, Japan, n. Alaska to n. Mexico, n. Atlantic Ocean

low intertidal to shallow subtidal

Some marine botanists define this brown alga as having branches less than 1 cm (0.3 in) wide and treat those specimens with broader (3–5 cm/1.3–3.3 in) but otherwise very similar branches, as another species, ▶wide acid weed, *Desmarestia munda*. Further study is needed to resolve whether there is one species or two. Photograph B shows close-up detail.

A Ucluth Peninsula, w. Vancouver Island, s. BC

B Bamfield, w. Vancouver Island, s. BC. Michael Hawkes photograph

Subtidal

SW57. OLD GROWTH KELP, walking kelp, pompom kelp, wing-bearing kelp, palm kelp
Pterygophora californica
to 2.3 m (7.6 ft) long
c. Alaska to n. Mexico
extreme low intertidal to 24 m (80 ft)
The strong, flexible stipe of old growth kelp is well adapted for either a surf-swept or high-current habitat. If individuals are attached to small boulders or large cobble, they can "walk" along the bottom in strong surf. This perennial species has annual growth increments in the stipe (stem-like structure) (photograph C), and studies of these have indicated a life span of at least 25 years, making old growth kelp one of the longest-living kelps.
A C Laura Point, Mayne Island, s. BC
B Plumper Islands, Weynton Passage, c. BC

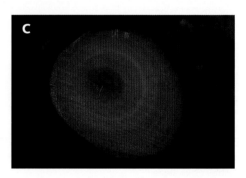

SW58. PALM KELP, southern sea palm, forked kelp
Eisenia arborea
to 2 m (6.5 ft) long
n. BC, s. California to n. Mexico
extreme low intertidal to 3 m (10 ft)
Until the 1950s, this species was not known north of California. Since then, populations have been recorded along the west coast of Vancouver Island and the Queen Charlotte Islands (Haida Gwaii). Increased search effort is definitely a contributing factor, but why is this kelp apparently absent from Washington or Oregon? Photograph C shows the juvenile, which looks very different from the adult.
A B Rainy Bay, Barkley Sound, s. BC
C Brooks Peninsula, w. Vancouver Island, c. BC

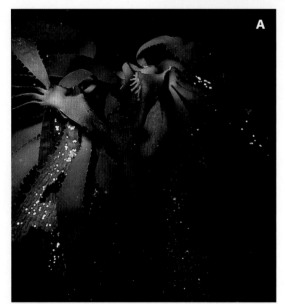

SW59. SMALL GIANT KELP, northern giant kelp, giant perennial kelp
Macrocystis integrifolia

to 30 m (100 ft) long
c. Alaska to c. California, west coast of s. America
extreme low intertidal to 15 m (50 ft)

Small giant kelp forms extensive underwater forests in nearshore coastal ecosystems, where it plays an important role as a major primary producer as well as providing shelter for young fish, invertebrates and marine mammals such as sea otters and juvenile gray whales. Photograph C illustrates a growing tip and photograph D depicts the creeping rhizome-shaped structure of the holdfast.

Populations of the very similar giant kelp, *Macrocystis pyrifera*, common and extensively harvested in California, are suspected to occur in BC and Alaska. Its holdfast is a tall, cone-shaped structure up to 1 m (39 in) across.

A B D Ucluth Peninsula, w. Vancouver Island, s. BC
C Wizard Islet, Barkley Sound, s. BC. Michael Hawkes photograph

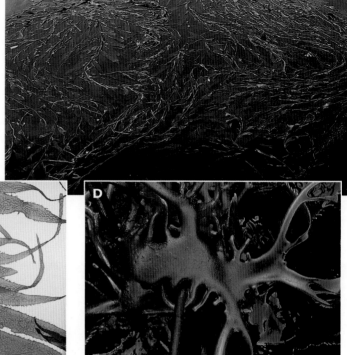

SW60. BULL KELP, bullwhip kelp, bullwhip, ribbon kelp
Nereocystis luetkeana

to 36 m (118 ft) long
n. Alaska to s. California
shallow subtidal to 20 m (65 ft)

This annual seaweed is very fast growing and reaches its full size by June. In early spring, young bull kelp may establish intertidally but do not survive there. This species is a vital component of the coastal ecosystem, forming important habitat for many other seaweeds and animals. The large, flask-shaped pneumatocyst (float) contains carbon monoxide and was used by coastal First Peoples as a storage container for water and eulachon (fish) oil. Kelp pickles can also be made from the pneumatocyst and stipe (stem-like structure).

A Anderson Bay, Texada Island, s. BC
B Plumper Islands, Weynton Passage, c. BC.
C Friday Harbor, San Juan Island, n. Washington

SW61. MERMAID'S GLOVES
Dictyota binghamiae
to 40 cm (16 in) long, typically much shorter in the northern portion of its distribution
Japan, n. BC to n. Mexico
shallow subtidal to 12 m (40 ft)
This delicate alga is most prominent during late winter and early spring. Most species in this genus live in warm temperate and tropical waters.
A God's Pocket Resort, Hurst Island, c. BC
B Dixon Island, Barkley Sound, s. BC. Michael Hawkes photograph

SW62. SEA COLANDER KELP, fringed sieve kelp
Agarum clathratum, *Agarum cribrosum*
to 1.3 m (4 ft) long
Japan, Siberia, n. Alaska to n. Washington
subtidal to 20 m (65 ft)
This kelp has a cylindrical stipe (stem-like structure) that is smooth and lacks any tooth-like projections, a feature that distinguishes it from *Agarum fimbriatum* (SW63). The blades of both species are perforate and tear very easily. Thick *Agarum* kelp beds frustrate the diver naturalist as their broad blades cover many interesting shelter-seeking creatures.
Eagle Point, San Juan Island, n. Washington

SW63. ▶FRINGED SEA COLANDER KELP, fringed sieve kelp
Agarum fimbriatum
to 1.3 m (4 ft) long
s. Alaska to Puget Sound, Washington, s. California and n. Mexico
subtidal to 20 m (65 ft)
This kelp differs only slightly from *Agarum clathratum* (SW62) in that its stipe (stem-like structure) is flattened and has tooth-like projections. Like many other algae, it represents an attachment site for a wide variety of marine invertebrates as well as other algae. Obviously the life span of these "hitchhikers" is defined by that of the host.
Sutton Islets, Egmont, s. BC

DIATOMS *Phylum OCHROPHYTA*

(Class Bacillariophyceae)

SW64. Colonies of single-celled diatoms, held together in a common mucilaginous matrix, can superficially resemble filamentous brown algae (SW21). Some types can be found growing on rock, or epiphytically on other algae, especially *Fucus gardneri* (SW23). These **colonial diatoms** are most prolific and visible in summer, when sunlight is strongest. A thin but noticeable coating on sandy substrate (see burrowing anemone, CN15, photograph B) patrolled by divers is likely formed by single-celled diatoms. Detailed identification of these algae requires microscopic examination.
Stanley Park, Burrard Inlet, s. BC

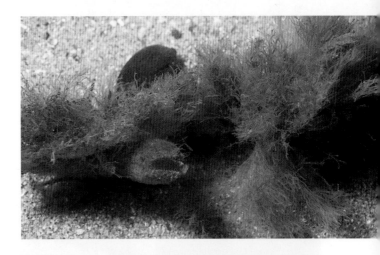

RED ALGAE *Phylum RHODOPHYTA*

Although a majority of these algae are indeed some shade of red, a wide variety of colours from yellow through blue to almost blackish hues are exhibited by various species. This colour variation results from the dominant accessory pigments phycoerythrin (red) and phycocyanin (blue), which mask the blue-green of chlorophyll a. Red algae absorb green, blue and red portions of the light spectrum and store fixed carbon in the form of floridean starch.

Unlike most other algal types, red algae have no motile reproductive stages—a factor that has not hindered their amazing proliferation. The cell walls of some red algae contain the complex polysaccharides agar and carrageenan, which have important commercial applications as emulsifiers and stabilizers in various food and industrial products.

Approximately 90 percent of the nearly 6,000 species worldwide live in the marine environment, and this group contains the deepest-dwelling alga—268 m (884 ft) for one Caribbean species. Approximately 370 Pacific Northwest red algae—many of which have attractive branching forms—are documented. The photograph features an undetermined species.

High Intertidal

SW65. BALD SEA HAIR, black sea hair
Bangia **spp**. (species in the Pacific Northwest remain unresolved; the names *Bangia fuscopurpurea* and *Bangia vermicularis* have sometimes been used)
to 10 cm (4 in) long
Japan, Korea, Siberia, n. Alaska to Costa Rica, n. Atlantic Ocean, southern oceans
high intertidal
The thin, hair-like strands of this red seaweed mock the thinning pates of many male naturalists. At times during the year, complete "baldness" occurs when this gamete-producing stage disappears from the rocks. It alternates with a microscopic, filamentous stage that lives in the calcareous matrix of mollusc shells and barnacle casings. This is a heteromorphic life history (the spore-producing and gamete-generating phases look different).
Sooke, s. Vancouver Island, s. BC. Michael Hawkes photograph

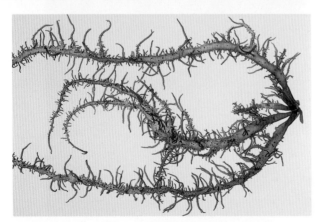

SW66. NORI, laver, including red laver, purple laver, brown laver, yellow laver, wild nori, California nori, black seaweed
***Porphyra* spp**. (approximately 22 difficult-to-separate Pacific Northwest species)
to 3 m (10 ft) long, most species typically 30 cm (12 in)
n. Alaska to n. Mexico, cosmopolitan
high intertidal to shallow subtidal
Nori has a heteromorphic life history. The bladed, gamete-producing phase (pictured) is only one or two cell layers thick and alternates with a microscopic, spore-producing phase that lives in calcareous structures like mollusc shells and barnacle casings. The bladed phase lasts just a few months: some species appear intertidally during the winter, only to disappear when low tides occur during daylight hours in spring. Most species of Nori can be distinguished only by microscopic examination of both vegetative and reproductive structures and determination of chromosome numbers. After Japan, BC has the greatest species diversity for *Porphyra*. Cultivated species in Japan are a multibillion-dollar-per-year industry and are used in the production of Nori, the seaweed wrapping around some types of sushi.
A Georgina Point, Mayne Island, s. BC
B Bremner Islet, Burnett Bay, c. BC
C Cape Beale, Barkley Sound, s. BC. Michael Hawkes photograph

SW67. NAIL BRUSH SEAWEED, nail brush, nailbrush, wire brush alga, brillo-pad seaweed, brillo-pad alga, sea moss
Endocladia muricata
to 8 cm (3.2 in) long
n. Alaska to n. Mexico
high intertidal
When dry, this red seaweed resembles an almost black scrub pad. The wiry, cylindrical branches are covered with short spines, a feature that distinguishes this bushy seaweed from the superficially similar *Gloiopeltis furcata* (SW68).
Friday Harbor, San Juan Island, n. Washington

SW68. ▶RED-BROWN MAT WEED
Gloiopeltis furcata
to 5 cm (2 in) long
Korea, Japan, Kuril Islands, n. Alaska to n. Mexico
high intertidal
Often forming extensive, turf-like mats, this species lives primarily along coasts exposed to direct Pacific surge. The slippery texture when wet and the lack of tiny spines distinguish this red alga from the bushier but somewhat similar *Endocladia muricata* (SW67).
Stanley Park, Burrard Inlet, s. BC

SW69. HAIRY SEAWEED
Cumagloia andersonii
to 90 cm (3 ft) long, typically much shorter
s. Alaska to n. Mexico
high intertidal
This red alga has a soft, slippery texture. It has a heteromorphic life history, with the large, gamete-bearing stage appearing in the early summer. This stage lasts for only a few weeks and alternates with a microscopic, filamentous stage—not shown—that produces spores.
Bamfield, w. Vancouver Island, s. BC. Michael Hawkes photograph

SW70. RUBBER THREADS
Nemalion helminthoides
to 1 m (39 in) long
Japan, n. Alaska to n. Mexico, Australia, New Zealand, n. Atlantic Ocean
high intertidal
This short-lived annual appears in the late spring to early summer, forming spaghetti-like masses on intertidal rocks. The gamete-bearing phase (shown) alternates with a microscopic, filamentous one.
Bamfield, w. Vancouver Island, s. BC. Michael Hawkes photograph

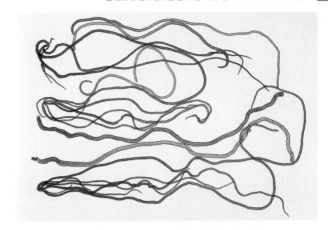

SW71. RED ROCK CRUST, rusty rock
Hildenbrandia **spp**., including *Hildenbrandia rubra, Hildenbrandia occidentalis*
indeterminate, irregular crusts
Alaska to Panama, Galapagos Islands, Atlantic Ocean
high intertidal to subtidal
Only two species in the Pacific Northwest, *Hildenbrandia rubra* and *Hildenbrandia occidentalis,* form red crusts on rock. The former species, illustrated in photograph A, forms thin, rusty red crusts in the high intertidal zone, whereas the latter species (photograph B) forms thicker, reddish black crusts and grows lower down the shore. Both often live where fresh-water runoff drains through the intertidal zone.
A Ucluth Peninsula, w. Vancouver Island, s. BC
B Newcastle Island, Nanaimo, s. BC. Michael Hawkes photograph

SW72. YELLOW SEAWEED, frilly turf seaweed
Mazzaella parksii, Mazzaella cornucopiae, Iridaea cornucopiae, Gigartina cornucopiae
typically to 5 cm (2 in) long
Japan, Kuril Islands, n. Alaska to c. California
high intertidal
A distinctive yellow-green colour and a turf-like growth pattern make this species easy to identify. Its surf-swept habitat should also assist the naturalist in determining its identity.
A total of 11 *Mazzaella* species occur along Pacific Northwest shores.
Frank Island, w. Vancouver Island, s. BC

SW73. BUSHY TURKISH WASHCLOTH
Mastocarpus jardinii, Gigartina agardhii
to 13 cm (5 in) long, 1.5 cm (0.5 in) wide
n. BC to s. California
high intertidal
All species of *Mastocarpus* have heteromorphic life histories. When exposed to air at low tide—often for long periods of time—the blades of this alga become even darker and harder than when it is submerged. Either way, it is a tough meal for grazers.
Frank Island, w. Vancouver Island, s. BC

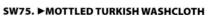

SW74. TURKISH WASHCLOTH / TAR SPOT SEAWEED
Mastocarpus papillatus, blade stage: *Gigartina papillata*; crust stage: *Petrocelis franciscana, Petrocelis middendorffii*
to 20 cm (8 in) long for blade stage
to 13 cm (5 in) across for crust stage
Japan, Siberia, n. Alaska to n. Mexico
high to mid-intertidal
This species is very common on both sheltered and wave-exposed coasts. A bladed, gamete-producing phase (photograph A) alternates with an encrusting, spore-producing phase known as 'Petrocelis' (photograph B). Initially, marine botanists believed them to be separate species, hence the two scientific names.
A Ucluth Peninsula, w. Vancouver Island, s. BC
B Cattle Point, San Juan Island, n. Washington

SW75. ▶MOTTLED TURKISH WASHCLOTH
Mazzaella oregona, *Gigartina heterocarpa, Iridaea heterocarpa, Mazzaella heterocarpa*
to 21 cm (8 in) long
s. Alaska to s. California
high to low intertidal
The oval, rubbery blades may have patches—1–4 mm (0.02–0.15 in) in diameter—of reproductive structures all over their surface, which gives them a distinctive mottled appearance. Look for this species on coasts directly exposed to Pacific surge.
Sekiu, Olympic coast, n Washington

SW76. ▶VERY SLENDER RHODOMELA
Rhodomela tenuissima, *Rhodomela lycopodioides*
to 15 cm (6 in) long
n. Alaska to Oregon
high intertidal
Look for this species in tide pools. It has a soft texture and sticks to paper on drying. *Neorhodomela larix* (SW77) is superficially similar but is stiff and cartilaginous to the touch and does not adhere to paper on drying.
Tongue Point, Olympic coast, n. Washington

SW77. BLACK PINE, black larch
Neorhodomela larix, *Rhodomela larix*
to 30 cm (12 in) long
Japan, Siberia, n. Alaska to n. Mexico
high to mid-intertidal
This red alga resembles a "dreadlocks" hairstyle on the rocks! Its dark brown to black coloration makes it easy to misidentify as a brown seaweed. At times, a dusty brown film—which is actually a layer of diatoms—may coat it; in other instances, *Leathesia difformis* (SW27) may attach to it.
Cattle Point, San Juan Island, n. Washington

SW78. ▶DARK BRANCHING-TUBE SEAWEED
Cryptosiphonia woodii
to 25 cm (10.5 in) long
n. Alaska to s. California
high to mid-intertidal
With a black to brownish colour, this alga does not look much like a red seaweed. However, it has a very distinctive shape and is easy to identify once you get to know it.
Dark branching-tube seaweed was first collected from Vancouver Island.
Dixon Island, Barkley Sound, s. BC. Michael Hawkes photograph

SW79. COARSE SEA LACE
Microcladia borealis
to 40 cm (16 in) long
n. Alaska to s. California
high to mid-intertidal—but low intertidal to subtidal in southern portion of its distribution
Close inspection of this alga reveals the characteristic inwardly curved tips on its branches, which are all located on one side of a primary axis. Sometimes this red alga grows as an epiphyte on various kelps.
Sekiu, Olympic coast, n. Washington

Mid-Intertidal

SW80. SEA SACS, sea sac, salt sacs, salt sac, sea nipples, condom-of-the-sea, deadman's fingers, dead man's fingers
Halosaccion glandiforme, *Halosaccion americanum*
to 30 cm (12 in) long, 4 cm (1.5 in) in diameter
n. Alaska to c. California
mid- to low intertidal
The water-filled sacs of this species look like rubber glove fingers and make wonderful water pistols! This species has a very unusual life history, in which the female, gamete-bearing specimens are microscopic discs, not large, hollow sacs like the male specimens. Diploid, spore-bearing individuals are also hollow sacs. The photograph shows what may be either sac-shaped type.
Sooke, s. Vancouver Island, s. BC. Michael Hawkes photograph

SW81. FILAMENTOUS RED SEAWEEDS

Throughout the Pacific Northwest, from the mid-intertidal and well into recreational diving depths, live a bewildering array (perhaps 60 or more species!) of finely branched, fuzzy-looking red algae. A majority of them reach a maximum size of 15 cm (6 in), and a few may be somewhat longer. Most are difficult to identify without the aid of a microscope.

We suggest that the reader use whatever vision-enhancing devices (a hand lens works well) are available and marvel at the intricate branching patterns of these beautiful seaweeds. They are truly a sight to behold. Photograph D features a finely branched species epiphytic on *Codium fragile* (SW16).

Common genera include: **Antithamnion, Antithamnionella, Callithamnion, Herposiphonia, Hollenbergia, Pterothamnion, Pleonosporium, Polysiphonia, Pterosiphonia** and **Scagelia**.

A Point Defiance, Puget Sound, c. Washington
B Cattle Point, San Juan Island, n. Washington
C Agamemnon Channel, Nelson Island, s. BC
D Dinner Point, Mayne Island, s. BC

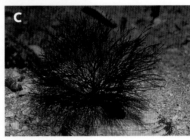

SW82. BEAUTY BUSH

Callithamnion pikeanum
to 20 cm (8 in) long
n. Alaska to s. California
mid-intertidal

Unlike the red algae represented above, this species is easily recognized by its dark colour and woolly appearance, reminiscent of a miniature fir tree lying on its side. Particularly noteworthy is the thickness of its branches, which are often overgrown by a thin coating of brown diatoms.

Frank Island, w. Vancouver Island, s. BC. Michael Hawkes photograph

SW83. NARROW IODINE SEAWEED, narrow bleach weed, iodine seaweed

Grateloupia americana, *Prionitis lanceolata*
to 35 cm (14 in) long
s. Alaska to n. Mexico
mid-intertidal to upper subtidal

Yellow colouration often dominates this red alga, especially in the summer months, when a shortage of nitrates in the surface water can cause a nitrogen deficiency that results in the yellow hue. Both this species and *Prionitis lyallii* (SW84) have a distinctive smell of bleach when they are crushed. This is probably a chemical defence against grazers. Recent unpublished molecular studies suggest that specimens in the local area that have been identified as *Grateloupia americana* may in fact be referable to *Prionitis lyallii* (SW84).

Frank Island, w. Vancouver Island, s. BC

SW84. BROAD IODINE SEAWEED, Lyall's iodine seaweed
Prionitis lyallii
to 35 cm (14 in) long
s. BC to n. Mexico
mid-intertidal to upper subtidal
This red alga is frequently found in tide pools. David Lyall, for whom this species is named, was a medical officer and naturalist for the Royal Navy. In 1858 his services were transferred to the Land Boundary Commission, which was charged with surveying the boundary between Canada and the United States on the west coast. It was during surveys of the Strait of Georgia that he collected this seaweed and sent it to Europe, where it was described by the Irish botanist William H. Harvey. Recent study resulted in the transfer of some Pacific Northwest *Prionitis* species to the genus *Grateloupia*; *Prionitis lyallii* may belong here too, but additional research is required.
Slip Point, Olympic coast, n. Washington

SW85. SEA BRAID, sea comb
Plocamium cartilagineum subsp. ***pacificum***, *Plocamium cartilagineum*, *Plocamium pacificum*, *Plocamium coccineum* var. *pacificum*
to 25 cm (10 in) long
n. Alaska to n. Mexico, Chile, Galapagos Islands, Australia, New Zealand, n. Atlantic Ocean
mid-intertidal to 20 m (65 ft)
Growing singly or in clumps, this red alga does not form mats. Photograph B shows the characteristic branching detail. Search through the profuse stands of this plant: you may see tiny white spots, which are a parasitic red algal species, *Plocamiocolax pulvinata*.

A Georgina Point, Mayne Island, s. BC
B Bamfield, Barkley Sound, s. BC. Michael Hawkes photograph

SW86. CRUSTOSE CORALLINES, pink rock crusts, encrusting coralline algae, rock crusts, mauve coralline algae
Clathromorphum, ***Lithothamnion***, ***Melobesia*** and ***Mesophyllum*** are common genera
indeterminate, irregular size
cosmopolitan, n. Alaska to n. Mexico
intertidal, typically to 30 m (100 ft)
Deposits of calcium carbonate in the cell walls of crustose coralline red seaweeds give them a hard texture. Despite this outer coating, these algae contain chlorophyll and are photosynthetic. Pink rock crusts may coat rocks, shelled animals and even other algae. The numerous species in this group are nearly impossible to identify without microscopic examination. The white spotting noticeable in photograph D indicates reproductive activity. These are the deepest-living algae in the Pacific Northwest.

A Slip Point, Olympic coast, n. Washington
B Annis Point, Kunghit Island, n. BC
C Sooke, s. Vancouver Island, s. BC. Michael Hawkes photograph
D Skyline Marina, Fidalgo Island, n. Washington. Charlie Gibbs photograph

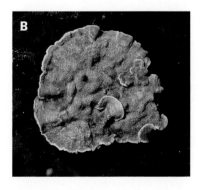

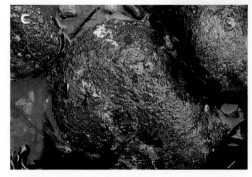

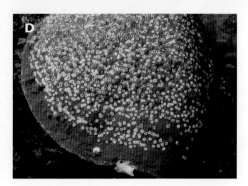

SW87. SURFGRASS CORALLINE SEAWEED, seagrass crust, circular pink alga
Melobesia mediocris
to 5 mm (0.2 in) across
n. BC to n. Mexico
low intertidal to shallow subtidal
This coralline seaweed grows as a disc-like epiphyte on the leaves of *Zostera marina* (SW2) and *Phyllospadix* spp. (SW4). A second species, *Melobesia marginata,* also occurs in the Pacific Northwest and grows epiphytically on various non-calcareous red algae.
Frank Island, w. Vancouver Island, s. BC

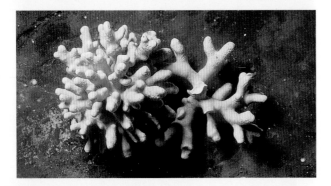

SW88. RHODOLITHS
Rhodoliths are crustose coralline algae that do not attach directly to the substrate but rather roll, in "tumbleweed" fashion, along the bottom until heavy enough to settle—usually forming beds. This worldwide phenomenon has been documented in the Pacific Northwest. Resembling toy jacks, some specimens as large as ping-pong balls have been collected and can establish beds nearly 60 m (200 ft) long. Precise rhodolith classification is incomplete but in Alaska at least, *Phymatolithon calcareum*—a North Atlantic species—is present. Another is potentially a new species similar to *Lithothamnion glaciale.*
Crosse Point, Barkley Sound, s. BC

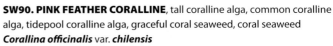

SW89. ARTICULATED CORALLINE ALGAE
In contrast to the crustose corallines (SW86), these are the upright, branching forms that as a group are referred to as the articulated coralline algae. Like their flattened crustose relatives, these vertically oriented species deposit calcium carbonate while retaining chlorophyll and the ability to photosynthesize. The hard "articulates" possess calcified segments called intergenicula, separated by non-calcified regions known as genicula. *Geniculum* means "knee"; consequently, an analogy exists here to our own skeleton, with the calcified segments equating to the bones and the non-calcified regions to the joints. For the articulated coralline algae, this characteristic provides both strength and flexibility to deal with surge and current. Common genera include ***Bossiella, Calliarthron, Corallina*** and ***Serraticardia***.
A Quarry Bay, Nelson Island, s. BC
B C Frank Island, w. Vancouver Island, s. BC

SW90. PINK FEATHER CORALLINE, tall coralline alga, common coralline alga, tidepool coralline alga, graceful coral seaweed, coral seaweed
Corallina officinalis var. ***chilensis***
to 15 cm (6 in) long
Korea, Japan, Siberia, c. Alaska to n. Mexico, Chile
mid-intertidal to shallow subtidal
Look for this coralline particularly on exposed, surf-pounded shores. It is usually very profuse and its large calcified segments are distinctively flattened.
Plumper Islands, Weynton Passage, c. BC

SW91. GRACEFUL CORALLINE, graceful coralline alga, coral seaweed
Corallina vancouveriensis
to 15 cm (6 in) long
n. Alaska to n. Mexico, Galapagos Islands
mid-intertidal to shallow subtidal
This species was first collected at Botanical Beach, BC, in 1901, by Professor
Kichisaburo Yendo, a Japanese botanist who was visiting the Minnesota
Seaside Station located there. Dr. Yendo named the species in honour of
Captain George Vancouver.
Frank Island, w. Vancouver Island, s. BC

SW92. CORAL LEAF SEAWEEDS, coral leaf algae, bead coral, coral leaf,
coral wing
***Bossiella* spp./*Calliarthron* spp**.
to 25 cm (10 in) long
n. Alaska to n. Mexico
low intertidal to subtidal
To distinguish the two genera listed here, specimens of the various
coral leaf algae must be reproductively active with visible pores called
conceptacles present. The five species of *Bossiella* have conceptacles on
the flat sides of the segments, whereas the two *Calliarthron* species feature
them on the segment edges. Photograph A illustrates specimens that
are not reproductively active, and therefore unidentifiable. Photograph
B features *Bossiella californica* subsp. *schmittii*, and photograph C shows
Calliarthron tuberculosum.
Another species, ▶feather-like coralline seaweed,
Serraticardia macmillanii, features a regular,
pinnate (feather-like) branching pattern.
The segments are hexagonal in shape, and
individual specimens usually lack branching
near the base, further enhancing the image of
a feather.
A Plumper Islands, Weynton Passage, c. BC
B Neah Bay, Olympic coast, n. Washington
C Sutton Islets, Egmont, s. BC

SW93. BLADED RED ALGAE
Marine botanists use the term "bladed" to describe a shape that is flat
and sheet-like. As a result of convergent evolution, many red algae have
a bladed shape but are not closely related. Microscopic examination of
vegetative and/or reproductive structures is usually required to identify
members of this group to genus and species.
A Sutton Islets, Egmont, s. BC
B Nakwakto Rapids, Slingsby Channel, c. BC
C Dixon Island, Barkley Sound, s. BC. Michael Hawkes photograph

SW94. ►LEATHERY STRAP SEAWEED
Dilsea californica
to 15 cm (6 in) long
n. Alaska to s. California
mid- to low intertidal
In this species, the blades are thick but not slippery, and the surface has a grained-leather texture. It has been reported to be one of the hosts for the rare endophytic green alga *Endophyton ramosum*—but this requires further study, and its presence would be difficult for the casual naturalist to detect without microscopic examination.
Frank Island, w. Vancouver Island, s. BC. Michael Hawkes photograph

SW95. ►TATTERED RED SEAWEED
Farlowia mollis
to 20 cm (8 in) long
Japan, Kuril Islands, c. Alaska to n. Mexico
mid-intertidal to subtidal
The specimen pictured here is a gamete-producing phase, which alternates with a crustose, spore-producing phase that lives subtidally. Note the alternate branching pattern that is flattened in the oldest sections. At the extremities or areas of most recent growth, the long tips are thin and cylindrical.
Chaatl Island, Queen Charlotte Islands (Haida Gwaii), n. BC. Michael Hawkes photograph

SW96. ►WIRY FORKED SEAWEED
Ahnfeltia fastigiata, previously misidentified: *Ahnfeltia plicata* (an Atlantic species)
to 5 cm (2 in) long, branches to 0.5 mm (0.02 in) or less in diameter
Korea, Japan, Siberia, n. Alaska to n. Mexico
mid- to low intertidal
This red alga and *Ahnfeltiopsis gigartinoides* (SW97) and *Ahnfeltiopsis linearis* (SW98) are associated with rock and cobble habitat that is heavily scoured by sand or gravel. Seasonal burial by these moving sediments can also occur. The very fine, wiry nature of this species contrasts with that of species SW97 and SW98—see maximum sizes listed for each as distinguishing characteristics.
Frank Island, w. Vancouver Island, s. BC. Michael Hawkes photograph

SW97. ►CYLINDRICAL FORKED SEAWEED
Ahnfeltiopsis gigartinoides, *Ahnfeltia gigartinoides*, *Ahnfeltiopsis pacifica*
to 20 cm (8 in) long, branches 0.5–1 mm (0.02–0.04 in) in diameter
c. Alaska to Mexico
mid- to lower intertidal
This dichotomously branched seaweed has cylindrical axes that are stiff and cartilaginous, making them abrasion resistant. It is attached to the bottom

by a creeping basal rhizome. This species inhabits exposed shores and grows in association with both the smaller *Ahnfeltia fastigiata* (SW96) and larger *Ahnfeltiopsis linearis* (SW98).
A Frank Island, w. Vancouver Island, s. BC. Michael Hawkes photograph
B Frank Island, w. Vancouver Island, s. BC

SW98. ▶FLAT-TIPPED FORKED SEAWEED

Ahnfeltiopsis linearis, *Gymnogongrus linearis*

to 18 cm (7 in) long, branches 5–8 mm (0.2–0.3 in) across, cylindrical near the base, slightly compressed near the tips

s. BC to c. California

low intertidal

Like *Ahnfeltia fastigiata* (SW96) and *Ahnfeltiopsis gigartinoides* (SW97), this red alga is tough and cartilaginous, and it associates with bedrock or boulders that are subjected to seasonal sand-burial—up to 90 cm (3 ft) deep! This is the largest, in terms of branch width, of the *Ahnfeltia/Ahnfeltiopsis* species.

Frank Island, w. Vancouver Island, s. BC. Michael Hawkes photograph

SW99. CALLOPHYLLIS-LIKE DULSE

Palmaria callophylloides, *Palmaria palmata* var. *sarniensis*

to 25 cm (10 in) long

n. Alaska to n. BC

mid- to low intertidal

Although it looks very different, this dulse is related to *Halosaccion glandiforme* (SW80) and they have similar life histories, in which spore-producing and male gamete-producing individuals are large blades and the female, gamete-bearing ones are microscopic discs. The specimen featured in the photograph is actually the Type Specimen designated in the original species description in 1986.

Langara Island, Queen Charlotte Islands (Haida Gwaii), n. BC. Michael Hawkes photograph

SW100. LEATHERY DULSE

Palmaria hecatensis

to 40 cm (16 in) long

n. Alaska to n. California

mid- to low intertidal

Restricted to wave-exposed coasts, this species has thick, leathery blades that arise from a broad, discoid holdfast, and it often forms extensive fringes on rocks in the low intertidal zone. In photograph A, the vast majority of specimens shown are leathery dulse.

A Tana Bay, Queen Charlotte Islands (Haida Gwaii), n. BC. Michael Hawkes photograph

B NW coast of Porcher Island, n. BC. Michael Hawkes photograph

Low Intertidal

SW101. THIN DULSE

Palmaria mollis, *Rhodymenia palmata* var. *mollis*, *Palmaria palmata* var. *mollis*

to 45 cm (18 in) long

n. Alaska to s. California

low intertidal to upper subtidal

Possessing a wedge-shaped blade that is irregularly split into lobes, this species usually grows in clumps. After overwintering, a surviving base may produce second-year growth. Dulse, *Palmaria palmata*, a related species in the north Atlantic Ocean, is eaten as a vegetable in the Canadian Maritimes and in Britain.

Sooke, s. Vancouver Island, s. BC. Michael Hawkes photograph

SW102. HAIRY POTTERY SEAWEED
Ceramium pacificum
to 18 cm (7 in) long
c. Alaska to n. Mexico
low intertidal
Assisting the naturalist's identification of this species is its characteristic habitat of shallow tide pools, containing water significantly warmer than the surrounding sea. A distinctive feature of all 10 Pacific Northwest *Ceramium* species is their forcipate branch tips—resembling tiny crab pincers (a good opportunity to use your hand lens!). Except for staghorn felt, *Ceramium codicola*, which grows only on *Codium fragile* (SW16), definitive species identification requires microscopic examination.
Point Defiance, Puget Sound, c. Washington

SW103. ▶BEAUTIFUL LEAF SEAWEEDS
Callophyllis spp., including *Callophyllis flabellulata*, *Callophyllis pinnata*, *Callophyllis violacea*, *Callophyllis heanophylla*
to 20 cm (8 in) long
n. Alaska to n. Mexico
low intertidal to 20 m (65 ft)
The blades of these red algae lack veins. To confirm that a specimen belongs to the genus *Callophyllis*, microscopic examination is required. Species identification can also be difficult and in most cases requires reproductive material. The most common species are listed above. Photograph A shows *Callophyllis heanophylla*; photograph B shows *Callophyllis flabellulata*.
A Ucluth Peninsula, w. Vancouver Island, s. BC
B Long Island, near Lopez Island, n. Washington

SW104. TURKISH TOWEL, Turkish towel alga
Chondracanthus exasperatus, *Gigartina exasperata*, *Gigartina californica*
to 1 m (39 in) long
c. Alaska to n. Mexico
low intertidal to upper subtidal
What kind of towels do they have in Turkey, anyway? Actually, rubbing one's body with Turkish towel removes dead skin. Photograph A features numerous smaller specimens, with red near the bases and yellow near the ends.
The ▶oval Turkish towel, *Chondracanthus corymbiferus*, oval in outline, may be yellowish pink intertidally and bluish red subtidally. It lives from s. BC to n. Mexico.
Five *Chondracanthus* species have been reported from the Pacific Northwest, but some species are restricted to the southern portion of this range.
A Clarke Island, Barkley Sound, s. BC. Michael Hawkes photograph
B Ucluth Peninsula, w. Vancouver Island, s. BC. Michael Hawkes photograph

SW105. IRIDESCENT SEAWEED, rainbow seaweed, rainbow leaf
Mazzaella splendens, *Iridaea splendens*, *Iridaea cordata* var. *splendens*
to 1.2 m (4 ft) long
s. Alaska to n. Mexico
low intertidal to shallow subtidal
Layering in the cell wall of this species gives it an iridescent, oily-blue sheen. Note also that the blades have a characteristic rubbery consistency. There are 11 *Mazzaella* species that may be encountered in the Pacific Northwest. One of the more common ones is ▶narrow, iridescent seaweed, *Mazzaella linearis* (photograph B), which is more slender and is found in areas of heavy surf along exposed outer shores.
A Ucluth Peninsula, w. Vancouver Island, s. BC
B Frank Island, w. Vancouver Island, s. BC

SW106. DELICATE SEA LACE
Microcladia coulteri
to 40 cm (16 in) long
n. BC to n. Mexico
low intertidal to shallow subtidal
Unlike *Microcladia borealis* (SW79), this species branches on both sides of the central axis. It may attach to other red algae, including *Chondracanthus* spp. (SW104), *Mazzaella* spp. (SW105), *Grateloupia americana* (SW83) and *Prionitis lyallii* (SW84), sometimes so thickly as to obscure the host alga. *Microcladia coulteri* is a choice species to press for making greeting cards!
A Ucluth Peninsula, w. Vancouver Island, s. BC. Michael Hawkes photograph
B Wizard Islet, Barkley Sound, s. BC. Michael Hawkes photograph

SW107. ▶SHAFT-BEARING IODINE SEAWEED
Grateloupia doryphora
to 45 cm (18 in) long
s. BC to Peru, n. Atlantic Ocean
low intertidal
A frequent inhabitant of tide pools, this species has blades that are thick, with a slippery texture. All *Grateloupia* species on this coast are poorly known and require further study.
Ucluth Peninsula, w. Vancouver Island, s. BC

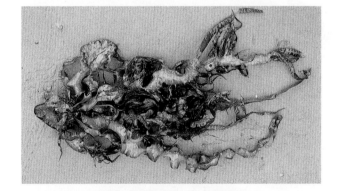

SW108. RUFFLED RED SEAWEED
Cryptopleura ruprechtiana, *Botryoglossum ruprechtianum*, *Nitophyllum ruprechtianum*
to 50 cm (19 in) long
s. Alaska to n. Mexico
low intertidal to upper subtidal
The blades of this species typically have ruffled or proliferous margins. Larger specimens can develop a thick mid-rib near the base. Such specimens in California are quite robust and some marine botanists treat them as a different species—*Botryoglossum farlowianum*. Small cabbage-like growths on this alga are the parasitic red alga *Gonimophyllum skottsbergii*.
Several other *Cryptopleura* species have been documented in the Pacific Northwest, including ▶hidden-ribbed red seaweed, *Cryptopleura lobulifera* and ▶delicate-veined red seaweed, *Cryptopleura violacea*.
Slip Point, Olympic coast, n. Washington

SW109. ▶BLACK-LINED RED SEAWEEDS
***Hymenena* spp.**
to 30 cm (12 in) long
n. Alaska to s. California
low intertidal to shallow subtidal
Not only are the species of *Hymenena* difficult to distinguish from one another but they are superficially much like the genus *Cryptopleura*. Reproductive material is required to make a positive identification.
Point Defiance, Puget Sound, c. Washington

SW110. RED SEA LEAF
Erythrophyllum delesserioides
to 50 cm (20 in) long
c. Alaska to s. California
low intertidal to shallow subtidal
This red alga has beautiful, rich red blades with a conspicuous mid-rib. Older plants may be lacerated. Look for it along wave-exposed outer coasts, where its lushness supplies a rich colour in surge channels. Specimens growing on kelps have been described as another species, *Erythrophyllum splendens* (not reported north of Oregon) but recent expert opinion questions the validity of this species.
A Frank Island, w. Vancouver Island, s. BC. Michael Hawkes photograph
B Fort Worden, Port Townsend, n. Washington

SW111. RED FAN, sea fern
Neoptilota asplenioides
to 30 cm (12 in) long
Japan, Siberia, n. Alaska to n. Washington
low intertidal to upper subtidal
This species has a very beautiful branching pattern, with both margins of the ultimate branches serrate (toothed). It is superficially similar to the two species of *Ptilota* that inhabit the Pacific Northwest.
Three other very similar *Neoptilota* species are recorded from the Pacific Northwest.
Sooke, s. Vancouver Island, s. BC. Michael Hawkes photograph

SW112. SEA BELLY
***Gastroclonium subarticulatum*,** *Gastroclonium coulteri*
to 30 cm (12 in) long
s. Alaska to n. Mexico
low intertidal to shallow subtidal
This red alga often forms extensive mats at the low-tide level along rocky shores exposed to direct Pacific surge. The tips of its tiny, sausage-shaped branches are hollow and filled with clear mucilage. Look for it growing on rock, other algae and the tubes secreted by various worms.
Ucluth Peninsula, w. Vancouver Island, s. BC

SW113. ▶JAPANESE RED SEAWEED
Lomentaria hakodatensis
to 13 cm (5 in) across
Korea, China, Japan, Siberia, s. BC to n. Washington, s. California to Costa Rica
low intertidal to shallow subtidal
Branch tips of this species are hollow and specimens form a turf. Pinch off a piece of this alga and clear mucilage will be exuded. This exotic alga is thought to have been introduced into our flora on oyster spat brought from Japan.

Bath Island, Gabriola Passage, s. BC. Michael Hawkes photograph

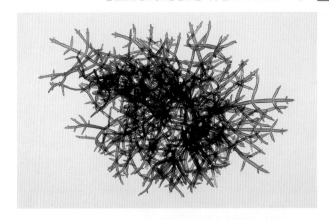

SW114. RED SPAGHETTI
Gracilaria/Gracilariopsis
to 1.5 m (5 ft) long
Japan, s. Alaska to n. Mexico
low intertidal to shallow subtidal
It is difficult to distinguish *Gracilaria* from *Gracilariopsis* unless specimens are at a particular reproductive stage. Microscopic examination is required. Habitat can be helpful, as *Gracilaria* is typically most common in sheltered, subtidal habitats, whereas *Gracilariopsis* prefers intertidal rocks in moderately exposed to exposed sand-bottom habitats. Similar and common species in the Pacific Northwest are *Gracilaria pacifica* (also reported as *Gracilaria verrucosa*), *Gracilariopsis andersonii* (also reported as *Gracilariopsis lemaneiformis*, but this species is restricted to Peru and Chile), *Gracilaria sjoestedtii* and *Gracilariopsis sjoestedtii*. A parasitic red alga, *Gracilariophyla*, occasionally appears as small warty cushions on *Gracilariopsis*.

A Georgina Point, Mayne Island, s. BC
B Agamemnon Channel, Nelson Island, s. BC

SW115. SEA BRUSH
Odonthalia floccosa
to 40 cm (16 in) long
n. Alaska to s. California
low intertidal
This red alga is easily mistaken for a brown one because of its brownish to almost black colour. It usually forms dense clumps and is also a frequent host for epiphytic algae such as *Leathesia difformis* (SW27) and *Soranthera ulvoidea* (SW29). Four other *Odonthalia* species occur in the Pacific Northwest.

Ucluth Peninsula, w. Vancouver Island, s. BC

SW116. ▶TOOTHED-TWIG SEAWEED
Odonthalia washingtoniensis
to 30 cm (12 in) long
c. Alaska to s. California
low intertidal to shallow subtidal
The characteristically flattened branches of this species feel very tough when touched. This seaweed was described in 1925 from collections made at Cattle Point, San Juan Island, n. Washington.

Cattle Point, San Juan Island, n. Washington

SW117. SEA LAUREL, pepper dulse

Osmundea spectabilis, *Laurencia spectabilis*
to 30 cm (12 in) long
s. Alaska to n. Mexico
low intertidal to shallow subtidal
The branches of this species are slightly flattened and have a firm, almost cartilaginous texture. The sea laurel contains brominated and chlorinated compounds. Crushing a piece of this alga produces a pungent odour characteristic of these chemicals. Occasional specimens may be infected by the parasitic red alga *Janczewskia gardneri,* which forms small, pale pink tuberculate growths (swellings or bumps).
Edith Point, Mayne Island, s. BC

SW118. SUCCULENT SEAWEED

Sarcodiotheca gaudichaudii, *Agardhiella coulteri, Neoagardhiella gaudichaudii, Agardiella tenera,* incorrect: *Neoagardhiella baileyi*
to 45 cm (18 in) long
s. Alaska to n. Mexico, Galapagos Islands, Peru, Chile
low intertidal to shallow subtidal
Resembling a cluster of translucent noodles that are reddish pink to brownish, this red alga is a common find for the beachcombing or scuba-diving naturalist. Look for it in shallow, sheltered bays. *Gardneriella tuberifera*, a parasitic red alga, grows between the cells in this species and forms an irregular-shaped mass (1–3 mm/0.04 in in diameter) that protrudes from the host's surface. *Note:* this parasite has not been reported north of California.
Ucluth Peninsula, w. Vancouver Island, s. BC. Michael Hawkes photograph

SW119. ▶CALIFORNIA ROSE SEAWEED

Rhodymenia californica
to 10 cm (4 in) long
n. BC to Mexico, Galapagos Islands
low intertidal to shallow subtidal
This species is one of many red algae that form part of the understorey beneath the larger and more obvious species, particularly the kelps. Like their counterparts in a rain forest, these species are adapted to grow with a reduced amount of light.
Wizard Islet, Barkley Sound, s. BC. Michael Hawkes photograph

SW120. ▶PACIFIC ROSE SEAWEED

Rhodymenia pacifica, *Rhodymenia lobulifera*
to 15 cm (6 in) long
n. BC to n. Mexico
extreme low intertidal to shallow subtidal
This red alga is a larger, more robust version of the *Rhodymenia californica* (SW119) and grows lower on the shore, typically in the shallow subtidal. Both this species and the preceding one can grow new blades vegetatively (asexually) from prominent horizontal stolons (stems).
Wizard Islet, Barkley Sound, s. BC. Michael Hawkes photograph

SW121. ▶CARTILAGE-WING SEAWEED

Pterochondria woodii

to 10 cm (4 in) long

s. Alaska to n. Mexico

low intertidal to shallow subtidal

This red alga is in a monotypic genus (it contains only one species). It grows epiphytically on *Cystoseira* spp. (SW49/50), *Macrocystis* spp. (SW59) and other large brown seaweeds. Several orders of alternating branches, arranged in two rows on opposite sides of the main axis, are distinctive. All of this fine branching is strongly flattened. A hand lens may be required to see it clearly.

Edith Point, Mayne Island, s. BC

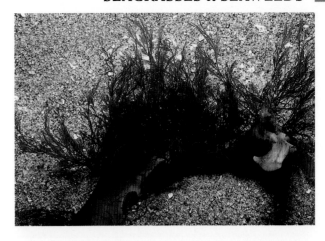

SW122. SLIMY LEAF

Schizymenia pacifica, *Haematocelis rubens*

to 60 cm (24 in) long

n. Alaska to n. Mexico

low intertidal to subtidal

This bladed alga, as shown in the photograph, is the gamete-bearing phase that alternates with a crustose, spore-bearing stage that was originally thought to be different and named *Haematocelis rubens*. Life history studies corrected this misconception. As the common name suggests, the blade has a very slippery texture—a feature not shared with all bladed red algae. Microscopic examination of blade cross-sections is required to identify most bladed red algae (SW93) with certainty.

Sutton Islets, Egmont, s. BC

SW123. RED FRINGE, seagrass laver

Smithora naiadum

to 5 cm (2 in) long

c. Alaska to n. Mexico

low intertidal to shallow subtidal

This species, which can only live as an epiphyte, grows on *Zostera marina* (SW2) or *Phyllospadix* spp. (SW4). The many red blades form a dramatic edging on these seagrasses. Photograph A shows *Smithora* growing attached to eelgrass in a sheltered area, and photograph B shows it living on surfgrass at an exposed site. The genus is named for Gilbert Morgan Smith, a famous botanist at Stanford University. Although it looks superficially like a species of *Porphyra* (SW66), it differs in reproductive details that can only be seen with a microscope.

A Stanley Park, Burrard Inlet, s. BC

B Botanical Beach, s. Vancouver Island, s. BC. Michael Hawkes photograph

SW124. KELP-FRINGING NORI, kelp-fringing laver

Porphyra gardneri, *Porphyrella gardneri*

to 7.5 cm (3 in) long

n. Alaska to n. Mexico

extreme low intertidal to shallow subtidal

This small Nori species grows only on other algae. In particular it prefers kelp, especially the blade margins of *Laminaria setchellii* (SW43). Important life-history details concerning sexual reproduction in the genus *Porphyra* were documented in this species by Dr. Michael Hawkes of the University of British Columbia, Vancouver, BC.

Whittlestone Point, Trevor Channel, s. BC. Michael Hawkes photograph

SW125. NETWORK RED SEAWEED, many veined red seaweed, crisscross network
Polyneura latissima
to 30 cm (12 in) long
Siberia, c. Alaska to n. Mexico
low intertidal to shallow subtidal
A characteristic feature of this species is the network of anastomosing (linking) veins and "crinkly" blades. Use a hand lens, or hold the blade in front of a bright light, to observe this feature clearly. Look for network red seaweed early in the spring, when it is at its best.
Point Defiance, Puget Sound, c. Washington

SW126. RED EYELET SILK
Sparlingia pertusa, *Rhodymenia pertusa, Rhodymenia stipitata*
typically to 1 m (39 in) long
to 20 cm (8 in) wide
Korea, Japan, n. Alaska to s. Oregon, Arctic Ocean, Greenland, Spitzbergen
low intertidal to 10 m (33 ft)
This is one of the largest red algae in the Pacific Northwest. The holes in the blade are a natural growth feature and not the result of invertebrate grazing.
Worlcombe Island, Howe Sound, s. BC

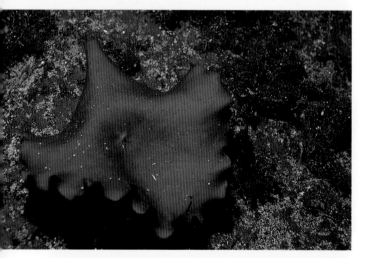

SW127. ▶GIANT CUP AND SAUCER SEAWEED
Constantinea subulifera
to 18 cm (7.2 in) tall, 30 cm (12 in) in diameter
Japan, Kuril Islands, n. Alaska to n. Washington
low intertidal to shallow subtidal
This species features umbrella-shaped blades borne on a cylindrical, branched stipe (stem-like structure). In addition, the blades are often split and feature conspicuous veins. This seaweed typically grows in sheltered locales.
Two other similar species of *Constantinea* live in the Pacific Northwest. The cup and saucer seaweed, *Constantinea simplex*, is found from n. Alaska to s. California in low intertidal to shallow subtidal regions. Smaller than its giant relative featured above, *Constantinea simplex* lives along exposed open-coast shorelines. Another subtidal species, ▶northern cup and saucer seaweed, *Constantinea rosa-marina*, occurs in Alaska and lacks veins in the blade.
Quarry Bay, Nelson Island, s. BC

SW128. WINGED RIB, baron delessert
Delesseria decipiens
to 50 cm (20 in) long
n. Alaska to s. California
low intertidal to shallow subtidal
This delicate, frilly species has a distinctive thick mid-rib with "leaflets" branching from it. It has an isomorphic life history—an alternation of identical-looking gamete-bearing and spore-bearing generations. It is common in the early spring and is most obvious as it hangs in clusters from rock walls.
Moore Point, Francis Peninsula, s. BC

SW129. ▶FEATHER-VEINED RED SEAWEED
Membranoptera platyphylla
to 10 cm (4 in) long
c. Alaska to s. California
low intertidal to shallow subtidal
This species attaches to rock, pilings or kelps by means of a discoid holdfast. It features very thin blades that have a prominent mid-rib. Delicate veins come off the mid-rib in a pinnate (feather-like) manner. Use a hand lens to fully appreciate the beauty of this species.
Dixon Island, Barkley Sound, s. BC. Michael Hawkes photograph

Subtidal

SW130. BULL-KELP NORI, bull-kelp laver
Porphyra nereocystis
to 3 m (10 ft) long
n. Alaska to s. California
shallow subtidal
Bull kelp Nori grows only on the stipes (stem-like structures) of *Nereocystis luetkeana* (SW60). It is one of the longest red algae in the world but is only one cell layer thick! Along the outer coast, this species appears on the stipes of bull kelp in November. However, in the Strait of Georgia it can be seen up to two months earlier. In both cases, it is found on senescent (old) *Nereocystis* specimens that have other epiphytes growing on their stipes. This Nori is present throughout the winter and spring.
Sutton Islets, Egmont, s. BC

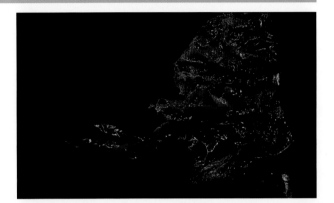

SW131. ▶THIN FORKED SEAWEED
Gymnogongrus chiton, *Gymnogongrus platyphyllus*
to 15 cm (6 in) long
s. BC to n. Mexico
subtidal
This is not a common species and superficially resembles some other flattened, dichotomously branched red algae. However in the details of its reproduction and life history, it is quite different and unusual.
Frank Island, w. Vancouver Island, s. BC

SW132. ▶FLESHY BUSH SEAWEED
Scinaia confusa, *Pseudogloiophloea confusa*
to 20 cm (8 in) long
s. Alaska to n. Mexico, Costa Rica, Galapagos Islands
low intertidal to 10 m (33 ft)
Like many other red algae, this species has a heteromorphic life history—one that features two very different forms. The gamete-bearing phase, shown in the photograph, is a spring–summer annual that is obvious to the naturalist. It alternates with a very tiny, filamentous, spore-bearing phase that is virtually impossible to find amid a vast array of other seaweeds. The cylindrical branches of this alga are soft to the touch. Break off a tiny piece and note the clear mucilage that is exuded—a distinctive feature of this species.
Ucluth Peninsula, w. Vancouver Island, s. BC

SW133. COMMON SEA OAK
Phycodrys riggii
to 15.5–20 cm (6–8 in) long
Japan Sea, Bering Sea, Aleutian Is., Alaska to n. BC
low intertidal to subtidal
Most common in Alaska, this red alga is a northern species of the Pacific Northwest flora. For some reason, or combination of reasons—possibly involving water temperature and herbivores—it has not colonized more southern coasts.
Annis Point, Kunghit Island, n. BC

SW134. ▶DELICATELY-BRANCHED RED SEAWEED
Bonnemaisonia nootkana, *Trailliella intricata*. Some researchers have recently suggested that *Bonnemaisonia californica* should be the name used for this species.
to 45 cm (18 in) long (gamete-bearing phase)
to 1 cm (0.3 in) long (spore-bearing 'Trailliella' phase)
c. Alaska to n. Mexico
subtidal to 20 m (65 ft)
One of the most beautiful Pacific Northwest red algae, this subtidal species has a heteromorphic life history. The obvious and attractive gamete-bearing stage, with its distinctive branching pattern, is shown. It does not in the least resemble the tiny, filamentous, spore-bearing stage known as the 'Trailliella' phase. Until the life cycle was studied, the two forms were believed to be two separate species. *Bonnemaisonia nootkana* was first collected at Nootka Sound, Vancouver Island, BC, by Archibald Menzies, surgeon naturalist on expeditions with both James Colnett (1787–1788) and George Vancouver (1791–1795).
Ross Islets, Barkley Sound, s. BC. Michael Hawkes photograph

SW135. PLUMOSE RED BRAID
Rhodoptilum plumosum
to 45 cm (18 in) long
Japan, s. Alaska to n. Mexico
subtidal
Another of the more attractive subtidal red algae, this species is not commonly encountered. Pity. Why is it not noticed more often? Have folks been looking in the wrong place? Whatever the case, the situation poses an interesting challenge for both the inquisitive naturalist and the knowledgeable expert.
A Cattle Point, San Juan Island, n. Washington
B Tzartus Island, Barkley Sound, s. BC. Michael Hawkes photograph

SW136. ▶BLUE BRANCHING SEAWEED
Fauchea laciniata

to 15.5 cm (6.2 in) across
c. Alaska to n. Mexico
very low intertidal to 10 m (33 ft)

The firm, fan-shaped blades of this species are slippery and exhibit an exquisite yellow-green or blue-violet iridescence, which is the result of light reflecting off gland cells embedded in a surface layer of cells. This seaweed frequently grows on worm tubes. Like many red algae, it has an isomorphic life history. Photographs A and B show a gamete-producing and a spore-producing specimen respectively. The cystocarps (tiny, swollen black dots) on the blade surface in photograph A are products of fertilization. A related species, ▶margined blue branching seaweed, *Fauchea fryeana*, has its cystocarps on the blade margin only, as shown in photograph C.

A Sekiu, Olympic coast, n. Washington
B Helm Point, Coronation Island, s. Alaska
C Whittlestone Point, Trevor Channel, s. BC. Michael Hawkes photograph

SW137. ▶ARCHED RED SEAWEED
Fryeella gardneri

to 21 cm (8.4 in) long
n. BC to n. Mexico
subtidal to 25 m (83 ft)

Hold a specimen up to the light and note the distinctive curving lines formed by internal partitions. In California this red alga has a blue iridescence, but farther north it does not. The reason for this difference is unknown. This species grows attached to worm tubes and other algae, as well as on rock. The genus is named for Dr. T.C. Frye, director of the University of Washington's Puget Sound Biological Station in the early 1900s (now Friday Harbor Laboratories). The species commemorates N.L. Gardner, who was a teacher at Whidbey Island, Washington, in 1897. His interest in the local marine algae grew into a long and fruitful collaboration on west coast seaweeds with William A. Setchell at UC Berkeley.

Edith Point, Mayne Island, s. BC

SW138. SEA GRAPES
Botryocladia pseudodichotoma

at least 15 cm (6 in) tall
n. BC to n. Mexico, Galapagos Islands
subtidal to 20 m (65 ft)

Aptly named, this succulent-looking seaweed has sacs that are actually filled with mucilage. Specimens found in more southerly regions, such as California, are often much larger than their more northern counterparts. The measle-like dots on the sacs obvious in photograph B are cystocarps, reproductive structures resulting from fertilization.

A Point Cowan, Howe Sound, s. BC
B Hutt Island, Howe Sound, s. BC

SW139. PRICKLY PEAR SEAWEED, red fan-shaped seaweed
Opuntiella californica, Cruoria profunda
to 30 cm (12 in) across
n. Alaska to n. Mexico
low intertidal to 20 m (65 ft)
This species' superficial resemblance to the prickly-pear cactus, genus *Opuntia*, results in both its scientific and common names. It has a heteromorphic life history. The large, obvious stage, which produces gametes and is featured in the photograph alternates with a microscopic crustose stage. So different was this minute spore-bearer that it was originally described as another species, known as *Cruoria profunda*.
Mutine Point, Barkley Sound, s. BC

SW140. ▶FURCATED FLESHY RED SEAWEED
Sarcodiotheca furcata
to 18 cm (7.2 in) long
s. Alaska to Costa Rica, Galapagos Islands
subtidal to 20 m (65 ft)
To gain an appreciation of how different closely related species of seaweed can look, compare this species with *Sarcodiotheca gaudichaudii* (SW118). Microscopic examination of both vegetative and reproductive structures is required to confirm that these two species belong in the same genus.
Agnew Passage, Nelson Island, s. BC

SW141. ▶FALSE MIDRIB SEAWEED
Stenogramma interrupta
to 15.5 cm (6.2 in) long
Japan, Korea, c. Alaska to n. Mexico, Galapagos Islands, New Zealand, Atlantic coasts of Europe
subtidal
What appear to be mid-ribs are actually lines of reproductive structures that characterize the female specimens of this alga. As one of the deeper-dwelling red algae in the Pacific Northwest, it is a likely sighting by the scuba diver, particularly as it is found at depths below the large, flat kelps that often cover much of the shallower sea floor.
Neah Bay, Olympic coast, n. Washington

Miscellaneous Marine Algae

Some red, green and brown algae that grow inside other plants are termed endophytic, and some of these are also parasitic. Others grow inside animals and are called endozoic.

One group of primitive organisms, Cyanobacteria, can also grow endophytically or endozoically. Microscopic examination is required for precise species identification, but specimens may be encountered by the casual naturalist.

Photograph A shows **SW142. red sponge growth** on a glove sponge (PO30) with what is likely a cyanobacterium—the red-coloured areas—infiltrating some of its "fingers."
Grainger Point, Samuel Island, s. BC

The **SW143. turquoise smudge**, obvious on the Lewis's moonsnail (MC225), shown in photograph B, is probably another species of cyanobacterium.

Oyster Bay, Mayne Island, s. BC

Photograph C shows a gaper clam shell (MC76/77) with a green colour. This **SW144. green shell alga** is likely a result of the microscopic phase of a green alga that lives inside the shell and alternates with a larger form (see green algae, SW5–19).

Dibrell Bay, Langara Island, n. BC

The green colour coating much of the cloud sponge (PO11) in photograph D may or may not be a green alga. The photograph of this **SW145. green sponge coat** was taken at about 25 m (80 ft)—deeper than most green algae live.

Anderson Bay, Texada Island, s. BC

Undetermined Seaweeds

In many instances, marine algae cannot be identified without microscopic examination of the specimen. The following photographs feature specimens that unfortunately were not retained for further study.

SW146. Undetermined seaweeds A and B. Photographs A and B were both taken very high in the intertidal zone along an exposed, surf-swept shoreline. On several occasions after the photographic session, Andy Lamb returned to the critical site but was unable to relocate the relevant growth.

A B Ucluth Peninsula, w. Vancouver Island, s. BC

SW147. Undetermined seaweed C. Photograph C shows an orange-coloured red alga, which indicates death through a breakdown in the pigment contained inside. It represents a very strange colour for what appears to be the red alga *Griffithsia pacifica*, although this is speculative until samples can be analyzed.

Anderson Bay, Texada Island, s. BC

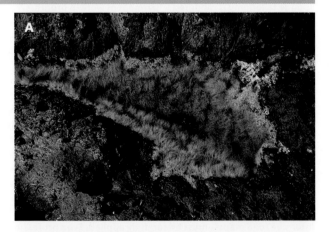

INVERTEBRATES

With a cast of characters so strange and bizarre that it would be the envy of any science fiction movie producer, the invertebrates—animals with no backbones—dominate the marine environment of the Pacific Northwest in terms of both diversity and total population. The fact that in a majority of species the tiny planktonic young bear little if any resemblance to the more recognizable adults further increases the seemingly endless array of unbelievable life designs. Most invertebrates are intimately associated with the sea floor or other submerged substrates for most of their lives, but spineless creatures frequent virtually every available space of the marine habitat that is our coast. This overwhelming assemblage of spectacular creatures may be biologically—though not necessarily easily—segregated into a number of phyla (singular: phylum).

Further Reading

Connor, Judith, 1993, *Seashore Life on Rocky Coasts*, Monterey Bay Aquarium, Monterey, CA, 64 pp.

Harbo, Rick M., 1999, *Whelks to Whales,* Harbour Publishing, Madeira Park, BC, 245 pp.

Kozloff, Eugene N., 1996, *Seashore Life of the North Pacific Coast*, University of Washington Press, Seattle, WA, 370 pp.

Kozloff, Eugene N., 1996, *Marine Invertebrates of the Pacific Northwest*, University of Washington Press, Seattle, WA, 539 pp.

Morris, Robert, Donald Abbott and Eugene Haderlie, 1980, *Intertidal Marine Invertebrates of California*, Stanford University Press, Stanford, CA, 652 pp.

O'Clair, Rita M., and Charles E. O'Clair, 1998, *Southeast Alaska's Rocky Shores*, Plant Press, Auke Bay, AK, 564 pp.

Ricketts, Edward, and Jack Calvin, 1985, *Between Pacific Tides,* Stanford University Press, Stanford, CA, 652 pp.

Sept, J. Duane, 1999, *The Beachcomber's Guide to Seashore Life in the Pacific Northwest*, Harbour Publishing, Madeira Park, BC, 235 pp.

SPONGES *Phylum PORIFERA*

Organized as a loose aggregation of various independent cells rather than via distinct tissue types, a sponge is essentially a water filtration device. Siliceous sponges (PO9–12) are an exception in that these cells are multi-nucleate (many central bodies with genetic material) without cell boundaries.

Central to this is a system of pores, canals and chambers, often with a complicated layout and lined with collar cells or collar bodies in one special group of sponges. These flagellate cells or bodies—each with a single hair-like structure—move seawater through the sponge while removing microscopic planktonic food. Sponges typically are supported by a skeletal framework of fibres often accompanied by glass- or chalk-like slivers called spicules. The photograph illustrates three specimens consisting of spicules.

Sponge classification and recognition is a most problematic and frustrating subject for a naturalist. Indeed, academic professionals who spend their careers studying the group are likewise challenged—a fact that leads to much uncertainty in scientifically oriented sponge publications. Historical inconsistencies and funding limitations overlay the fundamental difficulty of studying sponge anatomy. As such, sponge taxonomy is rendered a "permanent work in progress."

One approach to species identification of sponges is via their shapes, a standard used for most groups of organisms. This is workable in many instances, but numerous sponge species have few large, obvious diagnostic features. This is particularly true of encrusting forms that grow in mat-like carpets over whatever shape and type of surface is available. Environmental influences often dictate sponge growth patterns, further complicating this anatomical approach.

When applied with shape, colour can sometimes be an aid to sponge identification but must be considered only a factor of partial and limited value.

Traditional considerations of the aforementioned issues have led experts to focus on the "micro-anatomy" of sponges—namely the organization and types of fibres and/or spicules. The size and shape of these building blocks and their combinations have proven significant for identifying most species. Unfortunately, such precise determination involves microscopic examination of spicules, a task that most often must be preceded by sampling and preparation. Once spicule terminology is understood, complicated "keys"—jargon for intensive road maps—must be carefully applied. Even professional "spongophiles" have difficulty with such intricacies. As a result, numerous "forms" remain inadequately known, even nameless and essentially unclassified. Obviously this mitigates against successful identification of sponges by the beach-side naturalist or underwater explorer!

During preparation of this portion of the book, we became as confused as nearly everyone else about sponges and sought out Dr. Bill Austin of the Marine Ecology Centre in Sidney, BC—*the* acknowledged Pacific Northwest sponge guru. His invaluable assistance is greatly appreciated. Fundamental to his advice was that the understanding of sponges is in a state of flux and that caution should be exercised with respect to identification, particularly when samples are unavailable for inspection—as is the case for some entries presented here. When relevant, we mention such possibilities within a "species" account. The identification of some sponges that were photographed but not sampled proved hopeless, and a "best guess" would prove counterproductive. These sponges are presented at the end of this section.

At least 260 marine sponge species live in the Pacific Northwest, but as the preamble indicates, this is a tenuous number indeed!

CALCAREOUS SPONGES

PO1. TINY VASE SPONGES
Sycon **spp.**, *Scypha* spp.
to 5 cm (2 in) tall
Alaska to California
subtidal
Often inconspicuous in the silty, low-current locales they prefer, these sponges (probably a few nearly identical species) are not a highlight for the average scuba diver. An ancient group, sponges were well established and very diverse as far back as pre-Cambrian times, some 600 million years ago.
Ucluelet Harbour, w. Vancouver Island, s. BC

PO2. STALKED VASE SPONGE, urn sponge, urn-shaped sponge, stalked sponge, Nutting's sponge
Leucilla nuttingi, *Rhabdodermella nuttingi*
to 5 cm (2 in) tall
n. Alaska to n. Mexico
intertidal to 46 m (152 ft)
Usually found in clusters numbering less than 12, the stalked vase sponge is seen only with diligence: it is usually surrounded by other larger, more colourful creatures.
Laura Point, Mayne Island, s. BC

PO3. BRISTLY VASE SPONGE, spiny vase sponge, small tufted pear sponge, Heath's sponge, sharp-spined creamy sponge
Leucandra heathi, *Leuconia heathi*, *Scypha ciliata*
to 11 cm (4.2 in) tall
n. Alaska to n. Mexico
subtidal to 180 m (600 ft)
Usually living in small groups attached to vertical surfaces, the bristly vase sponge can be recognized by a fringe of spicules around each individual's tiny osculum (opening), together with a solid texture and large size.
Copper Cliffs, Quadra Island, s. BC

PO4. TUBULAR VASE SPONGE
Leucandra **sp.**
▶to 10 cm (4 in) tall
Alaska to BC
intertidal to subtidal
Obscured by a coating of sediment, the specimen appearing in the photograph may be one of several very similar species differentiated by the size and shape of their calcareous spicules. A ring of oxeas spicules (elongate and pointed at each end) is obvious around the osculum, the large opening through which seawater exits the animal.
Agamemnon Channel, Nelson Island, s. BC

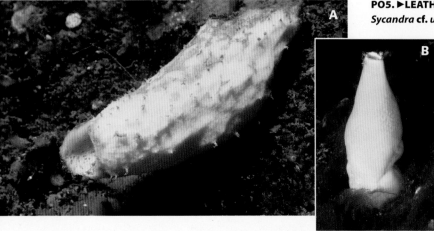

PO5. ►LEATHER BAG SPONGE
Sycandra **cf.** *utriculus*
to 15 cm (6 in) tall
BC
subtidal
This is a poorly understood sponge. Even its precise identity is in doubt, as indicated by "cf."—meaning "close to"—within the scientific name. The two very different-looking specimens featured in the photographs are leather bag sponges, according to sponge expert Dr. Bill Austin of Sidney, BC.
A Fraser Rock, Welcome Passage, s. BC. Neil McDaniel photograph
B Prominent Point, Knight Inlet, s. BC. Neil McDaniel photograph

PO6. LACY BALL SPONGE, organ pipe sponge, tube ball sponge
Leucosolenia eleanor, *Leucosolenia botryoides*
to 15 cm (6 in) colony diameter
Japan, n. Alaska to s. California
subtidal to 27 m (90 ft)
Usually extensively and confusingly branched, this animal obviously reminded someone of a musical instrument. A sponge has a very thin skin, only one cell thick, that is perforated to allow surrounding seawater to flow in.
Neah Bay, Olympic Coast, n. Washington

PO7. SPAGHETTI SPONGE, tube sponge
Leucosolenia nautilia, *Leucosolenia botryoides*
to 15 cm (6 in) across
BC to s. California
intertidal to subtidal
The spaghetti sponge resembles a ball of tangled yarn or thick string because of its convoluted growth pattern. Members of this genus, *Leucosolenia*—which includes several other species—are considered among the simplest sponges, being just hollow tubes lined by collar cells with one large outflow opening for each tube.
Green Bay, Nelson Island, s. BC

PO8. ►LATTICE-SKIN SPONGES
Clathrina **spp.**, *Leucosolenia* spp.
indeterminate, irregular size
BC to s. California
intertidal to subtidal
At least three species are believed to exist in the Pacific Northwest, but distinguishing them is nearly impossible. Two of these species have worldwide distribution, suggesting they are most adaptable.
Steep Island, Discovery Passage, s. BC. Neil McDaniel photograph

SILICEOUS SPONGES—(Hexactinellid sponges with some six-rayed spicules)

PO9. SHARP LIPPED BOOT SPONGE, boot sponge, chimney sponge
Rhabdocalyptus dawsoni, *Bathydorus dawsoni*
to 1.5 m (5 ft) tall
Alaska to s. California
subtidal, 10–500 m (35–1,650 ft) at least
Always heavily silted, this species has a thin osculum (opening) compared
to the round lipped boot sponge (PO10). The sharp lipped boot sponge is
further distinguished by the presence of thorns on the four-rayed spicules
projecting from the body. On your next dive, look inside a specimen. A
potentially boring dive may be transformed into an enlightening one,
thanks to the different creatures inhabiting these sponges.
Fearney Point, Agamemnon Channel, s. BC

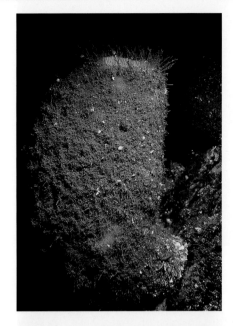

PO10. ROUND LIPPED BOOT SPONGE, boot sponge, chimney sponge
Staurocalyptus dowlingi, *Rhabdocalyptus dowlingi*
to 1.5 m (5 ft) tall
c. Alaska to s. California
subtidal to 924 m (3,050 ft)
Very similar to the sharp lipped boot sponge (PO9), the round lipped boot
sponge has a thick, rounded osculum (opening) as shown. Some specimens
are less folded over than others, so it may be difficult to differentiate this
species from the sharp lipped boot sponge. The presence of dagger-shaped
edges on at least some of the large, three-pronged spicules is the truly
definitive feature.
Agamemnon Channel, Sechelt Peninsula, s. BC

PO11. CLOUD SPONGE, clay pipe sponge
Aphrocallistes vastus, *Aphrocallistes whiteavesianus*
to 3 m (10 ft) either horizontally or vertically
Siberia, n. Alaska to n. Mexico
subtidal, 10–1,600 m (35–5,280 ft)
This spectacular sponge features cloud-like growths with a styrofoam
texture. The tips of specimens are usually palm-shaped but may be tubular.
The cloud sponge provides shelter for an amazing array of life. While we
were preparing this volume, we found it to be a virtual ecosystem unto
itself!
Anderson Bay, Texada Island, s. BC

PO12. FINGERED GOBLET SPONGE, goblet sponge, vase sponge
Heterochone calyx, *Chonelasma calyx*
to 90 cm (36 in) either horizontally or vertically
Japan to s. California
subtidal, 5–1,100 m (16–3,630 ft)
With much the same texture as the cloud sponge (PO11), this sponge has a much thicker wall and is often beautifully flared, like a goblet or vase. However, some grow straight and tall. Note the distinctive outgrowths. Giant **sponge reefs**, described as living fossils, exist in Hecate Strait, BC, between the Queen Charlotte Islands (Haida Gwaii) and the mainland coast at depths of 250 m (825 ft). These huge mound structures are composed primarily of three species, including the cloud sponge (PO11), fingered goblet sponge (PO12) and the lace sponge, *Farrea occa*—not likely to be encountered. These reefs are massive, but they are delicate and unique formations that cry out for protection from extraction activities, particularly destruction by trawls—nets that scrape the ocean floor in pursuit of bottom-dwelling seafood. The latest threat to the reefs could well be oil and gas drilling rigs.
Off west coast, Vancouver Island, s. BC

DEMOSPONGES

PO13. TENNIS BALL SPONGE, gray puffball sponge, gray puff ball sponge
Craniella villosa, *Tetilla villosa, Craniella arb ?, Tetilla arb ?*
to 25 cm (10 in) diameter
n. Alaska to n. Mexico
intertidal to 24 m (80 ft)
Dwelling primarily in rocky, high-current locales, this sponge usually resembles a softball-sized tennis ball, making it easy to identify.
Sutton Islets, Egmont, s. BC

PO14. SPINY TENNIS BALL SPONGE, spiny puffball sponge
Craniella spinosa, *Tetilla spinosa*
to 4 cm (1.5 in) diameter
n. Alaska to BC
subtidal
This smaller species looks whiter and appears much "hairier," because of more protruding spicules, than the tennis ball sponge (PO13). It is found mostly in lower-current locales and is often obscured by silt, which makes it a little more difficult to see.
Lions Bay, Howe Sound, s. BC

PO15. THICK WHITE PRICKLY SPONGE
Stelletta clarella, *Stelletta estrella*
at least 30 cm (12 in) across
s. Alaska to n. Mexico, Chile
intertidal to subtidal
An abundance of large projecting spicules give the thick white prickly sponge a plush texture adorning its dirty white colour.
Seymour Narrows, Discovery Passage, s. BC. Neil McDaniel photograph

PO16. ARMOURED BALL SPONGE
***Geodia mesotriaena**, Geodia agassizi, Geodia breviana, Cydonium muelleri*
at least 20 cm (8 in) across
s. Alaska to s. California
subtidal
Close inspection of the central white area—where the plush layer of long, brown spicules is absent—shows a "paving stone" appearance. Unfortunately, a hand lens or magnifying glass is usually required to see such detail.
Cyril Rock, Texada Island, s. BC. Neil McDaniel photograph

PO17. AGGREGATED NIPPLE SPONGE, many nipples sponge, aggregated vase sponge
Polymastia pachymastia
indeterminate, irregular size, but usually greater than 2.5 cm (1 in) across and 0.7 cm (0.3 in) thick
n. Alaska to s. California
intertidal to at least 55 m (182 ft)
Many seemingly "separate" individuals are part of a common thick carpet that forms a base. If this carpet is dusted off, it is the same creamy yellow underneath the surface. The smaller specimens in the photograph attached to the sponge are white examples of yellow social ascidians (CH24).
Lion Islets, Galiano Island, s. BC

PO18. AGGREGATED VASE SPONGE, western nipple sponge
Polymastia pacifica
indeterminate, irregular size
n. Alaska to California
intertidal to 180 m (600 ft)
Unlike the aggregated nipple sponge (PO17), this sponge's "nipples" are more pointed and laterally flattened. Usually when this sponge is located, only the protuberances are visible, the "mat" being hidden from view by silt. Another deep-water *Polymastia* species, with longer, more pointed "nipples," exists in the Pacific Northwest.
Tuwanek Point, Sechelt Inlet, s. BC. Charlie Gibbs photograph

PO19. ▶RETRACTABLE NIPPLE SPONGE
***Weberella* sp.**
at least 7.5 cm (3 in) across
BC
subtidal
Unlike many sponges, this species can expand/retract its extensions. When these "nipples" are protruding they are soft, but when contracted they become rubbery. Virtually nothing is known about its ecology.
Stubbs Island, Weynton Passage, c. BC. Neil McDaniel photograph

PO20. ▶MOUNDED NIPPLE SPONGE
Biemna rhadia
at least 7.5 cm (3 in) across
c. Alaska to n. Mexico
subtidal
In preparation of this sponge comment—as for numerous others—we searched the literature, which provided precious little information. The photograph and an accompanying sample were obtained many years ago as part of a field study of BC sponges that unfortunately did not receive sufficient funding.
Another *Biemna* species is also found in BC.
Gordon Islands, Goletas Channel, c. BC. Neil McDaniel photograph

PO21. YELLOW BORING SPONGE, boring sponge, sulphur sponge
Cliona californiana, *Cliona celata* var. *californiana*, *Pseudosuberites pseudos*
indeterminate, irregular size
n. Alaska to n. Mexico
intertidal to 120 m (400 ft)
This sponge is commonly associated with calcium "housed" barnacles, as shown in photograph A, and bivalves, particularly the giant rock scallop (MC48). Once the host dies, the yellow boring sponge causes the disintegration of the shells and barnacle housings, as shown in photograph C. Photograph B shows a close-up of the sponge.
A Moore Point, Francis Peninsula, s. BC
B Worlcombe Island, Howe Sound, s. BC
C Laura Point, Mayne Island, s. BC

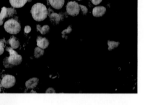

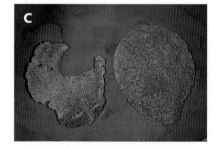

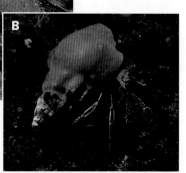

PO22. HERMIT CRAB SPONGE, hermit sponge
Suberites domuncula **forma** *latus*, *Suberites ?suberea* forma *latus* (the taxonomy of this creature is confused and awaits revision), *Suberites domuncula*, *Suberites latus*, *Choanites suberea*, *Choanites suberea* var. *lata*, *Ficulina lata*, incorrect: *Suberites ficus* (an Atlantic species)
▶to 25 cm (10 in) diameter
n. Alaska to s. California
intertidal to 36 m (120 ft)
In time this sponge completely replaces the original snail shell material and becomes the hermit's home. Sometimes it grows so large that one is tempted to feel sorry for the hermit. Photograph B shows sponge overgrowing a snail shell, and photograph A features two specimens, one overturned.
A Telegraph Cove, Vancouver Island, c. BC
B Anderson Bay, Texada Island, s. BC

PO23. PEACH BALL SPONGE
***Suberites montiniger**, Suberites concinnus*
to 30 cm (12 in) diameter
n. Alaska to n. Mexico
subtidal, 5–30 m (16–100 ft)
Soft texture and a smooth surface with few scattered oscula (holes) are distinctive for this sponge. A sponge is a non-selective particulate feeder, meaning that it may consume various prey provided they can pass through the tiny ostia (intake holes) in its body wall.
At least two other *Suberites* species exist.
Guide Islets, Cortes Island, s. BC

PO24. ORANGE ROUGH BALL SPONGE, orange puffball sponge, orange puff ball sponge, orange ball sponge, orange woody sponge, orange sponge
***Tethya californiana**, Tethya aurantia*
to 20 cm (8 in) diameter
s. Alaska to n. Mexico
intertidal to 440 m (1,460 ft)
Usually more or less spherical but with distinctive corrugations visible, this species may grow singly or cluster in small groups. Inside, it is a lighter colour.
Tyler Rock, Barkley Sound, s. BC

PO25. CHOCOLATE PUFFBALL SPONGE
***Sceptrella* sp. nov.**, *Latrunculia* sp.
to 10 cm (4 in) diameter
BC
subtidal to 20 m (65 ft)
This sponge has only recently been "discovered" and awaits a specific name. It is a confusing species, as it may appear turquoise or greenish when initially viewed underwater. Under artificial light, however, the chocolate puffball sponge looks totally different, as shown in the photograph. A lack of research into sponge pigments leaves this observation a mystery.
Sutton Islets, Egmont, s. BC

PO26. STALKED TRUMPET SPONGE, trumpet sponge, vase sponge
Stylissa stipitata
to 30 cm (12 in) tall
s. Alaska to Washington
subtidal to 30 m (100 ft)
Rarely, specimens that have double funnels are found, and others can lack the typical flare, making them more "flute-like." The external surface of the stalked trumpet sponge is relatively smooth, as compared to the uneven outer layer of the funnel sponge (PO27). Unfortunately, the only definitive way to distinguish the two is via spicule sampling and microscopic inspections. Further complicating matters, dorid nudibranch predators frequently alter both species' shapes through feeding activity.
Sutton Islets, Egmont, s. BC

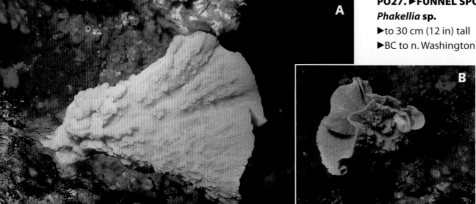

PO27. ▶FUNNEL SPONGE
Phakellia **sp.**
▶to 30 cm (12 in) tall
▶BC to n. Washington

subtidal
Similar to the stalked trumpet sponge (PO26) but usually with a deeply grooved or knobby outer surface, this sponge typically has a funnel shape. Without spicule sample and microscopic examination, though, identification should remain tentative. This sponge appears to prefer high-current locales and is also prey for dorid nudibranchs, particularly the noble sea lemon (MC291), as shown in photograph B.
A B Steep Island, Discovery Passage, s. BC

PO28. TOUGH YELLOW BRANCHING SPONGE
Syringella amphispicula
▶to 30 cm (12 in) across
BC to Washington
subtidal
The uneven surface of this sponge's projections give it a gnarled appearance. Look for it in silty, low-current locales, where it often provides shelter for small creatures. A sponge digests its food on a cellular level and does not secrete enzymes to assist the process.
Turn Island, San Juan Channel, n. Washington

PO29. ORANGE FINGER SPONGE, branched apically perforated finger sponge
Neoesperiopsis rigida, Isodictya rigida, Esperiopsis rigida
to 25 cm (10 in) tall
s. Alaska to n. California
subtidal, 3–30 m (10–100 ft)
A popular food source for some dorid nudibranchs, particularly the leopard dorid (MC298), this sponge may have a single or multi-tubed structure. Patches of brown alga sometimes grow over its surface. Several fish species lay their eggs inside this sponge.
Cotton Point, Howe Sound, s. BC

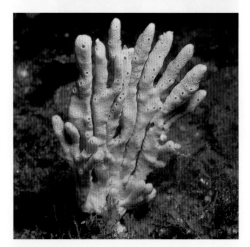

PO30. GLOVE SPONGE, branched laterally perforated finger sponge
Neoesperiopsis digitata, Isodictya digitata, Esperiopsis quatsinoensis
▶to 45 cm (18 in)
n. Alaska to Washington
subtidal
The glove sponge locates particularly on pronounced rocky outcrops, where the current is strongest. Note the numerous oscula (holes) where water exits the sponge.
Another similar species, the ▶small-spiculed glove sponge, *Neoesperiopsis vancouverensis,* also has abundant oscula (holes) along its branches, but its two spicule types are smaller.
Grainger Point, Samuel Island, s. BC

PO31. WHITE RETICULATED SPONGE

Iophon chelifer **var.** *californiana, Iophon chelifer*
▶to 60 cm (24 in) diameter
Alaska to n. Mexico
▶subtidal, 3–30 m (10–100 ft)
Occasional brown patches observed on some specimens are either a diatom (algal) growth or an area of the sponge that is dead. Intriguingly, specimens turn black when preserved in alcohol. Most species of sponge, including this one, are able to settle on a wide variety of hard surfaces. Another related species, the ▶piceus reticulated sponge, *Iophon piceus* var. *pacifica,* has spicules of different size and shape.
Sutton Islets, Egmont, s. BC

PO32. ▶MEMBRANE SPONGE

Hymeniacidon ungodon
at least 15 cm (6 in) across
BC to c. California
intertidal to subtidal
The photographed specimen was sampled and, through a spicule preparation and examination by Dr. Bill Austin, was determined to be this species.
Several other *Hymeniacidon* species exist, and the same involved process would be required to determine certain identification.
Stephenson Islet, Weynton Passage, c. BC. Neil McDaniel photograph

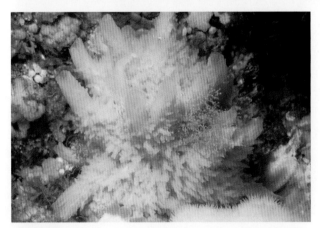

PO33. ▶THICK-STRAP SPONGES

Pachychalina **spp.**
size variable with species
BC
subtidal
The sponge illustrated in this photograph is one of several tough but spongy species that feature various growth forms. An osculum (exit hole) at each protruding end is an obvious feature. Unfortunately, much-needed studies of these sponges have not occurred.
Stubbs Island, Weynton Passage, c. BC. Neil McDaniel photograph

PO34. During preparation of this book, Bernie Hanby found and photographed this sponge off Gerald Island, Ballenas Channel, s. BC, at a depth of 20 m (65 ft). Originally categorized as an "unknown," it was tentatively labelled the ▶gnarled finger sponge. Fortunately Dr. Bill Austin, our sponge consultant, was able to determine that it is a **new species of** *Reniera*. Considerable time and effort will be needed to scientifically catalogue and name it so that it can be distinguished from several other *Reniera* species.
A Gerald Island, Ballenas Channel, s. BC
B Turn Island, San Juan Channel, n. Washington

PO35. ▶HARD GNARLED CLUMP SPONGE

Xestospongia hispida of Lambe
indeterminate, irregular size
s. Alaska to n. Mexico
▶subtidal, below 10 m (33 ft)
A hard species that prefers high current, this sponge grows either in large, beautifully sculptured forms or in low-profile mounds. Dr. Bill Austin of the Marine Ecology Centre in Sidney, BC, originally believed this sponge to be *Xestospongia trindanea* but now recognizes that there are two separate *Xestospongia* species. Confusion has existed since Dr. Lambe's original work in 1895.

Laura Point, Mayne Island, s. BC

PO36. SULPHUR SPONGE, yellow encrusting sponge

Myxilla lacunosa
indeterminate, irregular size
n. Alaska to s. BC
subtidal, below 10 m (33 ft)
Flaccid and easily crumbled, this usually mound-shaped species prefers high-current locales with an abundance of red soft coral (CN37). Within the mound-shaped structure is a very complex network of interconnecting tubes through which oxygen-rich and food-laden seawater passes. Photograph A shows a large, somewhat discoloured specimen; photograph B shows a close-up view of a clean one.

A B Browning Passage, Nigei Island, c. BC

PO37. BOWERBANK'S CRUMB OF BREAD SPONGE, crumb-of-bread sponge, crumb of bread sponge

Halichondria bowerbankia, has been confused with *Halichondria panicea*
indeterminate, irregular size
BC to c. California
subtidal
This sponge is most often found amid float and piling habitats. Because of its flaccid structure, it is easily dislodged by wave or current action, often leaving yellow-coloured debris under these man-made structures.

Egmont Marina, Egmont, s. BC

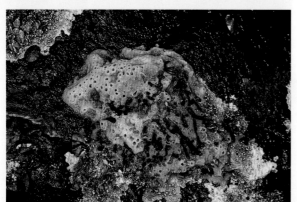

PO38. YELLOW-GREEN ENCRUSTING SPONGE, crumb of bread sponge, crumb-of-bread sponge, bread crumb sponge

Halichondria panicea
indeterminate, irregular size, 5 cm (2 in) thick
n. Alaska to n. Mexico
intertidal to 100 m (330 ft)
Living along exposed, rocky, surf-swept shores, this intertidal inhabitant is one of the few sponges that is readily seen by beachcombers. It appears to tolerate drying better than most other Pacific Northwest sponges.

Frank Island, w. Vancouver Island, s. BC

PO39. ▶BRISTLY YELLOW CLUMP SPONGE
Mycale **cf.** *toporoki*, *Mycale lingula*, *Esperella lingula*
▶to 10 cm (4 in) across
Japan, n. Alaska to Washington
subtidal
Supplied with a sample and a photograph, Dr. Bill Austin was able to identify this sponge as listed. Well, almost. The "cf." refers to uncertainty: this species does not quite match the diagnosis for *Mycale toporoki* in Japan.
Green Bay, Nelson Island, s. BC

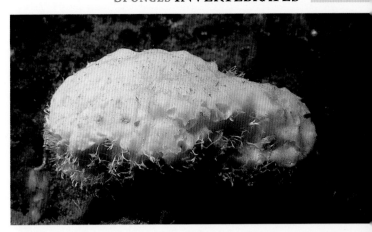

PO40. The creature shown here is a **"new species"** of *Stylinos*, referred to hereafter as the ▶**FLACCID SPONGE** due to its delicate, easily damaged body. It is a common though inconspicuous inhabitant of low-current locales in southern BC at least. Although scientifically discovered in the 1980s, it remains "new" primarily because of a lack of funding for the few capable scientists—such as Dr. Bill Austin—to carry out the laborious description required. Unfortunately, sponges are not perceived to be as interesting as whales or as economically important as salmon, and so they remain in relative obscurity.
Bowyer Island, Howe Sound, s. BC

PO41. Various factors make the study of sponge taxonomy challenging. Some of these are specific to sponges, others apply to all groups of plants and animals. One of these factors is the physical difference between adult and juvenile, which has often led to one species being classified as two. Dr. Bill Austin believes that the species shown here is the ▶**PAPILLA SPONGE**, *Laxosuberites* **sp. nov.** At only 5 cm (2 in) in diameter, it is also possibly a juvenile *Suberites* sp. A solution would be to note where a specimen was observed and return at a later date to assess any changes.
Nelson Island, Agamemnon Channel, s. BC

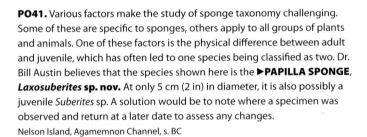

PO42. ▶PALE ORANGE CARPET SPONGE
Adocia **sp. ?**, similar to *Reniera foraminosa*
indeterminate, irregular size
▶BC to n. Washington
intertidal to subtidal
Confusion persists as to the precise identity of this sponge. It is, however, a very common species in areas with considerable current and literally carpets the bottom at some locales. The animal is spongy soft, and its colour is consistent throughout its thickness.
Laura Point, Mayne Island, s. BC

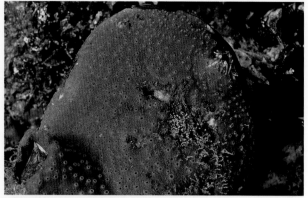

PO43. PURPLE INTERTIDAL SPONGE, purple encrusting sponge, violet encrusting sponge, violet volcano sponge, purple sponge, encrusting sponge

***Haliclona ? permollis**, Haliclona cinera, Reniera cinera, Reniera rufescens, Haliclona* species A of Hartman 1975

indeterminate, irregular size, 1.6 cm (0.7 in) thick

s. Alaska to s. California

intertidal to 6 m (20 ft)

Closely packed mini-mounds, each with an osculum (hole), are a typical form of this species, another of the few intertidal sponges. A very similar-looking sponge lives along the Atlantic coast of North America, but whether it is the same species is in doubt.

Frank Island, w. Vancouver Island, s. BC

PO44. ▶ORANGE CRATERED ENCRUSTING SPONGE

***Hamigera sp.**, Lissodendoryx kyma*

indeterminate, irregular size

BC to Washington

subtidal

Distinguished by closely packed mini-craters over its entire surface, this sponge is a prime site to find the Tara's dorid (MC296). Very little is known about this species.

Pasley Island, Howe Sound, s. BC

PO45. SLIPPERY ROSE SPONGE

***Aplysilla sp. nov.**, (Aplysilla glacialis* of authors in n.e. Pacific)

indeterminate, irregular size

▶BC to Washington

intertidal to subtidal

As in many other sponges, some of the skeletal support structures of this species are made up of special collagenous fibre called spongin. Large examples of these reinforced but loosely arranged fibres protrude from this sponge's surface, giving it a somewhat "hairy" appearance.

Booker Lagoon, Broughton Island, c. BC

PO46. SLIPPERY PURPLE SPONGE

Chelonaplysilla polyraphis

indeterminate, irregular size

w. Pacific Ocean, BC to c. California

intertidal to subtidal

This species, along with the slippery rose sponge (PO45), has been called the keratose sponge. The specific determinations are now more certain, and this "catch-all" name is now passé.

Tilly Point, s. Pender Island, s. BC

PO47. SLIPPERY WHITE SPONGE
Pleraplysilla **sp. nov.**
indeterminate, irregular size
▶s. Alaska to BC
subtidal
The slippery white sponge was originally believed to be a colour phase of a variable *Aplysilla* sponge. However, diligent taxonomic efforts have resulted in the splitting of this generalized *Aplysilla* into the three "slippery sponges" (PO45–47) shown here.
Benjamin Island, Lynn Canal, s. Alaska

PO48. THICK ENCRUSTING SCARLET SPONGE, red volcano sponge, red sponge
Acarnus erithacus
indeterminate, irregular size
s. Alaska to n. Mexico
intertidal to 700 m (2,300 ft)
Forming thick, bumpy mats on rocky bottoms subjected to high currents, this species is a popular "home" for the Cooper's dorid nudibranch (MC316). As shown in the photograph, the colour beneath the surface layer is somewhat lighter.
Laura Point, Mayne Island, s. BC

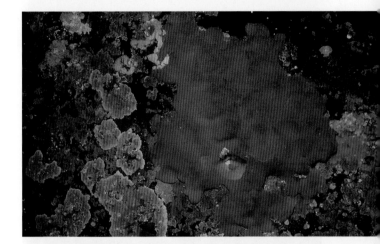

PO49. ▶RED-BROWN ENCRUSTING SPONGE
Anthoarcuata graceae, *Burtonanchora lacunosa*
indeterminate, irregular size
BC to c. California
subtidal
A thick, soft species that seems to prefer current-swept habitats, this encrusting sponge also often supplies food and shelter for the Cooper's dorid nudibranch (MC316). The outer surface is generally a darker hue than the internal layer.
Laura Point, Mayne Island, s. BC

PO50. BRIGHT RED SPONGE, red sponge, mucus sponge
Plocamia karykina
indeterminate, irregular size
BC to n. Mexico
intertidal to subtidal
Thick, hard textured and covered with few, irregularly spaced oscula (holes), this species can be confused with any of several other red encrusting sponges with spicules. Fortunately the bright red sponge can be distinguished by the copious amounts of mucus it secretes when touched.
Union Island, Kyuquot Sound, c. BC

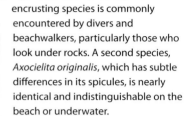

PO51. VELVETY RED SPONGES, including red encrusting sponge, scarlet sponge, red sponge
Ophlitaspongia pennata, *Desmacella pennata, Biemna pennata, Tylodesma pennata*
indeterminate, irregular size
Alaska to n. Mexico
intertidal to 90 m (300 ft)
The preferred "home" for the red sponge nudibranch (MC315), this thin encrusting species is commonly encountered by divers and beachwalkers, particularly those who look under rocks. A second species, *Axocielita originalis*, which has subtle differences in its spicules, is nearly identical and indistinguishable on the beach or underwater.
A Butress Island, Slingsby Channel, c. BC
B Tongue Point, Olympic coast, n. Washington

PO52. PIPECLEANER SPONGE
Asbestopluma occidentalis, *Asbestopluma lycopodium, Asbestopluma hadalis, Lycopodina occidentalis, Esperella occidentalis*
▶to 2.5 cm (1 in) tall
Siberia to s. California
subtidal
If a diver notices this diminutive species, its "non-sponge-like" appearance makes it readily identifiable. The pipecleaner and its relatives are unique among sponges for their lack of "plumbing" to produce feeding currents through their bodies. Instead, they trap minute animals by means of specialized hook-like spicules.
Agamemnon Channel, Nelson Island, s. BC

PO53. ROUGH SCALLOP SPONGE, bumpy pecten sponge, scallop sponge, rough encrusting sponge
Myxilla incrustans, *Myxilla parasitica, Myxilla rosacea, Myxilla behringensis, Myxilla barentsi, Ectodoryx parasitica*
to size of scallop shell or smaller
Japan, Arctic to s. California
subtidal
Lumpy with raised oscula (holes), the rough scallop sponge may be prey for various dorid nudibranchs.
Sutton Islets, Egmont, s. BC

PO54. SMOOTH SCALLOP SPONGE, smooth pecten sponge, smooth encrusting sponge
Mycale adhaerens, *Esperella adhaerens*
to size of scallop shell or smaller
Siberia to Washington
subtidal to 150 m (500 ft)
This species is similar to the rough scallop sponge (PO53) but smooth, with less obvious holes. Do both sponges benefit from living on scallops? Certainly their mobility is an option unavailable to most other sponges.
Cyril Rock, Texada Island, s. BC

PO55. SPOTTED GRAY SPONGE, salt and pepper sponge
Penares cortius
indeterminate, irregular size
s. Alaska to s. California
intertidal to subtidal
The spotted gray sponge grows in firm ridges or patches, often with open gaps of rocky substrate showing through. During rough weather, when potentially harmful silt and other debris is stirred up by wave action, many sponges can seal themselves off to keep harmful effects away from the delicate filtration system inside.
Gaviola Island, Flat Top Islands, s. BC

PO56. DEEP BLUE SPONGE, cobalt sponge
Hymenamphiastra cyanocrypta
indeterminate, irregular size
BC to n. Mexico
intertidal to 58 m (190 ft)
The photograph shows both colour phases of this unusual sponge. When it has a symbiotic bacteria living within, it is dark blue in colour. When the bacteria is missing, the deep blue sponge appears tan or pale orange.
Browning Passage, Nigei Island, c. BC

PO57. ▶TURQUOISE-TINGED SPONGE
Phloeodictyon **sp. nov.**
indeterminate, irregular size
BC
subtidal
Another of the "new species" of Pacific Northwest sponges that remain undescribed and incompletely named, this one is nonetheless obvious to the diver or naturalist. As one of the relatively few turquoise-coloured creatures living in these waters, it tends to be quite visible. The intriguing question is, why so little turquoise or blue?
Booker Lagoon, Broughton Island, c. BC

PO58. ▶BREAST SPONGE
Eumastia sitiens, *Halichondria sitiens*, *Pellina sitiens*
at least 15 cm (6 in) across
n. Alaska to BC
subtidal
This sponge is another little-known species with a scientific name (*Eumastia*) that refers to "breast," so our choice for a common name (as one could not be found in the literature) follows suit. Whether there is a resemblance is left for you to ponder.
Prominent Point, Knight Inlet, c. BC. Neil McDaniel photograph

PO59. ▶RICKETTS' SPONGE
Poecillastra rickettsi, perhaps *Volcanella tenuilamilaris*
at least 5 cm (2 in) across
BC, s. California
subtidal
This poorly known sponge is named for the pioneering naturalist Ed Ricketts of Monterey, California—a legendary figure in the Cannery Row saga written by John Steinbeck. Ed's legacy is the famous *Between Pacific Tides*—a wonderful, easily read book of which five editions have been published, each thoroughly updated by followers renowned in their own right.
Temple Rock, Pender Harbour, s. BC. Neil McDaniel photograph

PO60. YELLOW SPICULE-LESS SPONGE
***Hexadella* sp. nov.**
indeterminate, irregular size
s. BC
subtidal
One of the few local sponges with no spicules or skeletal elements, this species encrusts upon the hard remains of the cloud sponge (PO11), a site that supplies the animal with a rigid platform. Dr. Bill Austin determined this to be a new species, yet to be formally described. It is also the sponge that the capshell (MC283) feeds on.
Anderson Bay, Texada Island, s. BC

Undetermined Sponges—A Selection

During the preparation of this book, a sizable but incomplete collection of sponge photographs was assembled. Fortunately we were able to work with the authority on the topic—Dr. Bill Austin of the Marine Ecology Centre in Sidney, BC, an excellent educational facility that is open to the public and well worth a visit.

The Pacific Northwest sponge taxonomy is in a state of disarray. This has occurred for various reasons, primarily a lack of funding: the dedicated and competent scientists required to review the ever-increasing backlog of material are not being supported. The status quo is likely to persist, and sponge identification will continue to be a frustrating, often impossible task.

Through the following photographic presentation of essentially "unknown sponges" with the accompanying location data and descriptions, we hope to accomplish at least two things. The first is simply an appreciation and enjoyment of the wide variety of species in the Pacific Northwest. The second, perhaps more important, is an inspiration for progress in sponge classification. Motivated amateurs can be of great value—one need only consider the impact that keen underwater photographers and others have had with web sites.

PO61. Undetermined sponge A. Specimens are found subtidally as flat mounds of very firm texture, generally in locales with some current. It is tentatively categorized as a *Suberites* sp.
Fort Ebey, Whidbey Island, n. Washington

PO62. Undetermined sponge B. Specimens are found subtidally as small, fist-shaped, mauve-coloured mounds. The texture is rock hard; another similar-looking species is soft and spongy. It is tentatively categorized as an *Adocia* sp.
Ba Ucluth Peninsula, w. Vancouver Island, s. BC
Bb Cape Flattery, Olympic coast, n. Washington

PO63. Undetermined sponge C. Specimens are found intertidally encrusting the undersides of rocks. The texture appears slimy.

Ucluth Peninsula, w. Vancouver Island, s. BC

PO64. Undetermined sponge D. Specimens are found subtidally encrusting giant rock scallops (MC48) and giant acorn barnacles (AR171). This is a very thin, dull orange species.

Union Island, Kyuquot Sound, c. BC

PO65. Undetermined sponge E. Specimens are found subtidally encrusting rocky walls. This sponge appears very thin, almost like smudged yellow paint.

Tzoonie Narrows, Narrows Inlet, s. BC

PO66. Undetermined sponge F. Specimens are found subtidally as white flat mounds or thick encrustations. The texture is soft and spongy. It is tentatively categorized in the *Pellina* group.

Anderson Bay, Texada Island, s. BC

PO67. Undetermined sponge G. Specimens are found subtidally as large encrusting mounds. Texture is firm but spongy. It is tentatively categorized as sulphur sponge, *Myxilla lacunosa*, but this specimen seems different from the feature entry (PO36) for this species.

Booker Lagoon, Broughton Island, c. BC

PO68. Undetermined sponge H. Yellowish specimens are found intertidally on exposed rocky shorelines. The texture is firm but spongy. It is tentatively categorized as rough scallop sponge, *Myxilla incrustans*, but seems different from the feature entry (PO53) for this species.

Ha Slip Point, Olympic coast, n. Washington
Hb Frank Island, w. Vancouver Island, s. BC

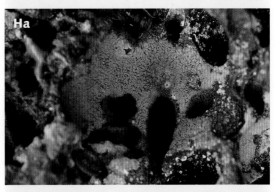

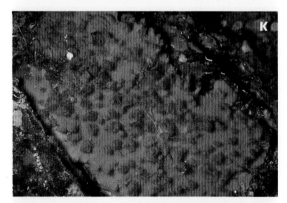

PO69. Undetermined sponge I. Resembling a yellowish suction cup extending into a tendril about 5 cm (2 in) long, this sponge could only be vaguely categorized by Dr. Bill Austin as similar to the non-sexual reproductive structures seen in a few species of sponges (*Tentorium*, *Polymastia*).

Agamemnon Channel, Nelson Island, s. BC

PO70. Undetermined sponge J. A cinnamon colour, this small, mound-shaped sponge is very hard to the touch. It is found subtidally in current-swept locales.

Laura Point, Mayne Island, s. BC

PO71. Undetermined sponge K. Bright orange and moderately thick, this soft encrusting sponge features gnarled protrusions. It usually forms irregular mats in areas of low to moderate current.

Anderson Bay, Texada Island, s. BC

PO72. Undetermined sponge L. Growing in an uneven mound, this large, yellow-orange sponge is firm to the touch and lives in locales swept by moderate current.

Turn Island, San Juan Channel, n. Washington

PO73. Undetermined sponge M. Generally similar to undetermined sponge L (PO72), this specimen features a lighter colour and smoother surface. Such differences may not be significant.

Bell Island, Orcas Island, n. Washington

PO74. Undetermined sponge N. An uneven mound sponge of bright yellow-orange, it has a soft texture and lives in strong-current areas.

Pearse Islands, Weynton Passage, c. BC

PO75. Undetermined sponge O. This sponge is similar to undetermined sponge N (PO74) in colour, shape, texture and size, and it was found in a similar habitat, but its surface structure appears different.

Browning Passage, Nigei Island, c. BC

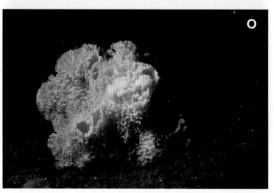

PO76. Undetermined sponge P. Another uneven, mound-shaped sponge, this soft, yellowish specimen was living on a steep wall in a low-current channel.

Butedale, Grenville Channel, n. BC

PO77. Undetermined sponge Q. Of similar texture to undetermined sponge P (PO76), this yellowish specimen growing as a thick, concentrated carpet has numerous oscula (holes). It was found at a low-current locale.

Link Island, Barkley Sound, s. BC

PO78. Undetermined sponge R. Growing in a small, uneven, greenish-grey mat, this firm sponge has numerous variously sized, unevenly spaced oscula (holes).

Diver Islands, Meares Passage, s. Alaska

PO79. Undetermined sponge S. A firm, yellow encrusting sponge, this specimen was growing on submerged and waterlogged bark where current is insignificant.

English Bay, Burrard Inlet, s. BC

PO80. Undetermined sponge T. This soft, white encrusting sponge has much surface detail in the form of tiny holes and trough-like markings.

Moore Point, Francis Peninsula, s. BC

PO81. Undetermined sponge U. This soft, yellow sponge shows some sculpture on its uneven surface. It was dwelling in very high-current habitat.

Johnson Point, Seymour Inlet, c. BC

PO82. Undetermined sponge V. This thin, yellowish encrusting sponge is overgrowing a dead cloud sponge (PO11).

Sabine Channel, Texada Island, s. BC

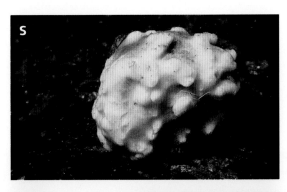

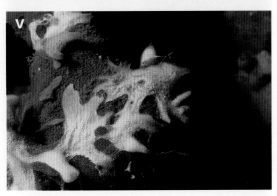

PO83. Undetermined sponge W. The encrusting specimens shown in these two photographs are similar enough that they are included here in the same entry. Both were living in high-current habitats.

Wa Josef Point, Gabriola Passage, s. BC

Wb Turn Island, San Juan Channel, n. Washington

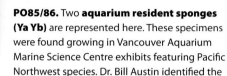

PO84. Undetermined sponge X. This encrusting sponge with rather tall protuberances was found subtidally in a moderate-current locale.

Baranof Hot Springs, Baranof Island, s. Alaska

PO85/86. Two **aquarium resident sponges (Ya Yb)** are represented here. These specimens were found growing in Vancouver Aquarium Marine Science Centre exhibits featuring Pacific Northwest species. Dr. Bill Austin identified the thin encrusting form as an *Oscarella* sp. and the thicker, uneven one as a *Desmacella* sp., perhaps one of the three Pacific Northwest species.

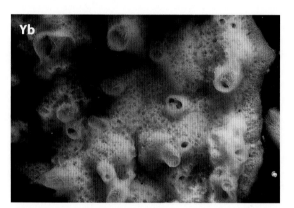

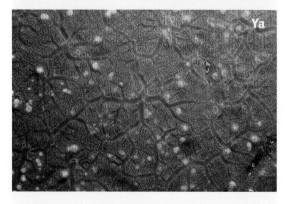

SEA ANEMONES, CORALS, HYDROIDS, HYDROCORALS, JELLIES AND OTHERS
Phylum CNIDARIA (aka Coelenterata)

Includes anemones, zoanthids, corals, gorgonians, sea pens, sea whips, hydroids, sea firs, hydrocorals and a variety of forms casually called "jellyfish" or "jellies."

Central to each cnidarian is a digestive system with one opening—yes, the mouth is also the anus! Ringing the opening is a circle of tentacles that have a definitive radial symmetry. The tentacles are festooned with millions of cells called cnidocytes, each of which has a tiny, harpoon-like mechanism. Prey capture is a common function of these specialized cells, many of which contain an associated toxin.

A cnidarian has one of two body types: the polyp or the medusa. The polyp, an example of which is shown in photograph A—rose anemone (CN8)—features a ring of tentacles and mouth/anus configuration atop a columnar body and exists either as a solitary entity or as part of a group with countless others.

In the case of sea anemones, these groups of polyps are clones, and members can be referred to as clone-mates. In the medusa body type, an example of which is shown in photograph B—sea nettle (CN91), a ring of tentacles and mouth/anus layout hang beneath a bell-shaped or pancake-shaped sac. This body form is usually free floating. Some cnidarian "rascals" have life cycles that alternate these two forms. More than 500 cnidarian species live in the Pacific Northwest.

Further Reading

Wrobel, David and Claudia Mills, 1998, *Pacific Coast Pelagic Invertebrates*, Monterey CA: Sea Challengers, 108 pp.

SEA ANEMONES

CN1. SHORT PLUMOSE ANEMONE, clonal plumose anemone, plumose anemone, frilled anemone, sun anemone, white plumed anemone, white-plumed anemone, white plume anemone, plumed anemone, powder puff anemone, orange anemone, fluffy anemone, sea pumpkin

Metridium senile

to 10 cm (4 in) tall
5 cm (2 in) across base
circumpolar, n. Alaska to s. California
intertidal to 300 m (1,000 ft)

This anemone's tentacular crown (oral disc) is not lobed. It prefers higher-current and shallow locales, where it often completely carpets the bottom.

Nakwakto Rapids, Slingsby Channel, c. BC

CN2. GIANT PLUMOSE ANEMONE, gigantic anemone, tall plumose anemone, white-plumed anemone, powder puff anemone, frilled anemone, sun anemone, frilled plumose anemone

Metridium farcimen

to 1 m (39 in) tall
n. Alaska to n. Mexico
subtidal to 300 m (1,000 ft)

Numerous large lobes enlarge this anemone's tentacular crown (oral disc). The animal appears to prefer lower-current locales and deeper water than the short plumose anemone (CN1). Photograph B shows a greatly retracted specimen with its acontia (defensive filamentous structures) extended from inside the gut.

A Agamemnon Channel, Nelson Island, s. BC
B Link Island, Barkley Sound, s. BC

CN3. CRIMSON ANEMONE, snakelock anemone, chevron-tentacled anemone
Cribrinopsis fernaldi
to 30 cm (12 in) tall
n. Alaska to Washington
subtidal to 300 m (1,000 ft)
Note the fine, irregular red banding on opaque tentacles, a feature readily visible on most crimson anemones. Specimens living in high-current

habitats usually appear more squat than those living in low-flow locales. Photograph B shows the pale form most prevalent on sandy bottoms.
A Agamemnon Channel, Nelson Island, s. BC
B Columbine Bay, Bowen Island, s. BC

CN4. The status of this **small pink anemone** is uncertain. It may be a small variant of the crimson anemone (CN3) that lacks the typical red banding on its tentacles, or it may be a distinct species. In any event, it was originally found some years ago by the diver/photographer Neil McDaniel of Vancouver, BC, while exploring the current-swept passages at the northeast end of Vancouver Island, BC.
A B Stubbs Island, Weynton Passage, c. BC

CN5. While helping out with the production of this book, diver/photographer Charlie Gibbs of Port Coquitlam, BC, found several specimens of this mysterious **white anemone** at about 30 m (100 ft) near Pender Harbour, BC. Bernie Hanby exposed a significant amount of film in order to get just the right exposure for this white, somewhat featureless animal—a photographic challenge.
For more than 35 years, Dr. Daphne Fautin, a sea anemone enthusiast and professor at the University of Kansas, has been diligently documenting and describing Pacific Northwest species. She has published numerous significant papers in various scientific publications, and her goal is to produce a comprehensive atlas of these colourful creatures. Her help with this portion of the book is most appreciated.
A B Agamemnon Channel, Nelson Island, s. BC

CN6. PAINTED ANEMONE, dahlia anemone, painted urticina, Christmas anemone, red and green anemone, red and green sea anemone, mottled anemone, northern red anemone, giant red sea anemone, painted tealia
Urticina crassicornis*
to 30 cm (12 in) tall
to 20 cm (8 in) column diameter
n. Alaska to s. California
intertidal to at least 30 m (100 ft)
Widespread and variably coloured, this species has long, banded tentacles. The banding is less obvious in tan individuals, as shown in photograph B. Photograph C features specimens of both primary colour variants from a current-swept locale.
*In many older references, the invalid genus name *Tealia* is used for the five *Urticina* species listed here.
A Fearney Point, Agamemnon Channel, s. BC
B Anderson Bay, Texada Island, s. BC
C Surge Narrows, Maurelle Island, s. BC

CN7. WHITE-SPOTTED ROSE ANEMONE, white spotted rose anemone, white-spotted anemone, spotted rose anemone, spotted red anemone, scarlet anemone, white spotted tealia, strawberry anemone, red sea anemone
Urticina lofotensis
to 25 cm (10 in) tall
to 15 cm (6 in) column diameter
n. Alaska to s. California
intertidal to 23 m (75 ft)
Irregular white spotting on a bright pink column is distinctive in this anemone, which is found in outer coast habitats.
Weld Island, Barkley Sound, s. BC

CN8. ROSE ANEMONE, fish-eating anemone, fish-eating urticina, velvety red anemone, fish-eating tealia
Urticina piscivora
▶to 30 cm (12 in) tall
to ▶30 cm (12 in) column diameter
n. Alaska to s. California
intertidal to 48 m (160 ft)
A deep maroon column with no markings and either a white or red oral disc are the distinctive features of this species. It is found in outer coast habitats. Juvenile specimens are much brighter and look quite different, as shown in photograph B.
A Baeria Rocks, Barkley Sound, s. BC
B Fox Islands, Slingsby Channel, c. BC

CN9. STUBBY ROSE ANEMONE, red-beaded anemone, beaded anemone, leathery anemone, stubby buried anemone, buried anemone, buried urticina, buried tealia
Urticina coriacea
to 15 cm (6 in) tall
to 15 cm (6 in) column diameter
Alaska to s. California
intertidal to 45 m (150 ft)
This species has stubby, lightly banded tentacles and a bright pink column. Two "forms" or perhaps species are shown: the one with the more pointed tentacles (photograph B) is an outer coast inhabitant; the other lives in sheltered, sandy regions.
A Lane Islet, Dawley Passage, s. BC
B Tongue Point, Olympic coast, n. Washington

CN10. SAND-ROSE ANEMONE, Columbia sand anemone, sand anemone, crusty red anemone
Urticina columbiana
to 25 cm (10 in) tall
to 1 m (39 in) column diameter
s. BC to n. Mexico
subtidal, 3–45 m (10–150 ft)
Raised white tubercles (bumps) in irregular rows on a pink column are distinctive in this sand-dweller. Unfortunately, one must excavate a little to see this obvious feature.
Mukilteo, Puget Sound, c. Washington

CN11. SWIMMING ANEMONE, cowardly anemone
Stomphia didemon
to 10 cm (4 in) tall
to 12 cm (5 in) across
Alaska to s. California
subtidal to 20 m (65 ft)
Some sea stars, especially the leather star (EC7), may elicit a "swimming" response from this anemone. Upon contact, the swimming anemone stretches upward, releasing itself from the bottom by making a cone shape of its adhesive base. By alternately contracting opposite sides of the column, it writhes about in an escape reaction.
Worlcombe Island, Howe Sound, s. BC

CN12. SPOTTED SWIMMING ANEMONE, swimming anemone
Stomphia coccinea
to 7.6 cm (3 in) tall
to 7.6 cm (3 in) across
n. Alaska to Washington
subtidal, below 10 m (35 ft)
Small white spots at the base of each tentacle, when viewed from above, forms a circle, distinguishing this species from the swimming anemone (CN11). Many thousands of cnidocytes (stinging cells) arm every anemone's tentacles, allowing the animal to disable its prey.
Telegraph Cove, n. Vancouver Island, c. BC

CN13. GREEN SURF ANEMONE, giant green anemone, giant green sea anemone, solitary green anemone, green sea anemone, green anemone, giant tidepool anemone, solitary anemone, rough anemone
Anthopleura xanthogrammica,
Cribrina xanthogrammica
to 30 cm (12 in) tall
to 30 cm (12 in) column diameter
s. Alaska to n. Mexico, perhaps Panama
intertidal to 30 m (100 ft)
This anemone prefers surge channels along surf-swept outer shores and tide pools, as shown in photograph B.
A B Frank Island, w. Vancouver Island, s. BC

CN14. PINK-TIPPED ANEMONE, pink-tipped green anemone, pink-tipped surf anemone, aggregating anemone, aggregate anemone, aggregate sea anemone, aggregated anemone, aggregate green anemone, clustering aggregate anemone, clonal anemone, elegant anemone, rough anemone, sandy anemone, surf anemone
Anthopleura elegantissima, *Cribrina elegantissima, Bunodactis elegantissima*
to 25 cm (10 in) across, 50 cm (20 in) tall
Alaska to n. Mexico
intertidal to 18 m (60 ft)
Although the green colour present in some specimens is produced by the animals themselves, this process can only occur when the unicellular symbiotic alga *Chorella* is residing in their tissues. Usually carpeting extensive rocky areas, colonies of clones actually war against each other. During her review of this book's sea anemone text, Dr. Daphne Fautin mentioned that the solitary "form" of the pink-tipped anemone has been accorded species status and is now known as the green anemone, *Anthopleura sola.* Currently documented from California, it may be found farther north in the future.
A B Dodd Narrows, Mudge Island, s. BC

CN15. BURROWING ANEMONE, green burrowing anemone, buried anemone, buried green anemone, buried sea anemone, buried moonglow anemone, beach sand anemone, moonglow anemone
Anthopleura artemisia, *Cribrina artemisia*
to 10 cm (4 in) across
s. Alaska to s. California
intertidal to 30 m (100 ft)
Look for this species particularly at a rock/sand interface, sometimes inhabiting holes excavated by rock-boring clams. In the intertidal zone, this anemone may be found with all its tentacles exposed and visible, or withdrawn as a less than obvious "blob" or even a puckered hole in the sand. Photograph B shows a green alga colouring the anemone.
A Eagle Harbour, West Vancouver, s. BC
B Irvines Landing, Pender Harbour, s. BC

CN16. STRAWBERRY ANEMONE, club-tipped anemone, pink anemone, strawberry corallimorpharian, corynactis anemone
Corynactis californica
to 2.5 cm (1 in) across
n. BC to n. Mexico
intertidal to 45 m (150 ft)
Vast carpets of this dazzling anemone are a "signature" at some high-current rocky locales, such as Discovery Passage, Campbell River, BC. Subtle colour variations, though, usually highlight the boundaries between many cloned individuals of two ancestors, like members of "opposing armies."
Quadra Island, Discovery Passage, s. BC

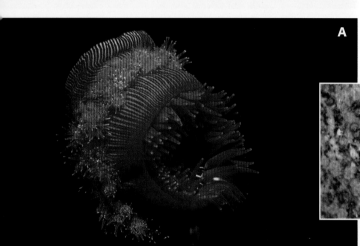

CN17. PROLIFERATING ANEMONE, brooding anemone, small green anemone
Epiactis prolifera
to 8 cm (3.2 in) across, 10 cm (4 in) tall
Alaska to s. California
intertidal to 18 m (60 ft)
After internal fertilization, embryos emerge, attach to the adult's column and develop into juveniles, as shown in the photographs. Eventually these young are "elbowed off" by growing siblings. This species also commonly dwells on eelgrass (SW2).
A Stephenson Islet, Weynton Passage, c. BC
B Tongue Point, Olympic coast, n. Washington

CN18. BROODING ANEMONE, proliferating anemone, giant brooding anemone
Epiactis lisbethae
to 8 cm (3.2 in) across, 4 cm (1.6 in) tall
s. Alaska to s. Oregon
▶intertidal to 30 m (100 ft)
Although tiny youngsters may adorn the column of the brooding anemone, their presence is often more difficult to detect than the young that festoon the proliferating anemone (CN17).
Appearing very flat when contracted and often under rocks, the ▶sand-accumulating brooding anemone, *Epiactis ritteri,* is similar but has adhesive pads on the lower part of its column that usually attract sand.
Superficially similar to the three preceding species proliferating anenome (CN17), brooding anemone (CN18) and sand-accumulating brooding anenome is the ▶warty-columned anemone, *Aulactinia incubans.* However, it differs significantly in the lengthwise rows of tubercles (bumps) on its column. This amazing anemone also broods its young internally and releases them through pores at the tips of its tentacles.
Eagle Point, San Juan Island, n. Washington

CN19. This obvious but **tiny orange anemone** is a common inhabitant of the rocky shores of islands at the northeast end of Vancouver Island. It lives in both intertidal and shallow subtidal zones. Underwater photographer/biologist Neil McDaniel was the first person to acknowledge its existence.
Lucan Islands, Browning Passage, c. BC

CN20. ORANGE-STRIPED GREEN ANEMONE, striped anemone, lined anemone
Diadumene lineata, *Haliplanella lineata, Haliplanella luciae, Sagartia luciae, Diadumene luciae*
to 3 cm (1.2 in) tall, 4 cm (1.6 in) across
Alaska to s. California, may have been introduced from the Orient
intertidal to shallow subtidal
Only keen-eyed "tidepoolers" find this tiny gem! Look in the high intertidal zone amid the barnacles.
Georgina Point, Mayne Island, s. BC

CN21. TEN-TENTACLED BURROWING ANEMONE, ten-tentacled anemone
Halcampa decementaculata
▶to 2.5 cm (1 in) across
s. BC to c. California
intertidal to 398 m (1,313 ft)
Only the small, cryptically coloured tentacle crown shows above the sand. This anemone's small, columnar body is somewhat worm-like if one is able to dig it out and retain it amid the cloud of billowing sand created during the process.
Sekiu, Olympic coast, n. Washington

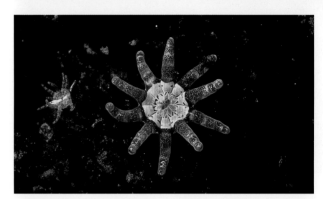

CN22/23. The **white-crowned burrowing anemones** shown in the two photographs are most likely two different species of ***Edwardsia***. One has nearly twice as many tentacles as the other. Dr. Meg Daley of Ohio State University is currently preparing formal descriptions and assigning species names. Slowness to retract distinguishes these tiny anemones from the various sand-dwelling tubeworms that share the sandy-bottomed environment.
A Stubbs Island, Weynton Passage, c. BC
B Discovery Passage, Campbell River, s. BC

CN24. ▶JELLY-DWELLING ANEMONE
Peachia quinquecapitata
▶to 2 cm (0.8 in) across
Japan, BC to s. California
pelagic (as a juvenile), intertidal to 161 m (531 ft)
After the larva of this anemone is ingested by a jelly, the tables are turned as it begins to feed on the host's internal organs. Eventually it transforms into an almost transparent anemone that hangs inside the jelly (photograph A). Ultimately the anemone drops off and assumes a bottom-dwelling existence in a mud/sand habitat. The fate of host jellies is not always predictable.
A Friday Harbor, San Juan Island, n. Washington. Phil Edgell photograph
B Miners Bay, Mayne Island, s. BC

CN25. This **small deepwater anemone** was collected from a depth of approximately 200 m (660 ft) off Bowyer Island, Howe Sound, s. BC, by Vancouver Aquarium staff as part of a trapping expedition. The two specimens captured, less than 5 cm (2 in) tall, were adhering to a length of rope that became tangled in the collecting gear. Unfortunately they perished before identification was made.

Bowyer Island, Howe Sound, s. BC

CN26. TUBE-DWELLING ANEMONE, tube anemone, burrowing anemone
Pachycerianthus fimbriatus, *Pachycerianthus torreyi*
tentacle crown to 30 cm (12 in) across
tube to 1 m (39 in) long
s. Alaska to n. Mexico
intertidal to at least 30 m (100 ft)
This anemone, the principal prey of and even a spawning site for the giant nudibranch (MC331), often forms huge fields on level soft substrates. Its buried tube is truly an ugly sight when exposed.

Mutine Point, Barkley Sound, s. BC

ZOANTHIDS

CN27. ORANGE ZOANTHID, yellow zoanthid, zoanthid, zoanthids
Epizoanthus scotinus
individuals to 5 cm (2 in) tall, form indeterminate, irregular colonies
Siberia, n. Alaska to s. California
intertidal to 54 m (180 ft)
This colonial creature usually prefers vertical and "undercut" walls swept by low to moderate currents. The beautiful, fluffy-looking underwater mats result from the prolific asexual budding of new individuals along the edge of the colony.
A Worlcombe Island, Howe Sound, s. BC
B Anderson Bay, Texada Island, s. BC

CN28. With polyps that appear smaller and somewhat more delicate than those of the orange zoanthid (CN27), this **deepwater zoanthid** has been found by Vancouver Aquarium Marine Science Centre divers while studying pink candelabrum gorgonian (CN46).

Agamemnon Channel, Nelson Island, s. BC

CN29. Pink with lighter stripes, this unidentified zoanthid was photographed at a depth of about 24 m (80 ft), where it lined a deep, narrow crevice in a steep rock wall. Only one sighting of this **pink zoanthid** was made in spite of several return visits to the site.

Quarry Bay, Nelson Island, s. BC

HARD CORALS

CN30. ORANGE CUP CORAL, orange-red coral, orange coral, cup coral, solitary orange cup coral, solitary coral, vivid orange-red solitary coral
Balanophyllia elegans
to 2.5 cm (1 in) across, 1.0 cm (0.4 in) tall
s. Alaska to n. Mexico
intertidal to 48 m (160 ft)
As in all hard corals, each polyp secretes and "sits on" a circular calcium disc, as seen in the photograph. This species is solitary, unlike its tropical reef-building relatives but like virtually all others in the Pacific Northwest.

Laura Point, Mayne Island, s. BC

CN31. BROWN OVAL CUP CORAL, tan cup coral, Stearn's cup coral
Paracyathus stearnsi
to 4 cm (1.5 in) across
BC to n. Mexico
subtidal, 9–90 m (30–300 ft)
The clear, pale brown tentacles (often with a green iridescence), oval shape and the calcium "seat" are distinctive in this solitary outer-coast species. In tropical reef-building species, each succeeding generation secretes its calcium skeleton on top of one where an animal has died. Over millennia, this stacking process, combined with horizontal expansion in all directions, creates the famous coral reefs of southern seas.

Lane Islet, Dawley Passage, s. BC

CN32. ▶TAN CUP CORAL
Caryophyllia alaskensis
to 3 cm (1.2 in) across
s. Alaska to s. California
subtidal to 15 m (50 ft)
Differing from the brown oval cup coral (CN31) in its round shape, this cup coral prefers moderate to low-current locales. If one carefully touches the polyp (living structure) of a cup coral, the hard calcium skeleton—a white disc-like base—can be felt underneath.

Point Cowan, Howe Sound, s. BC

CN33. The **branching white coral**, *Lophelia pertusa*, had been considered a North Atlantic species until 2004, when it was found by a remote-control submersible during a research cruise off the Olympic coast of Washington. The Pacific Northwest specimens observed were small in comparison to those featured in a photograph of Norwegian formations. Future studies may find larger colonies in Pacific waters.
▶Californian white coral, *Lophelia californica,* is also recorded from the Pacific Northwest.

Trondheim Fjord, Norway. Bo Lindstrom photograph

SOFT CORALS

CN34. PALE SOFT CORAL, octocoral
Clavularia **sp. A**
individuals to 2.5 cm (1 in) tall
small colonies of indeterminate, irregular size
BC to s. California
intertidal to 20 m (65 ft)
This coral is often obscured by other larger creatures, so its presence in small patches is easily overlooked. Unlike the "hard" corals, the various soft corals have only tiny calcium spicules (slivers) within their structure.

Browning Passage, Nigei Island, c. BC

CN35. ▶WHITE SOFT CORAL
Clavularia **sp. B**
individuals smaller than 1.2 cm (0.5 in) tall
forming tiny but distinct circular patches
BC
subtidal
When feeding, the extended polyps give a fuzzy appearance to the clustering colonies. Every polyp or individual of a soft coral has eight tentacles, each of which has many side branches. Most of the well-known tropical reef builders have a similar polyp design.

Barrow Point, Nakwakto Rapids, c. BC

CN36. Resembling a road map with tiny towns (horizontal branching stem-like structures linking feeding polyps) the ▶**road-map softcoral** was found in a display at the Vancouver Aquarium Marine Science Centre. From polyp anatomy it would appear to be a *Clavularia* species and to have arrived attached to its rock habitat collected somewhere in BC.
A B Vancouver Aquarium Marine Science Centre, Stanley Park, s. BC

CN37. RED SOFT CORAL, soft coral, sea strawberry, sea strawberry soft coral, sea raspberry
Gersemia rubiformis, *Eunephtya rubiformis*
to 30 cm (12 in) tall and across
Arctic, n. Alaska to n. California
▶intertidal to at least 36 m (120 ft)
Dominant in northern, high-current passages, this animal is a popular subject for underwater photographers. When the fully expanded colony retracts, it becomes a fraction of its size as virtually all the fluid is expelled, leaving mostly a tight red skin and compacted spicules.
Stubbs Island, Weynton Passage, c. BC

CN38. The attractive **pink soft coral** featured here was discovered and collected in spring and summer 2002, during two voyages of the MV *Nautilus Explorer*. Small amounts were observed during a Vancouver Aquarium Marine Science Centre excursion to the southern Queen Charlotte Islands and an abundance noted off Cape Ommaney, Baranof Island, s. Alaska, on a later charter. Samples were sent to Dr. Gary Williams, the soft coral expert at the California Academy of Sciences, who declared it a "new species" and very different from any other in the Pacific Northwest. Additional samples may provide enough material for a scientific description and a formal name.
Langara Island, Queen Charlotte Islands, n. BC. Marc Chamberlain photograph

CN39. ▶ORANGE SOFT CORAL
***Alcyonium* sp. ?**
▶to 20 cm (8 in) tall
BC
subtidal
Apparently never red or white, this poorly known species does not seem to coexist with the red soft coral (CN37). Whereas the red soft coral grows in massive profusion in many locales along the northeast coast of Vancouver Island, BC, this smaller, less profuse species appears to be restricted to a few select spots in the southern Gulf Islands.
Grainger Point, Samuel Island, s. BC

SEA PENS

Including the sea whip.

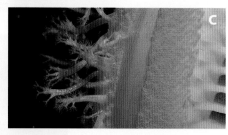

CN40. ORANGE SEA PEN, sea feather, fleshy sea pen, Gurney's sea pen, sea pen, stout sea pen
Ptilosarcus gurneyi, *Ptilosarcus verrilli, Ptilosarcus tenuis, Ptilosarcus quadrangulare, Leioptilus gurneyi, Leioptilus quadrangularis, Leioptilus quadrangulare*
to 48 cm (19 in) tall
n. Alaska to n. Mexico
subtidal to 135 m (445 ft)
The orange sea pen withdraws into its soft sediment habitat when disturbed. Try gently stroking one of these colonies on your next night dive, then turn out your light. Presto—a "natural" blue-green cyalume stick! Photograph C shows an unusual polyp formation on the "reverse side" of a specimen.
A B Lion Islets, Galiano Island, s. BC
C Martin Island, Pender Harbour, s. BC

CN41. WHITE SEA PEN
Virgularia sp., *Virgularia ? tuberculata*
to 30 cm (12 in) tall
s. Alaska to California
▶subtidal, below 10 m (35 ft)
A thin, rod-shaped skeleton made of calcium, is visible through this creature's tissues. Notice that this animal is colonial, with many feeding polyps serving the common good as connecting tissues provide nutritional benefits throughout.
Several other similar white sea pens, *Stylatula* spp. and *Acanthoptilum gracile,* have been documented in the Pacific Northwest. Proper identification of these poorly known species is yet to be done.
Daniel Point, Agamemnon Channel, s. BC

CN42. SEA WHIP
Halipteris willemoesi, *Balticina septentrionalis, Osteocella septentrionalis, Verrillia blakei, Pavonaria willemoesi, Balticina finmarchica ?*
to 2.5 m (8 ft) tall

s. Alaska to n. Washington, perhaps s. California
subtidal, below 20 m (65 ft)
With no branches, the polyps of the sea whip are horizontally oriented directly from a central "stem." Protruding from silty sediments and stiffened by a long, thin calcium skeleton, this species is probably unable to withdraw from view.
The ▶short sea whip, *Halipteris californica,* is smaller and has more sets of polyps.
A B Defence Islands, Howe Sound, s. BC

GORGONIANS

CN43. DWARF RED GORGONIAN, sea fan, gorgonian coral
***Swiftia torreyi**, Psammogorgia torreyi*
to 30 cm (12 in) tall
BC to s. California
▶subtidal, below 18 m (60 ft)
This animal is easily dismissed as a dark hydroid unless it is illuminated. At that point, its large, orange polyps, if open, and the overall red branching structure of the colony should indicate a gorgonian rather than a hydroid. This species appears to prefer the steep walls of protected fjords.
Fearney Point, Agamemnon Channel, s. BC

CN44. ▶SHORT RED GORGONIAN
***Swiftia spauldingi**, Psammogorgia teres, Psammogorgia arbuscula, Euplexaura marki*
▶to 25 cm (10 in) tall
n. Washington to s. California
▶subtidal, below 15 m (50 ft)
Preferring strong current and ocean surge, the short red gorgonian is a challenging quarry for a diver. It is readily distinguished from the dwarf red gorgonian (C43) by its white polyps, pinkish colour and more upright branching pattern, which resembles a candelabrum.
A B Cape Flattery, Olympic coast, n. Washington

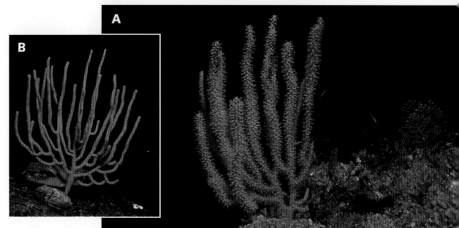

CN45. PINK GORGONIAN, pink sea fan, sea fan, gorgonian coral
Calcigorgia spiculifera
to 30 cm (12 in) tall
to 60 cm (24 in) across
s. Alaska to c. BC
subtidal, below 15 m (50 ft)
This species often has an interesting relationship with the basket star (EC46), as either a tightly entwined juvenile or a more loosely associated adult. Perhaps the gorgonian is acting as a "step ladder," allowing the basket star better access to the planktonic food they both seek.
A B Iphigenia Point, Langara Island, n. BC

CN46. PINK CANDELABRUM GORGONIAN, Kamchatka coral
***Paragorgia pacifica**, Paragorgia arborea (this synonomy is uncertain)*
▶to 2 m (6.6 ft) tall
Siberia, n. Alaska to s. BC
▶subtidal, below 38 m (125 ft)
This spectacular gorgonian is especially prolific in steep-walled fjords at depths below casual sport-diving limits. Viewing it, though, is well worth the effort for the experienced diver with proper equipment and a well-considered dive plan. Otherwise a submersible is in order.
Caldwell Island, Agamemnon Channel, s. BC

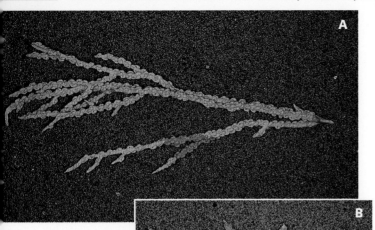

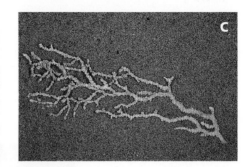

CN47. Frequently seen as decor items in Pacific Northwest dive shops, seafood restaurants and other businesses, are pieces—sometimes very large—of **deepwater gorgonians**. After considerable drying time to remove all offending live tissues and odour, what remains is a skeleton of compacted spicules coated with desiccated surface layers. Often they are species of *Primnoa* that have been brought to the surface as a bycatch of commercial fishing activities. The larger colonies, up to 2 m (6.6 ft) tall, can be very old and have growth rings similar to those of trees. Thanks to Dr. Bruce Wing of NOAA's Auke Bay Laboratory, near Juneau, Alaska, the specimens in these photographs can be identified as *Primnoa pacifica* (A), *Primnoa resedaeformis* (B) and *Primnoa willeyi* (C).

A B C Offshore, open-coast locales, BC

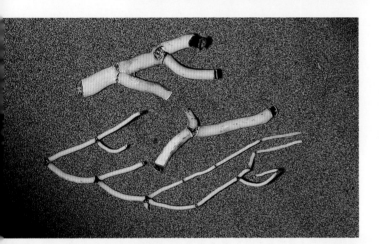

CN48. Popularly known as **bamboo corals**, for obvious reasons, these deep-water denizens are infrequently observed. They are occasionally dragged up as bycatch by trawlers fishing at great depths, but thanks to their very brittle structure, they rarely make a successful trip to the surface. The specimen in the photograph may be one of two species, *Isidella paucispinoa* or *Keratoisis profunda*. The black "nodes" suggest the former, but only careful examination of the red or orange polyps, from a fresh sample, would provide the answer.

After many decades of unrestricted trawling over deep, unseen and under-appreciated habitat, concern for the **"coral gardens"** that exist along the Pacific Northwest coastline has prompted a call for protection. Essentially an underwater version of old-growth forest, this virtually unknown habitat is no doubt valuable in many unforeseen ways—including as breeding and rearing areas for economically significant species.

Offshore, open-coast locales, BC

CN49. ▶DWARF WHITE GORGONIAN
Anthothela pacifica, *Clavularia pacifica*, *Sympodium armatum*
▶to 7.5 cm (3 in) tall
BC to s. California
▶subtidal, below 40 m (133 ft)
Look carefully for this tiny treasure at the base of the pink candelabrum gorgonian (CN46). Using specially designed and outfitted tanks at the Vancouver Aquarium Marine Science Centre, aquarists are researching several of these northern gorgonian corals in an attempt to define their requirements and ultimately produce a successful exhibit.

Caldwell Island, Agamemnon Channel, s. BC

HYDROCORALS

CN50. ENCRUSTING HYDROCORALS, purple encrusting hydrocoral, purple hydrocoral, purple stylasterine, purple carpet
***Stylantheca* spp.** including *Stylantheca petrograpta, Allopora petrograpta, Stylantheca porphyra, Allopora porphyra, Stylantheca sp., Allopora sp.*
indeterminate, irregular size
s. Alaska to s. California
intertidal to 30 m (100 ft)
A colony takes the shape of whatever it carpets in high-current areas. Several similar species are a source of great consternation to the experts. Fortunately Dr. Bruce Wing of Auke Bay, Alaska, was able to identify the species in these three photographs as *Stylantheca petrograpta*.
A Laura Point, Mayne Island, s. BC
B Useless Inlet, Barkley Sound, s. BC. Charlie Gibbs photograph
C Second Narrows, Vancouver Harbour, s. BC

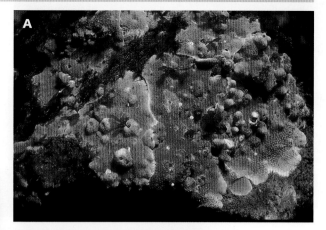

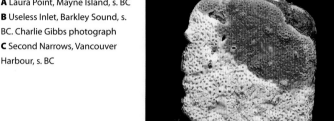

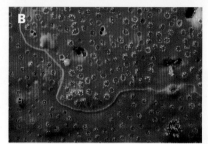

CN51. The **pink branching hydrocorals**, illustrated by these photographs, pose a confounding mystery that numerous experts have grappled with over the years. Whether they are subspecies or specimens that have grown differently in response to their environment (eco-types), the individual variation of their colony and pore design creates uncertainty. Only a few collected specimens are scattered between scientists, so it is no surprise that a definitive statement cannot be made. Sizes approaching 15 cm (6 in) across may be attained by specimens found from n. Alaska to s. California in the subtidal zone to 55 m (182 ft).
Dr. Bruce Wing, one of the leading experts in the field, suggests that specimens in the photographs are all ***Stylaster norvigicus*** and that they can be divided into the subspecies *Stylaster norvigicus californicus, Stylaster norvigicus venustus* and *Stylaster norvigicus verillii*. Doubtless this remains a source of debate.
Other scientific names that have been applied over the years include *Stylaster californicus, Allopora californicus, Stylaster verilli, Allopora verilli, Allopora norvegica, Allopora moseleyi, Stylaster venustus, Allopora venustus* and *Allopora venusta*.
A Cape Flattery, Olympic coast, n. Washington
B Sutton Islets, Egmont, s. BC
C Stubbs Island, Weynton Passage, c. BC

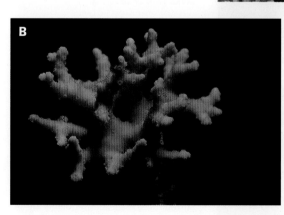

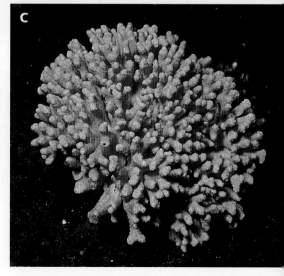

CN52. ▶WHITE BRANCHING HYDROCORAL
Stylaster campylecus, *Allopora campylecus*, *Stylaster boreopacifica typica*
at least 10 cm (4 in) tall
n. Alaska to Washington
▶subtidal below 15 m (50 ft)
Though this species is not as variable in form as the pink branching hydrocorals (CN51), Dr. Bruce Wing of Auke Bay, Alaska, also believes several subspecies or ecotypes are involved. Photograph B shows small specimens observed while diving in southeast Alaska; photograph A depicts a large one taken by a longline fisherman working in Hecate Strait, BC.
A Longlining territory, Hecate Strait, s. BC
B Benjamin Island, Lynn Canal, s. Alaska

HYDROIDS

Including sea firs.

CN53. OSTRICH-PLUME HYDROIDS, including ostrich plume hydroid, large ostrich-plume hydroid, ostrichplume hydroid, ostrich plume, feathery hydroid
Aglaophenia **spp.**, including *Aglaophenia struthionides*, *Aglaophenia latirostris*
to 15 cm (6 in) tall
Alaska to n. Mexico
intertidal to 160 m (525 ft)
Minute polyps, which are not readily noticeable, extend only on the "upside" of the branches of each feather-like colony. Reproductive polyps called gonothecae are clumped together to form specialized pod-shaped corbulae, structures visible in the photograph. This entry represents at least six species.
Butress Island, Slingsby Channel, c. BC

CN54. COARSE SEA FIR HYDROIDS, sea firs, fern garland hydroids, fernlike hydroids, sea spruces, cup hydroids
Abietinaria **spp.**
to 15 cm (6 in) tall
Alaska to s. California
intertidal to subtidal
The relatively large, flask-shaped polyps of coarse sea fir hydroids alternate from the two sides of colony branches, usually giving species of this genus a sawtooth appearance. At least 14 species are represented by this entry.
Sutton Islets, Egmont, s. BC

CN55. EMBEDDED SEA FIR HYDROIDS, sea firs, fern garland hydroids, fernlike hydroids, sea spruces
Thuiaria **spp.**
to 15 cm (6 in) tall
Alaska to s. California
intertidal to subtidal
The polyps and their associated coverings, located along the colony branches for *Thuiaria* species, are well buried or embedded in the surrounding tissue. Consequently, these hydroid species appear smoother than those of the coarse sea fir hydroids (CN54). As many as six species are covered by this entry.
Laura Point, Mayne Island, s. BC

CN56. GARLAND HYDROIDS
***Sertularella* spp., *Sertularia* spp.**
to 20 cm (8 in) tall
n. Alaska to s. California
intertidal to subtidal
The two genera featured in this entry can only be distinguished by counting the number of minute "tooth-like" structures located on the rim of each polyp—a chore requiring a microscope and much patience. At least 17 species are represented by this entry, and species determination is a specialized task. In general, a hydroid is a confusing creature because it is only one, albeit the dominant, stage of an alternating life form. Seasonally it produces countless tiny male and female, often mobile "jellyfish" that ultimately complete the cycle to create new hydroid colonies.

A B Frank Island, w. Vancouver Island, s. BC

CN57. ▶FISH-BONE HYDROID
***Selaginopsis* sp.**
▶to 20 cm (8 in) tall
BC to Washington
subtidal
The paired branches are the same length along nearly the whole main stem—a pattern that suggested its common name. The tiny polyps are arranged in at least two rows along the branches of this erect hydroid. At least five other selaginopsid species reside in the Pacific Northwest.

Laura Point, Mayne Island, s. BC

CN58. HORSE-TAIL HYDROID
Rhizocaulus verticillatus, *Campanularia verticillatus*, *Verticillina verticillatus*
▶to 10 cm (4 in) tall
Siberia, n. Atlantic, n. Alaska to c. California
subtidal
This hydroid resembles its namesake in the whorl-like branching pattern of the stems emerging from the main stalk. The fuzzy-looking tips are actually minute feeding polyps, which show best in photograph B.

A B Georgina Point, Mayne Island, s. BC

CN59. GLASSY PLUME HYDROID, little seabristle, decorator hydroid, delicate plume hydroid
***Plumularia setacea**, Corallina setacea*
▶to 15 cm (6 in) tall
s. Alaska to n. Mexico
intertidal to 133 m (450 ft)
Note the tiny, light-coloured, globular reproductive polyps attached to the main unbranched stems depicted in photograph A. Large clusters of the glassy plume hydroid often festoon kelp stipes (photograph B) or coat rocky outcrops in the shallows. Either way, this species is a delicately beautiful sight.
A Iphigenia Point, Langara Island, n. BC
B Stubbs Island, Weynton Passage, c. BC

CN60. DELICATE PLUME HYDROID
***Plumularia* sp.**
▶to 8 cm (3 in) tall
Alaska to n. Mexico
intertidal to subtidal
Note the extremely fine structure and greatly separated polyps on each feather-like colony. In this type of hydroid, the medusa or jellyfish is not released to pulse about, but rather it is retained, and reproduction is completed on site, at the hydroid. Ultimately ciliated (hairy) larvae crawl away and metamorphose into a new hydroid growth.
At least five other plumularid hydroids live in the Pacific Northwest.
Point Cowan, Bowen Island, s. BC

CN61. SURFGRASS HYDROID, furry hydroid
***Sertularia furcata**, Sertularia pulchella*
to 1 cm (0.4 in) tall
BC to s. California
intertidal to 50 m (165 ft)
This small hydroid primarily grows attached to surf grass (SW4) and consequently is found in abundance along exposed outer coasts. Enjoy the quest for this delicate beauty, but be mindful of the incoming tide and ever-present surge.
Frank Island, w. Vancouver Island, s. BC

CN62. ▶FIBRE-OPTIC HYDROID, fern hydroid, bushy colonial hydroid, hydroid
Abietinaria greenei misspelled: *greeni*
▶to 15 cm (6 in) tall
Siberia, n. Alaska to s. California
intertidal to 37 m (120 ft)
The distinctive lighter-hued growing tips inspire this hydroid's new-age common name. A colony grows in thick clusters of erect stems that sometimes branch.
Laura Point, Mayne Island, s. BC

CN63. WINE-GLASS HYDROIDS, bushy wine-glass hydroids, bushy wineglass hydroids, sea plumes
Obelia spp., including *Obelia dichotoma, Obelia longissima*
to 30 cm (12 in) tall
Siberia, n. Alaska to s. California, perhaps Chile
intertidal to at least 50 m (165 ft)
These usually large, long colonies hang from floats or algae, and the various species are all distinguished by the branching pattern. Visible with a magnifying glass, each polyp has a clear sheath around it—giving rise to the common name. Wine-glass hydroids reproduce sexually by releasing minute male and female jellies.
A Anderson Bay, Texada Island, s. BC
B C Agamemnon Channel, Nelson Island, s. BC

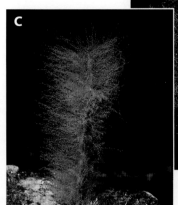

CN64. BROWN BUSHY HYDROID, California stick hydroid, California stickhydroid, sea-tree
Eudendrium californicum
to 15 cm (6 in) tall
s. Alaska to s. California
▶intertidal to at least 120 m (400 ft)
Clustering and thick-stemmed colonies feature alternating branches, each possessing small but readily visible pink polyps. Brighter pink spheres are reproductive bodies. As in most hydroids, each colony is either male or female, and sperm must drift by current to the female bushes.
At least six more *Eudendrium* species live in the Pacific Northwest.
Plumper Islands, Weynton Passage, c. BC

CN65. ORANGE HYDROID, brilliant orange hydroid, orange sea-tree
Garveia annulata
to 15 cm (6 in) tall
s. Alaska to s. California
intertidal to 120 m (400 ft)
This species' thick stems are strongly ringed or annulated, It is an easily distinguished hydroid, which has a life history somewhat similar to that of the brown bushy hydroid (CN64). The tiny round spheres obvious in the photograph contain several orange eggs, defining this specimen as a female. A nearby male orange hydroid colony would produce the required sperm.
Tzoonie Narrows, Narrows Inlet, s. BC

CN66. CREEPING ORANGE HYDROID
Garveia groenlandica
indeterminate, irregular size
Alaska to Washington
intertidal to 91 m (300 ft)
The creeping orange hydroid often grows on the undersides of rocks and grows so sparsely that it is easily overlooked. It is prominent in the photograph, but when other encrusting life is present, it may go completely undetected.
The Pacific Northwest is home to at least four other garveiaid species.
Kyen Point, Barkley Sound, s. BC. Charlie Gibbs photograph

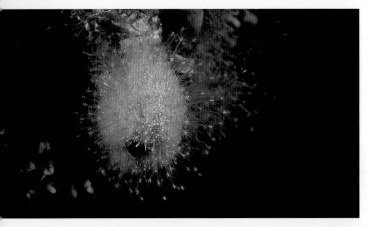

CN67. HEDGE-HOG HYDROID, hedgehog hydroid, fuzzy pink hydroid, Miller hydractinia
***Clavactinia milleri**, Hydractinia milleri*
colony to 8 cm (3.2 in) diameter
c. BC to s. California
intertidal to 25 m (80 ft)
The hedge-hog hydroid resembles a miniature "fireworks" display but is frequently oriented downward. The tall polyps, often called zooids, in this more encrusting type of hydroid rise from a base reinforced with calcium and beset with tiny spines.
Laura Point, Mayne Island, s. BC

CN68. SNAIL FUR HYDROID, snail fur
***Hydractinia sp.**, perhaps Hydractinia aggregata*
colony size restricted to area of host shell
BC to c. California
subtidal
This species usually appears as a "furry coating" on snail shells carried by hermits (hermit crabs). The photograph shows polyps retracted and forming little more than tiny knobs, but when they are actively feeding they very much resemble those of the barnacle fur hydroid (CN69). Much confusion exists concerning the species of *Hydractinia*.
Mukilteo, Puget Sound, c. Washington

CN69. ▶BARNACLE FUR HYDROID
***Hydractinia sp.**, probably Hydractinia laevispina*
indeterminate, irregular size
BC to Washington
subtidal
Particularly when the polyps are retracted, this hydroid often forms a "sandpapery" covering for clusters of the giant acorn barnacle (AR171). When extended, these same polyps give the hydroid a fuzzy appearance, as shown in the photographs. Fortunately Maria Pia Miglietta, a PhD student at Duke University in North Carolina, has been funded by a National Science Foundation grant under the Partnerships for the Enhancement of Expertise in Taxonomy (PEET) program to determine the taxonomic status of *Hydractinia* species.
A Booker Lagoon, Broughton Island, c. BC
B Cardigan Rocks, Browning Passage, c. BC

CN70. CLAPPER HYDROID
***Sarsia tubulosa**, Syncorne mirabilis, Corne mirabilis*
colony to 15 cm (6 in) diameter
Alaska to n. Mexico, perhaps s. America
▶intertidal to 20 m (65 ft)
Bushier than the bushy pink-mouth hydroid (CN71), a mini-bouquet of the clapper hydroid is composed of many usually unbranched and smooth stems. Sexual reproduction is accomplished via tiny, pelagic male and female medusae (jellies).
Stubbs Island, Weynton Passage, c. BC

CN71. BUSHY PINK-MOUTH HYDROID, pink-mouth hydroid, pink mouth hydroid, pink mouthed hydroid, pink heart hydroid, tubularian hydroid, oaten-pipe hydroid, bushy hydroid
Ectopleura crocea, *Tubularia crocea*, *Parypha crocea*
individuals to 12 cm (5 in) tall
colony to 30 cm (12 in) diameter
Arctic, n. Alaska to s. California
intertidal to 40 m (130 ft)
This hydroid consists of a bouquet of relatively large pink polyps, called hydranths, each attached to a straw-like stem. Each hydranth has two whorls of tentacles adorned by clusters of droplet-shaped reproductive sporosacs.
Stubbs Island, Weynton Passage, c. BC

CN72. SOLITARY PINK-MOUTH HYDROID, pink mouth hydroid, solitary hydroid
Ectopleura marina, *Tubularia marina*
to 8 cm (3.2 in) tall
BC to s. California
intertidal to 15 m (50 ft)
A more individualistic version of the bushy pink-mouth hydroid (CN71), this species has slightly different numbers of oral and aboral tentacles. Like most others, this hydroid is prey for the "bushy-back" or aeolid type of nudibranch. Inspect the photograph carefully to detect a pair of tiny red eyes betraying the presence of a commensal amphipod of unknown species.
Francis Point, Francis Peninsula, s. BC

CN73. GIANT PINK-MOUTH HYDROID, tall tubularian
Tubularia indivisa
to 10 cm (4 in) tall
s. Alaska to n. Washington
intertidal to subtidal
As a larger version of the solitary pink-mouth hydroid (CN72), this species is more viewer-friendly. Sometimes a "topless" specimen—with just a stalk and no "pink mouth"—is found. What happened? A predator, likely one of numerous aeolid nudibranchs, has availed itself of a meal. Details of intact specimens are readily seen in photograph B.
Several other very similar tubularian hydroids, including the
▶regal pink-mouth hydroid, *Tubularia regalis,* are recorded in the Pacific Northwest.
A Fidalgo Head, Fidalgo Island, n. Washington
B Pearse Islands, Weynton Passage, c. BC

CN74. WHITE HYDROID
Clava **sp.**
to 1.2 cm (0.5 in) tall, grows in indeterminate, irregular mats
BC to s. California
intertidal to subtidal
To a diver, the white hydroid appears to be very many separate, cup-shaped micro-polyps rather than the classic hydroid. However, they are all interconnected by a singular net-like stolon (branch-like stem) and form creeping colonies. Often this hydroid grows so densely that it mimics a "dusting of snow."
Sutton Islets, Egmont, s. BC

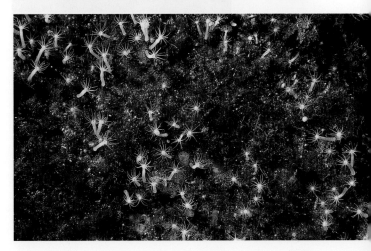

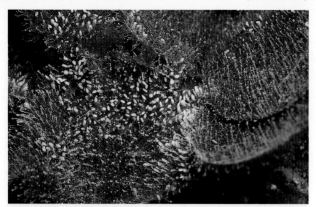

CN75. ▶SPIDER WEB HYDROID
Orthopyxis sp.
indeterminate, irregular size
Alaska to s. California
intertidal to subtidal
This creeping hydroid is particularly noticeable in summer on red and brown algae. The very tiny egg-shaped structures are reproductive polyps called gonangia. When released, the minute medusae have neither mouths nor digestive cavities—suggesting a brief existence.
Turn Island, San Juan Channel, n. Washington

CN76. RASPBERRY HYDROID
Corymorpha sp.
to 5 cm (2 in) tall
c. BC to c. California
subtidal
A large, solitary hydroid inhabiting current-swept passages, this species grows in clusters and is the primary food source of the pomegranate aeolid (MC360). Intriguingly, it has a thick stem that is composed of rather flimsy supportive tissue. The raspberry hydroid has been known since the 1960s, but it still awaits a formal scientific description and a designated species name.
Plumper Islands, Weynton Passage, c. BC

CN77. BOTTLEBRUSH HYDROID
Thuiaria thuja, Sertularia thuja, Salacia thuja
▶at least 15 cm (6 in) tall
n. Alaska to n. Washington
subtidal to 82 m (270 ft)
A most distinctive appearance, obvious in the photograph, gives the bottlebrush hydroid its name. It is often found growing among colonies of other hydroids in current-swept locales.
Long Island, Lopez Island, n. Washington

CN78. ▶LOOSE-SPIRAL HYDROID
Hydrallmania distans
▶at least 25 cm (10 in) tall
BC to s. California
intertidal to 45 m (146 ft)
This hydroid is most likely found in silty, low-current locales. We have encountered and recognized it widely during scuba-diving explorations. In younger colonies the polyps are arranged alternately, but in older specimens they are located only on one side of stems and branches.
Turn Island, San Juan Channel, n. Washington

CN79. MUFF HYDROID
Lafoea dumosa, *Lafoea gracillima, Lafoea fruticosa*
at least 15 cm (6 in) tall
n.w. Pacific Ocean, Alaska to n. Mexico, Atlantic Ocean, Antarctica
intertidal to 109 m (360 ft)
Muff hydroid colonies are usually erect but sometimes assume a creeping posture. The bright yellow swellings noticeable in photograph B are hermaphroditic reproductive structures called coppiniae. The minute feeding polyps are noticeable in photograph A and function like a sea anemone, except that their prey is minuscule.
At least two other *Lafoea* species live in the Pacific Northwest.
A B Anderson Bay, Texada Island, s. BC

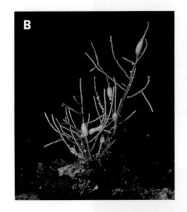

CN80. ▶SPINDLY EMBEDDED HYDROIDS
***Grammaria* spp.**
at least 10 cm (4 in) tall
n.w. Pacific Ocean, Alaska to BC, Atlantic Ocean
subtidal to 73 m (240 ft)
Sparsely branched and spindly, these hydroids are distinguished by tubular feeding polyps or hydrothecae in rows of four or more, which are almost completely buried in the stems. These features are difficult to see without a hand lens at least. Like the muff hydroid (CN79), this species also reproduces sexually via coppiniae.
Sutton Islets, Egmont, s. BC. Neil McDaniel photograph

CN81. ▶TUNICATE SIPHON HYDROID
Bythotiara huntsmani, *Endocrypta huntsmani, Ascidioclava parasitica*
to diameter of largest inhalant siphon of sea vase (CH3)
BC to Washington
intertidal to 100 m (330 ft)
By strict definition, this resourceful hydroid has a commensal as opposed to a parasitic relationship with its host. Rather than extracting nourishment directly from the tissues of the tunicate, this species shares in the planktonic prey being drawn in through the host's incurrent siphon. Photograph A features one noticeable colony as a "ring" inside a tunicate (at upper left) and photograph B shows individual polyps.
A Four Mile Point, Sechelt Inlet, s. BC
B Tuwanek Point, Sechelt Inlet, s. BC. Charlie Gibbs photograph

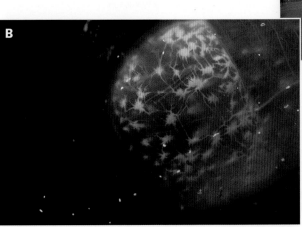

CN82. ▶CANDELABRUM HYDROID
Halecium beani, *Halecium scutum*
▶to 10 cm (4 in) tall
n.w. Pacific Ocean, Alaska to Ecuador, Atlantic Ocean
subtidal
The distinctive branching pattern of this species gave rise to its common name. Its main stem is composed of many tubes and collar-shaped polyps that alternately line its many branches. In general, a hydroid has a flexible exoskeleton, called a perisarc, that provides support for the colony. In some species it even surrounds the polyps; these hydroids are called thecate. If the perisarc encases only the stems, the creature is termed athecate.
Cape Flattery, Olympic coast, n. Washington

CN83. DENSE BUSHY HYDROID
Halecium densum
▶to 10 cm (4 in)
BC to Washington, s. California
subtidal to 50 m (165 ft)
Dense bushy hydroid colonies are erect and greatly branched, sometimes with two or three originating from the same point. The authors are most grateful to hydroid expert Dr. Lea-Anne Henry of Ottawa, Ontario, who was able to identify the colony in this photograph, but only after carefully working with the specimen.
At least 16 other *Halecium* species of hydroid have been recorded in the Pacific Northwest.
Annis Point, Kunghit Island, n. BC

A large number of hydroids inhabit the Pacific Northwest but many are difficult to identify without a microscope and the technical experience to use a jargon-intensive biological key. Even with specimens to examine, such a task is challenging. When only photographs are available, the process can be virtually impossible.

Therefore, the unsampled and undetermined hydroids in the following photographs appear with only captions and illustrate additional diversity within the group.

CN84. Undetermined hydroid A
Plumper Islands, Weynton Passage, c. BC

CN85. Undetermined hydroid B
Annis Point, Kunghit Island, n. BC

CN86. Undetermined hydroid C
Frank Island, w. Vancouver Island, s. BC

CN87. Undetermined hydroid D
Ucluth Peninsula, w. Vancouver Island, s. BC

CN88. Undetermined hydroid E
Quoin Island, Bate Passage, c. BC

JELLIES

Including schyphomedusae, hydromedusae, jellyfish, sea nettle and lion's mane (▶the by-the-wind sailor is a floating hydroid).

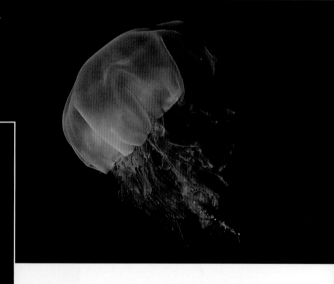

CN89. LION'S MANE, lion's mane medusa, lion's mane jelly, lion's mane jellyfish, sea blubber, red medusa, sea nettle
Cyanea capillata
to 2 m (6.6 ft) across, tentacles trail to 9 m (30 ft)
n. Alaska to Mexico
pelagic
Avoid stinging tentacles! But if you are stung, meat tenderizer is a handy antidote. Keep some in your dive bag or backpack. The sting does subside in a couple of hours and most fisher-folk "just tough it out." A spectacular planktonic creature, the lion's mane frequently provides shelter for the young and nimble of several fish species.
A Green Bay, Nelson Island, s. BC
B Anderson Bay, Texada Island, s. BC

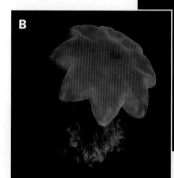

CN90. FRIED EGG JELLYFISH, eggyolk jelly, egg yolk jelly
Phacellophora camtschatica, *Phacellophora ambiqua*, *Phacellophora ornata*, *Phacellophora sicula*
to 60 cm (24 in) across
Japan, Siberia, n. Alaska to Chile
pelagic
The scalloped margin of the bell (body) is distinctive for this jelly. It also has that "freshly cracked in the pan" look. Unlike the lion's mane (CN89), it produces a relatively mild sting and primarily preys on other jellies.
Green Bay, Nelson Island, s. BC

CN91. SEA NETTLE
Chrysaora fuscescens, *Chrysaora helvola*
to 30 cm (12 in) across
Japan, Siberia, n. Alaska to c. California
pelagic
Avoid stinging tentacles of this open-coast wanderer, one of several large jellies that are successfully exhibited at the Oregon Coast Aquarium. Some confusion surrounds the distribution of this species and *Chrysaora melanaster*, a similar-looking species.
Off Newport, c. Oregon

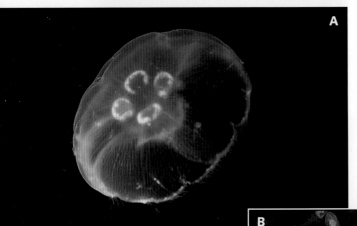

CN92. MOON JELLY, moon jellyfish, moon jelly fish, white sea jelly
Aurelia labiata, *Aurelia aurita* now deemed a separate species
to 40 cm (16 in) across
s. Alaska to s. California
pelagic
The four pinkish, yellow or purple "horseshoes" are this species' distinctive sex organs. Unfortunately, colour is not always a significant sexual characteristic. Spawning aggregations are often found in sheltered bays (photograph B). Photograph C shows the bottom-dwelling stage, called a scyphistoma, which may continually generate juvenile jellies.
A Quarry Bay, Nelson Island, s. BC
B Manson Bay, Cortes Island, s. BC
C Tzoonie Narrows, Narrows Inlet, s. BC

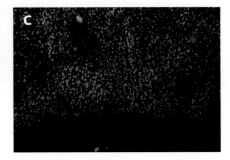

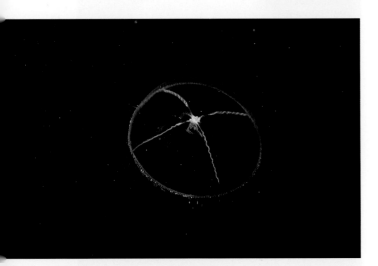

CN93. CROSS JELLYFISH, cross jelly fish
Mitrocoma cellularia, *Halistaura cellularia*, *Thaumantias cellularia*
▶to 10 cm (4 in) across
n. Alaska to c. California
pelagic
The shaggy "X marks the spot" structure is the distinctive feature of this creature, which has a large number of tentacles. A narrow, continuous, bioluminescent band circles the edge of the body.
Sekiu, Olympic coast, n. Washington

CN94. ▶SCALLOPED JELLIES including scalloped jellyfish, dinner plate medusa
Solmissus **spp.**
to 10 cm (4 in) across
worldwide, BC to tropics
pelagic
This jelly is named for the lobed structure of the bell-shaped body, with each lobe having one sinuous tentacle. Its simple mouth is located centrally and underneath, so it may drift about motionless or periodically pulsate. Experts are uncertain as to the number of species, with only subtle differences between types worldwide.
Plumper Islands, Weynton Passage, c. BC

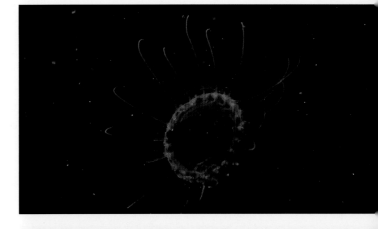

CN95. WATER JELLIES, water jellyfishes, water jelly fishes, many ribbed medusas, many-ribbed hydromedusas, many-ribbed jellyfishes
Aequorea **spp.**, including *Aequorea aequorea, Aequorea forskalea, Aequorea victoria, Aequorea flava*
to 17.5 cm (7 in) across
n. Alaska to n. Mexico
pelagic
This jelly resembles a bicycle wheel and its spokes. Photograph B shows the manubrium (mouth) in detail. More than one species may be represented in the photographs.
A Gerald Island, Ballenas Channel, s. BC
B Seven Mile Point, Sechelt Inlet, s. BC

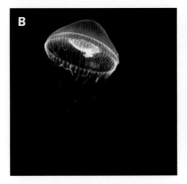

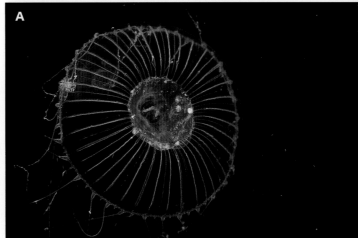

CN96. RED-EYE MEDUSA, penicillate jellyfish, redeye jellyfish, red-eye jellyfish, red-eye jelly fish, red-eyed jellyfish, bell medusa, bell-shaped jellyfish
Polyorchis penicillatus, Polyorchis montereyensis, Polyorchis miniatus
to 10 cm (4 in) bell height
Alaska to n. Mexico
pelagic
Minute red spots around the edge of the bell are light-sensitive eye-spots that help this jelly orient itself in the water column.
Ucluelet Harbour, w. Vancouver Island, s. BC

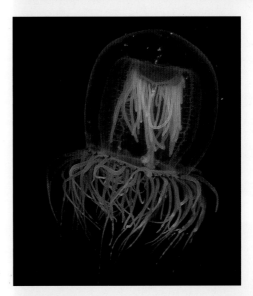

CN97. CLINGING JELLYFISH, orange striped jellyfish, orange striped jelly fish, orange-striped jellyfish, orange jellyfish, angled hydromedusa
Gonionemus vertens, Gonionemus murbachi
to 2.5 cm (1 in) across
Japan, Siberia, n. Alaska to s. California
pelagic
Tiny adhesive discs at the midpoints of the tentacles are definitive and allow this species to pause on solid substrate. The orange or brownish "X-shaped" sex-organ structure is also distinctive. In summer this jelly can be found clinging to eelgrass (SW2) and various algae.
Moore Point, Francis Peninsula, s. BC

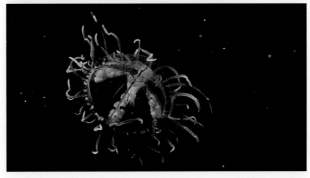

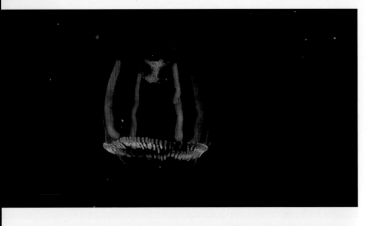

CN98. GREGARIOUS JELLYFISH, gregarious jelly fish
Clytia gregarium, *Phialidium gregarium*, *Phialidium languidum*
to 2.5 cm (1 in) across
n. Alaska to c. Oregon
pelagic
Particularly during late spring and summer, this tiny jelly is so abundant as to appear to be filling the ocean—an organism of cyclical plankton blooms. It feeds on smaller plankton and in turn is consumed by larger ones, including fellow jellies.
Cardigan Rocks, Balaklava Island, c. BC

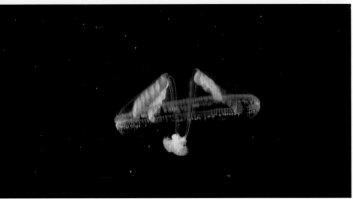

CN99. AGGREGATING JELLY
Eutonina indicans
to 4 cm (1.6 in) across
Japan, Siberia, n. Alaska to s. California
pelagic
The mouth of this jelly is distinctive in its four frilly lips at the end of a peduncle (stalk) that hangs well below the edge of the body and resembles the clapper of a bell. The thickenings on the four radial canals are the sex organs. Like the gregarious jellyfish (CN98), it is often very abundant in the warm spring and summer months, especially along the outer coast.
Arniston Point, Dundas Island, n. BC

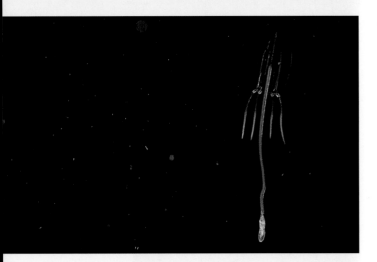

CN100. THIMBLE JELLYFISHES, including thimble jelly fish
Sarsia **spp.**
to 1 cm (0.4 in) across
n. Alaska to c. California
pelagic
Notice the four tentacles and extremely long manubrium (stomach), ending in the mouth, that hangs down well below the edge of the bell. At the insertion of each tentacle is an obvious ocellus (light-sensitive organ). This combination of features is distinctive in each of the very similar *Sarsia* species.
Anderson Bay, Texada Island, s. BC

CN101. ▶BLOB-TOP JELLY
Neoturris breviconis, *Leuckartiara breviconis*, *Perigonimus breviconis*, *Turris breviconis*
to 4.5 cm (1.8 in) tall
circumboreal, n. Alaska to c. California
pelagic
If you are a diver, watch for this and other jellies while you are relaxing on an anchor line doing a safety stop or decompressing. This potentially boring part of a dive can be a very worthwhile observation period, when you can easily see creatures you missed earlier while patrolling at greater depth.
Green Bay, Nelson Island, s. BC

CN102. ▶TALL-TOP JELLIES
***Leuckartiara* spp.**

to 2 cm (0.8 in) tall
BC to Washington
pelagic
Note the distinctive projection on the bell. This jelly can extend its tentacles to many times its body length. It is relatively short-lived—a month or two—and preys upon planktonic brethren of suitable size.
Kunechin Point, Sechelt Inlet, s. BC. Neil McDaniel photograph

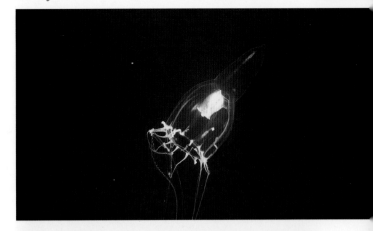

CN103. TINY RED SAUSAGE JELLIES
***Euphysa* spp.**, including *Euphysa flammea, Euphysa japonica*
to 1.2 cm (0.5 in) tall
n. Alaska to California
pelagic
The obvious red, sausage-shaped structure hanging in the centre is the creature's digestive tract, which has only one opening. As with all jellies, the mouth and anus are the same opening. A third very similar species, *Euphysa tentaculata,* has only three tentacles.
George Rock, Christie Passage, c. BC

CN104. FOUR TENTACLED JELLY
***Aegina citrea*,** *Aegina rosea*
to 5 cm (2 in) across
n. Alaska to s. California, all warm and temperate oceans
pelagic
This species is named for the four tentacles (though five or six may be present) that have their end portions rooted in the bell. It typically drifts with the tentacles pointed upward, as shown in the photograph—a behaviour that is not understood.
Egmont Marina, Egmont, s. BC

CN105. ▶HANGING STOMACH JELLY
Stomotoca atra
to 2.5 cm (1 in) across
n. Alaska to s. California
pelagic
In this species the four lips of the mouth are obvious, but the stomach, which literally hangs out of the bell, is not. This is because the folded sex organs are draped around it, obscuring it from view. Its two large tentacles (unfortunately withdrawn in the photographed specimen) are also characteristic. This jelly will "crumple" and sink when touched or disturbed.
Green Bay, Nelson Island, s. BC

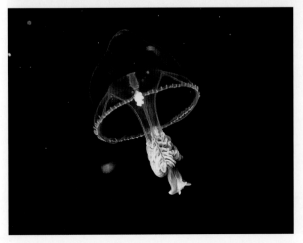

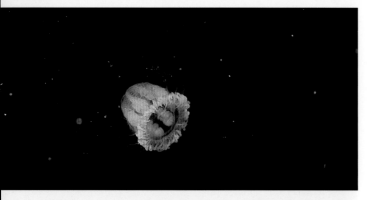

CN106. ▶EIGHT-STRAND JELLY
Melicertum octocostatum, *Melicertum georgicum*
to 1.4 cm (0.6 in) tall
n. Alaska to c. Oregon
pelagic
The eight radiating brown structures so visible in this species are the sex organs, which, together with extensions of the stomach, are attached to eight radial canals. This small jelly is a weak swimmer that frequently suspends upside down in the water column.
Hurst Island, Goletas Channel, c. BC

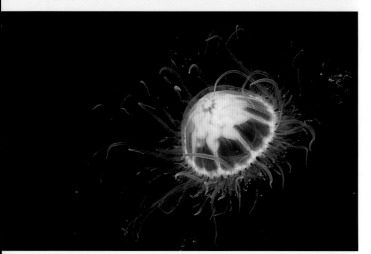

CN107. ▶FOLDED-STOMACH JELLY
Ptychogastria polaris
to 2.2 cm (0.9 in) across
Antarctica, north Atlantic, circumpolar, n. Alaska to c. California
pelagic
Generally this distinctive jelly rests on the bottom, attaching with its short, adhesive inner tentacles while it extends its long outside tentacles to capture prey. It may dwell as shallow as 10 m (33 ft) in boreal locales, but it lives much deeper in the Pacific Northwest.
Dynamite Beach, Resolute Bay, Nunavut. Danny Kent photograph

CN108. BY-THE-WIND SAILOR, by-the-wind-sailor, purple sailing jellyfish, sail jellyfish, sail jelly fish, purple sail jellyfish
Velella velella, *Velella lata*
to 10 cm (4 in) across
BC to c. California
cosmopolitan, coast-wide
Great numbers of these jellies are sometimes stranded on beaches of the outer coast. Much of the creature's rich blue remains for a day or so, but if stranded longer than that, only the transparent plastic-like sail and base float remain. This "jelly" is actually a floating hydroid.
Ucluth Peninsula, w. Vancouver Island, s. BC

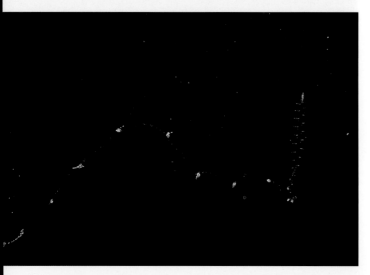

CN109. ▶TAILED JELLY
Nanomia bijuga, *Stephanomia bijuga* (*Nanomia cara* is another very similar species and the distribution of both requires further study)
at least 30 cm (12 in) long
BC to Oregon
pelagic
This distinctively bizarre creature is not soon forgotten. It gives rise to the "What's that?" question more than just about any other Pacific Northwest species. Technically it is a siphonophoran, a highly specialized jelly with numerous well-integrated structures. When undisturbed and "hunting," it spreads out its multi-branched fishing-line-like tentacles in spectacular array.
Sutton Islets, Egmont, s. BC

CN110. ▶BELL-HEADED TAILED JELLY

Praya **sp.**, *Nectodroma* sp.
to 135 m (446 ft)
▶c. BC to Mexico
pelagic

This jelly is reputed to be the world's longest animal. Parts of its "tail" may detach and survive for some time, either fulfilling a sexual function or just surviving damage, as in photograph A. Photograph B illustrates the anterior "head" end and a portion of the rest of the body. Such behaviour, coupled with its delicate construction, make this fascinating oceanic drifter a rare and confusing find.

A Cape Flattery, Olympic coast, n. Washington
B Sekiu, Olympic coast, n. Washington

At least 15 other species of small jellies have been documented from the Pacific Northwest. To sight any of these nomads drifting about in an incredibly huge oceanic expanse is truly serendipitous.

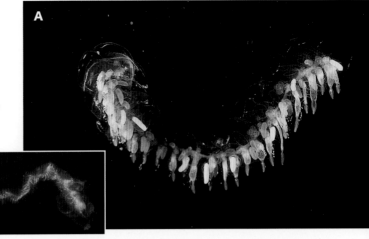

STALKED JELLIES

CN111. ▶OVAL-ANCHORED STALKED JELLY

Haliclystus stejnegeri
to 3 cm (1.2 in) across
n. Alaska to Washington
▶intertidal to 10 m (33 ft)

Identity crisis! A "jellyfish" reverting to a sedentary lifestyle? In the photograph, note the eight "bump-like" structures located between the more obvious eight multi-tentacled, brush-like arms. In this species, these "bumps" or marginal anchors are egg-shaped and without stalks. The trumpet stalked jellyfish, *Haliclystus salpinx,* has broad trumpet-shaped marginal anchors with conspicuous stalks.

Sekiu, Olympic coast, n. Washington

CN112. ▶RED STALKED JELLY

Manania gwilliami
▶to 5 cm (2 in) long
▶BC to c. California
intertidal to 10 m (33 ft)

This creature prefers surge-swept pinnacles or rocky outcrops along open-coast shores. It sways to and fro in the surge, capturing its tiny planktonic prey. It can slowly creep along, or even completely detach from its anchoring site and be swept to an alternate location.

Aguilar Point, Bamfield, s. BC

CN113. ▶WINDOWED STALKED JELLY, stalked medusa

Manania handi
to 8 cm (3.2 in) long
s. BC to Washington
shallow subtidal

Its colour and pattern make this species particularly difficult to find when attached to eelgrass (SW2). Various species of algae also serve as anchoring sites. When disturbed, a stalked jelly can contract its stalk. It may also use this ability to orient itself for prey capture. Apparently, small amphipods and copepods are preferred.

Sekiu, Olympic coast, n. Washington

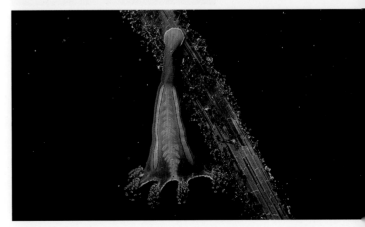

CN114. ▶HERRING-BONE STALKED JELLY
Manania distincta
to 5 cm (2 in) tall
Japan, Siberia, n. Alaska to Oregon
intertidal to subtidal
A little-known species that is seldom encountered, this jelly prefers the wave action of outer-coast shorelines. The underwater photographer wanting to test his or her skills, as both an image maker and a diver, should try shooting a stalked jelly. Just finding one is a challenge. Strong surge, dense plant growth, shallow depth and a reactive subject are a few of the complications in obtaining a good photograph.

Boas Islet, Hakai Passage, c. BC

COMB JELLIES *Phylum CTENOPHORA*

Includes the comb jellies, sea gooseberries and sea walnuts.

The gelatinous, transparent comb jellies superficially resemble the pulsating "jellies" or medusoid cnidaria, but it is their feeble but steady locomotion that truly sets them apart. This movement occurs via the rhythmic beating of countless tiny cilia (hairs) that are arranged in eight rows of ctenes (comb plates). Like lines of longitude upon a mini-globe, these rows adorn the usually spherical or oval body of each comb jelly, as shown in the photograph of a translucent comb jelly (CT5). Each ctene is essentially a tiny row of cilia fused at one end and protruding at the other, like the teeth of a mini-comb. Often sunlight (or artificial light at night) diffracted by these rows of beating cilia—a pulsating light show— is the only visual evidence of a comb jelly.

Fewer than 30 species of comb jellies or ctenophores live in the marine waters of the Pacific Northwest.

Further Reading

Wrobel, David, and Claudia Mills, 1998, *Pacific Coast Pelagic Invertebrates*, Monterey CA: Sea Challengers, 108 pp.

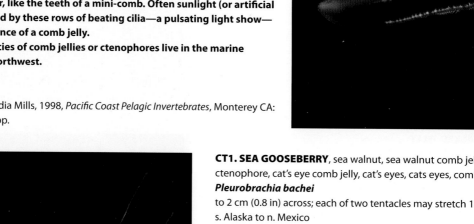

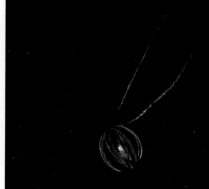

CT1. SEA GOOSEBERRY, sea walnut, sea walnut comb jelly, cat's eye ctenophore, cat's eye comb jelly, cat's eyes, cats eyes, combjelly, comb jelly
Pleurobrachia bachei
to 2 cm (0.8 in) across; each of two tentacles may stretch 15 cm (6 in)
s. Alaska to n. Mexico
pelagic
Massive numbers of this species may dominate the ocean's surface in spring. Although comb jellies are usually and conveniently found here, and in most books, next to the Cnidarians, they are not close relatives of the anemones or medusoid jellies.

Kleindale, Pender Harbour, s. BC

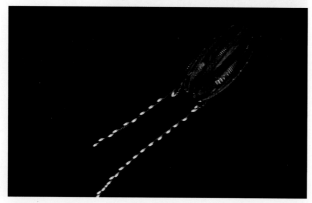

CT2. ▶OVAL SEA GOOSEBERRY
Euplokamis dunlapae
to 2 cm (0.8 in) long
BC to n. Washington
pelagic
Drifting along in the current, often near the surface, this species uses its tentacles as fishing lines, trolling for tiny copepod prey. Once the victim is ensnared by the tightly coiled tentilla (side branches), it is transferred to the mouth.

Sutton Islets, Egmont, s. BC

CT3. LOBED SEA GOOSEBERRY, fragile combjelly, fragile comb jelly
Bolinopsis infundibulum, *Bolinopsis septentrionalis*, *Bolina microptera*
to 15 cm (6 in) long
n. Alaska to s. California
pelagic
Distinctive front lobes are movable and open to consume drifting prey such as copepods and euphausids. It finds such food by ascending and descending in a drifting patrol.
Anderson Bay, Texada Island, s. BC

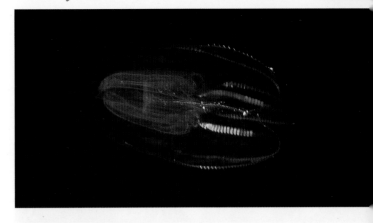

CT4. ▶ORANGE-TIPPED SEA GOOSEBERRY
Leucothea pulchra
to 25 cm (10 in) long
▶c. BC to n. Mexico
pelagic
Resembling a miniature dirigible, this species is a spectacular sight as it drifts by! Many years before this project was even considered, the authors found this specimen near Port Hardy, BC, during a week of exploration and underwater photography. The sighting remains one of the highlights of that adventure!
Browning Passage, Nigei Island, c. BC

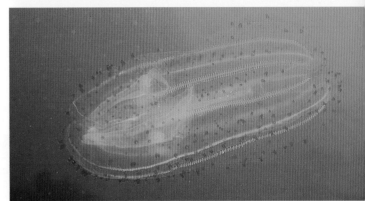

CT5. TRANSLUCENT COMB JELLIES
Beroe **spp.**, including *Beroe gracilis*, *Beroe abyssicola*, *Beroe forskalii*
to 3 cm (1.2 in) long
Alaska to s. California
pelagic
These comb jellies resemble tiny "prismatic" sausages and, for their small size, are quite easy to see. They feed on other comb jellies such as the lobed sea gooseberry (CT3), by opening their unbelievably large mouths and consuming them whole. From the prey's perspective, this activity is a scene from a horror movie.
Many other comb jellies inhabit the Pacific Northwest, but our understanding of these delicate creatures remains limited, due in large measure to their transient lifestyle. Scientists at the Monterey Bay Aquarium, who employ submersibles, are the acknowledged leaders in this fascinating field of research.
Egmont Marina, Egmont, s. BC

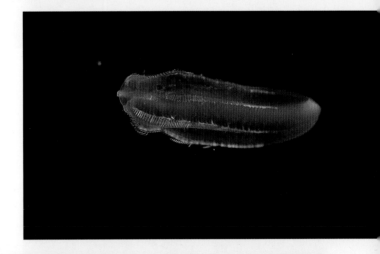

FLATWORMS *Phylum PLATYHELMINTHES*

This group includes the parasitic flukes and tapeworms, but further focus falls upon the free-living flatworms. "Dorso-ventrally challenged," or flattened top to bottom, these primitive, unsegmented flatworms slip along the substrate upon countless tiny cilia (hairs). The photograph shows the white flatworm (PL7). In each species, a simple or branched digestive tract is serviced by only one opening—the mouth doubling as the anus.

At least 126 species of free-living flatworms dwell in the marine waters of the Pacific Northwest, and doubtless many more remain to be discovered and recorded.

PL1. ▶SPOTTED FLATWORM
Eurylepta leoparda
to 2.5 cm (1 in) long
BC to Washington
intertidal to subtidal
Occasionally emerging en masse from beneath solid substrate, this species is often found inside the transparent tunicate (CH1). A flatworm's mouth is located near the midpoint of the underside, and it uses an evertable pharynx to seize and then draw the prey inside. Little is known about flatworm prey.
Halkett Point, Howe Sound, s. BC

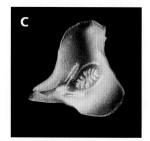

PL2. GIANT FLATWORM, giant leaf worm, large leaf worm, leaf worm
Kaburakia excelsa, *Cryptophallus magnus*
to 10 cm (4 in) long
s. Alaska to c. California
intertidal to subtidal
A flatworm glides along substrate on a self-produced "slime trail." Amazingly this species is also an accomplished, fluttering swimmer as shown in photograph C. Its digestive tract is also featured. Photograph B shows a swelled specimen, probably heavy with spawn and ready to reproduce.
A Stanley Park, Vancouver Harbour, s. BC
B C Passage Island, Howe Sound, s. BC

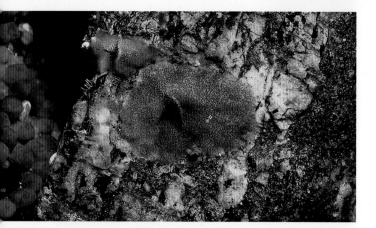

PL3. ▶SADDLEBACK FLATWORM
Notoplana sanguinea, *Notocomplana sanguinea*
▶to 2.5 cm (1 in) long
BC to Washington
intertidal and subtidal
The saddle-like red blotch on the back distinguishes this species. The pair shown here was found by overturning a rock during a dive—the only way to find some creatures. Be responsible and carefully return both rock and creatures as found. The larger of two animals is carrying a parasitic white copepod.
Sutton Islets, Egmont, s. BC

PL4. INTERTIDAL FLATWORMS, including tapered flatworm, brown flatworm, common flatworm, leaf worm
Notocomplana spp., including *Notocomplana actinicola, Notoplana acticola, Leptoplana acticola?*
to 6 cm (2.3 in) long
BC to c. California
intertidal to subtidal
Many flatworms are extremely difficult to identify, and this photograph is included to illustrate our dilemma.
Stanley Park, Vancouver Harbour, s. BC

PL5. ►CALIFORNIA FLATWORM
Stylochus californiensis
to 10 cm (4 in) long
►BC to s. California
►intertidal to 15 m (50 ft)
This species apparently lives with and feeds on bivalve molluscs, but the specimen photographed was one of a small group hiding under a piece of waterlogged bark in Agamemnon Channel, BC. Could they have been mating? This find extends the known range north from Oregon.
Green Bay, Nelson Island, s. BC

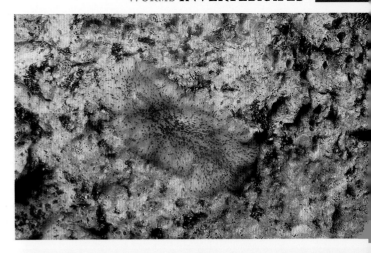

PL6. GREEN FLATWORM
Phylloplana viridis, *Triplana viridis*, *Stylochoplana viridis*
to 2.5 cm (1 in) long
s. BC to n. California
intertidal to subtidal
This species crawls about on eelgrass (SW2). So transparent is it that sand grains show through in the photograph. Many flatworms have light-sensitive eye-spots around the complete edge of the upper surface or at the tentacles, or possibly both.
Tuwanek, Sechelt Inlet, s. BC

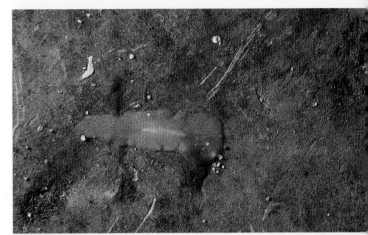

PL7. WHITE FLATWORM, polyclad worm
Pseudoceros luteus, *Ambylceraeus luteus*
to 5 cm (2 in) long
►s. BC to s. California
intertidal to subtidal
Though this attractive flatworm may crawl about on sea fir hydroids (CN54/55), it can also swim in a graceful, fluttering motion! The specimen in the photograph was found by Doug Swanston of Seacology, a BC-based marine life supply company. It was found near Tofino, BC, and represents a significant range extension for the species.
Lennard Island, Tofino, s. BC

PL8. STRIPED POLYCLAD WORM, polyclad worm
Eurylepta californica
to 3 cm (1.3 in) long
►c. BC to c. California
intertidal to 10 m (33 ft)
This specimen was photographed by Charlie Gibbs of Port Coquitlam, BC, as it crawled on kelp near Nootka Sound, Vancouver Island. This documentation is a significant range extension from the earlier northern Californian records. This species may superficially resemble a very thin dorid nudibranch, but it is easily distinguished by the lack of obvious gills.
Otter Island, Esperanza Inlet, s. BC. Charlie Gibbs photograph

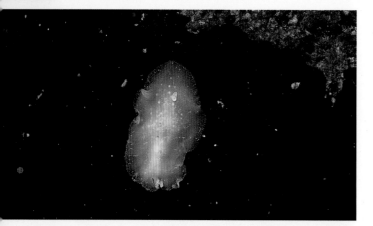

PL9. COMPOUND TUNICATE FLATWORMS
Pseudoceros canadensis/Stylostomum sanjuania
►to 1.2 cm (0.5 in) long
BC to s. California
intertidal to subtidal
After gathering and preserving a specimen of lobed compound tunicate (CH25), Andy Lamb found this specimen crawling about on the bottom of a collecting bucket. It could be either of the species listed above, as both apparently live with compound tunicates and they are difficult to tell apart.
Laura Point, Mayne Island, s. BC

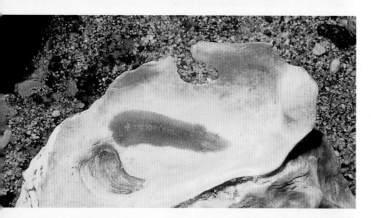

PL10. BIVALVE FLATWORM
Pseudostylochus ostreophagus, *Koinostylochus ostreophagus*
to 3 cm (1.2 in) long
Japan, s. BC to n. Washington
intertidal to shallow subtidal
Inadvertently introduced from Japan when oyster spat was first imported, this worm is now a predatory pest for local shellfish aquaculture interests. A special thanks to Barb Bunting of Island Scallops, Vancouver Island, BC, for supplying the photographed specimen. We know it won't be missed!
Island Scallops Inc., Qualicum, s. BC

PL11. ►PINK PARASITIC FLATWORM
Kronborgia pugetensis
length of coiled body difficult to assess
BC to Washington
intertidal to subtidal
Examine the Kincaid's shrimp (AR59) in the photograph carefully and note this flatworm inside. Eventually this strange worm leaves the host shrimp, drops to the bottom and forms a cocoon, which leads to reproduction. Unfortunately the shrimp usually does not survive the escape process.
Fidalgo Head, Fidalgo Island, n. Washington

RIBBON WORMS *Phylum NEMERTEA*

Slender, quite delicate and highly contractile, ribbon worms have a digestive system with a separate mouth and anus, as well as a circulatory system complete with blood vessels. Most unique, though, is the proboscis or food capturing device, shown in the photograph of a chevron ribbon worm (NE5). Like a fluid-filled, inside-out finger of a glove, the proboscis is either sticky or has a venomous, thorn-like stylet on the inside. On a massive muscular contraction of the proboscis, hydrostatic pressure everts it to envelop prey—often a segmented worm.

At least 87 species of ribbon worms live in the marine waters of the Pacific Northwest.

NE1. GREEN RIBBON WORM, green nemertean worm, green nemertean, green and yellow ribbon worm, mussel ribbon worm, mussel nemertean worm
***Emplectonema gracile**, Emplectonema viride, Nemertes gracilis*
to 50 cm (20 in) long
Japan, n. Alaska to n. Mexico, Chile
intertidal to subtidal
This species hides in barnacle/mussel clusters and is frequently found in entwined groups as shown. Barnacles are its primary prey.
Stanley Park, Vancouver Harbour, s. BC

NE2. ▶LEOPARD RIBBON WORM
Emplectonema purpuratum
to 1 m (39 in) long
▶BC to Washington
▶subtidal
Thick and robust, the leopard ribbon worm, like many nemertean species, can greatly expand and reduce its length. The dagger-like stylet on the end of its proboscis is used to immobilize prey before retracting it to the mouth. Annelid worms are a prime quarry for most ribbon worms.
Lions Bay, Howe Sound, s. BC

NE3. ▶MOTTLED RIBBON WORM
Emplectonema burgeri
▶at least 25 cm (10 in) long
Japan, n. Alaska to California
intertidal to subtidal
This species is often found in tangled clusters. Could it be a gathering stage for reproduction? This grouping and several others were found at Slip Point, Washington, during an intertidal excursion along the Olympic coast. They were found by overturning rocks during a low tide, well down the beach.
Slip Point, Olympic coast, n. Washington

NE4. PURPLE RIBBON WORM, Verrill's ribbon worm, lavender and white ribbon worm
***Micrura verrilli**, Lineus striatus*
to 50 cm (20 in) long
c. Alaska to c. California
intertidal to subtidal
Look under rocks or in the root mats of surfgrasses (SW4) to find this attractive creature showing through its clear mucus tube. Unlike the mottled ribbon worm (NE3), this one does not have a stylet on its proboscis but relies on the sticky quality of this organ.
The ▶salmon-pink ribbon worm, *Micrura alaskensis,* lives in similar haunts but grows much larger.
Eagle Point, San Juan Island, n. Washington

NE5. CHEVRON RIBBON WORM, two-spotted ribbon worm, two-spotted ribbonworm, chevron amphiporus, thick amphiporus, twisted brown ribbon worm, two-eyed ribbon worm
Amphiporus bimaculatus, Amphiporus angulatus
to 12 cm (5 in) long
n. Alaska to n. Mexico
intertidal to 137 m (450 ft)
Somewhat stubby with two dark head marks, this species mainly hides under rocks. The introductory photograph for Nemertea (see p. 116) depicts a specimen with its proboscis everted.
Tongue Point, Olympic coast, n. Washington

NE6. PINK-FRONTED RIBBON WORM, thin amphiporus, white nemertean
Amphiporus imparispinosus
to 7 cm (2.8 in) long
Siberia, n. Alaska to n. Mexico
intertidal to subtidal
A ribbon worm has a ciliated (hairy) skin, which it uses to glide along the substrate. In smaller species such as this one, mucus secreted by the epidermis lubricates the trail. This worm is likely to be in plain view when the weather is cool and moist rather than on hot, sunny days.
Frank Island, w. Vancouver Island, s. BC

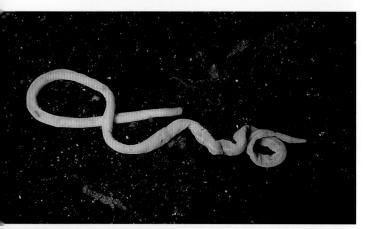

NE7. WHITE RIBBON WORM
Amphiporus formidibalis, Amphiporus exilis
to 30 cm (12 in)
Japan, Alaska to c. California
intertidal
This species has a slightly different proboscis than the pink-fronted ribbon worm (NE6)—a minor difference that requires dissection and microscopic examination to verify. Both are predators and each uses its proboscis to ensnare amphipods and other small invertebrate creatures.
When a ribbon worm is handled, it may literally divide its body into several sections in a process known as fragmentation. This is actually asexual reproduction, as each piece can become a complete worm by regenerating its missing parts.
Stanley Park, Vancouver Harbour, s. BC

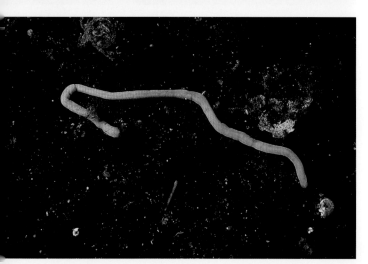

NE8. ▶MANY-EYED RIBBON WORM
Amphiporus cruentatus
to 4 cm (1.6 in) long
▶n. Atlantic Ocean, c. BC to s. California
▶intertidal to 20 m (65 ft)
This worm is distinguished by a longitudinal row of five to 10 eye-spots on each side of its head. Unfortunately they are tiny and difficult to see without a good-quality hand lens.
Browning Passage, Nigei Island, c. BC

NE9. MUD NEMERTEAN, wandering ribbon worm, wandering nemertean, restless worm, purple ribbon worm, purple-backed ribbon worm
Paranemertes peregrina
to 25 cm (10 in) long
Japan, Siberia, n. Alaska to n. Mexico
intertidal to subtidal
This small species may crawl about in the open intertidally when conditions are damp, but it is more often found under rocks in silty or muddy areas. In most ribbon worms, each animal is either male or female and the gametes (sex products) are shed into the surrounding water.
Stanley Park, Vancouver Harbour, s. BC

NE10. SIX-LINED RIBBON WORM, six-lined nemertean, lined ribbon worm
Tubulanus sexlineatus, *Carinella sexlineatus, Carinella sexlineata, Carinella dinema*
to 1 m (39 in) long
s. Alaska to s. California
▶intertidal to 15 m (50 ft)
This species is the ribbon worm most often found by the diver because it commonly moves about in the open over rocky, shallow subtidal locales. It is usually found completely stretched out but will readily retract if disturbed.
Long Bay, Gambier Island, s. BC

NE11. ORANGE RIBBON WORM, orange nemertean, red ribbon worm, primitive ribbon worm
Tubulanus polymorphus, *Carinella speciosa, Carinella rubra*
to 1 m (39 in) long
n. Europe, Mediterranean Sea, n. Alaska to s. California
intertidal to 50 m (165 ft)
Note the lack of stripes or bands, a distinctive feature for this bright-hued species. Perhaps the most spectacular ribbon worm commonly encountered by the beachcomber, it is often found stretched out and obvious.
Daniel Point, Agamemnon Channel, s. BC

NE12. ▶WHITE-RINGED RIBBON WORM
Tubulanus albocinctus, *Carinella albocinctus*
to 1 m (39 in) long
n. Alaska to s. California
subtidal
This attractive species is distinguished by the white body rings past the head area, with some slightly wider and more obvious than others. Unlike a flatworm, which only has one opening, a ribbon worm has a complete digestive tract with both a mouth and an anus.
Quarry Bay, Nelson Island, s. BC

NE13. ▶WHITE-LINED RIBBON WORM
Tetrastemma nigrifrons
▶to 75 cm (30 in) long
▶Japan, s. BC to c. America
subtidal
This species is distinctive in its orange colour with white head patch and white stripes along the entire body. Usually it is found coiled up but at times it stretches out and moves along using its surprisingly substantial musculature.

A denizen of shallower, seaweed-laden habitats is the ▶red-eyed ribbon worm, *Tetrastemma candidum*—a pale green species.

Kunechin Point, Sechelt Inlet, s. BC

NE14. ▶LIGHT-EDGED RIBBON WORM
Cerebratulus californiensis
to 15 cm (6 in) long
▶s. BC to n. Mexico
intertidal to 50 m (165 ft)
Divers venturing out at night sometimes see this broad ribbon worm lying on top of sand or mud. Usually it rests still on the bottom but it is capable of swimming—an amazing feat for this muscularly challenged creature.

A Treadwell Bay, Slingsby Channel, c. BC
B Stanley Park, Vancouver Harbour, s. BC

NE15. ROSE RIBBON WORM
Cerebratulus montgomeri
to 2 m (6.6 ft) long
Japan, Siberia, n. Alaska to California
intertidal to 400 m (1,320 ft)
Primarily seen at night, this gorgeous worm often extends its body from a burrow in the mud or sand but quickly retracts upon the slightest disturbance. This species may be able to follow its own slime trail to find its way back to its burrow following an extended excursion.

Point Atkinson, West Vancouver, s. BC

NE16. BLACK RIBBON WORM
Lineus spatiosus
▶to 12.5 cm (5 in) long
n. Japan, BC
subtidal
While diving near Tofino, BC, John Fisher, an aquarist at the Vancouver Aquarium Marine Science Centre, found this specimen living under a rock. After examining it, Dr. Fumio Iwata of Japan (by way of Friday Harbor, Washington) identified it as the same species that he had described nearly 50 years ago, from a single specimen taken in Hokkaido. An amazing story of a range extension!

Lennard Island, Tofino, s. BC

NE17. The yellow-orange unmarked body of this short, stocky species is usually obvious. Look for the **short orange ribbon worm** subtidally in depths greater than 20 m (65 ft) at low-current locales. Unfortunately its identity remains a mystery.
Garcin Rocks, Moresby Island, n. BC

NE18. The identity of this **subtidal white ribbon worm** may never be known, but we are convinced it is none of the worms mentioned here. This specimen was found subtidally, crawling about in the open. It is much larger than the pink-fronted ribbon worm (NE6) and the white ribbon worm (NE7).
Kunechin Point, Sechelt Inlet, s. BC

NE19. This **small tan ribbon worm** was found by John Fisher, an aquarist at the Vancouver Aquarium Marine Science Centre. After collecting eelgrass (SW2) plants for display, he noticed the small form (2.5 cm/1 in) on one of the green leaves. Whether it is a juvenile specimen or an adult of a diminutive species is unresolved.
Numerous cryptic and small ribbon worms are recorded from the Pacific Northwest, so keep your eyes open.
Cates Park, Indian Arm, s. BC

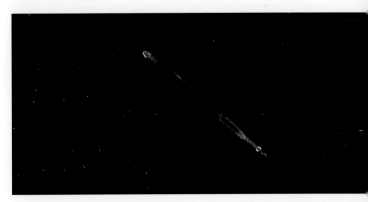

ARROW WORMS *Phylum CHAETOGNATHA*

Arrow worms or bristlemouth worms

Slender, tiny and transparent, the planktonic arrow worms present viewing problems even though they may be extremely abundant when in "bloom." Each species possesses a pair of lateral fins and a tail fin, but the worms swim by repetitive flexing of the central body area. This distinctive motion is an eye-catching hint of its presence. The most obvious anatomical feature of an arrow worm is a formidable pair of bristle-bearing "jaws" adjacent to its mouth.

Eighteen species of arrow worms are found in the marine waters of the Pacific Northwest.

CG1. ARROW WORM
Sagitta elegans
to 2.5 cm (1 in) long
cosmopolitan, Alaska to n. California
pelagic
This dominant member of zooplankton (floating animal) blooms is more prevalent in springtime. It may be seen hanging like a motionless sliver of glass, only to move by flexing at its midpoint. These factors, along with its diminutive size, make it a challenging photographic subject.
Sutton Islets, Egmont, s. BC. Charlie Gibbs photograph

PEANUT WORMS *Phylum SIPUNCULIDA*

Distinctively non-segmented, a peanut worm body consists of two vaguely defined regions. The extendable introvert (neck) has a tentacle-rimmed mouth designed for deposit feeding. The remainder of the body (trunk) is cloaked by a tough, rubbery wall. Extending into each region, the long coiled digestive tract culminates in a dorsally positioned anus, located just behind the mouth.
Approximately 21 species of peanut worms live in the marine waters of the Pacific Northwest.

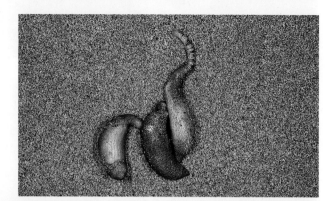

SP1. AGASSIZ'S PEANUT WORM, Agassi's peanut worm, dotted peanut worm, Pacific peanut worm, peanut worm
Phascolosoma agassizii, *Golfingia agassizii, Physcosoma agassizii*
to 15 cm (6 in) long
n. Alaska to n. Mexico
intertidal to 200 m (660 ft)
The striped introvert (neck) of this animal sometimes protrudes from under a rock. It is widely distributed along both exposed and sheltered shores.
Ucluth Peninsula, w. Vancouver Island, s. BC

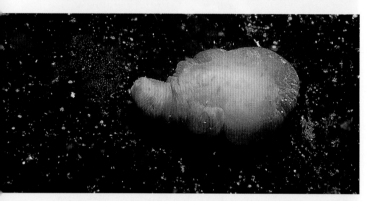

SP2. BROWN PEANUT WORM
Golfingia vulgaris, *Golfingia kolensis*
▶at least 15 cm (6 in) long
s. Alaska to Washington
subtidal
Usually noticeable as it protrudes from a crevice or beneath a rock, this peanut worm is a challenge to find. The specimen in the photograph appears in a state of contraction. Relaxed, it would be considerably longer and the orange anterior end and mouth would be more visible.
Another Pacific Northwest species is the ▶smooth brown peanut worm, *Golfingia pugettensis,* which can be differentiated by its darker colour, with a smooth and longer introvert (neck).
Porteau Cove, Howe Sound, s. BC

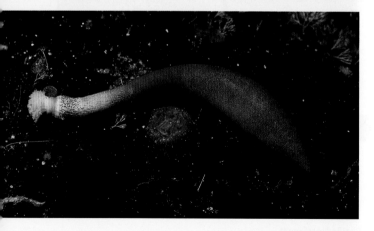

SP3. BURROWING PEANUT WORM, flowering peanut worm, tan peanut worm, rich brown peanut worm, bushy-headed peanut worm, common peanut worm
Themiste pyroides, *Dendrostomum pyroides, Dendrostoma pyroides, Dendrostomum petraeum, Dendrostoma patraeum*
to 20 cm (8 in) long
s. BC to n. Mexico
intertidal to subtidal
This creature resides primarily in the empty burrows of boring clams. The photograph shows a completely relaxed and extended specimen with its distinctive tentacles showing.
From Oregon south, the ▶southern burrowing peanut worm, *Themiste dyscrita,* might be encountered. Unlike the burrowing peanut worm, it has no spines on its introvert (neck).
Tongue Point, Olympic coast, n. Washington

SP4. Found in thick, compacted silt, this unidentified **white-necked peanut worm** was accidentally collected by John Fisher of the Vancouver Aquarium Marine Science Centre. He located it while gathering sea whips (CN42) for display purposes during a scuba dive at the Defence Islands. Unfortunately the specimen was lost before its identity could be ascertained.
Defence Islands, Howe Sound, s. BC

SEGMENTED WORMS *Phylum ANNELIDA*

Annulated (segmented) worms

The body of an annulated worm consists of a definitive, linear series of segments as illustrated in the photograph of a marine earthworm, p. 131 (Lumbrineridae). This external segmentation is reflected internally by the compartmentalization of various organ

systems. Each segmented worm possesses a body-length digestive tract with an anterior mouth and a posterior anus. Although virtually everyone's introduction to the segmented worms is via an encounter with the familiar backyard earthworm (an oligochaete) or the dreaded fresh-water leech, it is the polychaetes—"worms with many bristles"— that flourish in the marine environment. They are the "Cadillacs" of the annelid world! The diversity of segmented worms in the world has been estimated at more than 22,000 species, and at least 9,000 of these are polychaetes, the vast majority of which are marine.

Historically and for various reasons, annelids have received minimal attention in the popular press. Though there are many species of marine oligochaetes, it is a select group of leeches and polychaetes that are featured below. Additional introductory material for each family is included.

LEECHES

Although fresh-water leeches are common, species have been discovered more recently in both moist terrestrial and marine habitats. A most distinctive feature is the formidable suckers! The anterior sucker surrounds the mouth, and toward the posterior is a ventrally placed one. Some leeches use these suckers to move in "inchworm" fashion. Many leeches are free-living predators, some are scavengers and others are parasites.

AN1. This photograph represents a number of small bloodsucking leech species that use their suckers to attach to various Pacific Northwest fishes. **Fish leeches** (Piscicolidae) are difficult to distinguish without microscopic examination and expert knowledge. Sometimes they are so plentiful on fish, particularly flatfish species, that they give the appearance of fur. The individuals may appear red after feeding on the fishes' blood. Such an observation demonstrates that these creatures are parasites—more precisely ectoparasites because they attach and feed externally. Few fish leeches are active swimmers, because their muscles are poorly developed. They move about by looping movements over the substrate or host.
Vancouver Marine Science Centre, Stanley Park, s. BC. Donna Gibbs photograph

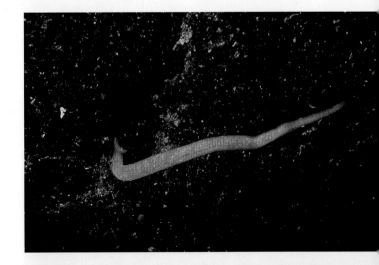

AN2. STRIPED SEA LEECH, striped sea-leech
Notostomobdella cyclostoma, *Notostomum cyclostoma*, *Carcinobdella cyclostoma*, *Carcinobdella cyclostomum*
to 15 cm (6 in) long
Japan, Arctic Ocean, n. Alaska to s. Alaska
subtidal to 366 m (1,200 ft)
Known to be a temporary parasite of fishes such as sharks and rays, this animal is also frequently found on the red king crab (AR134) and tanner crab (AR103). Close inspection of these crabs may reveal the black blister-like egg capsules (each containing a single young) deposited by this leech. Approximately 10 other species of leeches parasitize various fish and invertebrates that dwell in the Pacific Northwest.
Tristar Fisheries, Richmond, BC

POLYCHAETES

An estimated, accepted 9,000 species of polychaete worms, representing 81 families, have been recorded worldwide. To put this into perspective, global biodiversity estimates suggest the presence of only about 15,000 species of marine fish. Although estimates from 1985 place the Pacific Northwest as home to at least 836 polychaete worms, new species are continuing to be discovered and described. This is an impressive array, but much of the biology of polychaetes awaits study. Photographs and information for 79 species in 32 families of polychaetes are included herein.

Polychaete ("many bristles") worms are under-appreciated animals that are important in the marine environment. They are particularly significant as marine benthos (bottom dwellers) living on the seabed surface (epifauna) or within the seabed sediments (infauna). They can typically comprise 45 to 50% of the species diversity within a benthic community, and as much as 80% of the total individual animals! Like earthworms in a backyard garden, they are vital to the health of the sediments. By helping to decompose and bioturbate (turn over) the organic matter on the seabed, polychaetes actually recycle nutrients within the sediments as well as vertically into the water column. Many of these worms can rapidly recolonize and rehabilitate sediments drastically altered by waste-water disposal (such as sewage), oil spills, aquaculture-generated waste and even severe ocean storms.

A healthy polychaete community represents a major contribution to the food web. Polychaetes eat other polychaetes; other animals such as sea stars eat polychaetes; many demersal fish (those living at or near the bottom) eat polychaetes; gray whales eat polychaetes by the mouthful in sediments that they scoop from the bottom. The larvae of many polychaetes spend time in the plankton, feeding and developing to a particular stage before they can finally "settle out" onto the seabed and grow into adults. During this process, the larvae are a prime food source for other pelagic animals such as zooplankton, fish and baleen whales. Along the Pacific Northwest coastline, intertidal polychaetes are a nutritional resource for many shorebirds. And yes, there are even some species of polychaetes that are considered tasty morsels by humans in some parts of the world! What would our world be like without polychaetes?

Since the mid-1700s, the morphology (external characteristics) of polychaete worms has been used to describe and name the diversity of species. Gradually investigations shifted, and efforts focused on the relationships among these polychaete species and their families. One result of this process was an organizational scheme that divided the polychaete families into two major groups: the Errantia or errantiate polychaeta (free swimmers or burrowers) and the Sedentaria or sedentariate polychaeta (tube dwellers). This historic scheme is now considered to be an arbitrary and inconsistent division. The recent addition of research tools that incorporate evolutionary and molecular perspectives have greatly improved the understanding of polychaetes. Leading international experts have developed a new organizational scheme for polychaetes based on a combination of these perspectives that produces a more holistic approach.

According to this systematic approach, polychaetes are divided into three main groups. The **simple-bodied polychaete** has a noticeable head but it lacks obvious structures. The first segment is similar to all those that follow, bearing similar paired appendages for the entire body length as shown in photograph A, a Pacific Neapolitan lugworm (AN7). The **sensory-palp polychaete** has paired palps (anterior sensory outgrowths) but they are uniform, relatively short and positioned ventrally on the head. The usually visible, tapering and tactile palps are used for sensory perception. In addition, each member of this group of worms has a pair of antennae on the head. Finally, its parapodia (fleshy, flap-like appendages) are often well developed. Photograph B shows an example in the form of a red-and-white-banded sea-nymph (AN47). The **feeding-palp polychaete** has long palps on its head, in pairs, multiples or as a "tentacular" crown. Each of these palps has a ciliated (hair-lined), longitudinal groove that transports food to the mouth, as illustrated by the beautiful, delicate tentacular crowns of some tubeworms. Photograph C is an image of a feather-duster worm removed from its tube, p. 151.

Within these three categories, the polychaete worms are generally organized alphabetically by family, and within family groupings. Some exceptions apply where similar-looking polychaetes are grouped together for easier comparison. Where possible, the establishment of common names was based on the root derivative or origin of the scientific name.

In general, each segment of a polychaete worm is adorned with a pair of parapodia that bear the characteristic chaetae (bristles; occasionally written as "setae"). Often the parapodia are subdivided into two branches with the upper notopodia (near the back) carrying notochaetae, and the lower neuropodia (near the belly) carrying the neurochaetae. The individual shape of the chaetae, their combination and configuration, are usually species-specific. The anatomy of these bristly appendages is reflective of the lifestyle or "modus operandi" of each polychaete species.

Polychaete worms are a challenge to identify—living or preserved. In many cases, specific identifications require microscope examination, which unveils the fascinating and exquisite shapes of polychaete chaetae! However, the observant beachcomber or diver may, with some experience and the information here, recognize numerous commonly encountered species.

Further Reading

Beesley, P.L., G.J.B. Ross and C.J. Glasby, eds., 2000, *"Polychaetes & Allies: The Southern Synthesis," Fauna of Australia, vol. 4A: Polychaeta, Myzostomida, Pogonophora, Echiura, Sipuncula*, Melbourne: CSIRO Publishing, xii, 465 pp.

Blake, J.A., B. Hilbig and P.H. Scott, eds, *Taxonomic Atlas of the Benthic Fauna of the Santa Maria Basin and the Western Santa Barbara Channel, The Annelida*, vol. 4, part 1, 1997: 369 pp.; vol. 5, part 2, 1995: 378 pp.; vol. 6, part 3, 1996: 418 pp.; vol. 7, part 4, 2000: 348 pp.

Kozloff, E.N., 1996, *Marine Invertebrates of the Pacific Northwest*. With the collaboration of L.H. Price and contributions by other specialists. Seattle and London: University of Washington Press, 539 pp.

O'Clair, R.M. and C.E. O'Clair, 1998, *Southeast Alaska's Rocky Shores*, Animals, Auke Bay, AK: Plant Press, 559 pp.

Rouse, G.W. and F. Pleijel, 2001, *Polychaetes*. Oxford: Oxford University Press, 354 pp.

SIMPLE-BODIED POLYCHAETES

Bamboo-worms

Bamboo-worms (Family Maldanidae) are tube-building worms, whose bodies have long segments separated by nodes or joints, reminiscent of a bamboo plant. Each species usually has a fixed maximum number of segments and if part of its body is removed, the worm can regenerate the exact number of segments lost. Amazingly, bamboo-worms can regenerate the anterior or posterior ends—or both simultaneously. However, if the critical mid-body segments (usually 8 to 10) are lost, it proves fatal.

AN3. RED-BANDED BAMBOO-WORM, red-banded tube worm, bamboo worm, jointworm
Axiothella rubrocincta complex,* *Clymenella rubrocincta*
6–20 cm (2.4–8 in) long, tube longer than worm
Japan, s. Alaska to s. California
intertidal
At low tide, look closely in salt marshes and quiet bays, particularly where the muddy sand is hard-packed, to find small fields of fine-bored tubes. Only a short portion of a brittle tube protrudes above the surface, and very careful excavation will expose an intact worm. Each tube, probably used to brood juveniles, consists of a thin layer of coarse sand encrusting an interior of white parchment. It is not until the worm is removed from its tube that the striking pattern of red bands becomes apparent. On each of the anterior segments four to eight is a white glandular band preceding the bristles (chaetae) and a red band posterior to these structures. In the posterior segments, blotches of red surround the elevated bristles (seen in the photograph). The red-banded bamboo-worm has exactly 22 segments, 18 of which have bristles.
*For years taxonomists considered the presence of only one species of red-banded bamboo-worm along the coast but research in the 1980s revealed a complex of at least three species.
Crescent Beach, Delta, s. BC

AN4. ▶WINDMILL BAMBOO-WORM
Praxillura maculata
to 25 cm (10 in) long
tube to 30 cm (12 in) long (estimated)
BC to California
subtidal
The windmill bamboo-worm has developed a novel mesh-in-a-net method of suspension feeding. It builds 6 to 12 radial, windmill-like extensions or spokes at the end of its tube. The spokes project along a single plane about 2–7 cm (1–3 in) above the sediment. The worm produces strands of mucus that it drapes in web-like fashion from spoke to spoke. The mucus web gradually becomes clogged with tiny food particles, as illustrated in photograph B, and at certain intervals the worm emerges from its tube to consume both the net and trapped food. This unique method, rare for bamboo-worms, allows the worm to feed and minimizes its exposure to potential predators.
A Kyen Point, Barkley Sound, s. BC
B Mutine Point, Barkley Sound, s. BC. Charlie Gibbs photograph

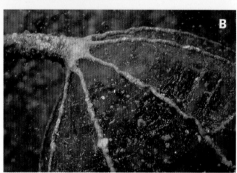

Bighead sludgeworms

There are two groups of polychaetes that, in shape, closely resemble familiar terrestrial earthworms (oligochaetes): bighead sludgeworms (Family Capitellidae, represented by the following species) and marine earthworms (Family Lumbrineridae, p. 131). They are all active burrowers. Bighead sludgeworms are opportunistic, often thriving in soft, organically enriched sediments or even black anoxic (low-oxygen) mud. Like their close relatives, bighead sludgeworms are a major component of the unseen benthic "labour force," bioturbating (ingesting, mixing and aerating) the sediments.

AN5. ▶THREAD SLUDGEWORM
Notomastus tenuis, *Notomastus lineatus balanoglossi*
to 20 cm (8 in) long
s. Alaska to s. California
intertidal to subtidal
Tiny black fecal castings on top of sediment provide the observant beachcomber with evidence of the worms hiding below. A shovelful of muddy sand will expose many thread-like bodies—so many as to practically bind the sediment together and so slender that they usually snap apart during the excavating process. Look carefully for their fertilized eggs, in pear-shaped, gelatinous masses 2.5 cm (1 in) long, attached to the sand's surface by tough, 10 cm (4 in) long strands of mucus.
Chesterman Beach, w. Vancouver Island, s. BC

Horn-headed worms

Little is known about the horn-headed worms (Family Scalibregmatidae) because they usually dwell at considerable depth and therefore are infrequently collected. Using the soft, eversible (can be turned inside out) proboscis, these sub-surface deposit feeders ingest fine particles.

AN6. ▶ PACIFIC HUMPBACK WORM
Hyboscolex pacificus, Oncoscolex pacificus
▶to 5 cm (2 in) long
BC to Mexico
intertidal to subtidal

The brilliant colour of the Pacific humpback worm overshadows its rather peculiar form. It has a T-shaped prostomium (head) with prominent horns, which may be used to manoeuvre the sediment within its burrow. Directly behind these horns are two pairs of very large black eyes. The anterior end of the worm is somewhat humpbacked before tapering toward the posterior. Note the rugged, uneven appearance of the skin, with each segment subdivided into smaller annulations—very unusual! Most likely this species broadcasts (free spawns) "en masse." The individuals emerge from the mud and metamorphose into epitokous (reproducing) individuals that swim about in the water column before releasing their gametes into the seawater. This specimen was trawled from a muddy bottom at approximately 100 m (330 ft), during an Environment Canada sampling cruise. Biologist Dixie Sullivan and her crew maintain a long-term monitoring program that assesses human impact upon the benthic environment at selected locations.
Mouth of Fraser River, Strait of Georgia, s. BC

Lugworms

Lugworms (Family Arenicolidae) were among the first polychaetes ever to be described. Some species of lugworms are such active diggers that an average-sized worm can irrigate its burrow by pumping water through at a rate of about 90 ml (3 oz) in 10 minutes. Most species of lugworms are mass spawners, though a few are known to brood juveniles in their burrows or produce mucus cocoons attached externally to the burrow by a stalk.

AN7. ▶ PACIFIC NEAPOLITAN LUGWORM, Pacific green lugworm,* Pacific lugworm, lugworm, lug worm
Abarenicola pacifica, Abarenicola pusilla (in part)
to 15 cm (6 in) long
Japan, Alaska to n. California
intertidal to subtidal

With an orange-red mid-body, greenish anterior and beige tail, this worm brings the image of Neapolitan ice cream immediately to mind. The species prefers protected muddy-sand bays, at high intertidal locations. Evidence of this burrower's presence at the beach is a coiled, tubular fecal cast (photograph B) on the surface of the sand. Its burrowing activity is much akin to "gardening," and it consumes tiny animals such as nematodes that require bacterial activity to digest. Such consumption increases bacterial production in the worm's intestines. Excess bacteria not ingested passes through the gut to enrich surface sediments through an excreted cast.
*"Pacific green lugworm" might more appropriately describe a purportedly warm-water species, *Arenicola cristata*, found in s. California and along the east coast of North America. The entire worm is a dark, velvety bottle-green colour. However, the discovery of suspicious-looking, tongue-shaped, gelatinous, stalked egg masses—15x7.5x2.5 cm (6x3x1 in)— in Boundary Bay, BC, and Willapa Bay, Washington, may also prove to be those of the Pacific green lugworm, *Arenicola cristata*. Species of lugworms can be reliably determined only through examination of internal structures.
A Tongue Point, Olympic coast, n. Washington
B Chesterman Beach, w. Vancouver Island, s. BC

AN8. ROUGH-SKINNED LUGWORM, black lugworm, lugworm
***Abarenicola claparedi* oceanica**, *Abarenicola vagabunda oceanica*,
Arenicola pusilla (in part)
to at least 16 cm (6.3 in) long or more
Japan, Siberia, Alaska to n. California
intertidal to subtidal
Large and black with very rough-looking skin, this "hard-working" burrower prefers to build its tube in clean sand, such as that found near the entrances of bays. Wave action in such areas not only supplies the worm's branchiae (bushy gills) with oxygen, it likely sweeps away any sign of the worm's telltale fecal cast. Digging this specimen from the sand brought back vivid youthful memories for Bernie Hanby. A very similar but much larger species, the blow lug, *Arenicola marina*, common on the beaches of Blackpool, England, was the popular bait item he used to catch bottom fish.
*The subspecies name *Abarenicola claparedi oceanica* is retained to distinguish this lugworm from a closely related one, the vagabond lugworm, *Abarenicola claparedi vagabunda*. Clarification of the exact number of species of lugworms in the Pacific Northwest is still not resolved, so it is important to keep the names of these apparent Pacific subspecies separate from the "parent" or stem species, *Abarenicola claparedii*, which occurs in European waters.
Crescent Beach, Delta, s. BC

Orbit-worms

The orbit-worms (Family Orbiniidae) are active burrowers, although they apparently do not feed while they excavate. The cylindrical, ragged appearance of their mid- to posterior ends is distinctive. The "raggedness" is a result of the increase in size of the paired, lateral branchiae (gills) that almost touch each other across the dorsal (upper) surface. As well, a transition of the parapodia (paired fleshy appendages) from a lateral orientation to a more dorsal position, produces a circular, almost tubular shape to the body in cross-section. About half of the orbit-worm species spawn freely into the seawater and the rest deposit their eggs into gelatinous (sometimes ribbon-shaped) masses or cocoons. For intertidal species, these cocoons apparently provide better protection for the eggs from predators, desiccation and salinity fluctuations.

AN9. ▶TUNNEL-TAIL ORBIT-WORM
Naineris dendritica, *Anthostoma dendriticum*, *Naineris laevigata* (in part)
to 8 cm (3.2 in) long
Alaska to s. California
intertidal
Although the bright orange anterior made this thick, robust specimen quite visible in the root mat of surfgrass (SW4), the tunnel-tail orbit-worm is generally brown. It is possible that the specimen in photograph A was a maturing female with developing eggs producing the orange colour in its anterior. Prior to their release, the mature gametes migrate to the worm's posterior region. Note the flattened shape of the anterior and the gradual change to a circular or tubular form toward the posterior, as shown in photograph B. The paired branchiae (gills) and parapodia (appendages) form a ragged-looking tunnel along the back of the worm. Its head is noticeably broad, flat and rounded, and when everted, the proboscis has numerous dendritic (tree-like) branches, resembling a ruffled rosette, for ingesting particles. The tunnel-tail orbit-worm is a common, shallow-water species.
Three other species are reported from the Pacific Ocean: the ▶slippery orbit-worm, *Naineris laevigata*, ▶four-point orbit-worm, *Naineris quadricuspida* and the ▶bent-hook orbit-worm, *Naineris uncinata*. All of the former are common arctic-boreal, Atlantic species and their records in the Pacific remain uncertain. Much confusion has apparently resulted from the misidentification of juveniles.
A Eagle Cove, San Juan Island, n. Washington
B Laura Point, Mayne Island, s. BC

Utility-worms

Utility-worms (Family Opheliidae) are active burrowers, contributing greatly to the bioturbation (aeration) of sediments. They all burrow head down in sand or mud. Their fusiform (cigar) shapes vary dramatically from grub-like forms, such as the pupa utility-worm (AN10), to those with a cylindrical design and enlarged head, like the sword utility-worm (AN11), or several other species that are slender and torpedo-shaped. The torpedo-shaped worms, *Armandia* species, are amazing swimmers, moving with lateral body undulations similar to that of salmon or sea snakes.

AN10. ▶PUPA UTILITY-WORM

***Travisia pupa**, Travisia carnea, Travisia foetida*
to 8.5 cm (3.4 in) long, 3 cm (1.2 in) wide
Alaska to Mexico
subtidal
The photograph shows the ventral (belly) side of this plump pupa-shaped worm. Note the wart-like beads on each of the segments, the size and position of which help to distinguish the nearly half dozen species of *Travisia* that inhabit the Pacific Northwest. Its finger-like branchiae (gills) and large mouth are also visible. This worm ingests food-laden mud as it burrows, digesting the nutritious components. When captured and handled, the pupa utility-worm emits a pungent, unpleasant odour, resulting in the moniker "stink worm"!
Imperial Eagle Channel, Barkley Sound, s. BC

AN11. ▶SWORD UTILITY-WORM, bloodworm, red worm

***Euzonus mucronata**, Ophelina mucronata, Thoracophelia mucronata*
to 10 cm (4 in) long
BC to n. Mexico
intertidal
A carpet of crowded, tiny holes in a well-defined zone of sand on exposed beaches is a definite clue for locating a colony of sword utility-worms. This worm, because of its bright red colour, has also been called a bloodworm—a common name applied in this book to another family of worms, Glyceridae (AN14). The red colour of the animal, though descriptive, is common to many polychaete species and results from a copious quantity of hemoglobin in the blood. The sword utility-worm feeds on organic matter adhering to surrounding sand grains. In turn, it is a primary food source for long-billed shorebirds, such as sandpipers, that forage along beaches during receding tides. Considering the size of this worm, it is difficult to imagine that in a limited strip of beach (1.6 km x 61 m x 0.8 m/1 mi x 200 ft x 2.6 ft) they are capable of "turning over" about 21 percent of the sand every year! Its sharply pointed head must be a definite asset in this activity.

Two other very similar utility-worms may be found to occur in the Pacific Northwest: the ▶pectinate-gill utility-worm, *Euzonus dillonensis*, and the ▶branched-gill utility-worm, *Euzonus williamsi*. Only examination of the branchiae (gills) and posterior ends of the worms can distinguish the three species. Interestingly, when all occur on the same beach, the sword utility-worm is the species found in the lower intertidal zone. All three species apparently spawn on or near the surface of the sand, and tiny larvae, which have only two chaetigers (bristle-bearing segments), develop rapidly to settle on the sand in less than 10 days.
Chesterman Beach, w. Vancouver Island, s. BC

SENSORY-PALP POLYCHAETES

Angled-jaw worms

Although the angled-jaw worms (Family Goniadidae) superficially resemble their close relatives, the bloodworms (Glyceridae), significant differences exist. Species in both families have a proboscis that is eversible (can be turned inside out), but the jaw apparatus for each is distinctive. Other important anatomical details, such as the shape of the appendages (parapodia) and their associated bristles (chaetae), must be examined in detail to distinguish the species. Little is known about the biology of these worms.

AN12. ▶MANY-JAWED WORM
Glycinde polygnatha
to 6.1 cm (2.4 in) long
Alaska to s. California
intertidal to 124 m (408 ft)
The sharply pointed head of this yellowish-brown worm is clearly visible in the photograph. What is not visible is the long proboscis, which, when everted, terminates in a pair of large, angled jaws called macrognaths. Between the macrognaths are two series of micrognaths (smaller jaws). About 20 micrognaths form the dorsal arc and three to five the ventral arc. Likely a carnivore, the many-jawed worm is considered an active burrower. This specimen was found hiding amid other float-bound creatures, though its preference is likely soft substrates.
At least five more species of angled-jaw worms live in the Pacific Northwest.
Miners Bay, Mayne Island, s. BC

Big-eyed Pelagic Worms

AN13. Big-eyed pelagic-worms (Family Alciopidae) are delicate worms with very thin bodies, usually about 7.5 cm (3 in) long. Although the shape and greenish yellow colour of the photographed specimen is suggestive of *Vanadis longissima*, found in the North Pacific, species determination requires careful examination—a tricky task even for the expert. Most noticeable are the worm's huge, red eyes. The eyes of alciopid worms are considered more sophisticated than those of any other polychaete worm. The complexity (presence of lens and retina) and function of this species' eyes have been compared to those of cephalopods (octopus) and vertebrates (such as humans)! The big-eyed pelagic-worms are carnivorous and spend their entire lives as part of the planktonic community, feeding on fellow floaters such as copepods and euphausids. Scientists speculate that males and females copulate and that the barely visible, modified parapodia (appendages) on the anterior of a female likely store small packages of sperm.
Sutton Islets, Egmont, s. BC

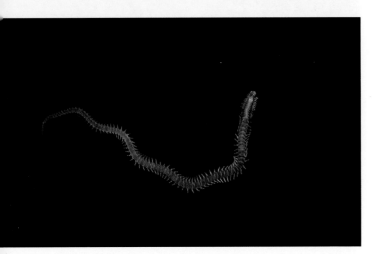

Bloodworms

The term "bloodworm" has been used to describe a number of different types of worms. No doubt the intense blood red colour of the sword utility-worm (AN11) is worthy of the name. But the term has traditionally been used as a common name for the Family Glyceridae. The red flesh colour of bloodworms may not always appear as vibrant as that in some utility-worms, but species from both families have copious amounts of hemoglobin in their blood. Regardless, the term "bloodworm" generally applies to the blood-red glycerid worm. At least two other explanations exist as well: the blood drawn from a human after a nasty bite to the arm—"bait digger's arm," or the blood flowing from a severed worm in the process of bring extracted from its burrow. Some of the larger bloodworm species in the world have been valued sport and commercial bait since the early 19th century.

AN14. ▶AMERICAN BLOODWORM, proboscis worm, corrugated worm, blood worm, beakthrower
Glycera americana
to 35 cm (14 in) long
s. Australia, New Zealand, BC to Chile
intertidal to 530 m (1,739 ft)

Upon capturing this colourful, iridescent species, a naturalist is generally startled as it rapidly everts a long, muscular, cylindrical proboscis with four fang-like jaws at the end. Whether to escape or burrow into soft sediment, the American bloodworm will thrust out the proboscis, anchoring it into the sediment before pulling the rest of the body in after it. The worm also uses the proboscis to capture worm or arthropod prey. Like most family members, the American bloodworm has venom glands at the base of the jaws that inject a neurotoxin into the prey. So be careful! A large worm can inflict a nasty pinch and cause inflammation and possible allergic reaction in humans.

As with other bloodworms, the American bloodworm has a curious feeding behaviour. After digesting its prey—usually other polychaetes such as scaleworms—it uses its proboscis to regurgitate the undigested remains of the food. These remains are deposited on the sediment surface in a small, tidy, membranous package. The bloodworm engages in this odd practice because it does not have a functional anus.

When an American bloodworm matures, various body changes occur, including a jettisoning of the proboscis, before the body fills up with gametes. This reproductive stage, called an epitoke, then swarms with many others of its species and spawning occurs either close to the bottom or in surface waters. The gametes are extruded through the mouth or ruptures in the body wall, and the reproducing individuals die shortly thereafter. Note the dorsal blood vessel in the photograph.

Ucluth Peninsula, w. Vancouver Island, s. BC

Marine earthworms

More than a dozen species of marine earthworms (Family Lumbrineridae) burrow in the muddy or sandy sediments of the Pacific Northwest. So closely do they resemble terrestrial earthworms (oligochaetes) that the oldest marine earthworm species was actually identified and named as an oligochaete species in 1776! Not unexpectedly, with rather featureless morphology, these marine earthworm species are difficult to identify without detailed examination of the parapodia (appendages), chaetae (bristles) and jaw structures. They likely live for several years. Some species apparently deposit their fertilized eggs in gelatinous egg masses. The marine earthworms may be easily confused with the bighead sludgeworms, p. 126.

AN15. ▶IRIDESCENT ZONEWORM, threadworm, thread worm
Scoletoma zonata, *Lumbrineris brevicirra, Lumbrineris zonata*
to 51 cm (20 in) long (usually less than half that size), 0.5 cm (0.2 in) wide
s. Alaska to n. Mexico
intertidal to 84 m (276 ft)

A search through surfgrasses (SW4) revealed various worms, including this one, nestled within the tight root mats. Considering the constant, crashing surf in which this plant thrives, its roots provide the iridescent zoneworm with a stable and sheltered environment. In addition, its jaws appear well designed for shredding the available food source: algae and marine plants. Generally solid brown in colour, this elongate worm can show brilliant blue/green iridescence or a bronzy orange-red, depending on the light. Dark reddish brown transverse bands highlight each segment's upper surface.

Eagle Cove, San Juan Island, n. Washington

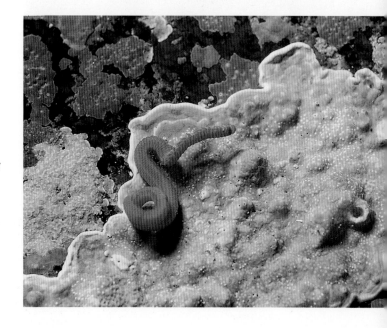

Hairy-hide worms

The jaw structures of some species of hairy-hide worms (Family Dorvilleidae) are peculiar in that they bear many tiny teeth, symmetrically arranged in several longitudinal rows. Fossilized versions of such jaws, dating back to Jurrasic and Cretaceous times, indicate that hairy-hide

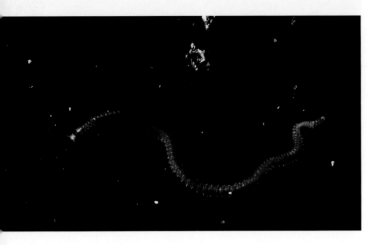

worms are an ancient group of polychaetes. A major part of this long-term success story may be the numerous and variable reproductive strategies of these worms. Most modern-day species are carnivorous, though some are known to be herbivorous. Many species are considered opportunists, able to thrive in organically enriched, even heavily polluted environments.

AN16. ▶FALSE RED HEADBAND WORM
Dorvillea pseudorubrovittata, *Schistomeringos pseudorubrovittata*
▶to 2.5 cm (1 in) long
Alaska to Oregon
intertidal to 46 m (150 ft)
This specimen crawled out from between giant acorn barnacles (AR171) to have its photograph taken. Like most polychaete worms, this one avoids predation by hiding from would-be consumers rather than attempting to defend itself or relying on a speedy escape. Although obviously small from a human perspective, this worm is actually quite large compared to other family members! The characteristic deep red headband is striking, as are the narrower red transverse markings on the segments that follow. Like many other hairy-hide worms, this worm apparently surrounds itself with copious amounts of mucus. It is not known to construct rigid tubes.
Passage Island, Howe Sound, s. BC

Maggot-worms
Aside from basic morphology and unconfirmed speculation, very little information about the maggot-worms (Family Sphaerodoridae) is available, likely because they are obscure—seldom seen or collected. The size and shape of these polychaetes varies from short, grub-like individuals to more elongate forms. Based on the content of their fecal deposits, maggot-worms are believed to feed on organic matter found in surface sediments of the sea floor.

AN17. ▶BALLOON-SKINNED MAGGOT-WORM
Sphaerodoropsis **sp**.
▶to 3 cm (1.2 in) long
Japan, Alaska to s. California
subtidal
The size and shape of minute, spherical balloon-shaped protuberances on the surface of the skin are keys to identifying this poorly known creature. The protuberances are usually arranged in distinct rows. The photograph primarily shows the ventral surface, where the spheres are less pronounced, although they are more obvious toward either end of the worm. The specimen was obtained in a fine-mesh trawl at a depth of at least 45 m (150 ft).
Mouth of Fraser River, Strait of Georgia, s. BC

Bobbit worms
Some naturalists are more familiar with tropical, coral reef species of Bobbit worms (Family Eunicidae), such as the palolo worm (*Palola viridis*)—famous not only for its spectacular spawning events but also as a gourmet delight for some indigenous people of the South Pacific islands. The largest of the Bobbit worms, usually found in warmer climates, attain lengths up to 6 m (20 ft). They are valued as bait but equally feared for the bites they inflict with their huge jaws! No doubt this is the reason why the term "Bobbit worm" has recently replaced the rather bland "mudworm" as a descriptive common name for the family.

AN18. ►WHITE-BANDED BOBBIT WORM, iridescent tubeworm
*Eunice valens**
to 20 cm (8 in) long
s. Alaska to c. California
►intertidal to 15 m (50 ft)

This worm secretes a parchment-like tube that is semi-transparent and often festooned with tiny adherent particles. It is usually found under rocky shelter. Near the anterior, the upper surface of this species is a purple-red colour and quite iridescent. Note the definitive broad, white band near the head. The worm ventures outside its tube in search of food, which includes both animal and vegetable matter. Closer examination of the photograph will reveal blood-red branchiae (gills) on the dorsal or upper surface of the parapodia (appendages). By mid-body, the comb-like gill filaments overlap across the worm's back.

*Of a possible six species of Pacific Northwest Bobbit worms, the ►Kobé Bobbit worm, *Eunice kobiensis,* appears to have characteristics most similar to those of the white-banded Bobbit worm. Distinguishing the two species in the past has been difficult, leaving it unclear as to whether one or both exist in the Pacific Northwest.

Tilley Point, s. Pender Island, s. BC

Necklace-worms

The necklace-worms (Family Syllidae) are a spectacular group whose complexity challenges species identification. Currently, many members of this family are in a state of taxonomic turmoil. Necklace-worms have remarkably diverse modes of reproduction, responding to many of the same internal and external cues that initiate spawning in the sea-nymphs, p. 144. However, unlike many sea-nymph species, most necklace-worms can reproduce more than once. Most necklace-worms are likely carnivorous. The muscular gizzard-like proventricle (glandular tube) is a unique aspect of the digestive system. Its pumping action is the main reason why the necklace-worm can feed by sucking. Less obvious is the proventricle's importance in hormone production, which in part regulates the worm's sexual development.

AN19. ►BROWN JEWEL NECKLACE-WORM
Trypanosyllis gemmipara
to 9.5 cm (3.5 in) long
Japan, s. Alaska to s. California
intertidal to subtidal

To find this worm, a diver must look under rocks, in sponges or amid kelp holdfasts. The specimen pictured here was living inside the pocket of a cloud sponge (PO11), where it had incorporated bits of debris in a slimy coating. The creature's spectacular pigment pattern consists of two purple-brown bands across the back of each segment and rings on each of the long, thick dorsal cirri (finger-like projections)—sharply contrasting with the pale yellow body. This worm reproduces by budding multiple stolons (individuals) simultaneously from a specialized area near its posterior. These stolons, produced by the bottom-dwelling parent stock individual illustrated in the photograph, are considered locomotive vessels that carry gametes into the pelagic environment. The stolons die after spawning, and the parent stocks, still on the bottom, survive and reproduce again. Another very similar species, the ►purple-stub necklace-worm, *Trypanosyllis ingens,* also lives in the Pacific Northwest.

Sutton Islets, Egmont, s. BC

AN20. ►OBTUSE SPONGE-DWELLING NECKLACE-WORM
Amblyosyllis **sp.**
►to 5 cm (2 in) long
BC
subtidal to 46 m (150 ft)

Wide but short, this delicate, amazing creature lives in the pockets of cloud sponge (PO11). It is a potential new species whose discovery is most exciting! Although the creamy colour blends well with its background, the obtuse sponge-dwelling necklace-worm appears to be completely vulnerable without the protection of the cloud sponge. The antennae, tentacular and dorsal cirri (finger-like projections) are extraordinarily long. They are often tightly coiled, but when extended they provide exceptional sensory and spatial contact with the worm's surroundings. Do these tendrils help seek out potential prey that also crawl about in the sponge, or is the sponge itself the food source? The size and structure of the worm's teeth suggest tiny prey. Most of the specimens collected were mature and swollen with gametes, except for the first few chaetigers (bristle-bearing segments), making the oddly trapezoidal segments look even more obtuse (photograph B). The exact mode of reproduction for the obtuse sponge-dwelling necklace-worm is not known, but it is likely different from the dramatic strategies of other necklace-worms. Perhaps as a response to the sponge habitat, the larvae are brooded before developing directly into crawling juveniles.

A B Sechelt Peninsula, Agamemnon Channel, s. BC

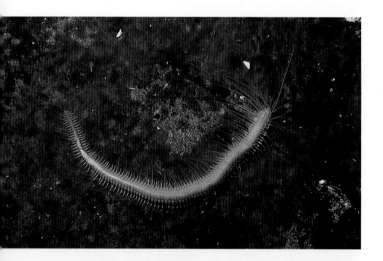

AN21. ►RED GIANT NECKLACE-WORM
Pionosyllis gigantea
►to 5 cm (2 in) long
Alaska to s. California
subtidal

The cloud sponge (PO11) seems to be an attractive haven for various necklace-worms. The red giant necklace-worm pictured here, which had secreted a slime coating laden with dark particulate matter, was found nestled in a sponge pocket. Its fragile body was swollen with eggs and it had swimming chaetae (bristles) toward the posterior end. Some species of *Pionosyllis* are known to brood their young on the ventral surface of the body. Possibly this specimen's slimy secretion is preparatory to the attachment and brooding of its embryos. Most species of necklace-worms are much smaller than this one.

Sechelt Peninsula, Agamemnon Channel, s. BC

AN22. While diving the Plumper Islands near Port McNeill, BC, we found this **mystery necklace-worm**. Significant numbers of this small (5 cm/2 in long) creature were crawling about in the open, completely exposed. Such behaviour would seem to invite predation. Unfortunately, without a specimen to accompany this photograph, accurate identification is not possible. Detailed examination of the palps, teeth, cirri (finger-like projections) and chaetae (bristles) are required for species determination. Some interesting observations can be made, however. The tentacular cirri near the head are much longer than their dorsal counterparts in the middle of the body: the latter appear to be shorter than the worm's body width. It is not clear, though, whether these cirri are annulated (ringed) or smooth. The specimen's eyes are evident as are some sensory organs located just behind them. Intriguing features are the two faint but obvious transverse structures on each segment that appear to be ciliated (hairy). It looks diminutive, but this mysterious worm is actually large compared to most necklace-worms.

Stubbs Island, Weynton Passage, c. BC

AN23. ▶NOBLE NECKLACE-WORM
Autolytus magnus
▶to 5 cm (2 in) long
Arctic, Bering Sea to Washington

These photographs provide a rare opportunity to observe the pelagic reproductive stages of this fascinating necklace-worm. The benthic male and female individuals (parent stock) produce epitokous (reproductive) forms or stolons that carry the gametes into the water column (schizogamy). Photograph A shows a sacconereis (female stolon); photograph B depicts the polybostrichus (male stolon). Stolons of both sexes are highly adapted for swimming, so that male and female stolons meet and perform a mating dance similar to that of the sea-nymphs, p. 144. What is different about the noble necklace-worms is that females deposit their eggs into external brood sacs or pouches located on their bodies' ventral surface, and fertilization likely occurs within these pouches. In some species, females may brood as many as 5,000 embryos per pouch (yellow in photograph A). Embryos are incubated for one to two weeks. Those in photograph A already have four chaetigers (bristle-bearing segments). After the larvae hatch, they assume a brief, near-bottom swimming phase before settling to the substrate. After spawning, the sacconereis and polybostrichus stolons die. The benthic parent stock, however, are essentially unchanged and able to generate stolons again.

Linking the pelagic epitokes (reproductive individuals) of *Autolytus* species to their bottom-dwelling counterparts is an ongoing challenge for polychaete taxonomists. Simply identifying the benthic forms can be difficult. Another six species of *Autolytus* are recorded from the Pacific Northwest. One, the ▶terminal-spawning necklace-worm, *Autolytus alexandri*, has yet a different reproductive mode (epigamy). Entire male and female benthic individuals transform into pelagic sexual epitokes similar in appearance to the true stolons of *Autolytus magnus*. However, as with the sea-nymphs, the body modifications are so extreme that the epitokes die, having reproduced only once. Most other necklace-worms that reproduce as epigamous epitokes do not undergo such severe body modifications as *Autolytus alexandri*, thereby surviving to spawn again.

A Sutton Islets, Egmont, s. BC. Charlie Gibbs photograph (female pelagic stolon)
B Steep Island, Discovery Passage, s. BC. Charlie Gibbs photograph (male pelagic stolon)

Paddleworms

At least seven very similar species of paddleworms (Family Phyllodocidae) inhabit the Pacific Northwest, and distinguishing them without detailed examination is difficult. The colour of paddleworms is often spectacular, reflecting iridescent tones of violet, purple, brown, yellow and green, or patches of pigments that form distinctive patterns. Many of the paddleworms swarm to the surface waters as epitokes (reproductive individuals) to release their gametes, although not all species undergo the dramatic transformations that occur in the sea-nymphs, p. 144. One species of *Phyllodoce* is known to form mucus egg masses, containing as many as 10,000 eggs!

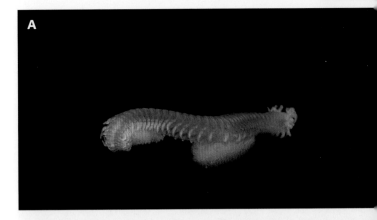

A

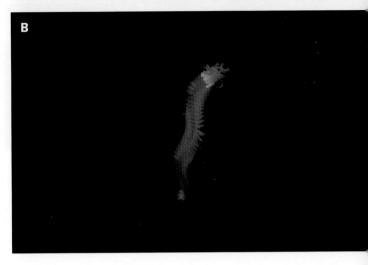

B

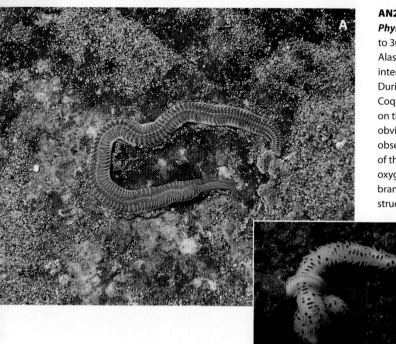

AN24. LEAFY PADDLEWORMS
***Phyllodoce* spp.**
to 30 cm (12 in) long
Alaska to Mexico
intertidal to 1,524 m (5,000 ft)

During a night dive, underwater photographer Charlie Gibbs of Port Coquitlam, BC, found this active specimen (photograph A) crawling about on the bottom of a shallow bay. Its posterior is noticeably smaller and obviously regenerating, suggesting a recent escape from a predator. Careful observation of a crawling leafy paddleworm will reveal a constant fluttering of the large dorsal cirri (finger-like projections). Such activity enhances oxygen exchange across the body surface. For many polychaete worms, the branchiae (gills) would fulfill this function, but paddleworms lack such gill structures. Compounding this fact, the hemoglobin present in the blood of paddleworms is colourless and not used in an oxygen transport role. Most paddleworms are apparently carnivores and some actually hunt by following mucus trails left on the mudflats by unsuspecting prey. Photograph B features a paddleworm species, likely another *Phyllodoce*, showing an impressive pigment pattern. If the head were visible in the photograph, species identification might be possible.
A Unkak Cove, Quadra Island, s. BC
B Tuwanek Point, Sechelt Inlet, s. BC. Charlie Gibbs photograph

Pelagic transparent-worms

Few polychaete worms live an entirely planktonic existence. The pelagic transparent-worms (Family Tomopteridae) and the big-eyed pelagic-worms (AN13) represent two of only seven families living this way. Compared with other gelatinous forms of zooplankton, pelagic transparent-worms have a higher protein, lipid and carbohydrate content in their tissues, perhaps suggesting a role as preferred prey items.

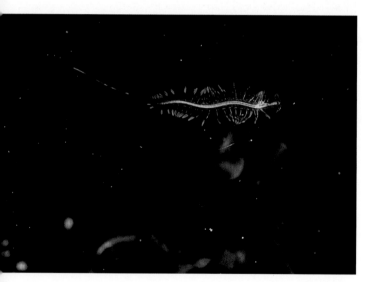

AN25. ▶TAILED PACIFIC TRANSPARENT-WORM
***Tomopteris pacifica*,** *Tomopteris renata*
to 5 cm (2 in) long
Japan, Siberia, n. Alaska to California
surface to 500 m (1,640 ft)

This agile swimmer is abundant in spring but nearly impossible to see: its body is so nearly transparent that if it is collected and put in a container of seawater, only its shadow may betray its presence! The long tail and rigid, whisker-like tentacular cirri (projections near the head) of this species are diagnostic. Does the tailed Pacific transparent-worm use these long cirri to sense and locate its favourite food items, such as arrow worms, p. 121, salps, p. 360, and fish larvae? From the prey's perspective, the approaching worm must look like a monster from the deep! Perhaps these cirri are also hydrodynamically important, assisting with buoyancy and swimming functions.

A smaller species, the ▶tailless northern transparent-worm, *Tomopteris septentrionalis*, also lives in the Pacific Northwest.

Agamemnon Channel, Nelson Island, s. BC. Christopher Pharo photograph

Porcupine-worms

The porcupine-worms (Family Euphrosinidae) are closely related to the more famous tropical fireworms (Family Amphinomidae). Fireworms have fragile chaetae (calcareous bristles) that when broken can lodge under the skin, causing considerable pain from an associated neurotoxin infection. The more benign porcupine-worms, however, apparently do not produce such secretions. Porcupine-worms are known to be carnivorous and have been reported to feed on sponges, bryozoans and coral. Relatively little information is available on the biology of porcupine-worms, especially those living in cold water.

AN26. ▶BRISTLY-BALL PORCUPINE-WORM
Euphrosine bicirrata*, Euphrosyne bicirrata*
to 3 cm (1.2 in) long
Alaska to Mexico
subtidal
Sometimes found in boot sponges (PO9/10), this porcupine-worm readily rolls up into a ball to maximize the protective value of its stiff calcareous chaetae (bristles). These hollow, fragile bristles have odd-shaped prongs that completely conceal the creature's branchiae (gills). The very long notochaetae (bristles of the upper branch of the appendages) practically cover the back of this species, and the associated neurochaetae (bristles of the lower branch of the appendages) are much shorter. This worm is probably a carnivore that feeds on the sponge itself or scrapes minute prey off its surface.
Agamemnon Channel, Nelson Island, s. BC

AN27. ▶MULTI-BRANCHED PORCUPINE-WORM
Euphrosine* cf. *multibranchiata
▶to 3 cm (1.2 in) long
▶BC
subtidal
pelagic epitoke
The specimen shown in photograph A was found drifting along in the water column by diver Donna Gibbs of Port Coquitlam, BC. Fortunately she was diving with the authors and this photograph was a result. The presence of long, thin modified swimming chaetae (bristles) indicate that this worm is a pelagic epitoke (reproductive individual), similar to a sea-nymph epitoke, p. 144, which has transformed from a bottom-dwelling adult (photograph B). The notochaetae (upper appendage bristles) do not cover the back of the worm, revealing several unusual vertebrae-shaped structures. Their significance is unknown. Just behind the tiny black eyes is an elongate, white ribbon-like structure called a caruncle that has a chemoreceptive function. The gills of this species have multiple finger-like filaments, a reflection of the possible species name *multibranchiata*.
A Sutton Islets, Egmont, s. BC
B Agamemnon Channel, Nelson Island, s. BC

Princess-of-Troy worms
    This group of worms (Family Hesionidae) was named after Hesione, Princess of Troy, who according to Greek mythology was rescued from a sea monster by Hercules. Typically, these dainty, fragile worms fragment and lose their long tentacular and dorsal cirri (finger-like projections) during collection. Some species are known to free spawn, others are hermaphroditic, still others are reported to have copulatory organs for transfer of sperm. Larvae of some species are known to remain in the plankton for several months. Surprisingly, some family members thrive in polluted, especially oxygen-deficient, environments. The methane iceworm, *Sirsoe methanicola* (not to be confused with the oligochaete species of snow and glacier iceworms), was discovered associated with icy cold methane seeps of energy-rich gas deposits on the Gulf of Mexico sea floor at 550 m (1,805 ft).

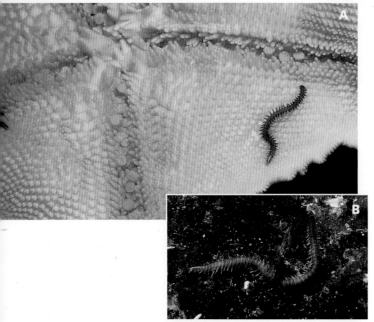

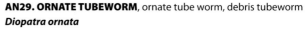

AN28. BAT STAR COMMENSAL WORM, bat star worm
***Ophiodromus pugettensis**, Podarke pugettensis*
to 4 cm (1.6 in) long
Japan, s. Alaska to s. California, Peru
intertidal to subtidal
This small, dark brown worm is very often commensal with the bat star (EC8, photograph A), but it also crawls about on the sea floor as a "solo act" (photograph B). Even without jaws the bat star commensal worm is an active carnivore, using its muscular proboscis to pump and suck in its prey. This worm uses its tactile palps (anterior sensory outgrowths), antennae and long cirri (finger-like projections) to detect and investigate food sources through the vibrations produced by the living prey. Calculations suggest that one close relative can consume about 8,300 copepods in one year, though scavenging is also practised. The bat star commensal worm is definitely attracted to potential sea star hosts by means of chemoreception and it is known to associate with nine sea star species.
A Beg Island, Barkley Sound, s. BC
B Tuwanek Point, Sechelt Inlet, s. BC

Quillworms and beachworms

The quillworms and beachworms (Family Onuphidae) are a varied group of polychaete worms with well-developed sensory structures on their heads. These structures are responsible for a reputed sense of smell. Some quillworms build tubes that are permanently anchored to the bottom; other species haul theirs along as they crawl upon the substrate. Still others secrete copious amounts of mucus to strengthen their burrows. The reinforcement material chosen and type of tube construction employed is often species specific.

AN29. ORNATE TUBEWORM, ornate tube worm, debris tubeworm
Diopatra ornata
to 25 cm (10 in) long, 2 cm (0.8 in) tube diameter
BC to n. Mexico
subtidal to 91 m (300 ft)
This subterranean quillworm uses a wide variety of bits and pieces of its environment to festoon the permanent tube that protrudes from the sediment—the only visible evidence of its presence. Foreign material used by the ornate tubeworm can include mud, sand, shell, seaweed and even the leaves of terrestrial plants. The inside of the tube is lined with a parchment-like layer. Occasionally, close inspection reveals the five well-developed sensory structures of its head (antennae and palps) protruding from the tube. In the unlikely event that the worm emerges even further from the tube, its large coiled branchiae (gills) may show. These spiralled structures are a unique characteristic of the ornate tubeworm.
Point Cowan, Bowen Island, s. BC

Scaleworms

Scaleworms (Family Polynoidae) are a unique group of polychaetes whose dorsa (backs) are covered by pairs of scale-like structures called elytra. The elytra are mounted on elytrophores (short stalks). Elytra are not found on every segment of the body (more or less on alternate segments), but generally the number of pairs of elytra is the same within a scaleworm genus. Scaleworms are carnivores, feeding on small arthropods, snails, polychaetes, sponges and hydroids. Immediately upon metamorphosis from a swimming planktonic larva to a bottom-dwelling juvenile (with only five or six pairs of scales), it becomes carnivorous. Many scaleworms are free-living, but others are commensal: living in an association with another creature whereby neither is harmed, but at least one receives some benefit.

AN30. ▶BRISTLY-TAIL SCALEWORM
***Hermadion truncata**, Harmothoe truncata, Eunoe spinicirris*
to 10 cm (4 in) long
Japan, n. Alaska to Oregon
intertidal to 203 m (670 ft)

The specimen pictured here could be mistaken for a fifteen-scaled worm (AN33), as it has the requisite number of elytra (paired scales), which show a similar colour pattern with a chocolate brown mid-dorsal, longitudinal band. However, the worm is only half-covered with these structures and the posterior is completely uncovered. The bristly-tail scaleworm has many thick, dark notochaetae (upper appendage bristles) with tips that appear to be broken off, but in the tail section these bristles spread out, almost touching each other across the back. This very impressive bristly tail is often encumbered with various tiny organisms.

Sutton Islets, Egmont, s. BC

AN31. ▶CILIATED SCALEWORM
Gattyana ciliata
▶to 8 cm (3.2 in) long
Japan, Alaska to Washington
subtidal

The elytral (scale) surfaces of this worm are covered by coarse papillae (fleshy projections), with the longer, denser ones fringing most of their outer edges. In addition, a few large, branching tubercles (bumps) and balloon-like structures can be found on these scales, often near their posterior edges. However, the tubercles are not nearly as large or sharply pointed as those of the thorny scaleworm (AN40). Considerable organic material may adhere to these tubercles and papillae, giving the ciliated scaleworm a furry appearance and likely camouflaging it from potential predators. Note the striking amber colour of the chaetae (bristles). The ciliated scaleworm wanders freely over mud, sand or gravel substrates, but it may also live amid algae or in mussel beds.

Two other species of *Gattyana* scaleworms may be encountered in the Pacific Northwest: the ▶cirrated scaleworm, *Gattyana cirrosa*, and the ▶fan-footed scaleworm, *Gattyana treadwelli*.

Sutton Islets, Egmont, s. BC

AN32. EIGHTEEN-SCALED WORM, armoured scale-worm, common scale worm, scaleworm, scale worm
***Halosydna brevisetosa**, Polynoe brevisetosa*
to 11 cm (4.3 in) long
c. Alaska to n. Mexico
intertidal to 545 m (1,788 ft)

This worm is very common along much of the Pacific Northwest coastline. It is the only resident scaleworm species that features eighteen pairs of elytra (scales). The strikingly shield-shaped scales vary considerably in colour but often appear to have white and/or black "eye-spots" against a brown background. Each eye-spot is generally located over the elytraphore (site of scale attachment). The notochaetae (upper appendage bristles) are considerably shorter than their ventral counterparts—hence the name *brevisetosa*. Free-living eighteen-scaled worms may live on old pilings, usually hiding among attached organisms, or shelter amid the roots of various seagrasses (SW2–4). Commensal forms often live with several other species, including the robust spaghetti-worm (AN75), the curly-head spaghetti-worm (AN74) and even the hooded nudibranch (MC340). In self-defence, a distressed eighteen-scaled worm will discard one or more scales. Even more remarkable, it is capable of regenerating new scales in five days! This voracious species preys on other worms.

Stanley Park, Burrard Inlet, s. BC

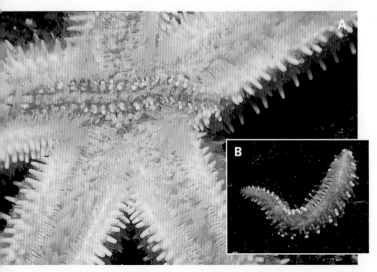

AN33. FIFTEEN-SCALED WORM, free-living scaleworm, scaleworm
Harmothoe imbricata
to 6.5 cm (2.6 in) long
n.w. Pacific Ocean, n. Alaska to s. California, circumpolar, Atlantic Ocean
intertidal to 3,710 m (12,172 ft)
Carolus Linnaeus, the father of the binomial system used in scientific taxonomy, described this species in 1767! It is one of the most widely distributed species of scaleworms and lives throughout the northern hemisphere. Readily identifiable with its 15 pairs of elytra (scales), it is an active swimmer that tolerates a wide range of salinities. It also frequents a variety of habitats: under rocks, amid eelgrass beds, in kelp holdfasts or in various soft substrates. The adult female broods fertilized eggs beneath her scales until the larvae are capable of swimming away, eventually settling on the bottom. As a solitary adult, the worm lies in wait. When its palps (anterior sensory outgrowths) sense telltale vibrations, it pounces on approaching prey. Though generally dominated by brown, the colour patterns are highly variable and possibly indicate differences between free-living and commensal individuals (those that live in non-harmful association with other species). The fifteen-scaled worm has been found living commensally inside the tubes of about six species of polychaetes. Two other species of deep-dwelling fifteen-scaled worms with finer, more delicate neurochaetae (lower appendage bristles) than the fifteen-scaled worm live in the Pacific Northwest: the elegant fifteen-scaled worm, *Bylgides elegans*, and the large-eyed fifteen-scaled worm, *Bylgides macrolepidus*.

A Sutton Islets, Egmont, s. BC

B Agamemnon Channel, Nelson Island, s. BC

AN34. ▶YELLOW AND BROWN SCALEWORM
Harmothoe extenuata, *Harmothoe bonitensis*, *Harmothoe triannulata*, *Lagisca extenuata*, *Lagisca rarispina*
▶to 2.5 cm (1 in) long
Arctic Ocean, n. Alaska to s. California
intertidal to 183 m (604 ft)
Look closely for this diminutive species—like most scaleworms, it hides very well. It can apparently be found on submerged pilings or in kelp holdfasts, but it may also choose clumps of barnacles and the northern horsemussel (MC35) as shelter. The worm's delicate, mottled-brown elytra (scales) are obvious, overlaying the pale yellow colour of the body beneath. As with some other scaleworms, the scales of this species are adorned with tubercles (bumps), which cannot be seen without magnification.
The Pacific Northwest is home to at least three other *Harmothoe* scaleworms: the ▶chocolate and white scaleworm, *Harmothoe fragilis*, the ▶hairy scaleworm, *Harmothoe hirsuta*, and the ▶many-bristled scaleworm, *Harmothoe multisetosa*. Some species formally in the Genus *Harmothoe* have recently been assigned to *Malmgreniella*.

Agamemnon Channel, Sechelt Peninsula, s. BC

AN35. ▶FRAGILE RUFFLED SCALEWORM, ruffled scale-worm, frilled commensal scaleworm, fragile commensal worm, fragile scaleworm, scale worm
Arctonoe fragilis, *Lepidonotus fragilis*, *Polynoe fragilis*
▶at least 8.5 cm (3.5 in) long
n. Alaska to s. California
intertidal to 275 m (910 ft)
The "fragility" of this species is reflected in the ease with which specimens fragment and lose their elytra (scales). The unusual ruffled or convoluted posterior margins of the thin, translucent scales are diagnostic. This scaleworm is commensal with at least nine species of sea stars. In these relationships, it usually crawls about on the undersurface (photograph A), among the tube feet, where it opportunistically gathers available food. The worm adapts its coloration to match that of its host: flesh to yellowish orange, reddish brown or pale green and often mottled with white (photograph B). The tubular dorsal cirri (projections) of its appendages appear to mimic the shape of the host's tube feet and spines.

A B Sutton Islets, Egmont, s. BC

AN36. RED-BANDED COMMENSAL SCALEWORM, yellow scale worm, scale worm

Arctonoe vittata, *Polynoe vittata*, *Halosydna lordi*
at least 10 cm (4 in) long
Japan, n. Alaska to n. Mexico, Ecuador
intertidal to 275 m (910 ft)

Of the three *Arctonoe* scaleworm species featured, this one possesses smooth rather than ruffled translucent elytra (scales). Another distinguishing feature is the solid, reddish brown, often faint, pigment band near the worm's anterior (photograph B). As it lives commensally with other species (beneficial to one or both), it may choose a variety of hosts, including sea stars, snails, sea cucumbers and even other polychaete worms. It is aggressive in defence of its host, such as the rough keyhole limpet (MC153), and may bite a potential predator—even an unsuspecting naturalist. The worm's jaws, however, are sized more appropriately for nipping the tube feet of the purple or ochre star (EC1) to drive it away. This scaleworm is fiercely territorial and will attack other members of its own species to prevent a second specimen living with the same host.

A Race Point, Porlier Pass, s. BC
B Agamemnon Channel, Nelson Island, s. BC

AN37. RED COMMENSAL SCALEWORM, dark-spotted scale worm, scale worm

Arctonoe pulchra, *Polynoe pulchra*
▶at least 7 cm (2.8 in) long
c. Alaska to n. Mexico
intertidal to 295 m (968 ft)

The red commensal scaleworm most commonly associates with the giant sea cucumber (EC54), although it has also been sighted on several species of sea stars, the rough keyhole limpet (MC153) and the giant Pacific chiton (MC30). As with most commensal scaleworms, this bright red species will vary its colour somewhat to match its host. The red commensal scaleworm clings to its giant sea cucumber host using sharply hooked neurochaetae (lower appendage bristles), usually nestling among the tube feet or near the head area, where it feeds on detritus. Apparently when the host is disturbed, this resourceful scaleworm crawls directly into the sea cucumber's mouth as it withdraws its tentacles.

Sutton Islets, Egmont, s. BC

AN38. ▶GIANT FLESHY SCALEWORM

Hololepida magna
▶at least 30 cm (12 in) long
Alaska to Washington, s. California
subtidal

Divers should look along sand/rock interfaces for this delicate giant of the scaleworm clan. Unique not only for its size, the giant fleshy scaleworm has gelatinous elytra (scales). However, only on the last half of the body are they paired on each segment, making this region look very crowded. Typical of scaleworms, it tends to hide by day and can only be found by overturning objects (please replace) or inspecting crevices. It also resides inside large boot sponges (PO9/10). At night this worm typically emerges to crawl gracefully along the bottom. It is a spectacular polychaete that may even be coaxed to swim about briefly, supplying a diver with a special logbook entry.

Lions Bay, Howe Sound, s. BC

AN39. ▶SNOW-SPECKLED SCALEWORM
Lepidasthenia longicirrata
to 12 cm (4.7 in) long
BC to s. California
intertidal to 330 m (1,083 ft)
Brilliant snowy white spots readily distinguish living specimens of this narrow scaleworm. The white spots are scattered over the surface of the elytra (scales) as well as on the long dorsal cirri (finger-like projections). The worm has more than 40 thin, smooth, translucent scales that lack tubercles (bumps) and marginal papillae (fleshy projections). Normally found free-living on mud, rocks or shell-strewn substrates, this scaleworm can also construct a parchment-like tube reinforced with sand or fine shell debris. The specimen in the photograph was found in a discarded beer bottle retrieved during a scuba dive. Edith Berkeley, in 1923, originally discovered this species in a sponge bed near Nanaimo, BC. Based at the Pacific Biological Station (Fisheries and Oceans Canada) in Nanaimo, she and her husband Cyril described many new species of worms from the Pacific Northwest. The taxonomic foundation for polychaete worms provided by these two pioneering scientists is monumental.
Passage Island, Howe Sound, s. BC

AN40. ▶THORNY SCALEWORM
Eunoe senta, *Gattyana senta*
▶to 4 cm (1.6 in) long
Alaska to s. California
subtidal, 5 to 346 m (16 to 1,335 ft)
Although several pale yellow specimens have been found crawling inside the cloud sponge (PO11), the thorny scaleworm also lives on sand and gravel substrates. Hard, sharp branching tubercles (bumps) or spines that resemble thorny bushes cover this worm's soft, thick elytra (scales). In addition, the spines become larger and more complex toward the posterior ends of the scales and of the worm. The margins of the scales and dorsal cirri (finger-like projections) are sparsely papillated (petit projections) and the worm's chaetae (bristles) occur in dense bundles. Overall, this combination of characters gives the thorny scaleworm a shaggy appearance.
Four other *Eunoe* scaleworms live in the Pacific Northwest: the ▶depressed scaleworm, *Eunoe depressa*, ▶rough-noded scaleworm, *E. nodosa*, ▶multi-pronged scaleworm, *E. oerstedi*, and ▶single-row scaleworm, *E. uniseriata*.
Agamemnon Channel, Sechelt Peninsula, s. BC

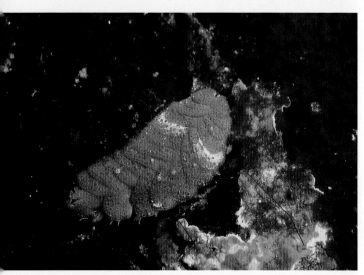

AN41. ▶WHITE-BANDED SCALEWORM
Gaudichaudius iphionelloides, *Gattyana iphionelloides*
to 3.5 cm (1.4 in) long
Siberia to Alaska to Washington, s. California
intertidal to subtidal
For the beachcomber or diver, only diligent searching of overturned objects or dense algal growth will reveal this scaleworm. It is a short, broad species that is found associating with eelgrass (SW2) or on muddy, rock-strewn bottoms overlain by scattered shell debris. The elytra (scales) of this worm are large, thick and brown. Close inspection of the scales will show irregular polygonal patches, each consisting of a flattened or slightly pointed tubercle (bump). These peculiar patches look like alligator skin—possibly evoking the scientific name of the species. Whitish foreign material often forms patches on the elytra or encrusts their papillated (petit projections) fringes. On the photographed specimen, distinctive white bands, reminiscent of closed eyelashes, decorate the fifth pair of scales.
Green Bay, Agamemnon Channel, s. BC

Sea mice
Pacific Northwest coastal waters provide habitat for several species of sea mice (Family Aphroditidae), stout, solid worms with oval-shaped bodies. Many species have a thick, often highly iridescent coat of "felt" covering their backs. Spiny notochaetae (upper appendage bristles) and fine silky fibres mesh together to produce the felt. Spinning glands weave these silky fibres, which in turn entrap silt particles or encrusting organisms,

making the worms look dirty. Probably solitary, sea mice live at a slow pace that contrasts with their aggressive feeding habits. Known to be active carnivores, they prey on large worms, small crustaceans, molluscs and even sea cucumbers. Without well-developed jaw structures, they use a muscular, eversible proboscis for feeding.

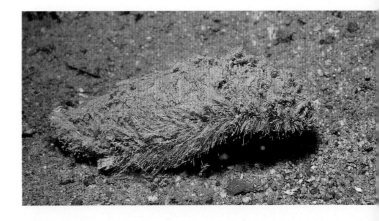

AN42. ▶DISHEVELLED SEA-MOUSE, bristle worm
Aphrodita negligens
to 8 cm (3.2 in) long
Japan, Siberia, n. Alaska to Washington, s. California to Mexico
shallow subtidal to 165 m (545 ft)
Initially this creature looks more like a furry mouse than a polychaete worm. Once overturned, however, its segmentation confirms its identity. Its dishevelled or neglected appearance likely evoked its species name, in odd contrast to the genus name—as Aphrodite is the goddess of love and beauty! As the myth is told, Aphrodite was born from sea foam—a wonderful segue to the fact that this particular specimen was found at low tide, completely exposed and crawling on the sand. Generally, though, the dishevelled sea-mouse remains unseen, buried in the mud.
Tongue Point, Olympic coast, n. Washington

Goddess-worms

The goddess-worms (Family Nephtyidae) can be difficult to identify, especially the small species. To the casual observer they are easily confused with sea-nymphs, p. 144. This has been a problem since 1817, when the Genus *Nephtys* was established to include some species that had previously been thought to be sea-nymphs. Years later in 1850, the Class Nephthydea, possibly in reference to an Egyptian goddess, was created to include the Genus *Nephtys*. The present family spelling of Nephtyidae is correct, as the initial spelling for *Nephtys* takes precedence over the subsequent class spelling of Nephthydea, where the final *h* was purposely or otherwise included. However, this does explain why these worms have occasionally been misspelled as *Nephthys*. Species of goddess-worms have been reported to reach great lengths—up to 40 cm (16 in). As with most polychaetes, there are separate male and female goddess-worms. Little is known concerning their reproductive habits, other than that they broadcast gametes into the seawater. After external fertilization, the larvae spend some time as part of the planktonic community. The transformation from larvae to juveniles apparently does not occur until they have settled into the sediment.

AN43. ▶GODDESS-WORMS (including shimmy worm, sandworm)
Nephtys spp.
to 30 cm (12 in)
intertidal to 1,600 m (5,249 ft)
Japan, Alaska to Peru
The goddess-worms tend to be pink to reddish brown in colour, but their iridescent cuticle (outer skin layer) is stunning! They are incredibly active burrowers, found at subsurface depths as great as 20 cm (8 in), but they do not construct permanent tubes. Their strong, muscular bodies use rapid sinusoidal (side to side) movements to swim quickly through the water. Unfortunately, goddess-worms are readily confused with sea-nymphs (below). The heads of goddess-worms are quite square and flat and generally have only one pair each of tiny antennae and palps. Such morphology is significantly different from the large palps (anterior sensory outgrowths) and long tentacular cirri (finger-like projections) on the heads of sea-nymphs. Also, the bodies of the goddess-worms are flattened and rectangular in cross-section, with the fleshy appendages fanning out from the four corners of each segment (notochaetae at the dorsal corners; neurochaetae at the ventral). The dorsal and ventral blood vessels are often clearly visible, extending the length of the body. Generally the goddess-worms are considered to be predators, using the relatively short, eversible proboscis to capture small arthropods, polychaetes and molluscs. Close to a dozen species of goddess-worms inhabit muddy or sandy sediments in the Pacific Northwest.
Sargeant Bay, Sechelt Peninsula, s. BC. J. Duane Sept photograph

Sea-nymphs

Members of the Family Nereididae are named after Nereus, a sea god and father of numerous sea nymphs. Sea-nymphs are among the most commonly encountered and widespread intertidal polychaete worms. Close to two dozen species live in the Pacific Northwest (at all depths). The intertidal species have been called ragworms. Upon attaining sexual maturity, nereids are well known for their precisely timed and choreographed "nuptial dance." The worms respond to internal cues (hormones and biological rhythm) as well as external environmental triggers to reach maturity. The environmental cues include seasonal or lunar cycles, tidal fluctuations, temperature, day length, light intensity and even salinity. As if by magic, all members of a species are able to reach sexual maturity simultaneously, as specialized forms called epitokes, and swim to the surface for spawning at exactly the same time and same place. The accompanying photograph of an undetermined species shows two sea-nymph epitokes, also known as heteronereids, exhibiting their highly transformed bodies, which are swollen with either eggs or sperm. Body transformations include increased size of the parapodia (fleshy appendages), greater swimming musculature, development of paddle chaetae (bristles) and enlargement of the eyes. These eyes are "programmed" to day length and light intensity, so it is not surprising that the epitokes can be falsely triggered and attracted to nearshore lights. Stimulated by self-produced, partner-attracting pheromones (chemical signals), the heteronereids perform intimate nuptial dances, jettisoning eggs and sperm into the surrounding sea but in close proximity to their partners. So extreme are these spawning modifications, along with a tendency for gamete release to occur through ruptures in the body wall, that spawning is inevitably followed by death. After fertilization the developing, non-feeding larvae inhabit the water column, ultimately being dispersed by tides and currents. Depending on the species, the larvae spend from hours to months as part of the plankton before settling out and onto the bottom. After completing metamorphosis, juveniles begin the journey to adulthood. Most, but not all, species of sea-nymphs exhibit this type of life cycle.

In the Pacific Northwest, late winter and spring is a magical time, when the reproductive activities of plants and animals occur at a frenzied pace and result in cyclical plankton blooms. Dockside observers and divers are treated to an amazing array of organisms congregating and breeding at or near the surface. Many of the sea-nymphs (Family Nereididae) join in the activity with their own unique reproductive method of broadcast (free) spawning.

AN44. ▶BANNER SEA-NYMPH, sand worm, piling worm, pile worm, large mussel worm, mussel worm, clam worm, clamworm
Nereis vexillosa
to 30 cm (12 in) long
Alaska to s. California
intertidal to subtidal
Hiding among barnacle and mussel clusters, the banner sea-nymph is a favourite bait for bottom-fish anglers. Raised high as if to mimic waving flags or banners are the elongate dorsal lobes located on each of this worm's posterior parapodia (appendages). The banner sea-nymph has a slightly different version of the basic reproductive cycle. Once a female epitoke or heteronereid detects the sperm of the male during the "nuptial dance," she releases her eggs along with a material that instantly agglutinates in the seawater. The doomed female and the fertilized egg mass then sink to the bottom, where the gelatinous unit gradually swells to the size of a chicken egg. This egg mass is bluish-green in colour and may be found on muddy sand at low tide. The rest of the banner sea-nymph's cycle follows the general family script.
A B Stanley Park, Burrard Inlet, s. BC

AN45. ▶GIANT PILING SEA-NYMPH/CLAM WORM, giant piling worm, giant pile worm, giant clam worm, giant mussel worm, clam worm, sand worm, sandworm
***Nereis brandti/Nereis virens**, Neanthes brandti*
to 1.5 m (5 ft) long
Siberia, n. Alaska to s. California
intertidal to subtidal
Two very large sea-nymphs potentially inhabit sandbars or mudflats in bays of the Pacific Northwest. One is the giant piling worm, *Nereis brandti*, the other is the clamworm, *Nereis virens*. These two worms can both reach great lengths and are very difficult to distinguish from each other without detailed examination of the paragnaths (tooth-like structures) located on the muscular proboscis (tongue). Although the clamworm (*Nereis virens*) inhabits the temperate waters of the North Atlantic Ocean, its status in the cold waters of the North Pacific remains yet to be definitively determined. It is not uncommon for some boreal species to occur in the northern regions of both the Pacific and Atlantic oceans. Both the giant piling sea-nymph and the clamworm are known for their massive jaws. The naturalist may be surprised to know that algae are a major component of their diet, and the jaws are used primarily in defence of territory.
Friday Harbor, San Juan Island, n. Washington

AN46. ▶LITTLE PILEWORM SEA-NYMPH, little pile worm, pile worm
Nereis procera
to 12.5 cm (5 in) long
s. Alaska to s. California
intertidal to 1,220 m (4,000 ft)
This sea-nymph is one of the smaller members of its family, but this status does not diminish its fierce predatory behaviour. It usually frequents pilings, mussel beds, eelgrass meadows, rocks or silty substrates. The central red stripe visible in the photograph is the worm's dorsal red blood vessel; a ventral counterpart may be visible along the underside. As in humans, the blood of sea-nymphs contains hemoglobin to convey oxygen throughout the body. Many sea-nymphs produce and live in flimsy mucus tubes from which they emerge to feed. If they stray too far from their shelters, these somewhat nomadic creatures will secrete new ones. Through active irrigation of their tubes, they can live in anaerobic (oxygen-free) intertidal areas.
Ucluth Peninsula, w. Vancouver Island, s. BC

AN47. ▶RED-AND-WHITE-BANDED SEA-NYMPH, red-and-white banded worm, hermit worm
Cheilonereis cyclurus
to 18 cm (7 in) long
n.w. Pacific Ocean, n. Alaska to s. California
intertidal to subtidal
This stunning red-and-white-banded worm has a special commensal relationship (beneficial to one or both) with large hermit crab species. Together they inhabit the shells of some large snail species, such as Lewis's moonsnail (MC225). Seldom does this sea-nymph emerge more than the length of its head, making detection of its presence difficult. Careful prodding was necessary to obtain complete exposure of the beautiful specimen in the photograph. The high, wrinkled collar partially enveloping the head helps to distinguish this species from other sea-nymphs.
Point Defiance, Puget Sound, n. Washington

FEEDING-PALP POLYCHAETES

Dumb-bell worms

The dumb-bell worms (Family Sternaspidae) are a small group of worms that burrow in the sediment. When partially contracted they can appear peanut-shaped, but when completely retracted they seem almost spherical or gourd-shaped. There is only one genus in this family and possibly only one species in the Pacific Northwest, although there are unresolved records. Historically, the ground-digger dumb-bell worm (AN48) living in the Pacific Northwest was determined as *Sternaspis scutata*, a species originally described from the Mediterranean Sea. However, recent investigations have equated this local worm with *Sternaspis fossor*, a species originally described from the Bay of Fundy on the east coast of Canada. Future investigations may change perceptions again. Another species is known to occur off California and perhaps yet a different one from Japan (or is it *Sternaspis scutata*?). Little is known about the reproduction or larval development of the dumb-bell worms, although their specialized genital papillae (fleshy projections) may be used for copulation.

AN48. ▶GROUND-DIGGER DUMB-BELL WORM
Sternaspis fossor, (as *Sternaspis scutata*)
to 2.5 cm (1 in) long , 1.5 cm (0.6 in) in diameter
s. Alaska to s. California
subtidal, 10–409 m (33–1,342 ft)—possibly to 2,800 m (9,186 ft)
An inhabitant of soft mud, this strange-looking worm is sometimes a bycatch for shrimp trawlers. But which end is which? The large, square amber to reddish-coloured "eyes" are not eyes at all but rather two stiff chitinized (tough, protective) shields or plates at the swollen posterior end. The narrower anterior end, where the real eye-spots and mouth are located, actually does the digging. This worm apparently lies just under the surface of the mud with its head directed downward and only its tiny branchiae (gills) protruding above the surface. In the photograph, note the rows of papillae (petit projections), appearing as tiny clusters of "pom-poms," on the top of each segment. About mid-body, two longer genital papillae are also visible. Often this chubby worm's surface is partially obscured by agglutinated bits of fine sand and mud. It is a treat to find, but alas, a rare one for most naturalists.
Mouth of Fraser River, Strait of Georgia, s. BC

Bristle-cage worms

The bristle-cage worms (Family Flabelligeridae) are variable of form, from short and grub-like to long and spindle-shaped. Their bodies are usually densely covered with papillae (petit projections) and adherent fine-grained sediment. These worms possess a green respiratory pigment in their blood called chlorocruorin—a feature shared by only a few other tube dwellers, such as the calcareous tubeworms, p. 147, and some spaghetti-worms, p. 156. Reproductive methods for bristle-cage worms are not well known but at least one close relative of the following species, reported from Antarctic seas, apparently broods its embryos in a thick layer of mucus along its back. Some other species have mass spawning episodes.

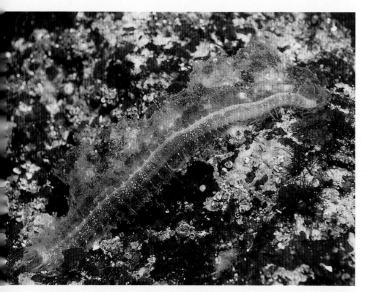

AN49. ▶SHEATHED BRISTLE-CAGE WORM
Flabelligera affinis, *Flabelligera infundibularis*
to 13 cm (5.1 in)
Japan, Arctic Ocean, Alaska to s. California, Atlantic Ocean
intertidal to 2,500 m (8,202 ft)
A "cage" is formed by two distinctive fans of very long chaetae (bristles) on either side of the head. Within this structure are sensory papillae (petit projections). Two grooved palps (anterior feeding appendages) protrude from the sides of the mouth and extend forward through this "cage" to gather sediment coated with organic matter. The tips of the palps are apparently sensitive to light and touch. The branchiae (gills), hidden beneath a hood near the mouth, may create water currents to facilitate the feeding process. When the worm is disturbed, the head retracts and the

two fans close around the head. The body of the worm is hidden within a white-speckled, transparent mucus sheath, secreted by glands near the mouth. Using hooked bristles that protrude through the sheath, the worm is apparently able to crawl around, carrying its shelter, somewhat like a caterpillar.

Sutton Islets, Egmont, s. BC

Calcareous tubeworms

Hard, rocky substrates tend to be the preferred sites for attachment of the calcareous tubeworms (Family Serpulidae), although various species also affix to algae and seagrasses, mollusc shells and arthropod exoskeletons. All calcareous tubeworms have tubes formed primarily of calcium carbonate and a matrix of mucus and carbohydrates. Specialized glands near their heads are responsible for tube production. When the mucus/carbohydrate mixture is secreted within the confined space of these glands, calcium carbonate is precipitated from the surrounding seawater. This mixture is then applied to the leading edges of the tubes. Consequently, as the worms grow, so do their encasements. The calcareous tubes immediately identify these worms and readily distinguish them from their close relatives, the feather-duster tubeworms, whose shelters consist of mucus/sediment combinations. As with the feather-duster tubeworms (AN60–67), the calcareous tubeworms have tentacular crowns that function in both feeding and respiratory activities. The tentacular crown is composed of two halves or lobes, each carrying a number of feather-like radioles (spoke-like branches), which have tiny lateral branches called pinnules. Calcareous tubeworms have as few as three pairs of radioles to 20 pairs or more. Most, but not all, calcareous tubeworms have the added benefit of an operculum (trap door) to seal off the tube entrance—presumably an anti-predator device. Each operculum is a transformed radiole (feather-like branch) of the tentacular crown and can be ornate, symmetrical or irregularly shaped, calcified or chitinized (tough, protective). Some species of calcareous tubeworms have achieved an economic status as significant fouling organisms on pilings, docks and boat hulls.

AN50. ▶PEARL-TOPPED CALCAREOUS TUBEWORMS
***Apomatus* spp.** (*Apomatus geniculata* and *Apomatus timsii*)
to 8 cm (3.2 in) long
Japan, BC to s. California
subtidal to 357 m (1,170 ft)
The gorgeous pearl-shaped operculum (trap door) carried on top of one of the radioles (feather-like branches) of the crown is unmistakable. The white crown (plume) is bilobed and fan-shaped. Two species, *Apomatus geniculata* and *Apomatus timsii,* are found in the Pacific Northwest, but only detailed microscope examination of their chaetae (bristles) can differentiate the two. The presence of the operculum and narrower tube of the pearl-topped calcareous tubeworm, however, readily distinguishes it from the white-crown calcareous tubeworm (AN51).

Quarry Bay, Nelson Island, s. BC

AN51. ▶WHITE-CROWN CALCAREOUS TUBEWORM
Protula pacifica
to 15 cm (6 in) long
Japan, Siberia, BC
subtidal to 250 m (820 ft)
An impressive-sized worm featuring a spectacular white crown with a large number (60 pairs) of tentacular crown radioles (branches) overshadows the fact that it is one of only a few calcareous tubeworms having no operculum (trap door). The two lobes of its tentacular crown are clearly spiralled. This tubeworm commonly cohabits with the similar-looking pearl-topped calcareous tubeworm (AN50), which does have an operculum. Easily gathered observations on the relative sizes and abundances of these co-occurring species could provide data for an interesting ecological study. Some species closely related to the white-crown calcareous tubeworm apparently brood their young in gelatinous masses near the mouths of their tubes.

A Agamemnon Channel, Nelson Island, s. BC

AN52. ►RED-TRUMPET CALCAREOUS TUBEWORM, colourful calcareous tubeworm, calcareous tubeworm, calcareous tube worm, limy tubed worm, limy-tubed worm, white-tubed worm, red tubeworm, red tube worm, serpulid worm, fan worm, plume worm
Serpula columbiana*
to 6.5 cm (2.5 in) long,** 0.6 cm (0.3 in) diameter
Alaska to California
intertidal to more than 100 m (330 ft)
The colour of this tubeworm is always brilliant! The characteristic sinuous, irregular coil of the chalky white tube is attached to the substrate over most of its length but the distal (head) end is usually elevated. There is no longitudinal keel on the tube. Photograph A shows a bright, distinctive tentacular crown arranged in two spiralled lobes that appear almost as complete circles. The bright colour of the crown is apparently produced by the presence of a special pigment, astaxanthin. The crown of this worm commonly occurs in various shades of red, orange or pink banded with white, but most stunning is its brilliant red, trumpet-shaped operculum (trap door). Photograph B illustrates this near-symmetrical, shallow funnel with many (55–160) tiny crenellations (teeth) along its edge and a constriction beneath where it attaches to the stalk. The red-trumpet calcareous tubeworm can colonize virtually any hard surface. It is a broadcast (free) spawner, releasing its gametes into the water column, where the developing larvae swim and feed on minute plankton before settling into bottom-dwelling adulthood.
*Until recently, much of the available literature accepted *Serpula vermicularis* as the only species of *Serpula* in the Pacific Northwest, and *Serpula columbiana* was considered a synonym. However, investigations indicate that *Serpula columbiana* applies to the Pacific Northwest species and *Serpula vermicularis* is likely restricted as a North Atlantic species.
**In the colder northern waters of Alaska and BC, there are records of gigantic red-trumpet calcareous tubeworms as long as 8–10 cm (4–5 in). It is yet to be determined whether these records represent an increase of maximum size for *Serpula columbiana* or whether they are another, larger northern species.
A Browning Passage, Nigei Island, c. BC
B Quarry Bay, Nelson Island, s. BC

AN53. ►THREE-BRANCH CALCAREOUS TUBEWORM, fragile tubeworm, fragile tube worm, orange tube worm
Salmacina tribranchiata*, *Salmacina dysteri tribranchiata
to 0.6 cm (0.3 in) long, 1 mm (0.04 in) tube diameter
colony to 20 cm (8 in) diameter
BC to s. California
intertidal to 82 m (270 ft)
The minute, extremely delicate nature of the clustering tubes of this species is surprising considering that it lives along exposed coastlines where the pounding of surf may be extreme. The intricate, convoluted shape of the colony is in part a result of asexual reproduction. Each new individual, cloned from the posterior end of its parent, makes a hole through the wall of the parent's tube and begins to secrete its own branch. Ultimately, there is the formation of a colonial mass of tangled tubes. The three-branched calcareous tubeworm is unique in having only three pairs of radioles (branches) forming its tentacular crown. The crown colour is primarily a shade of orange but can be almost colourless. This coral colour is also persistent in the developing eggs and even the emerging larvae.
Cape Flattery, Olympic coast, n. Washington

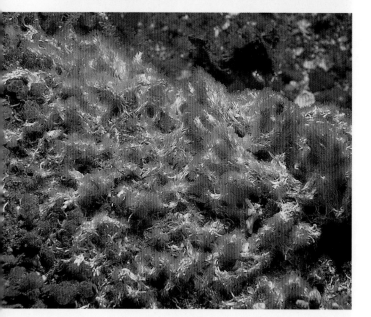

AN54. ▶WESTERN CALCAREOUS TUBEWORM, western serpulid
Pseudochitinopoma occidentalis, *Chitinopoma groenlandica* (in part)
to 1.2 cm (0.5 in) long
tube to 4 cm (1.7 in) long, 2 mm (0.1 in) wide
s. Alaska to s. California, Arctic Ocean
intertidal to 128 m (420 ft)

The very small-bored calcified tube of this species is not tightly coiled but meandering, and it has a noticeable dorsal keel (ridge) extending its complete length. The tiny, pinkish brown tentacular crown is not always visible. It has a small globular operculum (trap door) topped with a brown chitinous (tough, protective) plate. When feeding, this tubeworm filters phytoplankton and kelp detritus from the water column. After a relatively long planktonic existence, the larva metamorphoses into a juvenile that settles onto the bottom, its newly secreted tube barely 5 mm (0.2 in) in length! Some close relatives of this species reportedly brood their young inside their tubes or undergo asexual reproduction.

Passage Island, Howe Sound, s. BC

AN55. ▶YOKE-BEARER CALCAREOUS TUBEWORM
Crucigera zygophora
to 4.5 cm (1.8 in) long
Alaska to c. California
intertidal to 146 m (480 ft)

A close look at this worm indicates that its tentacular crown has about 30 pairs of tentacle crown radioles (branches). They are bright red at the base of the lobes, then gradually alternate with white bands toward their tips. An even closer inspection reveals a small, oddly shaped red operculum (trap door), which has a broad, open funnel situated on top of a stalk. The margin of the funnel has many crenellations that form ridges radiating into the centre. On the outside base of the funnel are three knobbed processes. The imaginative mind can visualize the knobs in the shape of a yoke turned on its side, with the funnel emerging through the opening—apparently the basis of the species name *zygophora* (yoke-bearer). This tubeworm is thought to be a broadcast (free) spawner.

The shape of the operculum's funnel and the number of bumps or knobs (not always visible) on the stalk below must be determined to distinguish this species from the similar ▶irregular calcareous tubeworm, *Crucigera irregularis*, a Pacific Northwest species that has two, not three, knobs below a laterally compressed funnel.

Halkett Point, Gambier Island, s. BC

AN56. ▶DWARF CALCAREOUS TUBEWORMS, tiny tube worms, spiral tubeworms, spiral tube worms, small spirorbid worms, snail worms
Pileolaria spp.
to 0.6 cm (0.3 in) tube diameter
BC to s. California
intertidal to subtidal

The name "dwarf calcareous tubeworm" is applicable to virtually any species of tiny, spirally coiled calcareous tube dweller. These worms, noticeable by the mere fact that their calcareous tubes are tiny and coiled, can be extremely common. Often they live in large crowded aggregations. The orange-red colour of the small tentacular crowns is obvious and highlighted by the white calcareous tubes. Observing their tiny opercula (trap doors), however, is a much greater challenge. A naturalist could spend considerable time determining whether the asymmetrical tubes in a patch are coiled clockwise or counter-clockwise—a characteristic important for species identification. Of particular significance is that these worms, unlike most polychaetes, are hermaphroditic: each worm carries both male and female reproductive systems, often in their abdomens. Even more fascinating, these worms brood their young in their trap doors! Once fertilization has occurred, the trap doors serve as brood chambers for the developing embryos. Depending on the species, these calcified trap doors may be in the form of an open cup or helmet-shaped chamber that can be used for more than one brood.

Sutton Islets, Egmont, s. BC

Dwarf calcareous tubeworms, also known as spirorbids, have at times been considered a separate family but are included here as Serpulidae. Their systematic status is debated, but some 130 described species of spirorbids are recognized worldwide, 30 of which occur in the Pacific from Alaska to Panama. Many of these species can be expected to inhabit the Pacific Northwest.

Curly filament-worms

The curly filament-worms (Family Cirratulidae) are a diverse group of polychaete worms that are reproductively fascinating. Most species, have both male and female worms that reproduce sexually through broadcast (free) spawning as epitokes (see sea-nymphs, p. 144). Brooding in jelly-like egg masses has been observed in some, possibly including the intertidal filament-worm (AN59), although other species of *Cirratulus* are known to reproduce both sexually and asexually. Both the coralline-encased filament-worm (AN57) and the fringed filament-worm (AN58), however, are masters of asexual reproduction. They are capable of fragmenting their bodies within their tubes and then regenerating the missing anterior or posterior ends. Colonies can contain both males and females or house only unisexual individuals. Life is not always what it appears!

AN57. ▶CORALLINE-ENCASED FILAMENT-WORM, coralline fringed tube worm
Dodecaceria concharum
to 5 cm (2 in) worm length, 3 mm (0.1 in) worm width
flat colonies, indeterminate, irregular size
BC to s. California
intertidal to 109 m (358 ft)
For a scuba diver, the first impression of these worms may be a cluster of tiny spiders perched on the surface of crustose coralline algae (SW86). On closer examination, the "spiders" are actually filaments, two thick palps (anterior feeding appendages) and three to six pairs of branchiae (gills) that are attached to the protruding head of each worm. The palps and gills are usually tan to yellow in colour but may appear reddish because of the presence of nearby blood vessels. The grooved palps of this filament-worm search out, collect and transport food to the mouth from the adjacent surface of the coralline algae. Although empty shells will also suffice, coralline-encased filament-worms typically bore into existing calcareous structures of crustose coralline algae, where they form U-shaped burrows.
Browning Passage, Barkley Sound, s. BC

AN58. ▶FRINGED FILAMENT-WORM, fringed tubeworm, Fewke's fringed worm, colonial tubeworm, honeycomb worm, cemented tube worm, black tube-building cirratulid worm
Dodecaceria fewkesi, *Sabella pacifica*, *Dodecaceria pacifica*, *Dodecaceria fistulicola*, misspelled: *Dodecaceria feweksi*
to 4 cm (1.6 in) long, 3 mm (0.1 in) wide
irregular, "reef-like" colony, at least 1 m (39 in) across
BC to s. California
▶intertidal to 24 m (79 ft)
The activities of this impressive colonial tube-dweller result in low-profile reefs that resemble hardened rock-like structures riddled with short tubes. The reefs generally cover rocky outcrops. The tubes protrude above the reef structure, making the "fringe factor" produced by this worm's filaments more obvious to the diver than those of the coralline-encased filament-worm (AN57). When viewed up close and under artificial light, each pair of palps (anterior feeding appendages) is usually dark brown to black in colour, and the gills (six to 11 pairs) are a lighter, yellow-brown hue. However, internal blood vessels may provide an overriding reddish hue (photograph A). When seen *au naturel* and from a distance (photograph B), fringing appears black.

A Browning Passage, Nigei Island, c. BC. Charlie Gibbs photograph
B Booker Lagoon, Broughton Island, c. BC

AN59. ▶INTERTIDAL FILAMENT-WORM

Cirratulus sp.* (possibly *Cirratulus cingulatus* or *Cirratulus robustus*)
▶to 7.5 cm (3 in) long
Alaska to c. California
intertidal

Look for aggregations of fine sand and mud under rocks when seeking this yellowish beige worm. The first impression is likely that of a multitude of long, writhing filaments on the surface of the sediment. These are the branchiae (gills) that are attached to each segment for most of the body's length. With the worm's body obscured by sediment, the gills protrude into the overlying water, where oxygen is in greater supply. The worm probably uses its dorsal palps (anterior feeding appendages), located near its head, to reach fine decaying matter or detritus prevalent on the surface. Cilia (hair)-lined grooves in the palps deliver the food to the mouth. Intertidal filament-worms are likely selective feeders, in terms of both particle size and composition.

*The taxonomy of *Cirratulus* species is difficult and has undergone recent revisions. For example, the large intertidal worm identified in previous guidebooks as *Cirratulus spectablilis* could be one of three species: ▶ringed filament-worm, *Cirratulus cingulatus*, ▶robust filament-worm, *Cirratulus robustus*, or ▶spectacular filament-worm, *Cirratulus spectabilis*. Based on size alone, the specimen in the photograph is unlikely to be *Cirratulus spectabilis*, as the documented maximum length of this species is only about 1 cm (0.4 in). Yet the species name, *spectabilis*, may have been intended to describe the spectacular size of the worm. Therein lies the conflict. Definitive species identification is virtually impossible without a microscope.

Fort Worden State Park, Port Townsend, n. Washington

Feather-duster worms

Taxonomically, the feather-duster tubeworms (Family Sabellidae) of the Pacific Northwest are in a state of flux because many species descriptions are based on specimens of European worms that may or may not exist along this coast. Gradually, research and new descriptions are determining the true identity of species in this group. As seen in the photographs, the feather-duster tubeworms are diverse. Their size range is also extreme, from less than 1 cm (0.4 in) to 2.1 m (7 ft)! The similarity of the tentacular crown structure and the household "feather duster" appears to be the common name's origin. To varying degrees, the tentacular crown (plume) serves the dual purpose of respiration and filter feeding, similar to the calcareous tubeworms, p. 147. The crown is bilobed and the spoke-like tentacular radioles (branches) that extend from each lobe have tiny lateral branches called pinnules. Feather-duster tubeworms have as few as two pairs of radioles to several hundred pairs. Both radioles and pinnules are grooved and ciliated. The cilia (hairs) effectively aerate the blood by circulating water up through the plume, while at the same time filtering out food items such as unicellular algae and planktonic larvae. Once captured, the food moves down the grooves of the radioles to the mouth. The feather-duster tubeworms have an amazing ability to sort and select particles by size, some obviously for ingestion and others for tube-building material. The action of giant nerve fibres within the ventral nerve cord enables these worms to retract inside their tubes rapidly when disturbed.

AN60. ▶MINUTE FEATHER-DUSTER

***Chone minuta**, Chone ecaudata* (in part)
to 1.5 cm (0.6 in) long
Alaska to s. California
intertidal to shallow subtidal

At first glance, the uninitiated beachcomber may think nothing of the many tiny, closely packed holes in shell-hash (crushed-shell) sediment adjacent to surfgrasses (SW4)—photograph A. However, on closer examination or even careful excavation, a multitude of tiny dark worms in tubes that are matted together like a tightly woven carpet, may be revealed. These worms represent some of the smallest members of the family. If it were not for the root system of the surfgrasses, which bind the tubes and sediments together, these tiny worms would probably not survive in their high-energy, open-coast environment. Photograph B illustrates several tiny plumes.

In the past, the names *Chone minuta* and *Chone ecaudata* were considered synonymous, but more recently, scientists recognize them as two distinct species: *Chone ecaudata* is generally found in soft sediments much deeper than the shallower water species, *Chone minuta*. Some evidence suggests that these tiny *Chone* species may brood their young in egg masses attached to their tubes. There are at least another half dozen species of this group of worms in the Pacific Northwest.

A Frank Island, w. Vancouver Island, s. BC
B Box Island, w. Vancouver Island, s. BC. J. Duane Sept photograph

AN61. ▶ORANGE FEATHER-DUSTER

Chone aurantiaca
to 20 cm (7.9 in) long (estimated), crown to 1.5 cm (0.6 in) long
BC to Washington
intertidal to subtidal

The attractive splash of this species' pink, orange, or infrequently white tentacular crown is eye-catching, but often only momentarily, to the alert diver patrolling sandy locales. This worm retracts its plume instantaneously upon the slightest disturbance, leaving no evidence of the brilliant orange-coloured body within the sediment. The crown is distinctively bilobed, twisted inward like a pair of ram's horns. An important feature is that the spoke-like radioles (branches) of the crown are connected over most of their length by a thin membrane. The lobes of the "ram's horns" lie very close to the surface of the shell-hash substrate.

A Browning Passage, Nigei Island, c. BC
B Deadman Island, San Juan Islands, n. Washington

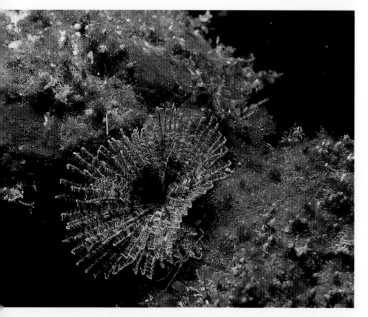

AN62. ▶PARASOL FEATHER-DUSTER

***Demonax medius**, Sabella media, Distylia rugosa, Sabella rugosa, Parasabella rugosa, Parasabella maculata, Sabella aulaconota, Potamilla californica*
to 10 cm (4 in) long
s. Alaska to c. California
intertidal to subtidal

A loner, this feather-duster tubeworm often lives within the clusters of the fringed filament-worm (AN58), a hint of which can be seen in the photograph. The two lobes of the crown resemble those of the orange feather-duster (AN61), insofar as they lie close to the substrate. However, the two lobes of the parasol feather-duster jointly expand to form a symmetrical, virtually unbroken circle. Apparently when reproducing, the mature female creates a jelly ring or cocoon around the tube opening. It is not until the eggs are deposited inside that a male fertilizes them. After leaving this maternal cocoon, the young larvae settle onto the substrate and begin feeding with only a few chaetigers (bristle-bearing segments) having developed.

Toquart Bay, Barkley Sound, s. BC

AN63. ▶**POLYMORPH FEATHER-DUSTER**, plume worm, feather-duster worm
Eudistylia polymorpha
to 17 cm (6.7 in) long, 1.2 cm (0.5 in) wide
Alaska to s. California
intertidal to 450 m (1,450 ft)
This worm is generally smaller and less frequently encountered in the Pacific Northwest than the Vancouver feather-duster (AN64). The colour of the tentacular crown (plume) of the polymorph feather-duster is variable. Any of the three distinct colour morphs—orange, brown and maroon— may also feature lighter alternating bands. Superficially these plume colours distinguish the species from the Vancouver feather-duster (AN64), but only microscopic examination provides the detail necessary for species differentiation. The polymorph feather-duster, Vancouver feather-duster and split-branch feather-duster (AN65) all have tiny, unpaired compound eyes on the outer margins of their spoke-like crown radioles (branches). An astute diver with a stealthy approach may notice these eyes on the bottom half of the branches before the creature retreats.
Monterey Bay, c. California. Daniel W. Gotshall photograph

AN64. ▶**VANCOUVER FEATHER-DUSTER**, feather duster worm, northern feather duster worm, plume worm, parchment tube worm
Eudistylia vancouveri, *Eudistylia plumosa*, *Sabella vancouveri*
to 25 cm (10 in) long, 1.2 cm (0.5 in) diameter
expanded crown to 6 cm (2.4 in) diameter
tube to 68 cm (26.8 in) long, 2 cm (0.8 in) diameter
Alaska to c. California
▶intertidal to 30 m (100 ft)
The parchment tube secreted by this feather-duster is thick and rubbery, providing excellent protection from current or wave action. The beautiful transverse banding of the crown, usually blueberry/green and maroon (photograph A), is striking! Initially, though, this colour appears to be black. Photograph C shows a possible but repeatedly encountered colour variant amid those of regular hue. Only bright sunlight or a beam from an artificial source exposes its true vibrancy. Most commonly found in large, entwined clusters (photograph B), this species may also live alone, but in a shorter tube. Pilings and floats are particularly favoured habitats. The Vancouver feather-duster was first described from Vancouver Island, and records from the early 1920s estimated that large groves contained as many as 375,000 to 500,000 individuals.
A Steep Island, Discovery Passage, s. BC
B Sekiu, Olympic coast, n. Washington
C Booker Lagoon, Broughton Island, c. BC

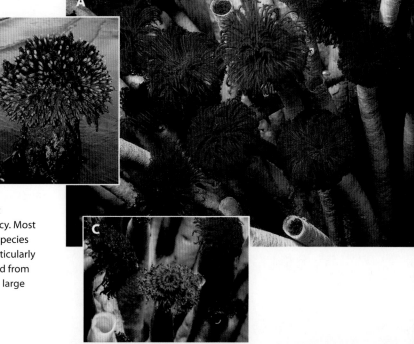

AN65. **SPLIT-BRANCH FEATHER-DUSTER**, split-plume feather-duster, feather duster worm, plume worm, fan worm
Schizobranchia insignis
15.8 cm (6.2 in) long, or greater—an Alaskan record 21.4 cm (8.4 in) long
tube to 20 cm (8 in) long
Alaska to c. California
intertidal to 46 m (150 ft)
The tentacular crown of this large tubeworm is uniformly coloured, often a pale pastel tan, orange, mauve or varying shades of green or brown. The observant naturalist will discern that the spoke-like radioles (branches) are dichotomously branched, with up to five forks—a key factor distinguishing this worm from the polymorph feather-duster (AN63) and Vancouver feather-duster (AN64). A common piling and float dweller, this feather-duster is very often intermixed with the latter, easily distinguished, species. The three feather-duster worms (AN63–65) likely free spawn their eggs and sperm into the water column, where fertilization occurs. Non-feeding larvae may live up to two weeks in the plankton, although larvae of many feather-duster species apparently are non-swimmers, settling quickly onto the bottom to grow into adults.
Edmonds, Puget Sound, n. Washington

AN66. ▶SLIME-TUBE FEATHER-DUSTER, slime tubeworm, slime tube worm, slime-dweller, slime feather duster, funnel plume worm, sabellid worm
Myxicola infundibulum
to 9 cm (3.5 in) long
crown to 3 cm (1.2 in) diameter
n. Alaska to California
intertidal to 425 m (1,400 ft)
Able to retract quickly enough to leave the slime tube "a-jiggling," this worm may live communally in rock crevices (photograph C) or as a solitary specimen, buried in sand or soft mud (photograph B). Different from most of the other feather-duster tubeworms, this one has a crown that forms a funnel, which has a membrane connecting the spoke-like radioles (branches) together over most of their length. This membrane is very effective at collecting food particles suspended in seawater (photograph A)—the feeding process is equivalent to filtering 286 mL (9.5 oz) in one hour. A snap contraction of the worm's giant nerve fibre (axon) not only initiates withdrawal of the feeding structure into its tube but also ensures that the accumulated waste materials are ejected well beyond the surface of the funnel. Even a worm can "keep its head clear"! Amputation of the crown by a predator, however, is usually lethal.

Another tube dweller, petit slime-tube feather-duster, *Myxicola aesthetica,* has been reported off the Pacific Northwest coast. Both species are of European origin and current investigations suggest that these local species are actually different from their European counterparts. New descriptions and names are likely to follow.
A B C Agamemnon Channel, Nelson Island, s. BC

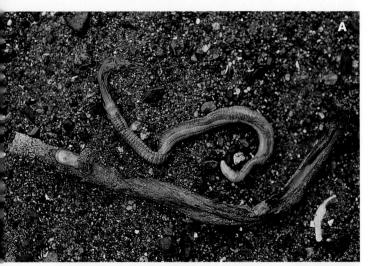

AN67. ▶TWIN-EYED FEATHER-DUSTER, plume worm, feather-duster worm
Bispira sp. (as *Sabella crassicornis*)
▶to 10 cm (4 in) long
▶crown to 5 cm (2 in) diameter
▶tube to 25 cm (10 in) long
Alaska to Washington, California, Arctic Ocean, Atlantic Ocean
subtidal to 421 m (1,380 ft)
This feather-duster tends to be a solitary tubeworm, preferring sandy substrates with some shell hash (crushed shell). Photograph A indicates the large size of the worm and parchment-like tube after extraction from sediment. The length of the tentacular crown is clearly visible. The crown is bilobed and spiralled, with about 25 pairs of spoke-like radioles (branches). Once the worm is detected, a careful, stealthy approach toward a fully extended crown could reveal a stunning sight—as many as 1,000 pairs of eyes staring back! Photograph C shows these small black eyes, paired at equal intervals along the outer edge and length of each radiole. These light-sensitive eyes alert the worm to potential danger, such as the shadow of an approaching predator. The retraction response of the worm is rapid, triggered by the giant internal nerve fibres. Some other feather-duster tubeworms have eyes, but they are more irregular in their placement and almost never in a paired sequence. Photograph B provides a close-up of a pair of short radiolar appendages rarely viewed in a live worm.
A Ucluth Peninsula, w. Vancouver Island, s. BC
B Deadman Island, San Juan Island, n. Washington
C Irvines Landing, Pender Harbour, s. BC

Ice-cream coneworms

Like methodical stonemasons, the resourceful ice-cream coneworms (Family Pectinariidae) build tubes from single grains of sand carefully bonded together with proteinaceous glue. Sand grains range from very fine to coarse, but the size of the grains increases as the worm grows, making tube composition alone insufficient for distinguishing species. The shape of the tube—straight or gently curved—remains unchanged with growth, but shape is not always reliable for identification if the posterior end is broken off. Generally, detailed examination of chaetae (bristles) is required. Ice-cream coneworms probably freely spawn their gametes into the seawater, where fertilization occurs. Curiously, the larvae are so predisposed to start digging that after several weeks in the plankton they metamorphose and secrete a larval tube while still floating in the water column! Soon thereafter they settle to the bottom to assume an adult existence.

AN68. ▶TUSK CONEWORM, ice-cream cone worm, cone worm, sandmason worm, tusk worm
Pectinaria granulata, *Cistenides granulata, Cistenides brevicoma*
to 3 cm (1.2 in) long
tube to 4 cm (1.6 in) long
s. Alaska to n. Mexico
intertidal to 165 m (540 ft)
Check in the muddy sand of low intertidal areas beneath cobbles or boulders to find coneworms. The tusk coneworm orients itself head first (large end of the cone) into the sediments; the posterior end of the tube may protrude slightly above the surface. The modified, broad, flattened paleae (bristles) on either side of the head dig and scoop sediment until the worm is almost completely buried. The two sets of bristles can overlap to form an operculum (trap door) to close off the mouth of the tube. The buccal (feeding) tentacles extend several centimetres beyond the head to select subsurface detritus that is moved to the mouth via ciliated (hair-lined) grooves. This worm's burrow is generally not permanent. After several hours of feeding in one spot, the worm moves on, dragging its tube along. The live specimen in the photograph (at top) features the flattened head paleae (bristles), looking very much like the long teeth of a comb; the other empty tubes indicate the tapering, gradual curve of the tube.
Two other species of ice-cream coneworms are recorded in the Pacific Northwest: ▶straight coneworm, *Pectinaria californiensis* (tube straight), and more rarely, ▶Moore's coneworm, *Pectinaria moorei* (tube curved).
Queen Charlotte Channel, Howe Sound, s. BC

Sandmason and honeycomb tubeworms

These worms (Family Sabellariidae) prefer to live in high-energy areas where the current or waves can provide them with abundant food along with sediment for building their tubes. The body shape is quite bizarre, but divers will only see the anterior ends protruding from the tubes. Close inspection may reveal various small structures, including opercula (trap doors) of modified bristles, branchiae (gills), buccal (feeding) tentacles and palps (anterior feeding appendages). These worms are thought to be suspension feeders that use their buccal tentacles to generate feeding currents and trap fine particles in boluses (mucus balls), before transporting them to their mouths. Both the buccal tentacles and grooved palps have the dexterity to capture and manipulate large particles. Depending on the type of particles gathered, the worms eat them, eject them or use them for tube building. In some areas of the world, sandmason and honeycomb tubeworms have built extensive reef systems that have had considerable impact on beach profiles, wave patterns and sediment distribution. Considering that their life span may be three to 10 years, their larvae can swim about in the water column for up to two months and 12,000 to 15,000 mature worms can live per sq metre (10 sq ft), their impact can be very significant! On subtidal reefs the two species pictured can apparently occupy distinct positions: the cemented sandmason tubeworm (AN69) forms the upper part of the reef and the stone-cave sandmason tubeworm (AN70) inhabits the lower portion.

AN69. ►CEMENTED SANDMASON TUBEWORM, cemented tubeworm, cemented colonial tubeworm, amber-topped honeycomb worm, California honeycomb worm, honeycomb worm
Neosabellaria cementarium, *Sabellaria cementarium*
to 7 cm (2.8 in) long, 0.6 cm (0.2 in) wide
tube to 7.5 cm (3 in) long
colonies of indeterminate, irregular size
n. Alaska to s. California
intertidal to 80 m (263 ft)
This species incorporates sand grains into its tubes and cements them, more often than not, to neighbouring tubes, ultimately forming intricate honeycomb structures. This tubeworm can be found in clusters of only a few individuals to massive gregarious colonies. A tube-building organ beneath each worm's mouth secretes the cement—composed primarily of protein materials, similar to a silk protein. The worm often collects and cements pebbles and shell fragments to the outside of the tube. The dark operculum (trap door), characteristically consisting of three rows of golden paleae (modified head bristles), plugs the tube when the worm withdraws. Each row of paleae has a distinctive, ornate shape. Note the mauve-coloured, ciliated (hairy) feeding tentacles in the photograph.
Keystone, Whidbey Island, n. Washington

AN70. ►STONE-CAVE SANDMASON TUBEWORM
Idanthyrsus saxicavus, *Idanthyrsus armatus, Idanthyrsus ornamentatus, Pallasia johnstoni*
tube to 9.5 cm (3.7 in) long
Japan, Siberia, n. Alaska to Mexico
intertidal to 150 m (492 ft)
Instead of a tentacular crown of "pretty plumes," this worm has a bilobed operculum (trap door), obvious in photograph A as pink wing-like structures protruding from its tube. Two types of golden-brown paleae

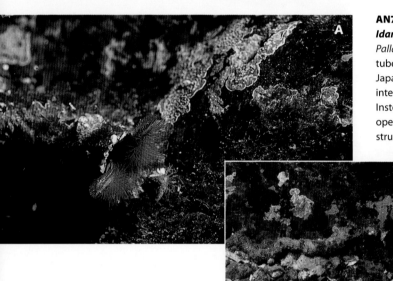

(modified head bristles) are arranged on the crown in an inner and outer row. The paleae in the outer row are coarsely barbed, and when the head projects outside the tube, a diver's first impression might be that the barbed operculum looks like a spiny "claw." The well-camouflaged tube, composed of sand grains and bits of shell embedded in a concrete-like matrix, is firmly attached to the substrate (photograph B). The tube is like a cave with only one opening. When the worm is contracted inside its tube, the trap door almost seals it off.
A B Lime Kiln, San Juan Island, n. Washington

Spaghetti-worms

The term "spaghetti-worms" is used to describe members of this family (Terebellidae) for good reason: their long buccal (feeding) tentacles resemble strands of spaghetti. These tentacles are grooved, and the edges of the grooves are lined with cilia (hairs). A thin layer of mucus secreted in the groove picks up fine surface particles and with the aid of the beating cilia, tiny packages of food-laden sediment are delivered to the mouth. So what's on the menu? Food items include detritus (organic material), unicellular algae and various small invertebrates. Using the cilia, the highly elastic tentacles engage in ciliary creeping—dancing and extending over the sediment surface, often causing the tentacles themselves to appear to be worms!

The spaghetti-worms are abundant, often very large and conspicuous marine worms. Some are known to host their commensal polychaete brethren, such as various scaleworm species. Mature male and female spaghetti-worms cannot be distinguished until just before spawning, when the developing gametes take on different colours: females loaded with eggs can be pinkish to greenish; males tend to be cream-coloured. A variety of modes of reproduction are known to occur, from broadcast (free) spawning of gametes, to brooding embryos inside the tube or inside a gelatinous mass.

AN71. ▶BASKET-TOP SPAGHETTI-WORM, basket-top tubeworm, fibre-tube worm, fibre tube worm, elongate terebellid worm
Pista elongata
to 21 cm (8.3 in) long
Japan, BC to s. California, Panama
intertidal to 63 m (207 ft)
The lifeless tube is misleading to an uninitiated observer. Looking much like a fibrous basket or reticulate, sponge-like network of fibres, the basket-top is comprised of two thick lobes. The basket-top of the worm in the photograph is festooned with green sea urchin spines (EC50). The lower part of the tube, where the worm resides, is coated with shell fragments and pebbles. Is the purpose of this extravagant tube solely to camouflage and protect the worm in its barren rocky habitat, or to increase its access to food? The worm extends its long tentacles through the basket to gather food particles selectively from the substrate. The basket-top may also function as a sieve, filtering out particles brought by currents. Elevating the tube above the rocky substrate may provide the elongate, and tree-like branchiae (gills), hidden inside the basket, with a good supply of oxygenated water.
Sutton Islets, Egmont, s. BC

AN72. ▶FRINGED-HOOD SPAGHETTI-WORM, tentacle-feeding worm
Pista pacifica
to 37 cm (14.6 in) long
BC to s. California
intertidal
Found in muddy sand substrates, this worm constructs an unmistakable tube: a vertical sandy tube that terminates in a bent, triangular hood fringed with numerous hanging "mini-tubes." Though it is the feeding tentacles that search the substrate for food particles, the hood likely also helps to trap particles suspended in the water column. Presumably the tube also protects the worm. The photograph features three tubes, but unfortunately, none reveal the beautiful red-wine colour of the worm's body. As with the basket-top spaghetti-worm (AN71), the worm is not usually seen unless it is excavated completely from the substrate and then removed from the tube.
Sekiu, Olympic coast, n. Washington

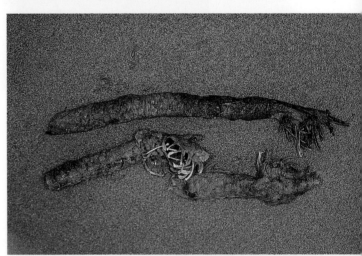

AN73. ▶BROWN INTERTIDAL SPAGHETTI-WORM
Eupolymnia heterobranchia, Eupolymnia crescentis,* Lanice heterobranchia
to at least 13 cm (5.1 in) long
Alaska to Mexico
intertidal
Look under rocks resting on coarse sand or shell hash (crushed shell) to find this worm's parchment-like tube, which is distinctively reinforced with sand grains and adorned with fragments of shell and sea urchin spines. Its tube appears to be a favourite retreat for various creatures such as the tube-dwelling pea crab (AR119) and the bat star commensal worm (AN28). This species' body is greenish to dark brown, with perhaps a hint of red, and its tentacles are brown. Like other spaghetti-worms, this one presumably feeds on detritus, microscopic algae and other small organisms that its flexible tentacles can readily manoeuvre from the surface of the sediment.
*There is still confusion in the literature with regard to the brown intertidal spaghetti-worm and several similar species. It may or may not be synonomous with *Eupolymnia crescentis, Lanice heterobranchia* or both. Only the examination of many more specimens, from many different depths, will resolve this dilemma.
Ucluth Peninsula, w. Vancouver Island, s. BC

AN74. ►CURLY-HEAD SPAGHETTI-WORM, coarse-tubed pink spaghetti worm, spaghetti worm, curly terebellid worm, curly terebellid, terebellid worm, shell binder worm, shell-binder worm, hairy gilled worm, hairy-headed terebellid worm
Thelepus crispus
to 28 cm (11 in) long
Alaska to s. California, India
mid- to low intertidal
This species is often one of the most common intertidal spaghetti-worms. However, because of competition for food, these worms appear to space themselves in the sediment carefully so as to avoid touching each other's feeding tentacles. An individual worm has three pairs of branchiae (gills), each with many slender, finger-like filaments. These are not tree-shaped like the gills found in the robust spaghetti-worm (AN75). Without their bright red colour (hemoglobin pigments), the gills would be difficult to distinguish from a multitude of curly, flesh-coloured feeding tentacles.

The curly-head spaghetti-worm's tube is composed of coarse sand and pebbles cemented together over a rigid membranous lining. Photograph A shows the feeding tentacles that, on their own, could represent any number of the spaghetti-worms. Photograph B shows the pink-brown bodies of two curly-head spaghetti-worms exposed at low tide.

Other Pacific Northwest species include the ►ringlet spaghetti-worm, *Thelepus cincinnatus*, the ►Japanese spaghetti-worm, *Thelepus japonicus*, the ►hooked spaghetti-worm, *Thelepus hamatus*, and the ►bristled spaghetti-worm, *Thelepus setosus*.

A Anderson Bay, Texada Island, s. BC
B Ucluth Peninsula, w. Vancouver Island, s. BC

AN75. ►ROBUST SPAGHETTI-WORM
Neoamphitrite robusta, *Amphitrite robusta*, *Amphitrite scionides dux*
to 15 cm (6 in) long
Alaska to s. California
intertidal to 1,980 m (6,496 ft)
The ivory-white feeding tentacles of this worm protrude from beneath the large, flap-like tentacular membrane visible in the photograph. The tentacles are an easy indicator of any spaghetti-worm, but distinguishing the features of the various species is more complicated. There are three pairs of arborescent branchiae (tree-shaped gills), but these are often intertwined in the tentacles. Subtle structural variations in body parts must be discerned to determine the different species of spaghetti-worms. The characteristic tube of this large, robust worm has very thick walls of mud.
Green Bay, Agamemnon Channel, s. BC

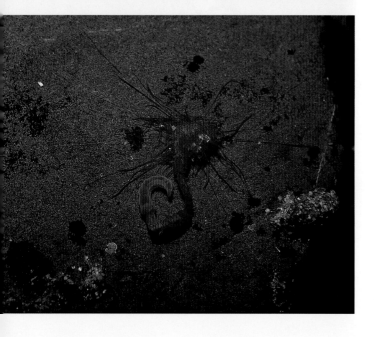
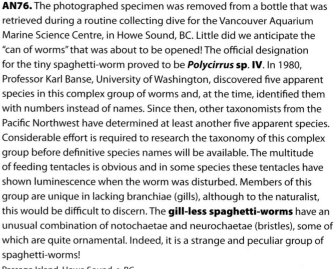

AN76. The photographed specimen was removed from a bottle that was retrieved during a routine collecting dive for the Vancouver Aquarium Marine Science Centre, in Howe Sound, BC. Little did we anticipate the "can of worms" that was about to be opened! The official designation for the tiny spaghetti-worm proved to be ***Polycirrus* sp. IV**. In 1980, Professor Karl Banse, University of Washington, discovered five apparent species in this complex group of worms and, at the time, identified them with numbers instead of names. Since then, other taxonomists from the Pacific Northwest have determined at least another five apparent species. Considerable effort is required to research the taxonomy of this complex group before definitive species names will be available. The multitude of feeding tentacles is obvious and in some species these tentacles have shown luminescence when the worm was disturbed. Members of this group are unique in lacking branchiae (gills), although to the naturalist, this would be difficult to discern. The **gill-less spaghetti-worms** have an unusual combination of notochaetae and neurochaetae (bristles), some of which are quite ornamental. Indeed, it is a strange and peculiar group of spaghetti-worms!
Passage Island, Howe Sound, s. BC

AN77. ▶GRAFT-HEADED SPAGHETTI-WORM
Scionella japonica
to 8 cm (3.2 in) long
Japan, BC to s. California
intertidal to 105 m (345 ft)
When the soft, thick, muddy tube of this specimen was opened, a colourful worm was found inside. The body was bright orange and was packed with what appeared to be the developing eggs of a female. The common name refers to the graft-like incisions around the anterior edge of the head with twig-like branchiae (gills) that appear as "newly inserted branches." The muddy tube of the graft-headed spaghetti-worm is sporadically encountered as unwanted bycatch in shrimp trawl nets. By contrast, the worm is no doubt popular with the many large bottom-dwelling predators.
Mouth of Fraser River, Strait of Georgia, s. BC

Three-section tubeworms

Three-section tubeworms (Family Chaetopteridae) have fragile bodies with three highly modified regions or sections: anterior (responsible for tube secretion and having tube-cutting bristles), middle (with surface of back specialized for feeding) and posterior (designed for gamete development). These unique suspension feeders strain seawater through mucus bags—a method that is very rare among invertebrates. For example, in the U-shaped parchment tubeworm (AN81), large, wing-like notopodia (dorsal branches of appendages) in the middle of the body secrete one large mucus bag within which suspended particles in the seawater are trapped. A cupule (small, cup-like structure) holds the tail end of the bag and, at short intervals, rolls the filled mucus bag up into a food bolus (ball). Posterior to the cupule, large fan-like notopodia that act like suction pumps or pistons move the water into and through the parchment tube. This action forces the water to flow through the mucus bag. Periodically the movement of water is reversed to assist the cilia (hairs) in the dorsal groove to transport the bolus forward to the mouth. For a U-shaped parchment tubeworm, the entire procedure of bag secretion and ball production takes approximately 18 minutes to complete. For the jointed three-section tubeworm (AN78), the process takes anywhere from 30 seconds to two minutes.

AN78. ▶JOINTED THREE-SECTION TUBEWORM, jointed tubeworm, jointed tube worm, jointed-tube worm
Spiochaetopterus costarum, *Leptochaetopterus pottsi*, *Telepsavus costarum*, *Spiochaetopterus costarum pottsi*, incorrect: *Telepsavis costarum*
to 48 cm (19 in) long
tube at least 63 cm (25 in) long, 3 mm (0.1 in) diameter
Japan, s. Alaska to s. California, n. Atlantic Ocean
intertidal to 150 m (492 ft)
Tubes of this worm are transparent, chitinous (tough, protective) and unbranched, with regular nodes or annulations (rings). Photograph A shows a close-up of the two long palps protruding from the tube. Their primary function is to remove waste products from the tube and to keep the tube clear of obstruction. The jointed three-section tubeworm feeds using a small-scale version of the method used by the U-shaped parchment tubeworm (AN81), detailed in "Three-section tubeworms," above. The jointed three-section tubeworm, however, produces at least eight tiny mucus bags, arranged in sequence between the dorsal appendages. Both the jointed three-section tubeworm and the prolific three-section tubeworm (AN79) use their cilia (hairs) to generate water current through their tubes. Photograph B features groups of jointed three-section tubeworms in their sandy environment.

A Point Cowan, Bowen Island, s. BC. Charlie Gibbs photograph
B Uganda Passage, Cortes Island, s. BC

AN79. ▶PROLIFIC THREE-SECTION TUBEWORM
Phyllochaetopterus prolifica
to 6 cm (2.4 in) long
tube to 15 cm (6 in) long, 0.2 cm (0.1 in) diameter
BC to s. California
intertidal to 457 m (1,500 ft)
Found among rocks or on rocky outcrops, this tubeworm forms massive colonies of entangled parchment-like tubes. These opaque tubes are long, sinuous and branched, although some tubes can be 15 cm (6 in) long before branching is evident. Newly formed sections of the tubes may also have weak, irregular annulations (rings). True to its name, this worm is prolific, both sexually and asexually. Immature worms readily fragment asexually and regenerate new individuals that may produce auxiliary branches from existing parent tubes. Such tightly matted colonies are havens for a host of tiny creatures, including juvenile sea stars. The prolific three-section tubeworm feeds using eight or more small mucus bags in a sequence to trap its food (see "Three-section tubeworms, p. 159), but it may adjust this method slightly. If it detects an increase in the amount of suspended particles while filtering seawater, it may produce an additional mucus rope. Extending well into the posterior part of the tube, this rope provides more surface area to collect particles not strained out by the mucus bags.
Ucluth Peninsula, w. Vancouver Island, s. BC

AN80. ▶TANGLED-STRAW THREE-SECTION TUBEWORM
Phyllochaetopterus claparedii
tube to 15 cm (6 in) long (a documented length of 1 m/39 in exists)
tube to 5 mm (0.2 in) diameter
matting colonies indeterminate, irregular in size
Japan, Philippines, Siberia, BC
subtidal, 14–3,100 m (46–10,171 ft)
A sandy underwater landscape that may appear devoid of life sometimes features extensive fields of this tubeworm. These stiff, string-like tubes may themselves appear lifeless as they protrude from the sand, because the heads of the worms are tiny and difficult to see. The chitinous (tough, protective), shiny metallic tubes of the tangled-straw tubeworm are noticeably greater in diameter than those of the prolific three-section tubeworm (AN79).
Helen Point, Mayne Island, s. BC

AN81. ▶U-SHAPED PARCHMENT TUBEWORM, parchment tube worm
Chaetopterus* species complex, formerly *Chaetopterus 'variopedatus'*
at least 25 cm (10 in) long, 1 cm (0.4 in) wide
tube at least 50 cm (20 in) long
BC to Washington, s. California to Mexico
intertidal to subtidal
The tips of this strange, U-shaped tube protruding from a sandy substrate are often the only indication of this worm's presence. When buried, the tube provides the worm with horizontal living quarters as well as two narrower, vertical shafts—one inhalant and one exhalant—leading to the surface. The parchment-like tube, produced by ventral (lower-surface) glands on the worm's anterior, is expanded and extended as the worm grows. It is not uncommon to find a tube that has three branches or even multiple tips. This alternative "design" may result from a worm that has encountered obstacles in the substrate, such as a large shell, which prohibits regular tube building. At this point, the worm creates a branch to circumvent the obstacle. Near the worm's head are heavy specialized chaetae (bristles) with blade-like edges, used to cut and modify tube walls. Such blades are characteristic of all of the three-section tubeworms. An empty tube lying on top of the substrate is likely either an abandoned, non-functional branch of the original U-shaped tube, or evidence of a deceased individual.
*The U-shaped parchment tubeworm, once considered a single cosmopolitan species, is now recognized as a complex of at least

several species—and perhaps as many as 10 North Atlantic forms. The
►collared parchment tubeworm, *Mesochaetopterus taylori*, and the U-
shaped parchment tubeworm are probably the two largest three-section
tubeworms living in the Northwest Pacific.

Saltery Bay, Sunshine Coast, s. BC

Worm tubes and other vermiforms

Periodically the observant beachcomber or diver may encounter a
small tubular structure that has been produced by an unknown Pacific
Northwest organism. Whether empty or occupied by a secondary tenant,
the original "builder's" identity is often a mystery. The assumption that
some species of an annelid worm is responsible might not be correct, as
other marine creatures also create tubes. These four photographs illustrate
this phenomenon.

Photograph A shows a tube reinforced with sand grains that was
empty, hard and cemented to the accompanying clamshell. These tube
sections appear to be constructed in a very similar manner to those of the
sandmason tubeworms, p. 155.

Point Cowan, Bowen Island, s. BC

Photograph B shows an empty tube festooned with boot sponge
spicules (PO9/10) that are carefully woven into its delicate structure.
Perhaps this is the handiwork of a species of quillworm, p. 138.

Agamemnon Channel, Nelson Island, s. BC

Photograph C shows a thin-bored tubular structure coiled around the
central stem of a hydroid. Its contents were examined and nothing was
revealed to suggest that it was a polychaete's tube or even some form of
"egg case" produced by another marine organism. There are many unusual
forms in the benthic marine environment that are still unknown or have an
unresolved identity. This appears to be one of them.

Annis Point, Kunghit Island, n. BC

Without doubt, photograph D features a section of a large,
reproductively mature polychaete worm, but most of the body is missing,
including the head. The long extensions of the parapodia (appendages)
would suggest that it was part of a giant fleshy scaleworm (AN38), whose
elytra (shield-like scales) are missing. Detailed examination, however,
reveals a hidden clue. When the parapodia are dissected, tiny, flattened,
comb-like chaetae (bristles) are embedded in the tissue. These structures
are not found in scaleworms but are located in calcareous tubeworms, p.
147. In this case, the fragment probably came from a rather large calcareous
tubeworm species.

Vancouver Aquarium Marine Science Centre, Stanley Park, s. BC. Donna Gibbs
photograph

SPOON WORMS *Phylum ECHIURA*

At the anterior end of an unsegmented, sac-like body, each echiuran has a grooved and extendable proboscis, a distinctive structure whose general spoon-like shape gives the group its common name. A pair of internal anal sacs, located near the terminal anus, further defines each echiuran.

A transient developmental segmentation along with the presence of a few setae (bristles) hints at an ancestor in common with the annelids (segmented worms).

Reclusive and preferring to burrow in sediments or lie in crevices, the spoon worms are particulate feeders that secrete mucus to envelop their food.

At least 18 echiurans live in the Pacific Northwest.

EH1. ▶PINK SPOON WORM
Aryhnchite pugettensis, *Aryhnchite californicus*
▶to 2.5 cm (1 in) long
▶BC to Washington
▶subtidal to at least 100 m (330 ft)
This specimen was trawled from a muddy bottom at a depth of approximately 65 m (200 ft). Apparently the species lives nearly completely buried in the substrate and, like other spoon worms, probably creates a burrow. A giant Californian species shares its burrow with other smaller creatures in a "group home" scenario.
Mouth of Fraser River, Strait of Georgia, s. BC

PHORONIDS *Phylum PHORONIDA*

The worm-like phoronid body is neither segmented nor bristled. Most conspicuous and definitive is a horseshoe-shaped crown of tentacles that surrounds the mouth. From there, a U-shaped digestive tract begins and loops through the body, culminating in an anus just below the tentacular crown, formally designated a lophophore. This anatomy can be seen in the large green phoronids (PH2) shown in the photograph (by Charlie Gibbs). Dwelling in self-made tubes, these filter-feeding creatures superficially resemble miniature polychaete worms of the feather-duster variety (see p. 151).

Only six species of phoronids live in the marine waters of the Pacific Northwest.

PH1. ▶WHITE COLONIAL PHORONID, twining phoronid
Phoronis ijimai, *Phoronopsis ijimai, Phoronopsis vancouverensis, Phoronis vancouverensis*
to 7.6 cm (3 in) long
colonies to indeterminate, irregular size
China, Japan, BC to California
intertidal to subtidal
Superficially, a cluster of this species resembles a small patch of tiny tubeworms. On close inspection, though, a diver should be able to note that the "crown" structure of each individual is quite different from that of a tubeworm.
Agamemnon Channel, Nelson Island, s. BC

PH2. ►LARGE GREEN PHORONID
Phoronopsis harmeri, *Phoronopsis viridis ?, Phoronopsis pacifica*
to 10 cm (4 in) long
BC to s. Oregon
intertidal to subtidal
Tiny plumes protruding from sand or shell-hash (crushed shell) bottoms indicate a field of many specimens. Phoronids are sometimes referred to as phoronid "worms" because of their elongate shape, but they are not actually worms at all. Because they possess lophophores, they are more closely related to the bryozoans (below).
Calvert Island, Hakai Passage, c. BC

MOSS ANIMALS *Phylum BRYOZOA (aka Ectoprocta)*

Existing as a colony of very tiny, nearly independent individuals called zooids, a bryozoan or moss animal is often symmetrical of pattern. The name "moss animals" results from the resemblance between encrusting bryozoans and thin patches of moss found on rock. Colonies are sessile (attached) and through asexual budding or "cloning" of zooids may spread out mat-like or stack up like a mini high-rise building, depending on the species. Superficially some bryozoans resemble other, very different organisms such as hydroids, hydrocorals or even seaweeds!

Three basic colony designs, shown here, are noticeable to the naturalist: encrusting or flat (photograph A, orange encrusting bryozoan BZ7), erect, branching and flexible (articulate) (photograph B, stick bryozoan BZ18) and erect, branching and calcified (inarticulate) (photograph C, fluted bryozoan BZ24).

Each zooid secretes an often highly ornamented house (chamber) made of calcium carbonate—species-specific of design—around itself. Normally the worm-like zooid body extends about halfway out of the house, revealing a ring of tentacles surrounding the lophophore. The filter-feeding lophophore uses millions of tiny beating hairs or cilia to propel tiny particles of food (such as bacteria, tiny algae and detritus) toward the gullet. The mouth is inside the incomplete circle of tentacles, and the anus is located outside and below—thus the name "ectoproct" (outside anus).

At least 300 species of bryozoans or moss animals live in the marine waters of the Pacific Northwest.

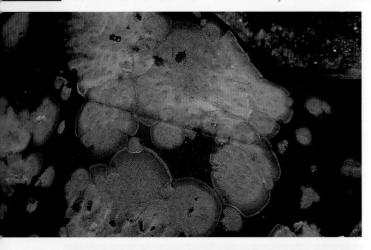

BZ1. KELP-ENCRUSTING BRYOZOAN, kelp encrusting bryozoan, kelp lace bryozoan, lacy-crust bryozoan, kelp lacy bryozoan, white-encrusting bryozoan, kelp lace, lacy crust, encrusting bryozoan, jackfrost bryozoan, tree bryozoan
Membranipora serrilamella, *Membranipora membranacea,* Membranipora villosa ?*
to 20 cm (8 in) across
s. Alaska to n. Mexico
intertidal to 180 m (600 ft)
Colony patch sizes increase all summer and may collectively all but engulf an alga. When the alga host dies, the attached specimens are doomed. However, this animal also encrusts other hard substrates, assuring long-term species survival.
*Originally used, this name correctly applies to another species not found in the Pacific Ocean.
Quarry Bay, Nelson Island, s. BC

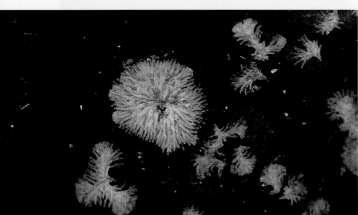

BZ2. CORAL BRYOZOANS
***Lichenopora* spp.**
▶to 2.5 cm (1 in) across
BC to California
intertidal and subtidal
Elevated tubes give a "deep" or hoar frost look to the small, generally circular colonies that most noticeably sprinkle various kelp species. The photograph shows various stages in colony development and represents one of two nearly identical species, *Lichenopora verrucaria* and *Lichenopora novae-zelandiae*.
Moore Point, Francis Peninsula, s. BC

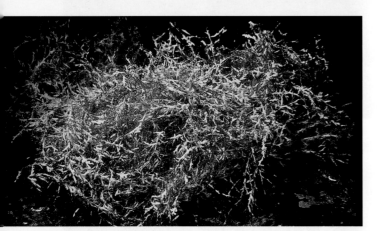

BZ3. ▶GLASSY-WHITE ENCRUSTING BRYOZOAN
Celleporella hyalina, *Hippothoa hyalina, Schizoporella hyalina*
indeterminate, irregular size
Atlantic Ocean, Alaska to n. Mexico
intertidal to subtidal
Colonies of this species usually grow over solid substrates in a thin layer. As shown overgrowing a hydroid in the photograph, this bryozoan may also produce thicker nodules. Inspection of this creature under a microscope would undoubtedly reveal numerous micro-predators.
Egmont Marina, Egmont, s. BC

BZ4. ▶PURPLE ENCRUSTING BRYOZOAN
Disporella separata
▶to at least 15 cm (6 in) across
▶BC to Washington, s. California
▶subtidal, below 10 m (33 ft)
Rock-hard to the touch with noticeable sculpture, this obvious species is found in high-current, rocky habitats. Although usually a small circular colony, its unusual royal purple hue attracts attention amid other brightly coloured encrusting life.
Turn Island, San Juan Channel, n. Washington

BZ5. ▶YELLOW ENCRUSTING BRYOZOAN
Rhynchozoon rostratum, Lepralia rostrata
▶to 7.5 cm (3 in) across
▶Alaska to Panama, Galapagos Islands
intertidal to 200 m (660 ft)
Distinctive markings on the thick, hard colony will aid in this species' recognition. However, precise identification—including separation from the very similar *Rhynchozoon tumulosum*—is a much more rigorous process, beyond the abilities of all but a few. Fortunately, biologist Valerie Macdonald and her staff at *Biologica Environmental Services*, in Victoria, BC, were able to provide us with this expertise.

Slip Point, Olympic coast, n. Washington

BZ6. DERBY HAT BRYOZOAN, rosy bryozoan, rose-colored bryozoan
Eurystomella bilabiata, Lepralia bilabiata
to 5 cm (2 in) across
s. Alaska to n. Mexico
intertidal to 237 m (782 ft)
The common name "derby hat bryozoan" results from the shape of the operculum (trap door) that protects the zooid after it has withdrawn into its chamber—a feature that may or may not be obvious, depending upon the naturalist's eyesight. A hand lens carried in a backpack or dive bag is always useful. Regardless, row upon row of these deep red derby or bowler hat-shaped opercula show against a pink background. Older, central portions are often white, indicating lifeless portions of a colony.

Moore Point, Francis Peninsula, s. BC

BZ7. ORANGE ENCRUSTING BRYOZOAN, orange crust bryozoan
Schizoporella unicornis, Lepralia unicornis
to 5 cm (2 in) across
virtually worldwide, BC to South America
intertidal to 60 m (200 ft)
Likely introduced from Japan with the Pacific oyster (MC50), this species has adapted well and is now the dominant encrusting bryozoan in much of the Pacific Northwest. The integrity of the Pacific Northwest's flora and fauna continues to be an issue, as an increasing number of invaders have established themselves. Long-term effects? An unfolding mystery.

Tilly Point, s. Pender Island, s. BC

BZ8. Perhaps following in the wake of the previous species is the **BLACK AND RED ENCRUSTING BRYOZOAN**, *Watersipora cucullata*. While visiting the John Wayne Marina, near Sequim, n. Washington, in the summer of 2004, Jennifer Ingram of Port Coquitlam, BC, noticed this attractive species growing in abundance on the floats. Photographs were forwarded to David Denning on Saltspring Island, BC, who kindly identified the animal. The find verified this non-native species' presence in the Pacific Northwest, but the where, when, why and how of the story await further investigation.

John Wayne Marina, Sequim, n. Washington

BZ9. TUBEWORM FUZZ
Bowerbankia **sp.**
irregular, indeterminate
BC to Washington
subtidal
Though most obvious as a skim on feather-duster worm tubes (AN64–65), it also coats solid surfaces. This species and its ilk spread by a network of stolons so tightly packed that a colony's growth pattern is not readily recognizable to the naturalist.
The identification of encrusting bryozoans is a difficult task not usually possible without access to specimens. A modest selection of the nearly 200 species was photographed without requisite specimen sampling; these appear at the end of this section.
Surge Narrows, Maurelle Island, s. BC

BZ10. SPIRAL BRYOZOAN, stiff stalk bryozoan, California moss animal, Pacific branching bryozoan
Bugula californica, *Bugula pacifica* ?
to 7.5 cm (3 in) tall
BC to Galapagos Islands, Hawaii
subtidal to 400 m (1,320 ft)
Each colony resembles a tiny evergreen tree—in shape, but not colour. Each colony is the result of budding or cloning from the original individual, itself having developed from a planktonic larva that settled—appropriately called the ancestrula. In the case of this species, the process is programmed as a spiral growth pattern.
Beg Islands, Barkley Sound, s. BC

BZ11. ▶PARASOL BRYOZOAN
Caulibugula californica, *Stirparia californica*, *Stirpariella californica*
▶to 3.5 cm (1.5 in)
BC to n. Mexico
intertidal to 231 m (762 ft)
Reminiscent of a miniature wind-blown umbrella, this distinctive species apparently prefers low-current, often silty locales. At such sites the parasol bryozoan is readily seen by an observant diver. Would it be noticed in high-current locales that are so often densely packed with life? Would it even exist there? This is yet to be determined.
Grey Rocks Island, Indian Arm, s. BC

BZ12. FAN BRYOZOAN
Dendrobeania murrayana
to 7.5 cm (3 in) tall
n. Alaska to n. Washington
subtidal to 140 m (462 ft)
Small, drab and growing amid silt, the fan bryozoan is often overlooked. It is distinguished by strap-like branches. When inspecting this animal, the naturalist may notice flexibility or lack of stiffness, which indicates much less calcification than in many of the following "hard to the touch" species. Under a microscope or hand lens, a living colony shows many tiny avicularia (individuals), which resemble bird beaks snapping protectively.
Turn Island, San Juan Channel, n. Washington

BZ13. LEAF CRUST BRYOZOAN, sea lichen bryozoan, sea-lichen
bryozoan, sea lichen, lichen bryozoan, leaf bryozoan, sea mat bryozoan
Dendrobeania lichenoides, Flustra lichenoides, Dendrobeania laxa?
frond to 2.5 cm (1 in) across
colony of indeterminate, irregular size
c. Alaska to c. California
subtidal to 100 m (330 ft)
The encrusting growth of this species with its upcurled edges likely
reminds the knowledgeable observer of terrestrial lichens.

Turn Island, San Juan Channel, n. Washington

BZ14. ▶WHITE TUFT BRYOZOANS
Crisia spp.
to 2.5 cm (1 in) tall
BC to Washington
subtidal
Many species of bryozoan are difficult to
identify simply by looking at their overall
structure. White tuft bryozoans have
smooth, white branches that are rather
heavily calcified, and the tiny holes from
which the zooids protrude are circular
and have no opercula (covering flaps)—
distinguishing features most noticeable
under some form of magnification.

A Sutton Islets, Egmont, s. BC

B Dillon Rock, Shushartie Bay, c. BC

BZ15. SPINY LEATHER BRYOZOAN, branch-spined bryozoan,
branched-spine bryozoan
*Flustrellidra corniculata, Flustrella cornicula, Alcyonidium
spinifera, Alcyonidium cervicorne, Flustrella cervicornis*
to 10 cm (4 in) tall
Alaska to n. California
intertidal to 75 m (250 ft)
The spiny leather bryozoan superficially resembles algae and is
usually found in close proximity to them. The tiny forked spines
are "leathery" and protrude from light yellow, flattened lobes.
This distinctive bryozoan lives on wave-swept outer-coast shores
and may be found at low tide by the adventurous beachcomber.

Frank Island, w. Vancouver Island, s. BC

BZ16. SMOOTH LEATHER BRYOZOAN
Alcyonidium pedunculatum
▶to 30 cm (12 in) tall
Alaska to c. BC
subtidal
Smaller colonies often appear pale pink or yellowish and not nearly as
"staghorn-like" as the specimen illustrated. This nondescript species
frequently confuses divers, who may think it is a sponge or even a plant.
Each tiny individual of the colony uses its minute tentacles to capture food
and therefore is considered a filter feeder.
The ▶gelatinous leather bryozoan, *Alcyonidium gelatinosum,* is a similar but
encrusting species.

Booker Lagoon, Broughton Island, c. BC

BZ17. SPINDLY RABBIT-EAR BRYOZOAN
Cellaria diffusa, *Cellularia diffusa*
to 10 cm (4 in) tall
BC to n. Mexico
intertidal to 216 m (713 ft)
The growth pattern, as emphasized at the tips, is reminiscent of the televison antenna called "rabbit ears" that graced 1950s sets. Usually living in low-current locales, this bryozoan has longer nodes (branch sections) than the stick bryozoan (BZ18) and they are circular rather than elliptical in cross-section. Promising research has shown that some bryozoans produce anti-cancer compounds.

Croker Island, Indian Arm, s. BC

BZ18. STICK BRYOZOAN
Microporina borealis
▶to 15 cm (6 in) across
circumpolar, n. Alaska to n. Washington
subtidal to 400 m (1,320 ft)
Though similar to the spindly rabbit-ear bryozoan (BZ17) in its growth pattern, this one is much bushier, more colourful and therefore more obvious. In most cases a bryozoan is a hermaphrodite, with each colony possessing both male and female capabilities, though fertilization is usually inter-colonial.

Boas Islet, Hakai Passage, c. BC

A

B

BZ19. LATTICE-WORK BRYOZOAN, lacy orange bryozoan, lacy bryozoan, lace-coral bryozoan, lace coral bryozoan, coralline bryozoan, lace coral, calcareous coralline bryozoan
Phidolopora pacifica, *Phidolopora labiata*, *Retepora pacifica*
to 22 cm (8.5 in) across
n. Alaska to Peru, Galapagos Islands
subtidal to 200 m (660 ft)
The peach-coloured colonies are very fragile, often with older central portions that are lifeless and white. Large colonies, as featured in photograph A, often have reuniting branches. A small, all-white lattice-work bryozoan specimen, common in protected inshore waters, is shown in photograph B.

A Tyler Rock, Barkley Sound, s. BC
B Point Cowan, Howe Sound, s. BC

BZ20. NORTHERN STAGHORN BRYOZOAN, staghorn bryozoan, false coral

Heteropora pacifica, *Tretocycloecia pacifica*, *Heteropora neozelanica*, possibly equivalent: *Heteropora magna*

▶to 45 cm (18 in) across
n. Alaska to s. California
subtidal to 27 m (90 ft)

On seeing northern staghorn bryozoan for the first time, most divers misidentify it as a coral, which it superficially resembles. Although it is highly calcified like coral, it is a very different animal. Photograph A features a typical yellow colony; photograph B records what is likely an unusual specimen—in both colour and shape.

A Outer Narrows, Slingsby Channel, c. BC
B Iphigenia Point, Langara Island, n. BC

BZ21. DELICATE STAGHORN BRYOZOAN

Heteropora alaskensis, *Heteropora pacifica alaskensis*, *Heteropora pelliculata*

▶to 5 cm (2 in) tall
BC to Oregon
subtidal

This species is usually an inhabitant of low-current locales. Perhaps this accounts for its more spindly and delicate structure, which contrasts with that of the northern staghorn bryozoan (BZ20). Note the pale tan growing tips of this delicate species.

Carlos Island, Gulf Islands, s. BC

BZ22. SOUTHERN STAGHORN BRYOZOAN, white branching bryozoan, coralline bryozoan

Diaperoecia californica, *Idmonea californica*, *Idmonea palmata*

to 25 cm (10 in) across
BC to n. Mexico, Costa Rica
intertidal to 185 m (610 ft)

This species is distinguished by projections created by rows of raised tubular openings along the main branches, and a more fragile makeup than the northern staghorn bryozoan (BZ20)—a species with which this one is often found. Indeed, in some Barkley Sound, BC, locations, they combine to create a coral reef-like ambience.

Laura Point, Mayne Island, s. BC

BZ23. RUSTY BRYOZOAN

Costazia ventricosa

to 15 cm (6 in) across
n. Alaska to n. California
intertidal to 100 m (330 ft)

Orange growing tips on very hard, stubby branches distinguish the rusty bryozoan from the preceding few species. Close inspection also reveals a rough, bumpy texture on these branches. Other creatures, notably the daisy brittle star (EC34), seek shelter in its colonies and may confuse the observer as to what creatures are being seen. Small growths of another, unidentified articulate bryozoan are also evident in the photograph.

Kyen Point, Barkley Sound, s. BC

BZ24. FLUTED BRYOZOAN, fluted coral bryozoan, sculptured bryozoan
Hippodiplosia insculpta, Schizoporella insculpta
▶to 15 cm (6 in) across
Alaska to n. Mexico, Costa Rica
intertidal to 235 m (775 ft)
This "sculpted" bryozoan is recognizable for the distinctive flat, curved branches of its calcium-reinforced colony. Note the yellow growing margins that contrast with the older, darker interior portions. Fluted bryozoan colonies may firmly encrust upon rocky substrates but can also adhere to algae.
Imperial Eagle Channel, Barkley Sound, s. BC

For some reason, conditions present at certain localities in Barkley Sound and other west coast Vancouver Island inlets are conducive for extra large and spectacular formations of the hard "coral-like" species of bryozoans (BZ18–23). Locales such as Kyen Point remind a diver of tropical coral reefs—minus the warm water!

The following two species of flexible, branching bryozoans were encountered and photographed during preparation of this book but were not identified.

BZ25. Undetermined branching bryozoan A. This bushy, flexibly branched bryozoan was found in abundance at a rocky locale subject to strong current at depths of 8–12 m (25–40 ft). Colonies were typically 7.5 cm (3 in) across.
Brooks Peninsula, w. Vancouver Island, c. BC

BZ26. Undetermined branching bryozoan B. Although this specimen has a branching pattern similar to that of the stick bryozoan (BZ18), it is somewhat smaller and quite delicate—subject to breakage when handled. It has been collected at several locales in the Gulf Islands, s. BC, at shallow, scuba-accessible depths.
Laura Point, Mayne Island, s. BC

Many encrusting bryozoans are not readily identified without keys and a powerful magnifying glass or dissecting microscope. Colonies are usually thin and consist of countless minute "boxes" abutting each other. The following selection of unidentified encrusting bryozoans found during the preparation of this book demonstrates that although some species are difficult to identify, their diversity can still be enjoyed and appreciated.

BZ27. Undetermined encrusting bryozoan A
Agamemnon Channel, Nelson Island, s. BC

BZ28. Undetermined encrusting bryozoan B

Point Cowan, Bowen Island, s. BC

BZ29 and **BZ30. Undetermined encrusting bryozoans C** and **D** (two species)

Hutt Island, Howe Sound, s. BC

BZ31. Undetermined encrusting bryozoan E

Hutt Island, Howe Sound, s. BC

BZ32 and **BZ33. Undetermined encrusting bryozoans F** and **G** (two species)

Tongue Point, Olympic coast, n. Washington

BZ34. Undetermined encrusting bryozoan H

Worlcombe Island, Howe Sound, s. BC

BZ35. Undetermined encrusting bryozoan I

Slip Point, Olympic coast, n. Washington

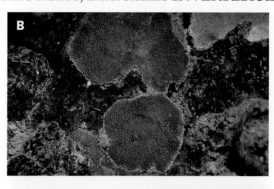

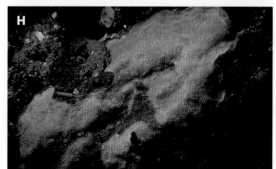

BZ36. Undetermined encrusting bryozoan J (on feather boa kelp, SW34)
Sekiu, Olympic coast, n. Washington

BZ37. Undetermined encrusting bryozoan K
Tongue Point, Olympic coast, n. Washington

BZ38. Undetermined encrusting bryozoan L (on cloud sponge, PO11)
Anderson Bay, Texada Island, s. BC

BZ39. Undetermined encrusting bryozoan M
Frank Island, w. Vancouver Island, s. BC

BZ40. Undetermined encrusting bryozoan N
Egmont Marina, Egmont, s. BC

BZ41 and **BZ42. Undetermined encrusting bryozoans O** and **P** (two species)
Baranof, Baranof Island, s. Alaska

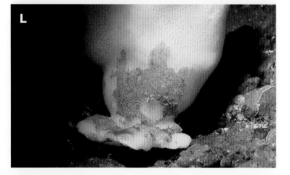

NODDING HEADS *Phylum ENTOPROCTA*

Subject to an "identity crisis," entoprocts so closely resemble bryozoans (moss animals) that the two groups have been lumped together. However, the most significant, distinguishing feature of an entoproct is the placement of its anus, which is located within the ring of feeding tentacles or calyx of each stalked individual. In contrast, the anus of the bryozoan is on the outside.

The many stalks of an entoproct colony bend very readily. This movement, coupled with the ability to roll the tentacles inward, produces a "nodding head"-like motion, hence the group's common name.

At least 13 entoprocts reside in the Pacific Northwest.

EN1. NODDING HEADS
***Barentsia* sp.**
colony to 5 cm (2 in) across
BC to California
intertidal to subtidal
Close inspection of this animal shows the characteristic "head" structure of each individual, which allows it to be distinguished from bryozoans or hydroids. Unlike a bryozoan zooid (individual) the "head" of this animal has no chamber to withdraw into and it can only shrink and curl its tentacles inward.
Quadra Island, Discovery Passage, s BC

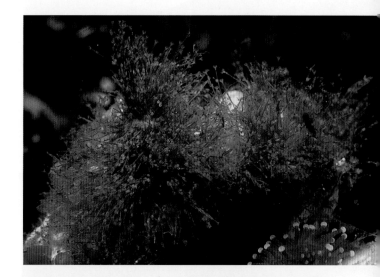

LAMPSHELLS *Phylum BRACHIOPODA*

A brachiopod (lampshell) looks like a small clam or mussel, but the resemblance is only superficial. Each brachiopod has a ventral and a dorsal shell rather than the right and left shells of a bivalve mollusc. Also, unlike clams and mussels, virtually all brachiopods are attached to something solid via a peduncle (stalk, featured in the photograph of a transverse lamp shell, BR1), through either a hole in the ventral shell or a gap between the two shells. Oddly, a lampshell often rotates upon its stalk, orienting itself "upside down" so that the ventral shell is uppermost. Finally, a brachiopod's internal anatomy is based on a large filter-feeding organ called a lophophore. This structure, powered by the movement of cilia (hairs), rests on a delicate calcareous "tray" supported by the ventral shell. A lampshell's anatomy is therefore fundamentally different from that of a clam.

Exclusively marine and solitary, lampshells were dominant in Cretaceous seas some millions of years ago, but today are relatively few in number.

Sixteen species of brachiopods have been documented from the Pacific Northwest. A majority live at great depths and are seldom encountered.

BR1. TRANSVERSE LAMP SHELL, scalloped lamp shell, common lampshell, common Pacific brachiopod, lamp shell, lampshell
Terebratalia transversa, *Terebratalia caurina*
▶to 7.6 cm (3 in) across
n. Alaska to n. Mexico
intertidal to 1,820 m (6,000 ft)
Whether smooth or ribbed, this species can be distinguished by the "smile"-like dip in the central area of shell confluence. The "smile" can be a "frown" if the animal is oriented upside down—an option that this stalked bivalve has!
Retreat Cove, Galiano Island, s. BC

BR2. CALIFORNIA LAMP SHELL, lampshell
Laqueus californicus, *Laqueus californianus*, *Laqueus vancouveriensis*,*
incorrect: *Megerlia jeffreysi*
to 5.3 cm (2.1 in) across
Japan, Alaska to s. California
intertidal to 1,500 m (5,000 ft)
An observant diver may see this oval bivalve rotate on its short, fleshy stalk as it orients to current flow. This mobility allows the animal, a filter feeder, to access its planktonic food source, which in part consists of single-cell algae called diatoms.
*A debate exists as to whether this is a separate species or merely a variation on the theme.
Croker Island, Indian Arm, s. BC

BR3. SNAKE'S HEAD LAMP SHELL, snake's-head lamp shell
Terebratulina unguicula
to 2.5 cm (1 in) across
Siberia, n. Alaska to n. Mexico
intertidal to 850 m (2,805 ft)
The common name refers to the shape of the shells when compared to a serpent's anterior end—at least from somebody's point of view! It is often plentiful when found, and individuals usually show tiny protruding hairs. If a specimen is opening or its shells are gaping, look inside and see the tiny feeding lophophore. The animal usually closes and rotates as one approaches, making such an observation difficult.
Very similar to the snake's head lamp shell (BR3) but rarely encountered is the ▶crenate lamp shell, *Terebratulina crossei*. It grows much larger, has pure white shells and is solitary.
Point Cowan, Bowen Island, s. BC

A

BR4. BLACK LAMP SHELL, black brachiopod
Hemithyris psittacea, *Rhynchonella psittacea*, misspelled: *Hemithiris psittacea*
▶to 2 cm (0.8 in) across
circumboreal, Greenland, Japan, n. Alaska to s. Oregon
intertidal to 400 m (1,320 ft)
Like all brachiopods, this one draws water in through the gaping shells at the sides and passes it over the filter-feeding lophophore before finally expelling it out the front. In photograph B, one can see the hole through which the fleshy peduncle attaches to a solid object. Apparently specimens from greater depths are likely to have coarser ribbing.
A B Vanderbilt Reef, Lynn Canal, s. Alaska

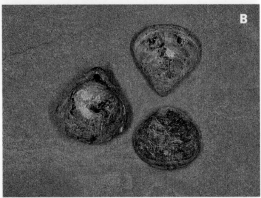

B

BR5. ▶DELICATE LAMP SHELL
Frieleia halli
▶to 2 cm (0.8 in) across
Japan, Alaska to s. California
subtidal, 170–2,200 m (560–7,260 ft)
The transparent or translucent appearance of this species' bi-lobed shape hints at the delicate nature of the shells. Unlike other Pacific Northwest brachiopod species that primarily affix to hard rocky substrate, this species seems to prefer organic material such as sponge or worm tubes as sites for attachment.
Royal British Columbia Museum, Victoria, BC

Each of the lampshells listed above (BR1–5) has two shells that have hinge teeth and sockets that form a joint, allowing for articulation. A second group, known as inarticulate brachiopods, have no such joints and their shells are held together only with body tissues. The flat brachiopod, *Crania californica*, lives in the Pacific Northwest. Because its lower shell is cemented directly to hard substrate, it superficially resembles the green false-jingle (MC54) rather than an articulate brachiopod. It usually lives affixed to large boulders in deep water and is unlikely to be encountered by most naturalists.

CHITONS, BIVALVES, UNIVALVES, BUBBLE SHELLS, NUDIBRANCHS, TUSKSHELLS, OCTOPUS, and SQUID *Phylum MOLLUSCA (Molluska)*

A superficial list includes chitons, mussels, scallops, oysters, clams, cockles, tellins, macomas, piddocks, shipworms, limpets, snails, abalones, dogwinkles, trophons, tritons, periwinkles, bittiums, turbans, olives, wentletraps, tusk shells, octopus, squid, bubble shells, sea hares and the various nudibranchs or sea slugs.

Each member of this large and conspicuous group has a soft, unsegmented body that includes a component called a mantle. This flap acts as a tent that envelops the remaining tissue—see photograph A, rough keyhole limpet (MC153) (upper) and spiny pink scallop (MC43). In the vast majority of species, for at least some portion of their life cycle, the mantle also constantly produces a calcareous secretion that hardens to form one or more shells. A typical snail shell is of hollow construction—see photograph B, wrinkled dogwinkle (MC167)—and provides space for the twisted body of the animal to grow continually. The muscular foot, another basic feature of every mollusc, may have evolved into one of many designs in response to a variety of functions.

Well over 1,600 species of molluscs live in the marine waters of the Pacific Northwest.

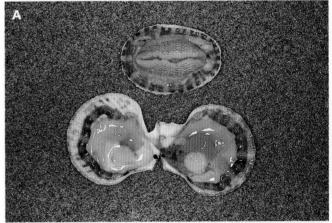

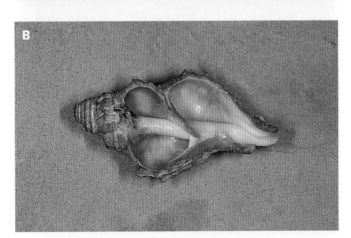

Further Reading:

Behrens, David W., and Alicia Hermosilla, 2005, *Eastern Pacific Nudibranchs—A Guide to the Opisthobranchs from Alaska to Central America*, Sea Challengers, Monterey, CA, 140 pp.

Coan, Eugene V., Paul Valentich Scott and Frank R. Bernard, 2000, *Bivalve Seashells of Western North America*, Santa Barbara Museum of Natural History, Stanford, CA, 764 pp.

Harbo, Rick M., 2001, *Shells and Shellfish*, Harbour Publishing, Madeira Park, BC, 271 pp.

CHITONS

Including mopalias and lepidozonas.

MC1. LINED CHITON, lined red chiton, the lined chiton
Tonicella lineata
to 5 cm (2 in) long
Japan, Siberia, n. Alaska to s. California
intertidal to 90 m (300 ft)
The lined chiton is distinguished by wavy lines found primarily on the extremities of each shell, although sometimes these lines are extremely faint. Seemingly endless colour variations exist. If dislodged, a chiton rolls into a ball to protect its soft underside, in a manner reminiscent of the familiar backyard wood bug.

A Sutton Islets, Egmont, s. BC

B Turn Island, San Juan Channel, n. Washington
C Plumper Islands, Weynton Passage, c. BC

MC2. BLUE-LINE CHITON, blue waved chiton
Tonicella undocaerulea
to 5 cm (2 in) long
c. Alaska to s. California
intertidal to 50 m (165 ft)
Brilliant blue zigzag lines on the orange or pink shells are distinctively attractive, separating it from the lined chiton (MC1). Like most chitons, this species uses its radula (file-like tongue) to scrape food from the substrate.
Kyen Point, Barkley Sound, s. BC

MC3. ▶LOVELY CHITON
Tonicella venusta
to 1.7 cm (0.7 in) long
s. Alaska to n. Mexico
intertidal to 140 m (462 ft)
Zigzag lines on terminal shells and light dash markings on the central areas of middle shells distinguish this species. The lovely chiton has only recently been separated taxonomically from the lined chiton (MC1) by the recognized authority Roger Clark, of Klamath Falls, Oregon. As a consequence, much of its biology remains to be studied—an opportunity for a willing naturalist.
Mountain Point, Ketchikan, s. Alaska. Alan Murray photograph

MC4. WHITE-LINE CHITON, white-lined chiton, red chiton, hidden chiton, remarkable red chiton
***Tonicella insignis**, Tonicella submarmorea, Tonicella submarmoreus*
to 6 cm (2.3 in) long
n. Alaska to n. Oregon
intertidal to 52 m (170 ft)
Narrow, wavy lines across the central triangle of each shell are definitive for this chiton. Its girdle—the band of visible tissue surrounding the base of the eight shells—is smooth. Photograph B shows a specimen with almost no white lines.
A Moore Point, Francis Peninsula, s. BC
B Anderson Bay, Texada Island, s. BC

MC5. WOODY CHITON, woody mopalia
***Mopalia lignosa**, Mopalia elevata*
to 8 cm (3.2 in) long
c. Alaska to n. Mexico
intertidal to subtidal
Tiny hairs originating from lighter spots on the girdle identify this chiton. The usually distinctive patterns on shells can be somewhat variable and are often most attractive.
Link Island, Barkley Sound, s. BC

MC6. MOSSY CHITON, mossy mopalia, bristly chiton
Mopalia muscosa
to 10 cm (4 in) long
s. Alaska to n. Mexico
intertidal to subtidal
Dark, bristle-like hairs growing thickly from the girdle readily distinguish this species of chiton. The interiors of the shells are blue. Photograph B shows a very worn specimen that was subject to greater pounding of surf in a more exposed habitat.
A Village Bay, Mayne Island, s. BC
B Frank Island, w. Vancouver Island, s. BC

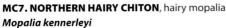

MC7. NORTHERN HAIRY CHITON, hairy mopalia
Mopalia kennerleyi
to 7.6 cm (3 in) long
n. Alaska to n. Mexico
▶intertidal to subtidal
Note alternating light/dark bands on a wide girdle and an obvious notch at the posterior. Most definitive, but difficult to see in the photograph, is the multitude of flattened brown hairs, with three rows of whitish spines at their bases, covering the girdle.
The "hairy chiton" is a species that has been recently split: this one has been separated from the southern hairy chiton, *Mopalia ciliata,* which is found in California.
Egmont Marina, Egmont, s. BC

MC8. SWAN'S MOPALIA
Mopalia swani, Mopalia swanii
►to 10 cm (4 in) long
n. Alaska to s. California
intertidal to 19 m (60 ft)

A usually pale, seemingly "hairless" girdle combined with plain, often light-centred shells mark this species. However, close inspection shows that the broad, fleshy girdle has very fine short hairs or setae.
A Laura Point, Mayne Island, s. BC
B Cactus Islands, New Channel, n. Washington

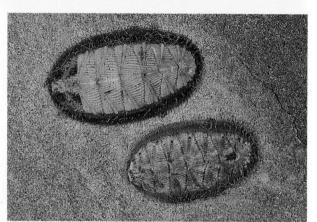

MC9. ►BRANCH-HAIRED MOPALIA
Mopalia imporcata
to 2.2 cm (0.9 in) long
s. Alaska to s. California
intertidal to subtidal
Like many mopalia chitons, this species is hairy. However, its hairs are thick and randomly scattered, and those that are branched have long secondary limbs. In the branch-haired mopalia the central portions of the valves or shells are heavily ribbed with a lattice-like pitting.
Brinnon, Hood Canal, c. Washington

MC10. HIND'S MOPALIA, encrusted hairy chiton
Mopalia hindsii, Mopalia hindsi, Mopalia wosnessenskii
to 10 cm (4 in) long
c. Alaska to n. Mexico
intertidal to subtidal
The Hind's chiton has a girdle with scattered slender hairs and a noticeable posterior notch. Chitons are reputed to be herbivorous, but this one, like most, is omnivorous and will graze any suitable attached organisms in its path. Note the variation of girdle markings in the two photographs.
A Nakwakto Rapids, Slingsby Channel, c. BC
B Butress Island, Slingsby Channel, c. BC

MC11. RED-FLECKED MOPALIA
Mopalia spectabilis, formerly confused with *Mopalia ciliata*
to 7 cm (2.8 in) long
c. Alaska to n. Mexico
►intertidal to 30 m (100 ft)
Shells with bright turquoise, orange and red-brown marks give this chiton a gaudy appearance. The girdle hairs have very dense branching secondary hairs resembling miniature bottle brushes. The shells, like those of other chitons, are sometimes colonized by other small animals.
Laura Point, Mayne Island, s. BC

MC12. SMOOTH MOPALIA, formerly confused with *Mopalia laevior*
Mopalia vespertina
to 8 cm (3.2 in) long
s. Alaska to c. California
intertidal to subtidal
The smooth chiton is distinguished by fine pitting in the centre of the green or brown shells, along with short girdle hairs. Carefully dislodge a specimen, turn it over and notice its muscular foot—the flat, sausage-shaped structure in the middle. In depressions on either side of this structure are rows of segments that are the gills.

Woodlands, Indian Arm, s. BC

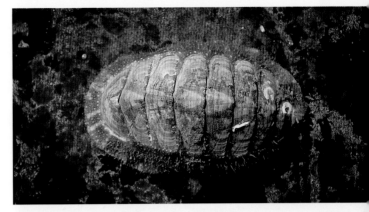

MC13. EGRET-PLUMED MOPALIA
Mopalia egretta
▶to 2.5 cm (1 in) long
Alaska to Washington
subtidal
With hairs on its girdle so fine as to appear velvety, the egret-plumed mopalia is usually obvious against a dark background. Chitons in the genus *Mopalia* are particularly frustrating to distinguish as the length and structure of the girdle hairs—the most diagnostic features—usually require at least a hand lens to verify.

Woodlands, Indian Arm, s. BC

MC14. FEATHERY MOPALIA
Mopalia phorminx
to 2 cm (0.8 in) long
c. Alaska to c. California
subtidal to at least 21 m (70 ft)
While trawling in English Bay at 21 m (70 ft), the collecting crew of the Vancouver Aquarium Marine Science Centre gathered a net full of waterlogged bark fragments. Careful inspection of these wood chips revealed a number of creatures, including this individual—a serendipitous unidentified find. Chiton guru Roger Clark of Klamath Falls, Oregon, who had never before encountered this species, identified the specimen and it is now part of his research collection.

English Bay, Burrard Inlet, s. BC

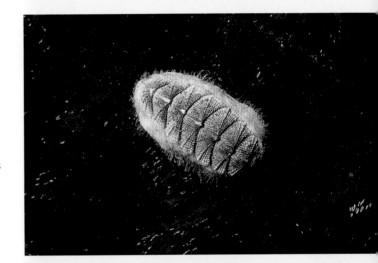

MC15. ▶DWARF HAIRY MOPALIA
Mopalia sinuata, *Mopalia goniura*, *Callistochiton aepynotus*
to 1.3 cm (0.5 in) long
Alaska to c. California
▶subtidal to at least 15 m (50 ft)
This species is almost impossible to detect. The only two specimens found by the authors were noticed after the creatures had crawled off their surroundings and onto the side of a Vancouver Aquarium Marine Science Centre holding tank.
The long-haired chiton, *Mopalia cirrata,* is very similar but it does not have branching girdle hairs. Its hairs are not especially recurved.

Point Atkinson, Burrard Inlet, s. BC

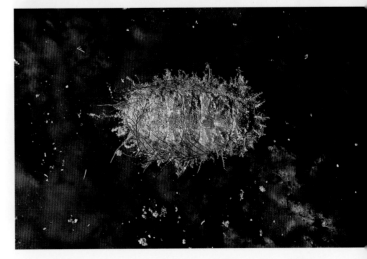

MC16. MERTEN'S CHITON, Mertens' chiton, mottled red chiton, red chiton
Lepidozona mertensi
to 5 cm (2 in) long
Japan, n. Alaska to n. Mexico
intertidal to 91 m (300 ft)
A granular and banded girdle surrounding the usually reddish shells typify this species, although purple ones are occasionally encountered. Found along all of the world's coastlines, chitons are often called sea cradles.
Sutton Islets, Egmont, s. BC

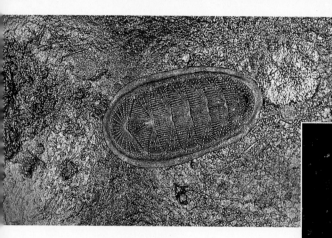

MC17. COOPER'S CHITON, dull brown chiton
Lepidozona cooperi, *Ischnochiton cooperi*
to 5 cm (2 in) long
►n. BC to n. Mexico
intertidal to 20 m (65 ft)
Very similar to Merten's chiton (MC16), the Cooper's chiton has a dull brownish hue and smaller girdle granules. Also, note the strong shell sculpturing that is obvious on the juvenile specimen in photograph A, less so on the well-worn, larger individual in photograph B.
A Sunset Bay State Park, Charleston, s. Oregon
B Ucluth Peninsula, w. Vancouver Island, s. BC

MC18. ►SMOOTH LEPIDOZONA
Lepidozona interstinctus, *Ischnochiton interstinctus, Ischnochiton radians*
to 2.5 cm (1 in) long
n. Alaska to s. California
►intertidal to 36 m (120 ft)
A tiny species that lacks obvious grooves and pits in its eight shells or plates, which give it a smooth appearance. Tiny tubercles (bumps), however, are present on all eight shells. The specimens in photograph A are of the *radians* variety or subspecies, according to Roger Clark, an authority on chitons.
A Browning Passage, Nigei Island, c. BC
B Bowyer Island, Howe Sound, s. BC
C Dibrell Bay, Langara Island, n. BC
D Boas Islet, Hakai Passage, c. BC
E Browning Passage, Nigei Island, c. BC

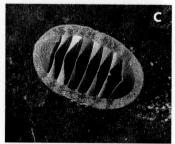
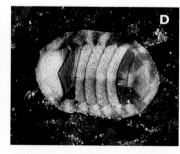

MC19. THREE-RIB CHITON

Lepidozona trifida, *Isnochiton trifidus ?, Tripoplax trifidus ?*
to 6 cm (2.3 in) long
n. Alaska to n. Washington
intertidal to 110 m (365 ft)
The reddish to orange-brown three-rib chiton has about 20 strongly radiating grooves on the first (head) plate and two similar grooves on the lateral areas of plates 2 through 7. Part of the temporary planktonic community, a microscopic larval chiton looks like a "spinning top" before it settles to the bottom and metamorphoses into a recognizable juvenile.
Woodlands, Indian Arm, s. BC

MC20. LITTLE LEPIDOZONA

Lepidozona retiporosa, *Lepidozona retiporosus*
to 2 cm (0.8 in) long
s. Alaska to n. Mexico
subtidal to at least 1,000 m (3,300 ft)
This chiton has longitudinal rows of shallow but noticeable pits in the central areas of plates 2 through 7. It is often found on the same rock as the Willett's lepidozona (MC21) and Golisch's chiton.
Lopez Island, San Juan Islands, n. Washington

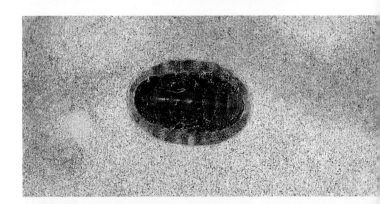

MC21. WILLETT'S LEPIDOZONA

Lepidozona willetti, *Ischnochiton willetti, Lepidozona catalinae*
to 3 cm (1.2 in) long
s. Alaska to s. California
subtidal
A reddish brown colour and larger maximum size help separate Willett's lepidozona from the little lepidozona (MC20) and Golisch's chiton. However, minor differences in the numbers of ribs and slits on the various valves as well as the relative size of girdle scales distinguish this species from the little lepidozona (MC20) and Golisch's chiton—an exercise ill suited to the beach or underwater.
Golisch's chiton, *Lepidozona scabricostata*, is nearly identical to the little lepidozona (MC20), but is usually a uniform orange-brown or creamy white.
Mountain Point, Ketchican, s. Alaska

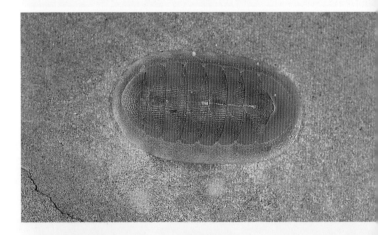

MC22. PAINTED DENDROCHITON

Dendrochiton flectens, *Leptochitona flectens, Basiliochiton flectens, Basiliochiton heathii, Trachydermon heathii, Leptochitona heathii, Mopalia flectens*
to 3 cm (1.2 in) long
s. Alaska to s. California
intertidal to 24 m (80 ft)
Very long, sometimes branching hairs protrude from the girdle of this red and white chiton, a feature that cannot be seen clearly in the photographs.
A Pearse Islands, Weynton Passage, c. BC
B Sechelt Rapids, Egmont, s. BC

MC23. GEM CHITON

***Chaetopleura gemma**, Ischnochiton marmoratus*
to 2 cm (0.8 in) long
s. BC to n. Mexico
intertidal

Although the colour may vary, the dark spot on the posterior shell or valve is distinctive for this small species. Also noteworthy for identification are tiny, transparent spines on the girdle—a feature that would require at least a magnifying glass to find. Good luck!

Garrapata State Beach, Monterey County, c. California. J. Duane Sept photograph

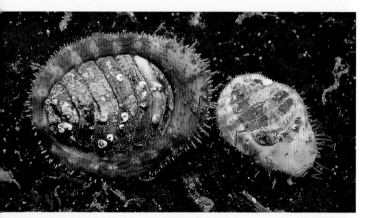

MC24. VEILED-CHITON, veiled Pacific chiton, veiled chiton, hooded-chiton, hooded chiton

Placiphorella velata
to 6 cm (2.3 in) long
c. Alaska to n. Mexico
intertidal to 20 m (65 ft)

An exclusively carnivorous chiton. When feeding, it raises its frontal flap, or veil, and pins any tiny mobile prey that blunders underneath. Amphipods, small shrimp and even tiny fish may fall victim. Noticeable dark bands on a light girdle and long bristles distinguish this species from the red veiled-chiton (MC25).

Ucluth Peninsula, w. Vancouver Island, s. BC

MC25. RED VEILED-CHITON, red veiled chiton, red hooded-chiton

Placiphorella rufa
to 5 cm (2 in) long
n. Alaska to s. Oregon
intertidal to 45 m (150 ft)

Usually distinguished by red shells on a white girdle, this chiton, like the veiled-chiton (MC24), is a carnivore. Female chitons usually lay jelly-coated eggs, each of which has a frilly membrane that in theory helps it float while awaiting fertilization by a sperm. Similar but with white shells, the ▶white veiled-chiton, *Placiphorella pacifica*, also inhabits the Pacific Northwest but usually lives in deeper subtidal haunts.

A Sutton Islets, Egmont, s. BC
B Butress Island, Slingsby Channel, c. BC

MC26. DWARF CHITON, tan chiton

***Leptochiton rugatus**, Lepidopleurus rugatus, Lepidopleurus cancellatus, Lepidopleurus internexus*
to 1.6 cm (0.6 in) long
n. Alaska to n. Mexico
intertidal

It takes a determined beachcomber searching the undersides of rocks resting on anoxic (low-oxygen) mud along exposed shorelines to find this inconspicuous animal. The dwarf chiton has rather smooth and rounded shells.

Slip Point, Olympic coast, n. Washington

MC27. GOULD'S BABY CHITON

Lepidochitona dentiens, *Lepidochiton dentiens, Isnochiton dentiens, Cyanoplax dentiens, Chiton dentiens, Ischnochiton dentiens, Cyanoplax raymondi*
to 2.7 cm (1.1 in) long
s. Alaska to n. Mexico
intertidal

This small, inconspicuous chiton usually lives high in the intertidal zone and is a challenging find for even the most observant naturalist. The girdle of Gould's baby chiton is usually banded or white spotted.

Another diminutive Pacific Northwest species, Fernald's baby chiton, *Lepidochiton fernaldi,* is very similar but has no banding on its girdle and usually shows eroded shells.

A Dinner Point, Mayne Island, s. BC
B Browning Passage, Nigei Island, c. BC

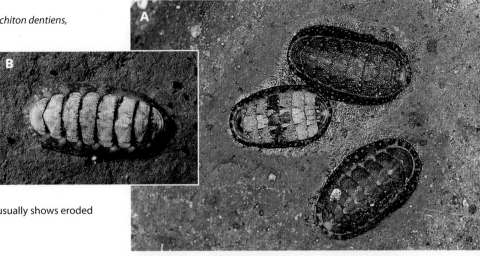

MC28. NORTHERN CHITON

Boreochiton beringensis
to 2.5 cm (1 in) long, at least
n. Alaska to s. Alaska
subtidal

Notice the light spots and sparse hairs on the dark pink girdle of this small, seldom-seen species. Diver Donna Gibbs of Port Coquitlam, BC, found this northern chiton specimen during a trip aboard the MV *Nautilus Explorer.*

Yasha Island, Chatham Strait, s. Alaska

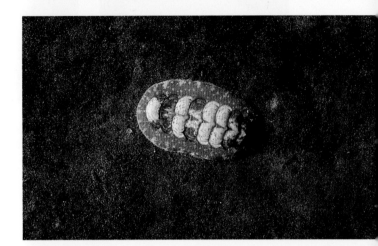

MC29. BLACK LEATHER CHITON, leather chiton, black chiton, black katy chiton, katy chiton, black katy, sea prune, small Chinese slippers, incorrect: gumboot chiton

Katharina tunicata
to 15 cm (6 in) long
Siberia, n. Alaska to s. California
intertidal to subtidal

This species, one of the larger chitons, was historically an aboriginal food source—a fact verified by archaeological research in ancient middens. The authors pass.

A Laura Point, Mayne Island, s. BC
B Tongue Point, Olympic coast, n. Washington

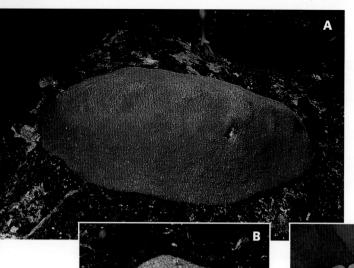

MC30. GIANT PACIFIC CHITON, giant chiton, gumboot chiton, giant gumboot chiton, giant red chiton, moccasin chiton, gum boot, Chinese slipper, butterfly shells
***Cryptochiton stelleri**, Amicula stelleri*
to 35 cm (14 in) long
Japan, n. Alaska to s. California
intertidal to 20 m (65 ft)
The largest chiton in the world! The giant Pacific chiton's eight shells are completely and cryptically overgrown by girdle. Photograph B shows a juvenile specimen and photograph C, a set of shells.
Additional chitons have been recorded from the Pacific Northwest, but most have centres of abundance farther south.
A B Agamemnon Channel, Nelson Island, s. BC
C Alcala Point, Galiano Island, s. BC

BIVALVES

Including mussels, philobryas, scallops, limas, oysters, jingles, clams, yoldias, diplodons, montacutids, bittersweets, astartes, cockles, gapers, geoducks, myas, tellins, macomas, lucines, venuses, rock dwellers, littlenecks, angelwings, nestlers, ship worms, entodesmas, pandoras, lyonsias, trapeziums, thracias and dippers.

Mussels

MC31. PACIFIC BLUE MUSSEL, common blue mussel, blue mussel, bay mussel, edible mussel, foolish mussel
Mytilus trossulus
to 11 cm (4.5 in) long
n. Alaska to n. Mexico, also introduced from Europe into many other regions
intertidal to 180 m (600 ft)
With the advent of DNA techniques, this historically misnamed mussel is now correctly categorized as *Mytilus trossulus*. However, confusion will no doubt continue, as the Mediterranean blue mussel (MC32) and blue mussel (MC33) have been introduced via aquaculture, and numerous complicating hybrids now exist.
A Irvines Landing, Pender Harbour, s. BC
B Point Cowan, Bowen Island, s. BC

MC32. The **MEDITERRANEAN BLUE MUSSEL** or Gallo's mussel *Mytilus galloprovincialis* attains 15 cm (6 in) in length and is readily available at many seafood markets courtesy of local suppliers. Capable of living both intertidally and subtidally, it was introduced from Europe. Its shells are black, triangular and fan-shaped with pointed anterior ends, but simple inspection of the shells is no guarantee of precise identification. Specimens were purchased at The Lobster Man, Granville Island Market, Vancouver, BC.

The Lobster Man, Granville Island, s. BC

MC33. The **BLUE MUSSEL** *Mytilus edulis* reaches a length of 11 cm (4.5 in) and is also a popular item for seafood gourmets. Introduced from the Atlantic coast of North America, this adaptable species may also dwell intertidally and subtidally. The straight or somewhat curved ventral margins of its shells are a distinctive feature, but exact determination is unlikely. Specimens were purchased at The Lobster Man, Granville Island Market, Vancouver, BC.

The Lobster Man, Granville Island, s. BC

MC34. CALIFORNIA MUSSEL, California sea mussel, Californian mussel, surf mussel, sea mussel, rock mussel, big mussel, ribbed mussel
Mytilus californianus, *Mytilus californicus*
to 25 cm (10 in) long
c. Alaska to n. Mexico
intertidal to 100 m (330 ft)
Heavy shells protect this bivalve in its exposed, surf-pounded habitat. In addition, the California mussel secretes tough byssus threads that attach to the bottom.
A Butress Island, Slingsby Channel, c. BC
B Frank Island, w. Vancouver Island, s. BC

MC35. NORTHERN HORSEMUSSEL, northern horse mussel, giant horse mussel, great horse mussel, horse mussel, common horse mussel, bearded mussel
Modiolus modiolus, *Volsella modiolus*, *Volsella modiola*, *Modiola modiola*
to 23 cm (9 in) long
circumpolar, to Japan, to New Jersey, to Mediterranean, n. Alaska to s. California
intertidal to 200 m (660 ft)
Specimens may bind together with gravel and sand, forming loosely aggregated mats.
Hurst Island, Goletas Channel, c. BC

MC36. STRAIGHT HORSEMUSSEL, straight horse mussel, fan-shaped horsemussel, fan-shaped horse mussel, fan horsemussel, fan mussel, fat horse mussel
Modiolus rectus, *Volsella recta, Modiola recta, Modiolus flabellatus, Volsella flabellatus*
to 23 cm (9 in) long
n. BC to Peru
intertidal to 45 m (150 ft)
Usually solitary, the straight horsemussel spreads attaching byssus threads and buries in sand or mud. Its shells are somewhat broader than those of the northern horsemussel (MC35).
Rosario Head, Deception Pass, n. Washington

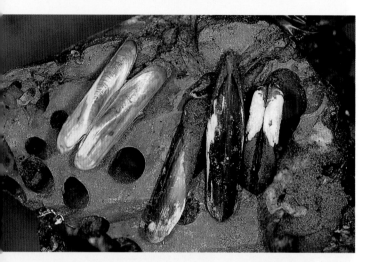

MC37. CALIFORNIA DATEMUSSEL, California date mussel, Californian date mussel, date mussel, California pea-pod shell, California pea-pod borer, California pea pod, pea-pod borer, pea pod borer
Adula californiensis, *Botula californiensis*
to 6 cm (2.5 in) long
n. BC to s. California
intertidal to 20 m (65 ft)
Using the rough ends of its shells, this creature bores into clay, shale or soft rock as shown in the photograph.
Two other *Adula* species are most likely to be encountered south of Washington state.
Sekiu, Olympic coast, n. Washington

MC38. DISCORDANT MUSSEL, discord mussel, discord musculus
Musculus discors, *Musculus leavigata, Musculus substriatus, Musculus substriata*
to 5.5 cm (2.3 in) long
n. Alaska to s. Washington
intertidal to 300 m (1,000 ft)
This species may nestle in sand or attach to other animals and therefore usually goes unnoticed. However, in more northerly locales, the discordant mussel attaches in clusters to kelp stipes or stems, making it much more obvious to the diver. Empty shells washed ashore by wave action are sometimes found by beachcombers.
Egg Harbor, Coronation Island, s. Alaska

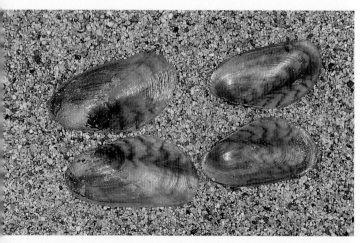

MC39. JAPAN MUSSEL
Musculista stenhousia, *Modiolus stenhousia, Musculus stenhousia, Volsella stenhousia*
to 4 cm (1.5 in) long
Japan, s. BC to c. California
intertidal to 20 m (65 ft)
Arriving incidentally with the Pacific oyster (MC50), this species exists at various sites but apparently prefers estuarine conditions. Wavy brown lines usually adorn the green periostracum (outer shell layer) of the Japan mussel, but a lack of bristles thereon is particularly distinctive.
Portage Inlet, Victoria, s. BC

MC40. BLACK MUSSEL, black musculus, little black mussel
***Musculus niger**, Musculus olivaceus, Musculus obesus, Musculus protractus*
to 8 cm (3.2 in) long
circumboreal, to New York, n. Europe, n. Alaska to c. California
intertidal to 300 m (1,000 ft)
The adult uses its byssus threads to create a cocoon for nestling in the substrate rather than as an attachment mechanism. Although called black, this species' shells are often an olive colour as shown in the photograph. Another similar but much smaller (8 mm / 0.3 in) species, Taylor's dwarf mussel, *Musculus taylori,* has thus far only been documented from the BC coast.
White Islets, Strait of Georgia, s. BC

MC41. PARTLY-SCULPTURED CRENELLA
***Vilasina seminuda**, Crenella seminuda, Modiolaria seminuda, Rhomboidella seminuda, Crenella grisea*
to 1.5 cm (0.6 in) long
Kuril Islands, n. Alaska to n. Washington
subtidal, 10–300 m (33–1,000 ft)
This species' thin, inflated shells, coated with a silky outer layer, are distinctive. Not surprisingly, this specimen was incidentally found attached to a cluster of hydroids, which was the prime collection objective. This serendipitous discovery is a great example of why a naturalist should always closely examine any find.
Arniston Point, Dundas Island, n. BC

MC42. HAIRY PHILOBRYA
Philobrya setosa
to 1.2 cm (0.5 in) across
c. Alaska to n. Mexico
intertidal to 73 m (240 ft)
A challenging species to find, it generally attaches to broken shells and coralline algae using its strong byssus threads. These threads, made of a special protein, are secreted by an organ located in the creature's hatchet-shaped foot.
Royal British Columbia Museum, Victoria, BC

Scallops

MC43. SPINY PINK SCALLOP, swimming scallop, Pacific pink scallop, Pacific spear scallop, pink rough-margined scallop, spiny scallop, pink scallop, pink pecten, spear scallop
***Chlamys hastata**, Chlamys hastatus, Pecten haustata, Chlamys hericia, Chlamys hericius, Chlamys hastata hastata, Chlamys hastata hericia, Chlamys hastata albida, Pecten islandicus pugetensis*
to 9.3 cm (3.7 in) across
n. Alaska to s. California
intertidal to 160 m (530 ft)
Sharp spines on radiating shell ridges are distinctive, but sponge growth usually obscures this feature. Photograph B shows a specimen covered by sponge; it could be this species or the smooth pink scallop (MC44).
A Laura Point, Mayne Island, s. BC
B Nelson Rock, Malaspina Strait, s. BC

MC44. SMOOTH PINK SCALLOP, pink smooth-margined scallop, smooth scallop, smooth pecten, swimming scallop, Hind's scallop, Hinds' scallop, reddish scallop, Pacific pink scallop, misspelled: smooth pectin
Chlamys rubida, *Pecten rubida, Chlamys rubidus, Chlamys hindsi, Chlamys hindsii, Chlamys kincaidi, Chlamys navaracha, Chlamys jordani*
to 8 cm (3.1 in) across
Siberia to n. Japan, n. Alaska to s. California
low-tide level to 300 m (1,000 ft)
Radiating shell ridges are smooth but usually obscured by thick sponge. The underside shell is usually paler than the uppermost.
A Finisterre Island, Bowen Island, s. BC
B Georgina Point, Mayne Island, s. BC

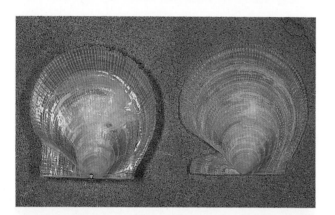

MC45. VANCOUVER SCALLOP, transparent scallop
Delectopecten vancouverensis, *Cyclopecten vancouverensis, Delectopecten randolphi, Cyclopecten randolphi, Delectopecten tillamookensi*
to 4.5 cm (1.8 in) across
Japan, Kamchatka, c. Alaska to n. Mexico
subtidal, 25–4,100 m (83–13,530 ft)
Distinguished by its shiny, translucent sheen, the Vancouver scallop often nestles with large sponges attached to rocks on muddy bottoms.
Off Willapa Bay, s. Washington

MC46. WEATHERVANE SCALLOP, weather-vane scallop, giant Pacific scallop
Patinopecten caurinus, *Pecten caurinus*
to 30 cm (12 in) across
n. Alaska to c. California
intertidal to 300 m (1,000 ft)
Like the spiny pink scallop (MC43) and the smooth pink scallop (MC44), the weathervane scallop can swim by "clapping" its shells together. This commercial species, harvested by trawling, is more often located at considerable depth and has a spotty distribution.
Sandy Cove, West Vancouver, s. BC

MC47. During the 1980s, the fledgling aquaculture industry, in conjunction with Fisheries and Oceans Canada, imported the **JAPANESE SCALLOP**, ***Mizuhopecten yessoensis***, to British Columbia. Reaching 18 cm (7.2 in) across, it has a lower white shell with rounded ribs rather than the flattened square ones of the weathervane scallop (MC46). Deemed to be a good candidate species for aquaculture, it was the subject of a research program. The result is a small but successful commercial enterprise at Island Scallops, near Qualicum Beach on the east coast of Vancouver Island. Specimens were purchased from The Lobster Man, Granville Island Market, Vancouver, BC.
The Lobster Man, Granville Island, s. BC

MC48. GIANT ROCK SCALLOP, giant rock-scallop, purple-hinged rock scallop, large rock scallop, rock scallop, purple hinge scallop, purple-hinged scallop, giant scallop, incorrect: oyster
Crassadoma gigantea, *Crassedoma giganteus*, *Crassedoma giganteum*, *Hinnites giganteus*, *Hinnites multirugosa*, *Hinnites multirugosus*, *Chlamys giganteus*, *Chlamys gigantea*, misspelled: *Crassedoma gigantea*, *Crassodoma gigantea*
to 25 cm (10 in) across
n. Alaska to n. Mexico
intertidal to 80 m (265 ft)
Orange mantles with many tiny black eyes are usually the only hint of life emanating from overgrown and obscured shells. Photograph A shows a giant rock scallop with paler mantles. The tiny juvenile is actually free-swimming. The shells of the adult have a purple stain on the inside where the hinge is located. Five or six species of glass-scallops live along Pacific Northwest shores but are tiny, deep-water denizens, unlikely to be encountered. Glass-scallops look like miniature swimming scallops but are grey and nondescript.
A Agamemnon Channel, Nelson Island, s. BC
B Anderson Bay, Texada Island, s. BC

MC49. HEMPHILL'S LIMA, Hemphill's file, Hemphill's fileclam, gaping file
Limaria hemphilli, *Lima hemphilli*, *Limatula hemphilli*, incorrect: *Lima orientalis*, *Lima dehiscens*, *Lima dihiscens*
to 2.5 cm (1 in) long
▶s. BC to Panama
intertidal to 100 m (330 ft)
Inclusion of this entry is courtesy of Kate Henderson and the Bamfield Marine Station, BC. It was dredged off Wizard Islet in Barkley Sound, s. BC, from approximately 15 m (50 ft). Unfortunately the specimen was lost before its exact verification was completed. It is remotely possible that it is an introduced species from Asia, rather than the one named above.
Wizard Islet, Barkley Sound, s. BC

Oysters and Jingles

MC50. PACIFIC OYSTER, giant Pacific oyster, Japanese oyster
Crassostrea gigas, *Ostrea gigas*
to 45 cm (18 in) long
native from Siberia to Pakistan, introduced from Japan to c. Alaska to c. California, also to Europe and Australia
intertidal to 6 m (20 ft)
A most successful aquaculture product raised on beaches, long lines and floating trays. Some suppliers claim beach-specific taste for their varieties, and photograph C shows Royal Miyagi on the top and Stellar Bay Gold on the bottom. Periodic "wild" population explosions provide the beach-going gourmet with a succulent windfall.
A Dinner Point, Mayne Island, s. BC
B Kleindale, Pender Harbour, s. BC
C The Lobster Man, Granville Island, Vancouver, BC

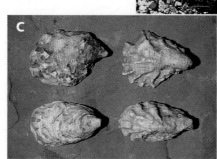

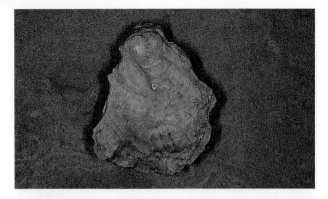

MC51. EASTERN OYSTER, Atlantic oyster, Virginia oyster, American oyster, eastern American oyster, blue point oyster, commercial oyster
Crassostrea virginica, *Ostrea virginica*
to 20 cm (8 in) long
native from Gulf of St. Lawrence to Brazil, introduced from east coast, s. BC to c. California
intertidal to 12 m (40 ft)
Unlike the Pacific oyster (MC50), the eastern oyster was introduced with little success. A spectacular exception is a thriving population in the estuary of the Serpentine River, BC, where it actually forms reefs on the silty bottom.
Royal British Columbia Museum, Victoria, BC

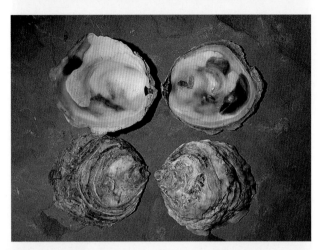

MC52. A global economy has affected the marine life of the Pacific Northwest in many ways. One of the more recent is the spread of the intertidal **EUROPEAN FLAT OYSTER**, *Ostrea edulis*, from aquaculture sites. Its white, tan, yellow or purplish shells reach 7.5 cm (3 in) across and have noticeable ribs with frilly growth margins. Economically driven decisions such as this introduction may prove impetuous and cause unforeseen impacts upon native fauna. Specimens were purchased from The Lobster Man, Granville Island Market, Vancouver, BC.
The Lobster Man, Granville Island, s. BC

MC53. OLYMPIA OYSTER, olympic oyster, native Pacific oyster, native oyster, lurid oyster, California oyster
Ostrea conchaphila, *Ostreola conchaphila*, *Ostrea lurida*, misspelled: *Ostrea conchapila*
to 9 cm (3.8 in) across
s. Alaska to Panama
intertidal to 50 m (165 ft)
Many aficionados claim this species is more gourmet than the Pacific oyster (MC50). The Olympic oyster is a challenging find for naturalists who search protected, inside waters. Recent studies suggest that subtidal and intertidal populations may actually be different subspecies.
Sargeant Bay, Sunshine Coast, s. BC

MC54. GREEN FALSE-JINGLE, green falsejingle, false Pacific jingle shell, false Pacific jingle, Pacific falsejingle, Alaska falsejingle, abalone jingle shell, abalone jingle, jingle money shell, jingle shell oyster, jingle shell, rock jingle, Pacific rock oyster, rock oyster, pearly monia, blister oyster, Madonna shell, money shell
Pododesmus macrochisma, *Pododesmus macroschisma*, *Pododesmus cepio*, *Pododesmus alope*, *Monia macroschisma*, misspelled: *Pododesmus machrochisma*, *Monia machroschisma*
to 13 cm (5.3 in) across
Siberia to n. Japan, Arctic Ocean, n. Alaska to n. Mexico
intertidal to 90 m (300 ft)
Attaches to the bottom permanently through a hole in the flattened lower shell. The green false-jingle is very common in low-current locales. See detail of lower shell in photograph B.
A Scotch Fir Point, Jervis Inlet, s. BC
B Grey Rocks Island, Indian Arm, s. BC

Clams

MC55. GUTLESS AWNING-CLAM, gutless awningclam
Solemya reidi
to 6 cm (2.3 in) long
s. Alaska to s. California
▶subtidal, 25–600 m (80–2,000 ft)
Amazingly, this clam does not have a digestive tract; bacteria living within its tissues provide it with food. The gutless awning-clam inhabits foul substrate types, notably near log storage and effluent outfall sites.
Mouth of Fraser River, Strait of Georgia, s. BC

MC56. DIVARICATE NUTCLAM, divaricate nut clam, castrensis nut clam, tent nutshell, nut clam, sculptured nut shell, sculptured nut, camp nut shell
Acila castrensis, Nucula castrensis
to 2 cm (0.8 in) across
n. Alaska to n. Mexico
subtidal, 5–400 m (16–1,320 ft)
This atypical bivalve has no siphons. It prefers mud or fine sand. The special shell sculpturing, termed divaricate, is diagnostic.
Queen Charlotte Channel, Howe Sound, s. BC

MC57. AXE YOLDIA, broad yoldia
Megayoldia thraciaeformis, Yoldia thraciaeformis
to 8 cm (3.5 in) long
circumboreal, to s. Japan, to n. Carolina, n. Alaska to c. California
subtidal, 25–760 m (80–2,500 ft)
The deep-dwelling axe yoldia clam has relatively thin shells. The specimen pictured was trawled from silty substrate during an Environment Canada sampling expedition.
Queen Charlotte Channel, Howe Sound, s. BC

MC58. WITNESS YOLDIA
Megayoldia martyria, Yoldia martyria
to 3 cm (1.2 in) long
s. BC to n. Mexico
▶subtidal, 100–330 m (330–1,080 ft)
Note the smooth shells with broadly rounded rear ends. Numerous species of yoldia clams live in the Pacific Northwest, at depths well beyond the range of most naturalists. Most of them look very similar to all but an expert in bivalve taxonomy.
Queen Charlotte Channel, Howe Sound, s. BC

MC59. OBLIQUE-LINED YOLDIA, oblique yoldia, crisscross yoldia, crisscrossed yoldia, halfsmooth yoldia, scissors yoldia
Yoldia seminuda, *Yoldia scissurata*, *Yoldia ensifera*
to 4 cm (1.8 in) long
Siberia to s. Japan, n. Alaska to s. California
subtidal, 15–375 m (50–1,233 ft)
The shells' shiny yellowish exterior and fine concentric lines are noteworthy features of this bivalve. The extent to which the rings cover the shell may vary.
Queen Charlotte Channel, Howe Sound, s. BC

MC60. CALIFORNIA NUTCLAM
Nuculana conceptionis, *Leda conceptionis*, *Perisonota conceptionis*
to 3 cm (1.2 in) long
n. Alaska to s. California
subtidal, 300–2,300 m (1,000–7,600 ft)
Although the California nutclam has a particularly long rostrum or pointed rear end to its shells, this design is noteworthy for the *Nuculana* species as a group. Like others in the group, the California nutclam is found in muddy, deepwater haunts.
At least nine *Nuculana* species dwell in the Pacific Northwest.
Off s. Vancouver Island, s. BC

MC61. ROUGH DIPLODON*
Diplodonta impolita
to 3.5 cm (1.5 in) across
n. Alaska to c. Oregon
intertidal to 100 m (330 ft)
Divers are likely to see empty shells on sand rather than living rough diplodons, which remain buried in sand. This species secretes a mucus channel to the surface.
*The species has been incorrectly referred to as the orb diplodon, *Diplodonta orbella*, a species found from Alaska to Puget Sound.
Tilly Point, s. Pender Island, s. BC

MC62. GIANT CLEFTCLAM, giant cleft clam, Pacific cleft clam, cleft thyasira
Conchocele bisecta, *Thyasira bisecta*, *Cryptodon bisecta*
to 11 cm (4.5 in) across
Okhotsk Sea to Japan, n. Alaska to n. California
subtidal, 7–750 m (24–2,475 ft)
This species has apparently also been documented in Colombia! The record seems out of place but is not questioned by experts in the field.
The Pacific Northwest provides shelter for several other small cleftclam species.
Royal British Columbia Museum, Victoria, BC

MC63. LITTLE HEART CLAM, little heart shell, Carpenter's cardita, Carpenter carditid
Glans carpenteri, *Cardita carpenteri, Glans subquadrata, Glans minuscala*
to 1.5 cm (0.6 in) across
s. Alaska to n. Mexico
intertidal to 100 m (330 ft)
This obscure nestler may also attach to the undersides of rocks. The little heart clam broods its young, and upon emerging, they usually attach to the underside of the parent's shell.
Several other heart clams inhabit the Pacific Northwest.
Royal British Columbia Museum, Victoria, BC

MC64. SUBORBICULAR KELLYCLAM, suborbiculate kellyclam, La Perouse kellyclam, kellyclam, Laperouse's kellia, smooth kelly clam, kelly shell, La Perouse's lepton, North Atlantic kellia
Kellia suborbicularis, *Kellia laperousi, Kellia laperousii, Kellia comandorica*
to 3.1 cm (1.3 in) long
circumboreal, south to Mediterranean, New York, c. Japan, n. Alaska to Peru
intertidal to 120 m (400 ft)
To find this adaptable animal, look for white siphons extending from narrow-neck bottles (photograph B) or holes in rock.
Two other small kellyclams reside in the Pacific Northwest but are seldom encountered.
A B Egmont Marina, Egmont, s. BC

MC65. MUD SHRIMP CLAM, wrinkled montacutid, wrinkled lepton
Neaeromya rugifera, *Pseudopythina rugifera, Orobitella rugifera, Pseudopythina myaciformes*
to 5 cm (2 in) across
c. Alaska to n. Mexico
intertidal to 56 m (187 ft)
This commensal clam attaches to the undersides of the blue mud shrimp (AR89) and the bristle worm (AN42). Tiny male mud shrimp clams live inside the mantle cavity of the adult female.
Hatfield Marine Science Center beach, Yaquina Bay, s. Oregon

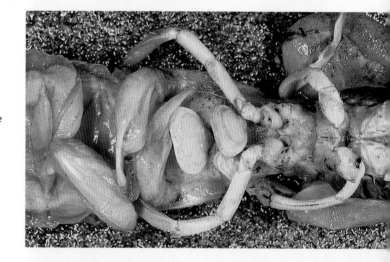

MC66. COMPRESSED MONTACUTID
Neaeromya compressa, *Pseudopythina compressa, Orobitella compressa*
▶to 2.5 cm (1 in) across
Alaska to Washington
subtidal, 10–700 m (33–2,300 ft)
Most bivalve molluscs use their gills to filter phytoplankton (floating algae) from the surrounding seawater. Scientists speculate that this clam lives in the burrows of the heart urchin (EC52).
One or two other smaller and less obvious *Neaeromya*-like species exist in the Pacific Northwest.
Royal British Columbia Museum, Victoria, BC

MC67. WESTERN BITTERSWEET, west coast bittersweet, Pacific coast bittersweet, northern bittersweet, California bittersweet, button shell
Glycymeris septentrionalis, *Glycymeris subobsoleta, Axinola subobsoleta*
to 4.5 cm (1.8 in) across
c. Alaska to n. Mexico
intertidal to 400 m (1,320 ft)
Observant divers patrolling over soft substrates will sometimes find the empty shells of the western bittersweet. Most living individuals burrow in large particulate sediments.
A second, rarely found species of bittersweet clam exists in the Pacific Northwest.
Tilly Point, s. Pender Island, s. BC

MC68. ELLIPTICAL ASTARTE, elliptical tridonta, Alaskan astarte, Alaska astarte, Alaskan tridonta, Alaska tridonta
Astarte elliptica, *Tridonta elliptica, Tridonta alaskensis, Astarte alaskensis*
to 5 cm (2 in) across
circumboreal, south to Massachusetts, Britain, c. Japan, n. Alaska to n. Washington
▶subtidal, 3–250 m (10–825 ft)
Note the distinctive rings on the dark shells. Sometimes live elliptical astartes lie exposed on the bottom—tempting fate? Numerous extinct astarte species have existed and may now be found as fossils.
Grey Rocks Island, Indian Arm, s. BC

MC69. COMPACT ASTARTE
Astarte compacta, *Astarte willetti*
to 3 cm (1.2 in) across
s. Alaska to n. Washington
subtidal, 10–200 m (33–660 ft)
This diminutive clam's shells have low, broad ribs and wavy inside edges. Female astarte clams apparently attach their eggs to the bottom.
A few other *Astarte* species are found in deep Pacific Northwest waters.
Royal British Columbia Museum, Victoria, BC

MC70. NUTTALL'S COCKLE, Nuttall cockle, Nuttall's heart cockle, basket cockle, heart cockle, cockle
Clinocardium nuttallii, *Clinocardium nuttalli, Clinocardium corbis, Cardium corbis*
to 14.6 cm (5.8 in) across
Kamchatka to n. Japan, n. Alaska to s. California
intertidal to 200 m (660 ft)
This animal can protrude its large, yellow foot and pole vault along the bottom when escaping from predators such as sea stars and moonsnails—a most interesting antic, as shown in photograph C.
A Georgina Point, Mayne Island, s. BC
B C Stanley Park, Vancouver Harbour, s. BC

MC71. HAIRY COCKLE, Iceland cockle
Clinocardium ciliatum, Ciliatocardium ciliatum, Cardium islandicum
to 8.5 cm (3.5 in) across
Siberia, circumpolar, n. Alaska to n. Washington
subtidal, 10–150 m (33–500 ft)
The hairy cockle prefers to live in a mud/sand substrate, so it is most often found by the naturalist as a pair of empty shells rather than as a living organism.
Royal British Columbia Museum, Victoria, BC

MC72. ALEUTIAN COCKLE, Bering Sea cockle, north Pacific cockle, California cockle
Clinocardium californiense, Cardium californiense
to 9 cm (3.8 in) across
▶Siberia to Japan, n. Alaska to s. BC (an early record from Puget Sound, Washington, proved to be *Clinocardium blandum*)
subtidal, 10–110 m (33–365 ft)
Historically correct and therefore unchangeable, the scientific name *californiense* is confusing because the Aleutian cockle does not inhabit that state.
Passage Island, Howe Sound, s. BC

MC73. LOW-RIB COCKLE, fucan cockle
Clinocardium blandum (has been synonomized with *Clinocardium fucanum*)
to 5 cm (2 in) across
n. Alaska to c. California
subtidal, 20–80 m (65–265 ft)
A diver who cruises over sandy or muddy bottoms may find the empty shells of this cockle. The shell shape of most cockles is variable.
Royal British Columbia Museum, Victoria, BC

MC74. HUNDRED-LINE COCKLE, hundred line cockle, hundred-lined cockle
Nemocardium centifilosum, Protocardia centifilosum, Nemocardium richardsoni, Cardium richardsoni
to 2.5 cm (1 in) across
c. Alaska to n. Mexico
subtidal, 2–150 m (7–500 ft)
The many very fine ribs radiating on the shells are a distinctive feature of this small cockle. Like most other cockles, it lives very close to the surface of the substrate.
Royal British Columbia Museum, Victoria, BC

MC75. GREENLAND SMOOTHCOCKLE, Greenland cockle
***Serripes groenlandicus**, Serripes protractus*
to 13 cm (5 in) across
circumboreal, south to New England, Japan, n. Alaska to n. Washington
intertidal to 100 m (330 ft)
The very smooth shells appear "un-cockle-like" but are definitive nonetheless. The cockles comprise a large family of approximately 170 living species.
Passage Island, Howe Sound, s. BC

MC76. FAT GAPER, gaper clam, northern gaper clam, fat horse clam, horse clam, horseneck clam, Alaskan gaper, summer clam, otter clam, rubberneck clam, blue clam, Washington clam, gaper, incorrect: Pacific gaper
***Tresus capax**, Schizothaerus capax*
to 28 cm (11 in) across
c. Alaska to s. California
intertidal to 30 m (100 ft)
Divers may see protruding siphon "shows" that slowly withdraw as the clam senses an approach. The fat gaper is a common bycatch for the clam digger and is sometimes mistaken for a Pacific geoduck (MC78). The fat gaper often hosts pea crabs in its mantle.
Ucluelet Harbour, w. Vancouver Island, s. BC

MC77. PACIFIC GAPER, gaper, southern gaper clam, gaper clam, Pacific horse clam, horse clam, horse neck clam, rubberneck clam, ottershell clam, otter-shell clam, big-neck clam, summer clam, otter clam, great Washington clam, Washington clam
***Tresus nuttallii**, Tresus nuttalli, Schizothaerus nuttallii, Tresus maximus*
to 23 cm (9 in) across, 1.8 kg (4 lbs)
c. Alaska to n. Mexico
intertidal to 80 m (265 ft)
Commercially more important than the fat gaper (MC76), the Pacific gaper has more elongate shells, and the finger-like projections on its incurrent siphon are dark green rather than gold.
Ucluelet Harbour, w. Vancouver Island, s. BC

MC78. PACIFIC GEODUCK, Pacific geoduck clam, geoduck clam, geoduck, geoduc, gweduc, gooeyduck, giant Pacific clam, king clam, giant panopaea
Panopea abrupta, *Panopea generosa*, mispelled: *Panope abrupta, Panope generosa*
to 23 cm (9 in) across shell, 9 kg (20 lbs)
Siberia to Japan, c. Alaska to c. California, Panama
intertidal to 100 m (330 ft)
Commercial harvesting of 70-year-old specimens is akin to logging old-growth forests. This species' lifespan of 168 years cries out for more No-Take Marine Protected Areas! The specimen in photograph B illustrates a siphon "show" and the one in photograph C is spawning.
A B C Ucluelet Harbour, w. Vancouver Island, s. BC

MC79. AMPLE ROUGHMYA, ample rough mya, false geoduck
Panomya ampla, *Panomya chrysis*
to 9 cm (3.8 in) across shell
Okhotsk Sea, n. Alaska to n. Washington
intertidal to 150 m (500 ft)
Rust-brown siphons sticking up above sand, gravel or mud substrate are often the only evidence of this creature's presence. The shell shape of the ample roughmya is highly variable, which also confounds the experts.
Royal British Columbia Museum, Victoria, BC

MC80. ARCTIC ROUGHMYA, Arctic rough mya, deepwater false geoduck
Panomya norvegica, *Panomya arctica, Panope arctica*
to 11 cm (4.5 in) across shell
circumpolar, south to New England, Britain and Japan, n. Alaska to s. California
subtidal, 20–640 m (65–2,100 ft)
This large clam lives in shallow burrows in sandy mud, out of sight of the beachcomber. The periostracum (outer shell layer) is very easily eroded.
A B Royal British Columbia Museum, Victoria, BC

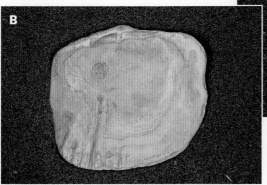

MC81. PACIFIC RAZOR-CLAM, Pacific razor clam, northern razor-clam, northern razor clam, razor clam, Pacific razor, giant razor
Siliqua patula
to 19 cm (7.5 in) long
c. Alaska to c. California
intertidal to 55 m (183 ft)
With its "digger foot," the Pacific razor-clam can outpace clam diggers. It is considered a gourmet clam and is most popular in Washington and Oregon, where open-coast sandy beaches are prevalent. Its shells are more elongate than those of the Alaska razor-clam (MC82).
Chesterman Beach, w. Vancouver Island, s. BC

MC82. ALASKA RAZOR-CLAM, Dall's razor clam, Alaska razor
Siliqua alta
to 20 cm (8 in) long
Kamchatka to n. Japan, n. Alaska to c. California
intertidal to 85 m (280 ft)
A narrow vertical rib inside each shell distinguishes this species from the preceding one, whose ribs slant backwards. The shells of this seldom-found species are also heavier and more robust.
Royal British Columbia Museum, Victoria, BC

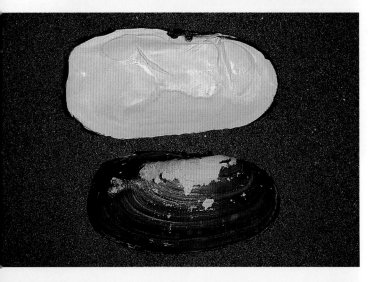

MC83. SICKLE JACKKNIFE-CLAM, sickle jackknife clam, sickle jackknife, sickle jacknife, blunt jackknife clam, fast jackknife clam, jackknife clam, sickle razor clam, blunt razor-clam, blunt razor clam, blunt razor
Solen sicarius, *Solen perrini*
to 12 cm (5 in) long
n. BC to n. Mexico
intertidal to 54 m (180 ft)
This clam thrives in mud and silt at depths usually greater than those hosting eelgrass beds (SW2), so the beachcomber is more likely to find its distinctive empty shells washed ashore on the substrate.
Navy Channel, Mayne Island, s. BC

MC84. HOOKED SURFCLAM, hooked surf clam
Simomactra falcata, *Spisula falcata, Symmorphomactra falcata*
to 10 cm (4 in) across
n. BC to n. Mexico
intertidal to 50 m (165 ft)
Usually buries near the surface in sand, primarily along sheltered beaches. Some surfclam species have symbiotic bacteria living within their tissues.
Royal British Columbia Museum, Victoria, BC

MC85. ARCTIC SURFCLAM, Alaska surf clam, Stimpson's surfclam, Stimpson's surf clam, Stimpson's mactra
Mactromeris polynyma, *Spisula polynyma, Mactra ovalis*
to 15.5 cm (6.2 in) across
circumboreal, south to Japan and Massachusetts, n. Alaska to n. Washington
intertidal to 110 m (365 ft)
Commercially harvested in Alaska, the Arctic surfclam may live 25 years and is a species that would benefit from No-Take Marine Protected Areas. It is a popular sashimi item. Distribution is poorly documented and its southernmost limit is in question.
Royal British Columbia Museum, Victoria, BC

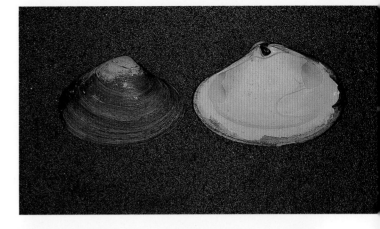

MC86. BODEGA TELLIN, Bodegas tellin, Bodega tellen, Bodega clam
Tellina bodegensis, *Moerella bodegensis, Tellina santarosae*
to 6 cm (2.3 in) across
s. Alaska to n. Mexico
intertidal to 100 m (330 ft)
Elongate, pointed shells with fine concentric lines define this bivalve, the largest of the local tellins. It usually dwells along exposed shores.
Chesterman Beach, w. Vancouver Island, s. BC

MC87. CARPENTER'S TELLIN, Carpenter tellin
Tellina carpenteri, *Angulus carpenteri, Tellina variegata, Tellina arenica*
to 2.5 cm (1 in) across
s. Alaska to Panama
intertidal to 823 m (2,700 ft)
Apparently an adaptable species, the carpenter's tellin lives in many sediment types from silt to coarse sand. Most tellins use their long in-current siphons to sweep up a fine detritus food source from the sea floor.
Aguilar Point, Bamfield, s. BC

MC88. PLAIN TELLIN, modest tellin, button tellin
Tellina modesta, *Angulus modesta, Tellina buttoni, Angulus modestus obtusus*
to 2.5 cm (1 in) long
c. Alaska to n. Mexico
intertidal to 100 m (330 ft)
Tellins, including this attractive species, are popular with shell collectors, who often use them as craft material. Let your imagination run wild.
Royal British Columbia Museum, Victoria, BC

MC89. SALMON TELLIN, salmon tellen, salmon-colored tellen, rose necklace clam
Tellina nuculoides, *Tellina nucleoides, Tellina salmonea*
to 2 cm (0.8 in) across
n. Alaska to s. California
intertidal to 155 m (510 ft)
Live salmon tellins leave "tracks" just under the sand's surface as evidence of their movement. Though primarily a coarse sand dweller, this tellin has also been recorded among rocks.
Royal British Columbia Museum, Victoria, BC

MC90. BENT-NOSE MACOMA, bent nose clam, bentnose macoma, bent-nose clam, bent-nosed clam, bent nosed clam, bentnosed clam, common macoma
Macoma nasuta, *Heteromacoma nasuta, Macoma kelseyi, Macoma tersa*
to 15 cm (6 in) across
c. Alaska to n. Mexico
intertidal to 50 m (165 ft)
A penchant for retaining sand makes this clam gritty and unappetizing. Too bad, as the bent-nose macoma is easily harvested and abundant in many accessible locales.
Navy Channel, Mayne Island, s. BC

MC91. POINTED MACOMA, stained macoma, polluted macoma, fouled macoma
Macoma inquinata, *Heteromacoma inquinata, Macoma irus, Macoma arnheimi*
to 6.6 cm (2.6 in) across
n. Alaska to c. California
intertidal to 50 m (165 ft)
The posterior of each shell of this clam is wedge-shaped and has a slight indentation. As in most clam species, a pair of muscles holds the two shells together.
Royal British Columbia Museum, Victoria, BC

MC92. BALTIC MACOMA, Balthic macoma, Balthica macoma, tiny pink clam, inconspicuous macoma, little macoma, Baltic tellin
Macoma balthica, *Tellina balthica, Macoma inconspicua*
to 4.5 cm (1.8 in) across
circumboreal, south to South Carolina, Spain and Japan, n. Alaska to s. California
intertidal to 40 m (130 ft)
Beachcombers find empty Baltic macoma shells a treasure! Experts suspect that Atlantic specimens may represent a different species. Detailed DNA profiling could verify this theory.
Crescent Beach, Boundary Bay, s. BC

MC93. WHITE-SAND MACOMA, white sand macoma, white sand clam, white macoma, giant macoma, butterfly clam, sand clam
Macoma secta
to 12 cm (5 in) long
s. Alaska to n. Mexico
intertidal to 50 m (165 ft)
Thin, glossy white shells with ridges at the rear are distinctive. The white-sand macoma buries deep in sandy substrates, which may be why its shells are not found by beachcombers in many areas. Rathtrevor Beach near Parksville, BC, is an exception.
Stanley Park, English Bay, s. BC

MC94. CHALKY MACOMA
Macoma calcarea, *Macoma sitkana*
to 6 cm (2.5 in) long
circumboreal, south to New York, Norway and Japan, n. Alaska to c. Oregon
intertidal to 500 m (1,650 ft)
The posterior end of each shell is slightly pointed and flexes to the right. Geological aging shows that the chalky macoma has lived in the Pacific Northwest for approximately 33 million years.
Royal British Columbia Museum, Victoria, BC

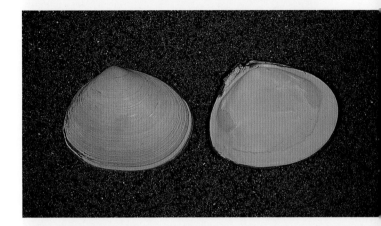

MC95. HEAVY MACOMA, brota macoma, Pacific brota, Pacific coast brota macoma, frail macoma
Macoma brota
to 7.5 cm (3 in) across
circumboreal, n. Alaska to n. Washington
subtidal, 10–260 m (33–853 ft)
The posterior (broader end) of each shell is squared and slightly flexed. The heavy macoma has heavier and thicker shells than other macoma clams, and thus is more likely to be found intact by the beachcomber.
Royal British Columbia Museum, Victoria, BC

MC96. CHARLOTTE MACOMA, Queen Charlotte macoma
Macoma carlottensis, *Macoma inflatula*, *Macoma quadrana*
to 3.3 cm (1.3 in) across
Arctic Ocean, n. Alaska to n. Mexico
subtidal to 1,550 m (5,100 ft)
The elongate shells have a glossy, greenish periostracum (outer layer). This layer flakes off with wear—a process that varies greatly between mollusc species.
Royal British Columbia Museum, Victoria, BC

MC97. EXPANDED MACOMA
Macoma expansa, Macoma liotricha
to 5 cm (2 in) across
n. Alaska to c. California
intertidal to 30 m (100 ft)
Apparently the expanded macoma prefers the surf-swept beaches of the exposed coast. It is believed that macoma clams originated during the Eocene Period, some 55 million years ago, and are particularly common in Arctic seas.
Royal British Columbia Museum, Victoria, BC

MC98. BEVELED MACOMA, file macoma
Macoma elimata
to 3.5 cm (1.5 in) across
s. Alaska to s. California
subtidal, 9–850 m (30–2,800 ft)
Silty or clay substrates are the habitat of choice for this bivalve. Evolutionary theorists believe that molluscs, including clams, share an ancestor with segmented worms.
Royal British Columbia Museum, Victoria, BC

MC99. ALEUTIAN MACOMA, Grant and Gale macoma
Macoma lama, Macoma planiuscula
to 4.5 cm (1.8 in) across
Arctic Ocean, n. Alaska to n. Washington
intertidal to 185 m (615 ft)
The clean sand of beaches directly exposed to surf provides shelter for this filter feeder. Scientists estimate that there are about 8,000 living species of bivalves (including clams) worldwide.
Royal British Columbia Museum, Victoria, BC

MC100. YOLDIA SHAPE MACOMA, yoldia-shaped macoma, yoldia macoma
Macoma yoldiformis
to 2.5 in (1 in) across
s. Alaska to n. Mexico
intertidal to 100 m (330 ft)
As the name of this clam suggests, its shell is similar in shape to that of the yoldia clams (MC57–59). The pencil mark in the photograph highlights the muscle scar on the inside of the shell.
Royal British Columbia Museum, Victoria, BC

MC101. PURPLE MAHOGANY-CLAM, dark mahogany-clam, dark mahogany clam, varnish clam
Nuttallia obscurata
to 7 cm (2.8 in) long
native to Korea and Japan, introduced, probably via ships' ballast, s. BC to c. Oregon
intertidal
Preferring sand/gravel locales with fresh-water seepage, this newcomer has made itself at home—so much so that it is now being marketed under the name of "savoury clam."
Stanley Park, Vancouver Harbour, s. BC

MC102. CALIFORNIA SUNSETCLAM, California sunset clam, sunset clam, sunset shell
Gari californica, *Psammobia californica, Psammobia rubroradiata*
to 15 cm (6 in) across
Kamchatka to Japan, n. Alaska to n. Mexico
intertidal to 280 m (925 ft)
A common "empty" find for the diver exploring sandy bottoms. Why not gather a few nicely coloured ones for a shell-collecting friend?
Dinner Bay, Mayne Island, s. BC

MC103. ROSE-PAINTED CLAM, rose-painted semele, rose-petal semele, rose petal semele, rock semele
Semele rubropicta
to 5 cm (2 in) across
n. Alaska to n. Mexico
intertidal to 100 m (330 ft)
Another pretty empty-shell find for the diver travelling over loose, coarse sediments. Classified as a deposit feeder, the rose-painted semele consumes material that has settled on the sea floor.
Eagle Point, San Juan Island, n. Washington

MC104. WESTERN RINGED LUCINE, ringed lucine, ringed lucina
Lucinoma annulatum, *Lucina annulata, Phacoides annulata, Phacoides annulatus, Lucinoma densilineata*
to 8.2 cm (3.3 in) across
Japan, c. Alaska to n. Mexico
intertidal to 750 m (2,500 ft)
Obvious growth rings on the shells of clams indicate age, though reading them is not always straightforward. These rings represent growth intervals, not necessarily years.
English Bay, Burrard Inlet, s. BC

MC105. FINE-LINED LUCINE, fine-line lucine, fine-lined lucina
Parvilucina tenuisculpta, *Lucina tenuisculpta, Lucinoma tenuisculpta,*
misspelled: *Parvalucina tenuisculpta*
to 1.5 cm (0.6 in) across
n. Alaska to n. Mexico
intertidal to 300 m (1,000 ft)
This clam has been found forming dense colonies in mud with high organic content. The shells of clams and other molluscs have been used to create artwork since the beginning of human history.
Royal British Columbia Museum, Victoria, BC

MC106. WASHINGTON BUTTER CLAM, butter clam, smooth Washington clam, Washington clam, giant rock-dweller
Saxidomus gigantea, *Saxidomus giganteus*
to 15 cm (6 in) across
n. Alaska to s. California
intertidal to 40 m (130 ft)
Exquisite for chowder, but heed red tide warnings when extracting it from your favourite clam-digging beach. Be considerate and obey conservation limits.
Georgina Point, Mayne Island, s. BC

MC107. PACIFIC LITTLENECK CLAM, native littleneck clam, littleneck clam, common Pacific littleneck, Pacific littleneck, common littleneck clam, common littleneck, little-neck clam, steamer clam, hardshell clam, rock venus, steamer, rock cockle, rock bay cockle, Tomales Bay cockle, ribbed carpet shell
Protothaca staminea, *Venerupis staminea, Paphia staminea*
to 13 cm (5.3 in) across
Siberia to n. Japan, n. Alaska to n. Mexico
intertidal to 40 m (130 ft)
Great steamed and dipped in melted garlic butter! Fortunately the Pacific littleneck clam is found on the same beaches as the Washington butter clam (MC106). Double pleasure.
Georgina Point, Mayne Island, s. BC

MC108. JAPANESE LITTLENECK CLAM, Japanese littleneck, Manilla clam, steamer clam, Filipino venus
Venerupis philippinarum, *Tapes philippinarum, Ruditapes philippinarum, Venerupis japonica, Tapes japonica, Protothaca japonica, Paphia japonica, Tapes semidecussata, Protothaca semidecussata*
to 7.5 cm (3 in) across
native from s. Siberia to China, introduced with oyster spat from Japan, n. BC to c. California
intertidal
Shells more elongate than Pacific littleneck clam (MC107), but the meat is equally gourmet.
Georgina Point, Mayne Island, s. BC

MC109. THIN-SHELL LITTLENECK, thin-shelled littleneck, thin-shelled little-neck, thin shelled little neck, thin-shelled littleneck clam, superlative rock venus, rock venus, finest carpet shell
Protothaca tenerrima, *Paphia tenerrima, Venerupis tenerrima, Protothaca restorationensis*
to 16 cm (6.3 in) across
s. Alaska to n. Mexico
intertidal to 50 m (165 ft)
Sometimes dug up and eaten by sea otters. Now these fellows know their seafood.
English Bay, Burrard Inlet, s. BC

MC110. MILKY VENUS, milky Pacific venus, deep water littleneck, translucent compsomyax
Compsomyax subdiaphana, *Marcia subdiaphana, Clementia obliqua, Saxidomus gibbosus*
to 8.5 cm (3.5 in) across
c. Alaska to n. Mexico
subtidal, 2–550 m (7–1,800 ft)
Apparently the milky venus makes a mucus nest in highly organic mud. As in scallops and many other bivalves, this species' sex organs are different in colour: white for males and red for females.
Royal British Columbia Museum, Victoria, BC

MC111. KENNERLEY'S VENUS, Kennerley's venus clam, Kennerley venus, Kennerley's rock venus, concentric ring clam, corrugated clam
Humilaria kennerleyi, *Venerupis kennerleyi, Marcia kennerleyi*
to 10 cm (4 in) across
c. Alaska to s. California
intertidal to 60 m (200 ft)
Exposed specimens that divers find have probably outlasted clam-digging sea star predators, which have given up and left to pursue easier prey. Perhaps Kennerley's venus has particularly strong muscles?
Laura Point, Mayne Island, s. BC

MC112. HEARTY ROCK DWELLER, hearty petricola, hearty rupellaria
Petricola carditoides, *Rupellaria carditoides, Rupellaria californica, Petricola denticulta*
to 6.3 cm (2.5 in) across
s. Alaska to n. Mexico
intertidal to 73 m (240 ft)
The bright purple siphons of this clam may protrude from empty piddock burrows colonized by the hearty rock dweller.
Royal British Columbia Museum, Victoria, BC

MC113. FALSE ANGELWING, false angel wing
Petricolaria pholadiformis, *Petricola pholadiformis*
to 7.1 cm (2.8 in) long
native from Quebec to Texas to Uruguay, Norway to the Black Sea, introduced to the west coast from the Atlantic and is established in s. Washington (Willapa Bay) and c. California
intertidal
A pair of shells, spread apart and observed from the outside, illustrate how this species' common name was derived. The false angelwing bores into intertidal peat in its native range.
Sea Rose Gifts & Shell Museum, Yachats, c. Oregon

MC114. SOFTSHELL-CLAM, soft-shell clam, softshell clam, soft shelled clam, soft-shelled clam, eastern soft-shell clam, eastern soft shell, softshell, soft clam, long clam, long-necked clam, steamer clam, mud clam, sand gaper, nanny nose
Mya arenaria, *Arenomya arenaria*
to 17 cm (6.8 in) across
circumboreal, south to Japan, Spain and n. Carolina, n. Alaska to c. California, introduced from east coast with Atlantic oysters
intertidal to 73 m (240 ft)
A successful import that is accessible to the clam-digging beachcomber. Great in chowder, too! Photograph B shows the chondrophore, the obvious protrusion at the hinge of mya clams.
A B Georgina Point, Mayne Island, s. BC

MC115. TRUNCATED SOFTSHELL-CLAM, truncate soft shell clam, truncated soft shell, truncate soft-shell clam, truncate softshell, truncated mya, blunt soft-shell clam, mud clam, mud gaper, blunt gaper
Mya truncata
to 8.5 cm (3.5 in) across shell
Japan, circumboreal, south to New England, south to Western Europe, n. Alaska to n. Washington
intertidal to 100 m (330 ft)
Divers often find empty shells complete with their rather tough siphon coverings still in place, lying on the bottom.
Green Bay, Nelson Island, s. BC

MC116. CALIFORNIA SOFTSHELL-CLAM, California softshell, California soft shell, California glass mya, Californian glass mya, glass mya, false mya
Cryptomya californica, *Cryptomya magna*
to 3.7 cm (1.5 in) across
n. Japan, c. Alaska to n. Peru
intertidal to 80 m (265 ft)
This resourceful bivalve lives in burrows excavated by the bay ghost shrimp (AR88) or the blue mud shrimp (AR89).
Ucluth Peninsula, w. Vancouver Island, s. BC

MC117. ARCTIC NESTLER, Arctic hiatella, Arctic saxicave, Arctic rock borer, nestling clam, nestling saxicave, Gallic saxicave, little gaper, red nose, boring clam
Hiatella arctica, Saxicava arctica, may equate to *Hiatella pholadis, Saxicava pholadis, Hiatella gallicana, Mya arctica*
to 7.8 cm (3.1 in) across
Arctic, Japan, south to deep cold waters of the Caribbean, n. Alaska to Chile, may have been spread south by human activity
intertidal to 1,190 m (3,930 ft)
The Arctic nestler, which attaches itself by strong byssus threads, is often found in algal holdfasts (root-like structures) or amid mussel mats. Consequently, only its orange siphons may be visible. Relatively few clams have byssus threads.
Hurst Island, Goletas Channel, c. BC

MC118. BORING SOFTSHELL-CLAM, checked softshell-clam, checked soft-shell clam, clay boring clam, checked borer, boring softshell, chubby mya, soft-shell clam, cross-barred broad tooth clam
Platyodon cancellatus
to 7.6 cm (3 in) across
n. BC to n. Mexico
intertidal to 100 m (330 ft)
Creates its own burrows in hard-packed clay substrates. Juveniles sometimes live in the holdfasts or root-like structures of some kelps.
Tlell, Graham Island, n. BC

MC119. FLAT-TIP PIDDOCK, flat-tipped piddock, flap-tip piddock, common piddock, piddock, left piddock
Penitella penita, Pholadidea penita, Pholadidea concamerata
to 9.5 cm (3.9 in) across
n. Alaska to n. Mexico
intertidal to 90 m (300 ft)
Working as a natural drill, this boring clam rotates its shells to create a snug hole in soft-rock and hard-clay bottoms. Note that each shell has two very different halves with the rough hind ends doing the abrading.
Sekiu, Olympic coast, n. Washington

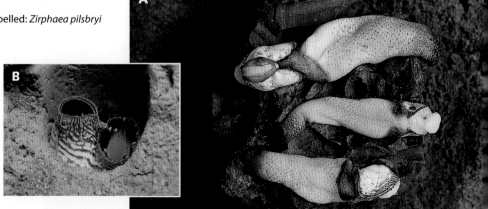

MC120. ROUGH PIDDOCK, Pacific rough piddock, Pilsbry's piddock, Pilsbry piddock, right piddock, boring clam
Zirfaea pilsbryi, Zirfaea pilsbryii, Zirfaea gabbi, misspelled: *Zirphaea pilsbryi*
to 15 cm (6 in) across shell
n. Alaska to n. Mexico
intertidal to 125 m (412 ft)
With a large body that does not completely fit between its protective shells, the rough piddock needs the protection of the hole it drills in its hard clay surroundings. Photograph B shows a typically coloured siphon protruding from the bottom.
A Shark Cove, North/South Pender Islands, s. BC
B Mukilteo, Puget Sound, c. Washington

MC121. ABALONE PIDDOCK, little piddock, Conrad's piddock
***Penitella conradi**, Pholadidea conradi, Navea conradi, Penitella parva, Pholadidea parva, Penitella subglobosa, Navea subglobosa, Navea newcombi, Martesia intercalata*
to 3.5 cm (1.5 in) long
n. BC to n. Mexico
intertidal to 20 m (65 ft)
This piddock primarily burrows into the shells of living northern abalone

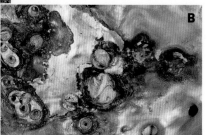

(MC165), a process not fatal to the "boree"—a very distinctive and particular habitat. Photograph A shows only the borer's handiwork; photograph B also shows several abalone piddocks.
A B Pile Point, San Juan Island, n. Washington

MC122. BEAKED PIDDOCK, rostrate piddock
***Netastoma rostratum**, Netastoma rostrata, Nettastomella rostrata, Pholadidea rostrata*
to 2 cm (0.8 in) long
s. BC to n. Mexico
intertidal to 30 m (100 ft)
Primarily a species that burrows in shale; this behaviour may lead to irregular shell formation. The beaked piddock is distinguished by the elongate posterior end and a swollen, gaping anterior.
Montana de Oro State Park, San Luis Obispo County, s. California

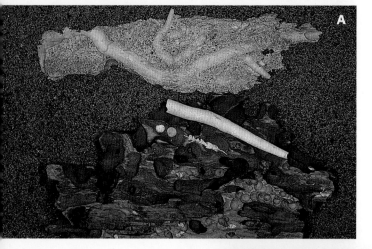

MC123. FEATHERY SHIPWORM, northwest shipworm, Pacific shipworm, shipworm, teredo
Bankia setacea
to 1 m (39 in) total length, 2.5 cm (1 in) in diameter
Japan, n. Alaska to n. Mexico
in wood exposed to saltwater, intertidal to 180 m (600 ft)
Historically and incorrectly called a worm, this creature is a boring clam responsible for the destruction of unprotected wood. Combatting this requires huge regular expenditures. Photograph A includes samples of the white clam burrow and boring activity; photograph B shows the results of boring. The **gribble**, *Limnoria lignorum*, is a tiny species of isopod (Phylum Arthropoda, p. 275) that, like this clam, consumes wood. Separately or together they remain a threat.
A Chesterman Beach, w. Vancouver Island, s. BC
B Agamemnon Channel, Nelson Island, s. BC

MC124. BILIRATE PANDORA

Pandora bilirata, *Pandora bicarinata, Pandora delicatula*
to 2 cm (0.8 in) across
Japan, c. Alaska to n. Mexico
subtidal, 5–308 m (16–1,020 ft)
A species with two different shells, this pandora is distinguished from others by one to three strong radial ribs on the left valve. Like other pandoras, its planktonic larval life is extremely short, usually less than one day!
Royal British Columbia Museum, Victoria, BC

MC125. THREADED PANDORA, western pandora

Pandora filosa
to 2.7 cm (1.1 in) across
c. Alaska to n. Mexico
subtidal, 20–300 m (65–1,000 ft)
Straight at both ends, the shells also have upturned and squared posteriors. Like all bivalves, the threaded pandora has two calcareous shells or valves connected by a chitinous (tough, protective) hinge called a ligament.
Royal British Columbia Museum, Victoria, BC

MC126. GLACIAL PANDORA, northern pandora

Pandora glacialis, *Pandora eutaenia, Pandora etaenia*
to 3 cm (1.2 in) across
Japan, Arctic Ocean, n. Alaska to n. Washington
subtidal, 5–350 m (16–1,155 ft)
Collecting an intact specimen of this clam is a challenge because of its fragile shells. Unlike most bivalves, pandoras are edentate, meaning they have no tooth-like structures in the hinge.
Royal British Columbia Museum, Victoria, BC

MC127. PUNCTATE PANDORA, dotted pandora

Pandora punctata, *Pandora punctatus, Heteroclidus punctatus*
to 7.6 cm (3 in) across
c. BC to n. Mexico
subtidal to 50 m (165 ft)
A pair of empty shells is an occasional find for a beachcomber roaming along exposed coastlines. Note the strong recurved upper edges of both shells that are characteristic of the punctate pandora.
Royal British Columbia Museum, Victoria, BC

MC128. GIANT PANDORA, grand pandora, Ward pandora
Pandora wardiana, *Pandora grandis, Pandora forresterensis*
to 7.6 cm (3 in) across
Siberia to Japan, n. Alaska to Oregon
subtidal, 5–400 m (16–1,320 ft)
This bivalve inhabits fine or silty sediments. It is also the largest living species of pandora.
Mouth of Fraser River, Strait of Georgia, s. BC

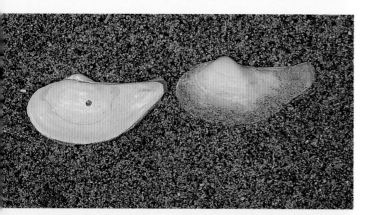

MC129. CALIFORNIA LYONSIA, Puget Sound lyonsia
Lyonsia californica, *Lyonsia haroldi, Lyonsia striata, Lyonsia gouldi, Lyonsia nesiotes, Lyonsia pugetensis*
to 4.2 cm (1.7 in) across
c. Alaska to n. Mexico
intertidal to 100 m (330 ft)
Sand often adheres to this species' very thin shells, particularly the thin brown periostracum (outer shell layer). A set of mucus-secreting glands provide for the adhesion of the sand.
Royal British Columbia Museum, Victoria, BC

MC130. BLADDERCLAM, sea bottle clam, sea-bottle clam, bottle clam, sea bottle shell, sea bottle, Nuttall's bladder clam, Nuttall's mytilimeria
Mytilimeria nuttalli
to 4.7 cm (1.8 in) across
s. Alaska to n. Mexico
intertidal to 70 m (230 ft)
The bladderclam is nearly always covered by compound tunicates, particularly the lobed compound tunicate (CH25), making it difficult to see. Look for gaping shells. The photograph shows both tunicate-covered specimens and a "clean" one.
Georgina Point, Mayne Island, s. BC

MC131. ROCK ENTODESMA, northwest ugly clam, ugly clam, rock-dwelling entodesma, rock-dwelling clam, rock-dwelling mytilimeria
Entodesma navicula, *Entodesma saxicola, Agriodesma saxicola, Lyonsia saxicola, Entodesma saxicolum, Mytilimeria saxicola*
to 15 cm (6 in) across
Japan, n. Alaska to n. Mexico
intertidal to 60 m (200 ft)
Divers may see this clam's obvious blue-tinged, orange-tipped siphons protruding from between rocks, but these twin holes can be mistaken for those of a tunicate. Close inspection should reveal the shells of the clam.
Josef Point, Gabriola Passage, s. BC

MC132. QUADRATE TRAPEZIUM

Neotrapezium liratum, *Trapezium liratum, Trapezium japonicum, Trapezium delicatum*
to 5.3 cm (2.2 in) long
Japan to Siberia, s. BC, California (?)
intertidal
Originally from the western Pacific Ocean, this nestling clam was found at the mouth of the Serpentine River by George Holm of Richmond, BC, in 1993. What is particularly fascinating is that here it strongly associates with the eastern oyster (MC51), a species introduced from North America's east coast.

Mouth of Serpentine River, Boundary Bay, s. BC

MC133. TRAPEZOIDAL THRACIA, trapezoid thracia, Pacific thracia, common Pacific thracia

Thracia trapezoides, *Thracia kanakoffi*
to 6.5 cm (2.5 in) across
c. Alaska to n. Mexico
subtidal, 11–200 m (36–660 ft)
This somewhat inflated bivalve has a larger right shell. The vast majority of bivalve species are herbivores, or algae eaters—underwater vegetarians. Three other *Thracia* species live in the Pacific Northwest.

Royal British Columbia Museum, Victoria, BC

MC134. FINE-RIBBED CARDIOMYA

Cardiomya planetica, *Cuspidaria planetica*
to 3 cm (1.2 in) long
Japan, n. Alaska to Panama and Galapagos Islands
subtidal, 25–3,000 m (83–10,000 ft)
One of the more attractive clams, the fine-ribbed cardiomya is a rare find for the average shell collector because of its small size and deep habitat. This species is distinguished by each shell having a long "beak" and more than 29 radial ribs.

Queen Charlotte Channel, Howe Sound, s. BC

MC135. RIBBED DIPPER, ribbed dipper shell, pectinate cardiomya, pectinate cuspidaria, Oldroyd's dipper shell, Oldroyd cardiomya

Cardiomya pectinata, *Cardiomya oldroydi, Cuspidaria californica*
to 4 cm (1.6 in) long
c. Alaska to c. California
subtidal, 5–1,000 m (16–3,300 ft)
The name "dipper" refers to this clam's resemblance to a liquid-delivering device. Living specimens of this strange-looking clam apparently nestle in sand or mud substrates.
Several other similar species, not likely to be encountered, live in deeper haunts.

Royal British Columbia Museum, Victoria, BC

UNIVALVES

Including limpets, puncturellas, snails, hoofsnails, slippersnails, abalones, dogwinkles, unicorns, hornmouths, mangelias, whelks, amphissas, drills, trophons, periwinkles, lacunas, nassas, bittiums, wentletraps, balcis, solarelles, margarites, turbans, olives, margin shells, spindle shells, tritons, oenopotas, caecums, lamellarids, earshells and iselicas.

Limpets and limpet-shaped snails

MC136. MASK LIMPET, masked limpet, speckled limpet, large variegated limpet
Tectura persona, *Notoacmaea persona, Notoacmea persona, Acmaea persona, Collisella radiata*
to 5 cm (2 in) across
n. Alaska to n. Mexico
intertidal
By day the mask limpet hides in damp/shaded crevices only to emerge at night, probably to feed. Note that the top of the shell or apex is significantly off centre.
Laura Point, Mayne Island, s. BC

MC137. PLATE LIMPET, Pacific plate limpet
Tectura scutum, *Notoacmaea scutum, Notoacmea scutum, Acmaea scutum, Acmaea testudinalis scutum, Acmaea patina, Acmaea pintadina*
to 6.4 cm (2.5 in) across
Japan, Siberia, n. Alaska to n. Mexico
intertidal to shallow subtidal
This limpet has a low, flat shell with an almost central top. However, the shell may be covered with sea lettuces (SW12/13).
Laura Point, Mayne Island, s. BC

MC138. SHIELD LIMPET, Californian shield limpet
Lottia pelta, *Collisella pelta, Acmaea pelta, Acmaea cassis pelta, Acmaea cassis, Acmaea olympica, Acmaea nacelloides*
to 5.4 cm (2.1 in) across
Siberia, n. Alaska to n. Mexico
intertidal
Distinguished by a tall shell with radiating bands, the shield limpet, like most other limpets, rasps marine algal growth from rock with its radula (file-like tongue).
A Outer Narrows, Slingsby Channel, c. BC
B Grice Bay, Tofino, s. BC

MC139. RIBBED LIMPET, fingered limpet, finger limpet, California finger limpet, hand limpet, mask limpet, digit limpet
Lottia digitalis, Collisella digitalis, Acmaea digitalis, Collisella austrodigitalis, Acmaea radiata
to 3.5 cm (1.5 in) across
n. Alaska to n. Mexico
intertidal
Note the pronounced ridges and off-centre, curved tip or apex of this univalve's shell. Look for the ribbed limpet in the high intertidal or splash zone amid acorn barnacles (AR164/165).
A B Laura Point, Mayne Island, s. BC

MC140. FENESTRATE LIMPET, chocolate limpet
Tectura fenestrata, Notoacmaea fenestrata, Notoacmea fenestrata, Collisella fenestrata, Acmaea fenestrata, Acmaea cribraria, Notoacmea fenestrata cribraria
to 2.6 cm (1 in) across
Alaska to n. Mexico
intertidal, may bury in sand at low tide
The apex or top of the white speckled shell is slightly off centre. Like all other limpets, this one grips the bottom tenaciously with its muscular foot.
Frank Island, w. Vancouver Island, s. BC

MC141. SPECKLED LIMPET, yellow limpet
Lottia ochracea, Collisella ochracea, Acmaea ochracea, Acmaea peramabilis, Acmaea patina
to 2 cm (0.8 in) across
s. Alaska to n. Mexico
intertidal
An active crawler, the speckled limpet often retreats under smooth rocks. Beachcombers in the southern Pacific Northwest are more likely to find this limpet, as it is most abundant from Oregon south.
Ecola State Park, Cannon Beach, n. Oregon

MC142. WHITECAP LIMPET, white-cap limpet, white cap limpet, white-capped limpet, dunce-cap limpet, dunce cap limpet, bishop's cap limpet, Chinaman's hat limpet, white cap, Chinaman's hat
Acmaea mitra
to 5 cm (2 in) across
n. Alaska to n. Mexico
intertidal to 60 m (200 ft)
This limpet is often coated with species of crustose corallines (SW86), sometimes with stubby nodes. Ironically, this very coralline algae is a major food source for the whitecap limpet.
A Turn Island, San Juan Channel, n. Washington
B Various Pacific Northwest locales

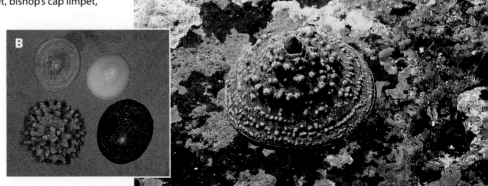

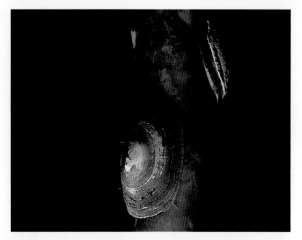

MC143. UNSTABLE LIMPET, unstable seaweed limpet, kelp limpet, rocking chair limpet
Lottia instabilis, *Notoacmaea instabilis, Collisella instabilis, Acmaea instabilis*
to 3.5 cm (1.5 in) across
n. Alaska to s. California
intertidal to 73 m (240 ft)
Very often this species resides on the stipes or stems of old-growth kelp (SW57), where its tight grip can leave a shallow scar.
Laura Point, Mayne Island, s. BC

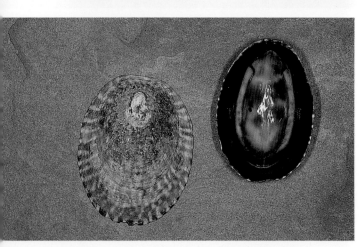

MC144. GIANT OWL LIMPET, owl limpet, owl shell
Lottia gigantea, *Scurria gigantea*
to 10 cm (4 in) across
n. Washington to n. Mexico
intertidal, along exposed shores
The shell is often polished for jewellery, and the flesh was a historic food source for coastal Aboriginal peoples. Giant owl limpet numbers in some locales are much reduced.
Royal British Columbia Museum, Victoria, BC

MC145. SEAWEED LIMPET, feather-boa limpet, kelp limpet
Discurria insessa, *Notoacmaea insessa, Notoacmea insessa, Collisella insessa, Acmaea insessa, Patella insessa*
to 2.2 cm (0.9 in) across
s. Alaska to n. Mexico
intertidal
A determined beachcomber may find this animal clinging to the central rib of the feather boa kelp (SW34), but the search might be time-consuming and unsuccessful.
Royal British Columbia Museum, Victoria, BC

MC146. FILE LIMPET, California file limpet
Lottia limatula, *Collisella limatula, Acmaea limatula*, misspelled: *Acmae limatula*
to 5 cm (2 in) across
s. BC to n. Mexico
intertidal
Minute overlapping scales on the strong ribs makes the shell characteristically rough to the touch. Though primarily a species that inhabits the exposed outer coast, the file limpet has also been taken in current-swept inside passages.
Seal Rock State Wayside, Newport, c. Oregon

MC147. BLACK LIMPET, black turban limpet, turban shell limpet, black seaweed limpet
Lottia asmi, *Collisella asmi, Acmaea asmi*
to 1 cm (0.3 in) across
s. Alaska to n. Mexico
intertidal
Very diligent searching of black turban snail shells (MC222) may uncover one or more of these tiny hitchhikers. Look closely: the black limpet's colour matches that of the black turban.
Royal British Columbia Museum, Victoria, BC

MC148. SURFGRASS LIMPET, chaffy limpet
Tectura paleacea, *Notoacmaea paleacea, Notoacmea paleacea, Collisella paleacea, Acmaea paleacea*
to 1 cm (0.3 in) across
s. BC to n. Mexico
intertidal
A very narrow body and a strong, muscular foot allows the surfgrass limpet to hang on to surfgrass leaves (SW4) even in heavy surge—an unstable environment!
Sunset Bay State Park, Charleston, s. Oregon

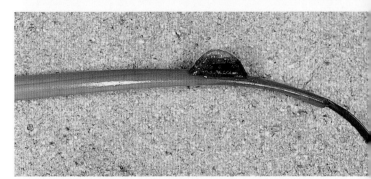

MC149. PACIFIC EELGRASS LIMPET, eelgrass limpet, bowl limpet
Lottia alveus paralella, *Lottia alveus, Collisella alveus, Acmaea alveus*
to 1.2 cm (0.5 in) across
s. Alaska to California
intertidal to shallow subtidal
As one might guess, this limpet lives on eelgrass leaves (SW2). The Atlantic eelgrass limpet, *Lottia alveus alveus,* a different subspecies, is apparently now one of the very few marine creatures officially declared extinct.
Ucluth Peninsula, w. Vancouver Island, s. BC

MC150. CORDED WHITE LIMPET
Niveotectura funiculata, *Acmaea funiculata*
to 2.5 cm (1 in) across
c. Alaska to n. Mexico
subtidal, 15–70 m (50–230 ft)
Somewhat atypical of most limpets, this species is commonly found at depths well below the intertidal zone. It is therefore more accessible to the diving naturalist.
Finisterre Island, Bowen Island, s. BC

MC151. RINGED BLIND LIMPET
Cryptobranchia concentrica, *Lepeta concentrica, Cryptobranchia caecoides*
▶to 2.3 cm (0.9 in) across
n. Alaska to c. California
intertidal to 60 m (200 ft)
Only very careful searching will uncover the ringed blind limpet hidden among its surroundings. The shells of this species, like those of all molluscs, have three distinct layers, the innermost being a smooth surface against the animal's body.
Royal British Columbia Museum, Victoria, BC

MC152. ▶PUSTULATE BLIND LIMPET
Lepeta caeca, *Lepeta alba, Cocculina cazanica*
to 1.5 cm (0.6 in) long
Arctic Ocean, n. Atlantic Ocean, n. Alaska to s. California
intertidal to subtidal
The radial striations show small pustules (pimples) where they meet the concentric growth rings—a feature that distinguishes this limpet from the ringed blind limpet (MC151). (The pustules do not show in this photograph.) This species often hides under rocks and consequently is seen infrequently.
Douglas Island, Stephens Passage, s. Alaska

MC153. ROUGH KEYHOLE LIMPET, keyhole limpet, rough keyhole, rough key-hole limpet
Diodora aspera, *Glyphis aspera*, misspelled: *Diadora aspera, Diadora murina*
to 7.6 cm (3 in) across
n. Alaska to Nicaragua
intertidal to 40 m (130 ft)
Often the shell is so overgrown with other life that the definitive round hole at the top is the only indication of this animal's presence.
A Surge Narrows, Maurelle Island, s. BC
B Josef Point, Gabriola Passage, s. BC

MC154. TWO-SPOT KEYHOLE LIMPET, two-spotted keyhole limpet
Fissurellidea bimaculata, *Fissurellidea bimaculatus, Megatebennus bimaculatus*
▶to 5 cm (2 in) across
s. Alaska to n. Mexico
intertidal to 33 m (100 ft)
The two-spot keyhole limpet's small shell is hidden below a covering body layer. This cryptic univalve nestles among compound tunicates, sponges or algal holdfasts. Photograph C shows a battered old intertidal survivor. Several other subtidal species of limpet occur in the Pacific Northwest but are rarely found.
A Tongue Point, Olympic coast, n. Washington
B Ucluth Peninsula, w. Vancouver Island, s. BC
C Stubbs Island, Weynton Passage, c. BC

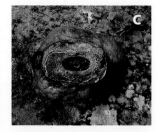
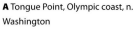

MC155. HOODED PUNCTURELLA, hood puncturella, helmet puncturella, ribbed keyhole limpet, hooded keyhole limpet, hooded keyhole
Cranopsis cucullata, *Puncturella cucullata, Puncturella multirugosa, Rimula cucullata*, misspelled: *Craniopsis cucullata*
to 4.2 cm (1.7 in) across
c. Alaska to n. Mexico
intertidal to 200 m (660 ft)
Note the strong ribs and puncture-like hole just off-centre on this limpet species. Frequently seen by divers.
Agamemnon Channel, Nelson Island, s. BC

MC156. MANY-RIBBED PUNCTURELLA, many-rib puncturella
Cranopsis multistriata, *Puncturella multistriata*
to 2 cm (0.8 in) across
n. Alaska to n. Mexico
intertidal to 91 m (300 ft)
Similar to the preceding species, but with a smooth basal edge and finer radial ribs. Each living limpet has a pair of tentacles (visible sensory organs) at the anterior end.
Royal British Columbia Museum, Victoria, BC

MC157. HELMET PUNCTURELLA
Puncturella galeata
to 2 cm (0.8 in) across
n. Alaska to s. California
subtidal, 19–137 m (60–450 ft)
This snail frequently adheres to empty shells of other molluscs with its strong muscular foot, an organ designed for a tight grip as well as for slow locomotion.
Several other *Puncturellas* exist in the Pacific Northwest, but they are unlikely to be found.
Royal British Columbia Museum, Victoria, BC

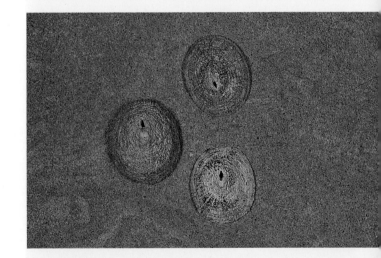

MC158. FLAT HOOFSNAIL, horse's hoofsnail, white hoofsnail, hoof snail, ancient hoof shell, Washington hoof shell, hoof shell
Hipponix cranioides, *Hipponix antiquatus, Hipponix serratus, Antisabia cranioides*, misspelled: *Hipponix cranoides*
to 2.5 cm (1 in) across
s. BC to n. Mexico
intertidal and subtidal
This creature sits on a calcareous slab secreted by its foot. Its shell is often overgrown with algae and other life, which complicates the beachcomber's search.
A second species, the tiny hoofsnail, *Hipponix tumens,* has only been found in s. BC.
Royal British Columbia Museum, Victoria, BC

MC159. WRINKLED SLIPPERSNAIL, wrinkled slipper shell, Pacific half-slippersnail, Pacific half-slipper shell, Pacific half-slipper, half-slipper snail, half-slipper shell
Crepipatella dorsata, Crepipatella lingulata, Crepidula dorsata, Calyptraea dorsata, Crepidula fissurata
to 2.5 cm (1 in) across
n. Alaska to Peru
intertidal to 100 m (330 ft)
This filter-feeding snail attaches to solid objects, including bottles and other man-made debris. Note the small shelf on the inside of the upturned shell.
Laura Point, Mayne Island, s. BC

MC160. CUP-AND-SAUCER SNAIL, Pacific Chinese-hat snail, Pacific Chinese hat, Pacific chinese-hat
Calyptraea fastigiata
to 2.5 cm (1 in) across
c. Alaska to s. California
intertidal to 137 m (452 ft)
A partial shelf on the inside of the shell (at right centre in the photograph) distinguishes the cup-and-saucer snail from the similar looking whitecap limpet (MC142). When both are viewed from above they are almost identical. The photograph shows a smaller specimen atop a larger one, together with an overturned individual.
Beg Islands, Barkley Sound, s. BC

MC161. NORTHERN WHITE SLIPPERSNAIL, white slipper snail, northern white slipper shell, western white slippersnail, western white slipper shell, western white slipper-shell, white slipper shell, white slipper, white slipper limpet
Crepidula nummaria, Crepidula fimbriata, and may be the same as Crepidula perforans and Crepidula nivea
to 5 cm (2 in) across
n. Alaska to Panama
intertidal to subtidal
As a shelled mollusc grows, an organ called a mantle secretes calcium along the edge of each shell.
Discovery Passage, Quadra Island, s. BC

MC162. HOOKED SLIPPERSNAIL, hooked slipper snail, hooked slipper shell, hooked slipper-shell, hooked slipper limpet, hooked slipper, turban slipper shell
Crepidula adunca
to 2.5 cm (1 in) across
n. BC to n. Mexico
intertidal to 19 m (60 ft)
Distinguished by the shell's bent apex (tip), this limpet commonly attaches to blue topsnail shells (MC210), as shown in the photograph. The photograph also features an upturned hooked slippersnail. Smaller male specimens frequently stack atop a large female, also shown.
Imperial Eagle Channel, Barkley Sound, s. BC

MC163. ▶ATLANTIC CONVEX SLIPPERSNAIL

Crepidula convexa, *Crepidula glauca*
▶to 2.5 cm (1 in) across
▶Atlantic Ocean, s. BC to s. California
intertidal

George Holm of Richmond, BC, a keen shell collector, first noticed and collected this tiny Japanese interloper inhabiting Boundary Bay, BC, in 1966. Perhaps it arrived with the eastern oyster (MC51). Note that the photograph shows the animal attached to the mudflat snail (MC202), itself an import from Japan.

Also introduced incidentally with oysters from the Atlantic coast, the Atlantic slipper, *Crepidula fornicata*, maintains itself in a few select Pacific Northwest locales. It looks similar to the hooked slippersnail (MC162) but grows much larger, and its pointed top or apex is folded over to one side. It often appears as a "group" with a larger female carrying a stack of smaller males.

Centennial Beach, Boundary Bay, s. BC

MC164. RETICULATE BUTTON SNAIL, reticulate button shell, reticulate gadinia, button shell

Trimusculus reticulatus, *Gadinia reticulata*
to 2 cm (0.8 in) across
n. Washington to n. Mexico, Chile
intertidal

Its habit of hiding in crevices, caves and even abandoned burrows of rock-boring clams (MC119/120) make this secretive snail a difficult quarry for the beachcombing naturalist. An air breather, it spends most of its time out of the water.

Montana de Oro State Park, San Luis Obispo County, s. California

Coiled snails

MC165. NORTHERN ABALONE, small northern abalone, pinto abalone, Japanese abalone, Kamchatka abalone, Alaskan abalone

Haliotis kamtschatkana, *Haliotis kamschatkensis*, *Haliotis assimilis*, *Haliotis smithsoni*, *Haliotis aulae*
to 18 cm (7 in) across
Japan, Siberia, s. Alaska to n. Mexico
intertidal to 35 m (116 ft)

Populations of this species have been obliterated by overharvesting and fisheries mismanagement. Even areas lightly harvested have many fewer individuals. Prospects for recovery are bleak indeed as illegal poaching activities outpace the many benefits of fishing closures.

A Laura Point, Mayne Island, s. BC
B Mutine Point, Barkley Sound, s. BC
C Anderson Bay, Texada Island, s. BC

MC166. FLAT ABALONE, northern green abalone
Haliotis walallensis
to 17.5 cm (7 in) across
Oregon to s. California
intertidal to 21 m (70 ft)
Distinguished by a flat, somewhat oblong shell with low ribs intersected with raised striations, the flat abalone is typically brick red. Historic reports indicate this species lives in BC, but no verifying specimens exist in reference collections. Look closely: you may be able to confirm its presence farther north.

In spite of some historic efforts to introduce it from California to Washington and BC, the red abalone, *Haliotis rufescens,* has not established itself in the Pacific Northwest north of Oregon. However, several years ago a few very large specimens were collected off the west coast of Vancouver Island, BC. Biologist Rick Harbo is at a loss to explain this find. Perhaps they drifted north on large kelp mats via an El Niño-related current? Red abalone shells were historically traded along the coast by First Nations peoples. The black abalone, *Haliotis cracherodii,* is another species not presently found north of Oregon.

Tichenor Rock, Port Orford, s. Oregon

MC167. WRINKLED DOGWINKLE, frilled dogwinkle, wrinkled dog whelk, wrinkled purple snail, wrinkled thais, wrinkled purple whelk, wrinkled whelk, frilled whelk, Roman purple snail, purple snail, purple whelk, wrinkled purple, dog whelk, oyster drill
Nucella lamellosa, Thais lamellosa, Thais lamellosa cymica, Thais lamellosa hormica
to 12.5 cm (5 in) long
n. Alaska to s. California
intertidal, to at least 10 m (33 ft)
Extremely variable shell colour, proportions and sculpturing often confuse the novice naturalist and expert alike. This species' unique egg cases, called sea oats, are shown in photograph C.

A White Islets, Strait of Georgia, s. BC
B Various Pacific Northwest sites
C Discovery Passage, Campbell River, s. BC

MC168. ▶NORTHERN STRIPED DOGWINKLE, striped dogwinkle, ribbed dogwinkle, emarginate dogwinkle, emarginate whelk, ribbed rock whelk, rock-dwelling thais, rock thais, short-spired purple snail, short-spired rock snail, short spired purple, short-spired purple, ribbed whelk, rock whelk
Nucella osterina, Nucella emarginata, *Thais emarginata,* misspelled: *Nucella marginata*
to 4 cm (1.6 in) long
n. Alaska to n. Mexico
intertidal
This attractive and readily noticeable snail prefers the pounding surf of the exposed rocky coast.
*Studies undertaken since the late 1990s have resulted in *Nucella emarginata* being designated as the ▶southern striped dogwinkle, found in s. California.

Frank Island, w. Vancouver Island, s. BC

MC169. CHANNELLED DOGWINKLE, channelled dogwhelk, channelled whelk, channelled purple snail, channelled purple, channelled thais
Nucella canaliculata, *Thais canaliculata*, *Purpura canaliculata*
to 4 cm (1.6 in) long
n. Alaska to c. California
intertidal
This carnivore uses its radula (drill-like tongue) to subdue and consume its barnacle prey. It also lays its characteristic yellow, somewhat urn-shaped egg cases amid barnacles.
Fox Islands, Slingsby Channel, c. BC

MC170. FILE DOGWINKLE, rough purple whelk, uniform purple snail, purple thais, rough purple
Nucella lima, *Thais lima*
to 5 cm (2 in) long
n. Alaska to n. BC
intertidal to subtidal
Very similar to the channelled dogwinkle (MC169) but it has fine ribs in between the heavy ones, a feature nicely illustrated in the photograph. Its egg cases are also slightly different.
Hungry Point, Petersburg, s. Alaska. Rick Harbo photograph

MC171. ANGULAR UNICORN, angular unicorn shell, angular thorn drupe, spotted thorn drupe, thorn snail
Acanthina spirata
to 4 cm (1.6 in) long
BC to n. Mexico
intertidal
An adult specimen has a sharp spine at the edge of the shell opening. Interrupted dark spiral bands also decorate the outside of the shell. This is only an occasional Pacific Northwest resident.
Royal British Columbia Museum, Victoria, BC

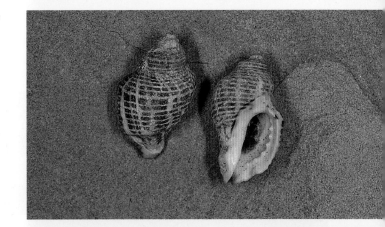

MC172. LEAFY HORNMOUTH, leafy hornmouth snail, foliate thornmouth, foliated thorn purple, foliate thorn purpura, leafy foliated thorn purpura, leafy thorn purpura, murex
Ceratostoma foliatum, *Ceratostoma foliata*, *Ceratostoma foliatus*, *Pterorytis foliatus*, *Purpura foliatum*, *Purpura foliata*, *Murex foliatum*
to 10 cm (4 in) long
c. Alaska to s. California
intertidal to 65 m (215 ft)
Large seasonal gatherings of this "winged" snail result in extensive masses of its distinctive egg cases, as shown in the photograph.
Sechart Channel, Barkley Sound, s. BC

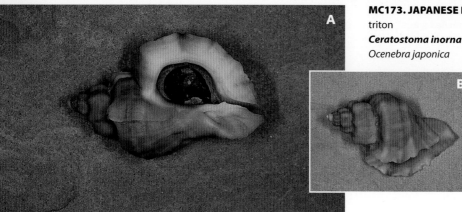

MC173. JAPANESE ROCKSNAIL, Japanese oyster drill, Japanese dwarf triton
Ceratostoma inornatum, *Ocenebra inornatum, Ocinebrina inornata, Ocenebra japonica*

►to 5 cm (2 in) long
Japan, introduced into BC, Washington and California
intertidal
This import preys upon native and non-native species of oyster. Its shell sculpture is somewhat variable.
A B Sea Rose Gifts & Shell Museum, Yachats, c. Oregon

MC174. DIRE WHELK, elongate dire whelk, spindle snail, spindle whelk, spindle shell
Lirabuccinum dirum, *Searlesia dira, Kelletia dira,* misspelled: *Searlisia dira*
to 5 cm (2 in) long
n. Alaska to s. California
intertidal to 35 m (115 ft)
This active snail is a scavenger that particularly prefers injured prey, which it locates with surprising speed. Its characteristic egg capsules are visible in the photograph.
Laura Point, Mayne Island, s. BC

MC175. WRINKLED AMPHISSA, wrinkled snail, wrinkled dove snail, Columbian amphissa
Amphissa columbiana
to 3 cm (1.2 in) long
n. Alaska to s. California

intertidal to 30 m (100 ft)
Aggregations of this univalve converge rapidly to scavenge the carcass of any unfortunate creature emitting body fluids. Variable shell dimensions and colour are shown in the photographs.
A Breakwater Island, Gabriola Passage, s. BC
B Green Point, Spieden Island, n. Washington

MC176. VARIEGATED AMPHISSA, variegate amphissa, variegated dove shell, varicolored amphissa, Joseph's coat amphissa, Joseph's coat dove shell
Amphissa versicolor, *Amphissa versicolor incisa, Amphissa incisa, Amphissa lineata*
to 1.9 cm (0.7 in) long
c. BC to n. Mexico
intertidal to 46 m (150 ft)
The ribs running at a notable angle to the shell's central axis distinguish the variegated amphissa from the wrinkled amphissa (MC175), which has parallel ones.
The much smaller reticulate amphissa, *Amphissa reticulata,* is a very rare subtidal find.
Royal British Columbia Museum, Victoria, BC

MC177. SCULPTURED ROCKSNAIL, sculptured rock snail, sculptured whelk, Carpenter's dwarf triton, sculptured rock shell
Ocinebrina interfossa, *Ocenebra interfossa, Tritonalia interfossa, Ocenebra atropupurea, Ocenebra clathrata, Ocenebra fraseri*
to 2.5 cm (1 in) long
Alaska to n. Mexico
intertidal to 100 m (330 ft)
This snail's attractive shell makes it a treasure for the shell-collecting beachcomber.
Steep Island, Discovery Passage, s. BC

MC178. LURID ROCKSNAIL, lurid rock snail, dwarf lurid triton, lurid dwarf triton, lurid rock shell, dwarf triton
Ocinebrina lurida, *Ocenebra lurida, Ocenebra lurida aspera, Ocenebra lurida munda, Urosalpinx lurida, Tritonalia lurida, Tritonium luridum, Ocenebra minor, Ocenebra munda, Ocenebra rotunda*
to 4 cm (1.6 in) long
c. Alaska to n. Mexico
intertidal to 200 m (660 ft)
A small but obvious inhabitant of strong-current locales, which are also preferred by many divers.
Laura Point, Mayne Island, s. BC

MC179. SCLERA ROCKSNAIL
Ocenebra sclera, *Urosalpinx sclera*
▶to 2.5 cm (1 in) long
n. BC to c. California
subtidal
This specimen was purchased from Sea Rose Gifts, the home of the Oregon Coast Shell Museum, near Yachats, Oregon. Drop by and see a wonderful collection.
Three other seldom-seen Pacific Northwest *Ocenebra* species round out this group of small snails fancied by shell collectors.
Sea Rose Gifts & Shell Museum, Yachats, c. Oregon

MC180. ATLANTIC OYSTER DRILL, eastern oyster drill, eastern drill, oyster drill
Urosalpinx cinerea, *Urosalpinx cinera, Urosalpinx cinereus*
to 4.3 cm (1.7 in) long
s. BC to c. California—incidentally introduced with the eastern oyster (MC51)
intertidal to 15 m (50 ft)
Primarily established in river estuaries where oyster culture occurs—obviously an unwelcome intruder. Specimens shown in the photograph are on an oyster shell, an animal that is its preferred prey.
Royal British Columbia Museum, Victoria, BC

MC181. SANDPAPER TROPHON
Scabrotrophon maltzani, *Trophon maltzani, Nipponotrophon maltzani,*
Trophonopsis lasius, Trophonopsis tenuisculptus, Trophon tenuisculpta,
Trophon subserratus, Trophonopsis subserratus, Nipponotrophon subserratus,
Nipponotrophon lasius
to 5 cm (2 in) long
n. Alaska to n. Mexico
intertidal to 1,000 m (3,300 ft)
The sandpaper trophon species has a very long aperture (shell opening),
through which its muscular foot protrudes.
Quarry Bay, Nelson Island, s. BC

MC182. WINGED TROPHON, Stuart's trophon
Boreotrophon stuarti, *Trophonopsis stuarti, Trophon stuarti, Boreotrophon*
smithi
to 6 cm (2.3 in) long
n. Alaska to s. California
intertidal to 100 m (330 ft)
This univalve's attractive shape and sculpturing make it a real prize for even
the casual beachcomber.
Kyen Point, Barkley Sound, s. BC

MC183. CORDED TROPHON, orpheus trophon, threaded trophon
Boreotrophon orpheus, *Trophonopsis orpheus, Trophon orpheus, Ocenebra*
orpheus, Ocenebra stuarti, Ocenebra smithi
to 2.5 cm (1 in) long
c. Alaska to s. California
subtidal to 150 m (500 ft)
The strongly ribbed shell of the corded trophon has a very long canal
protruding from the lower end of the shell opening.
Royal British Columbia Museum, Victoria, BC

MC184. RIBBED TROPHON, many-ribbed trophon
Boreotrophon multicostatus, *Trophon multicostatus, Trophonopsis*
clathratus, Boreotrophon pauciocostatus, Boreotrophon lamellosus
to 1.7 cm (0.7 in) long
c. Alaska to s. California
intertidal to 15 m (50 ft)
The complement of 11 thin, sharp-edged ridges on each whorl or turn
of the shell and the long, open siphonal canal at the shell's opening are
distinctive for this species.
Primarily northern and deep-dwelling, the trophon group is represented by
some other Pacific Northwest species.
St. Lazaria Island, Sitka Sound, s. Alaska

MC185. SITKA PERIWINKLE, Sitka littorine

Littorina sitkana, Littorina sitchana, Littorina atkana, possibly: *Littorina rudis, Littorina saxatilis*
to 2.5 cm (1 in) long
Japan, Siberia, n. Alaska to s. Oregon
intertidal
Seeking shade and moisture when exposed at low tide, the Sitka periwinkle often aggregates as shown in photograph B. Its squat shell is as wide as it is tall.
The similar eroded periwinkle, *Littorina keenae,* is unlikely to be encountered north of Oregon.
A Frank Island, w. Vancouver Island, s. BC
B Brown Island, Friday Harbor, n. Washington

MC186. CHECKERED PERIWINKLE, checkered littorine, checkered littorina

Littorina scutulata, Melarhaphe scutulata, Littorina scutellata
to 1.9 cm (0.7 in) long
n. Alaska to n. Mexico
intertidal
Only submerged for brief periods on the highest tides, the checkered periwinkle can actually drown if underwater too long. Look for it in the splash zone.
A Georgina Point, Mayne Island, s. BC
B Fort Worden State Park, Port Townsend, n. Washington

MC187. ▶SALT MARSH PERIWINKLE

Algamorda subrotunda, Littorina subrotunda, Algamorda newcombiana, Littorina newcombiana
to 0.8 cm (0.3 in) long
s. BC to n. California
intertidal
Distinguished by a thinner shell than that of the Sitka periwinkle (MC185) or checkered periwinkle (MC186), the salt marsh periwinkle also has a flange-like lip that partially covers its umbilicus, a hole into the columella (pillar) that the shell spirals around. Look for it amid salt marsh vegetation.
Crescent Beach, Boundary Bay, s. BC

MC188. ▶ORIENTAL CECINA

Cecina manchurica
▶to 0.8 cm (0.3 in) long
n.w. Pacific, s. BC to Washington
intertidal
A tiny but distinctive snail that was inadvertently introduced from the Orient, this species can be found on a beach walk even if it is not low tide. Look carefully amid marshy vegetation at the extreme high-tide level.
Birch Bay, Strait of Georgia, n. Washington

MC189. VARIABLE LACUNA, variegate lacuna, variegated lacuna, variegated chink-shell
Lacuna variegata
to 1.6 cm (0.7 in) long
c. Alaska to n. Mexico
intertidal to shallow subtidal
The variable lacuna is distinguished by its wide and flaring aperture or shell opening. It is available to the beachcomber, but its small size makes it a challenging quarry.
Cottam Point, Parksville, s. BC

MC190. WIDE LACUNA, wide chink shell, wide chink snail, wide chink-shell, wide-chink snail, common northern chink-shell, common northern chink shell, common northern lacuna, northern lacuna, northern chink shell, carinate lacuna, carinate chink shell, chink shell
Lacuna vincta, *Lacuna carinata*, *Lacuna carinata effusa*, *Lacuna carinata exaeauata*, *Lacuna divaricata*, *Lacuna solidula*, *Lacuna porrecta*
to 1.6 cm (0.7 in) long
n. Alaska to s. California
intertidal
This snail lays its eggs in tiny yellow doughnut-shaped clusters on various marine plants and algae, as shown in the photograph.
Long Island, near Lopez Island, n. Washington

MC191. CARINATE DOVESNAIL, carinated dove snail, keeled dove shell, keeled dove-shell, carinate dove shell, carinate dove-shell, keeled columbella
Alia carinata, *Mitrella carinata*, *Nitidella carinata*, *Columbella carinata*, *Mitrella californica*
to 1.1 cm (0.4 in) long
s. Alaska to n. Mexico
intertidal to 15 m (50 ft)
Though tiny, this univalve is easily and commonly seen on eelgrass (SW2) and various kelps.
Indian Cove, Shaw Island, n. Washington

MC192. SHAGGY DOVESNAIL, dovesnail, Gould's dove shell, common dove-mollusk
Astyris gausapata, *Alia gausapata*, *Mitrella gausapata*, *Columbella gausapata*, *Nitidella gausapata*, *Mitrella gouldi*, *Mitrella gouldii*, *Nitidella gouldii*, *Nitidella lutulenta*, *Collumbella dalli*, *Alia casciana*
to 1.3 cm (0.5 in) long
s. Alaska to n. Mexico
subtidal, 20–200 m (66–660 ft)
Along with the shaggy dovesnails in the photograph is a cluster of their transparent eggs.
Jericho Beach, English Bay, s. BC

MC193. ▶SWELLED DOVESNAIL
Alia tuberosa, *Mitrella tuberosa*
to 1 cm (0.3 in) long
s. Alaska to n. Mexico
intertidal to subtidal
Distinguished from the carinate dovesnail (MC191) by the swollen lower portion adjacent to the aperture (shell opening). A challenging quarry, even for the most accomplished observer searching mud flats.
Crescent Beach, Boundary Bay, s. BC

MC194. VIOLET-BAND MANGELIA
Kurtziella crebricostata, *Mangelia crebricostata, Kurtziella plumbea*
to 2 cm (0.8 in) long
c. Alaska to n. Washington
intertidal to 85 m (280 ft)
Only with great vigilance will the beachcomber notice this dweller of sandy substrates. Its attractive shell shape may make it worth the effort.
Departure Bay, Nanaimo, s. BC

MC195. WESTERN LEAN NASSA, western lean dogwhelk, lean western nassa, lean basketsnail, lean basket snail, lean basket shell, lean basket-shell, lean dog whelk, mud nassa, lean nassa
Nassarius mendicus, *Alectrion mendicus, Nassarius mendica, Alectrion mendica, Nassarius cooperi, Nassarius indisputabilis*
to 2.2 cm (0.9 in) long
n. Alaska to n. Mexico
intertidal to 75 m (250 ft)
This scavenger uses its tube-like siphon as a "taste" receptor to home in on its quarry. A silt covering may obscure specimens that live in low-current locales.
Sutton Islets, Egmont, s. BC

MC196. JAPANESE NASSA
Nassarius fraterculus
to 1.5 cm (0.6 in) long
Japan, s. BC to n. Washington
intertidal
This introduced snail was historically recorded from a few locales in Puget Sound. In 1985, George Holm of Richmond, BC, found specimens at Centennial Beach in Boundary Bay, s. BC. Is this population a result of an introduction there or the result of a northern advance out of Puget Sound?
Centennial Beach, Boundary Bay, s. BC

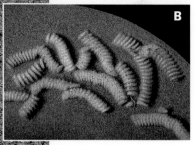

MC197. GIANT WESTERN NASSA, channelled nassa, channelled basket-whelk, giant western dogwelk, channelled dogwelk, channelled dog whelk, channelled basket snail, channelled basket shell, channelled basket-shell, basket shell, nassa
Nassarius fossatus, *Alectrion fossatus, Alectrion fossata, Nassa fossata*
to 5 cm (2 in) long
s. Alaska to n. Mexico
intertidal to 18 m (60 ft)
A prolific spawner, this sand-dwelling scavenger lays its characteristic egg masses on virtually any available solid object, including commercial traps and moonsnail egg collars (MC228), as shown in photograph B.
A B Snow Creek Marina, Olympic coast, n. Washington

MC198. BLACK DOG WHELK, eastern mud whelk, mud dog whelk, mud basket shell, eastern mud snail, eastern mudsnail, eastern mud nassa, mud snail, worn-out basket shell, worn out dog whelk
Ilyanassa obsoleta, *Ilyanassa obsoletus, Nassarius obsoleta, Nassarius obsoletus, Alectrion obsoleta, Desmondia obsoleta*
to 3 cm (1.2 in) long
s. BC to c. California, introduced from the Atlantic coast of North America
intertidal to shallow subtidal

Photograph A shows specimens with varying amounts of wear on their shells; photograph B shows two specimens with characteristic eggs on eelgrass (SW2).
Two other Pacific Northwest *Nassarius* species have been documented but are most likely found from Oregon south.
A Crescent Beach, Boundary Bay, s. BC
B Tokeland, Willapa Harbor, s. Washington

MC199. ▶MODEST LATTICEWORK SNAIL
Neoadmete modesta, *Admete modesta, Cancellaria modesta, Admete unalaskensis*
to 4 cm (1.6 in) long
s. Alaska to Washington
subtidal
The modest latticework snail is usually collected by subtidal dredging. Methodical sieving through dredged material must follow.
Five other species of cancellariid or latticework snails live in the Pacific Northwest.
Saxe Point, s. Vancouver Island, s. BC

MC200. THREADED BITTIUM, threaded snail, giant Pacific bittium, giant Pacific coast bittium, Eschrict's bittium, giant Pacific hornsnail, threaded horn snail, threaded cerith, screw snail, screw shell
Bittium eschrichtii, *Bittium eschrichti, Stylidium eschrichtii, Bittium icelum*
to 2 cm (0.8 in) long
s. Alaska to n. Mexico
intertidal to 54 m (180 ft)
A curious beachcomber may find small aggregations of this tiny, elongate snail by turning over rocks.
Sutton Islets, Egmont, s. BC

MC201. SLENDER BITTIUM, slender horsesnail, slender cerith
Bittium attenuatum, *Bittium attenuatum boreale*, *Lirobittium attenuatum*, *Bittium boreale*, *Bittium esuciens*, *Bittium latifilosum*, *Bittium multifilosum*
to 1.5 cm (0.6 in) long
s. Alaska to n. Mexico
intertidal to 70 m (230 ft)
More slender than the threaded bittium (MC200), this snail has faintly beaded spiral ridges.
Photograph B shows three specimens feeding on a sponge.
The beaded bittium, *Bittium munitum,* has very conspicuous beads around its shell.
A Laura Point, Mayne Island, s. BC
B Daniel Point, Agamemnon Channel, s. BC

MC202. MUDFLAT SNAIL, false-cerith snail, Japanese false cerith, Cuming's false cerith, false cerith, zoned cerith, screw shell, tall-spired snail
Batillaria cumingi, *Batillaria cumingii*, *Batillaria zonalis*, *Batillaria alterima*, *Batillaria attramentaria*
to 5 cm (2 in) long
Japan, s. BC to c. California, introduced from Japan
intertidal
On finding an abundance of these snails on a mudflat, it is difficult to believe that this is not a native species. Photograph B shows a specimen "carrying an Olympia oyster (MC53)" that settled on it as spat.
A Bennett Bay, Mayne Island, s. BC
B Mouth of Nicomekl River, Boundary Bay, s. BC

MC203. MONEY WENTLETRAP, Indian money wentletrap, Indian wentletrap
Epitonium indianorum, *Nitidiscala indianorum*, *Scalaria indianorum*, *Epitonium columbianum*, *Epitonium montereyensis*, *Epitonium montereyense*, *Epitonium regiomontanum*, *Scalaria regiomontana*, misspelled: *Scala indiorum*
to 3.8 cm (1.6 in) long
s. Alaska to n. Mexico
intertidal to 180 m (600 ft)
Yes, some First Nations peoples used this attractive shell as a medium of exchange.
Carlos Island, Gulf Islands, s. BC

MC204. TINTED WENTLETRAP, white wentletrap, painted wentletrap
Epitonium tinctum, *Nitidiscala tincta*, *Nitidiscala eelense*, *Epitonium subcornatum*, *Epitonium indianorum tincta*
to 3.2 cm (1.3 in) long
s. Alaska to n. Mexico
intertidal to 45 m (150 ft)
This tiny predator boldly feeds on the tentacles of the green surf anemone (CN13) and the pink-tipped anemone (CN14).
Chesterman Beach, w. Vancouver Island, s. BC

MC205. BOREAL WENTLETRAP, smooth wentletrap, northern opal-shell, northern opal shell, Wroblewski's wentletrap, Chace's wentletrap
Opalia borealis, *Epitonium borealis, Opalia wroblewskii, Epitonium wroblewskii, Opalia wroblewskyi, Opalia chacei, Acirsa chacei, Opalia gouldi*
to 3.2 cm (1.3 in) long
n. Alaska to n. Mexico
intertidal to 90 m (300 ft)
Like many wentletraps, this species is a predator of sea anemones. At least six other species of wentletraps live in the Pacific Northwest, though they are seldom seen, being both diminutive and deep dwelling.
Plumper Islands, Weynton Passage, c. BC

MC206. SHINING BALCIS, shining melanella, Carpenter's melanella
Balcis micans, *Balcis micans borealis, Eulimia micans, Melanella micans, Balcis comoxensis*
to 1.3 cm (0.5 in) long
c. Alaska to n. Mexico
subtidal, 16–100 m (50–330 ft)
Very difficult to notice on silty or sandy bottoms, even for the most observant diver.
Mukilteo, Puget Sound, c. Washington

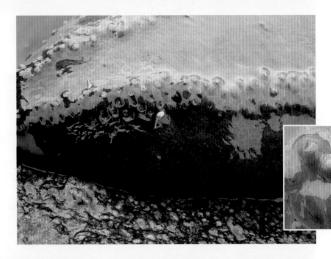

MC207. BRITISH COLUMBIAN BALCIS
Balcis columbiana
to 1 cm (0.3 in) long
s. Alaska to s. BC
intertidal to subtidal
Nicely illustrated in the photograph, this balcis associates with the giant black cucumaria (EC58). Many such hidden treasures await the naturalist who roams the shorelines or the reefs of the Pacific Northwest.
Several other smaller balcis species inhabit the Pacific Northwest, but most are intimately associated with sea stars and other echinoderms, making them difficult to find.
Wrangell Narrows, Mitkof Island, s. Alaska. Roger Clark photograph

MC208. PEARLY TOPSNAIL, lirulate margarite
Lirularia lirulata, *Lirularia lirulata conica, Lirularia lirulata obsoleta, Lirularia lirulata subelevata, Margarite lirulata, Lirularia funiculata, Margarites lacunata, Margarites lirulatus*
to 0.8 cm (0.3 in) across
s. Alaska to n. Mexico
intertidal to shallow subtidal
This species has a narrow slit-like opening on the underside of its shell. Very similar, but less commonly found, is the angular topsnail, *Lirularia parcipicta*, which has more pronounced spiral ridges.
Royal British Columbia Museum, Victoria, BC

MC209. TUCKED TOPSNAIL, tucked lirularia, tucked margarite, girdled margarite
Lirularia succincta, *Margarites succincta*, *Margarites succinctus*
to 0.8 cm (0.3 in) across
c. Alaska to n. Mexico
intertidal to shallow subtidal
This species differs from the pearly topsnail (MC208) by having a funnel-shaped slit on the underside of its shell.
Royal British Columbia Museum, Victoria, BC

MC210. BLUE TOPSNAIL, blue top snail, blue top shell, western ribbed top shell, western ribbed topshell, western ribbed top-shell, ribbed topsnail, western ridged top shell, costate top shell, costate top, Pacific top shell
Calliostoma ligatum, *Calliostoma ligatum caerulum*, *Calliostoma ligatum pictum*, *Calliostoma ligatus*, *Calliostoma costata*, *Calliostoma costatum*
to 3 cm (1.2 in) across
c. Alaska to s. California
intertidal to 30 m (100 ft)
A black algal growth sometimes covers the shell of this commonly seen snail, making its identity a little less obvious.
Mutine Point, Barkley Sound, s. BC

MC211. PURPLE-RINGED TOPSNAIL, purple-ringed top snail, purple-ring topsnail, ringed top snail, Pacific ringed top shell, ringed top shell, ringed topshell, purple ringed topsnail, purple ring top snail, purple-ringed topshell, purple ringed top shell, beaded top snail, ringed top-shell, ringed top, ribbed top-shell, jewelled top snail
Calliostoma annulatum
to 4 cm (1.6 in) across
n. Alaska to n. Mexico
intertidal to 42 m (140 ft)
Divers may find this beauty amid hydroids, one of its primary food sources. It is perhaps the Pacific Northwest's most spectacular shell.
A Turn Island, San Juan Channel, n. Washington
B Tilly Point, s. Pender Island, s. BC

MC212. VARIABLE TOPSNAIL, variegate topsnail, variegated top snail, variable top-shell, variable top, variegated top
Calliostoma variegatum
to 3.8 cm (1.5 in) across
s. Alaska to n. Mexico
intertidal to 182 m (600 ft)
Apparently this snail feeds on pink branching hydrocorals (CN51) and various bryozoans, so look for it nearby.
Sutton Islets, Egmont, s. BC

MC213. CHANNELLED TOPSNAIL, channelled top snail, channelled top shell, channelled top-shell, channelled top
Calliostoma canaliculatum, *Calliostoma canaliculata*, *Calliostoma doliarius*, *Calliostoma dolarium*
to 3.5 cm (1.5 in) across
c. Alaska to n. Mexico
intertidal to 25 m (83 ft)
This animal lives on and derives its nutrition from large species of kelp.
Sea Rose Gifts & Shell Museum, Yachats, s. Oregon

MC214. SILVERY TOPSNAIL
Calliostoma platinum
to 3.2 cm (1.3 in) across
s. Alaska to s. California
subtidal, 75–700 m (250–2,300 ft)
A rare and precious find for the serious shell collector—though some armchair enthusiasts buy it through dealers. The shell's spiral sections are called whorls by the shell aficionado.
Royal British Columbia Museum, Victoria, BC

MC215. LOVELY PACIFIC SOLARELLE, lovely solarelle, lovely top shell, lovely top
Solariella permabilis, *Solariella rhyssa*
to 2 cm (0.8 in) across
Japan, c. Alaska to n. Mexico
subtidal, 15–600 m (50–2,000 ft)
A thin, squat shell, it has a deep umbilicus (central hole). This structure is at the base of the columella (central axis).
Royal British Columbia Museum, Victoria, BC

MC216. NAKED SOLARELLE
Solariella nuda
▶to 1.6 cm (0.7 in) across
s. BC to n. Mexico
subtidal, 91–2,800 m (300–9,240 ft)
Similar to the lovely Pacific solarelle (MC215) species but with a beautiful "mother-of-pearl" finish. This layer increases in thickness as the snail ages and grows. Another rarity for the shell collector and one that would attract worldwide interest.
The very deep waters of the Pacific Northwest provide habitat for several other obscure solarelles and topsnails.
Royal British Columbia Museum, Victoria, BC

MC217. SPINY TOPSNAIL, Adam's spiny margarite, spiny top
Cidarina cidaris, *Lischkeia cidaris*
to 4 cm (1.5 in) tall
c. Alaska to n. Mexico
subtidal, 35–300 m (115–1,000 ft)
Note the distinctive beading on the rounded spiral ribs of this snail's shell. Information gathered during research sampling indicates that it prefers rocky or rubble bottoms.
Royal British Columbia Museum, Victoria, BC

MC218. BAIRD'S MARGARITE
Bathybembix bairdi, *Bathybembix bairdii*, *Lischkeia bairdi*, *Turricula bairdi*
to 4 cm (1.5 in) tall
n. Alaska to Chile
subtidal, 10–1,200 m (33–3,960 ft)
A more squat shell with a periostracum (outer layer) that is olive green in colour differentiates this species from the spiny topsnail (MC217). Baird's margarite also inhabits primarily deeper waters, with the result that it is less often seen.
La Pérouse Bank, w. Vancouver Island, s. BC

MC219. PUPPET MARGARITE, little margarite, margarite snail, pink topsnail
Margarites pupillus, *Margarites pupilla*, *Margarites salmoneus*
to 2 cm (0.8 in) tall
n. Alaska to s. California
intertidal to 100 m (330 ft)
The puppet margarite crawls about on kelp or rock. Areas of wear or damage to the outer layers of the shell are evidenced by exposed mother-of-pearl. Photograph B shows a specimen protruding its proboscis and pinwheel-like sensory structures.
A Brown Island, Friday Harbor, n. Washington
B Sechelt Inlet, Sunshine Coast, s. BC

MC220. HELICINA MARGARITE, smooth margarite, spiral margarite
Margarites helicinus, *Margarites helicina*, possibly *Margarites beringensis*, *Margarites marginatus*
to 1 cm (0.4 in) across
Arctic Ocean, n. Alaska to s. California
intertidal to 182 m (600 ft)
A tiny but active creature, the helicina margarite usually lives on eelgrass (SW2) or various algae, where it is surprisingly noticeable.
A number of other *Margarite* species dwell in the Pacific Northwest, but for some reason are not commonly encountered.
Pearse Islands, Weynton Passage, c. BC

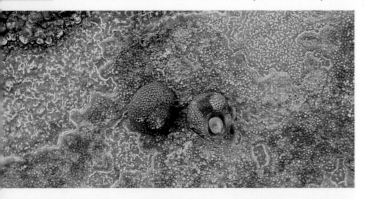

MC221. DWARF TURBAN, dark dwarf turban, dark dwarf-turban, Dall's dwarf turban, northern dwarf turban
Homalopoma luridum, *Homalopoma lurida, Homalopoma lacunatum, Homalopoma engbergi,* incorrect: *Homaploma carpenteri, Leptothyra carpenteri*
to 1 cm (0.4 in) across
s. Alaska to n. Mexico
intertidal to subtidal
Only by very careful searching will the beachcomber find this tiny gem. Two other similar Pacific Northwest *Homalopoma* species exist.
Tongue Point, Olympic coast, n. Washington

MC222. BLACK TURBAN, black turban snail, black turban shell, black tegula, California black tegula, black top-shell, black top
Tegula funebralis, *Tegula funebralis subaptera*
to 4.5 cm (1.8 in) across
n. BC to n. Mexico
intertidal to subtidal
Nearly every specimen has an eroded tip. Empty shells are quickly found and filled by several species of hermits (hermit crabs).
Ucluth Peninsula, w. Vancouver Island, s. BC

MC223. DUSKY TURBAN, dusky turban snail, dusky tegula, brown turban, northern brown turban
Tegula pulligo, *Tegula pulligo taylori*
to 4.3 cm (1.7 in) tall
s. Alaska to n. Mexico
intertidal to 3 m (10 ft)
Together with the black turban (MC222), the dusky turban lives only along exposed shores. It shelters among the rocks, clinging tightly to avoid being swept away.
The brown turban, *Tegula brunnea*, a similar species, is not likely to be encountered north of Oregon.
Ucluth Peninsula, w. Vancouver Island, s. B.C

MC224. RED TURBAN, red turban snail, red western turban, red top snail
Astraea gibberosa, *Lithopoma gibberosa, Lithopoma gibberosum, Astraea inaequalis, Astraea montereyensis*
to 11 cm (4 in) across
s. Alaska to n. Mexico
intertidal to 80 m (265 ft)
The red turban has a distinctive shell-like operculum (trap door). It is an herbivorous snail for which the small giant kelp (SW59) provides food and shelter.
Beg Islands, Barkley Sound, s. BC

MC225. LEWIS'S MOONSNAIL, Lewis's moon snail, Lewis' moon snail, Lewis' moon-shell, Lewis' moon shell, northern moon snail, western moon shell, moon snail, Lewis's moon
Euspira lewisii, *Polinices lewisii*, *Polynices lewisii*, *Lunatia lewisi*, *Lunatia lewisii*, *Polinices algidus*, *Natica lewisii*
to 14 cm (5.5 in) across shell
Japan, s. Alaska to n. Mexico
intertidal to 180 m (600 ft)
This carnivorous species preys on clams or other snails by drilling a single countersunk hole through one of its shells, as shown in photograph C.
Photograph B shows a specimen with its smooth egg collar.
Often moonsnails disappear into the substrate in a quest for prey.
A Tuwanek, Sechelt Inlet, s. BC
B Ucluth Peninsula, w. Vancouver Island, s. BC
C Crescent Beach, Boundary Bay, s. BC

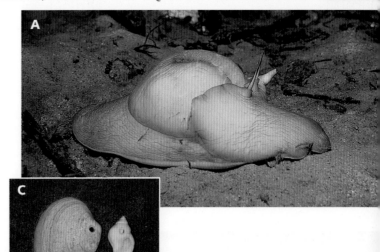

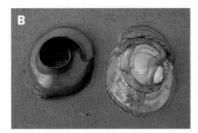

MC226. DRAKE'S MOONSNAIL, Drake's moon snail, Drake's moon-shell, Drake's moon shell, Drake's moon
Euspira draconis, *Polinices draconis*
to 9 cm (3.8 in) across
Alaska to n. Mexico
subtidal, below 19 m (60 ft)
The large, deep umbilicus (hole) narrows in a spiral staircase-like manner. Empty moonsnail shells are a favourite "mobile home" for various species of hermits (hermit crabs).
Imperial Eagle Channel, Barkley Sound, s. BC

A great deal of confusion exists with regard to which names apply to the following three species. A limited and hopefully correct synonymy is provided for each.

MC227. PALE NORTHERN MOONSNAIL, pale northern moon snail, pale northern moon-shell, northern moon snail, northern moon shell
Euspira pallida, *Euspira pallidus*, *Polinices pallidus*, *Lunatia pallida*
to 4 cm (1.6 in) across
circumpolar, n. Alaska to n. Mexico
intertidal to 500 m (1,650 ft)
The umbilicus (hole up the middle of the shell) is almost completely closed and the operculum (trap door) is brown and corneous (of horn-like material). The living pale northern moonsnail is a translucent white.
Queen Charlotte Channel, Howe Sound, s. BC

MC228. The species of **moonsnail** that produced the **egg collar** shown in this photograph unfortunately is **unidentified**. The collar was trawled off the mouth of the Fraser River, BC, but with no potential parent. Fisheries and Oceans Canada biologist Rick Harbo of Nanaimo, BC, who is currently studying North Pacific moonsnails, could not provide a certain identification but believes it is most likely from the pale northern moonsnail.

MC229. ALEUTIAN MOONSNAIL, arctic moonsnail, arctic moon snail, arctic natica, dwarf moon snail, closed moonsnail, bull's eye, northern moon shell, pale moonsnail, pale northern moon-shell, arctic moon
Cryptonatica aleutica, *Natica aleutica*
to 6 cm (2.3 in) across
n. Alaska to s. California
intertidal to 400 m (1,320 ft)
The body of the Aleutian moon snail is typically lighter than other Pacific Northwest species, with brownish spots or mottling and its operculum (trap door) is thick and calcareous. A white patch adjacent to the umbilicus (closed-over opening) at the bottom of the shell is characteristic.
Worlcombe Island, Howe Sound, s. BC

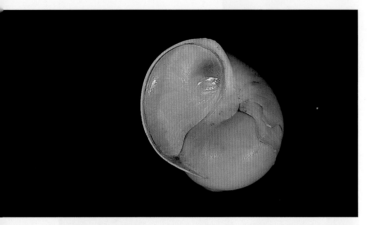

MC230. ARCTIC MOONSNAIL
Cryptonatica affinis, *Natica affinis*, *Natica clausa*, *Cryptonatica clausa*
to 2.5 cm (1 in) across
n. Alaska to n. Mexico
subtidal
Similar to the Aleutian moonsnail (MC229), the Arctic moonsnail has a creamy white body with no brownish markings. Like other species, this moonsnail often burrows beneath the surface of soft substrates searching for prey.
Off w. Vancouver Island, s. BC. Rick Harbo photograph

MC231. PEAR-SHAPED MARGIN SHELL, pear-shaped marginella, pear marginella
Granulina margaritula, *Cypraeolina margaritula*, *Marginella margaritula*, *Volutella margaritula*, *Granulina pyriformis*
to 0.3 cm (0.2 in) long
s. Alaska to Panama
intertidal to 91 m (300 ft)
Very mobile, this tiny snail crawls about amid gravel and associated plant and algal life. With its white-speckled grey body visible, the pear-shaped margin shell has been seen with the lined chiton (MC1).
Royal British Columbia Museum, Victoria, BC

MC232. PURPLE OLIVE, purple olive snail, purple olive shell, purple dwarf olive, purple olivella, olive snail
Olivella biplicata, *Olivella biplicata fucana*, *Olivella angelana*, *Olivella lapillus*, *Olivella fucana*, *Olivella parva*
to 3.5 cm (1.5 in) long
s. Alaska to n. Mexico
intertidal to 50 m (165 ft)
The purple olive is often noticed first as a "bump" at the end of a short, meandering sand trail on open coast beaches as shown in the photograph. Olives are carnivorous scavengers.
Chesterman Beach, w. Vancouver Island, s. BC

CHITONS, BIVALVES, UNIVALVES, NUDIBRANCHS, OCTOPUS AND SQUID **INVERTEBRATES**

MC233. BAETIC OLIVE, baetic olive snail, beatic dwarf olive, baetic olivella, beatic olive, brown olive, little olive, olive snail, San Pedro rice shell
Olivella baetica, *Olivella diegensis, Olivella intorta, Olivella mexicana, Olivella porteri, Olivella pedrona, Olivella boetica*
to 2.7 cm (1.1 in) long
n. Alaska to n. Mexico
intertidal to 60 m (200 ft)
Divers should look diligently on soft bottoms in low-current muddy/silty bottoms to find this species. Like other olives, the baetic olive typically buries itself.
Kyen Point, Barkley Sound, s. BC

MC234. ZIGZAG OLIVE, San Pedro dwarf olive
Olivella pycna, *Olivella pedroana*
to 1.5 cm (0.6 in) long
n. BC to n. Mexico
intertidal
Distinguished from the purple olive (MC232) and baetic olive (MC233) by the wavy lines on the shell, the zigzag olive is rare north of Oregon. Olive shells were popular with coastal First Nations people, who made necklaces with them.
Bamfield, w. Vancouver Island, s. BC

MC235. VIOLET SNAIL, round violet snail, common violet sea snail, common purple sea-snail, elongate janthina, common janthina, janthina, purple snail
Janthina janthina, *Janthina prolongata*
to 4 cm (1.6 in) across
BC to tropics
surface
An oceanic floater that occasionally washes ashore. Considering the fragility of the shell, it is unlikely to remain intact long enough to be found.
Open Pacific between Hawaii and Cape Flattery, n. Washington

MC236. PHOENICIAN WHELK
Neptunea phoenicia, *Neptunea phoeniceus, Neptunea staphylifius, Neptunea lyrata phoenicea*
to 11 cm (4.5 in) long
s. Alaska to c. Oregon
subtidal
Live specimens of this scavenging species are sometimes recovered clinging to prawn or crab traps. Photograph B shows distinctive egg cases and newborns.
A Ogden Point, Victoria, s. BC
B Mouth of Fraser River, Strait of Georgia, s. BC

MARINE LIFE OF THE PACIFIC NORTHWEST **237**

MC237. CHOCOLATE WHELK, common northwest neptunea, Smirnia neptune, Smirna neptune
***Neptunea smirnia**, Neptunea smirnius, Neptunea fukuae*
to 15 cm (6 in) long
Japan, n. Alaska to n. California
subtidal, 10–1,200 m (33–4,000 ft)
Apparently this scavenger prefers soft sediment bottoms. A resourceful chef who obtains a few specimens might consider them an escargot item.
Royal British Columbia Museum, Victoria, BC

MC238. RIDGED WHELK, ridged neptune, ribbed neptune, lyre whelk, northwest neptune, common northwest neptune
***Neptunea lyrata**,* Neptunea lyratus, Chrysodomus liratus, Neptunea nucea*
to 20 cm (8 in) long
n. Alaska to s. California
intertidal to 1,500 m (5,000 ft)
Shells of this "deep dweller" are sometimes carried to shallows by hermits (hermit crabs). A very similar subspecies, the New England neptune, *Neptunea lyrata decemcostata*, lives along the east coast of North America.
*This species name is currently under review and may be subject to change in the future.
Auke Bay, Favorite Channel, s. Alaska

MC239. PRIBILOF WHELK, Pribilof neptune
***Neptunea pribiloffensis**, Neptunea intersculpta pribiloffensis, Neptunea meridionalis, Chrysodomus vinosus*
▶to 20 cm (8 in) long
Alaska to Oregon
intertidal to 91 m (300 ft)
When sampled by Andy Lamb, the flesh of this primarily northern species was definitely a taste treat and verified the documented culinary data consulted. Most snails have an operculum (trap door) to seal off the shell and the photograph illustrates one for the Pribilof whelk, visible between the shells.
Auke Bay, Favorite Channel, s. Alaska

MC240. INFLATED WHELK, Stiles' neptune
Neptunea stilesi
to 11 cm (4.5 in) long
n. BC to Washington
subtidal, 60–250 m (204–820 ft)
A great deal of confusion exists concerning the deep-water whelks and the validity of some species. This "species" should probably receive DNA profiling to verify its legitimacy. The operculum (trap door) that seals the shell is readily evident in the photograph.
Sea Rose Gifts & Shell Museum, Yachats, c. Oregon

MC241. TABLED WHELK, tabled snail, tabled neptune
Neptunea tabulata, *Chrysodomus tabulata*
to 11 cm (4.5 in) long
Japan, s. Alaska to s. California
subtidal, 30–400 m (100–1,320 ft)
The very distinctive channelled shoulders on the handsome shell make it a collector's favourite and one of the most commonly encountered neptunes. Most of these whelks feed upon segmented worms or bivalve molluscs.
Sea Rose Gifts & Shell Museum, Yachats, s. Oregon

MC242. GIANT ELONGATE WHELK, Ithia neptune
Neptunea ithia
to 15 cm (6 in) long
s. BC to c. California
subtidal, 150–1,200 m (500–4,000 ft)
Unfortunately this attractive snail is seen by few observers other than those searching through museum collections. The Royal British Columbia Museum is an excellent resource.
Royal British Columbia Museum, Victoria, BC

MC243. KENNICOTT'S WHELK, Kennicott's neptune, Kennicott's beringius, Kennicott's buccinum
Beringius kennicottii, *Jumala kennicottii, Beringius incisus, Volutopsis rotundus, Beringion kennicotti*
to 15 cm (6 in) long
n. Alaska to n. Washington
subtidal, 3–50 m (9–165 ft)
Wavy longitudinal axial bands distinguish this attractive species. With its long proboscis, Kennicott's whelk is capable of locating and feeding on buried prey.
Royal British Columbia Museum, Victoria, BC

MC244. EYERDAM'S WHELK
Beringius eyerdami
▶to 12 cm (5 in) long
s. Alaska to c. California
subtidal to 180 m (600 ft)
Shell collectors and malacologists (students of molluscs) delight in finding this exquisite species. Hermits (hermit crabs) may be helpful by dragging shells into shallower, more accessible depths.
Royal British Columbia Museum, Victoria, BC

MC245. THICK-RIBBED WHELK, thick-ribbed buccinum, thick-cord whelk
Beringius crebricostatus, *Beringius crebricostata, Beringius undatus,*
Beringius undata
to 12 cm (5 in) long
n. Alaska to n. Washington
subtidal, 19–180 m (60–600 ft)
Few casual naturalists will find this seldom-encountered creature—so enjoy
the photograph.
Royal British Columbia Museum, Victoria, BC

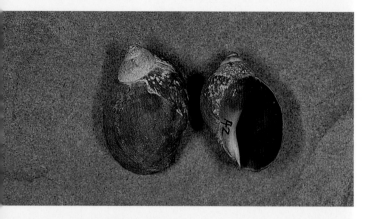

MC246. BIG-MOUTH WHELK, paper whelk, Alaskan volute, ample fragile
buccinum
Volutharpa ampullacea, *Volutharpa perryi,* possibly: *Volutharpa acuminata*
to 3.5 cm (1.5 in) long
Japan, n. Alaska to n. Washington
intertidal to subtidal
The periostracum (outer shell layer) of the big-mouth whelk is a distinctive
velvety green when the creature is alive. Less stable than the inner shell
layers, it may flake off with wear and tear.
Several other large whelks dwell in the deep waters of the Pacific
Northwest, but unfortunately these attractive shells are seldom seen.
Royal British Columbia Museum, Victoria, BC

MC247. ▶SMALL TALL WHELK
Exilioidea rectirostris, *Exilia rectirostris, Chrysodomus rectirostris,*
Tritonofusus rectirostris, Plicifusus rectirostris
to 3 cm (1.2 in) long
s. Alaska to n. Mexico
subtidal, 60–800 m (200–2,650 ft)
The very long siphonal canal (extension of the bottom of the shell) is
distinctive. It shelters the siphon, an organ that provides water-quality
information for the snail.
Royal British Columbia Museum, Victoria, BC

MC248. LYRE WHELK, sinuous whelk, plectrum whelk, lyre buccinum,
plectrum buccinum
Buccinum plectrum
to 10 cm (4 in) long
circumboreal, n. Alaska to n. Washington
intertidal* to 600 m (2,000 ft)
The photograph shows this species' speckled white tentacles and siphon.
The lyre whelk is a taste treat that has been commercially harvested in
Alaska and could have aquaculture potential.
*Biologist/author Rick Harbo of Nanaimo, BC, found the lyre whelk living
intertidally in Petersburg, Alaska.
Mouth of Fraser River, Strait of Georgia, s. BC

MC249. PERVERSE WHELK, perverse turrid

Antiplanes perversa, *Antiplanes major, Antiplanes catalinae, Antiplanes thalea, Antiplanes voyi, Pleurotoma catalinae, Pleurotoma perversa*

to 5 cm (2 in) long

n. BC to s. California

subtidal, 9–460 m (30–1,510 ft)

Note the distinctive reverse twisting of the shell in this species. The perverse whelk is one of the very few Pacific Northwest species that grows counter-clockwise.

Two other *Antiplanes* species live in the Pacific Northwest.

Royal British Columbia Museum, Victoria, BC

MC250. SPINDLE SHELL, Harford's spindle

Fusinus harfordi, *Fusinus harfordii*

▶to 5 cm (2 in) long

BC to n. California

subtidal

A bright orange body coupled with a nicely formed shell add up to an attractive species. As a minute member of the planktonic community, a larval snail bears no resemblance to the familiar adult. The photograph readily shows the operculum (trap door) in three of the four specimens. The tall spindle, *Fusinus barbarensis,* is not found north of Oregon.

Lanz Island, Cape Scott, c. BC

MC251. ▶SHOULDERED SPINDLE

Fusinus monksae, *Fusinus robustus, Fusinus kobelti monksae*

▶to 3.5 cm (1.5 in) long

n. BC to n. Mexico

subtidal, 36–180 m (120–600 ft)

This rarely found snail has a white body. Diver Phil Bruecker of Living Elements Research Ltd., Vancouver, BC, kindly supplied this specimen, which he found near Tofino, BC.

A B Lennard Island, Tofino, s. BC

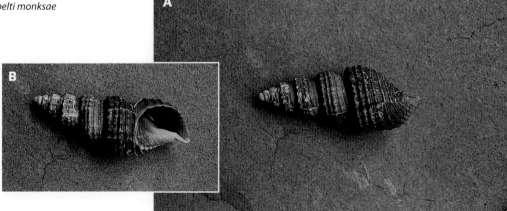

MC252. ALASKA VOLUTE, Stearn's volute

Arctomelon stearnsi, *Arctomelon stearnsii, Boreomelon stearnsi, Tractolira stearnsi, Sigaluta stearnsi*

to 12.5 cm (5 in) long

n. Alaska to Washington

subtidal, below 1,980 m (6,000 ft)

With a semigloss finish to its bluish white shell—most obvious when containing a living snail—the Alaskan volute is likely to be encountered live only by commercial fishers harvesting deep-dwelling seafood.

Amutka Pass, Aleutian Islands, n. Alaska

MC253. GRAY SNAKESKIN-SNAIL
Ophiodermella inermis, *Ophiodermella ophiodermella, Ophiodermella halcyonis, Ophiodermella incisa, Ophiodermella montereyensis, Ophiodermella ophioderma, Clathrodrillia incisa ophiodermella, Moniliopsis incisa, Moniliopsis incisa ophioderma, Pleurotoma inermis, Drilla incisa, Turris halcyonis*
to 4 cm (1.5 in) long
n. BC to n. Mexico
intertidal to 70 m (230 ft)
An anal notch at the upper part of its aperture (shell opening) is a distinctive feature of the gray snakeskin-snail.
Royal British Columbia Museum, Victoria, BC

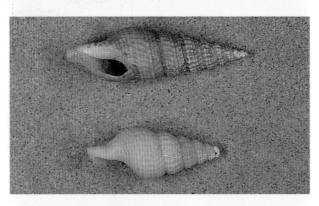

MC254. CANCELLATE SNAKESKIN-SNAIL
Ophiodermella cancellata, *Ophiodermella rhines, Pleurotoma vancouverensis*
to 1.3 cm (0.5 in) long
BC to s. California
subtidal, 50–500 m (165–1,650 ft)
Note the distinctive cancellate or latticework appearance of this snail's shell resulting from the crossing of axial and spiral ridges. It lives in silty or sandy areas where it hunts for small polychaete worms.
Ucluelet Harbour, w. Vancouver Island, s. BC

MC255. HALL'S WHELK, Hall's colus
Colus halli, *Colus errones, Colus jordani*
to 6 cm (2.3 in) long
n. Alaska to s. California
intertidal to 1,818 m (6,000 ft)
This whelk is a scavenger, which often swarms into prawn traps set in Alaskan waters and devours the bait. It uses its sensitive siphon as a locating device to home in on the chemical traces of food sources.
Queen Charlotte Strait, Howe Sound, s. BC

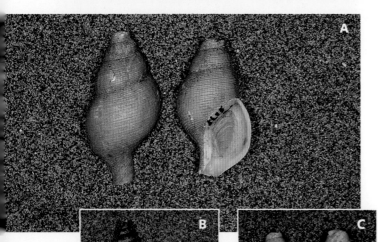

MC256. Colus Bolus illustrates the uncertainty of species determination, using whelks of the genus *Colus* as an example. Authorities on this subject disagree as to whether *Colus halidonus, Colus morditus, Colus severinus* and *Colus tahwitanus* are legitimate species or simply variations on a theme. As the years have passed, debates have continued and produced alternating documentation. Such uncertainty leaves most of us perplexed. Perhaps advances in technology, such as DNA fingerprinting, along with necessary research funding will solve the dilemma.
At least two other legitimate *Colus* species exist in the Pacific Northwest.
A *Colus halidonus*
B *Colus morditus*
C *Colus severinus*
D *Colus tahwitanus*
Royal British Columbia Museum, Victoria, BC

MC257. OREGON TRITON, hairy triton, Oregon hairy triton, hairy Oregon triton, Puget Sound whelk, whelk
Fusitriton oregonensis, Argobuccinum oregonensis, Fusitriton oregonense, Argobuccinum oregonense, Argobuccinum pacifica, Argobuccinum coosense, Ranella oregonense, Gyrineum corbiculatum
to 15 cm (6 in) long
Japan, n. Alaska to n. Mexico
intertidal to 180 m (600 ft)
The white eggs (photograph A) have outer transparent covers that appear almost plastic-like. Empty ones have hatched. Photograph B shows a "balding" specimen.
A B Long Island, near Lopez Island, n. Washington

MC258. CHECKERED HAIRYSNAIL, checkered hairy snail, cancellate hairysnail, cancellate hairy shell, cancellate hairy-snail, cancellated trichotropsis
Trichotropsis cancellata
to 4 cm (1.6 in) long
n. Alaska to Oregon
intertidal to 200 m (660 ft)
Apparently the checkered hairysnail feeds upon wastes generated by large calcareous tubeworms (AN50-55), so look for these worms when seeking this small snail. The photograph shows eggs, at left.
Three other Pacific Northwest subtidal *Trichotropsis* species are very rarely found.
Agamemnon Channel, Nelson Island, s. BC

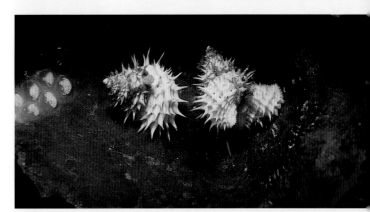

MC259. Oenopota overload
There are nearly 50 **species** of tiny snails in the genus *Oenopota*, a word that is composed of two Greek roots meaning "wine" and "drink." With maximum sizes usually much less than 2.5 cm (1 in), these univalves are difficult to find. In addition, distinguishing one from another is truly an exercise in patience, even if one has the appropriate biological key and at least a quality hand lens—an exercise likely to drive one to drink! A diversity of these snails is shown in the photograph.
We are much indebted to George Holm of Richmond, BC, for providing his excellent Pacific Northwest *Oenopota* collection for this project.

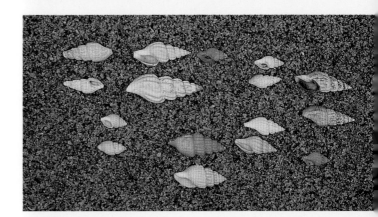

MC260. NORTHERN COMPACT WORMSNAIL, compact wormsnail, worm snail
Vermetus compactus, *Vermetus compacta, Petaloconchus compactus, Bivonia compactus*
to 0.3 cm (0.1 in) tube diameter, 2.5 cm (1 in) tube length
colony diameter: indeterminate, irregular
c. BC to n. Mexico
intertidal to 50 m (165 ft)
Colonies look like clusters of small calcareous tubeworms, but without colourful plumes. Only the brown, plug-like anterior ends of the snails can be seen.
Bellevue Point, San Juan Island, n. Washington

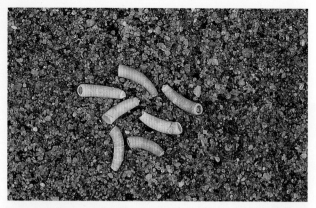

MC261. GIANT CAECUM
Caecum crebricinctum, *Micranellum crebricinctum*, *Caecum pedorense*,
Micranellum pedorense, *Caecum rosanum*, *Micranellum oregonense*,
Micranellum oregonensis, *Micranellum catalinense*, *Micranellum
profundicolum*, *Micranellum barkleyense*, *Micranellum rosanum*
to 0.6 cm (0.3 in) long
s. Alaska to n. Mexico
subtidal, 10–200 m (33–660 ft)
Very fine circular rings and a mucro (pointed tip) distinguish the giant
caecum from other smaller ones.
Royal British Columbia Museum, Victoria, BC

MC262. LEATHER LIMPET, northwest onchidella
Onchidella borealis, *Arctonchis borealis*
to 1.2 cm (0.5 in) long
n. Alaska to c. California
intertidal
This cryptic air breather lives under rocks or among algal holdfasts. Note
the eggs in the photograph. The leather limpet certainly feels "leathery," but
it is not closely related to the familiar limpets.
Dinner Point, Mayne Island, s. BC

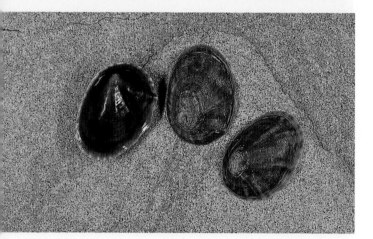

MC263. PACIFIC FALSELIMPET, Carpenter's falselimpet, Carpenter's false
limpet, siphon shell
Siphonaria thersites, *Liriola thersites*
to 3.1 cm (1.3 in) across
n. Alaska to n. Oregon
intertidal
This air breather most often lives among the rockweeds (SW22–24). The
Pacific falselimpet is hermaphroditic, meaning each specimen contains a
set of male and female organs, but self-fertilization does not occur.
Royal British Columbia Museum, Victoria, BC

MC264. SMOOTH VELVET SNAIL, velvet shell, baby's ear, elongate
lamellaria
Velutina prolongata
to 2.2 cm (0.9 in) across
n. Alaska to c. California
intertidal to 100 m (330 ft)
The bright orange-yellow rim and banded mantle around the shell are
distinctive of this snail. Its ear-shaped shell is visible but covered by a thin
layer of tissue.
Surge Narrows, Maurelle Island, s. BC

MC265. SPIRAL VELVET SNAIL, smooth velvet shell, velvet shell, smooth velutina, smooth lamellaria
Velutina velutina, *Velutina laevigata*, *Velutina plicatilis*, *Velutina sitkensis*, *Velutina cryptospira*
to 2 cm (0.8 in) across
circumpolar, n. Alaska to c. California
subtidal to 100 m (330 ft)
Usually found with its prey, especially the warty tunicate (CH10) and the hairy tunicate (CH15). Photograph B shows a spiral velvet snail laying its eggs on a glassy tunicate (CH4).
A Point Cowan, Bowen Island, s. BC
B Green Bay, Nelson Island, s. BC

MC266. This little treasure was not noticed until it was brought to the surface with some other creatures by Donna Gibbs while diving in Sechelt Inlet, s. BC. After this photograph was taken, the specimen was sent to Dave Behrens, who doubles as a resident expert on Pacific Northwest velvet snails and nudibranchs, in the hope that he could identify it. After much effort he determined that it is the **OBLIQUE VELVET SNAIL**, *Velutina plicatilis.*

Kunechin Point, Sechelt Inlet, s. BC

MC267. ▶RED VELVET SNAIL, red lamellaria
Velutina rubra
to 2.5 cm (1 in) across
▶c. Alaska to n. BC
▶intertidal to 20 m (65 ft)
This range-extending specimen was found by diver Sharon Jeffery of Vancouver, BC, who was participating in a Vancouver Aquarium Marine Science Centre expedition in the Queen Charlotte Islands aboard the MV *Nautilus Explorer*. Until then, the red velvet snail had only been found in Alaska and at shallower depths.

Iphigenia Point, Langara Island, n. BC

MC268. STEARN'S EAR SHELL
Marsenina stearnsi, *Marsenina stearnsii*, *Lamellaria stearnsii orbiculata*, *Lamellaria stearnsii*, *Marsenina orbiculata*
to 2 cm (0.8 in) across
c. Alaska to n. Mexico
intertidal to 19 m (62 ft)
Spends life intimately associated with compound tunicates, particularly the white glove leather (CH42). Spots on its body perfectly match the pattern of tunicate siphon openings.

Keystone, Whidbey Island, n. Washington

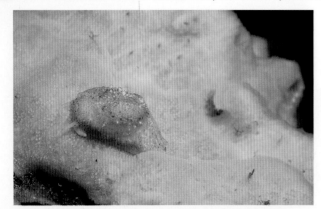

MC269. MARBLED LAMELLARID, rhombic lamellarid
Marsenina rhombica, *Lamellaria rhombica*
to 4 cm (1.6 in) long
s. Alaska to n. Mexico
intertidal to subtidal
A diver must look very carefully to spot this snail, which also is intimately associated with compound tunicates. These precise habitats offer food, shelter and even a place to spawn—a beautiful example of evolution.
Stubbs Island, Weynton Passage, c. BC

MC270. SAN DIEGO EAR SHELL, San Diego lamellaria
Lamellaria diegoensis, *Marsenina diegoensis*
to 2 cm (0.8 in) across shell
▶s. BC to n. Mexico
intertidal to subtidal
Like other Pacific Northwest members of this group, this cryptic snail associates with compound tunicates. Indeed, these specimens were incidentally found by Donna Gibbs of Port Coquitlam, BC, while collecting samples of California sea pork (CH34) for identification during this project.
Link Island, Barkley Sound, s. BC

MC271. PYRAMID SNAIL
Turbonilla **sp.**
to 1.2 cm (0.5 in) long
Alaska to California
subtidal
This photograph shows only one of many similar, difficult-to-distinguish species of pyramid snails. Most naturalists are satisfied just to find one of these tiny animals.
Departure Bay, Nanaimo, s. BC

MC272. OBTUSE ISELICA, obtuse fossarus, blunt iselica
Iselica obtusa, *Iselica laxa*, *Iselica obtusa laxa*
to 0.6 cm (0.2 in) across
s. BC to n. Mexico
intertidal to 45 m (150 ft)
Generally this tiny snail lives on a gravel or coarse sand bottom, often where there is shell and marine-plant cover. In some regions clam diggers can find the obtuse iselica crawling amid a jelly-like secretion on the Pacific littleneck clam (MC107) or the Japanese littleneck clam (MC108).
Hand Island, Barkley Sound, s. BC. Rick Harbo photograph

BUBBLE SHELLS, etc.

Including bubbles, aglajids, slugs, capshells, berthellas, pteropods, sea angels, sea cherubs, sea hares, alderias, sacoglossids, diaphanas and philines.

MC273. STRIPED BARREL SHELL, striped barrel snail, barrel-snail shell, barrel shell snail, barrel snail, barrel shell, Carpenter's baby bubble, Carpenter's baby-bubble, baby's bubble
***Rictaxis punctocaelatus**, Acteon punctocaelatus, Tornatella punctocaelata*
to 2 cm (0.8 in) long
s. Alaska to n. Mexico
intertidal to 100 m (330 ft)
Look closely on sand bottoms just deeper than beds of eelgrass (SW2) to find this tiny snail.
Cottam Point, Parksville, s. BC

MC274. SMALL BUBBLE
***Cylichna attonsa**, Cylichna propinqua,* possibly: *Cylichna culcitella*
▶to 1.2 cm (0.5 in) long
n. Alaska to n. Mexico
subtidal to 73 m (240 ft)
This species' shell has a sunken apex, which distinguishes it from the western barrel-bubble (MC275). The small bubble feeds upon minute creatures called foraminiferans that share its silty habitat.
The white chalice-bubble, *Cylichna alba,* also lives in the Pacific Northwest.
Queen Charlotte Channel, Howe Sound, s. BC

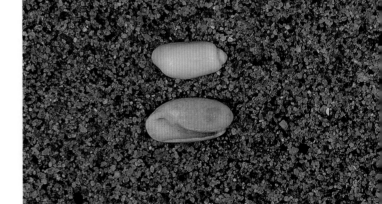

MC275. WESTERN BARREL-BUBBLE, pillow barrel-bubble, barrel bubble
***Acteocina culcitella**, Cylichnella culcitella, Torantina culcitella, Acteocina rolleri*
to 2.2 cm (0.9 in) long
c. Alaska to n. Mexico
intertidal to 46 m (150 ft)
The western barrel-bubble feeds upon various small snails, which it hunts in sand or mud bottoms. It probably spends most of its time just below the surface.
Three other similar but much smaller species, the grain barrel-bubble, *Acteocina cerealis,* the harp barrel-bubble, *Acteocina harpa,* and the ▶pleat-less barrel bubble, *Acteocina exima,* also inhabit the Pacific Northwest.
The tiny California diaphana, *Diaphana californica,* has been recorded from n. Washington. It resembles the western barrel-buble (MC275) but lives in kelp holdfasts, making it difficult to find.
Royal British Columbia Museum, Victoria, BC

MC276. WHITE BUBBLE SHELL, white bubble snail, blister paper bubble, blister glassy-bubble, white bubble, Gould's paper-bubble, Gould's paper bubble
Haminoea vesicula
to 2.5 cm (1 in) long
s. Alaska to n. Mexico
intertidal to shallow subtidal
In spring and summer, look among shallow-dwelling marine plants and algae to find the white bubble shell and its bright yellow eggs. The rest of the year it is essentially invisible. Note the delicate shell visible through a tissue layer in photograph A.

A Bennett Bay, Mayne Island, s. BC
B Crescent Beach, Boundary Bay, s. BC

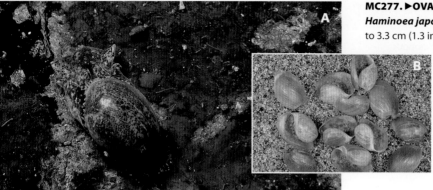

MC277. ▶OVAL BUBBLE SHELL
Haminoea japonica*, Haminoea callidegenita*
to 3.3 cm (1.3 in) long

▶s. BC to n. Washington
intertidal
Very similar to the white bubble shell (MC276), the oval
bubble shell has a narrower shell, white spots along the
body lobe margins and a deeply forked cephalic (head)
shield. It is a versatile animal, producing planktonic and
benthic young simultaneously. Such a reproductive
strategy does not put all the eggs in one basket.
A B Centennial Beach, Boundary Bay, s. BC

MC278. GREEN BUBBLE SHELL, green paper bubble, green glassy-
bubble, green bubble, Sowerby's paper-bubble, Sowerby's paper bubble
Haminoea virescens*, Haminoea olgae, Haminoea cymbiformis, Haminoea
rosacea, Haminoea strongi*
to 2 cm (0.8 in) long
Alaska to n. Mexico
intertidal
Only shell proportions accurately distinguish the green bubble shell from
the oval bubble shell (MC277). It lives in rocky, open-coast habitats.
Royal British Columbia Museum, Victoria, BC

MC279. DIOMEDES AGLAJID, Diomedes' aglajid, albatross aglaja
Melanochlamys diomedea*, Melanochlamys diomedia, Aglaja diomedea,
Aglaja diomedia, Doridium diomedia, Melanochlamys nana, Aglaja nana*
to 1.5 cm (0.6 in) long
Alaska to s. California
intertidal to 112 m (370 ft)
The jelly-like egg mass, seen at left in the photograph, may be readily
noticeable in spring on intertidal sand flats. This species has an internal
shell.
Cottam Point, Parksville, s. BC

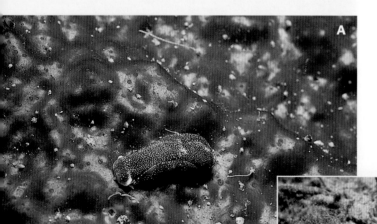

MC280. SPOTTED AGLAJID, spotted aglaja, yellow spotted aglaja, yellow-
spotted aglaja, eyespot aglaja
Aglaja ocelligera*, Doridium ocelligera, Doridium ocelligerum, Navanax
ocelligera, Chelidonura ocelligera, Aglaja phocae, Chelidonura phocae,
Doridium adellae*
to 2.5 cm (1 in) long
s. Alaska to s. California
subtidal to 20 m (65 ft)
This species lives in the same areas as the Diomedes aglajid (MC279), which
is also a prey item. Photograph B shows a line of spotted aglajids, likely
readying to spawn.
The ▶ear-like philine, *Philine auriformis*, which
resembles a creamy white version of the preceding
species, lives in the Pacific Northwest. It inhabits
muddy substrates from the intertidal zone to 6 m (20
ft) and reaches a length of 3 cm (1.2 in).
A B Cottam Point, Parksville, s. BC

MC281. WINGED SEA SLUG, winged bubble shell, Pacific wingfoot snail, Pacific batwing seaslug, Pacific bat-wing sea-slug, cloudy bubble shell
Gastropteron pacificum, *Gastropteron cinereum*, possibly: *Bullaria gouldiana*
to 4 cm (1.6 in) long
n. Alaska to n. Mexico, Galapagos Islands
intertidal to 425 m (1,400 ft)
A fine swimmer and easily seen when doing so, the winged sea slug often curls up on the bottom and may rest amid grape-like egg clusters. Photograph C shows benthic activity.
A B Green Bay, Nelson Island, s. BC
C Tuwanek Point, Sechelt Inlet, s. BC.
Charlie Gibbs photograph

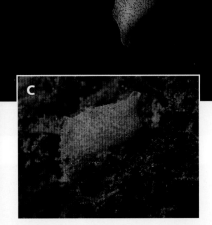

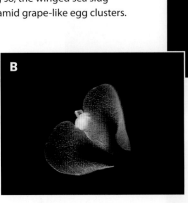

MC282. ZEBRA LEAFSLUG, Taylor's sea hare, green sea slug
Phyllaplysia taylori, *Phyllaplysia zostericola*, *Petalifer taylori*
to 8 cm (3.2 in) long
c. BC to n. Mexico
intertidal to subtidal
Careful inspection of eelgrass (SW2) may result in discovery of this cryptic animal. Search by gently separating the green leaves, as the zebra leafslug sometimes hides where they come together. The camouflage is obvious.
A Bennett Bay, Mayne Island, s. BC
B Egmont Marina, Egmont, s. BC

MC283. ►CAPSHELL
Anidolyta spongotheras, *Tylodinella spongotheras*, *Royo spongotheras*
to 2 cm (0.8 in) long
BC
subtidal, 25–360 m (80–1,200 ft)
This specimen was found crawling about on a dead cloud sponge (PO11) by Donna Gibbs of Port Coquitlam, BC. Historically this creature has been captured primarily by dredging, at depths far greater than a recreational diver might explore.
Cawley Point, Sechelt Inlet, s. BC

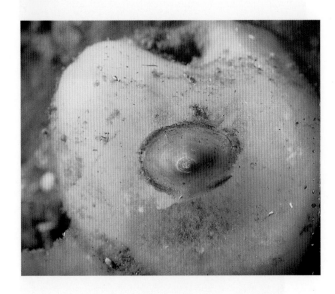

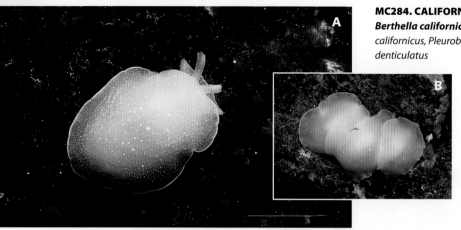

MC284. CALIFORNIA BERTHELLA, white berthella, California sidegill slug
Berthella californica, *Pleurobranchus californica, Pleurobranchus californicus, Pleurobranchus chacei, Pleurobranchus denticulatus, Berthella denticulatus*

to 5 cm (2 in) long
Siberia, s. Alaska to n. Mexico, Galapagos Islands (?)
intertidal to 33 m (110 ft)
The lack of a rose-shaped gill or branchial plume on its back distinguishes this species from the white dorid nudibranchs. Photograph B shows a ménage à trois. Half as large as the California berthella and having yellow spots, Strong's berthella, *Berthella strongi*, is rarely found north of California.
A B Sutton Islets, Egmont, s. BC

MC285. HELICID PTEROPOD
Limacina helicina, *Spiratella helicina, Limacina pacifica*
to 1.5 cm (0.6 in) across shell
Arctic Ocean, n. Alaska to n. Mexico
pelagic to 100 m (330 ft)
Note the coiled shell visible through the surrounding clear body. An active swimmer that beats its "wings" very rapidly, the helicid pteropod is often common in the spring plankton community. Northern specimens attain the largest size.
Egmont Marina, Egmont, s. BC. Donna Gibbs photograph

MC286. SEA ANGEL, common clione
Clione limacina, *Clione kincaidi, Clione elegantissima, Trichocyclus hansineensis*
to 8 cm (3.2 in) long
cosmopolitan in cold and temperate seas, n. Alaska to n. Mexico
pelagic to 600 m (2,000 ft)
Reproductive explosions or blooms of this amusing creature occur at the surface, usually during late winter. However, survivors may be seen anytime.
Sutton Islets, Egmont, s. BC

MC287. ▶SEA CHERUB
Cliopsis krohni
to 4 cm (1.6 in) long
temperate oceans of the world, BC to n. California
pelagic to 1,500 m (5,000 ft)
Not only did diver Charlie Gibbs of Port Coquitlam, BC, make this rare find off Mayne Island, BC, but he coined the excellent moniker "sea cherub." Indeed, it looks like a chubby and slow-swimming version of the sea angel (MC286).
Georgina Point, Mayne Island, s. BC

MC288. This ▶**KITE SEA ANGEL**, suspected to be a **Clio species**, was photographed during a trip aboard the MV *Nautilus Explorer*, when it anchored at Iphigenia Point, Langara Island, n. BC. Literally millions of these active swimmers were swarming at the surface, presenting an exciting and rare opportunity to photograph them. Unfortunately, by the next day they had completely disappeared with no specimens collected, so the identity of the species remains unknown.

Iphigenia Point, Langara Island, n. BC

MC289. HEDGPETH'S SEA HARE, Hedgpeth's elysia
Elysia hedgpethi, *Elysia bedeckta*
to 3.5 cm (1.5 in) long
s. BC to n. Mexico
intertidal to shallow subtidal
This creature's dark colour and small size make it difficult to find even when the naturalist or photographer knows it is there. It is intimately associated with sea moss (SW9) and sea staghorn (SW16).

Sutton Islets, Egmont, s. BC. Donna Gibbs photograph

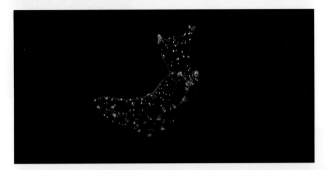

MC290. ▶**GREEN ALGA SACOGLOSSID**
Aplysiopsis enteromorphae, *Aplysiopsis smithi*, *Phyllobranchus enteromorphae*
to 2.5 cm (1 in) long
s. Alaska to n. Mexico
intertidal to subtidal
Small individuals, such as the one shown, are often darker than larger specimens. The colour of the green alga sacoglossid can also vary with the green algae that it is living with and feeding on.
A number of other small, cryptic and seldom-seen sacoglossid bubble shells inhabit the Pacific Northwest. They include the veined sacoglossid, *Placida dendritica*, the brown-streaked sacoglossan, *Stiliger fuscovittatus*, the modest alderia, *Alderia modesta*, Olive's sacoglossid, *Hermaea olivae*, Vancouver's sacoglossid, *Hermaea vancouverensis* and Hansine's sea slug, *Olea hansineenis*. For more detail, consult *Pacific Coast Nudibranchs* by David Behrens.

Quathiaski Cove, Quadra Island, s. BC. Neil McDaniel photograph

NUDIBRANCHS

Including sea lemons, sea goddesses, dorids, doris, cadlinas, adalarias, okenias, triophas, polyceras, anculas, roses, tritonias, dendronotids, dironas, flabellinas, shawls, aeolids and dotos.

MC291. NOBLE SEA LEMON, sea lemon, Pacific sea lemon, Pacific sea-lemon, sea lemon nudibranch, speckled sea lemon, lemon nudibranch, noble Pacific doris
Peltodoris nobilis, *Anisodoris nobilis*, *Montereina nobilis*
to 25 cm (10 in) long
c. Alaska to n. Mexico
intertidal to 228 m (750 ft)
Paler yellow tubercles (bumps) always show through dark patches and distinguish this nudibranch from the Monterey sea lemon (MC293). Photograph A shows a specimen with its coiled egg ribbon.
A Turn Island, San Juan Channel, n. Washington
B Discovery Passage, Quadra Island, s. BC

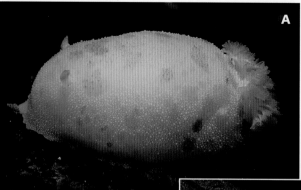

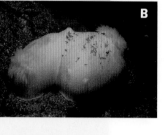

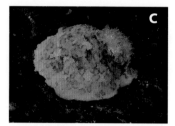

MC292. FRECKLED PALE SEA LEMON
Peltodoris lentignosa, Anisodoris lentignosa
▶to 23 cm (9 in) long
c. Alaska to s. Oregon
intertidal to 33 m (100 ft)
This species is distinguished by its slightly darker variable patches on a pale background. Nudibranchs are simultaneous hermaphrodites, meaning they function as male and female at the same time. Photograph B shows a pair exchanging sperm; this will result in each animal laying egg ribbons.
A B Anderson Bay, Texada Island, s. BC
C Tilly Point, s. Pender Island, s. BC

MC293. MONTEREY SEA LEMON, Monterey sea-lemon, Monterey dorid, Monterey doris, false sea lemon, sea lemon, false lemon peel nudibranch, dusty yellow nudibranch
Doris montereyensis, Archidoris montereyensis, Archidoris nyctea
to 15 cm (6 in) long
s. Alaska to s. California
intertidal to 256 m (845 ft)
At least a few tubercles (bumps) are tipped with black in this common and obvious dorid nudibranch.
Moore Point, Francis Peninsula, s. BC

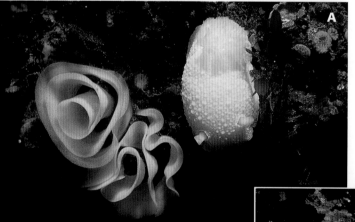

MC294. WHITE NUDIBRANCH, giant white dorid, snow white dorid, white dorid, white-knight nudibranch, white knight nudibranch, white knight doris, Odhner's dorid
Doris odhneri, Archidoris odhneri, Austrodoris odhneri
to 20 cm (8 in) long
n. Alaska to s. California
intertidal to 50 m (165 ft)
The white nudibranch typically has a circular, flower-shaped gill protruding from near the rear of an oval body. There are no dark markings on this nudibranch.
A Turn Island, San Juan Channel, n. Washington
B Laura Point, Mayne Island, s. BC

MC295. WHITE-SPOTTED SEA GODDESS, white speckled nudibranch, salted yellow doris, salted doris, white spotted porostome, yellow porostome

Doriopsilla albopunctata, *Dendrodoris albopunctata, Dendrodoris fulva, Doriopsis fulva*

to 6 cm (2.3 in) long

▶s. BC to n. Mexico

intertidal to 45 m (150 ft)

Distinguished by the white spots only on the tips of the small tubercles (bumps), this nudibranch was only recently found north of California.

Lovers Point, Monterey County, s. California. J. Duane Sept photograph

MC296. ▶TARA'S DORID

Aldisa tara

to 2.7 cm (1.1 in) long

s. BC

subtidal to 25 m (80 ft)

Tara's dorid nudibranch feeds on and lives in association with orange cratered encrusting sponge (PO44). Its limited documented geographic range is no doubt due to its recent discovery and small size. Expanding this distribution is an excellent opportunity for the sport diver to contribute to the study of marine biology.

Similar to Tara's dorid (MC296), Chan's dorid, *Hallaxa chani*, may be dull greyish or yellow, but has a series of large brown blotches down its midline.

Georgina Point, Mayne Island, s. BC

MC297. HEATH'S DORID, Heath's doris, gritty dorid, gritty doris

Geitodoris heathi, *Discodoris heathi, Discodoris fulva*

to 4.3 cm (1.7 in) long

c. Alaska to n. Mexico

▶subtidal to 20 m (65 ft)

The yellowish to white body is sprinkled with minute black or brown specks. Like all dorids, this nudibranch is capable of retracting its circular gills, leaving only a puckered hole as evidence. As with all dorids, it can also retract its two rhinophores (sensory organs).

Laura Point, Mayne Island, s. BC

MC298. LEOPARD DORID, leopard sea slug, ring-spotted dorid, ring spotted doris, ring-spotted doris, ring-spotted nudibranch, ringed doris, ringed dorid, ringed nudibranch, brown-ringed sea slug, brown spotted nudibranch, brown-spotted nudibranch, spotted nudibranch, tar spot nudibranch, San Diego dorid, San Diego doris, white nudibranch

Diaulula sandiegensis, *Discodoris sandiegensis*

▶to 12.5 cm (5 in) long

Sea of Japan, n. Alaska to n. Mexico

intertidal to 35 m (115 ft)

One might suspect from the photograph that two or three species are involved, but the distinct colour variations are "morphs" or types.

Mutine Point, Barkley Sound, s. BC

MC299. YELLOW-RIMMED NUDIBRANCH, yellow rimmed nudibranch, yellow edged nudibranch, yellow-edged nudibranch, yellow edged cadlina, yellow-edged cadlina, yellow-rim cadlina, yellow nudibranch, common yellow-margin nudibranch, yellow margin dorid, yellow-rimmed doris, pale yellow nudibranch

Cadlina luteomarginata, *Cadlina marginata*

▶to 8.3 cm (3.3 in) long

s. Alaska to n. Mexico

intertidal to 45 m (150 ft)

Stubby tubercles (bumps) tipped with yellow and a yellow rim distinguish this common species.

Laura Point, Mayne Island, s. BC

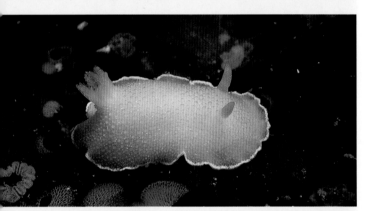

MC300. ▶WHITE-RIMMED NUDIBRANCH

Aldisa albomarginata

to 2.7 cm (1.1 in) long

s. BC

subtidal, 9–20 m (30–65 ft)

The greenish tinge of this species' body is distinct among Pacific Northwest dorid nudibranchs, and the white margin acts as a reflector for night divers. The very narrow parameters of this creature's distribution indicate its limited documentation to date. Perhaps your observations will expand the known geographic and depth range.

Agamemnon Channel, Nelson Island, s. BC

MC301. MODEST CADLINA

Cadlina modesta

to 4.5 cm (1.8 in) long

s. Alaska to s. California

intertidal to 50 m (165 ft)

Note the yellow spots that more or less ring the outer edge of the body's dorsal surface. The most forward of these extend ahead of the rhinophores (sensory organs). The modest cadlina's circular gills and rhinophores are

usually a pale yellow—a feature that may aid in its identification. Photograph B shows a specimen with gills withdrawn. A similar species, the yellow spotted cadlina, *Cadlina flavomaculata*, with black to dark brown rhinophores, also lives in the Pacific Northwest.

A B Moore Point, Francis Peninsula, s. BC

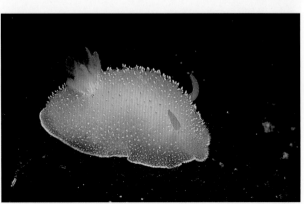

MC302. HUDSON'S DORID, Hudson's yellow margin nudibranch, Hudson's spiny doris, yellow margin dorid

Acanthodoris hudsoni

to 4 cm (1.5 in) long

s. Alaska to s. California

▶intertidal to 25 m (83 ft)

Long hair-like papillae tipped with yellow and a yellow rim are characteristic for this sea slug. The planktonic larvae of most nudibranchs are called veligers, and each possesses a tiny shell, which disappears when the larva metamorphoses into the adult form.

Sutton Islets, Egmont, s. BC

MC303. NANAIMO NUDIBRANCH, Nanaimo dorid, rufus tipped nudibranch, wine-plume dorid, wine-plumed doris, wine-plumed spiny doris, red gilled dorid, red-gilled dorid

***Acanthodoris nanaimoensis**, Acanthodoris columbina*

to 4 cm (1.5 in) long

c. Alaska to s. California

▶intertidal to 25 m (83 ft)

Similar to Hudson's dorid (MC302), this nudibranch has maroon tips on the gills and rhinophores (sensory organs) that are immediately recognizable. The amount of maroon can vary, as shown in photograph A. The Nanaimo nudibranch has a grey colour phase, as shown in photograph B.

A Ucluelet Harbour, w. Vancouver Island, s. BC

B Dinner Bay, Mayne Island, s. BC

MC304. PILOSE DORIS, hairy spiny doris

***Acanthodoris pilosa**, Acanthodoris pilosus*

to 2.7 cm (1.1 in) long (Atlantic specimens to 5.5 cm/2.1 in)

circumboreal, Iceland, Greenland to Morocco, Nova Scotia to Virginia, Sea of Japan, n. Alaska to c. California

intertidal to 270 m (890 ft)

This sea slug's body is covered with long, conical papillae (fleshy projections). It is listed as a circumboreal species, meaning it is found around the globe in Arctic regions. Many animal species have this designation but DNA research could alter this situation if cryptic or yet to be distinguished species are involved. Photograph B shows a spawning pair with egg ribbons.

A Sutton Islets, Egmont, s. BC

B St. Lazaria Island, Sitka Sound, s. Alaska

MC305. SANDALWOOD DORID, sandalwood scented dorid, yellow dorid, orange-peel doris

Acanthodoris lutea

to 3 cm (1.2 in) long

▶n. BC to n. Mexico

subtidal

This dorid apparently has the odour of sandalwood, a feature of little use to the diver. Its yellow hue and fine light speckling are distinctive. A lighter-than-normal specimen is shown in the photograph.

Best Point, Indian Arm, s. BC

MC306. BROWN NUDIBRANCH, brown dorid, cedar-scented dorid, brown thorned sea goddess

Acanthodoris brunnea

to 1.5 cm (0.6 in) long

s. BC to s. California

intertidal to subtidal

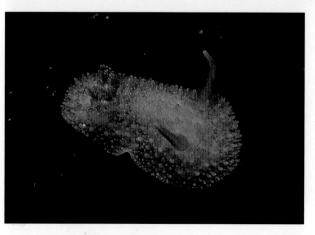

Differing from the barnacle-eating nudibranch (MC311), this gregarious species has fewer gills in its circular breathing structure, longer rhinophores (sensory organs) and pointed papillae (fleshy projections) instead of tubercles (bumps). The brown nudibranch produces a pungent cedar-like aroma when handled. The specimen shown here is one of several trawled from a shallow, sandy, wood chip-littered bottom in English Bay, Burrard Inlet, s. BC—a very different habitat from the shallow, rocky locales frequented by its barnacle-consuming look-alike.

English Bay, Burrard Inlet, s. BC

MC307. WHITE ADALARIA, yellow false doris
Adalaria proxima
to 2 cm (0.8 in) long (Atlantic specimens to 2.5 cm or 1 in)
circumboreal, Britain to Norway, Greenland to New England, Sea of Japan,
n. Alaska to s. BC
shallow subtidal
This species is readily found when living in groups on large, flat kelp, its
prime habitat. The tubercles (bumps) covering its back are long and club-
shaped.
Moore Point, Francis Peninsula, s. BC

MC308. JANNA'S ADALARIA
Adalaria jannae
to 1.5 cm (0.6 in) long
e. Russia, c. Alaska. to s. California
shallow subtidal
Other than having a more yellowish colour, smaller tubercles (bumps) and a
large, round tubercle behind the gills, Janna's adalaria is very similar to the
white adalaria (MC307). Many specimens typically gather together to lay
their tiny egg ribbons on kelp.
Tzoonie Narrows, Narrows Inlet, s. BC

MC309. There are several **tiny white dorids** in the genus *Adalaria* with
copious papillae (fleshy projections) covering their backs, that have yet
to be formally described and named. Nudibranch experts Sandra Millen
and Dave Behrens continue to grapple with this task. Meanwhile, amateur
naturalists periodically encounter specimens such as the one pictured here
during underwater forays or intertidal strolls.
Tzoonie Narrows, Narrows Inlet, s. BC

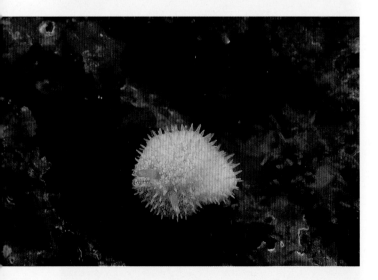

MC310. PORCUPINE DORID
Diaphorodoris lirulatocauda, Onchidoris hystricina
to 1.2 cm (0.5 in) long
s. Alaska to n. Mexico
intertidal to subtidal
Many long, slender papillae (fleshy projections) covering the back of the
porcupine dorid give it an appearance that inspired its common name. It
also has an abundance of opaque white flecks between the papillae that
are noticeable only on close inspection, and it has a long, trailing, ridged
tail.
Roche Point, Indian Arm, s. BC

MC311. BARNACLE-EATING NUDIBRANCH, barnacle-eating onchidoris, barnacle-eating dorid, barnacle nudibranch, rough-mantled sea slug, rough mantled sea slug, rough mantled doris, rough-mantled doris, many-gilled onchidoris

Onchidoris bilamellata*, Onchidoris fusca, Lamellidoris fusca*
to 3 cm (1.2 in) long (Atlantic specimens to 4 cm or 1.6 in)
circumboreal, w. Russia to France, Greenland to Connecticut, Sea of Japan, n. Alaska to n. Mexico
▶intertidal to 30 m (100 ft)

During spawning season, the snow-white egg masses are more obvious than the animal itself, as shown in photograph B. Photograph A features two typical mottled brown specimens and an unusual pale one. Yes indeed, it does feed upon barnacles, drilling in with its specialized radula (file-like tongue).

A Moore Point, Francis Peninsula, s. BC
B Sutton Islets, Egmont, s. BC

MC312. FUZZY ONCHIDORIS, muricate doris

Onchidoris muricata*, Lamellidoris muricata, Onchidoris hystricina, Onchidoris aspera, Onchidoris diaphana, Onchidoris varians, Diaphorodoris lirulatocauda*
to 1.4 cm (0.6 in) long
circumboreal, France to Russia, Greenland to Connecticut, n. Alaska to s. California
intertidal to 18 m (60 ft)

Living primarily on kelp and feeding upon associated encrusting bryozoans, this tiny species, which can also be cream or orange in colour, is usually only noticed when in groups.

Cape Neddick Lighthouse, York Beach, Maine. Charlotte Richardson photograph

MC313. FROST SPOT NUDIBRANCH, frost-spot corambe, Pacific corambe, frost spot, translucent gray nudibranch

Corambe pacifica*, Doridella pacifica, Gulinia pacifica*
to 1.5 cm (0.6 in) long
s. Alaska to n. Mexico
intertidal to subtidal

This species is similar to the cryptic nudibranch (MC314) but is distinguished by a notch at its posterior. Look for it on the kelp-encrusting bryozoan (BZ1), which supplies both its food and a spawning site.
The ▶white-ended nudibranch, *Loy thompsoni,* is very similar to the preceding species but is much darker and has striking white extremities. It lives on muddy substrates, is found from s. BC to c. Alaska and reaches 0.7 cm (0.3 in) in length.

Sekiu, Olympic coast, n. Washington

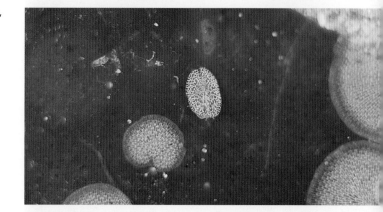

MC314. CRYPTIC NUDIBRANCH, Steinberg's dorid, Joan Steinberg's corambe

Doridella steinbergi*, Corambella steinbergi, Corambella bolini, Corambe mosaica, Suhinia steinbergi, Paracorambe steinbergi*
to 1.6 cm (0.7 in) long
c. Alaska to n. Mexico
intertidal to subtidal

By carefully searching colonies of the kelp-encrusting bryozoan (BZ1) (seen in photograph), a keen-eyed naturalist may find this animal and its white egg ribbons.

Stanley Park, Vancouver Harbour, s. BC

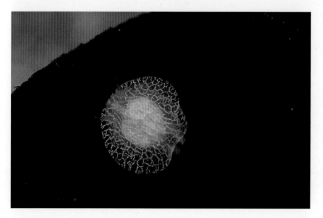

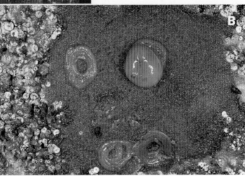

MC315. RED SPONGE NUDIBRANCH, red sponge doris, red nudibranch, bloody red dorid, crimson dorid, crimson doris, bright red nudibranch, MacFarlane's pretty doris
Rostanga pulchra
to 3.3 cm (1.4 in) long
s. Alaska to n. Mexico, Chile
intertidal to 100 m (330 ft)
As illustrated in photograph B, this nudibranch associates with and spawns on encrusting red sponges. Its coiled, red egg ribbons remain after its departure. Photograph A shows a specimen with its circular gill structure partially retracted.
A Long Island, near Lopez Island, n. Washington
B Ucluth Peninsula, w. Vancouver Island, s. BC

MC316. COOPER'S DORID, sea lemon
Aldisa cooperi, *Aldisa sanguinea cooperi*
to 2.5 cm (1 in) long
s. Alaska to n. California
intertidal to 23 m (75 ft)
The few black speckles along the midline of Cooper's dorid distinguish it from the red sponge nudibranch (MC315). The photograph shows a group of specimens that have deposited their egg ribbons on encrusting sponge, their primary food source.
The very similar red dorid, *Aldisa sanguinea,* is recorded from c. Oregon and south.
Laura Point, Mayne Island, s. BC

MC317. VANCOUVER'S OKENIA
Okenia vancouverensis, *Idalia vancouverensis, Cargoa vancouverensis*
to 1.8 cm (0.7 in) long
n. BC to s. BC
subtidal to 25 m (80 ft)
A dive in Sechelt Inlet, BC, by Donna Gibbs of Port Coquitlam, BC, resulted in this photograph. Perhaps one of your explorations will expand this species' known range. Be sure to contact us through the publisher.
Piper Point, Sechelt Inlet, s. BC

MC318. CLOWN NUDIBRANCH, sea-clown nudibranch, sea clown nudibranch, sea clown triopha, sea-clown triopha, clown dorid, Catalina triopha, Carpenter's doris, orange spotted nudibranch, orange-spotted nudibranch, common orange spotted nudibranch, orange-tipped nudibranch

Triopha catalinae, *Triopha carpenteri, Triopha modesta, Triopha eliota, Triopha scrippsiana*

to 15 cm (6 in) long

Sea of Japan, n. Alaska to n. Mexico

intertidal to 80 m (265 ft)

This nudibranch is an attractive favourite of diving photographers because it lives in shallow water and is readily found. The different-looking specimens in photographs B and C are unusual colour morphs of this species.

A Tyler Rock, Barkley Sound, s. BC

B Miners Bay, Mayne Island, s. BC

C St. Lazaria Island, Sitka Sound, s. Alaska

MC319. SPOTTED TRIOPHA, speckled triopha, maculated triopha, maculated doris, blue-spotted nudibranch

Triopha maculata, *Triopha grandis, Triopha aurantiaca*

to 18 cm (7 in) long

Siberia, s. BC to n. Mexico

intertidal to 33 m (110 ft)

This species, unlike most of the preceding dorid types, is more elongate and has processes on both the frontal veil and along the lateral ridge. Both this species and the clown nudibranch (MC318) feed on bryozoans.

Lennard Island, Tofino, s. BC

MC320. COCKERELL'S NUDIBRANCH, Cockerell's dorid, orange spotted nudibranch, lalia doris

Limacia cockerelli, *Laila cockerelli*

to 2.5 cm (1 in) long

s. Alaska to n. Mexico

intertidal to 35 m (115 ft)

The long papillae (fleshy projections) with bulbous, "dew-drop" tips are very distinctive on Cockerell's nudibranch, always a special find for the nudibranch enthusiast. Papillae shape, placement and colour may vary between northern and southern populations.

Long Island, near Lopez Island, n. Washington

MC321. SALT-AND-PEPPER NUDIBRANCH, salt-and-pepper doris, white knight nudibranch, white-spotted doris, small white nudibranch, white knight

Aegires albopunctatus

to 2.2 cm (0.9 in) long

s. Alaska to n. Mexico

subtidal to 30 m (100 ft)

This tiny white species is a great challenge for the underwater macro photographer. It is readily distinguishable by its oversized papillae (fleshy projections) and sparse black speckling.

Nelson Island, Agamemnon Channel, s. BC

MC322. THREE-COLORED POLYCERA, three-color polycera
Polycera tricolor
to 3 cm (1.2 in) long
s. Alaska to n. Mexico
subtidal to 60 m (200 ft)
Most common in the northern portion of its range, this distinctive species lives only along exposed shores and not in the protected waters of Puget Sound or the Strait of Georgia. Such an ecological niche is shared by many Pacific Northwest organisms.
Lane Islet, Dawley Passage, s. BC

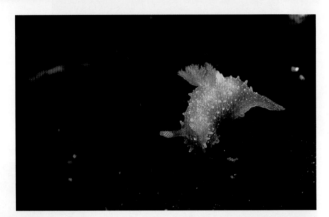

MC323. BANDED POLYCERA, eelgrass polycera
Palio dubia, *Polycera zosterae*, *Palio zosterae*
to 1.2 cm (0.5 in) long
circumboreal, s. Alaska to c. California
intertidal to subtidal
An easily overlooked species, the banded polycera feeds on encrusting bryozoans, particularly those coating the understory kelps and eelgrass (SW2). Many nudibranchs, particularly the smaller species such as this one, have a short life span—perhaps a year or less.
Butedale, Grenville Channel, n. BC

MC324. SORCERER'S NUDIBRANCH, orange-spike polycera, orange-spiked doris, black dorid, black polycera
Polycera atra
to 5 cm (2 in) long
▶c. Washington to n. Mexico
subtidal to 50 m (165 ft)
A "muck" dive by Andy Lamb under floats at Westport, Washington, resulted in a northern range extension for this species. It was interesting to find this richly coloured nudibranch in a silty, murky locale.
Westport Marina, Westport, c. Washington

MC325. PACIFIC ANCULA/ATLANTIC ANCULA
Ancula gibbosa, *Ancula pacifica*
to 1.6 cm (0.7 in) long (Atlantic specimens to 3.3 cm or 1.3 in)
circumboreal, Russia to the Mediterranean Sea, Greenland to Connecticut, c. Alaska to s. California
▶subtidal to 20 m (66 ft)
Are one or two species involved? This is sometimes a question when a species is described from the east coast of North America and a very similar one is found on the west coast. In this case, colour variations create further confusion. The tiny white "sausage" on the upper back of the photographed specimen is the egg package of a parasitic copepod.
Roche Point, Indian Arm, s. BC

MC326. HOPKIN'S ROSE, rosy-pink nudibranch, rose nudibranch
Okenia rosacea, *Hopkinsea rosacea*
to 3 cm (1.2 in) long
s. Oregon to n. Mexico
intertidal to 6 m (20 ft)
This species is another candidate for a northern range extension. Ocean currents from the south, affected by El Niño events, may deposit larvae along Pacific Northwest exposed shores. The authors would be interested to learn of any Pacific Northwest sightings.
James V. Fitzgerald Marine Reserve, San Mateo County, c. California. J. Duane Sept photograph

MC327. DIAMONDBACK NUDIBRANCH, diamond back nudibranch, diamondback tritonia, diamond back tritonia, festive nudibranch, festive tritonia, festive triton
Tritonia festiva, *Duvaucelia festiva*, *Lateribranchaea festiva*, *Tritonia reticulata*, *Sphaerostoma undulata*
to 10 cm (4 in) long
Japan, s. Alaska to n. Mexico
intertidal to 50 m (165 ft)
Small specimens, with their white line markings, are found dining upon red soft coral (CN37). The largest specimens often cruise sandy substrates, seeking various sea pens and sea whips (CN40–42) as prey. A pinkish hue indicates the colour of the latest meal of the individual in photograph B.
A B Meares Island, Clayoquot Sound, s. BC

MC328. This entry represents a serendipitous find associated with collection of specimens of the newly discovered pink soft coral (CN38) for the Vancouver Aquarium Marine Science Centre. After a Langara Island, n. BC, sample of the aforementioned coral was brought aboard the MV *Nautilus Explorer*, this tiny **mystery tritonid** nudibranch crawled out from between the polyps. Whether it is a strange variety of the diamondback nudibranch (MC327) or a new species is uncertain. At the time of publication, both the soft coral and the tritonid nudibranch were being investigated for possible species descriptions.
Dibrell Bay, Langara Island, n. BC

MC329. PINK TRITONIA, Diomedes tritonia, rosy tritonia, giant orange nudibranch, Diomedes' triton
Tritonia diomedea, *Sphaerostoma diomedea*, *Tritonia exulans*, *Duvaucelia gilberti*
to 22 cm (8.5 in) long
Sea of Japan, n. Alaska to Panama, Florida
intertidal to 656 m (2,165 ft)
Look for the pink tritonia on sandy bottoms, especially where its prey, sea pens and sea whips (CN40–42), are present. Photograph B shows a specimen with eggs.
A B Meares Island, Clayoquot Sound, s. BC

MC330. ORANGE-PEEL NUDIBRANCH, orange peel nudibranch, lemon-peel nudibranch, lemon peel nudibranch, giant orange tochni, tochni
Tochuina tetraquetra, *Duvaucelia tetraquetra*, *Sphaerostoma tetraquetra*, *Tritoniopsis tetraquetra*, *Tritonia aurantia*, *Tritonia gigantea*
▶to 50 cm (18 in) long
Siberia, n. Alaska to s. California
subtidal to 363 m (1,200 ft)

This nudibranch is supposedly edible, but we found it wanting. Photograph B shows a juvenile eating its way up a dwarf red gorgonian (CN43).
A Stubbs Island, Weynton Passage, c. BC
B Fearney Point, Agamemnon Channel, s. BC

MC331. GIANT NUDIBRANCH, giant dendronotid, giant frond-aeolis, giant frond eolis, rainbow nudibranch, rainbow dendronotid
Dendronotus iris, *Dendronotus giganteus*
to 30 cm (12 in) long
n. Alaska to n. Mexico
subtidal to 215 m (710 ft)
This variably hued nudibranch, with its white-rimmed foot, is an ideal underwater video subject, for either its feeding lunge at a tube-dwelling anemone (CN26) or its entrancing dance in the water column, well off the bottom.
A Quarry Bay, Nelson Island, s. BC
B Mitlenatch Island, Strait of Georgia, s. BC
C Anderson Bay, Texada Island, s. BC

MC332. RED DENDRONOTID, giant red dendronotid, red frond-aeolis, red frond eolis
Dendronotus rufus
to 28 cm (11 in) long
s. Alaska to n. Washington
subtidal
Gathering in small groups primarily in the spring, the red dendronotid produces distinctive egg "strings" that resemble tangled white yarn. Like all nudibranchs, each specimen is both male and female. Sperm is exchanged before individuals lay eggs.
Porteau Cove, Howe Sound, s. BC

MC333. DALL'S DENDRONOTID, Dall's frond-aeolis, Dall's frond eolis
Dendronotus dalli, *Dendronotus elegans*
to 14 cm (5.5 in) long
n. Alaska to n. Washington
subtidal
In this sea slug, the paired gills along the back are less bushy than in the giant nudibranch (MC331) and red dendronotid (MC332). This animal is a very capable swimmer once dislodged from the substrate.
Sutton Islets, Egmont, s. BC

MC334. MULTICOLOR DENDRONOTID, variable dendronotid, multicolor frond-aeolis, colored dendronotid
Dendronotus diversicolor
to 5 cm (2 in) long
s. Alaska to s. California
intertidal to 19 m (60 ft)
The pastel form of this nudibranch is readily found amid its sea fir hydroid prey (CN54–55) in spite of its small size. The various dendronotid species have unique cup-like sheaths around their rhinophores (sensory organs). The multicolor dendronotid usually has four pairs of gills. A pair laying egg ribbons is shown in photograph B.
A Eagle Point, San Juan Island, n. Washington
B Stubbs Island, Weynton Passage, c. BC

MC335. WHITE DENDRONOTID, white dendronotus, white frond-aeolis
Dendronotus albus
to 3.5 cm (1.5 in) long
c. Alaska to n. Mexico
intertidal to 30 m (100 ft)
The white dendronotid is difficult to distinguish from the white variant of the multicolor dendronotid (MC334). In this species the white stripe extends from between the fourth pair of gills or cerata (fleshy processes) to the tip of the tail, whereas in the multicolor dendronotid the stripe only extends from the last pair of cerata to the tip of the tail.
Laura Point, Mayne Island, s. BC

MC336. BUSHY-BACKED NUDIBRANCH, bushy-backed sea slug, frond-aeolis, frond eolis, leafy dendronotid
Dendronotus frondosus, *Dendronotus arborescens*, *Dendronotus venustus*, *Amphitrite frondosa*
▶to 10 cm (4 in) long
circumboreal, Europe, Siberia, Japan, south to New Jersey, n. Alaska to n. Mexico
intertidal to 400 m (1,320 ft)
Northern specimens can grow much larger, making them easier to find feeding upon their hydroid prey. This common dendronotid is distinguished by a lateral process protruding from each rhinophore's (sensory organ) stalk. It also has variable colouration. Photograph B shows a juvenile specimen.
A Miners Bay, Mayne Island, s. BC
B Tyler Rock, Barkley Sound, s. BC

MC337. STUBBY DENDRONOTUS, stubby frond-aeolis, subramose frond eolis, slightly branched dendronotid
Dendronotus subramosus
to 3.3 cm (1.3 in) long
s. BC to n. Mexico
intertidal to 120 m (400 ft)
If you seek the stubby dendronotus, look for its prey, the ostrich-plume hydroid (CN53). Once this is accomplished, carefully inspect the upright "plumes" and you may be rewarded with a sighting of this rarely found nudibranch.
Turn Island, San Juan Channel, n. Washington

MC338. ▶WHITE SPOTTED DENDRONOTID
Dendronotus albopunctatus
to 6 cm (2.3 in) long
▶n. BC to s. Oregon
subtidal
While participating in a MV *Nautilus Explorer* cruise to the Queen Charlotte Islands (Haida Gwaii), Andy Lamb found two of these nudibranchs at 15 m (50 ft) at Harriot Island. This find significantly extended the known range of this species. The bottom was extremely silty and this nudibranch's distinctively wide foot probably acts like a "snowshoe" to prevent it from sinking below the surface.
Harriot Island, Moresby Island, n. BC

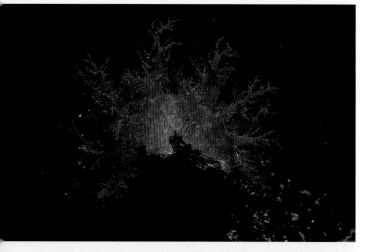

MC339. ▶LIGHT-SPECKLED DENDRONOTID
Dendronotus sp.
▶to 25 cm (10 in) long
s. Alaska to s. California
subtidal
Superficially similar to the bushy-backed nudibranch (MC336), the light-speckled dendronotid has no lateral process extending from the sheath of each rhinophore (sensory organ). Specimens have obviously been "found," but only a few have been photographed, and thus the light-speckled dendronotid remains scientifically and officially unnamed.
Treadwell Bay, Slingsby Channel, c. BC

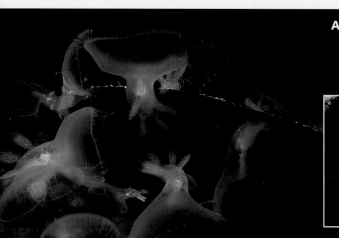

MC340. HOODED NUDIBRANCH, lion nudibranch, translucent nudibranch, melibe
***Melibe leonina**, Chioraera leonina, Melibe dalli, Chioraera dalli, Melibe pellucida*
▶to 17.5 cm (7 in) long
c. Alaska to n. Mexico
intertidal to 37 m (122 ft)
Reminiscent of a soft, underwater Venus flytrap, this strange nudibranch frequently detaches from its "site of rest" and flexes its way to and fro in the water column. A distinctive sweet smell, not unlike that of a watermelon, emanates from a hooded nudibranch when removed from water.
A Agamemnon Channel, Nelson Island, s. BC
B Irvines Landing, Pender Harbour, s. BC

MC341. BRITISH COLUMBIA DOTO, British Columbia's doto, Columbia doto
Doto columbiana
to 1.2 cm (0.5 in) long
n. BC to s. California
intertidal to 60 m (200 ft)
Only "blue ribbon" marine naturalists find the British Columbia doto hiding amid plumes of various sea fir hydroids (CN54/55). Its colour, design and diminutive size require its seeker to be very determined and have excellent eyesight.
Turn Island, San Juan Channel, n. Washington. Charlie Gibbs photograph

MC342. SEAL DOTO, dark doto
Doto kya, *Doto varians*
to 1 cm (0.4 in) long
s. BC to n. Mexico
intertidal to subtidal
This doto differs from the British Columbia doto (C341) in the dark blotches on its body and lack of dark rings on its rounded ceratal tubercles (bumps). Unfortunately these distinctive characteristics are not obvious without visual assistance—a magnifying glass at least.
Laura Point, Mayne Island, s. BC

MC343. ORANGE DOTO, hammerhead doto
Doto amyra, *Doto varians, Doto ganda, Doto wara*
▶to 2.5 cm (1 in)
s. Alaska to n. Mexico
intertidal to subtidal
The orange to almost white cores in the orange doto's bulbous cerata (fleshy processes) distinguish it from the British Columbia and seal dotos (MC341/342). Ongoing studies indicate there may be two or three species involved—stay tuned.
A Helm Point, Coronation Island, s. Alaska
B Baranof Hot Springs, Baranof Island, s. Alaska

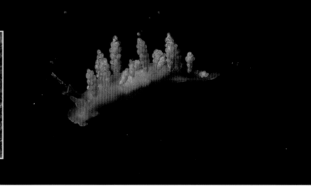

MC344. STRIPED NUDIBRANCH, striped armina, California armina, Californian armina, California arminid
Armina californica, *Pleurophyllidia californica, Armina columbiana, Armina digueti, Armina vancouverensis*
to 7.5 cm (3 in) long
n. Alaska to Panama
intertidal to 230 m (760 ft)
This predator plows through sand/mud looking for the orange sea pen (CN40), its primary prey. After the meal, all that may be left is the prey's long, slender calcium skeleton.
A Anderson Bay, Texada Island, s. BC
B Vivian Rock, Shearwater Passage, s. BC

MC345. FROSTED NUDIBRANCH, alabaster nudibranch, white-lined dirona, white-line dirona, chalk-lined dirona, chalk-line dirona, white-streaked dirona, white nudibranch
Dirona albolineata
to 18 cm (7 in) long
Japan, Siberia, s. Alaska to s. California
intertidal to 37 m (122 ft)
Irresistible to the underwater "paparazzi." When stressed, this delicate creature, named for the white edging that highlights its form, readily sheds its flattened cerata (fleshy processes).
A Miners Bay, Mayne Island, s. BC
B Moore Point, Francis Peninsula, s. BC

MC346. GOLDEN DIRONA, gold dirona, orange dirona
Dirona pellucida, *Dirona aurantia*
to 12 cm (5 in) long
Siberia, n. Alaska to c. Oregon
intertidal to subtidal
White speckling, particularly on the lower body, distinguishes the golden dirona from orange varieties of the frosted nudibranch (MC345). The spectacular leaf-shaped structures along its back are sites where the oxygen/carbon dioxide exchange occurs. Note that the shape and number of these leafy structures is quite variable.
A Booker Lagoon, Broughton Island, c. BC
B Sutton Islets, Egmont, s. BC

          C Point Cowan, Bowen Island, s .BC

MC347. ▶WHITE-AND-ORANGE-TIPPED NUDIBRANCH
Janolus fuscus, *Antiopella fusca,* formerly with *Antiopella barbarensis* or *Janolus barbarensis, Janolus aureocinta*
▶to 2.5 cm (1 in) long
Sea of Japan, s. Alaska to s. California
intertidal to 30 m (100 ft)
The brown-cored cerata (fleshy processes) of this species have orange ends with white tips. There is a red "racing stripe" on the head, but unlike the opalescent nudibranch (MC349), the cerata extend ahead of the rhinophores (sensory organs).
Ucluelet Harbour, w. Vancouver Island, s. BC

MC348. ▶FROSTY-TIPPED NUDIBRANCH
Janolus **sp. nov.**
▶to 3 cm (1.2 in) long
▶s. BC to Washington
▶subtidal, 6–20 m (20–65 ft)
One of the more exciting outcomes of this book's preparation was our discovery of this nudibranch at Quarry Bay, Nelson Island, s. BC, in 1995! Later collections of other specimens in nearby Sechelt Inlet will result in Sandra Millen's formal description and scientific naming.
Quarry Bay, Nelson Island, s. BC

MC349. OPALESCENT NUDIBRANCH, opalescent sea slug, opalescent aeolid, horned nudibranch, long-horned nudibranch, hermissenda nudibranch, hermissenda, thick-horned nudibranch, long-horned hermissenda, thick-horned aeolid
Hermissenda crassicornis, *Phidiana crassicornis, Hermissenda opalescens, Flabellina opalescens, Shinanoeolis opalescens, Shinanoeolis emurai*
to 8 cm (3.2 in) long
Sea of Japan, c. Alaska to n. Mexico
intertidal to 37 m (122 ft)
Note the bold stripe on the head, between the rhinophores (sensory organs) of this hydroid predator, which may also scavenge. Another extremely popular subject for underwater photographers.
A Butress Island, Slingsby Channel, c. BC
B Treadwell Bay, Slingsby Channel, c. BC

MC350. RED FLABELLINA, predaceous aeolis
Flabellina triophina, *Flabellina fusca, Coryphella fusca*
to 12 cm (4.9 in) long
Sea of Japan, s. Alaska to c. Oregon
subtidal to 65 m (215 ft)
The frilly cerata (gills) of the red flabellina have paler cores than those of the red-gilled nudibranch (MC351), and rather than being in clusters, they are continuous. These cores are extensions of the creature's digestive tract and provide extra surface area for this process. Note egg ribbons in the photograph.
Agamemnon Channel, Nelson Island, s. BC

MC351. RED-GILLED NUDIBRANCH, red-gilled aeolid, red verrucose nudibranch, verrucose aeolid, red-finger aeolis, red-fingered eolis
Flabellina verrucosa, *Coryphella rufibranchialis, Coryphella longicaudata, Coryphella verrucosa rufibranchialis*
to 10 cm (4 in) long
circumboreal, Britain, Norway, Iceland, Greenland to Maine, Sea of Japan, s. Alaska to n. Washington
intertidal to 300 m (1,000 ft)
Spawning on, as well as consuming, a variety of hydroids—particularly the pink-mouth hydroids (CN71–73) species—this colourful "cutie" usually lives in higher-current locales.
The ▶lovely nudibranch, *Flabellina amabilis,* nearly identical to this one, has so far only been found at the north end of Vancouver Island, BC, and the Sea of Japan. It lives with the brown bushy hydroid (CN64).
Irvines Landing, Pender Harbour, s. BC

MC352. THREE-LINED NUDIBRANCH, three lined aeolid, threeline aeolis, three-stripe aeolid
Flabellina trilineata, Coryphella trilineata, Coryphella piunca, Coryphella fisheri
to 3.6 cm (1.5 in) long
s. Alaska to n. Mexico
intertidal to 50 m (165 ft)
Though frequently found with the red-gilled nudibranch, this nudibranch is readily distinguished by its three obvious longitudinal stripes and clusters of cerata or (gills). An imminent predator–prey interaction is shown in photograph B.
A Plumper Islands, Weynton Passage, c. BC
B Sutton Islets, Egmont, s. BC

MC353. PEARLY NUDIBRANCH, pearly aeolid
Flabellina japonica
to 7.5 cm (3 in) long
circumboreal, Japan, Siberia, n. Alaska to s. BC
subtidal
White tips on numerous straw-coloured cerata (gills) are distinctive for this sea slug. These narrow, pointed cerata are the structures that define this group of nudibranchs: the aeolids. When disturbed, the pearly nudibranch readily sheds its cerata. Photograph B includes an egg ribbon.
A B Sutton Islets, Egmont, s. BC

MC354. SPANISH SHAWL, purple nudibranch, purple fan nudibranch, purple aeolis, elegant eolid, iodine eolis
Flabellina iodinea, Flabellinopsis iodinea, Coryphella iodinea, Coryphella sabulicola
to 9 cm (3.8 in) long
s. BC to n. Mexico
intertidal to 40 m (130 ft)
So brilliantly coloured is this nudibranch that any diving naturalist will notice it as a tiny "beacon." A somewhat rare sighting in the Pacific Northwest, the Spanish shawl apparently will swim when stimulated by a potential predator.
Cape Flattery, Olympic coast, n. Washington

MC355. PRICE'S AEOLID
Flabellina pricei, Coryphella pricei
to 2.5 cm (1 in) long
s. Alaska to s. California
subtidal
Yellow or greenish interiors of the white-tipped cerata (gills) together with this nudibranch's perfoliate rhinophores (feather-like sensory organs) are distinctive. Inspect delicate-looking hydroids when looking for this rarely observed species.
Steilacoom, Puget Sound, c. Washington

MC356. ISLAND AEOLID
Flabellina **cf.** *islandica*
to 2.2 cm (0.9 in) long
Sea of Japan, s. BC
shallow subtidal
Precise identification of this nudibranch is still in doubt—hence the "cf." designation. Found on muddy substrate in spring and summer, its stouter and wider shape—compared to other similar species—is believed to be an adaptation to such habitats.

Victoria Harbour, s. Vancouver Island, s. BC. Neil McDaniel photograph

MC357. BURROWING AEOLID
Cumanotus **sp. 1**, *Flabellina* sp. 1
to 1.4 cm (0.6 in) long
s. BC to s. California
subtidal
This reclusive nudibranch often buries itself in soft sediments. However, photographer/biologist Neil McDaniel of Vancouver, BC, reports that when it moves along the bottom, the creature uses its cerata (gills) in unison to and fro, resulting in a sculling motion—a method of propulsion atypical for nudibranchs.

Victoria Harbour, s. Vancouver Island, s. BC. Neil McDaniel photograph

MC358. RUSTIC AEOLID
Eubranchus rustyus, *Capellinia rustyus*, *Eubranchus occidentalis*
to 2.5 cm (1 in) long
s. Alaska to n. Mexico
intertidal to subtidal
The inflated cerata (gills) of this species each have two or three green to brown bands and are topped with a white tip. Specimens are likely to be found clustered and laying eggs on *Plumularia* hydroids (CN59/60). The similar-looking but smaller ▶olive aeolid, *Eubranchus rupium,* lays its eggs on wine-glass hydroids (CN63). Even tinier is the San Juan aeolid, *Eubranchus sanjuanensis*, which resembles the red-gilled nudibranch (MC351).

Copper Cliffs, Quadra Island, s. BC

MC359. BRITISH COLUMBIA'S AEOLID, BC aeolid
Catriona columbiana, *Cuthona columbiana*, *Catriona alpha*, *Catrena alpha*, *Cratena spadix*
▶to 2 cm (0.8 in) long
s. Africa, New Zealand, Japan, s. Alaska to s. California
intertidal to subtidal
Like many nudibranchs, this species is very particular about its food, preferring to dine on pink-mouth hydroids (CN71–73). It also uses these sites to lay its white egg ribbons.

Copper Cliffs, Quadra Island, s. BC

MC360. POMEGRANATE AEOLID
Cuthona punicea
to 2.5 cm (1 in) long
c. BC
subtidal, 12–30 m (40–100 ft)
Exclusively associated with the raspberry hydroid (CN76), this species lays its tiny white egg strings around the stalks of its host. So far the pomegranate aeolid has only been found along the northeast coastal area of Vancouver Island. You may change this with your observations.
Stubbs Island, Weynton Passage, c. BC

MC361. ROSE-PINK CUTHONA, Correa's aeolid
Cuthona divae, *Precuthona divae, Cuthona rosea,* Cuthona nana*
to 3.4 cm (1.3 in) long
s. BC to s. California
intertidal to 20 m (65 ft)
In this very bushy species, the first three rows of cerata (gills) begin ahead of its rhinophores (sensory organs). It feeds on hydractinid hydroids (CN67–69), whose colours it closely matches.
*This name applies to a nudibranch found in the Atlantic Ocean and the Sea of Japan that may be the same species.
Monterey Bay, c. California. Bruce Wight photograph

MC362. PUSTULATE AEOLID
Cuthona pustulata
to 2 cm (0.8 in) long
c. Alaska to s. BC
subtidal
A tiny but distinctive species, the pustulate aeolid has white speckles along its dark-cored cerata (gills). Note also the faint bands near the tips of the cerata. This nudibranch's brown jaws and white sex organs often show through its translucent body.
Boas Islet, Hakai Passage, c. BC

MC363. NEAT AEOLID, Trinchese's neat aeolid
Cuthona concinna, *Trinchesia concinna*
to 1.5 cm (0.6 in) long
circumpolar, n. Alaska to s. BC
subtidal
The cerata (gills) of this rather plain species can vary in colour intensity, those illustrated in the photograph being dark. Rather than looking for a tiny aeolid nudibranch, the thoughtful naturalist should examine hydroid colonies, where these creatures feed and breed.
The brown aeolid, *Cuthona cocoachroma*, is nearly identical but has only been recorded from Washington and south.
Brooks Peninsula, w. Vancouver Island, s. BC

MC364. GREEN AEOLID
Cuthona viridis
to 1.1 cm (0.4 in) long
w. Russia, s. Alaska to n. Washington
intertidal to subtidal
Just finding this tiny nudibranch is difficult, so distinguishing it from several others featured above, particularly during a dive or on a beachcombing trek, will be most problematic. It has white granulations on its tentacles and rhinophores (sensory organs).
Four other tiny cuthonid nudibranchs have been documented as far north as Washington. They are the white crusted aeolid, *Cuthona albocrusta*, the graceful aeolid, *Cuthona abronia*, the yellow-headed aeolid, *Cuthona flavovulta*, and the shiny aeolid, *Cuthona fulgens*.
Baranof Hot Springs, Baranof Island, s. Alaska

MC365. This photograph emphasizes the importance of having an actual specimen to examine when trying to identify a species that is very similar to several others. Although the detail of this **unidentified aeolid** is well illustrated, it is not enough to allow positive identification. The best hope is to find another specimen, collect it and ultimately complete this entry.
Pearse Islands, Weynton Passage, c. BC

MC366. SHAG-RUG NUDIBRANCH, shag rug nudibranch, shag rug sea slug, shag-rug aeolis, mossy nudibranch, shaggy mouse nudibranch, shaggy mouse, shaggy mouse aeolid, common grey sea slug, maned nudibranch, papillose aeolid, papillose eolis, sea mouse
Aeolidia papillosa, *Aeolidea papillosa*, *Aeolidia farinacea*
to 10 cm (4 in) long (Atlantic specimens to 12 cm or 5 in)
circumboreal, south to France, south to Maryland, Argentina, Falkland Islands, Sea of Japan, c. Alaska to n. Mexico, Chile
intertidal to 900 m (3,000 ft)
Not only does the shag-rug nudibranch feed upon various sea anemones, but amazingly, it stores the prey's undischarged stinging cells in its cerata (gills) for its own defence. Photograph B shows a specimen that has been feeding on orange zoanthids (CN27).
A similar but much smaller species, the
▶deepwater shag-rug nudibranch, *Aeolidia herculea*, lives in the Pacific Northwest but below 500 m (1,650 ft).
A Point Defiance, Puget Sound, c. Washington
B Whytecliff Park, Howe Sound, s. BC

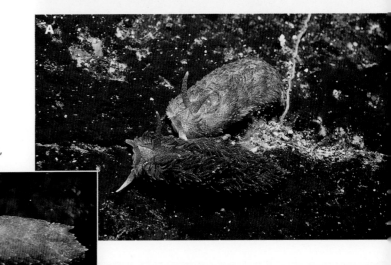

MC367. PELAGIC NUDIBRANCH, feathered fiona, fiona
Fiona pinnata
to 2.5 cm (1 in) long
cosmopolitan in northern seas, Chile
pelagic
Distinguished by its simple rhinophores (sensory organs) and sail-shaped cerata (gills), this nudibranch has a special relationship with its two primary and pelagic prey species. Those that live with and feed on the by-the-wind sailor (CN108) are purple, whereas those associating with the pelagic goose-neck barnacle (AR176) show as tan or brown.
Dibrell Bay, Langara Island, n. BC. Donna Gibbs photograph

MC368. Pacific Northwest naturalists, particularly scuba divers, frequently encounter what appear to be colourful coiled ribbons or loose yarn-like masses resting on the bottom. Often there is no animal in the vicinity to hint at what has produced this unknown entity. Such geometrical structures are **nudibranch egg ribbons**, three of which are depicted here. Other examples are shown with their parents in some of the preceding photographs. Indeed, so distinctive are these egg masses that the type of nudibranch responsible, if not the species, can be determined. Photographs A and B show two dorid egg ribbons, and photograph C features an aeolid or dendronotid mass.

A Quarry Bay, Nelson Island, s. BC
B Captain Island, Jervis Inlet, s. BC
C Cyril Rock, Texada Island, s. BC

TUSKSHELLS

MC369. WAMPUM TUSKSHELL, Indian money tusk, Indian-money tusk, Indian tooth shell, Indian's tooth shell, dentalia
Antalis pretiosum, *Dentalium pretiosum, Fustiaria pretiosum, Dentalium berryi, Dentalium watsoni*
to 5 cm (2 in) long
s. Alaska to n. Mexico
subtidal, 1–300 m (3–1,000 ft)
Yes, this species was used as an item of barter by some First Nations peoples. It also appears on ceremonial garb.
Ninstints, Queen Charlotte Islands, n. BC

MC370. WESTERN STRAIGHT TUSKSHELL, western straight tusk, straight tuskshell
Rhabdus rectius, *Dentalium rectius, Laevidentalium rectius, Fustiaria rectius, Dentalium watsoni, Dentalium dalli*
to 3 cm (1.2 in) long
Alaska to Peru
deep subtidal
When alive, this animal usually remains buried in sand or silt with its pointed end extended into the water column, allowing for seawater exchange. The western straight tuskshell apparently feeds on microscopic foods and fecal pellets.
Queen Charlotte Channel, Howe Sound, s. BC

OCTOPUSES and SQUIDS

MC371. GIANT PACIFIC OCTOPUS, giant north Pacific octopus, north Pacific giant octopus, giant octopus, Pacific octopus, common Pacific octopus, common octopus

***Enteroctopus dofleini**, Octopus dofleini, Octopus dofleini martini, Polypus dofleini, Octopus apollyon, Polypus apollyon, Paroctopus apollyon, Octopus hongkongensis, Polypus hongkongensis, Octopus punctatus, Octopus gilbertianus, Polypus gilbertianus,* possibly: *Octopus maorum*

to 7.3 m (24 ft) arm spread at least, 72.7 kg (160 lb) total weight at least
Japan, Siberia, n. Alaska to n. Mexico
intertidal to 1,500 m (4,950 ft)

The maximum size for the giant Pacific octopus species, listed conservatively above, is the subject of much anecdotal information. It is a fast-growing and -maturing animal: a female lives for only three years and dies after many weeks of tending her one and only batch of eggs. A male may survive an additional year. *Every* experienced diver has a special story about an interaction with this intelligent "dive buddy."

A Bellevue Point, San Juan Island, n. Washington

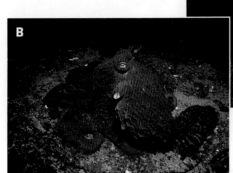

B Egmont Marina, Egmont, s. BC

MC372. PACIFIC RED OCTOPUS, red octopus

***Octopus rubescens**, Polypus rubescens,* some scientific names listed for the giant Pacific octopus have also been applied to this one

to 50 cm (20 in) arm spread, 0.4 kg (1 lb) total weight
c. Alaska to n. Mexico
intertidal to 300 m (1,000 ft)

Three tiny flaps or "eyelashes" below each eye and its muddy red colour distinguish the red octopus from a small specimen of the giant Pacific octopus (MC371). Although seldom sufficiently provoked, this animal can deliver a nasty bite, as can the normally docile giant Pacific octopus.

Irvines Landing, Pender Harbour, s. BC

MC373. SMOOTHSKIN OCTOPUS

***Benthoctopus leioderma**, Octopus leioderma, Polypus leioderma*

to 30 cm (12 in) arm spread
Siberia, n. Alaska to s. California
subtidal, 90–500 m (300–1,650 ft)

This deep-water denizen has very smooth skin with a ridge along each outer side of the mantle (body). Several were sighted during ecotourism submersible excursions off Hornby Island, BC, in the summer of 1999. This specimen was trawled during an Environment Canada benthic sampling exercise.

Mouth of Fraser River, Strait of Georgia, s. BC

MC374. STUBBY SQUID, Pacific bobtail squid, Pacific bobtailed squid, Pacific bob-tailed squid, north Pacific bobtail squid, eastern Pacific bobtail, short squid, bob-tail cuttlefish, bottle-tailed cuttlefish
Rossia pacifica, *Rossia borealis*
to 15 cm (6 in) long
Korea and Japan to Siberia, n. Alaska to n. Mexico
intertidal to 600 m (1,980 ft)
Sighting this active swimmer rising from the sand and releasing ink "blobs" is a night-diving highlight—especially when it instantaneously changes colour! Photograph B shows the distinctive eggs.
A Cotton Point, Keats Island, s. BC
B Columbine Bay, Bowen Island, s. BC

MC375. OPALESCENT SQUID, opalescent inshore squid, common Pacific squid, California market squid, market squid, opal squid, arrow squid, common squid, sea arrow, calamari, calamary
Loligo opalescens, *Loligo stearnsi*, *Loligo stearnsii*, *Loligo pealii*
to 28 cm (11 in) long
s. Alaska to n. Mexico
pelagic
The egg "sausages" (photograph C) result from massive spawning orgies, and the diver is more likely to see these eggs than the actual animal. In some Puget Sound locales, this squid's sporadic winter arrival in large swarms stimulates an avid recreational jig fishery.
A B Bargain Bay, Francis Peninsula, s. BC
C Bowyer Island, Howe Sound, s. BC

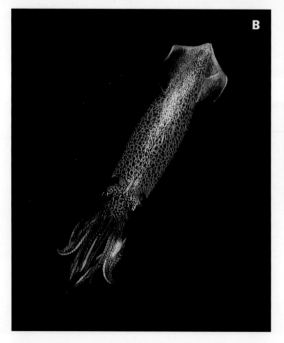

MC376. NORTH PACIFIC GIANT SQUID

Moroteuthis robusta, *Ommastrephes robusta*

to 3.35 m (11 ft) long

Atlantic Ocean, Indian Ocean, Japan, Siberia, n. Alaska to s. California

pelagic, surface to 600 m (2,000 ft)

Very occasionally a surprised beachwalker stumbles upon a giant squid that has washed ashore. Usually a spawned-out animal at the end of its normal life span, the specimen invariably proves to be *Moroteuthis robusta*. Such serendipitous discoveries occasionally are documented in local newspapers, often with an accompanying photograph.

Whidbey Island, Puget Sound, c. Washington. Roland Anderson photograph

MC377. Summer 2004—Humboldt squid invasion!

The first recorded occurrence of a southern denizen, the **HUMBOLDT SQUID**, *Dosidicus gigas*, in the Pacific Northwest happened in the summer of 2004, although stories of earlier sightings exist. Rather than just a specimen or two found at the southern extreme of the region, this unexpected incident was literally an invasion. Many adult specimens were either caught by surprised offshore fishers or found by amazed beachcombers—their fresh carcasses having washed ashore along coastal beaches. Jim Cosgrove, octopus and squid researcher at the Royal British Columbia Museum, Victoria, BC, correlated numerous reports, some from as far north as Kodiak Island and the Kamchatka Peninsula, c. Alaska, and many verified by photographs and specimens. This invasion may be linked with an unusual warm-water event, but studies continue, and observers are left to speculate about similar happenings in the future.

Approximately 30 other squids (including the neon flying squid, *Ommastrephes bartrami*) and octopuses inhabit the oceanic offshore waters of the Pacific Northwest—far from the vantage point of a shorebound naturalist.

Off Westport, Washington. Don Davenport photograph

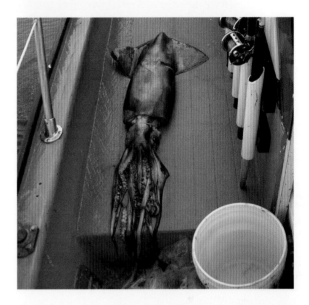

SHRIMPS, CRABS, HERMITS, BARNACLES, SEA FLEAS, SEA SPIDERS AND OTHERS
Phylum ARTHROPODA

Including shrimps, crabs, hermits, sea fleas, fish lice, whale lice, isopods, pill bugs, barnacles, mites and sea spiders.

Its entire body encased in a chitinous (tough, protective) exoskeleton or shell, an arthropod must periodically moult or shed this protective covering so it may grow (see photograph A: red rock crab, AR98). Growth-induced moulting occurs more frequently in early life. Before a replacement cuticle hardens around the body, it swells with seawater, providing space for gradual tissue addition—as a child grows into a new pair of shoes.

Mobility is possible because of strategically placed joints where the exoskeleton is much thinner and more flexible. Segmentation is always present but only readily obvious in some species, and may be externally obscured in others by the carapace, a large shell element. However, the presence of paired antennae, mouthparts, pincer claws and walking legs always shows body divisions. In addition, segmentation is visible on the abdomen, whether extended as in shrimps or folded under as in crabs. In some species, such as the Dungeness crab (AR 101), the appearance of the abdomen is a secondary sexual characteristic. Photograph B shows a female (wider, beehive-shaped) on the left side and a male (longer, lighthouse-shaped) on the right.

Approximately 2,000 species of arthropods live in the marine waters of the Pacific Northwest.

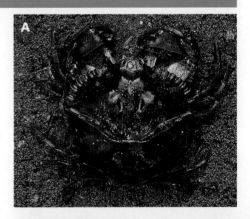

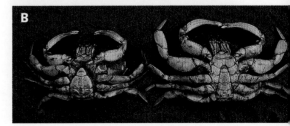

Further Reading

Hart, Josephine, 1982, *Crabs and Their Relatives of BC*, British Columbia Museum Handbook #40, Victoria, BC. 267 pp.

Jensen, Gregory, 1995, *Pacific Coast Crabs and Shrimps*, Sea Challengers, Monterey, CA, 87 pp.

MITES

AR1. RED VELVET MITE, red mite, intertidal mite
Neomolgus littoralis
to 0.3 cm (0.2 in) long
circumpolar, Japan, n. Alaska to n. Mexico
intertidal
This minute creature roams about in the splash zone, often amid decaying marine plants or over rocky substrates. Though hot red, the red mite is so tiny that it usually goes unnoticed by the casual beachcomber. A close relative of the spiders, it seeks out small flies, which it consumes by sucking out their juices.
Tongue Point, Olympic coast, n. Washington

AMPHIPODS

Including sea fleas, beach hoppers and skeleton shrimps. The featured species below are but a few of the very many that thrive in Pacific Northwest habitats.

AR2. ▶BLACK-AND-WHITE SEA FLEA, kelp flea
Chromopleustes oculatus, *Parapleustes oculatus, Neopleustes oculatus*
to 1 cm (0.4 in) long
▶BC to c. California
intertidal to subtidal
Large aggregations, stark markings and sporadic activity make this species obvious to the diver. A chemical defence exuded from this sea flea's mouth repels predators. The distinctive colouration apparently warns predators, such as sculpins, of its nasty taste.
Caldwell Island, Agamemnon Channel, s. BC

AR3. CALIFORNIA BEACH HOPPER, California beach flea
Megalorchestia californiana, *Orchestoidea californiana, Orchestoidea pugettensis*
to 2.7 cm (1.1 in) long
s. Alaska to s. California
high intertidal
This large species excavates burrows in sand underneath decaying plant material cast ashore along open-coast beaches. Pull aside a mass of this deteriorating shelter, which is also a moisture-laden food source, and one usually sees countless California beach hoppers leaping away.
Long Beach, s. Washington

AR4. ▶PALE BEACH HOPPER
Megalorchestia columbiana, *Orchestoidea columbiana*
▶to 2 cm (0.8 in) long
s. Alaska to c. California
high intertidal
Frequently found with the California beach hopper (AR3), the pale beach hopper differs in that it does not have the obvious red antennae but has fainter and more flattened "butterfly" marks on the dorsal (top) surface. A beach hopper springs away from predators by rapidly flexing and straightening its body—a behaviour that leads to the "sand flea" description.
Seaside, n. Oregon

AR5. SPLASH-ZONE BEACH HOPPER, small beach hopper, beach hopper, sand flea, sandhopper, kelp flea
Traskorchestia traskiana, *Orchestia traskiana*
to 2 cm (0.8 in) long
n. Alaska to n. Mexico
high intertidal
This is but one of innumerable, nearly identical species that populate the many habitats of this coast. Not only do many beach hopper species look similar, but male/female and juvenile/adult differences further confuse observers, including the experts.
Georgina Point, Mayne Island, s. BC.

AR6. PINK BEACH HOPPER
Maera danae, *Maera dubia*, *Maera loveni*
to 1.8 cm (0.7 in) long
Siberia, n. Alaska to s. California
intertidal to 100 m (330 ft)
The relatively colourful pink beach hopper seems to prefer the undersides of rocks that rest on mud. A few intertidal beach hoppers have a coating of wax on their bodies to resist drying out during long periods of exposure to air.
Hurst Island, Goletas Channel, c. BC

AR7. ▶KELP-DWELLING SEA FLEA
Peramphithoe humeralis, *Ampithoe humeralis*
▶to 2.5 cm (1 in) long
s. Alaska to n. Mexico
intertidal to subtidal
Like all amphipods, the female kelp-dwelling sea flea carries the developing eggs in her brood pouch. She also makes a "brooding cocoon" by secreting a sticky solution and stitching kelp around herself while she tends a batch of offspring after they hatch. Small giant kelp (SW59) is preferred by this sea flea, which broods its young much longer than most.
Brown Island, Friday Harbor, n. Washington

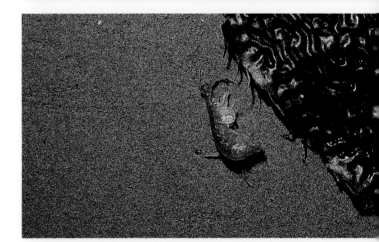

AR8. ▶SEA LETTUCE SEA FLEA
Ampithoe lacertosa, *Ampithoe scitulus*, *Ampithoe macrurum*, *Ampithoe stimpsoni*
to 2.5 cm (1 in) long
Alaska to n. Mexico
intertidal to shallow subtidal
Beautifully camouflaged in the emerald green sea lettuces (SW11–13), this amphipod is difficult to find. Such protective colouration helps this creature to avoid being consumed by its many potential predators. Look particularly among mature algae. Like the kelp-dwelling sea flea (AR7), the sea lettuce sea flea stitches together a brooding cocoon.
Skyline Marina, Fidalgo Island, n. Washington

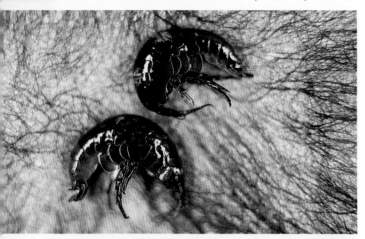

AR9. ▶DARK SEA FLEA

Hyale pugettensis, possible: *Allorchestes japonica*
▶to 1.2 cm (0.5 in) long
s. Alaska to n. California
intertidal to subtidal

Crouch down at a rocky tidepool high up in the intertidal zone and watch. Sooner or later you'll see a dark sea flea swimming quickly from one hideout to another. Between such sorties, it wedges its flattened body between various objects to conceal itself. This species tolerates very low salinities and consequently may live in river mouths or estuarine habitats.
Ucluth Peninsula, w. Vancouver Island, s. BC

AR10. ▶NEON SEA FLEA

Podocerus cristatus
to 1 cm (0.3 in) long
▶BC to n. Mexico
intertidal to subtidal

Literally a fluorescent, underwater "mini-beacon," this amphipod stands out like the proverbial sore thumb—unless it manages to find a matching background. Obviously the neon sea flea is successful, as it survives as a species. Perhaps, like the black-and-white sea flea (AR2), it is toxic to fish.
Bjorka Reef, Baranof Island, s. Alaska

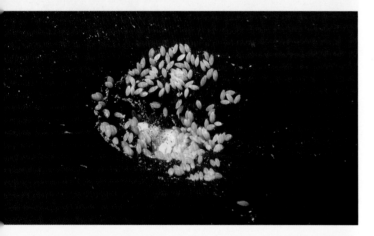

AR11. ▶GUT-COMMENSAL AMPHIPOD

Orchomene recondita, *Allogaussia recondita*
to 0.2 cm long (?)
▶BC to c. California
intertidal to subtidal

Documented as a commensal creature living within the digestive system of sea anemones, the gut-commensal amphipod is almost never encountered. However, this amazing photograph by Neil McDaniel of Vancouver, BC, shows some specimens on top of a retracted host anemone—likely having been ejected from the mouth.
Freshwater Bay, Olympic coast, n. Washington. Neil McDaniel photograph

AR12. ▶TUBE-DWELLING SEA FLEA

Ericthonius rubricornis, *Ericthonius hunteri*
▶to 15 cm (6 in) across colony
n. Alaska to s. California
intertidal to subtidal

This amphipod fabricates rubbery grey tubes to protect itself; as a result, the creature itself is very difficult to see. At best a diver may see its tiny reddish head peeking out as the tube-dwelling sea flea waits for a potential meal to drift past.
Georgina Point, Mayne Island, s. BC

AR13. Numerous small, **pelagic amphipods** or sea fleas live in the Pacific Northwest, and specimens are sporadically encountered by divers or dockside observers. Usually pale pink or white, these active animals will swim about quickly in a seemingly random fashion, then occasionally stop and drift for a brief period before resuming their odyssey. Identification is beyond the amateur, and the specimen in the photograph represents a group of species.

Agamemnon Channel, Nelson Island, s. BC

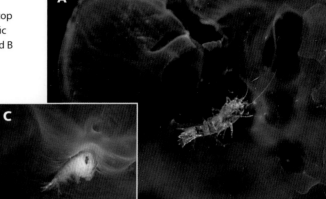

AR14. HITCHHIKING AMPHIPODS? Yes. Careful inspection of various jellies, such as the lion's mane (CN89), moon jelly (CN92), comb jellies (CT1–5) and other gelatinous drifters may reveal tiny sea fleas riding atop or inside. Apparently, at least 30 of these hyperiid amphipods are Pacific Northwest nomads. Photograph C features *Hyperia medusarum;* A and B show an unidentified species.

A B Green Bay, Nelson Island, s. BC
C Croker Island, Indian Arm, s. BC.
Neil McDaniel photograph

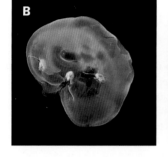

AR15. ▶GRAY WHALE LICE
Cyamus kessleri and *Cyamus ceti*, *Cyamus mysticeti*
▶to 2.5 cm (1 in) long
Alaska to n. Mexico
depth range of host
This large hitchhiking amphipod is beautifully adapted to its role as an ecto (external) parasite. Vital to its survival is an ability to cling tenaciously to the magnificent gray whale in sufficient numbers to allow successful procreation. Studies suggest that gray whale lice may actually benefit the host because they target areas of tissue damaged by parasitic barnacles: they initiate a healing process that results in the release of barnacles. Another similar-looking species, the humpback whale louse, *Cyamus boopis,* is a hitchhiking summer visitor in the Pacific Northwest.

Crescent Beach, Boundary Bay, s. BC. Doug Sandilands photograph

AR16. ALASKAN SKELETON SHRIMP, giant skeleton shrimp, caprellid amphipod, phantom shrimp
Caprella alaskana
to 4 cm (1.6 in) long
n. Alaska to c. California
intertidal to subtidal
The Alaskan skeleton shrimp is one of the largest and most obvious of numerous, very similar species. Sometimes they "hook" themselves onto the neoprene suits of scuba divers. Although usually unnoticed, they are often abundant.
Over a dozen other smaller, very similar species live in the Pacific Northwest.

Friday Harbor, San Juan Island, n. Washington

ISOPODS

Including sea slaters.

The featured species that follow are but a sample of a significant isopod fauna that thrives in the Pacific Northwest.

AR17. ▶SHRIMP PARASITIC ISOPOD
Bopyroides hippolytes
to 2 cm (0.8 in) long
n. Alaska to s. California
intertidal to subtidal
Visible as a "bulge" under the side of the host shrimp's carapace (shell), this organism does not look alive to the casual observer. It is found on most species of shrimp that are not in the *Crangon* group.
Hoskyn Channel, Read Island, s. BC

AR18. ▶GRAY SHRIMP PARASITIC ISOPOD
Argeia pugettensis
to 2 cm (0.8 in) across
Siberia, n. Alaska to s. California
subtidal to intertidal
Showing as a bulge that is very similar to that of the shrimp parasitic isopod (AR17), this one parasitizes the sand-dwelling crangonid shrimps. A parasite such as this lives off blood from the host's gills, but it almost never kills this nutritional source, as it would be doomed as well.
Stanley Park, Vancouver Harbour, s. BC

AR19. ▶MUD SHRIMP PARASITIC ISOPOD
Ione sp. (*Ione cornuta* no longer a valid synonym)
to 2 cm (0.8 in) long
BC to c. California
intertidal to subtidal
As seen in photograph A, the mud shrimp parasitic isopod illustrates a sexual dimorphism. Notice that the female is much larger and broader than the male. Both are housed in the same swelling (as with the gray shrimp parasitic isopod, AR 18), thus ensuring reproductive access and species viability. Photograph B shows a female inside a hairy-spined crab (AR129, a newly documented host) as opposed to the two in photograph A living in a blue mud shrimp (AR89).

Noticeable as a dark lump under the abdomen of various shrimp species, particularly the Sitka shrimp (AR66), is the ▶shrimp abdomen isopod, *Hemiarthrus abdominalis*. Superficially it resembles the shrimp parasitic barnacle (AR179).

A B Stanley Park, Vancouver Harbour, s. BC

AR20. ▶SQUAT LOBSTER PARASITIC ISOPODS
Munidon parvum/Pseudione galacanthae
▶to 2 cm (0.8 in) across
BC to n. Mexico
subtidal
Specific identification of either of these parasites is impossible without dissection of the "toothache"-like swelling and some jargon-intensive sleuthing using a biological key—an interesting academic exercise, but beyond most readers' fascination threshold.

Agamemnon Channel, Sechelt Peninsula, s. BC

AR21. ▶PINK PARASITIC ISOPOD
Rocinela propodialis
to 2.5 cm (1 in) long
Alaska to Washington
subtidal
This isopod is often parasitic on various species of fish, but readily leaves its food source and actively swims about—a process that requires the acquisition of a replacement host. Deep scars left behind are evidence of an attack by this ecto (external) parasite, even when it simply moves to another location on the same host.

Telegraph Passage, Prince Rupert, n. BC

AR22. SCAVENGING ISOPOD, dark-backed isopod, swimming isopod, Harford's greedy isopod, marine pillbug, dark-backed rock louse
Cirolana harfordi
to 2 cm (0.8 in) long
BC to n. Mexico
intertidal to subtidal
This active isopod scavenges among intertidal barnacles and mussels for whatever it can find. Often many individuals will swarm opportunistically when a significant "feast" is presented. Photograph B shows a subtidal specimen found inside a cloud sponge (PO11).

A Frank Island, w. Vancouver Island, s. BC
B Caldwell Island, Agamemnon Channel, s. BC

AR23.
While studying the Nakwakto goose-neck barnacle (AR174), Vancouver Aquarium Marine Science Centre divers encountered this secretive creature. Numerous completely unexpected disturbed specimens emerged from their barnacle-cluster hiding spots. Perhaps this is another commensal relationship. Unfortunately, the photographed specimen was lost during the process and a precise identification cannot be made. However, it has been designated as the **NOTCH-TAILED ISOPOD** and may be a species of ***Dynamenella***.

Nakwakto Rapids, Slingsby Channel, c. BC

AR24. SEA SLATER, northern sea roach, sea roach, rock louse
Ligia pallasi, *Ligia pallasii*, *Ligyda pallasi*
to 3.5 cm (1.5 in) long
n. Alaska to c. California
supralittoral (splash zone and above)
By day this nocturnally active creature is usually noticed only when scurrying along rocky outcrops in search of a dark crevice. An air-breather, the sea slater will drown if trapped in water. The larger specimen in the centre of the photograph is a mature female.
Ucluth Peninsula, w. Vancouver Island, s. BC

AR25. STUBBY ISOPOD, Oregon pill bug, pill bug,* pill-bug
Gnorimosphaeroma oregonensis, *Exosphaeroma oregonensis*, *Gnorimosphaeroma oregonense*, *Sphaeroma oregonense*, *Exosphaeroma oregonense*, *Neosphaeroma oregonense*
to 1 cm (0.4 in) long
Alaska to s. California
intertidal to subtidal
This isopod is usually found under rocks. When disturbed, it rolls into a ball, wood bug or pill-bug style.
*The term pill-bug is more correctly used in referring to terrestrial species and results from past times when people swallowed them like pills.
Sandy Cove, West Vancouver, s. BC

AR26. EELGRASS ISOPOD, concave isopod, cut-tailed isopod, seaweed isopod, kelp isopod, transparent isopod
Idotea resecata, *Idothea resecata*, *Pentidotea resecata*
to 4 cm (1.6 in) long
c. Alaska to n. Mexico
intertidal to 19 m (60 ft)
Though it usually clings tightly to leaves of the eelgrass plant (SW2), this manoeuvrable isopod is a very fast, accomplished swimmer! Dislodge one and see for yourself.
Bennett Bay, Mayne Island, s. BC

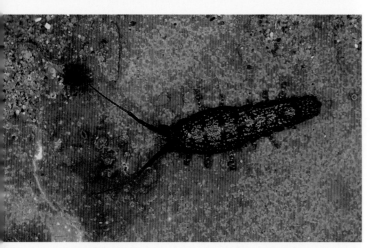

AR27. ▶SURFGRASS ISOPOD
Idotea kirchanskii, *Pentidotea kirchanskii*
to 1.5 cm (0.6 in) long
▶Washington to s. California
intertidal to subtidal
This tenacious surf-dweller holds on very tightly to surfgrass (SW4), literally defying removal. A female isopod broods its young in a pouch and eventually releases them as miniature versions of the adult, ready to fend for themselves.
Fort Ebey, Whidbey Island, n. Washington

AR28. ROCKWEED ISOPOD, olive green isopod, green isopod, kelp isopod, round-tailed isopod, Vosnesensky's isopod

***Idotea wosnesenskii**, Idothea wosnesenskii, Pentidotea wosnessenskii*

to 4 cm (1.6 in) long

Siberia, c. Alaska to n. Mexico

intertidal to 16 m (53 ft)

This slow creeper hides under rocks and usually occurs in groups. Please replace any disturbed rocks carefully to give these isopods a chance of survival. Photograph A shows a specimen taken from a rockweed (SW23) habitat; photograph B shows one found living in articulated coralline algae (SW89).

A Stanley Park, Vancouver Harbour, s. BC

B Frank Island, w. Vancouver Island, s. BC

AR29. MONTEREY ISOPOD

***Idotea montereyensis**, Pentidotea monteryensis, Idotea gracillima*

to 1.6 cm (0.6 in) long

c. Alaska to California

intertidal to 110 m (365 ft)

Commonly found clinging to surf grass (SW4), like other isopods, this one readily rolls up in a protective "ball" when disturbed. The numerous "shell-covered" segments protect the isopod's vulnerable underside.

Sunset Beach State Park, Charleston, s. Oregon

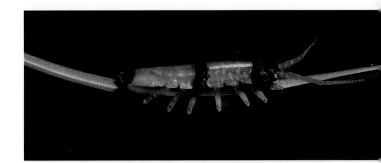

AR30. ▶FEATHER BOA ISOPOD

***Idotea stenops**, Pentidotea stenops*

to 4 cm (1.6 in) long

s. Alaska to n. Mexico

intertidal to subtidal

This robust species reputedly lives on the central rib of the feather boa (SW34). Hours of fruitless searching of feather boa kelp beds totally frustrated Andy Lamb. However, the feather boa isopod may simply hide in other brown-coloured shelter, as Kathy Moffett of Bellingham, Washington, discovered when she found the specimen in the photograph.

Eagle Point, San Juan Island, n. Washington

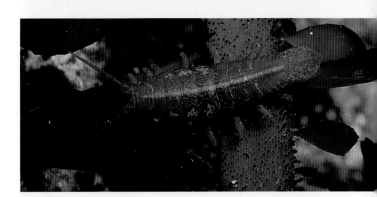

OPOSSUM SHRIMPS

AR31. A naturally occurring phenomenon commonly encountered by Pacific Northwest divers is the mysid swarm. These tiny, shrimp-like creatures, also called opossum shrimp because of the female's brood pouch, have feathery appendages adapted for swimming rather than walking. More than 50 species exist along this coast, but only a few **mysids** are encountered regularly en masse. Swarms can be single-species aggregations or mixed, and may be less than a hundred strong or so extensive as to seem like an underwater blizzard, stretching many square metres. Accompanying photographs show a swarm and two other individual species.

A Nelson Rock, Malaspina Strait, s. BC. Steve Martell photograph

B Fort Ebey, Whidbey Island, n. Washington. Charlie Gibbs photograph

C Bowyer Island, Howe Sound, s. BC. Charlie Gibbs photograph

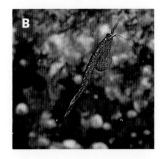
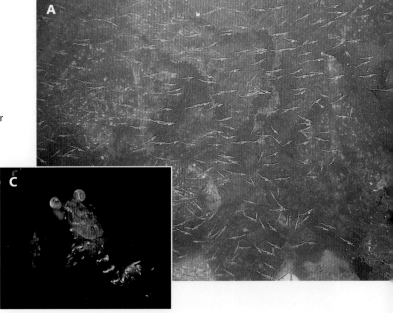

COPEPODS

Including sea lice.

As a group, the copepods are an important part of the marine ecology of the Pacific Northwest. The vast majority are free-living copepods and too tiny to be included in this volume—they appear as "jiggling" specks if noticed at all. Most are free-living and some are significant as part of the zooplankton, floating animal life that affects visibility for divers.

A significant number of the larger copepods are parasitic on fish and other marine animals and are popularly called sea lice. As a very small example, four **parasitic copepods** are illustrated here.

AR32. This photograph (A) features *Lepeophtherius* **species A**, probably *salmonis*. It commonly lives on the various Pacific salmon, particularly near the anus, and is thus often observed by sport anglers and commercial fishers.

Capilano River, West Vancouver, s. BC

AR33. Featured in this photograph (B) is *Lepeophtherius* **species B**, parasitizing the head of a lingcod. Without a specimen to examine, even expert Dave Whitaker of Nanaimo, BC (Fisheries and Oceans Canada), was unable to tell whether it is *Lepeophtherius pravipes* or *Lepeophtherius breviventris*.

Cotton Point, Keats Island, s. BC

AR34. This photograph (C) reveals a *Salmincola* **sp.**, probably *californiensis*, infesting the mouth of a coho salmon. Fortunately for the fish, this copepod is a fresh-water species and is only a factor at the very end of the salmonid life cycle.

BC Hydro Salmon Stream Project, Stanley Park, s. BC

AR35. Illustrated in this photograph (D) is *Phrixocephalus* **sp.**, a particularly "gruesome" creature that infests the arrowtooth flounder, *Atheresthes stomias* (*Coastal Fishes of the Pacific Northwest*, p. 202) by embedding its head in the eyeball of its host.

Mouth of Fraser River, Strait of Georgia, s. BC

EUPHAUSIDS (krill)

AR36. Perhaps most famous as the primary food source for many baleen whales, euphausids, popularly known as **krill**, are a vital part of the marine ecosystem in the Pacific Northwest. About 20 species of euphausids have been identified. Forming massive swarms, some species swim at great depths by day but head to surface layers at night—a phenomenon called diurnal migration.

The photo depicts a specimen whose identity is unknown. Night divers will be fortunate just to notice and distinguish specimens as euphausids while they zip about in a beam of light, as opposed to identifying individual species.

Grey Rocks Island, Indian Arm, s. BC. Charlie Gibbs photograph

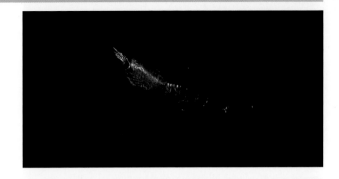

BRANCHIURA (fish lice)

AR37. ▶SURFPERCH FISH LOUSE
Argulus pugettensis, *Argulus niger*
▶to 1.1 cm (0.4 in) long
BC to California
intertidal to subtidal
An ecto (external) parasite, this fish louse prefers the various species of surfperch as hosts. It uses a pair of stalked suckers and various spines for attachment. Look for the surfperch fish louse on the fins or around the head and tail. A non-obligatory parasite, this adaptable arthropod may spend considerable time free-living away from a host. Its obvious eyes distinguish it from a copepod. A second species, the ▶flounder fish louse, *Argulus borealis,* may be encountered. It is usually smaller, light brown in colour and prefers various flounders as its hosts.
A B Keystone, Whidbey Island, n. Washington

SHRIMPS

Including argids, spinyheads, eualids, lebbeids and prawns.

AR38. COMMON ARGID
Argis alaskensis, *Nectocrangon alaskensis*
to 6.7 cm (2.7 in) long
n. Alaska to n. Oregon
subtidal, 18–221 m (60–730 ft)
Camouflaged beautifully for its surroundings, this elusive creature buries very rapidly and completely in sand or mud; consequently it is almost never seen by divers. This specimen survived being dragged along in a trawl net prior to its appearance and presentation here.
At least five other rarely found argids live in the Pacific Northwest.
English Bay, Burrard Inlet, s. BC

AR39. COMMON TWO-SPINED CRANGON
Crangon communis, *Neocrangon communis*, *Crago communis*
to 8 cm (3.2 in) long
Japan, n. Alaska to s. California
subtidal, 16–1,537 m (53–5,000 ft)
Only very close inspection will reveal the significant feature of two spines on top of the carapace (shell) of this shrimp. Commercial shrimp trawlers regularly take the common two-spined crangon as bycatch, but it is too small to be of any economic value.
Mouth of Fraser River, Strait of Georgia, s. BC

AR40. CALIFORNIA BAY SHRIMP
Crangon franciscorum, *Crago franciscorum*
to 8.4 cm (3.3 in) long
s. Alaska to s. California
intertidal to 180 m (600 ft)
This shrimp is apparently the subject of a recreational fishery in California, but is used mostly as bait rather than as an ingredient in a culinary masterpiece. Two subspecies occur, one living mostly in estuaries and the other inhabiting strictly marine locales.
English Bay, Burrard Inlet, s. BC

AR41. BLACKTAIL SHRIMP, blacktail gray shrimp, sand crangon
Crangon nigricauda, *Crago nigricauda*
to 5.3 cm (2.1 in) long
c. Alaska to n. Mexico
intertidal to 57 m (187 ft)
This shrimp is stockier and usually more brown than the grey-brown California bay shrimp (AR40). The common name is confusing in that it does not always have a black tail. It apparently awaits its amphipod prey while buried in sand—a manoeuvre that also helps it elude its own predators.
Miners Bay, Mayne Island, s. BC

AR42. NORTHERN CRANGON
Crangon alaskensis, *Crago alaskensis*
to 6.5 cm (2.5 in) long
n. Alaska to s. California
intertidal to 275 m (900 ft)
Very similar to the blacktail shrimp (AR41), the northern crangon is more slender. It also has a pair of antennal scales that are longer, narrower and slightly different in shape. This minor difference requires careful inspection to detect. Further complicating the problem is probable hybridization between these two species, which abundantly cohabit many areas.
Stanley Park, Vancouver Harbour, s. BC

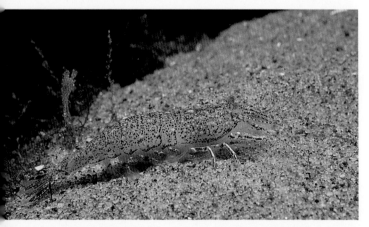

AR43. SMOOTH BAY SHRIMP, smooth crangon
Crangon stylirostris, *Lissocrangon stylirostris*, *Crago stylirostris*
to 6.1 cm (2.4 in)
s. Alaska to s. California
intertidal to 80 m (265 ft)
Preferring high-energy, wave-swept beaches, this species must quickly re-bury in shifting sands lest it become a meal for any of its predators. The smooth bay shrimp is one of the faster swimmers of the crangon clan.
Chesterman Beach, w. Vancouver Island, s. BC

AR44. SQUAT BAY SHRIMP
Crangon handi
to 5 cm (2 in) long
n. Washington to n. Mexico
intertidal to 55 m (180 ft)
Similar to the smooth bay shrimp (AR43), this cryptic shrimp is stouter and more boldly blotched. Look for it in sandy patches along rocky outer-coast beaches. In some locales the squat bay shrimp is found amid waterlogged concentrations of wood chips.
Several other cryptic crangonids live in the Pacific Northwest but are seldom seen.
Sekiu, Olympic coast, n. Washington. Greg Jensen photograph

AR45. HORNED SHRIMP, spike shrimp
Paracrangon echinata
to 7 cm (2.8 in) long
Alaska to s. California
subtidal, 7–200 m (23–660 ft)
Particularly when disturbed, this prickly-looking shrimp assumes a scorpion-like pose technically called the cataleptic position. In so doing it maximizes the defensive capabilities of its heavily spined body.
Woodlands, Indian Arm, s. BC

AR46. COASTAL SPINYHEAD
Metacrangon munita, Crago munita, Crangon munita
to 4.8 cm (1.9 in) long
c. Alaska to s. California
subtidal, 12–230 m (40–750 ft)
Very diligent searching of seemingly lifeless sand may reveal this cryptic, nocturnally active creature. The concentrated beam of a night diver's light offers the best hope of a sighting. Like other sand-dwelling shrimps, the coastal spinyhead can become an unfortunate and unwanted victim of shrimp trawls.
Helen Point, Mayne Island, s. BC

AR47. MINIATURE SPINYHEAD
Mesocrangon munitella, Crago munitella, Crangon munitella
to 2.2 cm (0.9 in) long
n. BC to n. Mexico
intertidal to 73 m (240 ft)
This slow mover apparently comes out to feed at night, so the comment for the coastal spinyhead (AR46) applies equally here—especially as this species is smaller! Your observational skills will be severely tested.
Queen Charlotte Channel, Howe Sound, s. BC

AR48. SADDLEBACK SHRIMP
Rhynocrangon alata, Sclerocrangon alata
to 4.5 cm (1.8 in) long
n. Alaska to c. California
subtidal, 11–167 m (36–550 ft)
Usually found resting motionless on rock walls, the saddleback shrimp has bright obvious colouration that may be obscured by a dusting of silt in low-current locales. These factors, combined with a thick, heavy exoskeleton, afford this shrimp protection from predators.
Chup Point, Barkley Sound, s. BC

AR49. TANK SHRIMP, sculptured shrimp
Sclerocrangon boreas
to 15 cm (6 in) long
circumboreal, n. Alaska to Washington
intertidal to 366 m (1,200 ft)
Unlike the vast majority of shrimps, juvenile tank shrimp do not hatch into a free-swimming stage. Rather, they attach to the pleopods (underside appendages of the female's "tail"). This shrimp is most abundant in the northern portion of its range and is not often found in the Pacific Northwest.
South Camp Jetty, Resolute Bay, Nunavut. Danny Kent photograph

AR50. GLASS SHRIMP
Pasiphaea pacifica
to 8.1 cm (3.2 in) long
Alaska to n. Mexico
subtidal
A delicate, pelagic species that rarely survives capture by the fine mesh nets of shrimp fishers. This hardy specimen was donated by biologist Brad Beaith of Nanaimo, BC, who collected it during research sampling. An opportunistic open-water photographic session followed.
Off Nanaimo, Strait of Georgia, s. BC

AR51. SHORTSCALE EUALID, short-scaled eualid
Eualus suckleyi, Spirontocaris suckleyi
to 7.9 cm (3.1 in) long
Siberia, n. Alaska to s. Washington
subtidal, 11–1,025 m (36–3,360 ft)
The abdomen (tail) of the shortscale eualid is banded with red. Particularly in living specimens, the white tips at the lower edge of each segment are noticeable and distinctive. Like most shrimps, this species is more likely seen at night in a beam of light.
Passage Island, Howe Sound, s. BC

AR52. TOWNSEND'S EUALID

Eualus townsendi, *Spirontocaris townsendi*
to 7.9 cm (3.1 in) long
Siberia, n. Alaska to s. Washington
subtidal, 38–630 m (124–2,066 ft)
Similar to the shortscale eualid (AR51), Townsend's eualid is more flattened side to side and has a larger "hump" on its abdomen. In colour, it resembles Kincaid's shrimp (AR59) but has no light stripe on the centre of its rostrum (head spike) and has more spines on its carapace (shell).
Burrows Bay, Fidalgo Island, n. Washington. Greg Jensen photograph

AR53. SPONGE EUALID

Eualus **sp. nov.**
to 2.5 cm (1 in) long
Alaska to n. Washington
subtidal, 18–55 m (60–180 ft) at least
This tiny shrimp commonly shelters inside large boot sponges (PO9/10) and cloud sponge (PO11). The silica spicules of these hollow structures may provide additional protection. The sponge eualid shown in photograph A is an adult male, distinguished by its very large third maxillipeds (structures used to spar with other males).
Photograph B shows a female with her developing green-coloured ovary.
The doll eualid, *Eualus pusiolus*, also found in the Pacific Northwest, is almost identical.
A B Fearney Point, Agamemnon Channel, s. BC

AR54. STRIPED EUALID

Eualus lineatus, *Eualus herdmani*
to 2.5 cm (1 in) long
s. Alaska to s. California
subtidal, 12–120 m (40–400 ft)
After painstaking examination of many museum specimens, Dr. Greg Jensen of the University of Washington redefined this species and separated it from the pygmy eualid (AR55)—a major job of taxonomic sleuthing.
Agamemnon Channel, Sechelt Peninsula, s. BC. Greg Jensen photograph

AR55. PYGMY EUALID

Eualus subtilis, *Eualus herdmani*
to 2.5 cm (1 in) long
s. BC to n. Mexico
intertidal to 74 m (244 ft)
As a result of the study that separated this species from the striped eualid (AR54), Dr. Greg Jensen found that pygmy eualid females are anatomically very different from the much smaller males. Colour variants are found.
Agamemnon Channel, Sechelt Peninsula, s. BC

AR56. BERKELEYS' EUALID
Eualus berkeleyorum
to 3.8 cm (1.5 in) long
n. Alaska to n. California
subtidal, 38–633 m (125–2,079 ft)
Note distinctive banding on the abdomen (tail) of Berkeleys' eualid.
Intriguing initial reports suggest that this shrimp may associate with the burrowing giant wrymouth, *Delolepis gigantea* (*Coastal Fishes of the Pacific Northwest*, p. 96).
At least six other eualid species live in the Pacific Northwest.
Helen Point, Mayne Island, s. BC

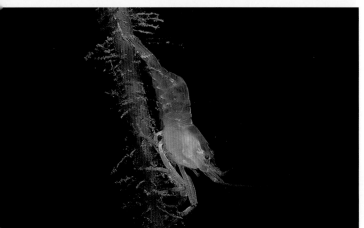

AR57. STOUT SHRIMP, stout coastal shrimp, shortspine shrimp, short-spined shrimp
Heptacarpus brevirostris, *Spirontocaris brevirostris, Hippolyte brevirostris*
to 6.2 cm (2.4 in) long
n. Alaska to s. California
intertidal to 128 m (420 ft)
Abundant among eelgrass (SW2) and algae-covered rocks, the stout shrimp, with its highly variable colour and pattern, is a master of disguise.
Stanley Park, Vancouver Harbour, s. BC

AR58. STIMPSON'S SHRIMP, Stimpson coastal shrimp
Heptacarpus stimpsoni, *Spirontocaris cristata, Hippolyte cristata*
to 3.3 cm (1.2 in) long
s. Alaska to n. Mexico
intertidal to 73 m (240 ft)
Light bands on the posterior edges of abdominal segments (tail sections)

are distinctive for this hard-to-find shrimp. Its usually drab coloration tends to blend in well with its normal surroundings. Photograph B shows a paler, less mottled phase.
A Mukilteo, Puget Sound, c. Washington
B Steilacoom, Puget Sound, c. Washington

AR59. KINCAID'S SHRIMP, Kincaid coastal shrimp, broken-back shrimp, broken back shrimp
Heptacarpus kincaidi, *Spirontocaris kincaidi*
to 3.5 cm (1.4 in) long
c. BC to s. California
subtidal, 10–180 m (33–600 ft)
Though very often associated with the crimson anemone (CN3), and in considerable numbers, Kincaid's shrimp is not always readily noticed. The white mid-rib along the pointed extension between the eyes or rostrum

(head spike) is distinctive. Photograph B shows an unusual colour variant that lives inside cloud sponges (PO11).
A Nelson Rock, Malaspina Strait, s. BC
B Agamemnon Channel, Sechelt Peninsula, s. BC

AR60. THREESPINE SHRIMP, threespine coastal shrimp
Heptacarpus tridens, *Spirontocaris tridens*
to 6.2 cm (2.4 in) long
s. Alaska to n. Washington
intertidal to 110 m (360 ft)
A very prominent abdominal hump and no central white stripe on the rostrum (head spike) distinguish this red-banded species from the Kincaid's shrimp (AR59). Look for it particularly near beds of the giant plumose anemone (CN2). The specimen photographed is a pale egg-bearing female.
Helen Point, Mayne Island, s. BC

AR61. SLENDER SHRIMP, slender coastal shrimp
Heptacarpus tenuissimus, *Spirontocaris gracilis*, *Hippolyte gracilis*, *Hippolyte amabilis*
to 4.3 cm (1.7 in) long
s. Alaska to s. California
subtidal to 137 m (450 ft)
An unbroken but uneven red line runs the length of the slender shrimp's body. Like many other small shrimps, this one often orients in a "head down" position on vertical surfaces.
Mukilteo, Puget Sound, c. Washington

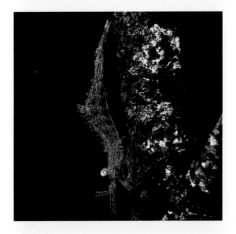

AR62. ELEGANT COASTAL SHRIMP
Heptacarpus decorus, *Spirontocaris decora*
to 6 cm (2.3 in) long
s. BC to s. California
▶subtidal, 40–313 m (133–1,045 ft)
Note that the last segment of the abdomen (tail) is longer than the telson (tail fin). While studying pink candelabrum gorgonian (CN46), Danny Kent and a collecting crew from the Vancouver Aquarium Marine Science Centre found this species amid branches of fans. The elegant coastal shrimp has also been found clinging to the orange sea pen (CN40).
Caldwell Island, Agamemnon Channel, s. BC

AR63. STILETTO SHRIMP, stiletto coastal shrimp
Heptacarpus stylus, *Spirontocaris stylus*, *Hippolyte stylus*, *Hippolyte esquimaltiana*
to 5.7 cm (2.2 in) long
n. Alaska to n. Washington
intertidal to 440 m (1,450 ft)
This master of disguise prefers to hide among marine algae. Its three prime colour phases match beautifully with the gold browns, wine reds and emerald greens of these plants. Two colour variants are shown.
A Brown Island, Friday Harbor, n. Washington
B Horton Bay, Mayne Island, s. BC

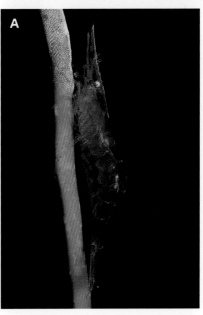

AR64. SMALLEYED SHRIMP, small-eyed coastal shrimp, smalleye shrimp, smalleye coastal shrimp
Heptacarpus carinatus, *Spirontocaris carinata*
to 6 cm (2.3 in) long
s. Alaska to s. California
intertidal to 27 m (90 ft)
This dazzling shrimp is nearly impossible to see when sheltering among green plant life. Once found, its small eyes and large curved spine on the third abdominal segment (tail) are distinctive.
Ucluth Peninsula, w. Vancouver Island, s. BC

AR65. BARRED SHRIMP
Heptacarpus pugettensis
to 2.5 cm (1 in) long
s. BC to c. California
intertidal to 15 m (50 ft)
This shy shrimp huddles under rocks and usually remains still when exposed. Eventually it slowly creeps around and hides again—tenaciously staying with its original shelter. Like other shrimp species, the barred shrimp is prey for a variety of fish and other creatures.
Roche Point, Indian Arm, s. BC

AR66. SITKA SHRIMP, Sitka coastal shrimp, red-banded transparent shrimp, common coastal shrimp
Heptacarpus sitchensis, *Spirontocaris sitchensis, Hippolyte sitchensis, Heptacarpus pictus*
to 2.7 cm (1.1 in) long
s. Alaska to n. Mexico
intertidal to 12 m (40 ft)
A master of the quick colour change, the Sitka shrimp is often transparent when seaweed is scarce. However, given the opportunity to nestle in algal tufts, it rapidly adopts its shelter's hue. Thin diagonal lines on the carapace (shell) distinguish this species. Pacific Northwest waters are home to at least four other heptacarpid shrimps.
Ucluth Peninsula, w. Vancouver Island, s. BC

AR67. GRASS SHRIMP, little green shrimp, kelp humpback shrimp
Hippolyte clarki
to 3.1 cm (1.2 in) long
c. Alaska to n. Mexico
intertidal to 30 m (100 ft)
As it hides among seaweeds, and particularly around wharves and floats, the grass shrimp is one that the inquisitive and observant non-diver has a reasonable chance of finding. Much patience is required, though, as it is a master of camouflage. Like other shrimps, this species is potential prey for many other creatures.
The California green shrimp, *Hippolyte californiensis,* with almost the same geographical distribution, is virtually identical to the grass shrimp. Its rostrum (head spike) is tipped with three minute spines, rather than two as in the grass shrimp.
Ucluth Peninsula, w. Vancouver Island, s. BC

AR68. ORIENTAL SHRIMP
Palaemon macrodactylus, Leander macrodactylus
to 6 cm (2.3 in) long
originally introduced from s.e. Asia; ▶s. BC to s. California
intertidal to subtidal
As this introduced species slowly spreads north, it seems to prefer hiding among plants in river estuaries. During the preparation of this book, Andy Lamb found this specimen at the mouth of the Nicomekl River, Boundary Bay, s. BC, well beyond its previous northernmost foothold of Willapa Bay on the southern coast of Washington.
Mouth of Nicomekl River, Boundary Bay, s. BC

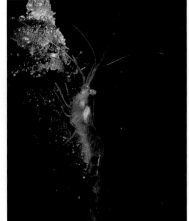

AR69. CANDY STRIPE SHRIMP, candy-stripe shrimp, candystripe shrimp, clown shrimp
Lebbeus grandimanus, Lebbeus grandimana, Hetairus grandimanus, Spirontocaris grandimana
to 4.5 cm (1.8 in) long
n. Alaska to n. Washington
subtidal, 6–180 m (20–600 ft)
Nearly always associated with the crimson anemone (CN3), the candy stripe shrimp is a favourite of the underwater photographer. However, getting *the shot* requires stealth and patience. Good luck!
Another similar but more northern species, the ▶polar shrimp, *Lebbeus polaris,* may be the same as the candy stripe shrimp.
Agamemnon Channel, Nelson Island, s. BC

AR70.
Hours spent peering into a microscope, in addition to complicated archival literature searches, are almost always required when a new species is formally described. Such was the formidable task of Dr. Greg Jensen of the University of Washington when he found that a shrimp known as the Okhotsk lebbeid, *Lebbeus schrencki,* is not a Pacific Northwest inhabitant. Remarkably, local specimens, originally identified as Okhotsk lebbeids, actually represent *two* completely new species! A scientific paper will soon document the **CLEANER LEBBEID**, *Lebbeus* **sp. 1** and the elusive lebbeid, *Lebbeus* sp. 2. It will supply them with officially sanctioned but as yet unusable species names. Scientific formalities must be maintained. The elusive lebbeid is very similar to the cleaner lebbeid but is orange and very secretive (no photograph). Without the initial observations by diver Donna Gibbs of Port Coquitlam, BC, these two new species would not have been discovered.
Ballenas Island, Strait of Georgia, s. BC

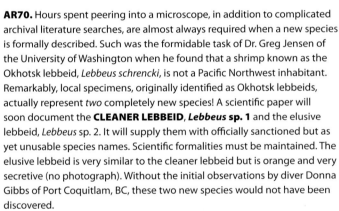

AR71. SPINY LEBBEID, king shrimp
Lebbeus groenlandicus, Spirontocaris groenlandica, Hippolyte groenlandicus, Astacus groenlandicus
to 10.7 cm (4.2 in) long
circumboreal, n. Alaska to n. Washington
intertidal to 520 m (1,700 ft)
The possessor of a relatively heavy exoskeleton (shell), this species may elevate its spiny abdomen (tail) when disturbed. The spiny lebbeid is sometimes a bycatch in prawn traps, particularly in more northern areas.
Georgina Point, Mayne Island, s. BC

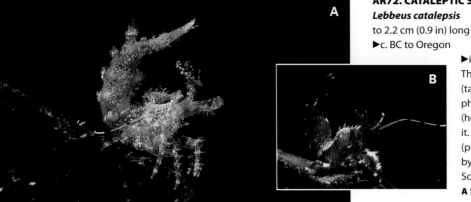

AR72. CATALEPTIC SHRIMP
Lebbeus catalepsis
to 2.2 cm (0.9 in) long
▶c. BC to Oregon

▶intertidal to 6 m (20 ft)
This newly described shrimp elevates its abdomen (tail) section in a cataleptic position, as seen in the photographs. This behaviour, plus a very short rostrum (head spike), should enable a naturalist to identify it. A subtidal specimen collected in the Scott Islands (photograph B) at the northern tip of Vancouver Island by Danny Kent of the Vancouver Aquarium Marine Science Centre was the first documented in Canada.
A Sekiu, Olympic coast, n. Washington
B Lanz Island, Cape Scott, c. BC

AR73. DEEP BLADE SHRIMP, deep-bladed shrimp, broken-back shrimp
Spirontocaris prionota, Hippolyte prionota, Spirontocaris macrodonta
to 2.7 cm (1.1 in) long
Japan, n. Alaska to n. Mexico
intertidal to 163 m (534 ft)
This slow plodder prefers the shell hash—finely broken shell fragments—that often accumulates at the base of walls or cliffs. Distinctive is the "sawtooth" edge of its broad rostrum (head spike). The species is extremely variable of hue and pattern. The blunt-bladed shrimp, *Spirontocaris tuncata*, is similar to the deep blade shrimp but lacks the many fine dorsal spines.
A Worlcombe Island, Howe Sound, s. BC
B Green Bay, Nelson Island, s. BC

AR74. DANA'S BLADE SHRIMP
Spirontocaris lamellicornis, Hippolyte lamellicornis
to 6.4 cm (2.5 in) long
n. Alaska to s. California
subtidal, 3–190 m (10–630 ft)
Large tooth-like spines along the entire top of the carapace (shell) separate this species from the deep blade shrimp (AR73). Divers may find Dana's blade shrimp living with the crimson anemone (CN3) or the sand-rose anemone (CN10).
Two other small northern shrimps, each with a large "bladed" rostrum (head spike), have been documented as far south as BC and Washington. The oval blade shrimp, *Spirontocaris ochotensis*, and the Rathbun's blade shrimp, *Spirontocaris arcuata*, are not only very similar but most difficult to locate.
Helen Point, Mayne Island, s. BC

AR75. SNYDER'S BLADE SHRIMP, Snyder blade shrimp
Spirontocaris snyderi
to 2.2 cm (0.9 in) long
c. B.C to n. Mexico
subtidal, 4–140 m (13–462 ft)
In Puget Sound at least, Snyder's blade shrimp intimately associates with the sand-rose anemone (CN10). Divers frequenting other locales might investigate further to confirm whether this relationship occurs over a more extensive geographic area.
Mukilteo, Puget Sound, c. Washington

AR76. SLENDER BLADED SHRIMP
Spirontocaris holmesi, Spirontocaris bispinosa
to 6.2 cm (2.4 in) long
Alaska to s. California
subtidal, 24–385 m (80–1,270 ft)
Like many diminutive species, this shrimp is potentially an unnoticed bycatch of commercial trawling operations—a most destructive harvesting method, not only because it destroys habitat but because it is non-selective.
The dagger-bladed shrimp, *Spirontocaris sica,* differs slightly in its rostral (head spike) spine complement.
Passage Island, Howe Sound, s. BC

AR77. COONSTRIPE SHRIMP, coon-stripe shrimp, coonstriped shrimp, dock shrimp, Dana's all-shining shrimp
Pandalus danae, Pandalus franciscorum, Pandalus gurneyi*
to 15 cm (6 in) long
n. Alaska to n. Mexico
intertidal to 183 m (610 ft)
Thin, diagonal stripes on the abdomen (tail) readily distinguish this species. It is popular with recreational harvesters, some of whom use ingenious capture techniques such as dip-netting at night. Variable amounts of red pigment occur.
*Incorrect synonymy. This is a valid species found in California.
A Sutton Islets, Egmont, s. BC
B Cactus Islands, New Channel, n. Washington

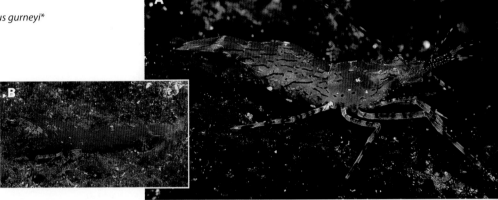

AR78. ROUGH PATCH SHRIMP, roughpatch shrimp
Pandalus stenolepis
to 8.3 cm (3.4 in) long
n. Alaska to Oregon
subtidal, 18–228 m (60–750 ft)
In living specimens, very bright blue dots are particularly noticeable. Red spots on the abdomen (tail), rather than the diagonal lines of the coonstripe shrimp (AR77), are a helpful identification aid, as is the smaller size of this species.
Lions Bay, Howe Sound, s. BC

AR79. HUMPBACK SHRIMP, king shrimp, coonstriped shrimp, coon-striped shrimp, coonstripe shrimp
Pandalus hypsinotus, Pandalus gracilis*
to 19 cm (7.5 in) long
Korea, Japan, n. Alaska to n. Washington
subtidal, 5–460 m (16–1,510 ft)
Wide, vertical abdominal bands and white body spots are species specific. The humpback shrimp is also a sporadic bycatch of prawn traps set in some locales. Fortunately for the gourmet, this shrimp tastes very similar to the well-known Pacific prawn (AR83).
*Incorrect synonymy. This is a valid species found in the western Pacific.
Grebe Islets, Howe Sound, s. BC

AR80. YELLOWLEG PANDALID
Pandalus tridens
to 12.3 cm (4.8 in) long
n. Alaska to c. Oregon
subtidal, 5–1,984 m (16–6,500 ft)
Banded legs and antennae, along with a lack of dark body markings and a long rostrum (head spike) with a three-pointed tip, are species specific. Like all shrimp species, the yellowleg pandalid can quickly dart backwards by flexing its muscular abdomen (tail), and thus confuse a potential predator.
Columbine Bay, Bowen Island, s. BC

AR81. SPINY PINK SHRIMP, Alaskan pink shrimp, pink shrimp, northern pink shrimp, northern shrimp, deepsea prawn
Pandalus eous, *Pandalus borealis*, *Pandalus borealis eous*
to 15 cm (6 in) long
Korea, Japan, n. Alaska to n. Oregon
subtidal, 16–1,400 m (53–4,500 ft)
Except for a spine on the top of the third abdominal segment, this shrimp is virtually identical to the oceanic pink shrimp, *Pandalus jordani*. Both are significant trawl targets. Photograph A shows a gravid female spiny pink shrimp carrying grey-coloured eggs on her abdomen; photograph B shows another female with developing blue gonads immediately behind the head.
A Copper Cove, Howe Sound, s. BC
B English Bay, Burrard Inlet, s. BC

AR82. HUMPY SHRIMP, flexed pandalid
Pandalus goniurus, *Pandalus dapifer*
to 7.8 cm (3.1 in) long
n. Alaska to n. Washington
subtidal, 1–450 m (3–1,485 ft)
Note the fine red lines angling up and back on the abdomen (tail). Like other pandalids, the humpy shrimp uses its legs to trap or cage its various tiny prey, preventing any escape. Keen-eyed night divers are most likely to see this species moving about on silty substrate.
A Copper Cove, Howe Sound, s. BC
B Popham Island, Howe Sound, s. BC

AR83. PACIFIC PRAWN, spot prawn, two spotted prawn, spot shrimp, prawn, spot
Pandalus platyceros, *Pandalus pubescentulus*
to 25 cm (10 in) long
n. Alaska to s. California
intertidal to 485 m (1,600 ft)
The two pairs of white spots on the abdomen (tail) and white lines on the carapace (shell) delineate this shrimp. Its solid, tasty flesh makes it a favourite for both commercial and recreational trapping. Young, often more greenish-hued Pacific prawns, as shown in photograph B, frequently hide under sea colander kelps (SW62/63), whereas adults prefer much deeper habitat.
A Point Cowan, Bowen Island, s. BC
B Agamemnon Channel, Nelson Island, s. BC

AR84. SIDESTRIPE SHRIMP, sidestriped shrimp, giant red shrimp
Pandalopsis dispar
to 20 cm (8 in) long
n. Alaska to Oregon
subtidal, 45–650 m (150–2,145 ft)
This economically important species, taken by trawl, has very long antennae and a white stripe along each side of the abdomen (tail). Though it is a typical bottom dweller, the sidestripe shrimp rises off the bottom to feed on planktonic prey drifting in the water column, as shown in photograph A.
A B Queen Charlotte Channel, Howe Sound, s. BC

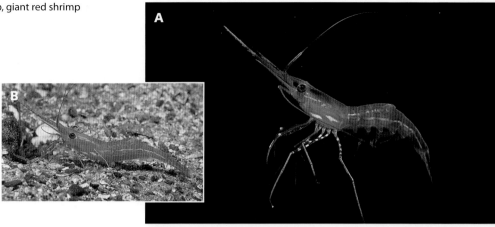

AR85. SPARKLING SHRIMP
Pandalopsis lucidirimicola
to 5 cm (2 in) long
c. BC to n. Washington
subtidal, 5–23 m (16–75 ft)
This spectacular species' penchant for crevices resulted in its very recent discovery in the 1990s. Led by Danny Kent, various members of the Vancouver Aquarium Marine Science Centre dive team assisted in the discovery and documentation. Young may hide beneath the spines of the red sea urchin (EC48).

Stubbs Island, Weynton Passage, c. BC

AR86. FUZZY HOODED SHRIMP
Betaeus setosus
to 2.5 cm (1 in) long
n. BC to c. California
intertidal to 19 m (60 ft)
Although this species is known to shelter with pairs of thickclaw porcelain crabs (AR124), its small size, transparency and habit of remaining still make the fuzzy hooded shrimp a tough find for the beachcomber. Perhaps this is another of those one-sided relationships, as the crab receives no apparent benefit.

Ucluth Peninsula, w. Vancouver Island, s. BC

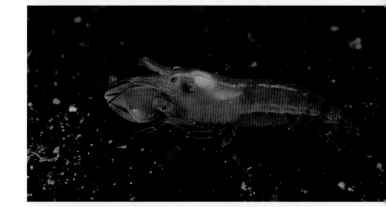

AR87. NORTHERN HOODED SHRIMP
Betaeus harrimani
to 3.5 cm (1.4 in) long
s. Alaska to s. California
intertidal
This cryptic species usually shares a burrow with the bay ghost shrimp (AR88), or the blue mud shrimp (AR89). However, the northern hooded shrimp sometimes wanders about on a solo nocturnal foray—an activity that would seem to make it more vulnerable to a wide array of sandy-bottom predators.

Stanley Park, Vancouver Harbour, s. BC

AR88. BAY GHOST SHRIMP, ghost shrimp, red ghost shrimp, pink sand shrimp, pink mud shrimp, California ghost shrimp, sand shrimp
***Neotrypaea californiensis**, Callianassa californiensis*
to 12 cm (5 in) long
s. Alaska to n. Mexico
intertidal to subtidal
Small mounds of sand, often in vast fields, are evidence of excavation activity. As a bait for steelhead, the bay ghost shrimp is so effective, it is banned in some locales. The photograph depicts a typical large-clawed male and a female.
The narrow-clawed ghost shrimp, *Neotrypaea gigas,* which has a longer rostrum, lives in similar locales. The male has a much longer and narrower dominant claw than the male bay ghost shrimp. This species may also dwell somewhat deeper and so is less often encountered by the casual naturalist.
Crescent Beach, Boundary Bay, s. BC

AR89. BLUE MUD SHRIMP, mud shrimp, Puget Sound ghost shrimp, marine crayfish
***Upogebia pugettensis**, Gebia pugettensis, Gebia californica*
to 15 cm (6 in) long
n. Alaska to c. California
intertidal
This resourceful creature digs tunnels that it shares with other animals. In turn, it is often uncovered by clam diggers seeking succulent bivalves. The blue colour phase is not often found.
Ucluth Peninsula, w. Vancouver Island, s. BC

AR90. A live seafood import from North America's east coast sporadically but increasingly is finding its way into Pacific Northwest marine habitats. In locales such as Indian Arm, near Vancouver, BC, the **AMERICAN LOBSTER,** *Homarus americanus,* is being released by misguided individuals. Ironically, sanctioned transplants by Fisheries and Oceans Canada in the 1950s did not succeed in establishing a viable population.
The Lobster Man, Granville Island, s. BC

AR91. PACIFIC MOLE CRAB, mole crab, Pacific sand crab, common sand crab, sand crab
***Emerita analoga**, Hippa analoga*
to 3.5 cm (1.5 in) long
c. Alaska to n. Mexico, Chile, Argentina
intertidal
Sightings north of Oregon are of young transients that apparently do not survive harsh winter conditions. Dimples in the sand indicate their presence to bait-seeking fishermen who wander exposed sandy beaches at low tide. Photograph B shows one burying abdomen first.
A B Neptune State Park, Cape Perpetua, c. Oregon

TRUE CRABS

AR92. GREEN SHORE CRAB, yellow shore crab, yellow shore-crab, hairy shore crab, hairy shore-crab, mud flat crab, mud-flat crab, mud crab, Oregon shore crab
***Hemigrapsus oregonensis**, Pseudograpsus oregonensis, Brachynotus oregonensis*
to 5 cm (2 in) across shell/carapace
s. Alaska to n. Mexico
intertidal
Nearly every coastal child's introduction to intertidal biology is turning over a rock and watching these creatures scurry off and under any adjacent shelter, including the child's own feet. Photograph B shows variably coloured juveniles. Tiny hairs on the green shore crab's legs are distinctive. Very occasionally, a naturalist strolling an open-coast beach might encounter a pelagic crab, *Planes* sp., stranded amid the flotsam. Somewhat similar to the green shore crab, it would have legs fringed with hairs designed for swimming.

A population of the Chinese mitten crab, *Eriocheir sinensis,* has established itself in San Francisco Bay, California. Whether this inadvertently introduced invader colonizes coastal areas farther north is a subject of debate. Perhaps more bizarre was the recent collection of a single specimen of the Japanese mitten crab, *Eriocheir japonica,* off the mouth of the Columbia River, Oregon.
A Ucluth Peninsula, w. Vancouver Island, s. BC
B Roche Point, Indian Arm, s. BC

AR93. PURPLE SHORE CRAB, purple shore-crab, purple beach crab, purple rock crab
***Hemigrapsus nudus**, Pseudograpsus nudus, Heterograpsus nudus, Brachynotus nudus*
to 5.7 cm (2.2 in) across shell/carapace
s. Alaska to n. Mexico
intertidal
A lack of hairy legs separates this species from the green shore crab (AR92) with which it is sometimes found. Except for an unusual green-coloured variant of this species, most purple shore crabs have purple spots on their pincers. This species prefers less muddy locales. Photograph B shows an unusual colour variant.
A Laura Point, Mayne Island, s. BC
B Ucluth Peninsula, w. Vancouver Island, s. BC

AR94. STRIPED SHORE CRAB, green-lined shore crab, lined shore crab, lined rock crab, rock crab
Pachygrapsus crassipes
to 4.8 cm (1.9 in) across shell/carapace
▶c. Washington to n. Mexico
intertidal
By day, this crab actively and aggressively scuttles about in the open, though it quickly retreats under cover when alarmed. The photographed specimen came from Westport, Washington, and represents a significant extension from earlier records in northern Oregon.
Westport Light State Park, Westport, c. Washington

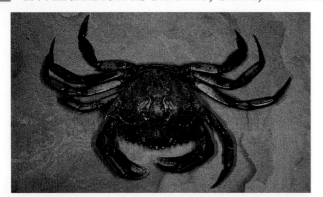

AR95. EUROPEAN GREEN CRAB, green crab, European shore crab
Carcinus maenas, Carcinides maenas
to 9.6 cm (3.7 in) across shell/carapace
s. BC to c. California, introduced from Europe
intertidal to 6 m (20 ft)
After a mysterious arrival in California, this potentially harmful species continues to spread northward. Well-meant eradication measures have resulted in the indiscriminate destruction of countless native crabs.
Nahcotta, Willapa Bay, s. Washington

AR96. BLACK-CLAWED CRAB, black clawed crab, northern black-clawed crab, black clawed mud crab, black-clawed pebble crab, black-clawed shore crab, blackclaw crestleg crab, black-fingered crab
Lophopanopeus bellus, Xantho bellus, Lophoxanthus bellus, Lophoxanthus diegensis, Lophopanopeus bellus bellus,* Lophopanopeus bellus diegensis*
to 4 cm (1.6 in) across shell/carapace
s. Alaska to s. California
intertidal to 80 m (265 ft)
Notice three "teeth" on each front corner of the carapace, beside the eye. In response to handling stress, specimens often stiffen with their claws extended.
*These names indicate two subspecies that some experts have distinguished.
Breakwater Island, Gabriola Passage, s. BC

AR97. PYGMY ROCK CRAB, pygmy cancer crab, Oregon crab, Oregon cancer crab, hairy cancer crab, Oregon rock crab
Cancer oregonensis, Trichocera oregonensis, Trichocarcinus oregonensis, Platycarcinus recurvidens, Trichocarcinus recurvidens, Trichocarcinus walkeri, Lophopanopeus somaterianus
to 5.3 cm (2.1 in) across shell/carapace
n. Alaska to s. California
intertidal to 436 m (1,430 ft)
Empty giant acorn barnacle casings (AR171) serve as "homes" for this stocky crab, which is distinguished by a thick, nearly circular carapace and very hairy legs.
Breakwater Island, Gabriola Passage, s. BC

AR98. RED ROCK CRAB, brick red cancer crab, red cancer crab, red crab
Cancer productus, Platycarcinus productus, Cancer perlatus
to 20 cm (8 in) across shell/carapace
c. Alaska to n. Mexico
intertidal to 91 m (300 ft)
BEWARE—powerful pincers may deliver a nasty nip. In many locales, where Dungeness crab (AR101) populations have dwindled, this black-clawed species faces increased recreational harvesting. More and continuing overexploitation? Photograph B illustrates a mating pair; photograph C shows two juveniles.
A Northeast Point, Texada Island, s. BC

B False Bay, San Juan Island, n. Washington
C Ucluth Peninsula, w. Vancouver Island, c. BC

AR99. SPOT-BELLIED ROCK CRAB, Pacific rock crab, red-spotted cancer crab, brown rock crab, red rock crab, common rock crab, edible rock crab, California rock crab, rock crab
Cancer antennarius, *Cancer antennaria*
to 17.8 cm (7 in) across shell/carapace
n. BC to n. Mexico
intertidal to 91 m (300 ft)
The characteristic reddish-coloured spotting of this heavily clawed crab is easily noticed by upending it, as seen in photograph B. Like most burying cancerid crabs, this species hides in sand/gravel under large rocks.
A B Ucluth Peninsula, w. Vancouver Island, s. BC

AR100. FURROWED ROCK CRAB, cancer crab
Cancer branneri, *Cancer gibbosulus*
to 7.5 cm (3 in) across shell/carapace
c. Alaska to n. Mexico
intertidal to 180 m (600 ft)
A very hairy species that is distinguished by spines on the upper edge of its top pincer "finger." Like most of the "astronomical" cancer crabs, this one uses its heavy claws not only to crush its prey but also to defend itself.
A Tongue Point, Olympic coast, n. Washington
B Egg Harbor, Coronation Island, s. Alaska

AR101. DUNGENESS CRAB, edible cancer crab, common edible crab, edible crab, Pacific edible crab, Pacific crab, market crab, commercial crab, misspelled: Dungeoness crab
Cancer magister, *Metacarcinus magister*
to 28 cm (11 in) across shell/carapace
n. Alaska to n. Mexico
intertidal to 230 m (756 ft)
This crab is arguably the most gourmet of all Pacific Northwest seafoods. Certainly it is an economically significant one, and one that is facing ever-increasing harvesting pressures. No-Take Marine Protected Areas are needed. Photograph B shows a mated pair actively digging and photograph C shows a juvenile.
A B Irvines Landing, Pender Harbour, s. BC
C Coal Harbour, Vancouver, s. BC

AR102. GRACEFUL CRAB, graceful cancer crab, graceful rock crab, slender crab, slender cancer crab
Cancer gracilis
▶to 12 cm (5 in) across shell/carapace
c. Alaska to n. Mexico
intertidal to 174 m (575 ft)
Preferring muddy/silty locales, this crab is more pink than the Dungeness crab (AR101). Both species are fast and may outpace a pursuing diver. Andy Lamb reports that the "graceful" one is also tasty.
Kleindale, Pender Harbour, s. BC

AR103. TANNER CRAB, Bairdi tanner crab, cobbler crab, snow crab
Chionoecetes bairdi
to 19 cm (7.5 in) across shell/carapace
n. Alaska to c. Oregon
subtidal, 6–475 m (20–1,550 ft)
Night divers find juveniles of this long-legged crab on open, sandy/muddy bottoms. It is an important commercial species in Alaska, where it is marketed as snow crab. Photograph A shows an adult; a juvenile is illustrated in photograph B.
A Point Atkinson, w. Vancouver, s. BC
B Woodlands, Indian Arm, s. BC

AR104. GROOVED TANNER CRAB
Chionoecetes tanneri
to 18.5 cm (7.3 in) across shell/carapace
Alaska to n. Mexico
subtidal, 29–1,944 m (97–6,415 ft)
Notice the deep, narrow groove in the centre of this crab's carapace. More orange than the preceding species, it is the object of a newly emerging fishery. Let's hope it will be managed better than most others.
The angled tanner crab, *Chionoecetes angulatus*, with its shiny carapace and inclined rostrum (head spike), is a deep-water denizen that is seldom seen.
Off Vancouver Island, s. BC

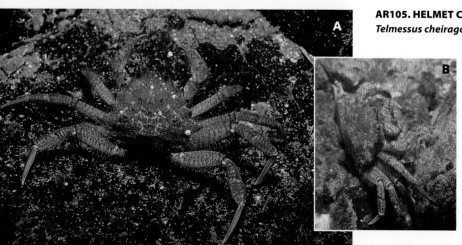

AR105. HELMET CRAB, horse crab, bristly crab, bristle crab
Telmessus cheiragonus, *Cancer cheiragonus, Platycorystes cheiragonus, Cheiragonus cheiragonus, Cheiragonus hippocarcinoides, Telmessus serratus, Platycorystes ambiguus*
to 12.5 cm (5 in) across shell/carapace
Japan, Korea, Siberia, n. Alaska to c. California
intertidal to 110 m (360 ft)
Coloured to match its surroundings, this crab hides in thick growths of eelgrass (SW2) and kelp, especially wireweed (SW51). It is one of the fastest moving Pacific Northwest crabs. Photograph B features a mating pair—this coupling may last several days.
A Bennett Bay, Mayne Island, s. BC
B Canoe Island, San Juan Islands, n. Washington

AR106. NORTHERN KELP CRAB, kelp crab, shield-backed kelp crab, shield back crab, spider crab
Pugettia producta, *Pugettia productus, Epialtus producta, Epialtus productus*
to 9 cm (3.8 in) across shell/carapace
s. Alaska to n. Mexico
intertidal to 75 m (250 ft)
The northern kelp crab's shell resembles a sheriff's badge. It uses its long legs to crawl about on various kelps or cling tenaciously to pilings. Kelp is also a food source for this crab.
Point Defiance, Puget Sound, c. Washington

AR107. GRACEFUL KELP CRAB, slender kelp crab, kelp crab, graceful spider crab, spider crab, graceful rock crab, slender crab
Pugettia gracilis, *Pugettia lordii, Pugettia quadridens gracilis*
to 4 cm (1.6 in) across shell/carapace
n. Alaska to n. Mexico
intertidal to 140 m (460 ft)
Black pincer claws tipped with orange define this variably coloured species. As shown in photograph A, the graceful kelp crab decorates itself.
A Plumper Islands, Weynton Passage, c. BC
B Fort Ebey, Whidbey Island, n. Washington

AR108. CRYPTIC KELP CRAB, kelp crab, spider crab
Pugettia richii, *Pugettia richi*
to 4.3 cm (1.7 in) across shell/carapace
s. Alaska to n. Mexico
intertidal to 100 m (330 ft)
This crab differs from the graceful kelp crab (AR107) in that its carapace is covered with spines. Spines on the edges of the carapace are more curved and project at sharper angles, and its pincers are tipped with white, not orange.
Ucluth Peninsula, w. Vancouver Island, s. BC

AR109. FOLIATE KELP CRAB, mimicking crab, foliate spider crab, sponge-covered kelp crab, sponge crab
Mimulus foliatus, *Pugettia foliata*
to 3.2 cm (1.2 in) across shell/carapace
n. Alaska to n. Mexico
intertidal to 128 m (420 ft)
Notice that the carapace is wider than it is long. Extremely variable of colour, this crab uses its hindmost legs to cling to surroundings while it grabs its food—bits of drifting kelp—with its pincers.
A Imperial Eagle Channel, Barkley Sound, s. BC
B Chrow Islands, Barkley Sound, s. BC

AR110. PACIFIC LYRE CRAB, lyre crab
Hyas lyratus, *Sayas lyratus*
to 8 cm (3.2 in) across shell/carapace
n. Alaska to n. Washington
subtidal, 9–640 m (30–2,100 ft)
This long-legged crab dwells on silty, somewhat drab-looking bottoms, where its colour is a good match. Like all arthropods, this crab must moult or shed its exoskeleton to grow, a process that occurs more often when the crab is young.
Treadwell Bay, Slingsby Channel, c. BC

AR111. SHARPNOSE CRAB, sharp-nose crab, sharp-nosed crab, sharp-nose spider crab, masking crab, sharp-nosed masking crab, intertidal masking crab
Scyra acutifrons
to 4.5 cm (1.8 in) across shell/carapace
Japan, n. Alaska to n. Mexico

intertidal to 220 m (725 ft)
This species uses sponge and colonial tunicates as low-relief decoration in an effort to confuse predators. Photograph B shows the smaller female with a male and his larger pincers.
A Stubbs Island, Weynton Passage, c. BC
B Laura Point, Mayne Island, s. BC

AR112. MOSS CRAB, masking crab, large masking crab
Loxorhynchus crispatus
to 12 cm (5 in) across shell/carapace
▶n. BC to n. Mexico
intertidal to 183 m (610 ft)
Only in the 1990s was the moss crab recorded north of California. Is this a range expansion, perhaps accelerated by several closely occurring El Niño events? It seems unlikely that such a large and obvious crab escaped detection over such a long coastal expanse. Photograph B shows a juvenile.
A Cape Flattery, Olympic coast, n. Washington
B Iphigenia Point, Langara Island, n. BC

AR113. GRACEFUL DECORATOR CRAB, slender decorator crab, decorator crab, spider crab

***Oregonia gracilis**, Oregonia longimana, Oregonia hirta*
to 5 cm (2 in) across shell/carapace
Japan, n. Alaska to c. California
intertidal to 436 m (1,430 ft)

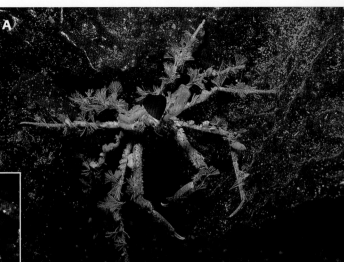

Decorator extraordinaire! Using virtually any material, this fastidious crab nips off pieces of its environment and then attaches them to its body. In captivity, if a specimen is moved to a different background, it will remove its old wardrobe and re-festoon.

The ▶split-nose decorator crab, *Oregonia bifurca,* lives at 500 m (1,650 ft) and deeper.

A Irvines Landing, Pender Harbour, s. BC
B The Gorge, Cortes Island, s. BC
C Baeria Rocks, Barkley Sound, s. BC

AR114. LONGHORN DECORATOR CRAB, decorator crab

***Chorilia longipes**, Hyastenus longipes*
to 4.5 cm (1.8 in) across shell/carapace
c. Alaska to n. Mexico
subtidal, 9–1,200 m (30–4,000 ft)

Unlike the graceful decorator crab (AR113), this species is a minimalist, using very little if any decorative material. Consequently, divers readily see its orange and white form clinging to walls or large cloud sponges (PO11).

Moore Point, Francis Peninsula, s. BC

AR115. MANTLE PEA CRAB, large pea crab, pea crab

***Pinnixa faba**, Pinnothera faba, Pinnotheres faba*
to 2.5 cm (1 in) across shell/carapace
s. Alaska to s. California
intertidal to 91 m (300 ft)

Although this species lives inside various bivalves as a juvenile, mature pairs dwell in the fat gaper (MC76), as shown in the photograph. These opportunistic crabs gather some of the microscopic plants that the clam filters from incoming seawater.

Crescent Beach, Boundary Bay, s. BC

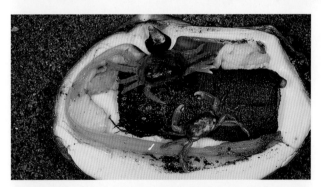

AR116. GAPER PEA CRAB, pea crab, messmate crab

Pinnixa littoralis
to 2.7 cm (1.1 in) across shell/carapace
c. Alaska to n. Mexico
intertidal to 91 m (300 ft)

The female of this species has a space between the pincer tips when they are closed, a feature that is not present in the female of the mantle pea crab (AR115). The male is more difficult to distinguish, although its third pair of legs is larger than those of the male mantle pea crab.

Ucluelet Harbour, w. Vancouver Island, s. BC

AR117. BURROW PEA CRAB, pea crab
Scleroplax granulata
to 1.3 cm (0.5 in) across shell/carapace
n. BC to n. Mexico
intertidal to 54 m (180 ft)
Distinguished by its oval carapace and red eyes, this crab shares the burrows of the bay ghost shrimp (AR88) and blue mud shrimp (AR89). Consequently it may be found by the observant clam digger. As part of a commensal relationship, this resourceful crab dines on food scraps, although it is also able to filter feed.
Hatfield Marine Science Center beach, Yaquina Bay, s. Oregon

AR118. GROOVED MUSSEL CRAB, mussel crab, clam crab, parasitic pea crab, pea crab
Fabia subquadrata, *Pinnotheres subquadrata*, *Raphnotus subquadrata*. *Pinnotheres concharum*, *Cryptophyrs concharum*, misspelled: *Faba subquadrata*
to 2.2 cm (0.9 in) across shell/carapace
n. Alaska to n. Mexico
intertidal to 220 m (720 ft)
The adult female grooved mussel crab is found inside the northern horsemussel (MC35), where she is fertilized by a male that apparently dies after mating.
Hurst Island, Goletas Channel, c. BC

AR119. TUBE-DWELLING PEA CRAB, polychaete worm pea crab, burrow crab, pea crab
Pinnixa tubicola
to 1.8 cm (0.7 in) across shell/carapace
s. Alaska to n. Mexico
intertidal to 57 m (187 ft)
Like several other very similar-looking species, this one lives inside certain tubeworm tubes. Here it not only avails itself of a steady food supply but it receives protection as well. Several other nearly identical species may also reside in such surroundings.
Ucluth Peninsula, w. Vancouver Island, s. BC

AR120. ▶SMOOTH TUNICATE CRAB
Pinnotheres pugettensis
to 1.3 cm (0.5 in) across shell/carapace
c. BC to c. California
subtidal, 6–64 m (20–212 ft)
This pea crab prefers tunicates that are not transparent, such as the bristly tunicate (CH9) shown. Its smooth, membranous carapace is distinctive, with an almost squarish outline.
Moore Point, Francis Peninsula, s. BC

AR121. ▶TUBERCULATE TUNICATE CRAB
Pinnotheres taylori
to 0.8 cm (0.3 in) across shell/carapace
c. BC to n. Washington
subtidal, 11–64 m (36–212 ft)
In contrast to the smooth tunicate crab (AR120), this one, which has two small tubercles (bumps) on the centre of its carapace, prefers translucent or transparent tunicates (CH3–5). Both species are examples of creatures that are no doubt present but seldom observed, due to their secretive lifestyle.
Worlcombe Island, Howe Sound, s. BC

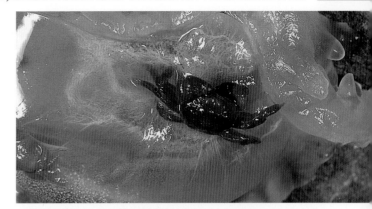

PORCELAIN CRABS

AR122. FLATTOP CRAB, porcelain crab, flat-topped crab, blue-mouth crab, porcellanid crab
Petrolisthes eriomerus
to 2 cm (0.8 in) across shell/carapace
n. Alaska to s. California
intertidal to 90 m (300 ft)
Blue mouthparts and blue spots at the thumb joints distinguish this species from the flat porcelain crab (AR123). However, mouth and claws must be open to show colouration. The subtidal distribution of this crab makes it one that divers who search under rocks might see.
Breakwater Island, Gabriola Passage, s. BC

AR123. FLAT PORCELAIN CRAB, smooth porcelain crab, porcelain crab
Petrolisthes cinctipes, *Porcellana cinctipes*, *Petrolisthes rupicolus*, *Porcellana rupicola*
to 2.5 cm (1 in) across shell/carapace
n. BC to n. Mexico
intertidal
Red mouthparts and red spots at the thumb joints are noticeable distinctions for this crab. However, the mouth and claws must be open to see these features. Beachcombers find this species under rocks in the intertidal zone.
Ucluth Peninsula, w. Vancouver Island, s. BC

AR124. THICKCLAW PORCELAIN CRAB, thick-clawed porcelain crab, thick clawed porcelain crab, rough mottled porcelain crab, lumpy porcelain crab, big-claw porcelain crab, thick clawed crab
Pachycheles rudis
to 1.9 cm (0.7 in) across shell/carapace
c. Alaska to n. Mexico
intertidal to 30 m (100 ft)
Male/female pairs live under various types of shelter with good water circulation, where they use their feathery mouthparts to filter feed.
Slip Point, Olympic coast, n. Washington

AR125. PUBESCENT PORCELAIN CRAB, hairy porcelain crab, porcelain crab
Pachycheles pubescens
to 2.2 cm (0.9 in) across shell/carapace
n. BC to n. Mexico
intertidal to 54 m (180 ft)
A dense covering of fine hairs on the claws and a pointed rostrum (head spike) distinguish this species from the thickclaw porcelain crab (AR124). After observing this creature, please ensure its security by replacing its cover.
Days Island, Puget Sound, c. Washington

GALATHEID CRABS

Including the squat lobster.

AR126. SQUAT LOBSTER or GALATHEID CRAB, pinch bug
Munida quadrispina
to 12.5 cm (5 in) long
s. Alaska to n. Mexico
subtidal, 12–1,463 m (40–4,800 ft)
A crevice or sponge dweller that extends its pincers in a threatening manner, this confusing creature is often a considerable nuisance as a prawn trap bycatch. Perhaps in the future, if other valuable species are overfished, the squat lobster could become more desirable as a rendered product. Several other similar-looking but technically different species live at great depths in the Pacific Northwest.
Lions Bay, Howe Sound, s. BC

LITHODE CRABS

AR127. GRANULAR CLAW CRAB, blue lithode crab, soft-bellied crab, hole-loving crab, papillose crab, paxillose crab
Oedignathus inermis, *Hapalogaster inermis, Oedignathus brandti, Hapalogaster brandtii, Oedignathus gilli*
to 3.5 cm (1.5 in) across shell/carapace
Japan, Korea, Siberia, c. Alaska to c. California
▶intertidal to 55 m (180 ft)
Look in empty casings of the giant acorn barnacle (AR171) at high-current locales for this impressive-looking crab.
Josef Point, Gabriola Passage, s. BC

AR128. HAIRY CRAB, fuzzy crab, tuft-haired crab, red-brown bristly crab, hairy lithodid, hairy lithode
Hapalogaster mertensii, Hapalogaster mertensi
to 3.5 cm (1.5 in) across shell/carapace
n. Alaska to n. Washington
intertidal to 54 m (180 ft)
This thin-bodied species prefers very narrow crevices in outcrops or similar spaces under rocks. Ensconced there, it consumes both animal and algal material, and may even filter feed. Photograph B features a juvenile found inside a cloud sponge (PO11).
The ▶blue-fingered hairy crab, *Hapalogaster grebnitzii*, is very similar to the above species except that the insides of its pincer fingers are blue with long hairs. It is a northern species primarily encountered in Alaska.
A Ucluth Peninsula, w. Vancouver Island, s. BC
B Agamemnon Channel, Sechelt Peninsula, s. BC

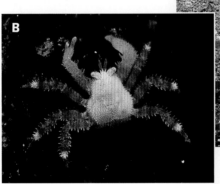

AR129. HAIRY-SPINED CRAB, red fur crab, fuzzy crab, spiny lithode crab, lithoid crab
Acantholithodes hispidus, Dermaturus hispidus
▶to 7.5 cm (3 in) across shell/carapace
n. Alaska to c. California
subtidal to 165 m (550 ft)
Distinguished by hair-tipped spines that cover the body and legs, this crab has orange-coloured claws that have white molar-like "teeth." These features are especially evident in adult specimens—like the one shown in photograph A. A juvenile is depicted in photograph B.
A Worlcombe Island, Howe Sound, s. BC
B Fearney Point, Agamemnon Channel, s. BC

AR130. RHINOCEROS CRAB, golf-ball crab, golf-ball lithode, gray-bearded crab
Rhinolithodes wosnessenskii
▶to 7.5 cm (3 in) across shell/carapace
c. Alaska to n. California
subtidal, 6–73 m (20–240 ft)
Note the triangular carapace with an obvious deep, semicircular orange and white groove. A dense covering of hairs coats all the appendages. This is a slow creeper that is well camouflaged amid its surrounding encrusting life.
Tzoonie Narrows, Narrows Inlet, s. BC

AR131. HEART CRAB, heart lithodid, spiny-leg lithode crab, flat spined triangle crab, flatspine triangular crab, papilla crab, lithoid crab
Phyllolithodes papillosus, *Phyllolithodes bicornis, Petaloceras bellianus*
▶to 10 cm (4 in) across shell/carapace
c. Alaska to s. California
intertidal to 183 m (610 ft)
Named for the raised heart-shaped pattern on its carapace, this crab has legs and pincers covered with prominent, hard spines. Like the rhinoceros crab (AR130), it is a fun find for the diver.

A Dodd Narrows, Mudge Island, s. BC
B Agamemnon Channel, Sechelt Peninsula, s. BC

AR132. PUGET SOUND KING CRAB, red box crab, box crab
Lopholithodes mandtii, *Lopholithodes mandti, Echinoceros mandti, Echinoceros cibarius, Ctenorhinus setimanus*
to 30 cm (12 in) across shell/carapace
s. Alaska to c. California
subtidal to 137 m (450 ft)
An underwater mini army tank, this crab starts out as a brightly coloured juvenile (photograph A) that grows into a more gnarly-looking dull red and purple adult (photograph B). Photograph C shows an intermediate stage.
A Stubbs Island, Weynton Passage, c. BC
B Nelson Rock, Malaspina Strait, s. BC
C Grebe Islets, Howe Sound, s. BC

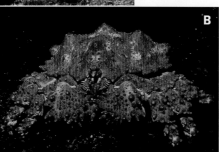

AR133. BROWN BOX CRAB, box crab, Oregon queen crab
Lopholithodes foraminatus, *Echinoceros foraminatus*
to 20 cm (8 in) across shell/carapace
c. Alaska to s. California
intertidal to 545 m (1,800 ft)
With its appendages folded, this box-shaped crab creates two obvious holes that provide access for clean water when the animal is routinely buried in soft bottoms. It is sometimes a bycatch in prawn traps. Because of its burying behaviour and dull colour, it is seen much less often than the rocky bottom-dwelling Puget Sound king crab (AR132).
Bowyer Island, Howe Sound, s. BC

AR134. RED KING CRAB, Alaska king crab, king crab, Kamchatka crab, Russian crab

Paralithodes camtschaticus, Paralithodes camtschatica, Lithodes camtschaticus, Lithodes camtschatica, Maja camtschatica, Paralithodes rostrofalcatus, Lithodes spinosissimus, Lithodes japonicus
to 28 cm (11 in) across shell/carapace, 11.8 kg (26 lbs)
Japan, Siberia, n. Alaska to n. BC
subtidal, 3–366 m (10–1,200 ft)

The more spiny juveniles may congregate in large groups called pods. Adults are targeted for a valuable fishery.
Similar to the red king crab is the blue king crab, *Paralithodes platypus*, found in Alaska and north.
A Tristar Fisheries, Richmond, s. BC
B Butedale, Grenville Channel, n. BC

AR135. GOLDEN KING CRAB

Lithodes aequispina, Lithodes aequispinus, Paralithodes longirostris
to 19.5 cm (7.8 in) across shell/carapace
Japan, Siberia, n. Alaska to s. BC
subtidal, 77–730 m (254–2,310 ft)

Only a slight difference in colour and a stout rostrum (head spike) with numerous spines differentiate this species from the red king crab (AR134). Both are commercial fishery targets, captured in huge traps fished in remote locales and often in perilous conditions.
A B Tristar Fisheries, Richmond, s. BC

AR136. SCARLET KING CRAB, deepsea king crab, deepsea red crab, deepsea crab

Lithodes cousei
to 10.5 cm (4.1 in) across shell/carapace
n. Alaska to s. California
subtidal, 258–1,829 m (850–6,030 ft)
This deep-water denizen has large spines of unequal size on its carapace, which is adorned anteriorly with an elongate spiny rostrum (head spike). Often a bycatch in more lucrative fisheries, this spindly crab is not a significant commercial species.
Esperanza Inlet, w. Vancouver Island, c. BC

AR137. ▶SHORTSPINE KING CRAB

Paralomis multispina, Leptolithodes multispina
to 8 cm (3.2 in) across shell/carapace
c. Alaska to s. California
subtidal, 830–1,665 m (2,750–5,465 ft)
Distinguished by many small spines and granules on its carapace, this crab is sometimes a bycatch of the sablefish (blackcod) trap fishery, which exploits great depths at the edge of the continental shelf. This magnificent specimen was supplied by Margot Elfert, a biological technician for Archipelago Marine Services of Victoria, BC.
Off Hippa Island, Queen Charlotte Islands, n. BC

AR138. ▶ABYSSAL KING CRAB
***Paralomis verrilli**, Pristopus verrilli*
to 11 cm (4.3 in) across shell/carapace
Siberia, n. Alaska to n. BC
subtidal, 1,238–2,379 m (4,060–7,803 ft)
Like the shortspine king crab (AR137), this crab has very spiny legs, but it lacks the copious short spikes on the carapace. Only a few commercial fishers or scientific sampling personnel such as Margot Elfert, a biological technician, are likely to encounter this long-legged crab. Thanks to her much-appreciated efforts, we are able to provide this insight into a hidden realm.
Off Hippa Island, Queen Charlotte Islands, n. BC

AR139. SCALED CRAB, scaly lithodid
***Placetron wosnessenskii**, Leiopus forcipulatus, Leiopus forcipatus*
▶to 7.8 cm (3.1 in) across shell/carapace
n. Alaska to n. Washington
intertidal to 110 m (365 ft)
This crab has spoon-like pincers and is named for the scale-like sculpturing on its legs and carapace. It often hides amid aggregations of the giant plumose anemone (CN2). Once found, however, it moves very quickly and may outpace a startled diver. A juvenile is featured in photograph B.
A Plumper Islands, Weynton Passage, c. BC
B Alcala Point, Galiano Island, s. BC

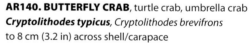

AR140. BUTTERFLY CRAB, turtle crab, umbrella crab
***Cryptolithodes typicus**, Cryptolithodes brevifrons*
to 8 cm (3.2 in) across shell/carapace
s. Alaska to s. California
intertidal to 45 m (150 ft)
This strange crab's distinctive shape is difficult to detect unless the creature moves—otherwise it resembles a piece of broken mollusc shell. A seemingly endless variety of colour patterns for this species adds to the difficulty of detection and subsequent enjoyment of the find. It is a hidden treasure. Photograph B shows the underside of this crab; photograph C shows colour variants.
A B C Stubbs Island, Weynton Passage, c. BC

AR141. UMBRELLA CRAB, umbrella-backed crab, flaring turtle crab, turtle crab, Sitka crab

Cryptolithodes sitchensis, *Cryptolithodes alta-fissura*

to 10 cm (4 in) across shell/carapace

s. Alaska to s. California

intertidal to 18 m (60 ft)

With a broader shell than the butterfly crab (AR140), this crab also has a rostrum (head spike) flared at the outer end, opposite to the butterfly crab. The umbrella crab is found only along exposed coasts and usually at shallower locales.

A Ucluth Peninsula, w. Vancouver Island, s. BC

B Eagle Point, San Juan Island, n. Washington

HERMITS (HERMIT CRABS)

Body-shell length refers to the measurement from the tip of the rostrum (head spike) to the rear of the thorax (posterior of trunk) where it joins the shell-less abdomen. This body-shell is visible when the hermit stretches out.

AR142. GRAINYHAND HERMIT, grainyhand hermit crab, grainy hermit crab, granular hermit crab, hermit crab

Pagurus granosimanus, *Eupagurus granosimanus*

to 2 cm (0.8 in) body-shell length

c. Alaska to n. Mexico

intertidal to 36 m (120 ft)

Notice the dark olive green colour with numerous light tiny granules covering the appendages. The body, hidden in the shell, is similarly marked. This hermit also has orange antennae. It prefers a large shell that seems almost too bulky to manage.

Ucluth Peninsula, w. Vancouver Island, s. BC

AR143. BLUEBAND HERMIT blueband hermit crab, blue-handed hermit crab, blue-clawed hermit crab

Pagurus samuelis, *Eupagurus samuelis*

to 2 cm (0.8 in) body-shell length

c. BC to n. Mexico

intertidal

An active, exposed-coast resident that prefers the shell of a black turban (MC222), although the specimen in the photograph has chosen otherwise. It has bright blue bands on olive-coloured legs, red antennae with no bands and a white striped carapace (shell).

Slip Point, Olympic coast, n. Washington

AR144. GREENMARK HERMIT, greenmark hermit crab

Pagurus caurinus

to 1 cm (0.4 in) body-shell length

n. Alaska to s. California

intertidal to 125 m (412 ft)

White leg banding, orange pincer tips and unbanded orange antennae distinguish this hermit. A beachcomber may conclude that it is a juvenile of another species because of its diminutive size.

Beg Islands, Barkley Sound, s. BC

AR145. HAIRY HERMIT, hairy hermit crab, hairy-legged hermit crab
Pagurus hirsutiusculus, *Eupagurus hirsutiusculus*, *Bernhardus hirsutiusculus*, *Eupagurus mertensi*, *Trigonocheirus hirsutiusculus*, *Pagurus hirsutiusculus hirsutiusculus*
to 1.9 cm (0.7 in) body-shell length
n. Alaska to s. California
intertidal to 110 m (365 ft)
An active species that prefers a tiny and easily abandoned shell, the hairy hermit relies primarily on speed to elude predators. It is distinguished by banded antennae and a hairy body and is very common intertidally.
A Ucluth Peninsula, w. Vancouver Island, s. BC
B Brown Island, Friday Harbor, n. Washington

AR146. ▶QUAYLE'S HERMIT
Pagurus quaylei
to 0.8 cm (0.3 in) body-shell length
s. Alaska to n. Mexico
intertidal to 97 m (320 ft)
This very small species has many tiny spines covering its claws and translucent antennae with dark brown bands. As in all hermits , its abdomen is soft and unprotected. Such vulnerability encourages the animal to acquire a shell or other hollow shelter.
Bremerton, Puget Sound, c. Washington

AR147. WHITEKNEE HERMIT
Pagurus dalli, *Eupagurus dalli*
to 1.8 cm (0.7 in) body-shell length
n. Alaska to Oregon.
intertidal to 275 m (910 ft)
This small, usually tan-coloured species crawls about on gravel, sand or muddy bottoms. It is readily distinguished from other hermits by the white or light markings on its "knees."
A Sutton Islets, Egmont, s. BC
B Ucluth Peninsula, w. Vancouver Island, s. BC

AR148. BERING HERMIT, Bering hermit crab
Pagurus beringanus, *Eupagurus beringanus*, *Pagurus newcombi*, *Eupagurus newcombi*
to 2.5 cm (1 in) body-shell length
n. Alaska to c. California
intertidal to 363 m (1,200 ft)
The Bering hermit prefers a large, thick shell into which it can withdraw completely. Pale bluish or grey walking legs banded with red at their joints are definitive. This is perhaps the most widespread subtidal hermit.
Quarry Bay, Nelson Island, s. BC

AR149. BLUESPINE HERMIT, bluespined hermit crab

***Pagurus kennerlyi**, Eupagurus kennerlyi*

to 4 cm (1.6 in) body-shell length

n. Alaska to n. Washington

intertidal to 275 m (910 ft)

The spines that cover the pincer claws are pale blue, but this colour is not usually obvious. This hermit generally carries a large shell, but it may also use a hermit crab sponge (PO22) instead. Photograph B shows a female bearing her typically black eggs.

A Georgina Point, Mayne Island, s. BC

B Alcala Point, Galiano Island, s. BC

AR150. ▶ORANGE HAIRY HERMIT

***Paguristes turgidus**, Pagurus turgidus, Eupagurus turgidus, Clibanarius turgidus*

to 3.3 cm (1.3 in) body-shell length

n. Alaska to s. California

subtidal, 5–465 m (16–1,525 ft)

A very slow plodder, this hirsute hermit prefers shells of the Oregon triton (MC257). It often dwells in rather silty locales, where it remains stationary for periods of time long enough that silt obscures the animal's orange colour.

Passage Island, Howe Sound, s. BC

AR151. FURRY HERMIT

***Paguristes ulreyi**, Paguristes occator*

to 2.2 cm (0.9 in) body-shell length

n. BC to n. Mexico

intertidal to 157 m (515 ft)

Note the short, stout antennae with a definite fringe of long hairs, which are used for filter feeding. Black tips on the pincers and the recurved ends of the walking legs are also definitive. This and the orange hairy hermit (AR150) are the only hermits occurring in the Pacific Northwest* with equal-sized chelipeds (pincer-bearing legs).

*The familiar geographic designation of Pacific Northwest is correct, at least from a North American perspective. It is also accurate to refer to the area in a more global way as the Northeast Pacific. Either may be used, although the latter most often appears in more technical or scientific references.

Iphigenia Point, Langara Island, n. BC

AR152. ▶ORANGE HERMIT, orange hermit crab, Pacific red hermit, red hermit crab

***Elassochirus gilli**, Eupagurus gilli, Pagurus gilli*

to 4 cm (1.6 in) body-shell length

n. Alaska to n. Washington

intertidal to 200 m (660 ft)

The orange hermit crab uses its large right claw as a door to seal off the shell when withdrawing inside. It is easily identified by its bright colour with no visible hairs. Divers tend to find specimens in rocky locales with some current. This species' yellow carapace (shell) is only noticeable when the creature extends itself, at least partially, from its protective shell.

Pile Point, San Juan Island, n. Washington

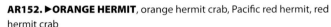

AR153. PURPLE HERMIT
Elassochirus cavimanus, *Pagurus cavimanus*, *Eupagurus cavimanus*, *Pagurus minitus*
to 3.2 cm (1.2 in) body-shell length
Japan, n. Alaska to Washington
subtidal, 30–252 m (100–825 ft)
Note the bright purple- and yellow-coloured claws and white spots covering the purple legs. Finding this specimen in s. Alaska for inclusion in this book was a "mission" for diver Donna Gibbs of Port Coquitlam, BC.
Auke Bay, Favorite Channel, s. Alaska

AR154. WIDEHAND HERMIT, widehand hermit crab, thin handed hermit crab, thin-hand hermit crab
Elassochirus tenuimanus, *Pagurus tenuimanus*, *Eupagurus tenuimanus*, *Bernhardus tenuimanus*
to 4.3 cm (1.7 in) body-shell length
n. Alaska to n. Washington
intertidal to 385 m (1,270 ft)
Carrying a large shell, this hermit wanders about on a wide variety of bottom types. The blue colour on the thighs (inner surfaces) of its appendages is a distinctive feature.
Auke Bay, Favorite Channel, s. Alaska

AR155. MAROON HERMIT, gold ring hermit crab
Pagurus hemphilli, *Eupagurus hemphilli*
to 2 cm (0.8 in) body-shell length
s. Alaska to s. California
intertidal to 50 m (165 ft)
An active denizen of the open coast, this hermit tends to use turban snail shells (MC222–224). Its deep red colour and black eyes with yellow rings are definitive. "Crazy eyes" commonly inhabits rocky tidepools or climbs about on kelp.
Tyler Rock, Barkley Sound, s. BC

AR156. STEVENS' HERMIT, Stevens hermit, Steven's hermit crab, sponge hermit crab
Pagurus stevensae
to 1.9 cm (0.7 in) body-shell length
n. Alaska to n. Washington
subtidal, 5–200 m (16–660 ft)
This uniformly coloured hermit has a very long, slender left claw. Although it apparently prefers the hermit crab sponge (PO22) as shelter, this species is often "bullied" by other hermits, losing this home in the process. Second choice is usually a discarded snail shell.
Chup Point, Barkley Sound, s. BC

AR157. ALEUTIAN HERMIT
Pagurus aleuticus, *Eupagurus aleuticus*
to 5 cm (2 in) body-shell length
n. Alaska to n. California
subtidal, 15–435 m (50–1,436 ft)
This large hermit has a groove on the tip of each walking leg and no dark red streaks near the cutting edges of its pincer claws. Its overall colour is reddish brown to orange. Hermits do not kill snails for their shells; they salvage vacant shells.
Three other large, reddish Pacific Northwest species are the ▶longhand hermit, *Pagurus tanneri,* the ▶hornyhand hermit, *Pagurus cornutus,* and the ▶knobbyhand hermit, *Pagurus confragosus,* which may be encountered by commercial trap or trawl fishers. Unfortunately these attractive deep-water dwellers are beyond reach for most of us.
Auke Bay, Favorite Channel, s. Alaska

AR158. BLACKEYED HERMIT, black-eyed hermit, armed hermit, armed hermit crab
Pagurus armatus, *Eupagurus armatus, Bernhardus armatus*
to 4.5 cm (1.8 in) body-shell length
n. Alaska to s. California
intertidal to 146 m (480 ft)
This hermit's large, almond-shaped black eyes are obvious and distinctive. It is usually observed on sandy bottoms. A male hermit may drag a female around for days, waiting for her to moult and thus be available for mating.
Point Defiance, Puget Sound, c. Washington

AR159. ALASKAN HERMIT, Alaskan hermit crab
Pagurus ochotensis, *Eupagurus ochotensis, Pagurus alaskensis, Eupagurus alaskensis*
to 5 cm (2 in) body-shell length
c. Alaska to s. California
intertidal to 385 m (1,270 ft)
This hermit is very similar to the blackeyed hermit (AR158), except that it has yellow-green eyes and its legs have a definite sheen. Like the blackeyed hermit, it prefers the shells of the Lewis's moonsnail (MC225).
Mukilteo, Puget Sound, c. Washington

AR160. SPLENDID HERMIT, splendid hermit crab
Labidochirus splendescens, *Pagurus splendescens, Eupagurus splendescens*
to 2.8 cm (1.2 in) body-shell length
Japan, n. Alaska to n. Washington
subtidal, 3–412 m (10–1,350 ft)
This is one hermit that relies primarily on a speedy escape rather than hiding in shelter. Consequently it prefers a tiny shell, which is often covered with hydroid growth as illustrated in photograph B. The sting from these hydroids may also deter predators.
A B Friday Harbor, San Juan Island, n. Washington

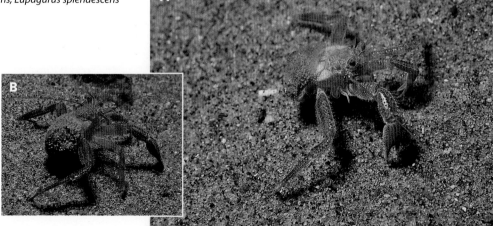

AR161. BRILLIANT HERMIT
Parapagurodes hartae
to 0.6 cm (0.2 in) body-shell length
c. BC to n. Mexico
subtidal, 6–640 m (20–2,100 ft)
The brilliant bluish-purple colour on the sides of the appendages readily distinguish this tiny hermit. Although it is often abundant and active at outer coast locales, it is often overlooked.
Tyler Rock, Barkley Sound, s. BC

AR162. TUBEWORM HERMIT, tube-dwelling hermit crab
Discorsopagurus schmitti, *Orthopagurus schmitti, Pylopagurus schmitti*
to 0.6 cm (0.2 in) body-shell length
s. Alaska to s. California
intertidal to 220 m (725 ft)
As this hermit has a straight abdomen (unlike all hermit species AR142–161), it is perfectly suited to hide in the empty tubes of various tubeworm species. Females live in attached tubes, but the wandering males use broken pieces, which allow for requisite conjugal visits. The calcareous tubeworms (AN50–56) are one species whose tubes are very often used.
Tyler Rock, Barkley Sound, s. BC

AR163. TOOTHSHELL HERMIT
Orthopagurus minimus, *Pagurus minimus, Pylopagurus minimus*
to 0.8 cm (0.3 in) body-shell length
BC to s. California
subtidal, 11–65 m (36–215 ft)
Very similar to the tubeworm hermit (AR162) but with no obvious banding on its legs, this hermit often uses the shell of the wampum tuskshell (MC369)—but not the specimen in the photograph, which has commandeered a calcareous tubeworm tube (AN50–56). This species usually extends its larger right claw ahead when moving about.
Beg Islands, Barkley Sound, s. BC

BARNACLES

AR164. SMALL ACORN BARNACLE, little acorn barnacle, little brown barnacle, brown buckshot barnacle, buckshot barnacle, small northern barnacle, Dall's barnacle, brown barnacle
Chthamalus dalli
to 0.8 cm (0.3 in) across
n. Alaska to s. California
intertidal
A splash-zone inhabitant, this barnacle is high and dry most of its life. It is able to retain moisture by remaining closed for long periods of time.
Sargeant Bay, Sunshine Coast, s. BC

AR165. COMMON ACORN BARNACLE, sharp acorn barnacle, acorn barnacle, white buckshot barnacle, common barnacle
***Balanus glandula**, Balanus glandulus*
to 2.2 cm (0.9 in) across
n. Alaska to n. Mexico
intertidal to subtidal
Very adaptable, this species can grow quite tall when crowded, or remain relatively squat given sufficient space. It is nearly ubiquitous when living in locales sheltered from direct open-coast wave action. Photograph B shows feeding specimens and an area "cleared" of individuals. The similar-looking Atlantic barnacle, *Balanus improvisus*, was incidentally introduced to the Pacific Northwest with eastern oysters (MC51) but is not common north of Oregon.
A Brown Island, Friday Harbor, n. Washington
B Moore Point, Francis Peninsula, s. BC

AR166. CRENATE BARNACLE
Balanus crenatus
to 2 cm (0.8 in) across
Japan, n. Alaska to s. California
intertidal to 180 m (600 ft)
This primarily subtidal species often settles on sunken bottles and other items dropped overboard. It is naturally quite squat, smooth and white. Along with most other barnacles, this one fouls the hulls of ships and consequently is an object of scorn for most boaters.
The similar-looking northern barnacle, *Balanus balanus,* is most prevalent north of BC.
Friday Harbor, San Juan Island, n. Washington

AR167. ROSTRATE BARNACLE
Balanus rostratus
▶to 5 cm (2 in) in height
Japan, n. Alaska to Washington
intertidal to subtidal
This barnacle's external appearance is highly variable. Photograph A shows a highly ridged, feeding specimen anchored to a swimming spiny scallop shell (MC43); photograph B illustrates a smooth form common in some low-current locales. Unfortunately this species is defined by an internal structure of casing plates, making it difficult to distinguish by a beachcomber or a diver.
A Georgina Point, Mayne Island, s. BC
B Passage Island, Howe Sound, s. BC

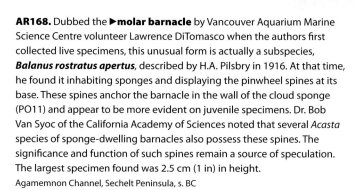

AR168. Dubbed the ▶**molar barnacle** by Vancouver Aquarium Marine Science Centre volunteer Lawrence DiTomasco when the authors first collected live specimens, this unusual form is actually a subspecies, ***Balanus rostratus apertus***, described by H.A. Pilsbry in 1916. At that time, he found it inhabiting sponges and displaying the pinwheel spines at its base. These spines anchor the barnacle in the wall of the cloud sponge (PO11) and appear to be more evident on juvenile specimens. Dr. Bob Van Syoc of the California Academy of Sciences noted that several *Acasta* species of sponge-dwelling barnacles also possess these spines. The significance and function of such spines remain a source of speculation. The largest specimen found was 2.5 cm (1 in) in height.
Agamemnon Channel, Sechelt Peninsula, s. BC

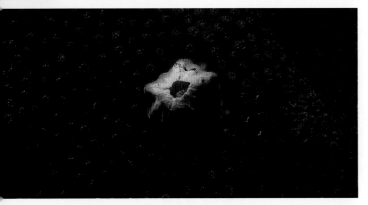

AR169. ▶HYDROCORAL BARNACLE
Solidobalanus engbergi, *Balanus engbergi*
to 1.9 cm (0.7 in) across
Alaska to c. Oregon
intertidal to subtidal
This small, primarily subtidal species is almost always associated with various hydrocorals (CN50–52), which usually overgrow most of the creature's casing. It has a very small opening, and the case ridging begins at the edge of this orifice.
Sutton Islets, Egmont, s. BC

AR170. SHELL BARNACLE
Solidobalanus hesperius, *Balanus hesperius*
to 2 cm (0.8 in) across
n. Alaska to s. California
intertidal to 65 m (215 ft)
This barnacle prefers to settle on mollusc and crab shells, usually those located subtidally. It has a square opening from which the living organism protrudes its cirri—feeding structures that are actually modified legs but resemble a feather-like claw that rapidly grabs at tiny planktonic prey.
Pillar Point, Olympic coast, n. Washington. J. Duane Sept photograph

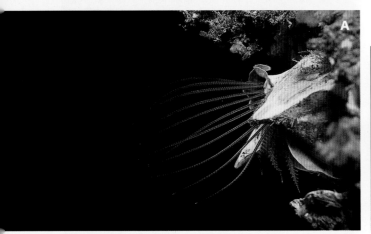

AR171. GIANT ACORN BARNACLE, giant barnacle, horse barnacle
Balanus nubilus, *Balanus altissimus, Balanus flos*
to 15 cm (6 in) across
s. Alaska to n. Mexico
intertidal to 91 m (300 ft)
This barnacle may be solitary or may aggregate, forming huge, reef-like structures. Its obvious pink cirri (claw-like feeding structures) protrude when the creature feeds, as shown in photograph A. Many animals may hide in the empty casings after the barnacles perish. Some fish species deposit eggs in these cavities.
A Edmonds, Puget Sound, c. Washington
B Sutton Islets, Egmont, s. BC

AR172. THATCHED ACORN BARNACLE, thatched barnacle, rock barnacle, horse barnacle
Semibalanus cariosus, *Balanus cariosus*
to 6 cm (2.3 in) across
Japan, n. Alaska to s. California
intertidal to 54 m (180 ft)
With its heavily ridged casing and black feather-like cirri (claw-like feeding structures), the thatched acorn barnacle is ideally suited to a surf-pounded habitat. It is the only acorn barnacle with a membranous base. However when crowded with limited horizontal space, this species, like some others, may grow with a significant vertical component instead.
The ▶ridge-less barnacle, *Semibalanus balanoides,* lives primarily in Alaskan and Atlantic waters.
Frank Island, w. Vancouver Island, s. BC

AR173. GOOSE-NECK BARNACLE, goose neck barnacle, Pacific goose barnacle, goose barnacle, leaf barnacle, stalked barnacle
Pollicipes polymerus, *Mitella polymerus*
to 15 cm (6 in) in height
s. Alaska to n. Mexico
intertidal to 30 m (100 ft)
This distinctive species grows in clusters (photograph A) along exposed shores, where it often attaches to the California mussel (MC34). The bright red meat inside the "stalk" tastes not unlike lobster.
A B Frank Island, w. Vancouver Island, s. BC

AR174. These photographs illustrate the spectacular formations of the **Nakwakto goose-neck barnacle**, a large and colourful variation of the goose-neck barnacle (AR173) found in Nakwakto Rapids, Slingsby Channel, c. BC. The glorious red colour is actually the hemoglobin in the barnacle's blood. The blood is obvious in subtidal specimens like these, which do not have the black pigment that protects the sun-exposed populations inhabiting shallow or intertidal zones. Familiar to an ever-increasing number of recreational divers, this unique and isolated population must be preserved via a No-Take Marine Protected Area.
A B Nakwakto Rapids, Slingsby Channel, c. BC

AR175. ▶MANY-PLATED GOOSE-NECK BARNACLE
Scalpellum columbianum, *Hamatoscalpellum columbianum*
▶to 2.5 cm (1 in) in height
s. Alaska to Washington
subtidal
Once considered a rare find, this deep-water species is seen more often in BC waters as a result of Fisheries and Oceans Canada's Commercial Fisheries Observer Program. Archipelago Marine Service staff such as Scott Buchanan periodically find this species while documenting trawl catches off the west coast of Vancouver Island. Most often, specimens are attached to snail shells, as shown in the photograph.
Off west coast of Vancouver Island, s. BC

AR176. PELAGIC GOOSE-NECK BARNACLE, goose neck barnacle, pelagic goose barnacle, common gooseneck barnacle, pelagic stalked barnacle, pelagic barnacle, common goose barnacle, blue goose barnacle
Lepas anatifera
to 20 cm (8 in) in height
cosmopolitan, Alaska to Mexico and s. America
pelagic; attached to floating objects
Mass population "crashes" of this barnacle occur when onshore winds force ashore the flotsam to which they are attached.
The ▶Pacific goose-neck barnacle, *Lepas pacifica,* and ▶Hill's goose-neck barnacle, *Lepas hilli,* also inhabit the open ocean off the Pacific Northwest.
Ucluth Peninsula, w. Vancouver Island, s. BC

AR177. ▶OWN-FLOAT GOOSE-BARNACLE, pelagic goose barnacle
Lepas fascicularis, *Lepas fascicularis aurivillii*
to 6 cm (2.3 in) in height
cosmopolitan, Alaska to s. California
pelagic; creates its own float
When young, this barnacle attaches to a very tiny floating object and then, using a cement gland, secretes an enveloping float that it may share with others as it grows. Like the pelagic goose-neck barnacle (AR176), it washes ashore after storms along the open coast.
The ▶jelly-dwelling goose-barnacle, *Alepas pacifica,* attaches to large jellies but would be a rare find in the Pacific Northwest.
Off Langara Island, Queen Charlotte Islands, n. BC. Danny Kent photograph

AR178. GRAY WHALE BARNACLE
Cryptolepas rachianecti
to 6 cm (2.4 in) across
Korea, n. Alaska to n. Mexico
pelagic (on the gray whale)
Generally abundant on the head and fins of its host, the gray whale barnacle is usually deeply embedded in the skin—a factor that ensures it is not easily dislodged. Consequently this barnacle is most readily observed on a beached gray whale.
Chesterman Beach, w. Vancouver Island, s. BC

AR179. ▶SHRIMP PARASITIC BARNACLE
Syon hippolyte
▶to 1.2 cm (0.5 in) across
Atlantic Ocean, BC to Washington
intertidal to subtidal
Resembling a small, sausage-shaped sac, this barnacle infects several species of shrimps that the naturalist may find. Many parasite species like this one are so highly modified to a specialized immobile existence that, as adults, they are little more than sacs of living reproductive tissue. The specimen photographed was living on the abdomen of a Kincaid's shrimp (AR59).
Agamemnon Channel, Sechelt Peninsula, s. BC

AR180. ▶BLACK-CLAWED CRAB PARASITIC BARNACLE
Loxothylacus panopaei
▶to 1.2 cm (0.5 in) across
w. Atlantic Ocean, Alaska to s. California
intertidal to 80 m (265 ft)
This creature is truly a "horror movie" come to life. At first, as a larva, it is similar to most barnacles. However, instead of settling on a rock or other solid substrate, it will inject itself into a crab. It spreads out into the crab, root-like, and absorbs nutrients from the host's blood. When mature, it produces the sac-like reproductive structure shown in the photograph. In spite of this gruesome infection, it is in the parasite's best interest for the host to survive.
A number of other fascinating parasitic barnacles infect various hermits and sea stars, so these obscure and often small creatures largely remain out of the naturalist's view.
Boas Islet, Hakai Passage, c. BC

SEA SPIDERS

AR181. ▶YELLOW HAIRY SEA SPIDER
Tanystylum anthomasti
▶to 1 cm (0.4 in) across
Japan, n. Alaska to Oregon
subtidal
This tiny creature, which seems to have a special association with red soft coral (CN37), is a worthy quarry for the diving naturalist looking for a challenge.
Browning Passage, Nigei Island, c. BC

AR182. ▶STUBBY OVAL SEA SPIDER
Pycnogonum stearnsi
to 1.3 cm (0.5 in) long
Japan, BC to s. California
intertidal
A smooth surface, short, thick legs and oval outline distinguish this parasitic sea spider. In California its preferred host is the green surf anemone (CN13), from which it withdraws cellular fluid sustenance.
Vancouver Aquarium Marine Science Centre, Vancouver, BC

AR183. ▶GIANT SEA SPIDER
Nymphon pixellae, Nymphon solitarium, Nymphon variatum
▶to 3.5 cm (1.5 in) across
BC to Mexico
subtidal
Finding the initial specimen of this sea spider is a real treat for the diver, as it is not only difficult to see but is also bizarre and unbelievable. Resembling the terrestrial daddy-long-legs spider, it moves very slowly and deliberately. Look on steep outcrop walls and concentrate particularly on boot sponges (PO9/10) or cloud sponges (PO11).
A White Islets, Strait of Georgia, s. BC
B Halkett Point, Gambier Island, s. BC

AR184. ▶SPINY-THIGH SEA SPIDER
Phoxichilidium femoratum
▶to 1.3 cm (0.5 in) across
Alaska to s. California
▶intertidal to 20 m (65 ft)
While preparing this book, the authors had the wonderful opportunity to work with Dr. Jason Gillespie of the University of Alberta. A sea spider enthusiast, he was creating a scientific key for Pacific Northwest species and kindly verified identifications—including this one, found climbing an anchoring chain at Egmont, s. BC, by Donna Gibbs of Port Coquitlam, BC.
Egmont Marina, Egmont, s. BC

AR185. This small **white sea spider** was living in a colony of hydroids collected at Boas Islet, Hakai Passage, s. BC, during an MV *Nautilus Explorer* cruise. It was not until after the dive that the tiny 0.7 cm (0.3 in) creature was noticed. Unfortunately the specimen was subsequently lost, and its identity remains a mystery.
Boas Islet, Hakai Passage, c. BC

Perhaps as many as 50 other species of sea spiders exist in the Pacific Northwest but remain largely unknown for several reasons: they are usually tiny and inconspicuous and often associate intimately with other creatures on which they can conceal themselves.

SEA STARS, BRITTLE STARS, FEATHER STARS, SEA URCHINS AND SEA CUCUMBERS
Phylum ECHINODERMATA

Including sea stars (starfish), brittle stars, basket stars, feather stars, sea urchins, sand dollars and sea cucumbers.

Each echinoderm has some manner of hard chalky skeleton within its skin, although the amount, size and compaction of these elements varies considerably. From fused, interlocking plates that are obvious in a sand dollar or a sea urchin, through the variably packed and often obvious ones of sea stars, to the tiny and widely separated ossicles (plate-like or spine-like skeletal structures) of most sea cucumbers, this internal skeletal system is a constant.

Radiating about a central mouth, the five rays (arms) of a typical sea star beautifully illustrate the definitive penta-radial (five-armed) symmetry of an echinoderm. This layout is also present in sea urchins, sea cucumbers and other echinoderms, although it is not as obvious.

Another definitive feature of each echinoderm is a water vascular system, which essentially comprises a single-opening, internal plumbing system with many interconnected fluid-filled canals. Rows of very many tube feet, extending over the body of each echinoderm, are the most obvious external evidence of this unique system, whose prime functions are breathing and supplying rigidity and locomotion.

The accompanying photograph illustrates a rainbow star (EC4), at left, regenerating two lost rays, a common occurrence. The other specimen, a cookie star (EC11), is "budding" a new arm near the tip of another—a very unusual event.

Nearly 300 species of echinoderms live in the marine waters of the Pacific Northwest.

Further Reading
Lambert, Philip, 2000, *Sea Stars of British Columbia, Southeast Alaska and Puget Sound*, Royal British Columbia Museum Handbook, UBC Press, Vancouver, BC, 186 pp.
Lambert, Philip, 1997, *Sea Cucumbers of British Columbia, Southeastern Alaska and Puget Sound,* Royal British Columbia Museum Handbook, UBC Press, Vancouver, BC, 166 pp.

SEA STARS

**New sea-star depth records for the giant pink star (EC2), rainbow star (EC4), sunflower star (EC28) and striped sun star (EC32) were supplied by the filmmaker/biologist Neil McDaniel of Vancouver, BC. While reviewing video footage taken from a submersible, he was able to correlate depths with species occurrence and use modern technology for a secondary biological purpose.

EC1. PURPLE STAR or OCHRE STAR, purple sea star, ochre sea star, ochre seastar, purple starfish, ochre starfish, Pacific sea star, common seastar, common sea star, common purple star, warty sea star, common starfish
Pisaster ochraceus, *Asterias ochracea,* misspelled: *Pisaster ochraceous*
to 50 cm (20 in) across
c. Alaska to n. Mexico
intertidal to 97 m (320 ft)
This star often forms huge winter spawning aggregations, as in photograph B. Photograph C shows a feeding individual. An old Pacific Northwest record for the giant star, *Pisaster giganteus,* is most likely this species.
A Frank Island, w. Vancouver Island, s. BC
B The Gorge, Cortes Island, s. BC
C Bremner Islet, Burnett Bay, c. BC

EC2. GIANT PINK STAR, spiny pink star, pink star, pink sea star, pink short-spined starfish, pink short-spined star, pink short-spined seastar, pink starfish, short-spined sea star, short-spined seastar, short-spined pisaster, knobby sea star
Pisaster brevispinus, *Asterias brevispina*
to 65 cm (25 in) across
s. Alaska to s. California
▶intertidal to 182 m (600 ft)**
Specimens that "belly down" in the mud/sand are using their extendable tube feet near their mouths to dig clams.
Sutton Islets, Egmont, s. BC

EC3. MOTTLED STAR, mottled sea star, mottled starfish, false ochre star, false ochre sea star, slender-rayed star, slender-rayed sea star, Troschel's star, Troschel's sea star, true star
***Evasterias troschelii**, Evasterias troscheli*
to 60 cm (24 in) across
Siberia, n. Alaska to c. California
intertidal to 75 m (250 ft)
A stiff species with proportionally long rays, this star preys primarily on mussels and barnacles. A feeding aggregation of many colour variants is depicted in photograph B.
A B Moore Point, Francis Peninsula, s. BC

EC4. RAINBOW STAR, rainbow sea star, long rayed star, long-rayed sea star, long-armed sea star, longrayed starfish, long-rayed starfish, red banded star, redbanded sea star, painted star, painted sea star, fragile star, fragile spiny seastar, rainbow starfish
***Orthasterias koehleri**, Asterias koehleri, Orthasterias columbiana*
to 60 cm (24 in) across
n. Alaska to n. Mexico
▶intertidal to 283 m (934 ft)**
Notice the rows of prominent spines and flexible body. An unusual solid red juvenile is pictured in photograph B.
A Agamemnon Channel, Nelson Island, s. BC
B Seapool Rocks, Barkley Sound, s. BC

EC5. ▶BLACK-SPINED SEA STAR
Lethasterias nanimensis
to 71 cm (28.5 in) across
n. Alaska to s. Alaska (doubtful historical BC record)
subtidal to 102 m (337 ft)
Unfortunately the southern distribution limit of this species is in doubt because of the creature's initial discovery. The "type" specimen, or the first one collected, is labelled as being from Departure Bay, near Nanaimo, BC. However, sea star expert and author Phil Lambert believes this is an error, as he has never encountered one south of Alaska. Neither have we.
Shrine Island, Juneau, Alaska. Lou Barr photograph

EC6. ▶VELCRO STAR, long-rayed star, long ray star, black star, black sea star, fish eating star, fish-eating sea star, fish-eating starfish
***Stylasterias forreri**, Asterias forreri*
to 67 cm (26 in) across
c. Alaska to s. California
subtidal, 6–545 m (20–1,800 ft)

This long-rayed, delicate star readily discards its arms when stressed. A neoprene-suited diver may find a specimen sticking to his or her suit by pedicellaria (minute but tenacious pincers) during a dive.
A Chup Point, Barkley Sound, s. BC
B Tyler Rock, Barkley Sound, s. BC

EC7. LEATHER STAR, leather sea star, leather starfish, garlic star, garlic sea star
Dermasterias imbricata, *Asteriopsis imbricata*
to 30 cm (12 in) across
c. Alaska to n. Mexico
intertidal to 91 m (300 ft)
This smooth-to-the-touch star has a very distinctive odour that some liken to garlic. It often causes the swimming anemone (CN11), a possible prey item, to swim. Like other five-rayed species, this one may sometimes have six or even (rarely) seven arms.
Moore Point, Francis Peninsula, s. BC

EC8. BAT STAR, bat starfish, broad disc sea star, broad-disc sea star, broad-disk starfish, sea bat, webbed star, webbed sea star, webbed starfish
Asterina miniata, *Patiria miniata*, *Asterias miniata*
▶to 25 cm (10 in) across
s. Alaska to n. Mexico
intertidal to 300 m (1,000 ft)
Primarily a herbivore (feeding on diatoms and other algae) and found only along exposed shores, this star, like others, protrudes its stomach outside its body to feed. Flip one over and check it out.
Beg Islands, Barkley Sound, s. BC

EC9. VERMILION STAR, vermilion starfish, red sea star, equal arm star, equal arm starfish, equal-arm star, misspelled: vermillion star
Mediaster aequalis
to 20 cm (8 in) across
n. Alaska to n. Mexico
intertidal to 500 m (1,650 ft)
Though it often feeds upon bryozoans, sponges and sea pens, this star will also consume detritus or fine matter derived from living organisms lying on the substrate.
The ▶Alaskan deepwater star, *Pseudarchaster alascensis,* resembles the vermilion star but has rays that appear longer and narrower, extending from a smaller central area. It is also paler. The Pacific Northwest represents the southern portion of this sea star's distribution.
Nile Point, Agamemnon Channel, s. BC

EC10. GUNPOWDER STAR, Swift's sea star
Gephyreaster swifti, *Mimaster swifti*
to 42 cm (17 in) across
n. Alaska to Washington
▶subtidal, 4–350 m (13–1,155 ft)
This odoriferous species appears to be a paler, larger and puffier version of the vermilion star (EC9). It feeds on sea anemones, particularly the short plumose anemone (CN1) and the spotted swimming anemone (CN12). Look for it in either rocky or sandy surroundings.
Doyle Island, Gordon Channel, c. BC

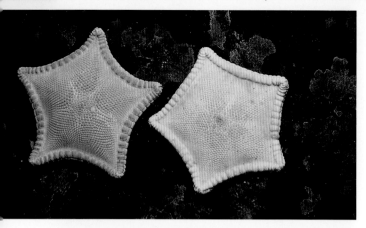

EC11. COOKIE STAR, cookie starfish, orange bat sea star
***Ceramaster patagonicus**, Pentagonaster patagonicus*, misspelled:
Ceremaster patagonius
▶to 20 cm (8 in) across
n. Alaska to s. Chile
subtidal, 10–540 m (33–1,785 ft)
Resembling a star-shaped shortbread cookie, this star prefers steep cliff faces in low-current locales. More than one subspecies or variety may be involved.
Agamemnon Channel, Nelson Island, s. BC

EC12. ARCTIC COOKIE STAR, arctic bat sea star
***Ceramaster arcticus**, Tosia arctica*, misspelled: *Ceremaster arcticus*
to 11 cm (4.2 in) across
n. Alaska to s. BC
intertidal to 186 m (620 ft)
A typical sea star, this species moves by pulling itself along with its thousands of tube feet, each of which has a suction cup that holds tight to the substrate.
Outer Narrows, Slingsby Channel, c. BC

EC13. SPINY RED STAR, spiny red sea star, spiny red starfish, spiny star, spiny starfish, thorny sea star
***Hippasteria spinosa**, Hippasterias spinosa*
to 34 cm (13.5 in) across
Siberia, n. Alaska to s. California
subtidal, 10–520 m (33–1,716 ft)
Note the monotone red colour of this species and its copious spines. One of its preferred prey items is the orange sea pen (CN40). This sea star looks significantly different as a juvenile (photograph B).
A McLeod Island, Ripple Passage, c. BC
B Cotton Point, Keats Island, s. BC

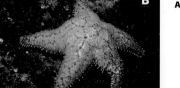

EC14. THORNY SEA STAR, spiny sea star
***Poraniopsis inflatus inflatus**, Poraniopsis inflata, Alexandraster inflatus*
to 20 cm (8 in) across
Japan, c. Alaska to s. California
▶subtidal, 8 to 366 m (26 to 1,207 ft)
This infrequently observed sea star differs from the spiny red star (EC13) in that its sparser, white-tipped spines are "linked" by lines of colour. A sea star has papulae (special skin gills)—a feature dramatically depicted in photograph B.
A B Tyler Rock, Barkley Sound, s. BC

EC15. CRESTED SEA STAR, yellow starfish
Lophaster furcilliger vexator, *Lophaster furcilliger, Sarkaster validus*
to 16.4 cm (6.5 in) across
n. Alaska to s. California, Galapagos Islands
subtidal, 12–2,000 m (40–6,600 ft)
The *vexator* subspecies is the shallow-dwelling one and therefore most likely to be seen by the diver. The tuft-like mini-spines of this star may cause it to adhere to a neoprene scuba suit.
Agamemnon Channel, Nelson Island, s. BC

EC16. SLIME STAR, slime starfish, cushion star, cushion sea star, fat sea star
Pteraster tesselatus, *Pteraster tesselatus arcuatus*
to 24 cm (10 in) across
Japan, n. Alaska to c. California
subtidal to 436 m (1,440 ft)
This species' short, stubby arms give it a cushion-like appearance. It readily produces large amounts of slime when stressed—either by a predator or an aquarium diver collecting it for display. Consequently it is always stored separately by collectors, lest its secretions suffocate other specimens.
A Moore Point, Francis Peninsula, s. BC
B Carlos Island, Flat Top Islands, s. BC

EC17. WRINKLED STAR, slime star, sea star
Pteraster militaris, *Asterias militaris*
to 15 cm (6 in) across
Japan, n. Alaska to n. Oregon
subtidal, 10–1,100 m (33–3,600 ft)
This star resembles the preceding species, but appears to have "been in a bathtub" far too long. Its rays are also noticeably longer. After receiving sperm through pores adjacent to her tube feet, a mature female broods at least some fertilized eggs within a body chamber. Up to 40 juveniles, each measuring about 1 cm (0.4 in) across, are ultimately released. Photograph B shows an unusual colour variant.
A Sutton Islets, Egmont, s. BC
B Seal Reef, Lasqueti Island, s. BC

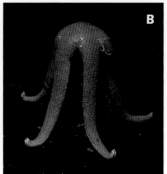

EC18. BLOOD STAR, Pacific blood star, blood sea star, blood red star, blood starfish, red sea star, Pacific henricia
Henricia leviuscula leviuscula, *Henricia leviuscula*, *Linkia leviuscula*
to 32 cm (13 in) across
Siberia, Japan, n. Alaska to n. Mexico
intertidal to 400 m (1,320 ft)
A number of subspecies reflect the considerable variation within the detailed anatomy of this species.
A sperm-spewing male exuding gametes from his "armpits" is shown in photograph B.
A Green Bay, Nelson Island, s. BC
B Agamemnon Channel, Nelson Island, s. BC

EC19. FAT BLOOD STAR, fat henricia, sanguine sea star, Atlantic blood star, blood star, blood sea star
Henricia sanguinolenta, *Henricia tumida*
to 26 cm (10.4 in) across
circumpolar, south to Massachusetts, n. Alaska to Washington
subtidal, 15–2,400 m (50–8,000 ft)
Creases at "armpits" give an overweight appearance to this species, which is nearly always white to pale orange on the Pacific coast. The female retains the fertilized eggs around her mouth, where brooding occurs before eventual transformation into juvenile sea stars.
Bowyer Island, Howe Sound, s. BC

EC20. RIDGED BLOOD STAR, sea star
Henricia aspera aspera, *Henricia aspera*
▶to 38 cm (15 in) across
Japan, n. Alaska to s. California
subtidal, 6–904 m (20–3,000 ft)
This stiff-armed star has a very noticeable coarse meshwork appearance that distinguishes it from other *Henricia* species. Reported as uncommonly seen in the Pacific Northwest—a statement that should challenge the diving naturalists of the region.
Moore Point, Francis Peninsula, s. BC

EC21. Currently known as the ▶**DWARF MOTTLED HENRICIA**, *Henricia* **sp. nov.,** a formal scientific designation for this species by Meg Strathman of Friday Harbor Laboratories, Washington, is pending. Its small size not only makes it difficult to find but initially suggests a possible juvenile status. Look for it under rocks in the intertidal zone along exposed shores. Specimens as large as 5 cm (2 in) have been found.
Two other representatives of this confusing group of sea stars, the ▶weak-mesh blood star, *Henricia asthenactis,* and the ▶longspine blood star, *Henricia longispina longispina,* have been documented in the Pacific Northwest but reside deeper than recreational diving depths.
Slip Point, Olympic coast, n. Washington

EC22. MUD STAR, mudstar
Ctenodiscus crispatus, *Asterias crispata*
to 10 cm (4 in) across
circumpolar, south to New England and Japan, n. Alaska to Panama, possibly Chile
subtidal, 10–1,890 m (35–6,240 ft)
This species is distinguished by the spined marginal plates around the edges of its arms and a raised central cone. It is classified as a non-selective deposit feeder, which means it ingests sediment and digests any edible matter.
Mouth of Fraser River, Strait of Georgia, s. BC

EC23. ▶PALE STAR
Leptychaster pacificus
to 10 cm (4 in) across
n. Alaska to n. Washington
subtidal, 10–435 m (33–1,436 ft)
This small star usually buries in sand and so is not often observed by divers—a minor disappointment because of the species' lack of colour. A spectacular opportunity for the underwater photographer it is not!
The ▶short-armed pale star, *Leptychaster anomalus,* and ▶Arctic pale star, *Leptychaster arcticus,* are more northern species found off the continental shelf in the Pacific Northwest.
Passage Island, Howe Sound, s. BC

EC24. SAND STAR, sandstar, sand starfish, spiny mudstar, mud star, mud sea star
Luidia foliolata, *Petalaster foliolata*
to 60 cm (24 in) across
c. Alaska to Nicaragua, Galapagos Islands
▶intertidal to 613 m (2,024 ft)
A rather dull-coloured species, this star has pointed tube feet adapted for travelling on soft substrates. Specimens often have small pointed tips on their arms, which indicate new growth after damage.
A George Fraser Islands, Barkley Sound, s. BC
B Treadwell Bay, Slingsby Channel, c. BC

EC25. SIX-RAYED SEA STARS—schizo-starburst!
Ever since the 1800s, when naturalists began seriously examining the six-rayed sea stars, the problem of how many species are involved and how each is defined has been debated and debated. The result is that species have been defined and redefined to the point where almost total confusion reigns as to "what is what." Phil Lambert, in his great book on sea stars (*Sea Stars of British Columbia, Southeast Alaska and Puget Sound*, p. 116), has summarized the current status.
Not wanting to make matters worse, we have listed all the names, both common and scientific, for the *species complexes* below and feature two species teased from the taxonomic "mess" following Phil's assessment.
To further confuse the issue, two other species of six-rayed sea stars that are primarily Arctic denizens have been recorded from the Pacific Northwest. They are the ▶rusty six-armed star, *Leptasterias coei,* and the ▶polar six-armed star, *Leptasterias polaris katherinae.*

Six-armed star, six-arm sea star, six-rayed seastar, six-rayed sea star, broad six-rayed sea star, knobless six-rayed sea star, six-rayed starfish, six-ray star, little six-rayed star, little six-rayed starfish, six-armed sea star, six armed star, six-arm starfish, delicate six-rayed sea star, brooding star, dainty six-rayed starfish

Leptasterias hexactis, Leptasterias aequalis, and their synonyms, *Leptasterias pusilla, Leptasterias alaskensis, Stenasterias macropora*

The photograph on p.331 presents specimens of both the following species complexes, namely the ▶drab six-armed star, *Leptasterias hexactis* and the ▶colourful six-armed star, *Leptasterias aequalis.*

Various Pacific Northwest locales

EC26. ▶DRAB SIX-ARMED STAR

Leptasterias hexactis species complex, including *Leptasterias hexactis hexactis, Leptasterias hexactis plena, Leptasterias hexactis siderea, Leptasterias hexactis regularis, Leptasterias hexactis aspera, Leptasterias hexactis vancouveri, Leptasterias hexactis epichlora*

to 10 cm (4 in) across
n. Alaska to n. Washington
intertidal to subtidal
Note the line of spines down the centre of each arm. Like other six-armed species, this one may occasionally have a complement of seven.
Not illustrated here is the ▶Alaskan six-armed star, *Leptasterias alaskensis,* species complex, which does not have a line of spines down the centre of each arm.
A B Frank Island, w. Vancouver Island, s. BC

EC27. ▶COLOURFUL SIX-ARMED STAR

Leptasterias aequalis species complex, including *Leptasterias aequalis aequalis, Leptasterias aequalis nana, Leptasterias hexactis* (in part)
to 10 cm (4 in) across
s. BC to s. California
intertidal to subtidal

Unlike most sea stars, the female six-rayed star broods her young underneath her arched body. Tiny, fully formed juveniles eventually crawl off to fend for themselves.
A Eagle Point, San Juan Island, n. Washington
B Nakwakto Rapids, Slingsby Channel, c. BC

EC28. SUNFLOWER STAR, sunflower sea star, sunflower starfish, many rayed star, twentyarm star, twenty-rayed star, twenty-rayed sea star, twenty-rayed starfish

Pycnopodia helianthoides, Asterias helianthoides
to 1 m (39 in) across, 5 kg (11 lbs) weight
n. Alaska to n. Mexico
▶intertidal to 314 m (1,038 ft)**
The speediest of sea stars, this voracious predator may consume virtually any living organism in its path. It is the largest sea star on the planet and may have up to 26 arms bearing a grand total of 15,000 tube feet!
Egmont Marina, Egmont, s. BC

EC29. ROSE STAR, rose sea star, rose starfish, snowflake star, snowflake sea star, spiny sun star, spiny sunstar, common sun star
***Crossaster papposus**, Solaster papposus, Asterias papposus*
to 34 cm (14 in) across
circumpolar, south to China and Japan, also south to New Jersey and Britain, n. Alaska to n. Washington
intertidal to 1,200 m (4,000 ft)
Extremely variable of pattern if not colour, the rose star is a denizen of low-current locales and almost always has 11 rays.
Moore Point, Francis Peninsula, s. BC

EC30. MORNING SUN STAR, morning sunstar, morning sun sea star, morning sun starfish, Dawson's sun star, Dawson's sea star
Solaster dawsoni
to 40 cm (16 in) across
China, Japan, Siberia, n. Alaska to c. California
intertidal to 420 m (1,386 ft)
A connoisseur of other sea stars, this predator will even pursue the larger sunflower star (EC28). The "small" predator chasing the larger prey is a strange sight indeed!
A Sutton Islets, Egmont, s. BC
B Laura Point, Mayne Island, s. BC

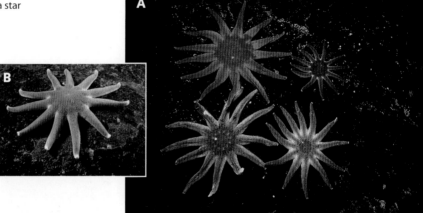

EC31. ORANGE SUNSTAR, evening sun sea star
Solaster paxillatus
to 37 cm (15 in) across
Siberia, Japan, n. Alaska to n. Oregon
subtidal, 11–640 m (35–2,112 ft)
The 8 to 10 quickly tapering rays of this star, together with its orange upper side and yellow underside, are the most obvious features. It is primarily a northern species, of which only a handful have been recorded south of Alaska.
Pearse Islands, Weynton Passage, c. BC

EC32. STRIPED SUN STAR, striped sunstar, striped sun starfish, Stimpson's sun star, Stimpson's sunstar, Stimpson's star, Stimpson's sea star, sun star, sun sea star, sun starfish, orange sun star
Solaster stimpsoni
to 50 cm (20 in) across
Japan, n. Alaska to c. California
▶intertidal to 201 m (663 ft)**
Dark stripes radiating from the centre to the tips of the arms that are narrower than those of the preceding species are distinctive. This feature may be difficult to see in a dark specimen as recorded in the photograph.
Turn Island, San Juan Channel, n. Washington

EC33. NORTHERN SUN STAR, northern sunstar, northern sun sea star, smooth sunstar, purple sun star
Solaster endeca, Asterias endeca
to 40 cm (16 in) across
circumboreal, south to Cape Cod and Britain, n. Alaska to n. Washington
intertidal to 475 m (1,550 ft)
Although this star closely resembles the morning sun star (EC30), creases at the "armpits" give it a puffy, overweight appearance. In the Pacific, this star's preferred prey are various sea cucumbers.
Eagle Point, San Juan Island, n. Washington

BRITTLE STARS

Including the basket star.

EC34. DAISY BRITTLE STAR, painted brittle star, painted brittlestar, painted serpent star, ubiquitous brittle star, rusty-red brittle star, serpent star
Ophiopholis aculeata
to 20 cm (8 in) across
circumpolar, n. Alaska to s. California
intertidal to 2,000 m (6,600 ft)
When extending its rays from under rocks or through sandstone holes, this brittle star is using them to catch small prey that drift with the current. It can also "mop up" detritus or decaying matter from the bottom with its mouth.
A Sutton Islets, Egmont, s. BC
B Agamemnon Channel, Sechelt Peninsula, s. BC

EC35. ►LONG-SPINED BRITTLE STAR
Ophiopholis longispina
►to 10 cm (4 in) across
BC to n. Mexico
subtidal, below 200 m (600 ft)
Over half of the Pacific Northwest brittle stars, including this species, live at depths in excess of 200 m (660 ft) and therefore are not accessible to most naturalists. Even those relatively few observers who might encounter them are unlikely to observe complete specimens of these easily damaged creatures.
Esperanza Inlet, w. Vancouver Island, c. BC

EC36. BLUNT-SPINED BRITTLE STAR, brittle star, serpent star
Ophiopteris papillosa
to 18 cm (7 in) across
s. BC to n. Mexico
intertidal to 140 m (462 ft)
This creature lives under rocks or hides in the holdfasts (root-like structures) of various large kelps. A surprisingly popular prey for various marine animals, brittle stars, like this one, are a food source for the China rockfish (VB38).
Monterey Bay, c. California. Daniel W. Gotshall photograph

EC37. LONG-ARMED BRITTLE STAR, snaky-armed brittle star
Amphiodia occidentalis, *Diamphiodia occidentalis*
to 37 cm (15 in) across
c. Alaska to s. California
intertidal to 360 m (1,200 ft)
This brittle star, which lives up to its common name, has extremely long rays that are easily broken off, even when the animal is carefully removed from under a rock. A lost appendage is readily regenerated by this and all brittle stars and their other echinoderm kin.
Miners Bay, Mayne Island, s. BC

EC38. DWARF BRITTLE STAR, small brittle star, small serpent star, serpent star, brooding brittle star, holdfast brittle star
Amphipholis squamata, *Axiognathus squamata*, *Amphiura squamata*
to 5 cm (2 in) across
cosmopolitan, Alaska to s. America
intertidal to 1,330 m (4,390 ft)
Look carefully for this tiny species under rocks set on sand or gravel. The writhing, serpent-like motion of a brittle star gives rise to the alternate name.
Tongue Point, Olympic coast, n. Washington

EC39. This **undetermined tiny brittle star** was found intertidally, living under rocks resting on a hard substrate in the same general habitat as the dwarf brittle star (EC38). Its identity could only be determined through close examination of its teeth, which unfortunately was impossible because the specimen was not retained.
Tongue Point, Olympic coast, n. Washington

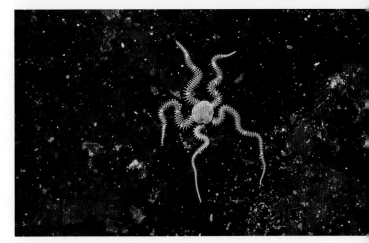

EC40. BLACK AND WHITE BRITTLE STAR, long armed brittle star, Puget Sound dwarf brittle star, dwarf brittle star
Amphipholis pugetana, *Axiognathus pugetana, Amphiura pugetana*
to 5 cm (2 in) across
Japan, n. Alaska to n. Mexico
intertidal to 604 m (1,993 ft)
This brittle star has very long arms that are 8 to 10 times the diameter of the disc-shaped body. It is known to eat tiny organisms called diatoms, as well as decaying matter or detritus.
Slip Point, Olympic coast, n. Washington

EC41. NOTCHED BRITTLE STAR, gray brittle star
Ophiura sarsii
to 15 cm (6 in) across
Japan, n. Alaska to c. California
subtidal, 3–3,000 m (10–10,000 ft)
Unlike a sea star that moves slowly by using thousands of tube feet, a brittle star pulls itself along the bottom using its flexible arms. This movement results from vertebrae-like ossicles down the centre of each arm. These articulating parts are linked by muscles that provide the locomotive power.
Helen Point, Mayne Island, s. BC

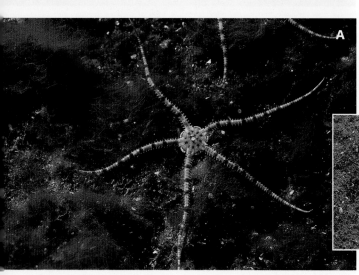

EC42. GRAY BRITTLE STAR
Ophiura lütkeni, *Ophiura luetkeni, Ophium luetkenii*
to 18 cm (7 in) across
n. Alaska to n. Mexico
subtidal, 9–1,265 m (30–4,185 ft)
Very similar to the notched brittle star (EC41), technically this brittle star differs only in the shape of minute spines on the edge of its arm comb, located at the top of each "armpit." Fortunately its banded arms with white spots appear to differentiate it.
A Point Cowan, Bowen Island, s. BC
B Agamemnon Channel, Nelson Island, s. BC

EC43. BURROWING BRITTLE STAR, long arm brittle star
Amphiodia periercta, *Diamphiodia periercta, Amphiodia urtica,* Amphiodia pelora, Amphiura urtica, Amphiodia barbarae, Ophiophragmus urtica*
to 30 cm (12 in) across
Siberia, BC to California
subtidal
Observant divers may notice the arms of this species protruding from silty or mud bottoms. Consequently it may not be recognized as a brittle star because the disc-shaped body is hidden from view. *Recent studies suggest that *Amphiodia urtica* is synonymous with this species.
Steilacoom, Puget Sound, c. Washington

EC44. ►TILE BRITTLE STAR
Ophiosphalma jolliense, *Ophiomuseum jolliensis*
to 12.5 cm (5 in) across
Japan, BC to Mexico
subtidal, 155–4,300 m (512–14,190 ft)
Unfortunately, only a few scientists have been inspired to study Pacific Northwest brittle stars, so minimal information on their biology is available. Phil Lambert of the Royal British Columbia Museum is one of these dedicated individuals and kindly identified several deep-water species, including this one.
Esperanza Inlet, w. Vancouver Island, c. BC

EC45. ►SNAKY BRITTLE STAR
Astroschema sublaeve
to 30 cm (12 in) across
BC to s. America
deep subtidal
The biology and life history of deep-water brittle stars remains a mystery, due primarily to their habitat and small size. Collecting and maintaining live specimens is challenging and expensive. Even with the advent of submersibles, it is nearly impossible to study them in their natural surroundings.
Esperanza Inlet, w. Vancouver Island, c. BC

EC46. BASKET STAR, common basket star
Gorgonocephalus eucnemis, *Gorgonocephalus japonicus, Gorgonocephalus caryi, Gorgonocephalus stimpsoni, Astrophyton eucnemis*
to 75 cm (30 in) across
Japan, Siberia, Greenland to Cape Cod, Spitzbergen, n. Alaska to s. California
►subtidal, 10–1,850 m (33–6,115 ft)
A close inspection of this spectacular creature shows that it has five arms that repeatedly branch "ad infinitum." When totally extended in a feeding posture, these appendages form a basket-like cage that ensnares planktonic prey, as shown in photograph A.
A Stubbs Island, Weynton Passage, c. BC
B Quadra Island, Discovery Passage, s. BC

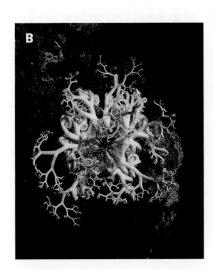

FEATHER STARS

EC47. FEATHER STAR, sea lily
Florometra serratissima, *Heliometra serratissima, Antedon serratissima, Florometra perplexa, Antedon perplexa*
to 25 cm (10 in) across
n. Alaska to n. Mexico, perhaps to s. America
subtidal, 10–1,252 m (33–4,108 ft)
This star is essentially an "upside-down brittle star" that feeds on plankton. If a diver dislodges one it will likely "walk up an invisible staircase" in the water column—an excellent subject for the underwater videographer. A stalked juvenile is portrayed in photograph C.

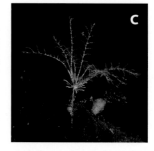

At least three other deep-dwelling sea lilies have been documented from the Pacific Northwest.
A Egmont Marina, Egmont, s. BC
B Sutton Islets, Egmont, s. BC
C Agamemnon Channel, Nelson Island, s. BC. Charlie Gibbs photograph

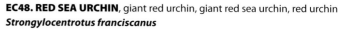

SEA URCHINS

Including the sand dollar.

EC48. RED SEA URCHIN, giant red urchin, giant red sea urchin, red urchin
Strongylocentrotus franciscanus
to 30 cm (12 in) across
Japan, n. Alaska to n. Mexico
intertidal to 125 m (412 ft)
Both divers and beachcombers may find the globular, spineless test (shell) that remains after this creature's passing (photograph B). In many locales where few of its predators remain, this herbivore's population can

completely overtake its algal food sources, resulting in overgrazed areas called urchin barrens.
A Sutton Islets, Egmont, s. BC
B Rebecca Rock, Algerine Passage, s. BC

EC49. PURPLE SEA URCHIN, purple urchin, purple spined sea urchin
Strongylocentrotus purpuratus
to 15 cm (6 in) across
c. Alaska to n. Mexico
intertidal to 65 m (215 ft)
Using its short, heavy spines, this urchin can excavate holes in "soft" rock—an activity that protects it from the crashing surf of the open coast. In this

scenario the urchin depends on drift algae for subsistence. Photograph B shows exposed intertidal specimens, including an unusual red one.
A Turn Island, San Juan Channel, n. Washington
B Tongue Point, Olympic coast, n. Washington

EC50. GREEN SEA URCHIN, green urchin
Strongylocentrotus droebachiensis
to 9 cm (3.6 in) across
circumpolar, Japan, n. Alaska to n. Washington
intertidal to 1,138 m (3,800 ft)
With much finer spines than the purple sea urchin (EC49), this species lives in locales away from direct surge. Sea urchins are active grazers that seek out various marine algae. Individuals browse with their five teeth, visible on the underside. These teeth are operated by a jaw-like structure called Aristotle's lantern.
A Point Cowan, Bowen Island, s. BC
B Vanderbilt Reef, Lynn Canal, s. Alaska

EC51. WHITE SEA URCHIN
Strongylocentrotus pallidus, Strongylocentrotus echinoides, Strongylocentrotus sachalinicus
to 9 cm (3.6 in) across
n. Atlantic Ocean, n. Alaska to Oregon
subtidal to 1,600 m (5,280 ft)
Pale tube feet and sparser, whitish spines distinguish this variably coloured species from the green sea urchin (EC50), with which it may coexist. The white sea urchin is also somewhat flatter. Like all sea urchins it uses its five teeth when browsing.
A B Turn Point, Stuart Island, n. Washington

EC52. HEART URCHIN
Brisaster latifrons, Schizaster latifrons, Brisaster townsendi
to 8 cm (3.2 in) long
Japan, n. Alaska to c. America
subtidal, 9–2,817 m (30–9,200 ft)
This deep-water sea urchin, which buries completely in soft sediments, is only seen as a bycatch of trawling or similar activities. The heart urchin's test (shell), more elongate than those of other sea urchins, is very delicate. As a result this detritus feeder seldom reaches the surface undamaged.
Trincomali Channel, Gulf Islands, s. BC

EC53. EXCENTRIC SAND DOLLAR, Pacific sand dollar, west coast sand dollar, common sand dollar, sand dollar, sand cookie, sea biscuit
Dendraster excentricus, Echinarachnius excentricus
to 10 cm (4 in) across
s. Alaska to n. Mexico
intertidal to 90 m (300 ft)
The smooth white tests (shells) of dead specimens are a favourite beachcombing treasure. Less often found are the rough, dark purple living ones. Like its "cousin" the sea urchin, the sand dollar is a vegetarian. Expeditions undertaken to sample the deep-water fauna off the coastal areas of the Pacific Northwest have documented at least 10 species of sea urchins and sea urchin-like creatures. These obscure animals await meaningful study.
Departure Bay, Nanaimo, s. BC

SEA CUCUMBERS

EC54. GIANT SEA CUCUMBER, giant red sea cucumber, giant red cucumber, California sea cucumber, California cucumber, large red cucumber, common sea cucumber, California stichopus
Parastichopus californicus, *Stichopus californicus*, *Holothuria californica*
to 50 cm (20 in) long
c. Alaska to n. Mexico
intertidal to 250 m (825 ft)
The giant sea cucumber uses its stubby white tentacles like dust mops to gather up its diet of decaying matter or detritus. When stressed by a predator, it can use its five longitudinal muscle bands to writhe about and escape. Many colour variants are shown in photograph A, and a juvenile is shown in photograph C.
A Sutton Islets, Egmont, s. BC
B Agamemnon Channel, Nelson Island, s. BC

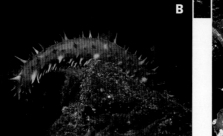

C Irvines Landing, Pender Harbour, s. BC

EC55. ▶LONG-SPINED SEA CUCUMBER
Synallectes challangeri, *Stichopus challangeri*
to 20 cm (8 in) long
Atlantic Ocean, s. Alaska to Chile
subtidal
Similar to the giant sea cucumber (EC54), the long-spined sea cucumber has longer "spines" and is a much more subdued pinkish grey in colour. The soft but formidable-looking spines may influence visual predators but are of little value against those without eyes.
Ocean Falls, Cousins Inlet, c. BC. Neil McDaniel photograph

EC56. GIANT ORANGE SEA CUCUMBER
Parastichopus leukothele
to 38 cm (15.2 in) long
n. BC to c. California
▶subtidal, 18–285 m (60–941 ft)
A special and rare find for a diver! To the touch, a sea cucumber is soft with no hint of the "spiny skin" nature of other echinoderms. However, embedded in its skin are countless tiny, well-spaced skeletal elements called ossicles.
Chup Point, Barkley Sound, s. BC

EC57. RED SEA CUCUMBER, red cucumber, orange sea cucumber, orange burrowing cucumber, red burrowing cucumber, vermilion sea cucumber, red sea gherkin

Cucumaria miniata, *Cladodactyla miniata, Stereoderma miniata, Cucumaria japonica, Cucumaria albida*
to 25 cm (10 in) long
n. Alaska to n. Mexico
intertidal to 225 m (743 ft)
Finely branched tentacles protrude from a tubular body that is usually

lodged under rocks or
other shelter. A feeding
specimen with a food-
laden tentacle inserted
in its mouth is shown in
photograph C.
A Turn Island, San Juan
Channel, n. Washington
B Barrow Point, Nakwakto
Rapids, c. BC
C Castle Point, Deserters
Island, c. BC

EC58. GIANT BLACK CUCUMARIA

Cucumaria frondosa japonica, *Cucumaria frondosa*
to 30 cm (12 in) long
Arctic Ocean, s. Alaska to c. BC
subtidal, 25–130 m (83–430 ft)
A black or grey body and tentacles are characteristic of this species, which is most common in the northern portion of its range. When disturbed, it swells into a football shape. Some debate continues as to whether the term *japonica* represents a species or subspecies designation.

Mouth of McMaster River, Resolute Bay, Nunavut. Danny Kent photograph

EC59. PALE SEA CUCUMBER

Cucumaria pallida
to 25 cm (10 in) long
s. Alaska to s. California
intertidal to 91 m (300 ft)
This pale species has more delicate-looking white tentacles when compared to those of the similar red sea cucumber (EC57). Many sea cucumber species are most obvious in summer, when their tentacles are actively capturing abundant planktonic prey. During winter months, when food is scarce, these creatures appear to "hibernate."

Agamemnon Channel, Nelson Island, s. BC

EC60. STIFF-FOOTED SEA CUCUMBER, stiff-footed cucumber, white sea cucumber, white cucumber, white sea gherkin, white gherkin

Eupentacta quinquesemita, *Cucumaria quinquesemita, Cucumaria chronhjelmi*
to 10 cm (4 in) long
Japan, s. Alaska to n. Mexico
intertidal to 55 m (183 ft)
The tube feet of this species are stiff to the touch because of abundant ossicles (skeletal elements) within the skin and tube feet. A second nearly identical species, the false white sea cucumber, *Eupentacta pseudoquinquesemita*, has more flexible tube feet.

Turn Island, San Juan Channel, n. Washington

EC61. AGGREGATING SEA CUCUMBER

Pseudocnus lubricus*, Pseudocnus lubrica, Cucumaria fisheri astigmata*
to 4 cm (1.6 in) long
 s. Alaska to c. California
intertidal to 78 m (257 ft)
Although nearly identical anatomically to the black sea cucumber *Pseudocnus curatus* EC67, this species is often white as shown in the photograph. If specimens are dark, species determination requires DNA study and detailed inspection of ossicles (skeletal elements).
Long Island, near Lopez Island, n. Washington

EC62. ▶U-SHAPED WHITE SEA CUCUMBER

Pentamera pseudocalcigera*, Cucumaria calcigera*
to 10 cm (4 in) long
s. Alaska to n. Mexico
subtidal, 13–448 m (43–1,478 ft)
This species, with its more tapering posterior, is one of several in the genus *Pentamera*. Technically, only close inspection of the tiny calcareous ossicles (skeletal elements) in its skin enables precise identification. Its U-shaped body suggests that it lives in mud or silt with both ends at the surface. Three other small, white sea cucumbers that are similar to the U-shaped white sea cucumber live in the Pacific Northwest. They are the ▶rough-plated sea cucumber, *Pentamera trachyplaca*, the ▶abundant sea cucumber, *Pentamera populifera*, and the ▶smooth-plated sea cucumber, *Pentamera lissoplaca*.
Mouth of Fraser River, Strait of Georgia, s. BC

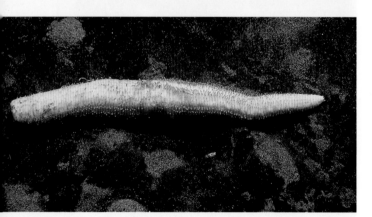

EC63. ▶ELONGATE WHITE SEA CUCUMBER

Pseudothyone levini
to 14 cm (5.5 in) long
n. BC to n. Washington
intertidal to 70 m (231 ft)
Since his excellent book on sea cucumbers (*Sea Cucumbers of British Columbia, Southeastern Alaska and Puget Sound*) was published in 1997, Phil Lambert has formally described this species. In a further update, his *Pentamera* species A is now designated as *Pentamera rigida* (▶rigid white sea cucumber) and *Pentamera* species B is now officially *Pentamera pediparva* (▶small footed white sea cucumber).
Point Defiance, Puget Sound, n. Washington

EC64. BURROWING SEA CUCUMBER, skin-breathing cucumber

Leptosynapta clarki*, Leptosynapta inhaerens, Synapta inhaerens, Leptosynapta albicans, Synapta albicans, Leptosynapta roxtona*
to 14.6 cm (5.8 in) long
n. BC to c. California
intertidal to 73 m (240 ft)
With its characteristic feeding tentacles withdrawn, the burrowing sea cucumber looks more like a worm than a sea cucumber. Its five distinctive muscle bands usually show through its transparent skin. This species prefers to nestle amid eelgrass roots (SW2).
A second species, the ▶subtidal burrowing sea cucumber, *Leptosynapta transgressor,* is very similar but lives at greater depths.
Skyline Marina, Fidalgo Island, n. Washington

EC65. ▶BENT SEA CUCUMBER
Thyone benti, *Havelockia benti*
to 15 cm (6 in) long
n. BC to n. Mexico
subtidal to 135 m (446 ft)
This rarely found sea cucumber is distinguished from most others by its tube feet, which are scattered along its body rather than forming five distinct rows. This feature, combined with its 10 feeding tentacles, is definitive of the bent sea cucumber.
Queen Charlotte Channel, Howe Sound, s. BC

EC66. SALT AND PEPPER SEA CUCUMBER, peppered sea cucumber
Cucumaria piperata, *Pentacta piperata*, *Pseudocnus piperata*, *Cucumaria nigricans*
to 13 cm (5.3 in) long
n. BC to n. Mexico
intertidal to 250 m (825 ft)
Dark speckling on the tentacles and black spots on the whitish body are distinctive for this sea cucumber. Usually it is concealed under cover, with only tentacles exposed, as shown in photograph B.
A Moore Point, Francis Peninsula, s. BC
B Gerald Island, Ballenas Channel, s. BC

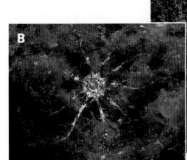

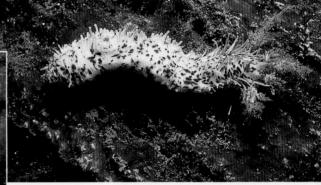

EC67. BLACK SEA CUCUMBER, tar spot
Pseudocnus curatus, *Cucumaria curata*
to 3 cm (1.2 in) long
Alaska/BC border to c. California
intertidal to 20 m (66 ft)
Extensive fields of this species may cover rock outcrops, and when feeding, they give the bottom a dark plush appearance as illustrated in photograph A.
A B Eagle Point, San Juan Island, n. Washington

EC68. TAR SPOT SEA CUCUMBER
Cucumaria pseudocurata
to 3.5 cm (1.5 in) long
n. BC to c. California
intertidal
This sea cucumber is similar to the black sea cucumber (EC67), but it most often associates with the California mussel (MC34). Look for it nestling with or nearby this bivalve. To be certain, though, examine the tentacles. The tar spot sea cucumber usually has eight large and two small ones, rather than 10 equal-sized structures as in the black sea cucumber (EC67).
Butress Island, Slingsby Channel, c. BC

EC69. ▶TINY BLACK SEA CUCUMBER

Cucumaria vegae

▶to 4 cm (1.6 in) long

Japan, n. Alaska to n. BC

intertidal

Externally the tiny black sea cucumber is virtually identical to the tar spot sea cucumber (EC68), and only careful inspection of the ossicles (skeletal elements buried in the skin) can distinguish them. Fortunately, distribution appears to help: specimens found north of the Queen Charlotte Islands (Haida Gwaii), BC, are this species.

Point Lena, Juneau, s. Alaska

EC70. ▶FURRY SEA CUCUMBER

Thyonidium kurilensis, *Duasmodactyla kurilensis*

to 20 cm (8 in) long

Kuril Islands, Russia, and c. Alaska to n. Washington

subtidal, 10–228 m (33–750 ft)

The shallow-dwelling specimens in the photograph were found in angular gravel, with only the bushy tentacles protruding from the central individual. Twenty tentacles, a high number for a sea cucumber, look particularly dense. The animal's copious and scattered tube feet allow for positive identification.

The ▶northern furry sea cucumber, *Ekmania diomedeae,* is similar but rarely encountered in the Pacific Northwest.

Cactus Islands, New Channel, n. Washington

EC71. ▶WHITE-DOTTED SEA CUCUMBER

Chiridota albatrossii, *Chiridota laevis*

to 30 cm (12 in) long

Japan, Siberia, s. Alaska to Oregon

▶subtidal, 10–732 m (33–2,316 ft)

Shrimp trawlers, who use fine-meshed nets, sometimes drag their gear over thick beds of this sea cucumber and completely clog their bag-like equipment. Observant scuba divers venturing over mud bottoms may occasionally see this species as well.

Several other species of *Chiridota* have been described but their validity is under review.

Grey Rocks Island, Indian Arm, s. BC

EC72. SWEET POTATO SEA CUCUMBER

Molpadia intermedia, *Trochostoma intermedium*

to 43 cm (17 in) long

s. Alaska to s. America

subtidal, 7–2,900 m (23–9,570 ft)

This "blimp" or sausage-shaped sea cucumber burrows in mud or silt, from which it probably extracts its nourishment. The specimens shown in the photograph were collected as part of Environment Canada's ongoing monitoring of ocean dump sites and were obtained courtesy of biologist Dixie Sullivan.

Rarely encountered, the rattail sea cucumber, *Paracaudina chiliensis,* is distinguished by its very long tail-like posterior.

Mouth of Fraser River, Strait of Georgia, s. BC

EC73. CREEPING PEDAL SEA CUCUMBER, creeping pedal cucumber, armored sea cucumber, armored cucumber, creeping armored sea cucumber, creeping armored cucumber, slipper sea cucumber
Psolus chitonoides, *Psolus californicus*
to 7 cm (2.8 in) long
Japan, n. Alaska to n. Mexico
intertidal to 250 m (825 ft)
Flip a specimen from a rock and notice the tube feet on the flat pad underneath. This feature readily separates this strange sea cucumber from the somewhat similar-looking chitons. Photograph B shows an individual with its tentacles retracted.
A Agamemnon Channel, Sechelt Peninsula, s. BC
B Agamemnon Channel, Nelson Island, s. BC

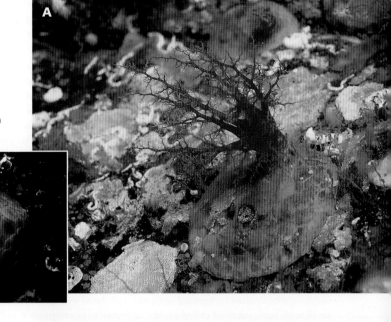

EC74. PALE CREEPING PEDAL SEA CUCUMBER
Psolidium bidiscum, incorrect: *Psolidium bullatum*
to 3 cm (1.2 in) long
s. Alaska to c. California
intertidal to 220 m (725 ft)
A miniature version of the creeping pedal sea cucumber (EC73), this one is pink instead of orange. With its tentacles withdrawn, it hardly resembles a sea cucumber at all. In late spring and summer, a brown diatom layer may grow over this creature and hide it from view, especially when its tentacles are withdrawn.
Tuwanek Point, Sechelt Inlet, s. BC

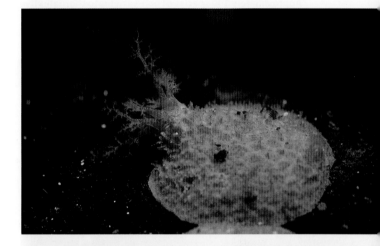

EC75. ▶WHITE CREEPING PEDAL SEA CUCUMBER
Psolus squamatus, *Cuvieria squamatus*, *Psolus pauper*
to 13 cm (5.3 in) long
Norway, n. Alaska to s. Chile
subtidal, 37–1,061 m (122–3,500 ft)
Sport scuba enthusiasts, particularly "techies" (technical divers), may find this sea cucumber on very deep sorties, most likely in steep-walled fjords. Its white tentacles and white or pinkish white body are definitive. Photograph B depicts a specimen with withdrawn tentacles.
The number of sea cucumbers included here seems impressive, but nearly as many living within Pacific Northwest waters are not included. These species exist in very deep waters and many have only been collected once or twice.
A B Caldwell Island, Agamemnon Channel, s. BC

TUNICATES, SALPS, ACORN WORMS AND OTHERS *Phylum CHORDATA*

Includes tunicates or sea squirts, sea porks, ascidians and salps as well as the vertebrates.

A hollow nerve cord supported by a firm but flexible notochord (stiffening rod) defines this group. Throat slits called stigmata or pharyngeal perforations, features common to chordates, are only found in the earliest life stages of all advanced members of the group. In the vertebrates (p. 361) this brief stage steadily gives way, through embryological development, to a more complex and recognizable adult anatomy. With tunicates and salps, on the other hand, this early stage—called a tadpole larva—metamorphoses into a totally different adult form, as a caterpillar turns into a butterfly. In tunicates the stigmata divide many times and form a large filtering sac for feeding on tiny plankton.

Essentially an adult tunicate is a fine-mesh filtering sac and associated internal organs within a tough external sac made of a cellulose-like material called tunicin. The basic tunicate is attached to something solid and has two openings at the top called siphons. Two different species of solitary tunicates illustrating this basic design are featured in photograph A: yellow-coloured disc-top tunicate (CH16) and orange broadbase tunicate (CH7). Plankton-laden seawater enters through the in-current siphon, filters through the mesh bag and exits through the ex-current siphon. Colonial versions, often called compound tunicates, consist of variously interdependent but small basic tunicate units called zooids, as shown in photograph B: red ascidian (CH35).

Approximately 100 species of non-vertebrate chordates live in the marine waters of the Pacific Northwest.

SOLITARY TUNICATES

Including sea squirts, ascidians, sea vase, sea blisters and sea peach.

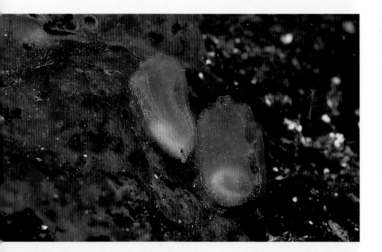

CH1. TRANSPARENT TUNICATE, transparent sea squirt, solitary tunicate
Corella willmeriana, *Corella rugosa*
to 7.5 cm (3 in) tall
s. Alaska to s. California
subtidal to 75 m (250 ft)
So transparent is this tunicate that the internal anatomy can be seen through its outer tunic, the layer that gives the creature its common name. Notice the rectum filled with waste products—the most noticeable part of its anatomy. The spotted flatworm (PL1) is also often visible inside this tunicate.
Moore Point, Francis Peninsula, s. BC

CH2. BROODING TRANSPARENT TUNICATE, transparent tunicate, solitary tunicate
Corella inflata
to 5 cm (2 in) tall
n. BC to n. Washington
intertidal to 50 m (165 ft)
A more cubic shape distinguishes this species from the transparent tunicate (CH1). The brooding transparent tunicate is most likely found shallower than 10 m (33 ft) and commonly attaches to floats and pilings. An adult retains its young in an enlarged brood chamber, further differentiating this one from its non-brooding look-alike. Look closely to see the embryos— even without magnification.
Agamemnon Channel, Nelson Island, s. BC

CH3. SEA VASE, smooth sea bottle, simple tunicate, yellow-green sea squirt
Ciona savignyi, incorrect: *Ciona intestinalis*
to 15 cm (6 in) tall
cosmopolitan, n. Alaska to s. California
intertidal to 500 m (1,650 ft)
More elongate and delicate than the transparent or brooding transparent tunicate (CH1/2), the sea vase is often found in crevices or holes. Unique populations in Sechelt Inlet, BC, are particularly spectacular, forming huge clusters that carpet the rocky bottom (photograph B).
A Moore Point, Francis Peninsula, s. BC
B Four Mile Point, Sechelt Inlet, s. BC

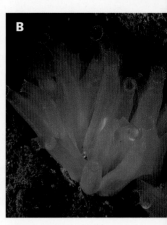

CH4. GLASSY TUNICATE, glassy sea squirt, warty sea bubble
Ascidia paratropa, *Ascidiopsis paratropa*
to 15 cm (6 in) tall
n. Alaska to c. California
intertidal to 100 m (330 ft)
This large, obvious tunicate has an opaque appearance with pointed "bumps" and is waxy to the touch. Each solitary tunicate has two siphons, an in-current one that brings in the food-laden water and an ex-current one that expels the filtered product.
Moore Point, Francis Peninsula, s. BC

CH5. SEA BLISTERS, flattened sea squirts
Ascidia columbiana/Ascidia callosa, *Ascidiopsis columbiana*, perhaps *Ascidiella griffini*
to 5 cm (2 in) across
Kamchatka, n. Alaska to Washington
intertidal to 20 m (65 ft) at least
Earlier publications unknowingly included this species in the *Ascidia callosa* designation. In 2001, after much diligent work, tunicate expert Dr. Gretchen Lambert demonstrated that *Ascidia columbiana* is a legitimate species. It differs by having a dense circle of papillae (fleshy projections) around each siphon. Specimens found south of Alaska are likely *Ascidia columbiana*; northern populations are probably *Ascidia callosa*.
Another similar species, the California sea squirt, *Ascidia ceratodes,* is most likely encountered south of the Pacific Northwest.
Point Cowan, Bowen Island, s. BC

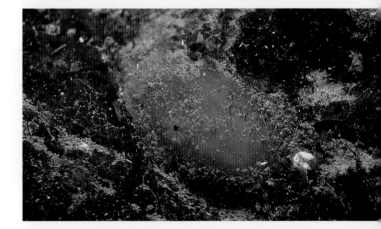

CH6. ▶TINY WHITE TUNICATE
Bathypera feminalba, possibly: *Bathypera ovoida*
to 2 cm (0.8 in) across
s. BC to c. California
▶subtidal, 20–100 m (65–330 ft)
Especially when its siphons are closed, this tiny species is difficult to recognize as a tunicate. Close inspection will show not only the tiny slits, but a pattern of interwoven white lines that give the creature a mesh-like appearance due to a covering of tiny, spined calcareous spicules embedded in the tunic.
Worlcombe Island, Howe Sound, s. BC

CH7. BROADBASE TUNICATE, broad-base sea squirt, broad base sea squirt, shiny red tunicate, red sea squirt, shiny orange sea squirt, brilliant red hide tunicate, solitary tunicate, Finmark's tunicate
Cnemidocarpa finmarkiensis, *Cnemidocarpa joannae, Styela stimpsoni, Polycarpa finmarkiensis, Styela finmarkiensis, Styela elsa, Tethyum finmarkiensis*, misspelled: *Cnemidocarpa finmarchiensis*
to 5 cm (2 in) across
circumboreal, Japan, s. Alaska to c. California
intertidal to 50 m (165 ft)
This tunicate is identified by its squat stature, square-shaped siphon openings and smooth red tunic.
Pasley Island, Howe Sound, s. BC

CH8. PACIFIC SEA PEACH, sea peach
Halocynthia aurantium, *Tethyum aurantium*, misspelled: *Halocynthia auvantium*
to 15 cm (6 in) tall
Japan, Siberia, n. Alaska to California
subtidal to 100 m (330 ft)
A very distinctive species. Nearly all tunicates are hermaphroditic, meaning that each adult specimen has both male and female organs. However, self-fertilization, usually a reproductive disadvantage, is avoided by eggs and sperm being released at different times.
Mutine Point, Barkley Sound, s. BC

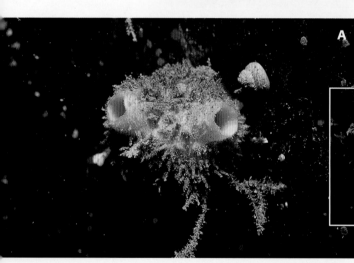

CH9. BRISTLY TUNICATE, spiny sea squirt, sea hedgehog
Halocynthia igaboja, *Halocynthia hispida, Halocynthia hilgendorfi, Halocynthia hilgendorfi igaboja*
to 10 cm (4 in) tall
Japan, s. Alaska to s. California
intertidal to 165 m (550 ft)
In low-current locales, the distinctive flexible bristles of this tunicate may be so silted that the animal is nearly undetectable, especially when the telltale orange siphons are collapsed. The two photographs show variation within this species.
A Pasley Island, Howe Sound, s. BC
B Nelson Rock, Malaspina Strait, s. BC

CH10. WARTY TUNICATE, warty sea squirt, wrinkled sea squirt, wrinkled seapump, decorator tunicate, solitary tunicate, solitary sea squirt
Pyura haustor, *Halocynthia haustor, Halocynthia johnsoni, Halocynthia washingtoni, Cynthia haustor*
to 8 cm (3.2 in) tall
n. Alaska to s. California
intertidal to 200 m (660 ft)
This tunicate is often obscured by other creatures growing on its wrinkled body. Its long, pink or red siphons are the best indicator of its presence. A cluster of specimens and a solitary individual (at left) show in the photograph.
Moore Point, Francis Peninsula, s. BC

CH11. ▶ALADDIN'S LAMP TUNICATE
Pyura mirabilis
to 10 cm (4 in) across
Japan, Korea, BC to s. California
intertidal to 60 m (200 ft)
Search for this strange-looking tunicate, with its horizontally protruding siphons, either in crevices or under rocks. A tunicate can respond to touch, light, temperature and chemical stimuli, but to date no specialized receptors for these inputs have been found by those who study this group. Photographer and author Bernie Hanby provided the common name.
Croker Island, Indian Arm, s. BC

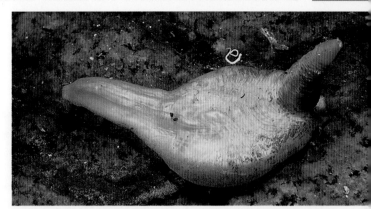

CH12. BROWN TUNICATE, peanut sea squirt, sea peanut, short-stalked baseball club tunicate
Styela gibbsii, Styela gibbsi, Cynthia gibbsii
to 4 cm (1.5 in) tall
BC to s. California
intertidal to 91 m (310 ft)
A tunicate is your closest invertebrate relative?! This sac with two holes actually has a tadpole-like larva with a notochord—a primitive version of a spine. This suggests that a common ancestor may exist in our distant past. The ▶leathery tunicate, *Styela coriacea,* is attached by its basal side and has a wrinkled and brown exterior.
Lee Bay, Pender Harbour, s. BC

CH13. CLUB TUNICATE
Styela clava, Styela barnharti
to 15 cm (6 in) tall
Australia, Japan, Asian North Pacific Ocean, n.w. European harbours, Atlantic Canada, s. BC to s. California
intertidal to 25 m (80 ft)
Native to the western Pacific, this adaptable tunicate has only recently taken hold in a few Pacific Northwest harbours—a probable result of transport by ship from the Orient. Distinguished by its short, broad stalk and tubercles (bumps), it is a prized seafood in Korea called mideuduck. A very similar species, the corrugated sea bottle, *Styela yakutatensis,* thrives farther north in Alaska. It has apparently also been found in BC waters. It varies from the club tunicate (CH13) in its bright red siphons and fewer tunic tubercles. Brooding larvae can usually be found in its atrial cavity.
A B Blaine Marina, Blaine, n. Washington

CH14. STALKED TUNICATE, Monterey stalked tunicate, stalked simple tunicate, Monterey stalked sea squirt, long-stalked sea squirt, stalked sea squirt, baseball club tunicate, Monterey tunicate, tidepool tunicate, California styela
Styela montereyensis
to 30 cm (12 in) tall
c. BC to n. Mexico
intertidal to 30 m (100 ft)
Look intertidally along exposed, surf-swept shores for this slender, long-stalked version of the club tunicate (CH13). It may be encrusted with other life, as shown in photograph A.
A Denny Island, Lama Passage, c. BC
B Frank Island, w. Vancouver Island, s. BC

CH15. HAIRY TUNICATE, spiny-headed tunicate, strawberry sea squirt, hairy sea squirt, stalked hairy sea squirt, bristly tunicate, shaggy tunicate
Boltenia villosa, *Halocynthia villosa*, *Cynthia villosa*
to 10 cm (4 in) tall
s. Alaska to s. California
intertidal to 100 m (330 ft)

Usually but not always "stalked," this species is often silted over when located in low-current areas.

Another similar species is the spiny-tipped tunicate, *Boltenia echinata*. It differs from the hairy tunicate (CH15) in that it is never stalked and has few hair-like spines. More important, each spine has a circle of four to eight tiny "spinelets" at the top. The spiny-tipped tunicate appears to be less common than the hairy tunicate, but this observation is likely a result of sampling bias.

A Quarry Bay, Nelson Island, s. BC
B Laura Point, Mayne Island, s. BC

CH16. DISC-TOP TUNICATE, flattop sea squirt, horseshoe sea squirt, horseshoe ascidian
Chelyosoma productum
to 2.7 cm (1.1 in) across

c. Alaska to s. California
intertidal to 50 m (165 ft)
This squat tunicate has triangular "flaps," which seal off siphon openings when disturbed. It may live as a solitary individual or carpeting vast areas of rocky walls. Like other tunicates, its outer body wall consists of a cellulose-like substance called tunicin. Photograph B shows more rounded individuals.

A Barrow Point, Seymour Inlet, c. BC
B Carter Bay, Princess Royal Channel, n. BC

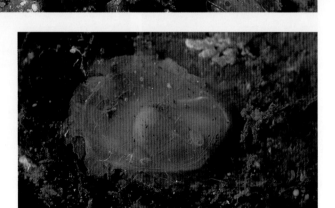

CH17. ▶TRANSPARENT DISC-TOP TUNICATE
Chelyosoma columbianum
▶to 2.5 cm (1 in) across
BC to c. California
subtidal
Somewhat flatter and more transparent than the disc-top tunicate (CH16), this tunicate is for some reason less commonly observed by divers. An adult tunicate attaches to a solid object by means of small villi (spreading processes). An unidentified juvenile tunicate is growing on top of the specimen pictured here.
Agamemnon Channel, Nelson Island, s. BC

CH18. GLOBULAR ASCIDIAN
Molgula pacifica
to 2.5 cm (1 in) tall
▶s. Alaska to Washington
intertidal to subtidal
If undisturbed, this small tunicate, with one orange siphon extending much farther than its companion, is noticeable. With siphons retracted, the globular ascidian is virtually invisible because its body is usually festooned with tiny bits of shell or sand. Specimens of a small unidentified tunicate are also visible in photograph A, to the left of the pertinent species. Photograph B shows the complete body of a globular ascidian with its siphons retracted.

A Laura Point, Mayne Island, s. BC
B Baranof Hot Springs, Baranof Island, s. Alaska

CH19. ►EASTERN GLOBULAR ASCIDIAN
Molgula manhattensis
to 2.5 cm (1 in) tall
Australia, China, Japan, n. Atlantic Ocean, c. Washington to s. California
(introduced to many areas including the Pacific Northwest)
intertidal to subtidal
During a dive at Westport, Washington, in 2005, this interloper, a rather
plain species that originated in the Orient, was found in abundance
attached to marina floats. Previously it had been documented only as far
north as California.

Westport Marina, Westport, c. Washington

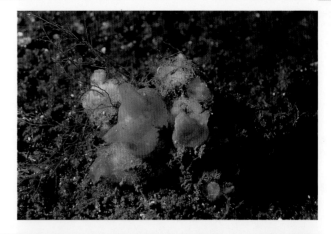

SOCIAL TUNICATES

CH20. ORANGE SOCIAL TUNICATE, orange social sea squirt, orange social
ascidians, red sea buttons, Taylor's colonial tunicate, colonial tunicate
Metandrocarpa taylori
to 2 cm (0.8 in) tall
s. Alaska to s. California
►intertidal to 30 m (100 ft)
Crowded together but appearing separate,
individuals are interconnected by thin strands
of tissue. Photograph B illustrates that in spite
of the name, individuals may occasionally be
yellow or yellow-green.
A Sutton Islets, Egmont, s. BC
B Keystone, Whidbey Island, n. Washington. Charlie
Gibbs photograph

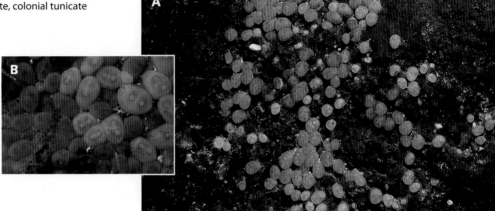

CH21. FUSED ORANGE SOCIAL ASCIDIAN
Metandrocarpa dura
to 0.6 cm (0.2 in) tall
BC to s. California
subtidal
In contrast to the orange social tunicate (CH20), individuals of this tunicate
are tightly packed within a common layer. The fused orange social ascidian
is much more likely to be found in the southern portion of its range and
normally occurs in regions of heavy surf.

Monterey, s. California. Daniel W. Gotshall photograph

CH22. YELLOW SOCIAL TUNICATE, sea grapes, yellow-green creeping
tunicate
Perophora annectens
to 0.6 cm (0.2 in) tall
s. Alaska to s. California
intertidal to 30 m (100 ft)
Single specimens are much smaller and more transparent than yellow
individuals of the orange social tunicate (CH20). Amazingly, a tunicate
heart can pump in either direction. Two mauve-coloured juveniles of the
mushroom compound tunicate (CH27) are located at centre-left of the
photograph.

The Gorge, Cortes Island, s. BC

CH23. LIGHT-BULB TUNICATE, light bulb tunicate, lightbulb tunicate, light bulb ascidian, social tunicate
Clavelina huntsmani
to 5 cm (2 in) tall
s. BC to n. Mexico
intertidal to 30 m (100 ft)
This tunicate, which almost always grows in clusters along coastlines directly exposed to the open ocean, is easily recognized by the two luminescent pink lines that resemble the glowing filaments of a light bulb. These structures are part of the food-collecting pharynx in this filter feeder.
Fox Islands, Slingsby Channel, c. BC

CH24. YELLOW SOCIAL ASCIDIAN, social tunicate
Pycnoclavella stanleyi
to 2 cm (0.8 in) tall
s. BC to n. Mexico
intertidal to 20 m (65 ft)
Each tiny transparent individual has a horizontally oriented, swirl-like structure inside. This structure is the pharynx. Bright yellow-orange individuals are also common, and the colour variants form common assemblages. Individuals are much smaller than those of the light-bulb tunicate (CH23).
Laura Point, Mayne Island, s. BC

COMPOUND TUNICATES

Including ascidians, sea pork, white crusts and glove leathers.

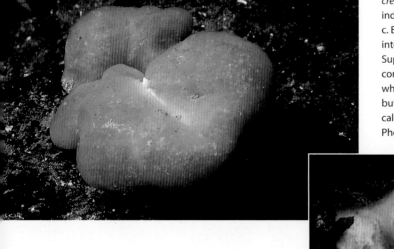

A

B

CH25. LOBED COMPOUND TUNICATE, lobed tunicate, lobed ascidian
Cystodytes lobatus, *Distoma lobatus*, *Eudistoma lobatum*, *Cystodytes cretaceus*
indeterminate, irregular size
c. BC to n. Mexico
intertidal to 200 m (660 ft)
Superficially sponge-like, this species has a slick, "wet leather" feel. A compound tunicate comprises countless tiny individuals called zooids, which are basically the same design as the yellow social ascidian (CH24) but interconnected and enveloped in a common matrix. Tiny disc-shaped calcareous spicules in the tunic form a cup around each zooid's abdomen. Photograph B shows a small developing colony.

A Laura Point, Mayne Island, s. BC
B Stubbs Island, Weynton Passage, c. BC

CH26. ▶MAUVE LOBED COMPOUND TUNICATE
***Eudistoma purpuropunctatum**, Archidistoma* sp.
indeterminate, irregular size
▶s. Alaska to n. Washington
subtidal
Superficially this species resembles the lobed compound tunicate (CH25)—except for its colour and the fact that it lacks spicules. Unfortunately, this second factor is of little help to most diving naturalists.
Tyler Rock, Barkley Sound, s. BC

CH27. MUSHROOM COMPOUND TUNICATE, mushroom tunicate, mushroom ascidian, club tunicate, western distaplia, colonial tunicate
***Distaplia occidentalis**, Distaplia californica*
to 12.5 cm (5 in) across colony
s. Alaska to s. California
intertidal to 20 m (65 ft)
Comprising "mushroom-like" zooid clusters, coloured with multiple pastel shades, this species is perhaps the most beautiful of all the Pacific Northwest tunicates.
Laura Point, Mayne Island, s. BC

CH28. ▶PALE MUSHROOM COMPOUND TUNICATE
***Aplidiopsis pannosum**, Polyclinum pannosum*
to 5 cm (2 in) across colony
n. Alaska to n. Washington
subtidal
For the amateur naturalist who uses external anatomy to identify species, it is very difficult to distinguish many of the compound tunicates. For example, this one appears as a colourless, somewhat flaccid version of the mushroom compound tunicate (CH27). Identification, using this photograph and specimen, was made by Dr. Gretchen Lambert, a tunicate expert.
Worlcombe Island, Howe Sound, s. BC

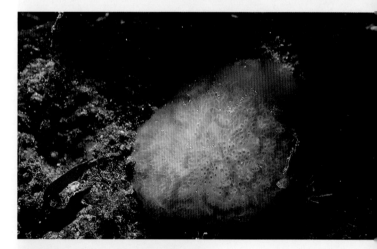

CH29. STALKED COMPOUND TUNICATE, paddle ascidian, Smith's distaplia
Distaplia smithi
to 10 cm (4 in) tall
c. Alaska to c. California
intertidal to 15 m (50 ft)
Living along exposed shores, this species' distinctive stalked, club-like colonies sway back and forth with the constant ocean swell. The more exposed the locale, the more abundant this tunicate seems to be, suggesting that there are certain, as yet unknown, conditions present that this tunicate requires.
Butress Island, Slingsby Channel, c. BC

CH30. ▶CLUBBED COMPOUND TUNICATE
Distaplia **sp.**
▶to 4 cm (1.6 in) tall
▶BC to Washington
▶subtidal to 20 m (65 ft)

Unfortunately for the amateur naturalist, compound tunicates are difficult to identify without dissection, access to a microscope and detailed jargon-intensive identification keys—all of which are impractical for the diver or beachcomber. Below the orange and tan clubbed compound tunicates in the photograph are a number of fringed filament-worms (AN58).
The ▶tunic-band compound tunicate, *Euherdmania claviformis*, which is primarily a California species, has been documented from Friday Harbor, n. Washington. Its elongate, almost transparent lobes distinguish it from the clubbed compound tunicate (CH30).

Outer Narrows, Slingsby Channel, c. BC

CH31. ▶ORANGE COMPOUND TUNICATE
Ritterella pulchra, *Distoma pulchra*, *Sigillinaria pulchra*
to 4 cm (1.6 in) tall, colonies irregular, indeterminate size
c. Alaska to s. California
intertidal to shallow subtidal

This hardy exposed-coast species is accessible to the adventurous beachcomber. However, it prefers the surf zone, where stormy weather can create dangerous wave action. Consequently sand grains often become embedded in its colonies.

Frank Island, w. Vancouver Island, s. BC

CH32. ▶RED MUSHROOM COMPOUND TUNICATE
Ritterella rubra
to 3 cm (1.2 in) tall, colonies irregular, indeterminate size
BC to c. California
intertidal to shallow subtidal

Another of these "nasties" that defy on-site identification or later determination via a photograph. Fortunately, expert Val Macdonald of *Biologica Environmental Services*, Victoria, BC, had access to a sample and completed the identification.
Another similar species, the ▶orange mushroom compound tunicate, *Ritterella aequalisiphonis,* lives over virtually the same range.

Seapool Rocks, Barkley Sound, s. BC

CH33. In the Pacific Northwest and other cool northern regions, many colonial tunicates regress in winter, reabsorb the thorax and digestive system and store energy in the postabdomen. This results in a **resting phase**. In spring they grow a new thorax and abdomen from their food stores. Having examined the specimen pictured here, Dr. Gretchen Lambert believes it to be a species of ***Ritterella***—perhaps one of the three preceding species—shown in its dormant phase.

Baranof Hot Springs, Baranof Island, s. Alaska

CH34. CALIFORNIA SEA PORK, sea pork

***Aplidium californicum**, Amaroucium californicum*
indeterminate, irregular size
Alaska to n. Mexico, Galapagos Islands
intertidal to 85 m (280 ft)
This flaccid species spreads out over the substrate and other associated animals. After metamorphosing from a tadpole larva, a compound tunicate begins the benthic (bottom-dwelling) stage of its life as a single entity. Subsequently it buds asexually to produce additional tiny opaque zooids (individuals) accumulating under a common tunic. Photographs show two colour variants.
A Sechart Channel, Barkley Sound, s. BC
B Chibahdehl Rocks, Olympic coast, n. Washington

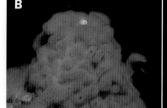

CH35. RED ASCIDIAN

***Aplidium solidum**, Amaroucium solidum*
to 20 cm (8 in) across colony
s. BC to s. California
intertidal to 40 m (130 ft)
One of the most vexing problems for the amateur naturalist is to distinguish compound tunicates from encrusting sponges. Often members of both groups lack an obvious structure and/or they have a similar "hole-bearing" appearance. We share your angst. Photograph B shows a nearly white colony.
A Waadah Island, Neah Bay, n. Washington
B Sekiu, Olympic coast, n. Washington

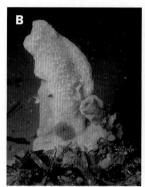
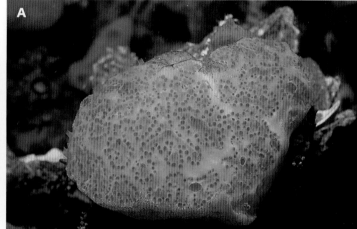

CH36. ▶SAND-EMBEDDED COMPOUND TUNICATE

***Aplidium propinquum**, Amaroucium propinquum*
to 5 cm (2 in) lobe length
▶c. BC to s. California
▶intertidal to 15 m (50 ft)
During a research expedition to Kyuquot Sound on the west side of Vancouver Island, Donna Gibbs of Port Coquitlam, BC, discovered a significant subtidal population of this species at Lookout Island. Until this find, the northern range limit of the species had been n. Washington. The ▶small sand-embedded compound tunicate, *Aplidium arenatum*, looks very similar but has more rounded lobes and is more diminutive.
Lookout Island, Kyuquot Sound, s. BC

CH37. ▶STUBBY STALKED COMPOUND TUNICATE
***Eudistoma** probable new species*
▶to 20 cm (8 in) across colony
▶n. BC
▶subtidal to 20 m (65 ft)
Superficially at least, this species is recognizable as a cluster of bulb-tipped stalks. After careful inspection and a thorough microscopic examination by Dr. Gretchen Lambert, an authority on Pacific Northwest tunicates, the specimen in this photograph was declared a probable new species. More specimens will be required before it can be properly described and receive a scientific name.
Boas Islet, Hakai Passage, c. BC

CH38. ▶RED-DOTTED COMPOUND TUNICATE
Eudistoma molle, *Archidistoma molle*
to 10 cm (4 in) across lobe
BC to c. California
intertidal to 10 m (33 ft)
The opaque white lobes with red-ended zooids showing through are distinctive for this species. Compound tunicates reproduce sexually and asexually. Once a sexually produced tadpole larva has settled and metamorphosed to start the colony, it grows larger by asexual budding.
A Weld Island, Barkley Sound, s. BC
B Sechart Channel, Barkley Sound, s. BC

CH39. LEATHERY COMPOUND TUNICATE, hard sheet tunicate
Eudistoma psammion, *Archidistoma psammion*
to 20 cm (8 in) across
▶c. BC to s. California
intertidal to 30 m (100 ft)
Formations of this species may often be riddled with sand, particularly populations encrusting rock outcrops adjacent to surf-swept sandy beaches. This photograph was taken during a dive trip along the Olympic coast, Washington, aboard the MV *Puffin*, captained by Steve Boothe.
Neah Bay, Olympic coast, n. Washington

CH40. ▶GRAY ENCRUSTING COMPOUND TUNICATE
Diplosoma listerianum, (formerly *Diplosoma macdonaldi*)
indeterminate, irregular size
c. BC to s. California
intertidal and subtidal
Like many other compound tunicates, this species not only encrusts rocks but creatures with hard outer coatings such as bivalves, solitary sea squirts and barnacles. It has also been found thriving on the exoskeleton of the sharpnose crab (AR111), after having been attached by the "host." The crab benefits from camouflage and the tunicate obtains mobility.
Link Island, Barkley Sound, s. BC. Charlie Gibbs photograph

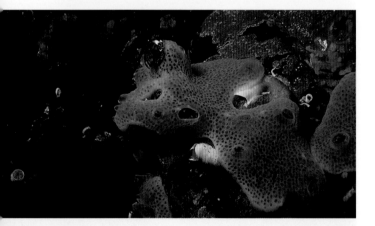

CH41. PACIFIC WHITE CRUST, colonial tunicate
Didemnum carnulentum
to 12.5 cm (5 in) across colony
c. BC to Panama
intertidal to 30 m (100 ft)
Many small openings and a few larger ones adorn the small, rounded, grouped colonies of this species. The colonies are reinforced by secreted globular calcareous concretions that have pointed tips—a feature useful for identification only if a microscope is available.
Fox Islands, Slingsby Channel, c. BC

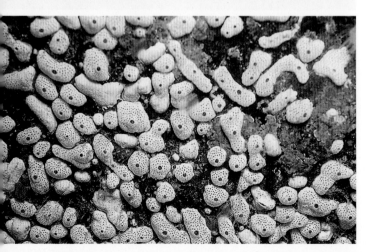

CH42. WHITE GLOVE LEATHER

Didemnum/Trididemnum complex

indeterminate, irregular size

n. Alaska to California

intertidal to subtidal

As one might guess from the scientific name, species identification for this entry is most problematic. The gross anatomy visible from the photograph does not provide enough data, even for experts like Dr. Gretchen Lambert, let alone the authors. The colony in the photograph was identified as a *Trididemnum* species, primarily on the basis of microscopic examination of its tiny spicules and the number of rows of stigmata (perforations in the pharynx).

Ucluelet Harbour, w. Vancouver Island, s. BC

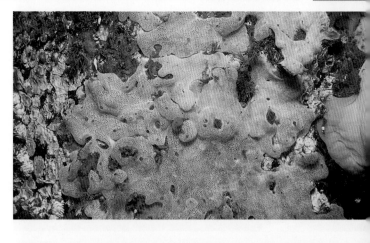

CH43. Although marine organisms originating in other parts of the world have increasingly been a factor in the Pacific Northwest, few have established themselves as quickly or with such potentially devastating effects as the **INVASIVE COMPOUND TUNICATE.** Originally from Europe, this rapidly growing species established itself significantly on the east coast of North America before it was first recorded in Puget Sound, Washington, at the Edmonds Marine Park in 2004. Subsequently the authors and other divers have found significant populations at several locales in Agamemnon Channel, s. BC, subtidally to approximately 12 m (40 ft). Here, mats not only carpet the substrate (photograph C) but overgrow many other attached organisms, such as the fringed sea colander kelp (SW63), illustrated in photograph B. Dr. Gretchen Lambert, a tunicate expert, originally believed it to be *Didemnum* **cf.** *lahillei* but now refers to it more generally as *Didemnum* **sp.**

A B C Agamemnon Channel, Nelson Island, s. BC

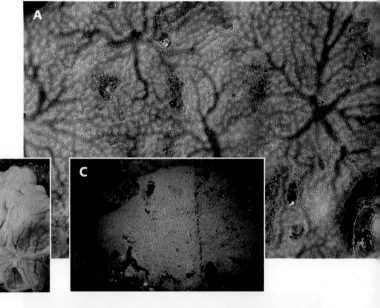

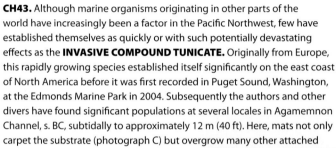

CH44. ▶SPECKLED COMPOUND TUNICATE

Trididemnum alexi

indeterminate, irregular size

▶BC to Washington

subtidal

Many little openings or siphons and a few larger holes on a tan or mauve background allow this tunicate to be identified to a generic level. This species was only recently described and little is known about it. Compound tunicates such as this one usually encrust rocky substrates but can colonize virtually any solid surface.

A Long Island, near Lopez Island, n. Washington

B Anderson Bay, Texada Island, s. BC

C Seymour Inlet, c. BC. Charlie Gibbs photograph

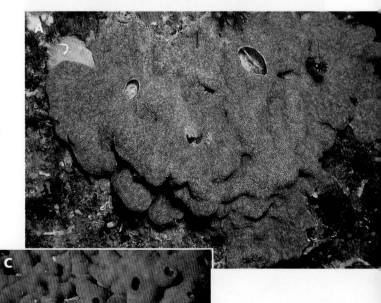

CH45. HARBOUR STAR ASCIDIAN
Botryllus schlosseri
indeterminate, irregular size

n.e. US Atlantic coast, s. BC to n. Baja California (introduced from the east coast)

intertidal to subtidal

Notice the large central hole in the middle of each star or flower-shaped section within the overall structure of this compound tunicate. This is a communal "water exhaust" servicing the associated zooids (individuals), each of which has its own intake siphon. Among the colour variations is a chocolate brown.

Sutton Islets, Egmont, s. BC

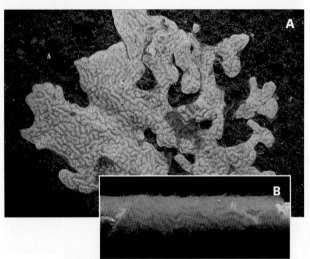

CH46. LINED COMPOUND ASCIDIAN
Botrylloides violaceus
indeterminate, irregular size

Japan, Atlantic coast of North America, BC to n. Baja California (introduced into the Pacific Northwest from the Orient)

intertidal to subtidal

The individual zooids are arranged as a labyrinth of intricate windings, reminiscent of a maze, which encrust any available solid substrate, including many marine algae. The obvious patterns of this and the harbour star ascidian (CH45) help in distinguishing them from encrusting sponges.

A Green Bay, Nelson Island, s. BC
B Egmont Marina, Egmont, s. BC
C Coal Harbour, Stanley Park, s. BC

CH47. ELEPHANT EAR TUNICATE, flat-bulbed tunicate
Polyclinum planum, *Glossophorum planum*
to 20 cm (8 in) across

▶n. Washington to n. Mexico

intertidal to 30 m (100 ft)

The broad, flat structure of this species is attached to the substrate by a short, slender stalk. Not only does this allow it to sway to and fro in the current but it provides the naturalist with a key to its identity. This species is definitely a rarer sighting in the northern portion of its range.

Waadah Island, Neah Bay, n. Washington

CH48. ▶YELLOW MOUND COMPOUND TUNICATE
Synoicum jordani
indeterminate, irregular size

n. Alaska to Washington

subtidal

The specimen in the photograph was collected and preserved, enabling Dr. Gretchen Lambert to identify it to species. There are a number of other similar northern species in the genus *Synoicum*, and the entire group is in a state of taxonomic disarray. Only painstaking additional collecting combined with expert examination will provide solutions.

Denny Island, Lama Pass, n. BC

CH49. ▶PEACH-COLOURED COMPOUND TUNICATE
Synoicum parfustis
indeterminate, irregular size
BC to c. California
subtidal
The taxonomic issues discussed for the yellow mound compound tunicate (CH48) apply to this tunicate, and its physical appearance, shown here, results in additional confusion. The small, dark spots embedded in the overall matrix are living commensal creatures—the ▶**compound tunicate amphipod**, *Polycheria osborni*. This amphipod lives within various compound tunicates from BC to n. Mexico.
Laura Point, Mayne Island, s. BC

Species CH50–52 are a selection of compound tunicates that were photographed without samples being obtained. This was indeed unfortunate, because without such material, tunicate expert Dr. Gretchen Lambert was unable to confirm their identities.

While the authors work to correct this oversight, the photographs and location information are included to illustrate the diversity of the group and record additional species that readers might encounter.

CH50. Undetermined compound tunicate A
Masset Harbour, Graham Island, n. BC

CH51. Undetermined compound tunicate B
Helm Point, Coronation Island, s. Alaska

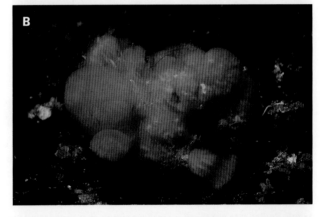

CH52. Undetermined compound tunicate C
Fox Islands, Slingsby Channel, c. BC

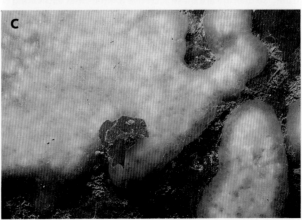

SALPS

Including beach bubblewrap.

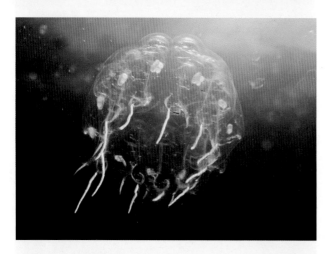

CH53. BEACH BUBBLEWRAP, beach bubble wrap, pelagic tunicate, salp
Salpa fusiformis
to 5 cm (2 in) long as a solitary individual, 1 m (39 in) long as a colony
Japan, n. Alaska to s. America
pelagic
This floating creature may live as an individual unit or be connected in long colonies. A salp is essentially an unattached version of a tunicate, and most species are primarily open-sea wanderers. In contrast to tunicates, salps generate their internal water flow (and locomotion) by muscles rather than hair-like cilia.

Beg Islands, Barkley Sound, s. BC

CH54. ▶FLABBY CIRCLE SALP
Cyclosalpa bakeri
to 15 cm (6 in) long as a solitary individual, 20 cm (8 in) in diameter as a colony
temperate and tropical oceanic waters, north to c. Alaska
pelagic
A fast-growing species that can exist as separate individuals or, as shown in the photograph, a ring-shaped colony. In the latter state it is more easily recognized.
Less common is the ▶solid circle salp, *Cyclosalpa affinis,* which often forms a chain of three or more circles when colonial.

Monterey Bay, c. California. David Wrobel photograph

ACORN WORMS Phylum HEMICHORDATA

With a name indicating a tenuous link to chordates and thus ultimately to ourselves, the hemichordates ("half-chordates") are obscure marine creatures popularly known as acorn worms. Most live in burrows and are direct deposit feeders, meaning that they scuffle about in mud or sand, gathering whatever nutritional benefits are available. Often the only evidence of their presence is fecal castings at the burrow entrances.

Each acorn worm has a three-part body consisting of a large, somewhat bulbous proboscis, a short, narrow collar and a long, sac-like trunk. So delicate are these secretive animals that excavating complete specimens for study and description is very challenging!

A small size, combined with the previously mentioned factors, makes even a simple species tally for the Pacific Northwest difficult. Dr. Chris Cameron, a post-doctoral fellow at the Bamfield Marine Sciences Centre in Bamfield, BC, who studies these creatures, has recently completed taxonomic work involving several species and this information is shared below.

HC1. ORANGE ACORN WORM
Saccoglossus pusillus, *Dolichoglossus pusillus*
to at least 25 cm (10 in) long
c. BC, s. California
intertidal to subtidal
Evidenced subtidally by its long, bright orange proboscis, which extends upon its crushed shell/sand habitat, the orange acorn is a surface deposit feeder. It excavates a U-shaped, mucus-lined burrow into which it can retract its proboscis rather quickly. This behaviour will help the naturalist distinguish this species from the orange ribbon worm NE11.
While five other acorn worm species from the Pacific Northwest have been officially described, several other potential additions, in the US National Museum of Natural History collection, await study.

Beg Islands, Barkley Sound, s. BC

SELECTED VERTEBRATES

Here we depart from the phylum-only introductions presented throughout this book and give vertebrates (a subdivision of the chordates) a similar, if brief, mention. This departure is due to custom and humankind's penchant for self-importance. We fancy ourselves as intelligent and thus the "most advanced" vertebrate.

Fishes and reptiles are included in this volume, but marine birds and mammals are not, because many excellent references may be found for them. No marine amphibians exist.

The section on fish is offered primarily as an updated augmentation of *Coastal Fishes of the Pacific Northwest*, the second reference listed below. We have included photographs that illustrate duplicated species differently, by featuring colour variations or different poses. A few additional fish species, found and photographed during this book's preparation, are included.

Further Reading

Humann, Paul, 1996, *Coastal Fish Identification, California to Alaska*, New World Publications Inc., Jacksonville, FL, 205 pp.

Lamb, Andy, and Phil Edgell, 2010, *Coastal Fishes of the Pacific Northwest, Revised and Expanded Second Edition*, Harbour Publishing, Madeira Park, BC, 352 pp.

Love, Milton S., 2011, *Certainly More Than You Want to Know About The Fishes of The Pacific Coast*, Really Big Press, University of California, Santa Barbara, CA, 672 pp.

Mecklenberg, Catherine W., T. Anthony Mecklenberg and Lyman Thorsteinson, 2002, *Fishes of Alaska*, American Fisheries Society, Bethesda, MD, 1,037 pp.

VB1. SPINY DOGFISH, Pacific dogfish, grayfish, dog-fish
Squalus acanthias, Squalus suckleyi
to 1.6 m (5 ft) long
n. Atlantic Ocean, s. Pacific Ocean (not tropical), Siberia, n. Alaska to n. Mexico
intertidal to 1,244 m (4,105 ft)
A very common but usually unwanted catch, this shark has rows of small but sharp teeth and dorsal spines that should be avoided when a writhing specimen is handled. If skinned and prepared promptly, its flesh is truly gourmet.
Waddington Channel, Desolation Sound, s. BC

VB2. BIG SKATE, Pacific great skate, barndoor skate
Raja binoculata
to 2.4 m (8 ft) across
E. Bering Sea, n. Alaska to n. Mexico
subtidal to 800 m (2,650 ft)
Note the distinctive "bull's eye" pattern on each of the huge pectoral fins or "wings." Divers and anglers are most likely to encounter this sandy-bottom denizen, but the beachcomber may find its dark, rectangular egg case, called a mermaid's purse, cast up on a beach (photograph B).
A Agamemnon Channel, Nelson Island, s. BC
B Cottam Point, Parksville, s. BC

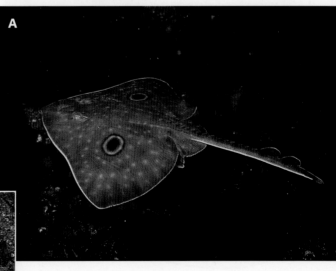

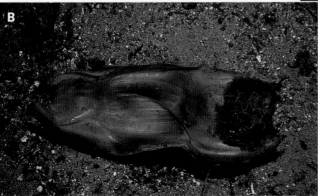

VB3. LONGNOSE SKATE, long nose skate
Raja rhina
to 1.4 m (4.5 ft) across
s. Alaska to n. Mexico
▶intertidal to 680 m (2,250 ft)
Along with many other fish species, this skate is a frequent bycatch of various commercial fishing operations. It is usually discarded, but if

market factors are appropriate, skate "wings" can show up as a relatively inexpensive but tasty item. Photograph B shows an egg case.
A Stanley Park, Vancouver Harbour, s. BC
B Point Cowan, Bowen Island, s. BC

VB4. SPOTTED RATFISH, ratfish, rat-fish, chimaera, rabbit fish
Hydrolagus colliei
to 1 m (39 in) long
c. Alaska to n. Mexico
intertidal to 925 m (3,085 ft)
To the diver, the spotted ratfish is a beautifully grotesque companion. To the surprised bait-fishing angler, it is a strange encounter. When first brought into captivity, females often jettison empty spindle-shaped egg cases (photograph B)—perhaps the result of collection stress.
A Agamemnon Channel, Nelson Island, s. BC
B Sutton Islets, Egmont, s. BC

VB5. PACIFIC SARDINE, pilchard
Sardinops sagax, *Sardinops caerulea*, *Sardinia caerulea*
to 41 cm (16.3 in) long
s. Africa, s. Pacific Ocean, Japan, Siberia, n. Alaska to Mexico
surface to 150 m (500 ft)
The presence of fine striae (lines) on the gill covers, triangular flaps on the caudal (tail) fin and black spots along the sides distinguish this species from the Pacific herring, *Clupea pallasi*. After many years of apparent decline, Pacific Northwest populations of the valuable Pacific sardine show a noticeable, albeit fluctuating, increase.
Off Barkley Sound, w. Vancouver Island, s. BC

VB6. AMERICAN SHAD, shad
Alosa sapidissima
to 76 cm (30 in) long
4.2 kg (9.3 lbs)
s. Labrador to s. Florida, introduced to Pacific coast, Siberia, n. Alaska to n. Mexico
pelagic
A deep body and the presence of enlarged scutes (scales) along the belly area distinguish this successfully introduced fish from the Pacific sardine (VB5). A popular game fish when migrating to spawn in several large Pacific coast rivers, it is also considered a fine seafood item. This fish has inhabited the Pacific Northwest since the 1890s, and its effect on native species is debatable.
Off Barkley Sound, w. Vancouver Island, s. BC

VB7. THREESPINE STICKLEBACK, three-spined stickleback
Gasterosteus aculeatus
to 10 cm (4 in) long
Hudson's Bay to Chesapeake Bay, Japan, Siberia, n. Alaska to n. Mexico
intertidal to 27 m (90 ft)
This adaptable fish thrives in fresh, brackish and salt water. Indeed, in some of the island lakes, located in the Strait of Georgia, BC, the isolation of populations has accelerated the evolutionary process. Several "new species" significantly different than the familiar one that appears here have evolved.
Kleindale, Pender Harbour, s. BC

VB8. TUBESNOUT, tube-snout
Aulorhynchus flavidus
to 18 cm (7 in) long
c. Alaska to n. Mexico
subtidal to 30 m (100 ft)
Commonly observed forming large schools, this "stretched-out" but armourless version of the threespine stickleback (VB7) is a plankton feeder. During the late winter, spring and summer breeding season, solitary aggressive males develop black and fluorescent blue snouts and entice prospective mates to lay small clusters of amber-coloured eggs upon suitable seaweed.
Edmonds, Puget Sound, c. Washington

VB9. BAY PIPEFISH, pipe-fish
Sygnathus leptorhynchus, Sygnathus griseolineatus
to 39 cm (15.6 in) long
c. Alaska to n. Mexico
▶intertidal to 30 m (100 ft)
A stretched-out but tailed version of the familiar seahorse, this pipefish shares a reversed role in reproductive strategy. After the eggs are fertilized, the female deposits them in the male's brood pouch and he carries them until the young are born.
Agamemnon Channel, Sechelt Peninsula, s. BC

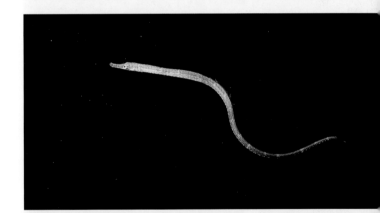

VB10. PACIFIC SAND LANCE, sand-lance, sandlaunce, needlefish, sand eel, incorrect: candlefish
Ammodytes hexapterus, Ammodytes tobianus personatus
to 28 cm (11 in) long
w. Canadian Arctic Ocean, Japan, n. Alaska to s. California
intertidal to 100 m (330 ft)
This active species lives a dual existence. At times it buries completely in sand or gravel; at others, it swims in huge schools. Both beachcomber and diver may be fortunate enough to see it during the emergence/burying period.
A Turn Island, San Juan Channel, n. Washington
B Tongue Point, Olympic coast, n. Washington

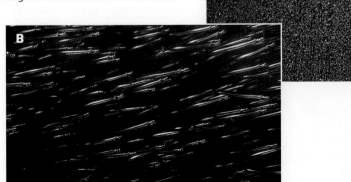

VB11. PACIFIC COD, true cod, grey cod, gray cod
Gadus macrocephalus
to 1.2 m (4 ft) long
Korea, Japan, China, n. Alaska to n. Mexico
subtidal to 900 m (3,000 ft)
A long barbel (chin whisker) and a vermiculate (worm-like) pattern on the sides are distinctive. Like many species of long-harvested fish, this cod's size has decreased over time. The progression of this shrinking-fish scenario will ultimately have a devastating effect on the species and the fishery.
Sunset Marina, Howe Sound, s. BC

VB12. WALLEYE POLLOCK, Pacific pollock, Alaska pollack, whiting
Theragra chalcogramma
to 91 cm (36 in) long
Japan, Korea, Siberia, n. Alaska to c. California
subtidal to 970 m (3,200 ft)
Divers and dockside observers see only the juveniles, but commercial trawlers target the valuable adult—the bulk ingredient in "artificial" crab. With the overfishing of many other species, the walleye pollock has become the target of a major international harvesting effort in the north Pacific.
Copper Cove, Howe Sound, s. BC

VB13. BLACKBELLY EELPOUT, black-bellied eel-pout
Lycodopsis pacifica
to 46 cm (18 in) long
n. Alaska to n. Mexico
subtidal, 15–400 m (50–1,320 ft)
Divers, look for this elongate bottom dweller during your next nocturnal sortie over a sandy substrate. It is easily recognized as an eelpout, primarily because its dorsal, anal and caudal (tail) fins are all linked together or confluent. Of the numerous eelpout species, this is virtually the only one encountered at shallow, readily accessible depths.
Cotton Point, Keats Island, s. BC

VB14. BLACKEYE GOBY, crested goby, bluespot goby
Rhinogobiops nicholsii, *Coryphopterus nicholsi*
to 15 cm (6 in) long
s. Alaska to n. Mexico
intertidal to 640 m (2,112 ft) for adults, 2,234 m (7,372 ft) for larvae.
This small, aggressive fish prefers a mixed bottom of rock and sand, where it excavates a sheltering burrow. A breeding male often rises vertically, up to 15 cm (6 in) off the bottom, in a mating ritual that apparently attracts the female.
A Francis Point, Francis Peninsula, s. BC
B Hospital Bay, Pender Harbour, s. BC

VB15. BAY GOBY, finescale goby, fine scaled goby
Lepidogobius lepidus
to 10 cm (4 in) long
s. Alaska to n. Mexico
intertidal to 210 m (700 ft)
Unlike the blackeye goby (VB14), this ghostly goby inhabits vast expanses of open sand or silt. It usually maintains a "safe" distance between itself and a diver and, when stressed, retreats into a burrow. As a result, the bay goby is a challenging subject for the underwater photographer.
A Kleindale, Pender Harbour, s. BC
B Hospital Bay, Pender Harbour, s. BC

VB16. NORTHERN RONQUIL, ronquil
Ronquilus jordani
to 20 cm (8 in) long
n. Alaska to c. California
subtidal to 275 m (910 ft)
Readily distinguished from either of the preceding goby species by its single long dorsal fin, the northern ronquil often shares similar habitats. A breeding male has a bright turquoise anal fin, which is no doubt an attractant for a willing female. Photograph B depicts a juvenile.
A Green Bay, Nelson Island, s. BC
B Nile Point, Agamemnon Channel, s. BC

VB17. ALASKAN RONQUIL
Bathymaster caeruleofasciatus
to 30 cm (12 in) long
Siberia, n. Alaska to n. BC
subtidal to 95 m (314 ft)
More robust and having a larger mouth than the northern ronquil (VB16), this ronquil is also much darker. The Alaskan ronquil readily confronts a diver—an activity that usually makes it easier to find. A male is shown in photograph A, a female in photograph B.
A B Iphigenia Point, Langara Island, n. BC

VB18. HIGH COCKSCOMB, cockscomb prickleback, crested blenny
Anoplarchus purpurescens
to 20 cm (8 in) long
n. Alaska to s. California
intertidal to 30 m (100 ft)
Most of the squirming "eels" found by beachcombers who overturn intertidal rocks are this species. It is an anguilliform (eel-shaped) fish that has spiny fin supports or rays along its back that are prickly to the touch. True eels have no spines anywhere on their bodies. This is an unusual colour variant—the species is generally a mottled brown or grey.
Ucluth Peninsula, w. Vancouver Island, s. BC

VB19. ROCK PRICKLEBACK, rock blenny, rock-eel
Xiphister mucosus
to 58 cm (23 in) long
c. Alaska to s. California
intertidal to 20 m (66 ft)
If a beachcomber can quiet a squirming specimen long enough, dark bands with light centres that radiate from its eyes should be obvious. The black prickleback (VB20) is the reverse. First, though, one must overturn algae-covered intertidal rocks or look carefully subtidally to find this secretive fish.
Ucluth Peninsula, w. Vancouver Island, s. BC

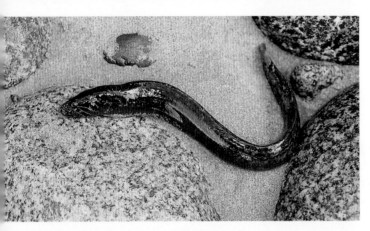

VB20. BLACK PRICKLEBACK, black blenny
Xiphister atropurpureus, *Epigeichthys atropurpureus*
to 32 cm (13 in) long
c. Alaska to n. Mexico
intertidal to 10 m (33 ft)
Black bands with thin, white edging radiate from the eyes of this species. It also has a whitish vertical band where the tail fin connects with the body. It lives in virtually the same habitat as the rock prickleback (VB19). The two may even coexist under the same rock.
Ucluth Peninsula, w. Vancouver Island, s. BC

VB21. RIBBON PRICKLEBACK, belted blenny
Phytichthys chirus
to 20 cm (8 in) long
n. Alaska to s. California
intertidal to 13 m (43 ft)
An inhabitant of rocky shores along more exposed locations, this secretive fish may be found by turning over rocks on a stroll at low tide. Please be considerate and replace the shelter as you found it, as the organisms living on top and on the underside locate this way for a reason.
Fort Worden State Park, Port Townsend, n. Washington

VB22. MOSSHEAD WARBONNET, mosshead prickleback, ornamented blenny
Chirolophis nugator
to 15 cm (6 in) long
n. Alaska to s. California
intertidal to 80 m (265 ft)

This "crewcut" species often hides under rocks or in the empty casings of the giant acorn barnacle (AR171). An organized group of beachcombers, suitably equipped, may find this fish by bailing out a tidepool. Select a pool in the lower intertidal zone that can be bailed out. This method is eco-friendly, as the returning tide quickly restores the habitat.
A Cactus Islands, New Channel, n. Washington
B Hussar Point, Browning Passage, c. BC

VB23. DECORATED WARBONNET, decorated prickleback, decorated blenny
***Chirolophis decoratus**, Chirolophis polyactocephalus*
to 42 cm (16.5 in) long
n. Alaska to n. California
subtidal to 91 m (300 ft)
This species is usually encountered by divers who look in crevices or inside sponges such as the two boot sponges (PO9/10). More extensive festooning cirri (tentacle-like projections), highlighted by the tree-like bush between its eyes, distinguishes this warbonnet from the mosshead warbonnet (VB22). There has been much speculation concerning the function of the cirri, but as yet, no definitive answers are available.
A Brockton Island, Quatsino Sound, c. BC
B Strawberry Islet, Malaspina Strait, s. BC

VB24. PACIFIC SNAKE PRICKLEBACK, snake prickleback, eel-blenny
***Lumpenus sagitta**, Lumpenus anguillaris*
to 50 cm (20 in) long
Japan, Siberia, n. Alaska to n. California
intertidal to 425 m (1,400 ft)
Most commonly observed in summer and fall, this denizen of sandy or muddy shallows, unlike the other elongate species illustrated, rests with its body relatively straight. The structure and alignment of its vertebrae prevent a curling position. The term "prickleback" refers to the many tiny spines that support its dorsal fin.
Treadwell Bay, Slingsby Channel, c. BC

VB25. PENPOINT GUNNEL, penpoint blenny, pen-point blenny
Apodichthys flavidus
to 46 cm (18 in) long
c. Alaska to s. California
intertidal to 18 m (60 ft)
The three colour phases of this cryptic but attractive fish beautifully match the basic algal colours: wine red, emerald green and golden brown. Don Wilkie, former director of the Scripps Aquarium in La Jolla, California, linked this phenomenon to its similarly coloured amphipod prey.
Ucluth Peninsula, w. Vancouver Island, s. BC

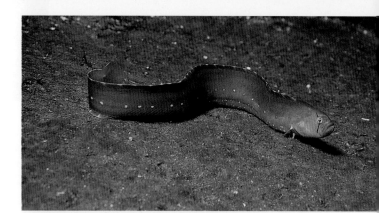

VB26. CRESCENT GUNNEL, bracketed blenny
Pholis laeta
to 25 cm (10 in) long
Siberia, n. Alaska to n. California
intertidal to 73 m (240 ft)
During summer, this gunnel commonly entwines itself with various seaweeds. In winter, when this shelter is less available, the fish may hide in a discarded bottle with only its head poking out. We do not advocate "creating" such habitat, but many creatures capitalize on such opportunities.
Bennett Bay, Mayne Island, s. BC

VB27. SADDLEBACK GUNNEL, saddled blenny
Pholis ornata
to 30 cm (12 in) long
s. BC to c. California
intertidal to 36 m (120 ft)
The "saddles" of this fish supposedly differentiate it from the "crescents" along the back of the crescent gunnel (VB26), but this subjective difference may be a difficult call. Anal fin ray counts are the ultimate determining factor. The two species reside in similar territory and frequently cohabit.
Bennett Bay, Mayne Island, s. BC

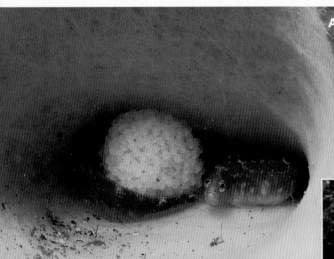

VB28. LONGFIN GUNNEL
Pholis clemensi
to 12.5 cm (5 in) long
s. Alaska to n. California
subtidal, 7–64 m (23–210 ft)
This diminutive gunnel may display either a bright or dull colour variation. Like many of the other elongate fishes covered here, the guarding parent coils around the eggs and fans them with its pectoral fins. Photograph A shows this activity occurring inside a boot sponge (PO9/10).
A Green Bay, Nelson Island, s. BC
B Agamemnon Channel, Nelson Island, s. BC

VB29. QUILLFISH, quill-fish
Ptilichthys goodei
to 34 cm (13 in) long
Japan, Siberia, n. Alaska to Oregon
subtidal to 360 m (1,290 ft)
Whereas a diver may spot an adult "snaking" over a sandy bottom, a nocturnal dockside observer may see the amazing larvae of this fish. The late Dr. Charlie Moffett of Friday Harbor, Washington, employed a submersible "night light" during calm summer nights to attract this bizarre creature.
Moresby Passage, Portland Island, s. BC

VB30. WOLF-EEL
Anarrhichthys ocellatus
to 2.4 m (8 ft) long
c. Alaska to s. California
subtidal to 225 m (740 ft)

Readily "tamed" to accept handouts by divers, this magnificent creature represents the ultimate in non-human "dive buddies." However, its tasty flesh sometimes finds its way to seafood shops, resulting in "user" group conflict. Pioneering work in breeding this species at the Vancouver Aquarium Marine Science Centre, together with a subsequent aquaculture experiment, may provide a solution. Photograph A shows an adult male, photograph B an adult female, photograph C a sub-adult and photograph D a juvenile.

A Long Island, near Lopez Island, n. Washington
B Nelson Rock, Malaspina Strait, s. BC
C Worlcombe Island, Howe Sound, s. BC
D Anderson Bay, Texada Island, s. BC

VB31. PROWFISH
Zaprora silensis
to 1 m (39 in) long
n. Japan, Siberia, n. Alaska to California
subtidal to 675 m (2,228 ft)

A high, blunt snout, an absence of pelvic fins, and pores on the head ringed with white are distinguishing characteristics of this species. This noteworthy photograph was taken by Terry Whalen of Friday Harbor, Washington, while visiting the wreck of the SS *Princess Sophia*, near Juneau, Alaska. A rarely seen and even more rarely photographed fish, it has been observed in significant numbers at the Bowie Seamount, west of the Queen Charlotte Islands.

Wreck of the SS *Princess Sophia*, Juneau, s. Alaska. Terry Whalen photograph

VB32. STRIPED SEAPERCH, striped perch, blue seaperch, blue sea-perch
Embiotoca lateralis, *Taeniotoca lateralis*
to 37 cm (15 in) long
s. Alaska to n. Mexico
subtidal to 30 m (100 ft)

Electric blue stripes on a coppery background make this fish one of the most colourful in the Pacific Northwest. An active species, the striped perch is most easily photographed at night, when it is more approachable. Photograph B illustrates a juvenile threesome.

A Keystone, Whidbey Island, n. Washington
B Edmonds, Puget Sound, c. Washington

VB33. PILE PERCH, pile seaperch, dusky perch, dusky sea-perch
Rhacochilus vacca, Damalichthys vacca
to 45 cm (18 in) long
s. BC to n. Mexico
subtidal to 80 m (265 ft)
Like all members of the surfperch family, a mature female pile perch bears large, live young during summer months. As many as 36 are jettisoned into the weed-choked shallows. Later, fertilization of the next batch occurs when male and female quiver, belly to belly, turning upward in the process. A juvenile is shown in photograph B.
A Nile Point, Agamemnon Channel, s. BC
B Eagle Harbour, w. Vancouver, s. BC

VB34. SHINER PERCH, yellow shiner, shiner surfperch, seven eleven perch
Cymatogaster aggregata, Cymatogaster aggregatus
to 20.3 cm (8 in) long
s. Alaska to n. Mexico
intertidal to 146 m (480 ft)
This species may be the embodiment of precociousness, as a newborn male is physically capable of mating immediately. However, they most likely would not get a chance, as aggressive and blackened veteran males dominate the scene. By day this species forms large schools, and by night the schools break apart, leaving individuals to hug the bottom.
Eagle Harbour, w. Vancouver, s. BC

VB35. KELP PERCH, kelp seaperch, brown perch, brown sea-perch
Brachyistius frenatus, Brachyistius brevipinus
to 22 cm (8.5 in) long
s. Alaska to n. Mexico
subtidal to 30 m (100 ft)
Usually found hovering among large kelps, this well-camouflaged fish unfortunately falls victim to kelp-harvesting operations in California. It has been documented in the southern part of its range as a cleaner species (removing parasites from larger fish), but this behaviour has not been seen in the north.
Anderson Bay, Texada Island, s. BC

VB36. COPPER ROCKFISH, copper rock-fish, incorrect: rockcod and rock cod
Sebastes caurinus, Sebastodes caurinus
to 66 cm (26.4 in) long
c. Alaska to n. Mexico
intertidal to 183 m (603 ft)
Steadily and alarmingly, Pacific Northwest populations of this once-abundant species are declining. The main reasons are the commercial "live rockfish" fishery, combined with increasing pressure from salmon-starved recreational anglers. Fishery managers, facing political pressure from consumers, appear powerless to stop it.
A Captain Island, Jervis Inlet, s. BC
B Irvines Landing, Pender Harbour, s. BC

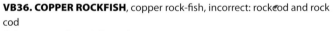

VB37. QUILLBACK ROCKFISH, yellow-backed rockfish, orange-spotted rock-fish, speckled rockfish, incorrect: rock cod, rockcod
Sebastes maliger, Sebastodes maliger
to 60 cm (24 in) long
c. Alaska to s. California
subtidal to 275 m (900 ft)
Like other rockfish, this species is easily caught by novice anglers. Extraction activities, which continue unabated, can lift virtually every specimen from a reef. This fish, which can live as long as 95 years, has had only three strong reproductive year classes in the last century in BC waters.
A Captain Island, Jervis Inlet, s. BC
B Moore Point, Francis Peninsula, s. BC

VB38. CHINA ROCKFISH, yellowstripe rockfish, yellow spotted rockfish, yellow rockfish, yellow-striped rock-fish, (incorrect: rockcod and rock cod)
Sebastes nebulosus, Sebastodes nebulosus
to 45 cm (18 in) long
s. Alaska to s. California
subtidal to 128 m (420 ft)
The black background colour of the china rockfish presents a special challenge for the underwater photographer. Light-coloured surroundings are needed to make the subject stand out, but they present exposure difficulties that must be overcome for a "crisp" shot.
Hunt Rock, Gordon Channel, c. BC

VB39. BROWN ROCKFISH, brown rock-fish, bolina, incorrect: rockcod, rock cod
Sebastes auriculatus, Sebastodes auriculatus, Sebastodes dallii
to 56 cm (22.4 in) long
c. Alaska to n. Mexico
subtidal to 135 m (444 ft)
Various shades of brown mottling, a dark spot on each operculum (gill cover) and a pink chin make this rockfish recognizable. Strangely, its presence in the Pacific Northwest is uneven.
Tzoonie Narrows, Narrows Inlet, s. BC

VB40. BLUE ROCKFISH, priest-fish, priestfish, (incorrect: sea bass)
Sebastes mystinus, Sebastodes mystinus
to 53 cm (21 in) long
s. Alaska to n. Mexico
intertidal to 550 m (1,800 ft)
This species, one of the schooling rockfishes, may gather in huge numbers and seldom rest on the bottom. Like the china rockfish, it is not present in the protected waters of Puget Sound or the Strait of Georgia. It frequently forms mixed aggregations with any of the four following rockfish (VB41–44).
Beg Islands, Barkley Sound, s. BC

VB41. DUSKY ROCKFISH, Alaska black rockfish
Sebastes ciliatus, Sebastodes ciliatus
to 46 cm (18.4 in) long for grey colour phase, 53 cm (21.2 in) long for brown
colour phase
Japan, Siberia, n. Alaska to c. BC
subtidal to 525 m (1,750 ft)
Although different rockfish are found throughout the northern oceans, the waters along North America's Pacific coast provide habitat for the greatest species diversity. The photographs may show two species or simply two colour variants.
A Arniston Point, Dundas Island, n. BC
B Boas Islet, Hakai Passage, c. BC

VB42. BLACK ROCKFISH, black rock-fish, bass rockfish, incorrect: sea bass, black bass
Sebastes melanops, Sebastodes melanops
to 69 cm (27.6 in) long, 5 kg (11 lbs) weight
n. Alaska to n. Mexico
intertidal to 366 m (1,200 ft)
This species' habit of breaking surface in pursuit of prey makes it an interesting quarry for the adventurous fly fisher—and, on light tackle, a lot of fun! In this situation, when the rockfish's gas-filled swim bladder is not overfilled, it makes a great candidate for catch and release.
A Booker Lagoon, Broughton Island, c. BC
B Van Anda Point, Texada Island, s. BC

VB43. YELLOWTAIL ROCKFISH, yellow-tail rockfish, yellow-tailed rock-fish, incorrect: sea bass
Sebastes flavidus, Sebastodes flavidus
to 66 cm (26 in) long
n. Alaska to s. California
intertidal to 549 m (1,812 ft)
The yellowtail rockfish is virtually identical to the black rockfish (VB42), except that it appears "washed over" with yellow, particularly on the fins. It is easily distinguished in mixed schools. Like all other rockfish, this species is a live bearer: each pregnant female produces a huge number of tiny transparent larvae, which are incompletely developed at birth.
Plumper Islands, Weynton Passage, c. BC

VB44. WIDOW ROCKFISH, brown bomber, soft brown, incorrect: widow rockcod, rockcod, bass
Sebastes entomelas, Sebastodes entomelas
to 59 cm (23.6 in) long
c. Alaska to n. Mexico
subtidal to 800 m (2,640 ft)
This species is an active schooling fish that often pursues prey such as herring at the surface. Though seen by divers at some inshore locales, it is one of a number targeted by offshore trawlers and comes to market in the general category of "rockfish fillets."
Boas Islet, Hakai Passage, c. BC

VB45. PUGET SOUND ROCKFISH
Sebastes emphaeus
to 18 cm (7 in) long
c. Alaska to n. California
subtidal to 365 m (1,200 ft)
This small species may form massive schools or hide in small groups in crevices. Its small size suggests that it is a prey species. In recent years some divers have remarked on its growing abundance. Is this true? If so, perhaps it is because of the relative reduction of other, larger predatory rockfish and lingcod.
A Stubbs Island, Weynton Passage, c. BC
B Laura Point, Mayne Island, s. BC

VB46. CANARY ROCKFISH, orange rockfish, orange rock-fish, fantail rockfish
Sebastes pinniger, *Sebastodes pinniger*
to 76 cm (30 in) long
s. Alaska to n. Mexico
intertidal to 838 m (2,765 ft)
A large black blotch on the dorsal fin that marks a juvenile, fades in the sub-adult. Like most rockfish, this species is difficult to release successfully after capture because on removal from greater depths its swollen swim bladder prevents a life-saving descent.
A Beg Islands, Barkley Sound, s. BC
B Sekiu, Olympic coast, n. Washington

VB47. VERMILION ROCKFISH, vermilion rock-fish
Sebastes miniatus, *Sebastodes miniatus*
to 76 cm (30 in) long, 6.8 kg (15 lbs) weight
c. Alaska to n. Mexico
subtidal to 436 m (1,440 ft)
This rockfish usually forms very small schools, but individuals occasionally infiltrate schools of canary rockfish (VB46). In the latter scenario, the interlopers stand out like the proverbial "sore thumb"! Both species orient more to the bottom as juveniles than as schooling adults.
A Beg Islands, Barkley Sound, s. BC
B Treadwell Bay, Slingsby Channel, c. BC

VB48. YELLOWEYE ROCKFISH, rasphead rockfish, red rockfish, goldeneye rockfish, incorrect: red snapper
***Sebastes ruberrimus**, Sebastodes ruberrimus*
to 90 cm (36 in) long, 11.3 kg (25 lbs) weight
n. Alaska to n. Mexico
subtidal, 15–550 m (50–1,800 ft)
Like many rockfishes, the juvenile of this species (photograph B) looks very different from an adult, which is almost solid pale orange. Tragically the larger, older females, capable of producing over a million young each, are being harvested or caught as bycatch everywhere, unabated—an underwater version of clear-cutting old-growth forests! Yelloweye rockfish are known to live longer than 100 years. Photograph A, taken in 1984, shows a pair of sub-adults that were part of a small group—a circumstance now rarely observed in the Pacific Northwest.
A Nelson Rock, Malaspina Strait, s. BC
B Anderson Bay, Texada Island, s. BC

VB49. TIGER ROCKFISH, blackbanded rockfish, banded rock-fish
***Sebastes nigrocinctus**, Sebastodes nigrocinctus*
to 60 cm (24 in) long
c. Alaska to s. California
subtidal, surface to 298 m (984 ft)

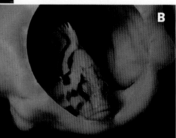

This territorial rockfish is never far from its "home" crevice. Traditional fishery management efforts have failed miserably to protect and sustain rockfish populations. No-Take Marine Protected Areas, where no extraction activities of any kind are allowed, offer hope if and when established.
A Nelson Rock, Malaspina Strait, s. BC
B Anderson Bay, Texada Island, s. BC

VB50. GREENSTRIPED ROCKFISH, green-striped rock-fish, strawberry rockfish, striped rockfish, poinsetta
***Sebastes elongatus**, Sebastodes elongatus*
to 43 cm (17.2 in) long
c. Alaska to n. Mexico
subtidal, 12–495 m (40–1,632 ft)
Unlike most other rockfish species, the greenstriped inhabits primarily sandy, open substrates where relatively little solid shelter is available. As a consequence this smallish species is an unwanted bycatch of shrimp-trawling activities. Alternative methods that prevent such waste should be developed and utilized.
Tzoonie Narrows, Narrows Inlet, s. BC

These three photographs illustrate a problem that faces all amateur fish watchers and photographers: even when good images are available, the subtle physical characteristics that differentiate one species from another may be obscure. The exact identity of the **rockfish** pictured here will almost certainly remain a **mystery**, for without the actual specimens to examine, we do not have enough information. Speculation about species from deeper water and hybridization has challenged us. Even the rockfish expert Milton Love (see Further Reading, p. 361) was hesitant to make positive identification.
VB51. A Mukilteo, Puget Sound, c. Washington

VB52. B Moore Point, Francis Peninsula, s. BC

VB53. C Rainy Bay, Barkley Sound, s. BC

VB54. KELP GREENLING

Hexagrammos decagrammus, Chiropsis decorammus
to 60 cm (24 in) long
n. Alaska to s. California
intertidal to 45 m (150 ft)

The female, which looks very different from the male, frequently lays her eggs in the empty casing of a giant acorn barnacle (AR171). The kelp greenling is often the only large fish found at Pacific Northwest dive sites. Is this species the next one to be designated for slaughter, as fishers, politicians and fisheries managers look for another underutilized species to exploit? Photographs C and D show juveniles, photograph A an adult female and photograph B an adult male.

A Breakwater Island, Gabriola Passage, s. BC
B Worlcombe Island, Howe Sound, s. BC
C Green Bay, Nelson Island, s. BC
D Tyler Rock, Barkley Sound, s. BC

VB55. ROCK GREENLING, fringed greenling

Hexagrammos lagocephalus, Hexagrammos superciliosus, Lebius superciliosus
to 60 cm (24 in) long
Yellow Sea, Japan, Siberia, n. Alaska to c. California
intertidal to 80 m (264 ft)

Surprisingly this garish greenling blends well with its shallow, exposed surroundings—and is therefore seldom seen by divers. Pity. Historically it has been "protected" by its remote, inhospitable habitat and non-aggregating behaviour.

Plumper Islands, Weynton Passage, c. BC

VB56. WHITESPOTTED GREENLING, white-spotted greenling
Hexagrammos stelleri
to 48 cm (19 in) long
Japan, Siberia, n. Alaska to s. Oregon
intertidal to 175 m (578 ft)
A darkened male (photograph A) is extremely aggressive in defence of

his "nest" of bright turquoise or mauve-coloured eggs. A diver who blunders into such a situation may be circled, pestered and even nipped at by this Lilliputian guardian. A juvenile whitespotted greenling is the first catch for many a novice youthful angler in the Pacific Northwest.
A Millers Landing, Bowen Island, s. BC
B Point Cowan, Bowen Island, s. BC

VB57. LINGCOD
Ophiodon elongatus
to 1.5 m (5 ft) long, 47.7 kg (105 lbs) weight
c. Alaska to n. Mexico
subtidal to 2,000 m (6,600 ft)
Overfishing has reduced virtually every population of this species, which appears tailor-made for a No-Take Marine Protected Area solution. In recent years, concerned and motivated divers have been participating

in lingcod egg-mass counts every February (photograph B). Through this enjoyable annual activity, amateurs are contributing to a greater understanding of this valuable resource. Interested people can contact the Research Department of the Vancouver Aquarium Marine Science Centre.
A B Moore Point, Francis Peninsula, s. BC

VB58. PAINTED GREENLING, convictfish
Oxylebius pictus
to 25 cm (10 in) long
c. Alaska to n. Mexico
intertidal to 50 m (165 ft)
The characteristic and normal banded pattern of this species is obscured in breeding males by an overall darkening. If you are confronted during a dive, stop and inspect the area carefully—you may find a cluster of orange-coloured eggs.
Sutton Islets, Egmont, s. BC

VB59. LONGSPINE COMBFISH, long-spined greenling
Zaniolepis latipinnus
to 30 cm (12 in) long
s. BC to n. Mexico
subtidal, 18–180 m (60–600 ft)
An unusual member of the greenling family, the longspine combfish dwells on sandy or muddy bottoms rather than the rocky habitats preferred by others. However, like most greenlings, the male becomes much darker and more aggressive, and his mouth becomes noticeably more pointed, at breeding time.
Tuwanek Point, Sechelt Inlet, s. BC

VB60. FLUFFY SCULPIN, cirriated sculpin
Oligocottus snyderi
to 9 cm (3.5 in) long
c. Alaska to n. Mexico
intertidal
Very cryptic in its exposed and surf-swept rocky habitat, this active sculpin hides either in emerald-green surfgrass (SW4) or amid pink coralline algae (SW89–92). Look for it in tidepools of the lower intertidal zones. Be safe and stay vigilant of an incoming tide and crashing surf.

A B Frank Island, w. Vancouver Island, s. BC

VB61. TIDEPOOL SCULPIN, tide pool sculpin, tidepool johnny, rockpool johnny
Oligocottus maculosus
to 10 cm (4 in) long
c. Alaska to s. California
intertidal
The most widespread and commonly encountered of the tidepool-dwelling sculpins, this species may be found in nearly any tidepool or even under exposed, seaweed-covered rocks.

A Georgina Point, Mayne Island, s. BC
B Chesterman Beach, w. Vancouver Island, s. BC

VB62. SCALYHEAD SCULPIN, plumose sculpin, white-spotted sculpin
Artedius harringtoni
to 10 cm (4 in) long
n. Alaska to s. California
intertidal to 30 m (100 ft)
This species is a classic example of how coloration is often virtually useless as a tool for identification. Extreme variation is the norm. An adult male scalyhead sculpin, as illustrated in photograph B, has a large cirrus (flap of skin) behind each eye. Females and juveniles are difficult to distinguish, a phenomenon that also applies to other sculpin species.

A Surge Narrows, Maurelle Island, s. BC
B Laura Point, Mayne Island, s. BC

VB63. SMOOTHHEAD SCULPIN, flathead sculpin
Artedius lateralis
to 14 cm (5.5 in) long
Siberia, n. Alaska to n. Mexico
intertidal to 14 m (46 ft)
The "popular" male shown in photograph B had several willing partners, resulting in obvious clutches of eggs for his intertidal nest. As a reward for his prowess he is left to guard and aerate the fertile eggs until they hatch. At this time they drift away, becoming temporary members of the planktonic community.

A Stanley Park, Vancouver Harbour, s. BC
B Tongue Point, Olympic coast, n. Washington

VB64. PUGET SOUND SCULPIN
Ruscarius meanyi, *Artedius meanyi*
to 6 cm (2.3 in) long
s. Alaska to n. California
intertidal to 82 m (270 ft)
The Puget Sound sculpin is most often found hiding in narrow rock crevices. However, during the preparation of this book, several specimens were found while searching through cloud sponge (PO11) specimens.
Fearney Point, Agamemnon Channel, s. BC

VB65. LONGFIN SCULPIN, bandeye sculpin
Jordania zonope
to 15 cm (6 in) long
c. Alaska to c. California
intertidal to 38 m (125 ft)
This slender sculpin has light, wavy vertical lines below each eye. It is an active fish, which an observant diver might see moving up and down over vertical walls or "hanging" upside down on cavern ceilings. Very dark individuals are sexually active males looking for partners and/or guarding eggs.
Sutton Islets, Egmont, s. BC

VB66. THORNBACK SCULPIN
Paricelinus hopliticus
to 20 cm (8 in) long
n. BC to s. California
subtidal, 20–183 m (65–604 ft)
Although sculpins are found worldwide in cool northern waters, they flourish along Pacific Northwest shorelines. Here, many forms have evolved to take advantage of diverse habitats. This small, inconspicuous species is one of several elongate ones whose ecology is still poorly understood.
Agamemnon Channel, Sechelt Peninsula, s. BC

VB67. MOSSHEAD SCULPIN, globe-headed sculpin, round-headed sculpin
Clinocottus globiceps
to 19 cm (7.5 in) long
n. Alaska to s. California
intertidal
As a youthful collector employed by the Vancouver Aquarium, Andy Lamb encountered this amphibious sculpin leaving its tidepool for an adjacent exposed rock at Chesterman Beach. It was the noise of its splashing that alerted him to this unexpected activity. The moment will always remain a magical one, forever imprinted.
Frank Island, w. Vancouver Island, s. BC

VB68. ROSY-LIP SCULPIN, rosylip sculpin, rosy-lipped sculpin, incorrect: bullhead
Ascelichthys rhodorus
to 15 cm (6 in) long
c. Alaska to c. California
intertidal to 15 m (50 ft)
This sculpin is very easy to identify if the naturalist can collect a specimen and turn it on its back, as it has no pelvic fins (the pair normally located on the belly, just behind the gills). Holding it will also demonstrate another distinctive feature: its smooth, scaleless body. After your encounter, please return the fish gently to the place of capture.
Slip Point, Olympic coast, n. Washington

VB69. CABEZON, giant marbled sculpin, giant sculpin, incorrect: bullhead
Scorpaenichthys marmoratus
to 1 m (39 in) long, 13.5 kg (30 lbs) weight
s. Alaska to n. Mexico
intertidal to 75 m (250 ft)
An adult male guarding the green, mauve or purple eggs of his mate(s) can be quite aggressive. More than a few divers have been startled when charged and bumped by a large individual. For the exotically inclined gourmet, **beware—this sculpin's eggs** (photograph B) **are toxic!**
A Stubbs Island, Weynton Passage, c. BC
B Seymour Bay, Bowen Island, s. BC

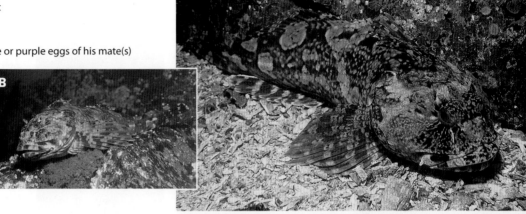

VB70. RED IRISH LORD, red Irish lord sculpin, spotted Irish lord, red sculpin, incorrect: bullhead
Hemilepidotus hemilepidotus
to 50 cm (20 in) long
Siberia, n. Alaska to c. California
intertidal to 50 m (165 ft)
So confident is this sculpin in its camouflage and its capacity for concealment, it is easily picked up by a diver. A resourceful underwater photographer may turn this behaviour to advantage by placing a specimen on a suitable background.
A Plumper Islands, Weynton Passage, c. BC
B Stubbs Island, Weynton Passage, c. BC

VB71. BROWN IRISH LORD, incorrect: bullhead
Hemilepidotus spinosus
to 29 cm (11.3 in) long
c. Alaska to s. California
intertidal to 97 m (318 ft)
The brown Irish lord is observed much less frequently than the red Irish lord (VB70), perhaps because it generally hides in caves along outer, exposed coasts. Close inspection will show horizontal bands, six to eight scales wide, under the dorsal fin instead of the four or five bands of the red Irish lord.
Iphigenia Point, Langara Island, n. BC

VB72. PACIFIC STAGHORN SCULPIN, staghorn sculpin, incorrect: bullhead
Leptocottus armatus
to 48 cm (19 in) long
n. Alaska to n. Mexico
intertidal to 90 m (300 ft)

Often this sculpin remains undetected because it is usually buried in sand, even in the brackish waters of river estuaries. A common but unwanted catch for the casual angler, its characteristic "stag antler-shaped" preopercular (cheek) spines can inflict a nasty wound. Photograph B shows the burying action.
A B White Cliff Point, Howe Sound, s. BC

VB73. BUFFALO SCULPIN, buffalo fish, incorrect: bullhead
Enophrys bison
to 37 cm (15 in) long
c. Alaska to c. California
intertidal to 20 m (65 ft)
Usually motionless and always well camouflaged, this fish is easily overlooked, even by experienced diving naturalists. One of many seemingly identical sculpins, this one has a pair of long, heavy preopercular (cheek) spines and a series of large, raised plates along each lateral line. Photograph A shows a colourful male guarding eggs.
A Copper Cliffs, Quadra Island, s. BC
B Discovery Passage, Campbell River, s. BC

VB74. LEISTER SCULPIN
Enophrys lucasi
▶to 37 cm (15 in) long
n. Alaska to c. BC
subtidal to 17 m (56 ft)
Very small spines, perpendicular to each of the main heavy preopercular (cheek) spines, as well as tiny lip flaps, distinguish the Leister sculpin from the buffalo sculpin (VB73). Like most other sculpins, this cryptic species is an ambush predator. It waits motionless for prey to venture near and then darts quickly to seize its victim.
Plumper Islands, Weynton Passage, c. BC

VB75. GREAT SCULPIN, incorrect: bullhead
Myoxocephalus polyacanthocephalus
to 75 cm (30 in) long
Japan, Siberia, n. Alaska to n. Washington
intertidal to 775 m (2,558 ft)
How exciting! Another sculpin. A drab fish living in drab, silty surroundings. Indeed, it illustrates the classic characteristics of the group: a large head with preopercular (cheek) spines, a relatively small, tapering body and a pair of large fan-like pectoral fins protruding from just behind the head.
Uganda Passage, Cortes Island, s. BC

VB76. FRINGED SCULPIN
Icelinus fimbriatus
to 19 cm (7.5 in) long
BC to s. California
subtidal, 20–265 m (65–870 ft)
Unfortunately, to most observers one sculpin looks just like the next. Subtle characteristics distinguish one from another. This species has cirri (tufts) at the rear of its upper jaw and a fringe-like tip on the cirrus of the nasal spine. Also it has a double row of scales along each upper side, just below the dorsal fins, which extend to the space between these fins and the tail fin—or the caudal peduncle (wrist).

A B Tuwanek Point, Sechelt Inlet, s. BC

VB77. SPINYHEAD SCULPIN, wooly sculpin, incorrect: bullhead
Dasycottus setiger
to 23 cm (9 in) long
Japan, Siberia, n. Alaska to n. Washington
subtidal, 15–140 m (50–462 ft)
A denizen of soft bottoms, this inconspicuous species is one of many creatures politely referred to as bycatch by commercial shrimp trawlers. Night divers venturing into silty situations are the only other folks likely to encounter its well-camouflaged form.

Sandy Cove, Burrard Inlet, s. BC

VB78. ROUGHBACK SCULPIN
Chitonotus pugetensis
to 23 cm (9 in) long
n. BC to n. Mexico
subtidal, 9–140 m (30–462 ft)
A common, nocturnally active sculpin, it thrives on sandy or silty bottoms. Adult specimens are usually easy to sex. A male often displays bright or noticeable "eye caps" and always has a large anal papilla—an organ analogous to the penis (not visible in the photograph).

Point Cowan, Bowen Island, s. BC

VB79. GRUNT SCULPIN, gruntfish, pigfish
Rhamphocottus richardsonii, *Rhamphocottus richardsoni*
to 8.9 cm (3.7 in) long
Japan, c. Alaska to s. California
intertidal to 200 m (660 ft)
This atypical sculpin is intimately associated with the giant acorn barnacle (AR171), specifically the empty casings in which it hides. When showing its snout from a casing, it mimics a live quiescent barnacle. When protruding its orange tail, it produces the effect of a feeding barnacle.

A Browning Passage, Nigei Island, c. BC
B Dodd Narrows, Mudge Island, s. BC

VB80. SAILFIN SCULPIN, sailorfish
Nautichthys oculofasciatus
to 20 cm (8 in) long
c. Alaska to s. California
intertidal to 110 m (365 ft)
Nocturnally active naturalists have access to this attractive and sinuous swimmer. Dockside observers occasionally notice it clinging to pilings, and divers frequently see its straightened form, propelled by a series of fin waves.
Columbine Bay, Bowen Island, s. BC

VB81. SILVERSPOTTED SCULPIN, silverspot sculpin, silverspot
Blepsias cirrhosus
to 20 cm (8 in) long
Japan, Siberia, n. Alaska to n. California
intertidal to 47 m (155 ft)
Whether resting in or fluttering slowly amid marine plants and algae, this very cryptic sculpin mimics perfectly a piece of kelp. These photographs are

the product of a rare night dive encounter, during which Bernie Hanby determinedly followed the featured fish in shallow water for more than 75 minutes while exposing two rolls of film.
A B Edmonds, Puget Sound, c. Washington

VB82. CRESTED SCULPIN
Blepsias bilobus, *Histiocottus bilobus*
to 27 cm (10.5 in) long
Japan, Siberia, n. Alaska to c. BC
subtidal to 190 m (627 ft)
A much more robust fish than the silverspotted sculpin (VB81), this species is distinguished by the lack of a notch in the first dorsal fin and smaller snout cirri (whiskers). Watching a specimen swim is almost entrancing, for it uses its large pectoral fins like an old-time fan dancer to manoeuvre while propelling itself slowly with more typical tail strokes.
Meyers Island, Cleveland Peninsula, s. Alaska

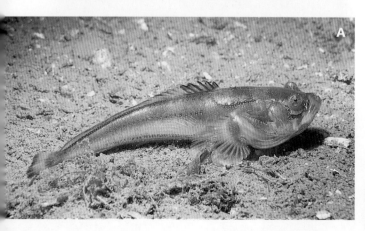

VB83. PLAINFIN MIDSHIPMAN, midshipman, singing toadfish, singing fish, grunting fish
Porichthys notatus
to 38 cm (15 in) long
c. BC to n. Mexico
intertidal to 365 m (1,200 ft)
This widespread species commonly buries in soft substrates (photograph B). In summer, a protective adult male may be found under intertidal rocks guarding developing eggs or newborns, both of which are attached to the

underside of the solid shelter. At any time of year, huge numbers are an unwanted bycatch in commercial shrimp trawling activities.
A B Passage Island, Howe Sound, s. BC

VB84. NORTHERN CLINGFISH, flathead clingfish, common cling fish
Gobiesox maeandricus, *Sicyogaster maeandricus*
to 16 cm (6.5 in) long
s. Alaska to n. Mexico
▶intertidal to 20 m (65 ft)
Turn over rocks in the intertidal zone and you are likely to find this tenacious inhabitant attached to its shelter. The sucking disc on its underside results from modifications to the fish's pelvic fins. Rather than pulling directly, try sliding the fish off for a close look. Please return it gently to the same spot.
Ucluth Peninsula, w. Vancouver Island, s. BC

VB85. KELP CLINGFISH, slender clingfish
Rimicola muscarum, *Rimicola eigenmanni*
to 7 cm (2.8 in) long
s. Alaska to n. Mexico
intertidal to 18 m (60 ft)
This narrow fish has evolved beautifully to match its eelgrass or kelp habitat. Its suction disc, formed from modified pelvic fins, provides stability. If you are lucky enough to find one, look closely to see its tiny red heart beating. If it is a mature female, eggs may also be visible.
Ucluth Peninsula, w. Vancouver Island, s. BC

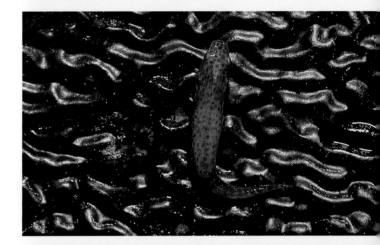

VB86. RIBBON SNAILFISH
Liparis cyclopus
to 11.4 cm (4.5 in) long
Siberia, n. Alaska to n. Washington
intertidal to 183 m (610 ft)
This fish may be the unknown species referred to as #156 in *Coastal Fishes of the Pacific Northwest*. At the time of its publishing, the renowned ichthyologist Dr. Norman Wilimovsky was uncertain as to the identity of the fish in the *Coastal Fishes* photograph. Subsequent studies by his protege, Dr. Jeff Marliave of the Vancouver Aquarium Marine Science Centre, suggest it is indeed this fish.
Stanley Park, Vancouver Harbour, s. BC

VB87. MARBLED SNAILFISH, Denny's liparid
Liparis dennyi
to 30 cm (12 in) long
n. Alaska to n. Washington
subtidal, 10–225 m (33–743 ft)
Of all the groups of fishes present in the Pacific Northwest, the snailfishes are the most difficult to recognize at a species level. A thorough review of these species is long overdue, but it is so daunting a project that investigators have yet to step forward.
Queen Charlotte Channel, Howe Sound, s. BC

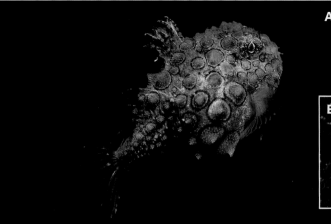

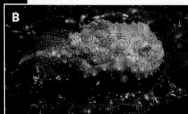

VB88. PACIFIC SPINY LUMPSUCKER, spiny lumpsucker, spiny lump-sucker
Eumicrotremus orbis
to 12 cm (5 in) long
Japan, Siberia, n. Alaska to n. Washington
intertidal to 575 m (1,900 ft)

A delightful but very occasional discovery for the observant underwater explorer, this stubby species *has* to qualify as a "cute" fish. It is most likely seen when it "huffs and puffs" about, like an out-of-shape, finned couch potato. Photograph B shows one sitting on kelp.
A B Stanley Park, Vancouver Harbour, s. BC

VB89. NORTHERN SPEARNOSE POACHER, windowtail poacher, window-tailed sea-poacher
Agonopsis vulsa, *Agonopsis emmelane, Averruncus emmelane*
to 20 cm (8 in) long
c. Alaska to c. California
subtidal, 5–180 m (17–600 ft)
This nocturnally active creature is easily picked up by a curious night diver. Like many of its fellow poachers, this species usually remains in a curled position when replaced on the sea floor. Is it playing possum? Photograph B shows a juvenile.
A Quarry Bay, Nelson Island, s. BC
B Friday Harbor, San Juan Island, n. Washington

VB90. SMOOTH ALLIGATORFISH, smooth poacher, smooth sea-poacher
Anoplagonus inermis
to 15 cm (6 in) long
n. Alaska to n. California
subtidal, 5–133 m (16–435 ft)
Like all poachers, this species has abutting, bony scutes (modified scales) that render it stiff as well as offering protection. Also, like other elongate family members, it moves its stiff, rudder-like body with sculling movements of its pectoral fins. Dark brown is a typical colour for this fish.
Friday Harbor, San Juan Island, n. Washington

VB91. STURGEON POACHER, sturgeon-like sea-poacher
Podothecus accipenserinus, *Agonus acipenserinus*
to 30 cm (12 in) long
Siberia, n. Alaska to n. California
intertidal to 300 m (1,000 ft)
One has only to look at the head of this fish to see how it acquired its name. Like its namesake, it has "taste buds" on the bushy tendrils protruding from the underside of its head. These structures allow it to recognize its invertebrate prey as it rummages through the sand or silt of its habitat.
Mouth of Capilano River, West Vancouver, s. BC

VB92. TUBENOSE POACHER, tubesnout poacher
Pallasina barbata, *Pallasina barbata aix*
to 20.8 cm (8.3 in) long
Korea, Japan, Siberia, n. Alaska to c. California
intertidal to 27 m (89 ft)
Resembling an "armoured" tubesnout (VB8), this cryptic fish also swims with a sculling motion of its pectoral fins. A beachcombing naturalist might find a juvenile trapped in a tidepool, and a keen-eyed scuba diver is more likely to encounter the deeper-dwelling adult. Either way, one's observational skills are put to the test.
Frank Island, w. Vancouver Island, s. BC

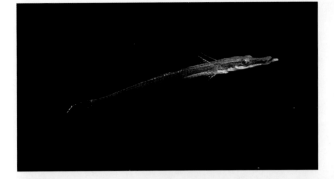

VB93. KELP POACHER
Agonomalus mozinoi
to 8.9 cm (3.5 in) long
n. BC to c. California
intertidal to 11 m (36 ft)
This stubby poacher uses its tail and lower fins to creep slowly along the bottom. It is truly a contradiction as it lives in the rocky shallows directly exposed to the pounding surf of the open Pacific, where a strong swimming ability would seem most advantageous.
A Frank Island, w. Vancouver Island, s. BC
B Tofino, w. Vancouver Island, s. BC

VB94. ROCKHEAD, deep-pitted poacher, deep-pitted sea-poacher, pitted poacher, pithead poacher
Bothragonus swanii, *Bothragonus swani*
to 9 cm (3.5 in) long
c. Alaska to c. California
intertidal to 20 m (65 ft)
The rockhead is almost impossible to find in exposed coastal tidepools. Like the kelp poacher (VB93), it relies on camouflage as its primary survival strategy. As yet, nobody has determined the reason for the pit in the top of its head.
A Frank Island, w. Vancouver Island, s. BC
B Eagle Point, San Juan Island, n. Washington

VB95. STARRY FLOUNDER, grindstone, leatherjacket, emerywheel
Platichthys stellatus
to 90 cm (36 in) long
Korea, Japan, Siberia, Canadian Arctic Ocean, n. Alaska to s. California
intertidal to 375 m (1,238 ft)
A larval starry flounder, like all baby flatfish, is symmetrical. However, during an amazing metamorphosis, the young fish's skull twists and one of its eyes migrates to the other side of its body, which along with other changes produces the typical adult form.
Irvines Landing, Pender Harbour, s. BC

VB96. C-O SOLE, popeye sole, spot flounder, muddy flounder
Pleuronichthys coenosus
to 36 cm (14.5 in) long
s. Alaska to n. Mexico
subtidal to 350 m (1,155 ft)
Though usually indistinct, the "C" and "O" markings on the tail give this flounder its name. Its protruding eyes, which move independently, provide this small-mouthed species with a unique view of its surroundings. Photograph B shows an unusual colour phase adorning a specimen that likely resides amid coralline algae.
A Worlcombe Island, Howe Sound, s. BC
B Egmont Marina, Egmont, s. BC

VB97. ENGLISH SOLE, lemon sole, pointed-nosed sole, common sole, California sole
Parophrys vetulus, *Pleuronectes vetulus*
to 61 cm (24 in) long
n. Alaska to n. Mexico
intertidal to 550 m (1,815 ft)
An elongate diamond outline and a lateral line that arches high over each pectoral fin distinguish this flounder from several other similar-looking species. Like other small-mouthed flatfishes, this one feeds primarily on small invertebrate prey.
Stanley Park, Vancouver Harbour, s. BC

VB98. WANDERING GARTER SNAKE, western garter snake
Thamnophis elegans
to 1 m (39 in) long
along coast, from BC to c. California
terrestrial and intertidal
An excellent swimmer, this snake routinely visits the beach at low tide to prey on intertidal creatures, particularly small fish. Summer, when the sun's rays energize this basking reptile, is the optimal time for the beachcomber to look for it.
Brown Island, Friday Harbor, n. Washington

VB99. BEACHCOMBER
Homo sapiens "intertidalus"
to 2.1 m (7 ft) tall—at least!
worldwide
terrestrial and intertidal
Some individuals of this species are hunter/gatherers; others are non-consumptive observers. It is vital that this supposedly intelligent creature not only realize that its environment and associated organisms are threatened, but that it aggressively lobby its fellow "subspecies" to take action. The beachcomber can no longer be simply an interested bystander.
Egmont Marina, Egmont, s. BC

VB100. SCUBA DIVER
Homo sapiens "subaqueous"
to 2.1 m (7 ft) tall—at least!
worldwide
terrestrial, intertidal and subtidal
Once primarily focussed on harvesting, this creature has become increasingly conservation-oriented. Truly the "underwater eyes of humanity," he or she bears witness to the devastation being wrought by the overharvesting of marine species. As members of this "subspecies," the authors hope this publication will help spur long-overdue remedial action.
Quarry Bay, Nelson Island, s. BC

GLOSSARY

aboral Opposite end or side from which the mouth is located.

agar A red algal gum that has many uses including meat packaging and microbiological media.

annulation Marked or formed of rings or segments.

antenna (plural antennae). In polychaete annelids, a slender sensory projection arising from the top, sides or front of the prostomium (head area), often in pairs. In arthropods, the first (and sometimes second) head appendage.

aperture In snails, the opening in the shell from which the animal's body protrudes.

atrial cavity In tunicates, the central body cavity.

avicularium (plural avicularia). In bryozoans, a specialized zooid that resembles the beak of a bird.

benthic Referring to the sea floor.

bioturbating Reworking and aerating sediments via the activities of living organisms.

branchia (plural branchiae). Structure, usually with blood vessels, that functions as a gill.

carapace Hard shield or section of the exoskeleton on the back of a crab or shrimp that protects the head and thorax.

caudal fin A propulsive and stabilizing structure at the rear of fish.

cerata (singular ceras). In nudibranchs (sea slugs) and their relatives, fleshy processes on the back that contain diverticula (branches) of digestive glands.

cf. Species unknown or new but most closely compared with that listed.

chaeta (plural chaetae). In polychaete annelids, a chitinous bristle emerging from or embedded in the parapodium (appendage). **Seta** (setae) is an equivalent, outdated spelling.

chaetiger Any segment of a polychaete annelid that bears chaetae (bristles). **Setiger** is an equivalent, outdated spelling.

cheliped In crabs, shrimps and their relatives, a leg with a pincer at its free end.

chitin A polysaccharide (carbohydrate whose molecules consist of long chains of simple sugars) forming the major constituent of an arthropod exoskeleton, a polychaete annelid worm bristle or some polychaete annelid tubes.

chloroplast A small organelle, containing a green pigment responsible for light absorption, within a cell undergoing photosynthesis.

chondrophore In bivalve molluscs, a spoon-shaped structure, often projecting from the hinge plate.

cilia Microscopic hair-like processes used in locomotion, food gathering and other functions.

cirrus (plural cirri). Soft, fleshy projection ranging in shape from hair-like, finger-like, cylindrical to leaf-like; generally sensory in nature.

cnidocyte (nematocyst). In sea anemones, corals, jellies and their relatives, the microscopic stinging organ usually found on the tentacles.

collar cells In sponges, the flagellate (long lash-like appendage) cells that line the body cavities.

columella In many snails, the central axis of the shell around which the shell and the body of the snail spirals or coils.

commensalism An association between two species that live together, which benefits individuals of one species without harming those of the other.

ctenes In comb jellies (sea gooseberries), the bands of fused cilia that form individual comb plates, which, in long series, form the eight characteristic combs defining the animal.

demersal Being or living near the sea bottom.

detritus Debris containing organic matter, often of decomposed organisms, recycled as a major food source for many organisms.

dorsal fin A stabilizing structure on the back of fish.

elytra (singular elytron). In some polychaete annelids, a shield-like plate on the back of the worm.

elytron (plural elytra). A shield-like scale or plate on the dorsum (back) of scaleworms, polychaete annelids; notably in pairs.

elytrophore A stalk that attaches the elytron to the back of the scaleworm.

epidermis Outer cell layer of the skin.

epifauna Benthic organisms living on or above the surface of the sediment.

epigamy In some polychaete annelids, a structural modification of an entire adult individual into an epitoke or reproductive stage, ready to leave the bottom for swarming and spawning.

epiphyte A plant or alga growing on, but not parasitic on, another.

epitoke In some polychaete annelids, a structurally modified individual, pelagic sexual stage, that leaves the bottom to reproduce; includes epigamous epitokes and schizogamous epitokes.

exoskeleton The chitinous, rigid outer covering of a crab, shrimp or other arthropod.

forma Of a particular morphology but without a particular ecological or genetic rationale or reason.

fucan A sulphated polysaccharide (carbohydrate whose molecules consist of long chains of simple sugars) that is a common structural component of the cell wall of many brown algae.

gamete A mature germ cell, i.e. egg or sperm, able to unite with another cell in sexual reproduction.

gametophyte A gamete producing form of an organism that has alternation of generations with the asexual form.

gonangium (plural gonangia). In hydroids (sea firs), a polyp for production of medusae.

hemoglobin A red oxygen-carrying pigment, containing iron and protein, present in red blood cells or body fluids.

heteromorphic Of dissimilar forms, e.g. existing in different forms in a life cycle.

heteronereid Modified pelagic, reproductive stage or epitoke of a mature sea-nymph, polychaete annelid.

holdfast In large algae, a root-like structure that seaweeds use to attach to the substrate or other solid objects.

holistic Describes the view of an entire system as a whole rather than by its separate parts.

hydranth In colonial hydroids (sea firs), a polyp designed for feeding.

infauna Benthic orgamisms living within the sediment.

introvert In peanut worms, a portion of the body that can be retracted by being pulled inside itself.

lophophore In moss animals (bryozoans), lampshells and phoronids, a circular or horseshoe-shaped fold or ridge on the body wall that bears ciliated tentacles used for respiration and food collection.

mantle In molluscs, the interior sheet of tissue that encloses the rest of its soft body. The shell (or shells), if present in the mollusc, are secreted by the edge of the mantle.

manubrium In jellies, the stalk on which the mouth is located.

medusa A jelly. The free-swimming life history stage of some cnidarians. (The term **jellyfish** is outdated and considered a misnomer.)

moult In arthropods, the cast-off exoskeleton resulting from a growth increment.

neurochaeta In polychaete annelids, a chaeta (bristle) protruding from the neuropodium.

neuropodium (plural neuropodia). In polychaete annelids, the lower lobe of the parapodium (appendage).

notochaeta (plural notochaetae). In polychaete annelids, a bristle protruding from the notopodium.

notochord Particularly in larval tunicates (sea squirts), a primitive type of skeletal rod.

notopodium (plural notopodia). In polychaete annelids, the upper lobe of the parapodium (appendage).

ocellus A simple eye or eyespot.

operculum In most snails, the trap door attached to the foot, which covers and seals off the shell opening. Present, in modified form, in some polychaete annelids.

oral disc In sea anemones and their relatives, the rounded top, ringed with tentacles, that contains the central mouth/anus.

osculum (plural oscula). In sponges, the excurrent opening by which water is pumped from an individual cell.

ossicle In echinoderms, a calcareous skeletal structure, often plate-like or spine-like.

palea (plural paleae). In some polychaete annelids, a specialized, modified chaeta (bristle), broad and flat or ornate and hooked, located near the head.

palp In some polychaete annelids, one of a set of paired structures arising from the specific areas of the head or prostomium: short, conical or cushion-like sensory structures in some; long, grooved feeding structures in others.

papilla (plural papillae). A tiny, fleshy projection from the body wall or other structures, usually sensory in nature.

papulae In sea stars, the thin-walled, sac-shaped gills that form as out-pocketings of the body wall on the back (aboral) surface of the animal.

parapodium (plural parapodia). In polychaete annelids, the flap-like appendages on each side of most segments, from which chaetae (bristles) arise.

pectoral fins A pair of stabilizing and propulsive structures on the belly, one on each side immediately behind the head of a fish.

pedicellaria In sea stars and sea urchins, tiny pincer-like structures on the body's surface.

peduncle In lampshells, a stalk that anchors the animal to the substrate.

pelagic Belonging to the water column of the ocean.

pelvic fins A pair of stabilizing structures located on the belly area of a fish.

periostracum In molluscs, the organic material, often fibrous, that coats the outside of the shell.

photosynthesis The process by which the energy of sunlight is used by organisms (especially plants) to synthesize or create carbohydrates from carbon dioxide and water.

plankton Free-floating aquatic organisms whose mobility is essentially controlled by currents.

pleopod In crabs, shrimps and their relatives, a paired, two-branched appendage found on the ventral (under) side of the abdomen.

polybostrichus In some necklace-worms (polychaete annelids), a male version of a stolon.

polyp In cnidarians, an individual, often part of a colony, with one end comprising a mouth surrounded by tentacles and the other end attached to the substrate.

proboscis (plural proboscises). In ribbon worms, an anterior cylindrical sensory, defensive and offensive organ that can evert itself. In some polychaete annelids, the anterior, eversible part of the digestive tract.

prostomium In polychaete annelids, the head, without segments and anterior to the mouth; sometimes bearing eyes, antennae, and/or palps.

proventricle In some polychaete annelids, a muscular, glandular, gizzard-like tube forming part of the digestive tract posterior to the proboscis; involved in food processing.

radiole In sabellid and serpulid tubeworms (polychaete annelids), one of several to many feather-like and spoke-like branches of the tentacular crown.

radula In snails, limpets and nudibranchs (sea slugs), a tooth-like file, located in the mouth, used to rasp food from hard surfaces.

rays In sea stars, the appendages or "arms" radiating from the central disc.

rhinophore In nudibranchs (sea slugs) and bubbleshells, a paired sensory organ located on the head.

rhizome A root-like stem bearing both roots and shoots.

rostrum In shrimps and some other arthropods, the spine-like anterior projection on the carapace.

sacconereis In some necklace-worms (polychaete annelids), the female stolon.

schizogamy In some polychaete annelids, a structural modification of part of an adult individual by budding off sexual epitokes, or reproductive stages (i.e., stolons), that leave the bottom for swarming and spawning.

scyphistoma In some jellies, a sessile polyp that produces and ejects young medusae (jellies).

siphon Either of two tubes in bivalve molluscs and tunicates: the inhalent tube draws water into the mouth and gills; the exhalent tube ejects wastewater. In some snails, the siphon is a single tube that is sensory.

siphonal canal In some coiled snail species, a canal, located at the extreme end of the aperture or opening, from which the siphon protrudes.

sp. Species identity undetermined.

spicule In sponges and some other animals, the skeletal building block that stiffens the body.

sp. nov. A species that is not yet formally described.

spore Specialized reproductive cell of many plants, algae and micro-organisms.

spp. More than one species undetermined.

ssp. Subspecies.

stigmata In tunicates (sea squirts), perforations in the pharynx (internal filtering sac).

stolon In some polychaete annelids, a secondary individual, budded off from a parent individual or stock, that forms a pelagic reproductive, sexual stage.

stylet In some snails and some ribbon worms, a slender pointed structure for piercing prey.

taxonomy The science of classification of living and extinct organisms; in specific terms the identification, describing and naming of species.

tentacular crown In sabellid and serpulid tubeworms (polychaete annelids), the array of feather-like radioles on the head used for feeding and respiration.

tentilla (singular tentillum). In some cnidarians, the contractile branches on a long, hollow feeding tentacle that bear stinging cells.

test In sea urchins and sand dollars, the rigid, calcareous protective container formed from fused ossicles.

tubercle A small bump, or knob-like projection, on the skin of some invertebrates.

tunicin In tunicates (sea squirts), the leathery outer covering of the body.

umbilicus In snails, the hole or opening in the shell that is visible at the base of the columella (central axis). The hole is formed because the whorls are not closely wound against each other at either end of the axis.

var. Variety or subspecies.

villi Numerous short slender hair-like projections on some membranes.

whorl In many snails, a turn or twist of the shell spire. The largest and newest whorl is the body whorl, which provides the aperture through which the foot and head protrude.

zooid In bryozoans (moss animals), colonial tunicates (sea squirts) and hydroids (sea firs), individual members of a colony that are structurally continuous, usually in box-like, cup-like or tube-like units.

ACKNOWLEDGEMENTS

We are truly thankful for the very special efforts of many people, without whom production of this book would not have succeeded. The following lists are not exhaustive, but they acknowledge particular invaluable contributions.

Identification of Pacific Northwest marine organisms is the primary focus of this book, and we were most fortunate to have numerous experts, leading academics in their chosen areas, perform and/or validate species determinations. They undertook detailed examination of specimens, which often involved dissection and microscopic inspection of samples. As well, many of them reviewed text and photographs and shared their knowledge and experience. They also provided fascinating, often newly discovered background information and vital scientific editing. These experts are: Dr. Roland Anderson (octopuses and squids), Dr. William Austin (sponges), David Behrens (velutinas, bubble shells and nudibranchs), Dr. Anita Brinkman-Voss (hydroids), Sheila C. Byers (polychaete worms), Dr. Christopher Cameron (acorn worms), Roger Clark (chitons), Dr. Marymegan Daly (sea anemones), David Denning (moss animals), Dr. Daphne G. Fautin (sea anemones), Jayson Gillespie (sea spiders), Rick Harbo (chitons, univalve and bivalve molluscs), Leslie Harris (polychaete worms), Dr. Michael W. Hawkes (seaweeds), Dr. Lea-Anne Henry (hydroids), George Holm (chitons, univalve and bivalve molluscs), Dr. Fumio Iwata (ribbon worms), Dr. Gregory Jensen (shrimps, crabs, hermits and other arthropods), Dr. Charles Lambert (tunicates), Dr. Gretchen Lambert (tunicates), Philip Lambert (sea stars, brittle stars, feather stars, sea urchins, sea cucumbers, flatworms and ribbon worms), Neil McDaniel (invertebrates), Valerie Macdonald (invertebrate identification), Dr. Jeff Marliave (fishes), Sandra Millen (bubble shells and nudibranchs), Claudia E. Mills (jellies), Dr. Christopher Pharo (lampshells), Perry Poon (amphipod and isopod identification), Eugene Ruff (polychaete worms), Dr. Paul V. Scott (bivalve molluscs), Dr. Robert Van Syoc (barnacles), David Whitaker (copepods), Dr. Gary Williams (corals) and Dr. Bruce Wing (corals).

The tedious task of copy editing was willingly completed by Charlie Gibbs, Donna Gibbs, Catherine Po and Sheila C. Byers.

Numerous chores, including the collection and transportation of living specimens for photography, were a major and time-consuming requirement for this book. The following people diligently assisted with these activities: Mike Atkins, Esther Baumann, Patti Beer, Brian Bingham, Philip Bruecker, Scott Buchanan, Glenn Budden, the late Dave Christie, Renate Christie, Bill Coates, Verleen Coates, Elizabeth Darby, Ralph Delisle, Doug Deproy, Bill Ebert, Margot Elfert, John Fisher, Leah French, Chris Gehlen, Charlie Gibbs, Donna Gibbs, Mackenzie Gier, Dr. Ian Hass, Julia Hass, Morgan Hass, Sarah Hass, Kate Henderson, Herb Herunter, Jeremy Heywood, Lorne Hildebrand, Chris Homan, the late Albert Hull, Jennifer Ingram, Sharon Jeffery, Keith Kartzewski, Danny Kent, Alec Lamb, Susan Lamb, Virginia Lamb, Ian Lamont, Joanne Lamont, Sonja Melo, Cathy Moffett, the late Dr. Charles Moffett, Takuji Oyama, John Rawle, Kelly Sendall, Dusty Sept, J. Duane Sept, Jerry Stauber and Doug Swanston.

Logistical support was very kindly supplied by Norma Alonzo, Steve Boothe, Jim Borrowman, Bud Bowles, Barbara Brooks, George Brooks, Margaret Butschler, Penny Carrigan, Tony Carrigan, Leah Commons, Kal Helyar, James Hollis, Mike Lever, Bill McKay, John MacLeod, Cam Montgomery, Linda Newcombe, Bill Pappajohn, Mike Richmond, Trevà Ricou, Tom Sheldon, Pete Sweetnam, Bart Van Herwaarden, Bill Weeks and John Zavaglia.

The following institutions and businesses generously assisted through their facilities and services: Abyssal Dive Ventures, All Seasons Dive Charters, Aquatica, Biologica Environmental Services, Biomedia Associates, Brooks Wet Suits Ltd., Dunne & Rundle Foto Source, Eagle Harbour Yacht Club, Egmont Marina Resort, God's Pocket Resort, Great Pacific Diving Co. Ltd., Lever Diving, Living Elements Research Ltd., The Lobster Man, M&P Mercury Sales, Nootka Sound Divers, Oregon Coast Aquarium, Pender Harbour Resort Ltd., Porpoise Bay Charters, Puffin Adventures, Rendezvous Dive Ventures, Royal British Columbia Museum, Seacology, Seymour Inlet Lodge, Sirius Charters, Stubbs Island Charters, Tristar Fisheries, Vancouver Aquarium Marine Science Centre and West Vancouver Laboratory (Department of Fisheries and Oceans, Canada).

Without the outstanding technical support of computer wizard Charlie Gibbs, this project would have been exceedingly more challenging to complete.

So important, integral and inspiring was Donna Gibbs' contribution to this project that it is nearly impossible to acknowledge fully. She assisted with virtually every facet of the process.

We also acknowledge the invaluable encouragement and support of our wives, Virginia Lamb and Sue Hanby, over the years during which the concept of this book was realized.

Thanks must be expressed for the support, again over at least a twelve-year period, to Howard White, who recognized the need for a comprehensive work in this area. We also thank Vici Johnstone and Peter Read at Harbour Publishing for production coordination, Peter Field at Agile Media for image scanning, Roger Handling at Terra Firma for book design and Mary Schendlinger for editing.

Over the years, Bernie Hanby's boating pursuits and base of operations in the Pender Harbour, BC, area proved invaluable. We were able to access preferred dive sites and respond quickly when photographic opportunities arose. Andy Lamb's position as School Program Coordinator at the Vancouver Aquarium Marine Science Centre and access to live holding facilities were also extremely beneficial.

All the photography presented within these pages was produced by Bernie Hanby, with the following noted exceptions. Those who generously provided images are gratefully acknowledged as follows:

Roland Anderson, MC376

Lou Barr, EC5

Marc Chamberlain, CN38

Roger Clark, MC207

Don Davenport, MC377

Phil Edgell, CN24A

Charlie Gibbs, PO18, CN50B, CN66, CN81B, PL8, CG1, AN4B, AN23A, AN23B, AN24B, AN58A, AN78A, MC281C, MC341, AR31B, AR31C, AR36, EC47C, CH44C, Phoronids (intro)

Donna Gibbs, p. 15, MC285, MC289, MC367, AN1, WA4

Daniel W. Gotshall, AN63, EC36, CH21

Rick Harbo, MC170, MC230, MC272

Dr. Michael W. Hawkes, SW4C, Marine Algae (intro B), SW5, SW15B, SW19A, SW22, SW26, SW27, SW29, SW30, SW41, SW43A, SW44, SW48, SW50, SW55B, SW56B, SW59C, SW61B, SW65, SW66C, SW69, SW70, SW71B, SW78, SW80, SW82, SW85B, SW86C, SW93C, SW94, SW95, SW96, SW97A, SW98, SW99, SW100A, SW100B, SW101, SW104A, SW104B, SW106A, SW106B, SW110A, SW111, SW113, SW118, SW119, SW120, SW123B, SW124, SW126, SW129, SW134, SW135B, SW136C

Dr. Gregory C. Jensen, AR44, AR52, AR54

Danny Kent, CN107, AR49, AR177, EC58

Bo Lindstrom CN33

Neil McDaniel, PO5A, PO5B, PO8, PO15, PO16, PO19, PO20, PO32, PO33, PO58, PO59, CN80, CN102, MC290, MC356, MC357, AR11, AR14C, EC55

Dr. Steve Martell, AR31A

Jeff Mondragon, SW36

Alan Murray, MC3

Dr. Christopher Pharo, AN25

Charlotte Richardson, MC312

Doug Sandilands, AR15

J. Duane Sept, AN43, AN60B, MC23, MC295, MC326, AR170

Terry Whalen, VB31

Bruce Wight, MC361

Dave Wrobel, CH54

Doug Pemberton, Sue Hanby and Donna Gibbs provided the author images.

INDEX

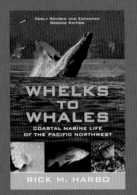

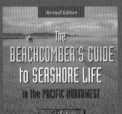

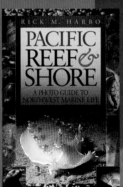
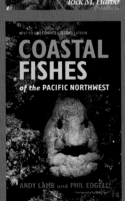